Handbook of
Wage and Salary
Administration

Handbook of Wage and Salary Administration

MILTON L. ROCK *Editor-in-Chief*

Managing Partner, Edward N. Hay & Associates

McGRAW-HILL BOOK COMPANY

New York   St. Louis   San Francisco   Düsseldorf   Johannesburg
Kuala Lumpur   London   Mexico   Montreal   New Delhi
Panama   Rio de Janeiro   Singapore   Sydney   Toronto

Library of Congress Cataloging in Publication Data

Rock, Milton L
    Handbook of wage and salary administration.

    Includes bibliographical references.
    1. Wages—Handbooks, manuals, etc.   2. Wage pay-
ment systems—Handbooks, manuals, etc.   I. Title.
HD4926.R6   658.32   71-167499
ISBN 0-07-053348-2

666 book pages

HANDBOOK OF WAGE AND SALARY ADMINISTRATION

    9 10 11 12 13   VBVB   8 9 8 7 6 5 4 3 2

The coordinating editor for this book was
Virginia S. Albrecht, the editors were Dale L. Dutton,
W. Hodson Mogan, and Don A. Douglas, the designer
was Naomi Auerbach, and its production was
supervised by Teresa F. Leaden. It was set in
Caledonia by Monotype Composition Co., Inc.

To the next generation, especially Liza Devon Herzog.
May their contribution fulfil this generation's aspirations
for them.

M. L. R.

Editorial Advisory Board

Contributors

H. PAUL ABBOTT   *Manager, Personnel and Administration, INA Corporation, Philadelphia, Pennsylvania (Chapter 20)*

WILLIAM ABOUD   *Wharton School of Finance and Commerce, University of Pennsylvania, Philadelphia, Pennsylvania (Chapter 19)*

R. C. ALBRIGHT   *The American Bankers Association, Washington, D.C. (Chapter 24)*

F. ELLIOTT AVERY   *Manager of Equal Opportunity, Southern California Edison Company, Rosemead, California (Chapter 16)*

ALVIN O. BELLAK   *Partner, Edward N. Hay & Associates, Philadelphia, Pennsylvania (Chapter 42)*

EUGENE J. BENGE   *Benge Associates, Pompano Beach, Florida (Chapter 10)*

ALFRED R. BRANDT   *Senior Wage Practices Specialist, Western Electric Company, Inc., New York, New York (Chapter 2)*

HAROLD N. CHADWICK   *Manager, Executive Financial Counseling Service, Edward N. Hay & Associates, Philadelphia, Pennsylvania (Chapter 46)*

C. S. DADAKIS   *Manager, Salary Administration, Union Carbide Corporation, New York, New York (Chapter 45)*

JAMES H. DAVIS   *Manager, Organization and Compensation, Aluminum Company of America, Pittsburgh, Pennsylvania (Chapters 1 and 48)*

WILLIAM F. DINSMORE   *General Partner, Edward N. Hay & Associates, Philadelphia, Pennsylvania (Chapter 36)*

J. A. ENGEL   *Director, Executive Compensation Service, American Management Association, New York, New York (Chapter 15.2)*

GLENN L. ENGELKE   *Corporate Personnel Director, Addressograph Multigraph Corporation, Cleveland, Ohio (Chapter 14)*

D. H. EVEREST   *Manager, Industrial Engineering, Western Steel Operations, United States Steel Corporation (Chapter 12.2)*

GLENN T. FISCHBACH   *Director of Engineering Services, American Association of Industrial Management, Melrose Park, Pennsylvania (Chapter 12.3)*

F. L. FLETCHER   *Managing Partner, F. L. Fletcher & Associates, Philadelphia, Pennsylvania (Chapter 35)*

R. L. FORD   *Manager, Manpower Planning & Development, Kennecott Copper Corporation, New York, New York (Chapter 26)*

RONALD G. FOSTER   *Vice President, Marketing, Worthington Pump International, Mountainside, New Jersey (Chapter 27)*

RICHARD C. FREMON   *Director, Salary Administration, Bell Telephone Laboratories, Incorporated, Murray Hill, New Jersey (Chapter 50)*

LLOYD E. FULLER   *Manager, Compensation Department, Sandia Laboratories, Albuquerque, New Mexico (Chapter 40)*

RICHARD C. GERKEN, JR.   *Staff Organization Analyst, Aluminum Company of America, Pittsburgh, Pennsylvania (Chapter 1)*

GINO P. GIUSTI   *Employee Relations Manager, Texas Gulf Sulphur Company, New York, New York (Chapter 29)*

WILLIAM GOMBERG   *Wharton School of Finance and Commerce, University of Pennsylvania, Philadelphia, Pennsylvania (Chapter 19)*

TIMOTHY P. HAWORTH   *General Partner, Edward N. Hay & Associates, Philadelphia, Pennsylvania (Chapter 33)*

R. E. HOLLERBACH   *Director, Compensation and Personnel Development, Parke, Davis & Company, Detroit, Michigan (Chapter 17)*

WILLIAM H. HRABAK   *Director, Total Compensation, Owens-Illinois, Inc., Toledo, Ohio (Chapter 49)*

A. W. HUDOCK   *Director, Compensation and Benefits, Scott Paper Company, Philadelphia, Pennsylvania (Chapter 3)*

CHARLES L. HUGHES   *Director of Corporate Industrial Relations, Texas Instruments Incorporated, Dallas, Texas (Chapter 11)*

BERNARD INGSTER   *Senior Principal, Edward N. Hay & Associates, Philadelphia, Pennsylvania (Chapter 23)*

RAYMOND JACOBSON   *Director, Bureau of Policies and Standards, United States Civil Service Commission, Washington, D.C. (Chapter 12.1)*

R. G. JAMISON   *Corporate Manager of Compensation, General Mills, Inc., Minneapolis, Minnesota (Chapter 38)*

GRADY E. JENSEN   *Director of Organization and Manpower Development, American Express Company, New York, New York (Chapter 37)*

H. L. JUDD   *Director of Personnel, United States Gypsum Company, Chicago, Illinois (Chapter 25)*

DENNIS S. KENNEDY   *Insurance Company of North America, Philadelphia, Pennsylvania (Chapter 20)*

ALAN LANGER   *Associate, Edward N. Hay & Associates, Boston, Massachusetts (Chapter 39)*

L. EARL LEWIS   *Chief, Division of Occupational Wage Structures, Bureau of Labor Statistics, U.S. Department of Labor, Washington, D.C. (Chapter 15.3)*

H. W. LIEBER   *Assistant Manager, Industrial Engineering, Western Electric Company, New York, New York (Chapter 34)*

W. O. LORY   *General Manager, Personnel Services, Aluminum Company of America, Pittsburgh, Pennsylvania (Chapter 48)*

ROBERT E. LUCE   *Director, Training and Communications, Edward N. Hay & Associates, Philadelphia, Pennsylvania (Chapter 51)*

JAMES E. McELWAIN   *Director, Compensation, National Cash Register Company, Dayton, Ohio (Chapter 47)*

EDWIN D. MEADE   *Principal, Edward N. Hay & Associates, Philadelphia, Pennsylvania (Chapter 35)*

GEORGE E. MELLGARD   *Manager, Personnel, Pittsburgh Coke & Chemical Company, Pittsburgh, Pennsylvania (Chapter 13)*

LAWRENCE WM. MUTH   *Director, Corporate Economic Research and Statistical Reporting, Johnson & Johnson, New Brunswick, New Jersey (Chapter 32)*

KEITH OCHELTREE   *Public Personnel Association, Chicago, Illinois (Chapter 41)*

CHESTER C. PAYNE   *Director, Corporate Compensation, The Dow Chemical Company, Midland, Michigan (Chapter 21)*

ROBERT E. RADLEY   *Director, Salary Administration, Sperry Rand Corporation, New York, New York (Chapter 44)*

HENRY C. RICKARD   *Director, International Compensation Coordination, Edward N. Hay & Associates, Philadelphia, Pennsylvania (Chapters 15.1, 15.4 and 15.5)*

KENNETH H. ROSS   *President, Huggins & Company, Inc., Philadelphia, Pennsylvania (Chapter 30)*

THOMAS S. ROY   *Senior Analyst, Salary Administration Department, Armstrong Cork Company, Lancaster, Pennsylvania (Chapter 6)*

WILLIAM T. RYAN   *Senior Consultant, Edward N. Hay & Associates, San Francisco, California (Chapter 28)*

HENRY A. SARGENT   *Principal, Edward N. Hay & Associates, Philadelphia, Pennsylvania (Chapter 9)*

FRED E. SCHUSTER   *Associate Professor of Management, and Assistant Dean, College of Business and Public Administration, Florida Atlantic University, Boca Raton, Florida (Chapter 22)*

ROBERT H. SELLES   *Huggins & Company, Inc., Philadelphia, Pennsylvania (Chapter 30)*

EDWARD B. SHILS   *Chairman, Department of Industry, Wharton School of Finance and Commerce, University of Pennsylvania, Philadelphia, Pennsylvania (Chapter 7)*

DONALD R. SIMPSON   *Director, Noncash Compensation Services, Edward N. Hay & Associates, Philadelphia, Pennsylvania (Chapter 31)*

C. IAN SYM-SMITH   *Vice President, Edward N. Hay International, Inc., Paris, France (Chapter 43)*

FREDERIC L. TAYLOR   *Department Chief, Industrial Engineering Research, Western Electric Company, New York, New York (Chapter 34)*

DONALD R. THOMPSON   *Vice President, Industrial Relations, Warner Gear/Warner Motive, Muncie, Indiana (Chapter 18)*

CHARLES W. G. VAN HORN   *General Partner, Edward N. Hay & Associates, Philadelphia, Pennsylvania (Chapter 12.4)*

ROBERT P. VORHIS   *Manager, Salary Administration, Armco Steel Corporation, Middletown, Ohio (Chapter 5)*

KENNETH O. WARNER   *Executive Director, Public Personnel Association, Chicago, Illinois (Chapter 41)*

CARL S. WEBBER   *Senior Principal, Edward N. Hay & Associates, Philadelphia, Pennsylvania (Chapters 4 and 46)*

CHESTER L. WILHELM   *General Manager, Salary Administration Department, Armstrong Cork Company, Lancaster, Pennsylvania (Chapter 6)*

RICHARD E. WING   *Director, Compensation, Corporate Compensation and Benefits Department, Eastman Kodak Company, Rochester, New York (Chapter 8)*

Preface

Management's challenge is to create an environment which stimulates people in their jobs and fosters company growth, and a key aspect of the environment is compensation. Its dramatic impact is felt not only in the area of costs but also in the area of individual motivation. Motivation, in turn, is an essential prerequisite to top corporate as well as individual performance. A company's reward system and its application indicate explicitly just how highly a person and his contributions are valued. The attributes and visible accomplishments of the individuals who are recognized with larger and more frequent pay and promotional increases tangibly communicate to employees at large what kind of behavior is needed and desired.

Viewed from this perspective, compensation is more than pay. It is a total reward system involving incentives and noncash benefits, performance appraisal, and manpower development as well as base wages and salaries. Thus, in addition to providing for material needs, the compensation administrator must consider the employee's need for self-realization—the need to feel that he is having a real impact on the organization. While money, in one form or another, is a major source of satisfaction and motivation, other factors can be equally important to employee morale. These include the nature of the work, the organizational environment and style of management, and the company's past performance and its outlook for the future.

As a total package, compensation is an integral part of the art and science of management. It involves people, job design, organization design, and corporate effectiveness. Compensation policies must therefore accurately reflect the organization's style and philosophy as well as attract the type of people suited to that style and philosophy.

The *Handbook of Wage and Salary Administration* has been written to help managers create a compensation process which meets these needs. Intended as a practical reference work for managers who want to improve their effectiveness, the Handbook sets forth the concepts, techniques and processes which are basic to good wage and salary administration. These include the work, the products, the ideas, services, and end results for which jobs are created, leading inevitably to the *people* who fill the jobs. People, not jobs, get rewarded for their contributions to the organization. Therefore, a company that cares about its employees needs a systematic, organized vehicle for wage and salary administration which will minimize subjectivity and be equitable to all.

Our underlying belief in planning this Handbook has been that no element of the pay system stands alone; each is a part of the whole and all are affected by the design and administration of the others. In keeping with this fundamental idea, the Handbook is organized to guide the reader through the compensation process, showing how the principles and procedures are coordinated to build a solid foundation for an *integrated total compensation program*. The first sections, therefore, are devoted to those elements which provide the foundation for a company's base pay policy—job design and description (Part 1), job evaluation (Part 2), and surveys of competitive pay practices (Part 3). Part 4 discusses ways in which this information is applied, in the light of company goals and philosophy, to develop a base pay structure or policy. Next we turn to performance appraisal (Part 5), which provides the means for turning policy into practice. Performance appraisal also, because it is closely related to manpower development, represents the primary link between the compensation program and the broader management system. Noncash benefits (Part 6) and incentives (Part 7) complete the total compensation package. Part 8 discusses out-of-the-ordinary compensation problems; and Part 9 deals with the day-to-day concerns of compensation program administration.

To get the best thinking on this entire process, we have brought together a group of authors who are experts in wage and salary administration. These professionals represent a number of the major corporations and financial institutions of the United States as well as influential universities, trade associations, and the government. Despite their varying backgrounds and environments, they share the objectives common to wage and salary administration: that the system of pay be equitable, sufficient to attract and retain the talents and capabilities a company needs, and motivating to employees.

The concept of equity is multidimensional. Our feeling is that, in most cases, equity is best established and maintained by calculating pay according to job content—that is, according to the job's functions and ac-countabilities and its relative importance to the organization. The job content approach is based on the idea that the job's importance and impact are inherent in its content, and, therefore, the job can be evaluated in terms of content.

We also recognize, however, that for some jobs the job content approach by itself is not sufficient. Although the experience and education required to fill the job can be specified, the job's potential contribution and value to the organization are harder to define. For example, one research chemist may do a perfectly acceptable job for years, while the man in the next lab may discover Nylon. Their relative value to the organization is inherent not in the content of the job but is in their performance, which cannot be predicted very precisely because the range of possibilities is so wide. Hence, pay for these jobs cannot be based solely on job content. Chapter 40 discusses one means of handling jobs of this nature.

In addition, many professionals see a trend toward broader definitions of jobs. They believe people will have roles, rather than jobs, in an integrated process aimed at specific end results. These roles will change continuously as goals are achieved and individuals move on to new projects; and pay will be related to performance and contribution in these varying roles. This concept is dealt with in Chapters 11 and 25.

Recognizing the diverse needs a total compensation program must satisfy, we have designed the Handbook to provide a conceptual and practical basis for dealing with compensation issues related to all kinds of jobs in all kinds of situations. Also, we feel that the material in the Handbook is applicable in all economic situations. It is our firm belief, after years of experience in this field, that a wage and salary program that is inherently sound and flexible will provide a strong foundation from which management can respond to the difficulties of an economic downturn, inflation, price and wage controls, etc. As a matter of fact, even in good times, a company cannot administer compensation effectively without a formal, flexible, and fair program.

Looking at the future, we recognize that American society is changing rapidly and that industry, commerce, and government structures must at least accommodate themselves to these changes, if not lead them. Many younger workers view companies and jobs in the broad context of society's needs. Moreover, having grown up in relative affluence, they tend to be less concerned with money and security than their elders and more concerned with self-expression. It appears to us that this pattern is widespread and not, as some would have it, confined to disaffected and politically radical young people. Among those who enter business, the trend will manifest itself in their desire to make an immediate and visible contribution to any endeavor in which they are engaged.

Thoughtful managers have always known that involving people in something—giving them the sense that they are making a real impact—is the key to motivating them. The difference now is that people are less willing to serve long apprenticeships before they can make their presence felt. Hence, jobs will have to be redesigned to allow incumbents more autonomy in choosing how they carry out their responsibilities, and new relationships will have to be established among jobs within an organization so that employees have an opportunity to influence results on a broader plane. In addition, a career path development factor will be built into more jobs: few will stand alone, unrelated to any other jobs. Instead, a job's design will recognize preconceived extensions or relationships both with surrounding jobs and with jobs that may logically lie ahead of each employee. Second, more and more professionals will come to recognize compensation as a total, integrated system rather than a bundle of discrete elements. It is no longer news that noncash compensation is growing in importance and in proportion to total payroll expense (for the company) and total income (for the employee). The reasons for this are well documented and include inflation, tax laws, union activities, and a number of changes in the thinking of the general public about how it wants to be paid. One aspect of this trend will be the growing emphasis on the cafeteria style in executive compensation, in which the individual is given a choice among various forms of payment. An outgrowth of the cafeteria style will be a real need for expert financial counseling for executives to assist them in selecting the compensation alternatives best suited to their unique needs (Chapter 46).

Third, wage and salary administration will be woven even more tightly into the general management process. This means more stress on performance standards, performance measurement, and accountability management and a drive for greater efficiency through interrelating functions and accountabilities. Organizations will devote greater effort to appraising the potential of employees in the light of future organizational needs, and they will follow up by developing employees on a career basis to fill those needs. Furthermore, there will be a heightened awareness of the subtle implications of management style coupled with a more sophisticated use of internal communications to foster employee understanding of and commitment to the corporation's philosophy and goals.

Fourth, wage earners are going to demand that the modern techniques developed for salary administration be applied in determining their pay structures. Wage inequities resulting from poor evaluation techniques or procedures will have to be corrected. Wage earners and unions will place greater emphasis on the total compensation package, as have their salaried counterparts. We find more interest in individual and group incentives. The benefits package will expand and take in many new areas. Pressure will continue for weekly or monthly guaranteed wages.

Finally, when all is said and done, base salary or wages in the form of cash will continue to be the core of the compensation package. We've already conceded that cash equivalents—pensions, health and life insurance, disability income, etc.—will grow in importance and that higher-paid executives will pay increasing attention to incentive plans and tax-minimizing measures. But cash will continue to be the largest single compensation element, as well as the element that sets the tone for the entire package. It is not likely that this will change during the time that people refer to this Handbook.

This Handbook represents the contributions of many people. To avail ourselves of the best thinking in the field, we brought together an Editorial Advisory Board of distinguished authorities on compensation. Board members provided valuable ideas in planning the Handbook and also in selecting knowledgeable, experienced authors for each chapter. To the Editorial Advisory Board for their advice and to the authors for their willingness to share their knowledge and ideas with others, I express my sincere thanks.

I am also grateful for the professional contribution of the Coordinating Editor, Virginia S. Albrecht, who handled the editorial aspects of the Handbook. And to Betty McHugh, my deep appreciation for valuable administrative assistance and support. Thanks also to Frances Markmann for her competent handling of the proofreading.

To all who participated goes my deep appreciation. Without their help this book would not have been possible.

MILTON L. ROCK
Editor-in-Chief

Contents

Part 3   Surveys

Part 4   The Pay Structure

Part 5   Performance Appraisal

Part 6   Noncash Compensation

Part 7   Incentives

Part 1

Job Content

chapter 1

Designing Jobs

JAMES H. DAVIS   *Manager, Organization and Compensation, Aluminum Company of America, Pittsburgh, Pennsylvania*

RICHARD C. GERKEN, JR.   *Staff Organization Analyst, Aluminum Company of America, Pittsburgh, Pennsylvania*

WHY JOB DESIGN?

To ask why the manager should concern himself with job design is really to ask whether he should concern himself with how things get done in his organization and who does them.   In any organization, be it the neighborhood hardware store or an international corporation, jobs must be designed in some manner or other, with or without the attention of the manager.   In other words, job content will be fixed by some means.   The process may be elementary, for example, hiring another salesman; or it may be extremely complex, involving a wide range of organization restructuring and performance implications.   A job's design may evolve from the myriad influences in and on the organization.   Or conversely, it may be the product of caprice or expediency and therefore relatively insensitive to circumstances with which it should be reconciled.

So the question really is not whether jobs will be designed or not.   If jobs exist, they will be designed in some way—even if the design process appears to be more of a "happening" than anything else.   The question to be decided, then, is the extent to which the manager should involve himself in this inevitable process.   To what extent and how should he endorse, influence, and direct the process?

Few would quarrel with the manager's responsibility to make the best and most productive use of all his resources, including materials, intangibles, and workers.   In many industries, the people portion of the manager's resources represents the major cost area.   In most industries, it is at least a very significant cost area. Thus, if the manager is to fulfill his total responsibility, he must be interested in any management technique that promises better utilization of his people resources and contributes to making each job as productive and meaningful as possible. An active, conscious effort to analyze and design jobs is just such a technique.

DESIGN OR DESCRIBE?

Webster defines the word *design* in these terms: "To contrive, to project with an end in view, to decide upon and outline the main feature of; to plan." That's quite a different thing from *describe,* which is defined: "To tell or write about, to picture in words." The main difference is the element of planning that is integral to the design process. Planning is generally accepted as a *sine qua non* of the management process. By the same token, it is the very essence of job design.

Active designing must be an analytical and creative process. For example, the decision to hire an additional salesman hardly taxes the analytical skills of the manager. It does, nevertheless, represent the result of a decision-making process that gave at least fleeting attention to such questions as whether another salesman is really needed, where he will be assigned, what he will be selling, and whether his job is to be similar in all respects to the jobs of other salesmen already on the payroll. To that extent, some designing took place, but not necessarily the kind that truly warrants the label of a specific management technique. If managers are to use job design as a significant tool for utilizing human resources, a seat-of-the-pants approach will not suffice. By comparison, most managers deal with questions of major capital expenditures in the most probing and analytical manner. These are questions of the allocation of money resources. The alternatives can be quantified. Further, the validity of the choice is frequently measurable within a specific time period.

Likewise, a prudent manager will allocate and control the organization's people resources in the same probing and analytical manner, although, unlike the capital expenditure, people often elude precise quantification. This is particularly true when it comes to those whom Peter Drucker calls the "knowledge workers." They simply cannot be assigned to work or their duties defined in the same way as assembly line workers. In short, people are complex resources, difficult to deal with, and, what's more, their complexity is ever changing—often in unpredictable ways.

Many good managers possess a charisma or leadership style that truly inspires people to unusual achievement. But they know that inspiration will not, of itself, consistently produce results—especially over the long pull of managing a successful enterprise. Planning is required. If workers are inspired or well motivated, the manager has accomplished a great deal. But it will go for naught if the workers lack a sense of individual direction and an appreciation of their individual role in the larger scheme of things. They will find it difficult to succeed if they do not know what constitutes success. And the manager will find himself spending a great deal of time on short-range direction of their efforts.

Thus, good job design should be looked upon as a critical ingredient of the management process at all levels of the organization. It can preclude the need for constant or excessive supervision and free the supervisor to pursue broader, longer-range accountabilities. The justification for management time and effort spent in designing jobs, therefore, is not different from the justification for any other kind of planning. The fact that job design deals with the complexities of human behavior simply places it in a distinct category of planning and one requiring specialized techniques.

PERSPECTIVE ON JOB DESIGN

Job design has existed as long as man. Even the lone hunter set himself a task and then, on the basis of his experience, modified the way he performed it each time. And, to those to whom the word *job* connotes a specific task-oriented relationship between two or more people, the history of job design is every bit as ancient.

The basic circumstance of some men performing tasks in response to the direction of other men has never really changed. What is continually changing is the nature of the tasks, the manner in which they are performed, and the relationship between subordinate and superior. This is not to say that these changes have occurred to the same degree and in the same manner in all facets of our society. For example, military organizations still insist on rigid obedience within a fixed hierarchy of command. But goals and objectives have changed markedly, as have the kinds of duty assignments made to military personnel.

It was the industrial revolution that engendered the sort of division of labor we think of today as designed jobs. For years prior to the industrial revolution, work activity was specialized to a degree. The farmer, the craftsman, and the merchant all went about their affairs in their own ways. But it was the marriage of technology and money in mid-eighteenth-century England that brought numbers of workers together under one roof.

The factory—the place where a single source of mechanical energy could be put to use—was not simply a collection of craftsmen. It became, especially between 1760 and 1790, a production system requiring coordination of specialized work by both men and machines.

The industrial revolution produced a dramatic change in man's view of work. The interdependence of their labors increased sharply when men became factory employees instead of independent producers. The machine emerged as the center of attention. No longer was it a curiosity of the inventor—it was an immensely productive and profitable device. And, by its nature, the machine required a highly specialized but repetitive function from each of its parts. So it was with the worker who tended the machine. It is not surprising that job design in this context was almost as mechanistic in approach as machine design.

The cost of labor may have been modest in the beginnings of the industrial revolution, but it increased steadily over the years and commanded more and more of management's attention. World War I, with its attendant inflation and worker shortage, forced industrial management to look in earnest for better ways to manage the cost of labor. Thus, the work of Frederick Taylor and others became quite pertinent. In their work was the beginning of industrial engineering concepts, especially time and motion study, standardization of tasks, and highly structured jobs. Scientific management was the byword, promising a truly analytical approach to the human element in the productive process.

The adoption of scientific management filled a real need, and today's industrial engineering discipline owes a great deal to the concept. Half a century later, however, the original approach appears to many observers to be too mechanistic and too prone to ignore worker psychological factors not directly related to such basic elements as heat, light, and fatigue. So, while scientific management was far more sophisticated than the techniques used by eighteenth-century England's factory bosses, the resulting job design tended toward the mechanistic specialization of tasks.

TODAY'S JOB DESIGN ENVIRONMENT

Today, a growing number of behavioral scientists, management consultants, and commentators find the mechanistic or overspecialized approach to job design at cross purposes with the goals of the organization. Much has been written about the effect of impersonal and standardized work situations on the worker's attitude and, in turn, the effect of the worker's atttitude on productivity. In fact, the whole broad area of worker motivation and how it is influenced by job and organization design and leadership style has received considerable attention from such authors as Chris Argyris, Rensis Likert, Frederick Herzberg, and Douglas McGregor.

Concepts of job design which feature job enlargement and increased latitude for the employee are presented as desirable alternatives to the traditional approach of maximum specialization. This is not to say that the ultimate goal is a jack-of-all-trades assignment for everyone. Good, solid expertise in specialized fields is more in demand today than ever before. But jobs which are designed to utilize expertise need not necessarily restrict their incumbents to the practice of that expertise alone. Moreover, the rate of technological change and the evolutionary growth of most organizations can make the specialist obsolete with little warning. So today's manager is cautioned to seek out an approach to job design that broadens the worker's horizon rather than limits it.

There is another reason, in addition to productivity, for designing jobs so that they satisfy the worker as well as utilize him. It is a simple reason: the worker wants it that way and he has learned how to get what he wants.

Perhaps it would be more accurate to speak of society's wants instead of just the worker's. Certainly, the events of the past few years have demonstrated that industry can no longer confine itself to the profit motive. Protests, both active and passive, by important segments of the citizenry are quite explicit about their concern for broad quality-of-life issues. Their message carries authority, and industry is well aware of this. So, regardless of what any individual manager may feel about the importance of job meaningfulness to the individual versus the enterprise, he has little choice but to listen and respond. The plain fact is that today's corporate recruiters frequently encounter a disenchantment with business among the very people industry needs for its own sustenance.

THE DESIGN PROCESS

The actual process of designing jobs is not necessarily a fixed sequence. There are, however, two basic activities that must take place. The first is identifying the need to either design a new job or redesign an old one. Once it has been established that the need is real, the second activity must be undertaken: job content must be developed.

Identifying the Need to Design a New Job. When a new activity or function is introduced into some part of the organization, the manager must make a judgment as to whether or not conditions suggest that a new or revised job should be designed. This is the point where job analysis can be most valuable, so, in making this decision, the manager can consider some of the questions discussed below.

Is the need current and valid?   Normally, there is a sense of permanency in the business of establishing and filling new jobs—at least, the incumbent tends to view it that way.   A new job assignment, and especially a promotion, is usually not undone painlessly.   Without being an obstructionist, the manager can be a stabilizing influence and insist that the proposal for a new job in fact represents a valid need.

Are the job specifications realistic?   One excellent technique to determine whether a valid need exists is to state the job's duties or objectives *in writing.* Better yet, have the supervisor who is requesting the new job write the statement.   This need not be a complete description; an informal list of duties will suffice.   If the proposed job function is only a hazy idea, the supervisor will have considerable difficulty setting down that list of duties.   Experience has demonstrated that a job that cannot be described usually cannot be performed. The very least this technique contributes to the process of job design is to force the concerned parties to be analytical rather than expedient, thus avoiding costly errors.

What about permanency?   Thus far, job design has been discussed in terms of relatively permanent functions in the organization.   However, there are many occasions, such as during peak work loads or vacation periods or when specialized technical help is required, when a critical but *temporary* function needs to be performed.

Several avenues are open to the manager in filling temporary needs.   Temporary personnel may be hired from an agency specializing in this field or the function may be contracted to another firm.   Also, the function may be assigned temporarily to an existing employee within the organization.   The project-oriented task force often used in larger organizations is a good example of this alternative.   Existing employees are assigned full- or part-time to a specific critical but temporary project.   One advantage of this method is that, as permanent employees, task force members are particularly well motivated to accomplish the objective—a motivation that might be lacking in an outside group.

The important point is that temporary jobs be identified as such and not treated as new permanent assignments.   To do otherwise is to create conditions that become untenable.

Where should the job be placed?   The tendency toward empire building can be quite innocent, especially in a large organization.   When a department head believes he needs an accountant or engineer, he may really mean he wants his own accountant or engineer.   The proposed job may pass with flying colors the test of having its duties set out in writing.   There may be no question of the need for the function to be performed.   The real question may be— where?

Here again, the manager's duty is to take the overall organizational viewpoint.   He may be in the best position to know that an accountant or an engineer performing an identical function but with a meager work load already exists in another part of the organization.   The possibilities for shopping within the organization for help should not be overlooked.

If it's only work load. . . .   When the need for a new job is based on work load alone, and the increased work load has all the appearances of permanency, the solution seems evident: hire another for whatever job is in short supply of help!   It may not be quite that simple.   And, equally important, circumstances may present an opportunity for some organizational creativity.

For example, a growth situation requiring frequent hiring and assigning of more of the same kinds of jobs will eventually reach the point where all of the "sames" can no longer be properly supervised by the existing boss. At this point (or in anticipation of this point) the organizational structure should be examined for job design possibilities such as the creation of "working supervisors." An alert management will seek such opportunities for organizational structure change and job design in a growth situation not only to maintain a smoothly functioning organization but also to provide sound promotional routes.

The Incumbent's Judgment. Designers of jobs should keep in mind that their designs inevitably are judged by an astute critic—the incumbent in the job. The ultimate test of a job's viability is whether it can be performed by a qualified incumbent. He will know whether it passes the test soon after being assigned to it, and his judgment should be considered a significant contribution to the design process. If job design problems are not corrected as they are discovered, their cost to the organization, both monetary and intangible, could become substantial. Avoidance of this damage is the real reward for thoughtful attention to good job design.

Developing Job Content. The second basic activity in job design is developing job content. Once the need for a new job has been identified, the manager can address himself specifically to its content. Consideration of the checkpoints and guidelines discussed below may be helpful to him.

Sources of Design Information. One important source of design information is the person who wants the job designed. This is often the person who will supervise the work to be performed. A skillful interviewer will be alert to the particular strengths and weaknesses of information provided by the job's creator. That person may be able to express the job specifications without precisely identifying how the job contributes to the organization's objectives. Or, in contrast, he may have the need for the job clearly in mind and not be able to express the job's specifications.

Industry sources, salary surveys, reference material, and articles about the performance of certain functions provide excellent guidelines for the design of jobs that fit into certain recognized patterns. Jobs of similar content within the organization are another source of design information. The job candidate may provide a particular insight into the design of a job that is not available from any other source. Involving the proposed incumbent in the construction of job content is, in itself, important not only to achieve the objectives of the organization, but to assure a strong commitment by the incumbent.

Compatibility. Compare the goal of the job to be designed and the goal of the organization. It is easy to concentrate so completely on design information that a job could be designed which is not compatible with the goals of the parent organization. The manager should satisfy himself that the position being designed will meet the test of compatibility.

Realistic Objectives. The objectives of the designed job must be attainable and realistic. The manager should avoid the frustration that comes from proposing objectives which simply cannot be achieved. For example, to require a safety director to achieve a zero injury goal would provide him with a virtually impossible task in most industrial and commercial situations. Job design provides the opportunity to identify realistic objectives.

Can the job be filled or refilled? In some cases, the first incumbent is on hand when the job is being designed. Even in these circumstances the question of whether the job can be filled should be answered if there is a likelihood of turnover in the job. Generally, jobs should be built with a sensitivity to the traditional disciplines in the industry or business where the job is found. The requirement for bizarre or unusual combinations of skills or duties should be avoided if the job must be refilled routinely.

Combinations of several disciplines or skills reduce dramatically the candidates for a job. For example, if typing is the principal skill required, the job might be filled by a large number of applicants; if typing and shorthand both are required, the number shrinks significantly; and if typing, shorthand, and the ability to read a particular foreign language are all requirements, the number of available candidates would be limited.

Legal Implications. Certain positions are identified by their titles or organizational placements with certain legal responsibilities. For example, the general duties of the secretary and the controller of a corporation are often included in the bylaws. It is important that job design not usurp or compromise the legal responsibilities vested in those jobs.

Contractual Agreements. Job content can be the subject of union agreement. In certain industries jobs are designed, and their content approved, by both management and the bargaining union. In this situation, it is important to distinguish between the type of work covered under the bargaining agreement and that which is excluded from it. With this precaution, jobs will be designed so that they do not cross the line between bargained and nonbargained work, thereby forestalling the possibilities of union grievance or incorporation into the bargaining unit of work that had previously been excluded.

Judgment. The range of discretion, judgment, or original thinking to be exercised in a job should be clearly understood by the designer of the job. It is essential that these elements of job content be compatible with and supported by the job's required level of know-how or experience.

Management Style. Consider the management style prevalent in the hierarchy over the job. For example, if the style is typically participative, a job designed to be most effective in an autocratic environment might be literally unperformable.

Clarity. Avoid stereotypes and clichés. Confine the description to meaningful words and rigorously exclude excessive language which tends to describe the general environment but does not clarify the situation in which the job is performed.

The Job and the Incumbent. It is appropriate, in certain circumstances, to design the job around the incumbent. This is a useful technique to make the best use of some specialized expertise or available talent. The job may be built around a particular person whom the supervisor hopes to attract to the job, and the design may take in some of that person's particular interests as an incentive to make the job look interesting.

Designing a job around the incumbent is a most effective device for solving certain personnel problems such as those resulting from health or performance deficiencies. It provides an opportunity to assure that each incumbent can fill his job with dignity and that the position is not a burden but rather an asset to the rest of the organization.

Some jobs are designed specifically to develop or train the incumbent. This specification is most appropriate when the time available for training is limited and the job must establish a particular training environment. Most managers agree, however, that given enough time, the best design is one that includes definite accountabilities beyond "being trained."

Prototypes. The prototype is a generalized description that is useful for positions held by large numbers of people, usually performing rather similar tasks. A prototype often selects gradient language to describe a series of levels in a hierarchy of skills. Words like *simple, routine, difficult,* and *complex* appear in prototypes to create the band of job levels that cover a range of skills or other characteristics that are difficult to describe precisely.

Prototypes are valuable to describe points along a continuum, and generally they simplify the administrative process that attends job descriptions, job evaluation, and salary administration. They are, however, subject to abuse. There is a tendency for employees to become misclassified in prototypes either because supervisors, not recognizing the speed at which subordinates attain proficiency, fail to upgrade them promptly, or because supervisors are reluctant to discuss a subordinate's limitations frankly with him and therefore they advance him to a position along the continuum beyond his performance or ability.

Titles. Titles are often regarded as the frosting on the cake of job substance, but it is sometimes difficult to recognize the cake without the frosting. The title given to a position represents one more opportunity for an organization to display its management style. If it prefers vague or imprecise job descriptions, it would probably prefer imprecise titles. In an organization where the descriptions of jobs tend to be very precise, the titles are usually more descriptive. In addition, the title's status implications, both inside and outside the organization, must be considered.

MAINTENANCE AND REDESIGN

In most organizations the elements that affect job design are subject to change. For example, a company's business objectives, its organization structure, the level of technology, and the general economy all change and bring different emphases to the design of jobs. Accordingly, jobs must be reviewed constantly and changed if they are to be kept current.

Redesign is usually initiated in the same way as new design; that is, the need is identified and the job content is established. Redesign can be initiated by reviewing the evaluations or the descriptions of jobs that are in place. Sometimes it is a chain reaction: the impact from the design or redesign of related or similar jobs triggers an examination of other jobs. The guidelines for redesign and the elements of concern are the same as those for original job design.

As with most activities that merit the manager's attention, maintaining a current job design program requires constant effort. The program's usefulness rests not only on the technique employed at its inception, but equally on its being kept up to date. With a sound introduction and a conscientious maintenance effort, the job design program can be one of the manager's indispensable tools.

BIBLIOGRAPHY

Argyris, Chris: *Personality and Organization*, Harper & Row, Publishers, Incorporated, New York, 1957.

Dale, Ernest: *Planning and Developing the Company Organization Structure*, American Management Association, Inc., New York, 1952. (Contributions by F. W. Taylor.)

Likert, Rensis: *New Patterns of Management*, McGraw-Hill Book Company, New York, 1961.

McGregor, Douglas: *The Human Side of Enterprise*, McGraw-Hill Book Company, New York, 1960.

Odiorne, George S.: *Management by Objectives*, Pitman Publishing Corporation, New York, 1965. (Contributions by Rensis Likert and Douglas McGregor.)

Sutermeister, Robert A.: *People and Productivity*, 2d ed., McGraw-Hill Book Company, New York, 1963. (Contributions by Chris Argyris, Frederick Herzberg, Douglas McGregor, and Rensis Likert.)

chapter 2

Describing Hourly Jobs

ALFRED R. BRANDT   *Senior Wage Practices Specialist, Western Electric Company, Inc., New York, New York*

USES OF HOURLY JOB DESCRIPTIONS

No single instrument is as important to effective wage and salary administration as the job description.   Yet there is evidence that it receives far less attention than it requires to assure either that it is properly prepared in the first place or that its uses are properly understood or directed.

To begin with, there is considerable confusion as to what a job description really is.   In literature relevant to management practices, a variety of terms are used for this particular instrument—"job analysis," "job specification," "job evaluation sheet," etc.   To provide a firm foundation for this discussion some definitions would seem to be in order.   L. B. Michael defines a job as "a recognized, normal, recurring set of duties and responsibilities, assigned to a particular employee or to a number of employees as their part in the whole work or service function."[1]   A job description, then, is simply a narrative statement or listing of these duties and responsibilities (sometimes referred to as *functions*). In actual practice, the job description format generally includes for identification purposes a job title and, usually, some sort of code number.   Depending on its use, this may be the limit of information involved, or the description may be incorporated into a more comprehensive document called a "job specification" (or "job grade specification").   Typically included in job specifications is information about tools, equipment, products or processes involved, amount·of supervision provided, responsibility for directing efforts of other employees, job conditions, and occasionally such items as the identity of the organization and job supervisor and the number of employees covered by the specification.

[1] L. B. Michael, *Wage and Salary Fundamentals and Procedures*, McGraw-Hill Book Company, New York, 1950, p. 52.

If used in connection with job evaluation, the specification may include, either on the same or a separate page, evaluation-supporting information under the heading of "substantiating data sheet" or "job evaluation sheet."

The job description, when properly developed to meet specific needs, has vast potential for a wide variety of administrative applications.

1. *Training:* as a guide to new job incumbents and job supervisors in explaining functions, sequence of actions, and nature of overall work load, and in planning training programs.

2. *Hiring:* as a guide in assessing qualifications of applicants and explaining jobs to them.

3. *Placement (Promotion, Demotion, or Lateral Transfer):* for matching qualifications of individuals to specific jobs, planning of force adjustments, development of employee movement systems, and posting of job openings (usually in compliance with the union contract).

4. *Test Development:* for information about job content and requirements in devising tests of aptitude and proficiency.

5. *Personnel Statistics:* for various management planning and control purposes and manpower usage reports to the government.

6. *Engineering Planning:* in preparing job layouts, specifying labor requirements, automating operations, improving methods, and making wage incentive applications.

7. *Health and Safety:* in identification of hazardous operations and development of protective equipment and preventive measures.

8. *Labor Relations:* in resolving questions of job overlap, pay treatment, and proper recognition of responsibilities.

9. *Man Rating:* for performance appraisals and establishment of performance standards and objectives.

10. *Organization Planning:* for alignment of functions, determination of manpower requirements, proper utilization of skills, job enrichment, and development of manning tables or tables of organization.

11. *Accounting Effort:* in establishing expense ratios, cost estimating, and budget control.

12. *Miscellaneous Personnel Concerns:* for employee morale (explanation of job changes), equal employment opportunity planning and control, and counseling.

While extensive, this list is not all-inclusive. However, a survey conducted by the author in January, 1969, of over 70 nationally known companies showed that, aside from hiring and placement, over 40 percent of these organizations made little use of job descriptions for other than wage administration. A possible explanation of this may lie in two factors (1) the language and format of most job descriptions tend to be tailored to wage administration needs, thus limiting their value for other applications, and (2) a general failure to instruct and encourage supervisors and management specialists in the use of this tool.

The latter problem can be solved by education and a conviction by upper management as to the value of this tool. Altering language and format, however, will be accomplished only when companies choose to take a broader systems approach to job analysis and conduct much more comprehensive studies to answer a wide variety of questions about work.

The job description's role in the wage determination process varies from company to company. In companies which do not have a formal job evaluation program, the description is most commonly used to rank jobs internally, as a basis for comparison in an industry or area wage survey, or as the basis for bargaining job rates with the union. Usually such descriptions are rather brief and general. Sometimes they are little more than a title definition as found in the *Dictionary of Occupational Titles* prepared by the United States Employment Service.

In more sophisticated applications, the job description usually becomes a part of the job grade specification. These descriptions tend to be more comprehensive, more delineative of differences in jobs, and supportive of evaluation statements. In some cases, the description is the basis or backbone of the evaluation. In others, both the evaluation and the description are developed from more detailed information contained in a job analysis booklet or a job study folder. Since job descriptions of this type are used more extensively for comparisons in the job evaluation procedure and for job administration by line supervisors, it is essential that they be prepared by individuals who are properly selected and trained for this activity.

SELECTING AND TRAINING JOB ANALYSTS

Since very few companies employ persons for the sole purpose of writing descriptions, the observations that follow apply to the occupation most commonly identified as *job analyst* (also variously known as "job evaluation engineer," "job grader," "wage practices specialist," "compensation specialist," etc.). The importance of this position is indicated by the findings of the 77-company survey mentioned earlier. In over 40 percent of the companies surveyed, job descriptions are written by the job supervisor individually or in cooperation with some specialist trained for this work; almost all the other respondents rely on a job analyst. Also, in almost all instances the job analyst function is performed as part of a more comprehensive responsibility as reflected in the more descriptive titles mentioned above. This is important when one considers the qualifications and training required for these jobs.

Criteria for Selecting Job Analysts. Major factors to be considered in choosing people to act as analysts are formal education, previous work experience, and personal qualifications. Specific requirements in these areas are discussed in the following paragraphs.

Education and Experience. Ideally, analysts should have a degree either in industrial engineering or in business administration with an industrial management major. Either discipline would provide the desired background in industrial measurement and control theories and techniques. This should be supplemented by a broad exposure to varied kinds of work. A person who lacks a degree might be acceptable if he has the equivalent of two years of college credit and a significant breadth of work experience.

This combination of formal education and work experience will give the analyst an appreciation of how jobs are designed and how work is organized—for example, that some work by its very nature is repetitive or sporadic, short- or long-cycle, etc. It will enable him to understand the terminology of the field of work—both legitimate technical terms and the accepted language of the shop (so-called "trade jargon"). It will also enable him to comprehend the significance and *relative* importance of facts picked up in the job study.

In addition, this background is important in fulfilling the analyst's major responsibilities:

1. Planning the job study or investigation, conducting interviews and any preliminary or corroborative research, observing operations, and obtaining supportive information and exhibit material.

2. Evaluating the job on the basis of the evaluation plan and comparisons with what one knows about other jobs and other kinds of work.

3. Writing the description to assure that functions are given their proper emphasis.

4. Where applicable, assisting or advising in the design of jobs and alignment or assignment of functions and responsibilities.

Personal Qualifications.   Personal qualifications are of vital importance, since analyst jobs involve extensive contacts with all types of people, at all levels in the company, and in a wide variety of circumstances and situations.   Most job information is gleaned through observation and interview, so that the analyst must possess tact, empathy, and a liking for people in order to frame questions that will not irritate or arouse unwarranted suspicions.   At the same time, he must be dispassionate so that emotions do not interfere with his objectivity. He must be able to instill in supervisors, employees, and union representatives confidence in his ability to be objective, fair, and thorough and to comprehend the significance of information he obtains in his job study.

Writing Ability.   Analysts should be able to prepare a narrative statement of job functions that is clear, concise, and free from redundancy.   Furthermore, because the description is used to compare a particular job with others, writers should be able to use modifiers and delineative phrases that will facilitate such comparisons.   Style is not a consideration, since description preparation by design tends to follow a stereotyped form.

Training Job Analysts.   Methods of training analysts will vary considerably according to specific job requirements and the emphasis that a company gives to this effort. Indoctrination in the mechanics of job analysis, evaluation, and description writing generally begins by having the new analyst study the company's evaluation plan and the procedures of its application.   Familiarization with the plan and how it has been used on some selected jobs ordinarily requires a relatively short interval.   If a union is involved, this study period should include familiarization with the applicable portions of the union contract.   Finally—and the importance of this cannot be overstated—the analyst should be thoroughly instructed in company policies and organizational structure.   It is essential for him to know what departments make what products or perform what services.   He must also know the company philosophy on job enrichment versus job simplification, at what level and by what procedure functional conflicts are resolved, and how to handle problems which may arise —for example, finding that a supervisor's design of a particular job is not in the best interests of the company.   This understanding of the company is a vital ingredient in the broad systems approach to job analysis that was mentioned earlier.

After the trainee has familiarized himself with the company and the evaluation plan, he is teamed with an experienced analyst for the second phase of training.   This phase usually involves:

1. Accompanying the experienced analyst as he makes a job study.   In this phase, the experienced man explains his actions during the interview and observation of the job and provides an analysis of the resulting evaluation and job description.

2. A joint study effort in which the experienced analyst conducts the interview and the trainee takes his own notes, records his own observations, and prepares an evaluation and job description independently, all of which is followed by a comparison with the findings and conclusions of the experienced analyst and discussion of results.

3. A job study performed by the trainee with the experienced man observing, analyzing, and commenting on the results.

Any of these steps should be repeated as often as necessitated by the progress of the new analyst.

After the new analyst is judged capable of performing on his own, his efforts should be reviewed closely for six to twelve months, primarily for assuring consistency of his treatment of his findings with existing job grade descriptions and evaluations. It is this period which is the most significant of his training.

Since the application of his knowledge to the description and evaluation of jobs takes place in a comparative context, the mastery of the required skills can be achieved only through exposure to a wide variety of jobs. It is obvious that, except under most unusual circumstances, this learning process will take considerable time.

KINDS OF JOB DESCRIPTIONS

Job descriptions in current use vary widely, ranging from very brief (no more than an occupational title definition) to extremely lengthy and detailed with much supplementary information. The 77-company survey found that there is little or no apparent correlation between the character of the description and its intended usage or the size or type of company involved. In fact, it was found in several companies that differences prevail between plants or divisions in both the type and the use of descriptions.

Length or detail in descriptions depends on the type of job involved. Jobs involving functions, tasks, or operations which are familiar to everybody concerned and/or which do not entail any significant variation or range of difficulty can be described briefly with a minimum of embellishment. Where some of the same terminology might be used for a lot of different job situations, so that a condition of ambiguity could evolve, or where there is a definite range of difficulty, then more descriptive or delineative language will be required to bring out the distinctive features of the job for evaluation or comparison purposes.

Aside from differences in length and amount of detail, job descriptions may be classified generally as specific or individual, standard or general. As the name implies, the *specific or individual description* is a statement of *all* the duties and responsibilities assigned to one or more individuals in the job. The specific description is usually rather detailed and comprehensive, providing good support for evaluation and serving as a useful document in comparing the relative requirements of jobs. On the other hand, because of its exactness, this type of description demands a thorough job study, considerable care in preparation, and active prosecution of effort in maintaining the description. Consequently, while this is probably the soundest type of job description to use, it is also likely to be the most costly. Figures 1, 2, and 3 are examples of good specific descriptions for low-, intermediate-, and higher-level jobs.

Standard and *general* descriptions are similar in that they both apply to varying job situations and are designed to permit more flexibility in application and to be less sensitive to changes in duties and responsibilities. The *standard description* is usually a rather brief, very broadly written listing of functions. It is designed to cover multiple applications of essentially the same functional combinations which would evaluate at the same level. When properly written, it should be based on a fairly thorough study of several job situations. All too often such studies are omitted. Problems are then compounded by making only a superficial analysis of the tours of functions to which it is subsequently applied.

Most commonly, the standard description omits references to specific product codes, model numbers of equipment, details about procedures, or modifying words or phrases which pin down difficulty or complexity. It is the easiest, quickest, and least costly description to apply, gives the supervisor the greatest

Figure 1.   Specific description for a low-level job.

JOB GRADE SPECIFICATION
(SHOP-TYPE JOB)

JOB TITLE: Assembler

JOB FUNCTION: Assemble spacers and select bars to crossbar switches. Work is performed from detailed directions and part is positioned in positive locating fixture.

JOB DUTIES AND PROCEDURES: Obtain switch from hold or staging area and place switch on bench with contact side down. Assemble and set spacers using proper hand tool. Place switch in holding fixture, obtain appropriate number of select bars, lubricate with proper oil, and assemble the select bars to the crossbar switch frame.

Remove the switch carrier from the switch and position check fixture on switch. Align bearing blocks, run in pivot screws on both sides of switch, and tighten lock nuts on right side of switch. Remove the checking fixture, replace the switch carrier, and place switch on conveyor.

Detail switches for select bar lubrication, as required.

Perform related material handling, when required.

Notify supervisor or other designated personnel when unusual conditions occur.

Post record of daily output.

TYPICAL PRODUCTS INVOLVED: Crossbar switches, spacers and select bars.

MACHINES AND EQUIPMENT INVOLVED:	Oper- ate	Change Tools	Adjust	Set Up
Switch carriers	Use			
Select bar positioning fixture	Use			
Oil containers	Use			
Holding fixtures	Use			

TOOLS AND GAGES USED: Oil, spin wrench, and other general-purpose hand tools.

SOURCE OF METHODS AUTHORITY: Detailed verbal instructions.

---

amount of administrative latitude, and is least demanding in terms of maintenance effort. At the same time, its use assumes a knowledge in depth by the analyst (not always true) of each application situation, and it provides the weakest support for evaluations, lends itself most readily to misadministration, and is most vulnerable to union challenge.

The *general description* is a compromise between standard and specific descriptions. It covers a basic combination of functions and responsibilities common to several jobs and requires a thorough study of each job involved. It is written broadly enough to allow for some variations in product, equipment, or procedure as long as the evaluation is not affected. Also, the general description might include some functions performed by one or more of the jobs but not necessarily all of them, a fact which imposes constraints on its preparation and use. Because these descriptions are broadly written and allow for different combinations of functions, their language must be properly qualified to forestall the assignment of functions to individuals in a manner contrary to the evaluations.

The general description can be a useful tool, but it is not as good as the specific description for making comparisons. Furthermore, experience has shown that it can generate administration problems and union grievances if not properly written in the first place or if a supervisor chooses to ignore the

Figure 2.   Specific description for an intermediate-level job.

JOB GRADE SPECIFICATION
(SHOP-TYPE JOB)

JOB TITLE: Saw Operator (Power Equipment)

JOB FUNCTION: Set up and operate table saws and special cutting machines to cut panels, piece parts, and details from rod, bar, and sheet stock.

JOB DUTIES AND PROCEDURES: Read and interpret drawings, cutting tickets, layouts, and shop orders to determine requirements such as size of material, equipment to be used, and number of parts and details to be cut.

Lay out and scribe material for proper size and notching so that waste is held to a minimum.

Set up and operate machines to cut and notch metal stock and to cut and bevel asbestos panels.   Involves setting stops, making adjustments to maintain setups, and changing saw blades and cutting and beveling wheels.

Wash off asbestos panels after cutting and clean drainage outlet tank.   Perform hand cutting operations such as sawing cutouts in asbestos panels and removing burrs and rough edges by filing.

Keep records of parts and details cut.   Perform associated handling of material, using hand truck as necessary.

TYPICAL PRODUCTS INVOLVED: Various-size asbestos panels and metal stock used in the manufacture of power equipment.

MACHINES AND EQUIPMENT INVOLVED:	Oper- ate	Change Tools	Adjust	Set Up
Cochrane-Bly Semiautomatic Power Saw	x	x	x	x
Patch Wagner Cutting Machine	x	x	x	x
Oliver Table Saws	x	x	x	x
Hand Trucks	x			
Water Hose	x			
Hand and Electric Hoists	x			

TOOLS AND GAGES USED: Hacksaw, scale, files, square.

SOURCE OF METHODS AUTHORITY: Verbal instructions; simple piece part drawings, cutting tickets, and shop orders.

ACCURACY REQUIREMENTS AND DIFFICULTY OF MEETING THEM: Tolerances of normally $\frac{1}{32}''$ on asbestos panels and $\frac{1}{64}''$ on metal details are not difficult to maintain.

limitations built into the description.   Although the time required to make a job study (per job) for a general description is nearly the same as it is for a specific description, and although description writing time may actually be a little longer, the per-job cost of coverage should be lower, since it will be spread over several jobs.   Finally, it takes more care and skill to prepare a *good* general description than any other kind.   Figure 4 is an example of a good general description for a low-grade-level job.

PREPARATION OF DESCRIPTIONS

Description writers are advised to strive for brevity, since excessive detail makes a description unwieldy. Certainly, a description is unnecessarily cluttered with phrasing such as "it is the duty of ——," "a —— should be able to ——," and "a —— must be thoroughly familiar with ——." Also, a descrip-

Figure 3. Specific description for a higher-level job.

JOB GRADE SPECIFICATION
(Shop-type Job)

JOB TITLE: Machine Setter (Wire-forming and Cutting Machines)

JOB FUNCTION: Set up and operate wire-cutting and forming machines, and collaborate with engineers and supervisors in overcoming operational difficulties to produce a large variety of metal piece parts.

JOB DUTIES AND PROCEDURES: Obtain, read, and understand manufacturing information to determine requirements and procedures involved in setting up and operating wire-cutting and forming machines for producing small, delicate, metal piece parts to close tolerances.

Set up and adjust wire-cutting and forming machines for production of metal piece parts to close tolerances by performing operations such as changing camming surfaces, referring replacement of cams to machine repair organization, mounting and making multiple, accurate, interrelated adjustments to forming tools, mandrels, strippers, feed rate, cutoff position, and wire straightener. Collaborate with product engineers and toolmakers in the setup and prove-in of new and repaired tools and discuss problems concerning their operating characteristics and acceptability. Remove and sharpen cutoff tool as required. Make trial runs and check quality of piece parts with the aid of a microscope, optical comparator, go–no-go gages, vernier calipers, dial indicator gage, micrometer, and scale.

Diagnose and clear job difficulties such as failure of product to meet close tolerances or frequent jamming of machine. Devise mucket arrangements as necessary to clear difficulties. Clean and lubricate machines and equipment as required. Report unusual conditions to supervisor and maintenance organization. Record production and quality obtained and compute and post information on control charts. Receive work orders and schedule work as required to meet demands. Order, obtain, and maintain the necessary supply of wire and ribbon. Instruct machine operators in the setup and operation of the equipment involved.

TYPICAL PRODUCTS, PROCESSES, AND CHARACTERISTICS INVOLVED: Cut and form wire and ribbon piece parts such as base tabs, clips, folded armatures, pole pieces, heater connectors, springs, slugs. *This tour is limited to not more than one employee per shift.*

MACHINES AND EQUIPMENT INVOLVED:	Oper-ate	Change Tools	Adjust	Set Up
"Bundgens" Wire Cutoff Machine, "Nilson" Multi-Slide Press #S2F, "Nilson" 4-Slide Press #0 and #00	x	x	x	x
Stacking Machine	x		x	
Pedestal Grinder	x			

TOOLS AND GAGES USED: Vernier calipers, go–no-go gages, micrometer, dial indicator gage, metal scales, weighcount scales, toolmakers' microscope, optical comparator, and associated gage charts and common-use hand tools.

SOURCE OF METHODS AUTHORITY: Verbal instructions; layouts, piece part drawings.

ACCURACY REQUIREMENTS AND DIFFICULTY OF MEETING THEM: Considerable accuracy required to set up and adjust wire-cutting and forming machines to produce small, delicate, metal piece parts to tolerances of 0.0005".

---

tion should not be regarded as a manufacturing layout specifying "how to" for every task.

On the other hand, the description should contain enough detail to assure its effectiveness as an instrument of wage administration. The aim should be both

Figure 4.   General description for a low-level job.

JOB GRADE SPECIFICATION
(Shop-type Job)

JOB TITLE: Material Handler (General)

JOB FUNCTION: Handle and transport piece parts, assemblies, equipment, tools, and miscellaneous materials and supplies between storerooms, storage areas, work positions, inspection, and other designated areas.   Maintain quantities of supplies on hand and perform associated handling, stacking, sorting, packing, and counting duties.

JOB DUTIES AND PROCEDURES: Refer to tab cards, delivery tickets, packing and stock lists, identification tags, and similar information in order to identify and verify quantities of items required for transport.

Transport various items between storerooms, storage areas, and work positions.   Maintain levels of stock consistent with needs of individual work positions and available storage space.   Increase or decrease quantities provided as instructed by responsible personnel.   Requisition items as required.

Supply individual work positions with necessary parts, materials, supplies, and containers.   Remove completed work from work positions and transport to subsequent work, inspection, or storage areas.   Store items on multiple-tiered racks using hi-lift truck.   Assist operators in loading, unloading, and handling materials and parts.

Perform associated duties, such as sorting and arranging items in storage area; weighing, counting, packing, unpacking, stamping, loading, and unloading parts and materials; cleaning parts in solutions; and removing burrs from parts.   Perform stock selecting and bench and degreasing operations where instructions and demonstrations are provided by designated personnel.   Post records of stock on hand and in process.   Take inventory of items in stockrooms and storage areas on a periodic basis.   Record quantities of items on hand, using a programmed teletype machine and keep punched teletype tape and printout for disposition by others.

Maintain storage areas in a clean and orderly condition.   Dispose of empty cartons, boxes, scrap, and similar items.

MACHINES AND EQUIPMENT INVOLVED:

	Operate
Walkie-type hi-lift fork truck and hand transporter	x
Hydraulic hand-lift truck, tea carts, floor-controlled electric bridge crane, shelf trucks, and similar material-handling equipment, steel strapper and tape dispenser, storage racks, cargotainers, containers, trays, and skids, weight scales	
	Use
Blakeslee degreaser, vacuum cleaner, and teletype machine	x

TOOLS AND GAGES USED: Pliers, screwdriver, wrenches, files, band and wire cutters, tapers, brushes, brooms, and similar items.

SOURCE OF METHODS AUTHORITY: Detailed verbal instructions; identification tags, packing and stock lists, material requisitions, scrap tickets, delivery tickets, tab cards, and similar information.

---

to reflect the intent of the job (the reason for its existence) and to delineate its content in such a way as to support the evelution of the job, facilitate comparisons with other jobs, and minimize the supervisor's job administration problems.   The following sections discuss the description format, arrangement, and style which best help achieve these aims.

Format.   Except for the very brief descriptions, it is common for descriptions to have two parts.   The first, frequently designated the "job function" or "job summary," is a concise summation in one or two sentences of the job's main functions intended to reflect the purpose of the job. The second is a more detailed series of statements about the functions, labeled "major job duties" or "work performed" or something similar. In some formats, this section will include the products, equipment, and sources of instruction as an integral part of the description. In others, separate sections will be set aside for this information.

Arrangement.   Functions are most commonly arranged in one of the following sequences:

1. In order of importance, i.e., the main reasons for the existence of the job regardless of the amount of time involved or the effect on evaluation

2. Chronologically, i.e., the sequence in which the functions are performed

3. For their significance to the evaluation of the job, i.e., highlighting those functions which have greatest impact on main evaluation factors

4. According to the proportion of time spent out of the full tour

Occasionally these sequences may coincide, but when they do not, evaluation significance is the preferred arrangement. However, it is often impossible to determine the significance of a particular function. When this is the case, proportion of time is usually preferred, although order of importance is equally acceptable.

Style.   Comments on style found in various texts generally recommend terse or concise sentences built around action verbs. One company goes a bit farther in its instruction manual by providing word lists wherein those grouped in list 1 are relatively clear as to meaning while those grouped in list 2 are somewhat ambiguous and require supplementary explanation. To facilitate understanding, every effort should be made to quantify the description. Where it is necessary to use words such as *large* or *complex*, the terms should be defined by concrete examples. Writers should avoid negative language and, wherever possible, such terms as *simple* and *minor importance*, which would demean the job in the mind of the incumbent.

EMPLOYEE'S ROLE IN WRITING AND MAINTAINING JOB DESCRIPTIONS

The role of the employee in description writing is almost universally kept to a minimum. Of the 77 companies surveyed in 1969, only four involved the employee in writing the job description, and in all cases it was in collaboration with either the job supervisor or the analyst. This is understandable, since description writing for wage administration application requires skill in using meaningful language and in organizing descriptions for effective comparisons. Attempts have been made to involve the employee through the use of questionnaires and a rather elaborate set of instructions. However, experience has shown that results from the questionnaire approach are generally unsatisfactory. In most instances, the job description is the logical follow-up of a job analysis by a specialist. To bring the analyst into the picture at some later point would either impair the effectiveness of his efforts or result in a wasteful duplication of effort.

Of course, this does not preclude employee involvement in the job study as an interviewee, but in companies with a wage incentive plan, some unions have ruled out even this kind of participation as an interference with the employee's earning process.

In the area of job description maintenance, employee participation is almost always a matter of self-interest. For example, when changes occur in their own jobs or nearby jobs, employees may question either the job supervisor or the union representative about the adequacy of their job description (and grade level).

PROCEDURES FOR APPROVALS OF JOB DESCRIPTIONS

Approval procedures vary according to the kind of responsibility vested in job supervisors and wage administrators, the extent to which a company uses administrative controls, the extent to which job descriptions are used for other purposes, and the terms of union contracts relative to approvals.

Since it is a management responsibility to organize work and design jobs, job incumbents are seldom involved in the approval process. An exception to this may occur where there is an inexperienced supervisor and job study information has been obtained from the employee. In such cases, confirmation is obtained as to accuracy and completeness of the write-up of the job study information, but not in the approval of the job description.

Depending on the authority given the job supervisor, he may have approval over the entire job grade specification or he may be limited to approval of the job description alone or of the job study information (the job analysis write-up). In some cases, while he may not have approval authority per se, he may have the right to challenge the accuracy of the job grade specification within a specified period.

Because the design of jobs occasionally involves questions of functional alignment and delegation of responsibility, most companies require the approval of upper supervision of the line organization. In the wage administration organization, approval of upper-level supervision is generally required relative to the acceptability of the job description and evaluation.

Except where the job description is actually used in bargaining a grade level or pay rate, union involvement is generally in terms of challenging the accuracy of the job grade specification within a specified period.

An ideal arrangement would involve:

1. Job supervisor's agreement that the job analysis write-up is a comprehensive, error-free representation of the job

2. Job supervisor's agreement that the job description is complete, accurate, and a usable administrative document

3. Upper-level line supervision's agreement as to functional alignment and responsibility delegations

4. Wage administration supervision's agreement as to the acceptability of the job description and evaluation

5. Where several plants use the same job evaluation plan and grade structure, corporate wage administration approval as to consistency of plan application

6. Union review and approval as to completeness and accuracy of job grading specification

SEPARATING THE MAN FROM THE JOB

In most hourly jobs, the procedure or technique employed by the operator is rather rigidly prescribed with little opportunity for him to personalize the job. Designing jobs to get maximum use of the talents of a particular employee is not too uncommon in more complicated jobs which require the employee to solve problems—for example, to identify causes of defects and to propose remedial measures or to improvise tooling or methods for accomplishing tasks.

There is nothing seriously wrong with this beyond the resulting dependence on that individual. Should the incumbent leave the job, his successor might not have the same ability, and considerable difficulty and inconvenience might be experienced in obtaining the desired coverage of the functions in question.

Occasionally an employee will describe his job in terms of what he does or can do rather than of what he is expected to do. However, as mentioned earlier, few companies involve the employee in the process of obtaining hourly job information, and even where they do, the information about job content is subject to supervisory confirmation.

The problem lies not so much in identifying job functions as in forming an accurate opinion of the difficulty of the functions either for evaluation purposes or to properly reflect this difficulty in the language of the job description.

It takes experience and judgment on the part of the job analyst to ascertain the extent to which the skill of the operator makes functions appear easier or more difficult than they really are. This calls for an appreciation of both the relative requirements of a wide variety of jobs and what constitutes normal operator proficiency on various kinds of tasks, as well as some knowledge of the things employees can do and sometimes do to distort the appearance of what the job really entails.

THE IMPORTANCE OF UPDATING JOB DESCRIPTIONS

If job descriptions are of any significance to a company's wage and salary administration or to any other area of management control, then it is essential that they be kept up to date. Changes in jobs take many forms and occur for a variety of reasons. For example:

1. A change in physical facilities or surroundings might affect the comfort, fatigue, or hazard factors of a job, creating or eliminating the need for protective garments or equipment and/or altering the way in which functions are performed.

2. A technological change either in the product itself or in the process or equipment used to manufacture, test, transport, or pack the product could affect the environmental factors mentioned above. It might make the job easier or more difficult to perform. It might create or eliminate a need for special knowledge. It might also affect the time needed to perform a particular function, so that the employee would be required to operate several machines or processes instead of one, or the function might now be combined with other functions in order to fill out the job tour.

3. A change in supervisors might result in a realignment of several jobs into completely new combinations of functions which could entail an increase or decrease of difficulty and/or responsibility of any given job. Some of this restructuring might be a reflection of current interest in job enrichment or of a companywide drive for more efficient use of manpower. The same consequences might result from changes in the corporate structure, product lines, or volume of business.

Some changes are abrupt and quite marked, clearly calling for a review of the job and a revision of the description. Others are more gradual or more subtle and frequently go unnoticed. Also, it is sometimes difficult to decide when a change in a job has enough significance to merit the time and effort involved in rewriting a job description. Often minor changes are ignored. Occasionally, however, even though the change may be only a minor one, pressure from job supervision or the union may force a description rewrite. Some companies cope with minor changes by issuing a supplement sheet noting the changes. Another method is to reissue the job description, noting the change and coding the sheet as a revision. Sometimes the change is merely noted in the study folder with nothing being done to the job description until a major change occurs. Any of these approaches is adequate; the important point is that the change has been recognized and recorded.

The issue of job description maintenance entails several questions of urgency, importance, and responsibility. What are they and how should they be handled?

The need for prompt action in description maintenance relates to the nature of the change. Anything affecting the rate of pay (labor cost) for a job or personnel movement considerations should be dealt with as soon as possible. Experience has shown that where updating action is put off for an extended period after the change, job descriptions tend to lose their effectiveness as a management tool. Moreover, if the change affects the employee's rate of pay adversely and a union is involved, it is almost impossible to regrade the job.

Changes which have no effect on the evaluation of the job can be processed on an as-time-permits basis, but even these should not be unduly postponed.

What are the potential effects of a change? Pay check and placement considerations have already been mentioned. Very closely related to these are employee morale and motivation. The change and/or a failure to recognize it might generate complaints or claims from employees on other jobs. Where a union is involved, the change could offer the union a means of demonstrating to employees that it is guarding their interests. It could also be the basis for unwanted militancy and might provide an item of leverage in negotiating contracts. From the company's standpoint, aside from labor costs and the preservation of employee morale, changes affect the planning of schedules, functional alignments, organization structures, personnel movements, training and hiring needs, etc.

It is obvious then that description maintenance is everybody's concern. But what about the responsibility for initiating action? Since it is management's responsibility to organize work, it follows that the job supervisor should arrange for a review of the job. All too often, though, the supervisor is ignorant of this responsibility—or he may be inclined to put self-interest before company interest, hoping to avoid an unpleasant personnel situation, the need to train a replacement at a lower level, or the creation of a high-turnover job. Naturally, if he sees it working to his advantage, he is quite likely to take prompt action.

Also, it is certain that employees and the union will be quick to call attention to changes that could result in increased pay for the job.

What can be done to assure that everybody's interest is protected when changes occur? Basic to everything is executive-level support of the company's wage administration program. Next, and almost as important, is education. Supervisors, employees, and the union must all understand the importance the company attaches to description maintenance. In particular, supervisors should know they will be held accountable for any undesirable consequences of inaction. Two other protective measures can be taken by the wage administration organization: (1) a program of periodic audits designed not only to ascertain if any unrecorded changes have occurred, but also to detect any breaches of supervisory responsibility in wage administration; and (2) where feasible, job analysts should have a close working relationship with the line organization so that they are aware of changes taking place and, if necessary, can remind the supervisor of his responsibility. Various other ways might be explored, such as requiring product planning or manufacturing engineers to keep the wage administration organization informed of anticipated technological changes.   Regardless of the techniques employed, the important point is that everybody should be functioning as a team to preserve the integrity of the wage administration program.

BIBLIOGRAPHY

Berenson, Conrad, and Henry O. Ruhnke: "Job Descriptions: How to Write and Use Them," *Personnel Journal*, Swarthmore, Pa., 1967.

Jones, Philip W.: *Practical Job Evaluation*, John Wiley & Sons, Inc., New York, 1948.

Lytle, Charles Walter: *Job Evaluation Methods*, 2d ed., The Ronald Press Co., New York, 1954.

Michael, Lionel B.: *Wage and Salary Fundamentals and Procedures*, McGraw-Hill Book Co., New York, 1950.

National Industrial Conference Board: "Job Descriptions," Studies in Personnel Policy no. 72, New York, 1946.

————: "Preparing the Company Organization Manual," Studies in Personnel Policy no. 157, New York, 1957.

Otis, Jay L., and Richard H. Leuhart: *Job Evaluation*, Prentice-Hall, Inc., Englewood Cliffs, N.J., 1948.

Patton, John A., C. A. Littlefield, and Stanley Allen Self: *Job Evaluation—Text and Cases*, 3d ed., Richard D. Irwin, Inc., Homewood, Ill., 1964.

Riegel, John W.: *Salary Determination*, Report no. 2, University of Michigan Press, Ann Arbor, Mich., 1940.

Roscoe, Edwin Scott: *Organization for Production*, Richard D. Irwin, Inc., Homewood, Ill., 1967.

Russel, Richard S.: "How to Describe a Job?" *Supervisory Management*, May, 1966, pp. 14–18.

Smyth, Richard C., & Associates and Matthew J. Murphy: *Job Evaluation and Employee Rating*, McGraw-Hill Book Co., New York, 1946.

chapter 3

Describing Salaried Jobs

A. W. HUDOCK *Director, Compensation and Benefits, Scott Paper Company, Philadelphia, Pennsylvania*

Although in the past descriptions of salaried jobs were typically summarizations of job duties, used primarily for job evaluation, this is no longer the case. The art and science of management have become more complex and, as a result, a simple list of responsibilities is no longer sufficient to describe realistically the content of management jobs. Further, management has recognized that job descriptions can be useful in meeting a variety of organizational needs beyond the traditional job evaluation applications.

Today the job description format recognizes that management jobs exist, not to perform a prescribed set of duties but to play a part in managing the total enterprise by being accountable for the accomplishment, either personally, through the supervision of others, or through the managing of functions, of some objectives of the enterprise.

A marketing vice president, for example, is accountable for moving goods profitably from the factory floor into the hands of the consumer. A plant manager is accountable for the timely production of a given volume of goods which meet prescribed quality standards at a budgeted cost while maintaining his equipment properly. Each is accountable for the safety, development, and motivation of his work force.

The environment within which management jobs operate will vary from company to company, depending upon the degree of delegation or centralization of authority and to some extent on individual incumbents, but the basic reason for a management job to be on the payroll—to accomplish some desired end result—is the same.

PURPOSES AND USES OF JOB DESCRIPTIONS

Considering the breadth of responsibility of management jobs, the descriptions of these jobs can serve as a vital management tool not only in job evaluation but also in:

1. *Organization Analysis.* Job descriptions provide a solid foundation for examining job relationships, exposing overlaps and omissions in accountabilities, and highlighting the critical aspects and needs of each job.

2. *Performance Appraisal.* The job description's list of accountabilities (end results) can be used to develop short-term objectives against which individual performance can be measured.

3. *Selection and Training.* Whether it be for hiring or promotion, a good job description provides the essential requirements of a job, against which the applicant's qualifications can be measured. Once an individual has been selected, the job description provides him with an overall charter of his position.

4. *Management Development.* By focusing attention on the know-how and problem-solving elements of a job, management can determine the development needs of present and potential job incumbents. Job descriptions, together with a management audit, followed up by a training or recruitment program, are the prime ingredients of a management continuity program.

5. *Career Planning.* Job descriptions, together with job evaluation, form the basis for a planned career development program, including a promotional path through successive levels of job accountability as well as exposure to various management functions.

To serve these multiple functions, as well as to provide the basic information needed for job evaluation, the description must specify:

1. *Why the Job Exists:* its general function and primary objective. In addition, the description should list the important end results (accountabilities) which the incumbent must achieve to fulfill his function and attain the job's primary objective.

2. *The Kind of Job It Is:* the general framework and environment in which it operates; its role in the organizational scheme; its relationship with and dependence upon other functions and jobs; its important external relationships; and the basic challenges of the job. Additionally, the description must bring out the general nature of technical, managerial, problem-solving, and human relations skills required by the job.

3. *The Job's Freedom to Act:* the nature and source of controls limiting the incumbent's ability to make final decisions and take action.

4. *The Job's Impact:* how the job's primary objective affects major corporate objectives; how significant the job's impact is.

5. *The Job's Magnitude:* the general dollar size of the area most clearly affected by the job. A distinction should be made here between dynamic dollars (sales quota, budget expenditure, etc.) versus static dollars (assets, money managed, etc.). Usually, manufacturing organizations are concerned with dynamic dollars while financial institutions are involved with static dollars.

6. *The Job's Supporting Staff:* the size, scope, and nature of each major function reporting to the job.

SELECTING JOB ANALYSTS

It is apparent that the job assigned the accountability to develop management job descriptions itself requires considerable management skills. The job analyst must be of management caliber, with enough managerial know-how to understand how the various parts of the enterprise function and interact. He must be sufficiently familiar with his management's philosophy and his organization's climate and objectives so that he can extract the essence and ignore the frills of management jobs. He must be perceptive enough to distinguish between why a job exists and how it operates, and to identify the content of the job as distinct from a particular individual's handling of the job. He must be a persistent but tactful interviewer, always keeping in mind that he is dealing with a sensitive area, ultimately associated with compensation level. He must have analytical ability and the integrity to use it, coupled with the ability to write with clarity and precision.

CONDUCTING THE INTERVIEW

Preparing a job description requires a high order of integrity and objective thinking by the job analyst, both in interviewing the job incumbent and in writing the description. The job analyst should always keep in mind that he is concerned with the job and what it is intended to accomplish, and not with the person in the job.

This is not easy. One person will aggressively overstate the role he performs, while another will depreciate the role of his job. The job analyst can best avoid either extreme by being prepared with a checklist of questions which will keep the interview focused on facts.

During the interview, the job analyst should give the incumbent his full attention, since this is the incumbent's "day in court." Detailed notes should be taken, but not in a fashion which disrupts the incumbent's chain of thought. The interview can be kept on track by following an outline prepared beforehand; for example:

1. Please give me a brief description of your overall function.

2. What is the overall end result expected from your job?

3. What annual dollar dimensions (budgets, sales, payroll, etc.) does your job impact upon?

4. Sketch briefly for me your departmental organization, showing the functions and persons reporting to you and the person and function to whom you report.

5. Describe briefly the types of policies you initiate, interpret, or work within.

6. Give me some examples of the types of procedures you initiate, interpret, or work within.

7. Give me some examples of the planning you do to carry out your job. Do these plans include other functional areas?

8. Tell me the makes or breaks (principal accountabilities) of your job. What are the end results which your boss expects you to accomplish? Which of these do you do yourself and which are delegated to subordinates?

9. What accountability do you have for establishing, approving, or recommending budgets, quotas, work performance standards, etc.?

10. What maximum dollar approval authority do you have?

11. Describe the type of guidance, direction, or supervision you receive.

12. What do you feel is needed in the way of formal education and/or experience to do your job in an acceptable manner?

13. What human relations skills does your job require? Describe for me some typical people relationships in your job—with subordinates, with other departments, with people outside the company.

WRITING THE JOB DESCRIPTION

The written job description should help the reader grasp the essential and significant facts—"the guts"—of the position. Extraneous details should be avoided.

The description should be written on the basis of how the job is being done *now*, not how the job incumbent thinks it should be done, nor how it was done in the past, nor how it might be done in the future. In the vast majority of cases, the truly significant facts concerning any job can be recorded in no more than two pages. In fact, establishing two pages as the maximum length for a management job description forces precise and clear thinking as to what facts are truly relevant and encourages crisp, concise writing. The description's usefulness is also enhanced by the adoption of a uniform format and writing style.

The analyst's job is to record significant facts, not to reach conclusions concerning them. For example, a statement such as "This position requires a high degree of aptitude in dealing with people" is an opinion and should be avoided. Instead, state factually *just what is involved in dealing with people*, to provide the reader with facts from which he can draw his own conclusions. Similarly, if a need for a knowledge of electronics is claimed, indicate why the need exists.

Use figures whenever possible instead of less precise phrases such as *few, many, very large, very small,* etc. Where the amount fluctuates, show the range. Let the reader decide, within the context in which he is working, whether 20 or 2,000 is "a few," "many," or "a large amount."

In summary, in writing a job description the job analyst should:

1. Focus on important, significant facts, stated in objective terms.
2. Follow a uniform outline.
3. Write in clear, concise language, using a uniform style.
4. Avoid repetition and trivia.

JOB DESCRIPTION FORMAT

After a standard heading which would include job title, name of incumbent, department or division in which the job is located, date, and the name of the job analyst, a good job description should begin with a capsule statement which in two or three sentences tells why the job is on the payroll. This section should give the reader a quick grasp of the specific end results the job is intended to accomplish. Other sections normally included in a written job description are described below.

Dimensions. This section should summarize in broad terms all statistics pertinent to the job, giving the reader a clear picture of the magnitude of the end results affected by the job. Magnitude is measured in terms of money on an *annual* basis, whether operating budget, sales volume, cost of wages and salaries, assets or funds managed, or other aspects significant to the job. To provide additional perspective, pertinent items other than money, e.g., number of subordinates, unit volumes, number of plants, etc., should be included.

Nature and Scope. This section is the real meat of a job description. It should be written in narrative fashion and should tell the reader what the job is all about. This section should describe the following facets of the job:

1. How the job fits into the organization, including reference to significant internal and external relationships.
2. The general composition of supporting staff, including a short summary of each function supervised, if any.
3. The general nature of technical, managerial, and human relations know-

how required.   If this is a marketing job, for example, the narrative should describe what is sold, how it is sold, the nature of the distribution, what promotional techniques are used, the nature of the competition, and the other major challenges of the job.

4. The nature of the problem solving required.   The narrative should describe the key problems that accrue to the job, including problems dealt with by the job incumbent and problems referred to higher authority.

5. The nature and source of controls on the job's freedom to solve problems and take action.   Controls on any job's freedom to act will exist to some degree in the form of established policy and procedures, in supervisory relationships, or inherently in the job itself.   A cost accountant in a manufacturing operation, for example, may analyze and pinpoint the reason for a variance in production costs but is not free to take corrective action.   Even the chief executive officer of a company has constraints on his freedom to act in the form of his board of directors, shareholders, federal and state laws, etc.

Principal Accountabilities.   This section is a listing of the important end results which the job exists to achieve.   These will vary in number from perhaps four to as many as eight or ten.   Each statement should be a concise "do" statement, accompanied by a "why" statement or clause.   Each statement should pinpoint an accountability against which some measure of performance can be applied.   The following checklist will help ensure complete coverage of the broad managerial areas for which a job might possibly be held accountable:

1. *Organization.*   What accountability, if any, does the job incumbent have for (1) planning the structure of his organization; (2) manning his organization; (3) developing and motivating his organization, including selection, training, appraisal, wage and salary administration, hiring and firing, etc.?

2. *Strategic Planning.*   What accountability, if any, does the job have for long-range planning?   Does the job have an accountability to establish policy objectives, set long-range goals and targets, or establish quality standards of people, equipment, and product?   Obviously, only top-level jobs have an accountability for long-range planning.

3. *Tactical Planning, Execution, and Directing the Attainment of Objectives.* What accountability does the job have for managing, supervising, or performing activities on a day-to-day basis in order to carry out assigned functions effectively?

4. *Review and Control.*   What accountability does the job have for assessing the effectiveness of the organization in achieving its objectives?   What key controls are available to the job to give warning signals when things go wrong?   If there are none, should there be?

It is worth reemphasizing here that an accountability is an end result or objective which the job exists to achieve.   In contrast, a duty or responsibility is the means by which end results are achieved.   Management job descriptions should concern themselves with the former, not the latter.   Whether a sales manager keeps his sales force effective and enthusiastic by means of group meetings, memos, or personal visits to the field is immaterial; one of the end results expected of a sales manager is to maintain an effective and enthusiastic sales force.

Thus, the total job description should tell the reader in two typewritten pages or less:

1. *Why* the job is on the payroll
2. *What* there is to do
3. *How* and *under what conditions* these things are done

Sample job descriptions for exempt and nonexempt salaried jobs appear at the end of the chapter.

JOB DESCRIPTION APPROVAL

The foregoing discussion assumes that information about each job has been obtained by means of an interview conducted by the job analyst with the job incumbent. This is without doubt the best method, although it is time-consuming. Alternatively, the job incumbent may be given a set of instructions and asked to write his own job description subject to clarification and editorial revision by the job analyst, or he may be asked to complete a questionnaire, the responses to which are used by the job analyst to develop a job description.

In any event, once the job description has been developed by the job analyst, it should be reviewed with the job incumbent and approved by at least the immediate supervisor. Differences of opinion as to how the job is perceived are ironed out and the final description is prepared.

Here, too, the job analyst must function as an analyst and not as a mere recorder of opinion. If two persons have laid claim to the same accountability, for example, the analyst should point out the overlap to the supervisor and resolve the matter. Frequently the overlap of accountabilities involves more than one department. For example, the accountability for new-product development may well be claimed as a primary role by the sales department, the market planning department, and the research department. In such an instance, the job analyst can play a major role in organizational clarity by having the matter resolved by top management.

KEEPING JOB DESCRIPTIONS CURRENT

Having installed a job evaluation system, a procedure for maintaining current job descriptions and evaluations must be established. Since the job description focuses on end results and not duties, there is no need to revise the job description and reevaluate the job unless significant job changes occur. Nonetheless, departmental, divisional, and corporate reorganizations do occur. New jobs are created and existing jobs are combined with others. Additionally, minor changes take place which cumulatively amount to a significant change over time.

Whenever a new job is created, preferably before the job is filled, a job description should be written for it. Frequently, there is resistance to writing a job description at this juncture, based on the assumption that the job won't jell until it has been operative for a few months. Balderdash! If the need for a new job is perceived so clearly that management has authorized the expenditure of additional payroll dollars to have that perceived end result accomplished, the job can be reduced to a written job description. The day that the new job incumbent appears on the scene, someone must know enough about what he is to do to get him started. If that much is known, the job can be described in a job description.

In fact, the intellectual exercise of developing a description for a new job frequently results in a much better understanding of how the new job is to function and what it really is intended to accomplish. The existence of a written job description is a valuable aid to the new incumbent, giving him a quick understanding of the role he is to play and reducing wheel-spinning and frustration to a minimum. Finally, since the job ultimately will be evaluated, and a salary range established in any event, it is far better to have these facts in hand before the job is filled rather than after the incumbent is placed in it and a salary level agreed upon. The job may change somewhat after it has been operative for a time, and if this happens, the job description and evaluation can be revised accordingly.

Whenever a major change occurs in an existing job, the job should be re-analyzed and a new description written. In a large organization, jobs are restructured rather frequently as employees are promoted or retire and managers rearrange accountabilities to fit the talents of the work force. Periodically, major reorganizations occur to meet new or changed conditions within or outside the organization. In each case, the changed jobs should be reanalyzed and described and a new evaluation made.

Additionally, all job descriptions should be reviewed periodically, perhaps at two- or three-year intervals, to take into account minor changes which may have occurred. The "dimension" portion of the job description is particularly likely to change over time. The job description should be updated as required and a judgment made as to whether the change is significant enough to warrant reevaluation.

In all cases of new jobs or restructured jobs, the job analyst can and should play a significant management role by being alert to duplication and overlap of accountabilities and by assuring that the problem is resolved at the appropriate management level. In most cases, duplication of accountabilities occurs, not as a result of any deliberate attempt at empire building on the part of individual managers, but simply because an individual manager perceives a need to be met and develops a capability to meet it. Unknown to him, another manager perceives the same need and develops a capability in his department to meet it. The job analyst is in a unique position to detect such overlaps and to call them to the attention of top management for clarification as to where in the organization the accountability should be placed.

NONEXEMPT SALARIED JOBS

Nonexempt salaried jobs are those which, because of their routine nature, fail to meet the test for exemption from the overtime requirements of the Fair Labor Standards Act. Typically, such jobs perform secretarial, clerical, or technician functions.

While nonexempt salaried jobs are more limited in scope and freedom to act than are exempt jobs, the format of the job description can be essentially the same. The emphasis, however, is on duties and skills rather than on broad accountability for end results. A sample description of a clerical job also is included with this chapter.

SAMPLE JOB DESCRIPTION—EXEMPT

JOB TITLE: Manager of Compensation   DATE:
                 and Benefits
INFORMATION PROVIDED BY:
JOB ANALYST:
DIVISION/PLANT:
DEPARTMENT:
REVIEWED BY:

Accountability Objectives

Plans and directs the development and implementation and audits the administration of programs in salaried job evaluation, salary administration, incentive compensation, and employee benefits which enable the company to attract, motivate, and retain high-caliber employees within the bounds of competitive costs.

Dimensions

Total Salary Payroll $_____
Retirement Plan Costs $_____
Group Insurance Costs $_____
Stock Plans Costs $_____
Budget $_____
Persons Supervised   _____ exempt
                               _____ nonexempt

Nature and Scope of Position

This position reports to the Vice President—Industrial Relations. This position is expected to keep informed of developments in compensation and benefits among leading companies in the national industrial community and to develop total compensation programs tailored to the needs of the company which will enable it to attract, retain, and motivate high-caliber employees. The incumbent directs and personally performs research in salary administration, management bonus plans, stock option plans, group insurance plans, pension plans, stock purchase plans, etc., and works with consultants, actuaries, and insurance carriers to develop new programs or changes to existing programs as well as internal policies and procedures to keep the company at a competitive level in total compensation. Detailed recommendations, including costs, are reviewed by the Vice President—Industrial Relations prior to presentation to the Chief Executive Officer. Once programs have been approved, the incumbent directs their implementation through the various divisional personnel organizations.

The incumbent serves as a consultant in compensation and benefits to all divisions and audits their ongoing administration of compensation and benefits programs. The incumbent secures all required Internal Revenue Service approvals and directs the filing of annual D-2 and related reports and the maintenance of corporatewide salary records. The incumbent serves as Secretary of the Retirement Board and works closely with the Vice President—Industrial Relations and the Executive Compensation Committee in the administration of such programs as the Management Incentive Plan, the Stock Option Plan, and executive salary reviews. The incumbent participates in labor negotiations as an employee benefits expert as required.

This position maintains close working relationships with the Law, Controller, Treasurer, and Tax Departments. Outside contacts are maintained with actuaries, insurance consultants, and compensation consultants. This position maintains membership and participates in associations of professional compensation and benefits administrators.

The principal challenge of this position is to develop and recommend programs of compensation and benefits, appropriately balanced between direct and indirect compensation, which will maintain a total compensation climate at a sufficiently competitive level to enable the company to develop and maintain a highly talented and motivated managerial staff and a skilled and company-oriented work force and to minimize the cost of such programs by the use of effective funding methods and by the avoidance of duplication and errors in administration, both internally and with insurance carriers and actuaries.

Reporting to this position are:

Employee Benefits Analyst. This position performs research and develops recommendations for changes in all employee benefit programs—group insurance, pension plans, and stock purchase plans. The incumbent serves as a consultant to the operating divisions in the administration of these programs corporatewide and audits the effectiveness of the programs and their administration.

Compensation Analyst. This position conducts salary surveys and performs research in other forms of direct compensation and develops recommendations. The incumbent audits the administration of the salaried job evaluation program corporatewide.

Principal Accountabilities

1. Directs the development of compensation and benefits policy and programs which will enable the company to attract, retain, and motivate high-caliber employees within the bounds of competitive cost.

2. Keeps informed, through research and participation in professional associations, of current trends and levels in compensation and benefits to assure that the company's programs are maintained at competitive levels.

3. Serves all profit centers as a consultant in compensation and benefits to assure accurate and equitable administration.

4. Participates in labor negotiations as a pension and insurance expert as required to assure that the required expertise on these matters is available to the management bargaining team.

5. Directs the development of booklets, brochures, and other communications devices to communicate the company's compensation and benefits programs to all employees.

6. Keeps informed on laws and Internal Revenue regulations dealing with compensation and benefits matters to assure that all programs achieve maximum effectiveness within federal, state, and local regulations.

7. Selects, trains, and develops department personnel to ensure excellent current performance and the opportunity for future growth and development.

SAMPLE JOB DESCRIPTION—NONEXEMPT

JOB TITLE: Salary Records Clerk   DATE:
INFORMATION PROVIDED BY:
WRITTEN BY:
DIVISION/PLANT:
DEPARTMENT:
REVIEWED BY:

Accountability Objectives

Maintains and updates companywide salary records and compiles salary information for the preparation of surveys and special studies.

Nature and Scope of Position

This position reports to the Compensation Analyst.

The Salary Records Clerk is responsible for maintaining salary records for all exempt salaried employees. This is accomplished by posting from personnel status forms received from all divisions to salary record cards. Tabulating cards used for maturity studies and for annual salary reviews are updated weekly. Any changes made on these cards must be accurate, for these records are the central storehouse of salary information.

The Salary Records Clerk extracts information from these salary records for the preparation of surveys and special studies. These surveys and special studies require some arithmetical calculations, such as percentages and averages. These studies require approximately half of the incumbent's time.

In addition, the incumbent prepares monthly stock distribution award lists and major employment anniversary lists; collects data for periodic reports of salary administration activity and assists with the general typing work load in the department.

This position requires clerical and typing skills and some familiarity with the use of the keypunch machine. Accuracy in record keeping and arithmetical calculation is important in preparing reports and studies.

This incumbent is in contact with staff and plant personnel departments, department heads, and executives concerning salary information.

Principal Accountabilities

1. Maintains salary records for all exempt salaried employees. Prepares maturity study and salary review tabulating cards.

2. Extracts data for salary surveys and special studies and performs necessary arithmetical calculations.

3. Assists with general typing work load.

chapter 4

Collecting Data
through Standard Descriptions

CARL S. WEBBER   *Senior Principal, Edward N. Hay & Associates, Phila-delphia, Pennsylvania*

Standard job descriptions are the simplest, most generalized descriptions in use. They are not based on audited job content or generated to reflect one *specific* position. They represent a compromise: not so general as to be meaningless nor so specific that the description applies to only a small number of closely related positions. Companies may write their own standard descriptions or may use those in the *Dictionary of Occupational Titles*.

Since they do represent a compromise, standard descriptions are best used for lower-level jobs, where more detailed descriptions would be impractical. They are an effective vehicle for gathering a maximum amount of external salary information from a large number of participants at a minimum cost. Such surveys can provide personnel departments with statistically sound median pay data. In addition, companies lacking the money to carry out internal surveys based on job content can use standard descriptions internally, but this practice is less common.

It is perhaps worth noting briefly, by means of a simple example, the differences between three common means of identifying a job: the job specification, the job duty, and the end results expected of a job. Suppose the position is that of a company driver who transports visitors from the main gate to various office buildings around the large facility. The *specification* might read: "Must hold a valid driver's license for the Commonwealth of Pennsylvania." An example of an *activity or duty* might be: "Drives a passenger car or limousine on company property." And the job's *objective* might read: "The timely, safe, and courteous chauffeuring of visitors on the company's property."

The shortest and most general job description, on the other hand, is a mere *job title,* such as "telephone operator." Because this is a relatively simple job and widely known, the job title is almost a satisfactory job description in itself. Job titles alone are commonly used in all job title comparison salary surveys because they are the most economical way to obtain large amounts of salary data at a minimum cost. As is so often the case, however, one gets what one pays for. Even at this level, the title may well be too general and may fail to pick up differences which are more important than the similarities which it does include.

For most serious compensation studies, one should know whether the switchboard is manual or automatic, single or multipositional, centrex-connected, the number of trunk lines and extensions, whether the operator also serves as a receptionist, and, if so, to what extent and with what kind of public, and whether she is also used as a clerk-typist during off periods. These kinds of questions could be asked:

1. Size and difficulty of switchboard operations
3. Degree and kind of receptionist work
3. Amount of typing and related work

The failure of most standard descriptions to pick up this kind of data may be seen from the following example from the *Dictionary of Titles* (Volume I, Third Edition):

> Telephone Operator (Clerical) Number 235-862 Control Board Operator; P.B.X. Operator; Private-Branch Exchange Operator; Switchboard Operator; Telephone-Switchboard Operator. Operates cord or cordless switchboard to relay incoming, outgoing, and interoffice calls; pushes switch keys to make connections and relay calls on cordless switchboard. On cord-type equipment, plugs cord in jacks mounted on switchboard. *May* supply information to callers and record messages. *May* keep record of calls placed and toll charges. *May* perform clerical duties such as typing, proofreading, and sorting mail. *May* operate system of bells or buzzers to call individuals in establishment to phone. [Emphasis supplied.]

This type of standard description creates problems by including a great variety of actual job content. Even if a more sophisticated standard job description were used, however, the problem of interpreting the compensation data would still remain. Obviously, performance level requirements vary from organization to organization, and one organization may pay significantly more than another organization for identical job content. The point is that a survey based on standard job descriptions should include enough participants to ensure that extremes at either end of the pay scale, as influenced by performance, do not unduly distort the picture of average compensation related to a standard of average performance.

Of course, such data must be analyzed and interpreted with care before they can be applied to the compensation practice of any one organization. The surveying organization must determine, as it does with exempt positions, the standards of performance it requires for the surveyed positions and do its best to relate these standards to the marketplace.

Although, as we have seen, standard descriptions can be useful in a variety of situations, this usefulness can be undermined by external factors. For example, if employer-employee relations are strained, management may use standard descriptions as a form of protection. In an adversarial environment, employers have a natural tendency to want to include in job content almost any reasonably related duty or activity in order to prevent an employee from refusing to do something "because it is not in my job description." The more adversarial the climate, the more management is likely to include protective clauses such as "and all other duties related to the position." The drawback to this is obvious: *important elements* are harder to see.

Interunion rivalry, which leads to jurisdictional disputes among unions over who has the "right" to perform certain kinds of activities, has led, in some cases, to standard job descriptions so general that they become almost pointless. Often agreements reached between various unions are not the same everywhere, so that duties or activities properly included in a standard job description for one employer may prove totally inappropriate for another employer.

Another drawback to standard job descriptions involves their use by unions to *interpret* competitive compensation practices. Because these descriptions are so broad, unions seeking the highest-paid salary comparisons can point to the highest-paid job which bears any relationship to the standard description.

Employers can counter this approach on a number of grounds, including local competitive compensation practices, performance requirements' variance among employers, and, perhaps most usefully of all, on the basis that the positions have been evaluated as internally equitable with all other positions in the organization.

Another problem arises when both public and private employers are included in a survey based on standard descriptions. Public and private employers generally are not comparable: they deal with different types of jobs and different salary scales, situations, and problems. Public employers, i.e., federal, state, and city governments, are nonprofit organizations. They have no surplus wealth, to use crude Marxian language, for "workers and bosses" to fight over. In addition, the public employer is a service organization. Any interruption of these services is often intolerable to citizens as a whole, so that the ultimate threat of strike by employees is often forbidden. This places an even higher responsibility upon the *public* employer to be a *good* employer. Data based on surveys including both public and private employees must be interpreted with great sensitivity to these facts. Civil service regulations also have some effect on the comparability of standard job descriptions.

In general, standard job descriptions are useful only if they cover a sufficiently large sample of employers and if the positions covered lend themselves at least moderately well to a standardized description. Clearly, the latter requirement is easier to meet at lower levels of job content. As soon as we begin to reach that jagged gray area which separates exempt from nonexempt positions, we see jobs whose variety, even under the same title, is often so great that the differences become as important as, or more important than, the similarities.

chapter 5

Collecting Data
through Questionnaires

ROBERT P. VORHIS *Manager, Salary Administration, Armco Steel Corporation, Middletown, Ohio*

The use of questionnaires to obtain information for position descriptions for hourly paid and salaried clerical people has not been very successful. Companies that have tried this method of gathering facts about the jobs being studied have found that the primary objections are as follows:

1. It is difficult to design a standard questionnaire that will elicit vital information.

2. Hourly and clerical employees are not trained to write paragraphs that give the analyst the information that he will need to properly describe and classify the position.

3. Some descriptions will be brief and sketchy and of little use, while others will be too long and will require additional study to identify the useful information.

4. The shop or clerical employee will not take enough time to analyze his position and answer the questions properly.

5. Some employees resent the questionnaire approach and suspect that their job rate might depend on what they write and not on what they do.

However, some companies have used the questionnaire method successfully to gather facts about a job, and they use it as a reference source in writing position descriptions. Questionnaires are particularly useful in large-scale evaluation studies where individual interviews would be impractical. Department store sales clerks, skilled hourly positions such as maintenance repairmen or machinists, and many office clerical positions are examples of jobs that have been described by using the questionnaire approach. Companies who have used this method report that best results may be obtained if these rules are followed:

1. The questionnaire should contain questions that employees will relate to their own jobs. Thus, a sales clerk's questionnaire may ask questions about pricing stock, writing sales slips, making change, and balancing a cash register, while a maintenance repairman's questionnaire may ask about equipment that is repaired, tolerances permitted, and type of supervision he receives from his foreman.

2. The form should contain easily understood questions that require short, factual answers.

3. The employee should sign the questionnaire and submit it to his supervisor for approval to ensure that all information reported is a factual representation of the employee's position.

A typical questionnaire for a maintenance repairman is shown in Figure 1.

Questionnaires should always be meaningful in terms of the specific occupation about which facts are desired. When the true facts and statistics are reported on the above description, a clear and accurate job description could be obtained that can be used to classify and rate the maintenance repairman.

Figure 1.   Job questionnaire (maintenance repairman).

JOB QUESTIONNAIRE (Maintenance Repairman)

I. *To the Employee*:   You are requested to describe your job on this questionnaire. To help you cover all important points, a number of questions are included. Use plain English in answering these questions, avoiding needlessly long words and involved sentences.

II. *Job Identification*:
   1. Your name.
   2. Your immediate supervisor's name.
   3. Your department.
   4. Today's date.

III. *Description of Your Job*:
   1. What do you do and how do you do it?
      a. List the kinds of equipment you repair. (For example: Hallden Shear, Temper Mill, Conveyors, etc.)
      b. List the assemblies you repair. (For example: Bearings, Shafts, Motor Boxes, etc.)
      c. For each assembly which you repair, list two typical repair jobs which you do.
      d. List the tools and equipment which you use.
   2. How and how much are you supervised?
      a. Do you receive instructions orally, by written work order, or both?
      b. Do you have to read and use blueprints, drawings, or repair instructions in your work? Explain.
      c. How often does your supervisor review your work?

Check one.

(1) Frequently   _____
(2) Seldom   _____
(3) Upon completion of work only   _____

   3. Do you supervise other workers? If so, list their job titles and the number in each title.
   4. If you believe there are other pertinent facts about your job, describe them on the attached blank sheet of paper.

Employee Name_____

Approved, Immediate Supervisor_____

Suppose the family of jobs to be described is a large clerical group in a typical accounting department. The questionnaire, besides identifying the employee, the section, and the immediate supervisor, would also ask questions about the work performed, the equipment used, and the type of supervision received that would provide the same basic information about the accounting clerk that was obtained about the maintenance repairman. When questions are written in terms familiar to the employee, he will understand them and be able to answer them to everyone's satisfaction.

In a typical study using questionnaires to gather information from large sections or departments, the analyst reviews the jobs to be studied to determine the type of questions he should ask to gather the required information. He must become familiar with the department organization and must know how each job relates to the ones above it and below it in the normal organization structure.

The analyst should visit the department supervisors and review the positions to be studied. He should work with these supervisors to develop the questionnaire. This is particularly true in departments that have functions or technical positions with which the analyst is not familiar.

After a rough draft of the questionnaire has been developed, the department supervisor should review it to spot any weaknesses or questions that might be misunderstood. When this step is completed, plans should then be made to distribute the final questionnaire to the employees to be studied. Best results will be obtained if the supervisor discusses the need for the survey and how it is to be completed, and then answers any questions the employee might have about the forms to be completed. At this time, the supervisor should instruct the employee to complete the questionnaire and return it to him for final approval.

When the questionnaires have been returned to the supervisor, he should review them for accuracy. In the case of inaccurate statements or important items forgotten, the supervisor will discuss areas in question with the employee and together they will correct the questionnaire. After the questionnaires have been approved and signed, the supervisor will send them to the analyst in charge of the study.

After all questionnaires have been received, the analyst should review them to determine whether they provide complete information. The final questionnaires are now ready to be analyzed and used to develop position descriptions for the department.

Many companies have used questionnaires to obtain job-related information about high-level positions, including all exempt management positions, principal division heads, and elected officers of the company. At this level, questionnaires have the following advantages:

1. Where time is a factor, more jobs can be analyzed in the same amount of time through questionnaires than through personal interviews.

2. The questionnaire can be organized so that the employee will think about his job in a systematic and logical manner.

3. Problems dealing with cross-divisional responsibilities can be identified and corrected.

4. The executive will have a clearer idea of his duties and responsibilities when he reviews his questionnaire with the president.

Several major companies have completed their salary studies of management positions in record time by following this method. A questionnaire used by one of these companies is shown in Figure 2.

Several major companies have successfully used a questionnaire similar to

Figure 2. Exempt position description questionnaire.

EXEMPT POSITION DESCRIPTION QUESTIONNAIRE

This is a preliminary step in the preparation of a position description covering your job. After completing this questionnaire, discuss it with your supervisor or department head. He will pass it on to the analyst responsible for preparing position descriptions for your area. A rough draft of the position description will be returned to you for your comments. Use the back page if there is not sufficient space to complete questions.

Your Name_____Date_____

Present Title_____

    Location_____ Department_____

    Section_____

1. What is the primary purpose of the job? (I.e., What is it accountable for? Why does it exist?)
2. What dollar amounts represent areas this position most clearly impacts? (I.e., conversion costs, department operating cost, approximate dollar size of payroll supervised, money spent, sales made, etc.) Write a statement explaining each.
3. What is the immediately superior position?
4. What functional direction, if any, is received? (I.e., reports to the Controller, but receives some assignments from Works Manager; or reports to Works Manager, but receives functional guidance from Corporate Traffic.)
5. What procedural controls are adhered to? (I.e., standard operating practices, sales goals, budgets, cost standards, etc.) Write a statement explaining how, what deviations are made, etc.
6. List positions supervised or directed and number of incumbents.
7. What are the positions or departments with which there are primary working relationships and contacts? What is the nature of these?
8. Describe those activities which are accomplished through the supervision or direction of others.
9. Describe those activities which are performed directly. (Don't overlook planning, scheduling, coordinating, expediting, approving, etc.)
10. Describe anything else applicable to the position not covered elsewhere. (Equipment responsible for; geographical area covered; external contacts; committees and outside organizations and assignments *required* by the job, etc.)
11. What special kinds of problems other than those clearly implied in previous statements are encountered?
12. Comments and approval by immediate supervisor or department head.

                  Approved_____

                  Date_____

the one shown in Figure 2. They report that after the questionnaire is completed and approved by the president, the analyst usually conducts a personal interview with the executive to clear up any statements made that might not be understood. From this questionnaire, accurate job descriptions can be written.

Armco Steel Corporation uses either a questionnaire or a Position Guide Format, depending on whether a trained analyst or the incumbent is to write the position description. The questionnaire presents pertinent information so that a trained analyst may write a position description without conducting lengthy interviews with the incumbent. The Position Guide Format (see Figure 3) has been developed so that the individual can write his own position description. Since Armco classifies jobs in terms of three factors—know-how, problem solving, and accountability—the questions on the format have been designed to clarify items related to these three factors.

Using the Position Guide Format, job information and job descriptions can

Figure 3.   Position guide format.

POSITION GUIDE FORMAT

I. ACCOUNTABILITY OBJECTIVE(S)
   1. Write a general statement of the primary function of the job that will be a *capsule statement of its end results.*
      a. The statement should reflect what the job is accountable for and explain its reason for existence.
      b. This will normally be a one-sentence statement and should be as brief as possible.

II. NATURE OF THE POSITION
   1. This section should be a series of *narrative* statements, in paragraph form, that describe:
      a. Nature or character of the job; areas of principal concern.
      b. Scope as to technical depth; i.e., as applicable:
         (1) Product responsibility
         (2) Territorial coverage
         (3) Customers—competitors
         (4) Type and numbers of equipment
         (5) Manufacturing processes
         (6) Division, plants, or departments serviced
         (7) And the like
      c. Principal organization relationships outside of own department or unit:
         (1) List departments or specific positions as appropriate and describe the nature of them.
         (2) Relationships outside the corporation, important to the position.
      d. Problem-solving requirements for original self-starting thinking.   This is the frame of reference for applying job knowledge in decision making, analyzing, evaluating, exercising judgment, and the like. It should include those kinds of problem solving *primarily unique* to the position.
      e. Number and kind of organization and personnel supervised or managed, if any. Positions reporting directly, and other key positions, should be stated by job title.

III. PRINCIPAL ACTIVITIES TO ATTAIN ACCOUNTABILITY OBJECTIVES
   1. This section is a series of numbered paragraphs, each sentence of which begins with an action verb which is typed in full caps.   These paragraphs should include, in the following order:
      a. Statements covering managerial or supervisory responsibilities in own area for organizational structuring, employee selection, personnel development and appraisal, and recognition.
      b. Statements covering activity in, or responsibility for, development of practices, procedures, or policies (policies are corporate) and for approving or recommending and/or implementing them.
      c. Statements (several) covering activities which are typical and inherent to the function of the job. These should be an explanation of Section I, "Accountability Objectives," and they should be the specifics of those generalities described in Section II, "Nature of the Position."
      d. Special activities required of the position, i.e., committee memberships and outside organizations.

COMMENTS:
1. Confine the description to the limits of the two-page format.
2. A position guide should be a perceptive critique of external and internal conditions and objectives, rather than a repetitive, classified listing of generalities.
   a. In addition to pertinent supporting data, a sales description should explain: what is sold, where and how it is sold, what are the competitive conditions, selling and distribution practices, and the like.
   b. In addition to pertinent supporting data, an operating description should explain what are the raw materials received, what processes, through what kinds of

Figure 3 (continued).
    equipment, by which kinds of employees, produce what kinds of finished products, for what uses.

  c. In addition to pertinent supporting data, a staff position should explain what support functions it provides to what organizations, through what kinds of programs, to achieve what kinds of objectives. It should enumerate the extent of its advisory activities and carefully state any control functions delegated by line management.

---

be gathered from remotely located units of the company, and travel time of an analyst is kept at a minimum. Salary studies have been successfully completed in overseas operations by supplying the foreign manager with do-it-yourself kits which include well-written sample job descriptions of an operating job, an administrative job, and a sales job, blank job description forms, and a Position Guide Format. By following the format and reading the sample descriptions, even an employee untrained in writing descriptions can write an acceptable description of his own position.

One overseas division of the company translated the Position Guide Format and the sample job descriptions into the language of the country, instructed the employees to write their descriptions in their native language, then translated the approved position descriptions into English for the salary committee. The manager thought the resulting position descriptions were better than those completed in English by another unit of his company.

Questionnaires can be used to gather job information if they are designed for the jobs to be studied. Obviously, you cannot use a questionnaire developed for a clerical position to gather information about a management position. If the questionnaire is developed carefully, reviewed with the department head, and answered honestly by the employee, the questionnaire method can be used to gather information for writing position descriptions.

chapter 6

Collecting Data through Interviews and Observations

CHESTER L. WILHELM *General Manager, Salary Administration Department, Armstrong Cork Company, Lancaster, Pennsylvania*

THOMAS S. ROY *Senior Analyst, Salary Administration Department, Armstrong Cork Company, Lancaster, Pennsylvania*

The preceding chapters discussed the collection of data on job content through the use of standard descriptions and questionnaires. These are probably the least expensive and most expeditious techniques that can be employed for this purpose. They do, however, have severe limitations. A complete review of a total operation, division, or company requires a broad range of descriptions and questionnaires. Moreover, using questionnaires with hourly factory workers is generally impractical, as many workers simply are not able to adequately describe and place proper emphasis in writing on the duties involved in their work. Even supervisors are often unfamiliar with the duties of subordinates. Further, these approaches to the collection of data often are considered too impersonal and mechanized, and they generally presume considerable knowledge and understanding of the jobs being studied.

Generally, the interview and the observation, used alone or in combination, are considered the best means of gathering complete information to develop a job description. These techniques are time-consuming and costly, but the quality of the data generated usually justifies the additional investment of time and money.

The observation technique is best suited to factory jobs. The observation usually is carried out by an industrial engineer as part of his more general responsibilities, and the observation often is the primary—even the sole—source of information used in developing the job description. Interviews are used for higher-level jobs, and they are conducted by interviewer-analysts specially selected and trained to fill this function. Interviews may serve as the exclusive source of job information or they may be buttressed by additional study—for example, of the job's position in the organization structure.

OBSERVATION

Observation is the gathering of information by physically watching workers as they perform their tasks. Its major advantage is that information is gathered firsthand, thus eliminating omissions and permitting a thorough understanding of the work. The analyst can familiarize himself with the working conditions, process flow, required skills, and equipment and materials involved.

This method is most widely used in the factory for hourly jobs and is most successful for those clerical jobs that are repetitive and require relatively little skill. It is also best applied where the cycle of work is brief enough to permit the analyst to observe the entire job in a relatively short time. Observation of administrative or managerial jobs is considered impractical; its use for most clerical jobs is generally tedious and lengthy and is therefore often restricted to studies of clerical systems and procedures.

The steps involved in preparing for and carrying out an observation include the following:

1. *Review purpose of observation.* The beginning point for any procedure requiring personal contact is to gain the cooperation of the people involved and to remove any suspicions. It is important to review the purpose of the study with the supervisory personnel so they may understand what information is required and why, and to communicate the purpose to the workers being observed. Often a departmental meeting is held for this purpose.

2. *Gain overall picture.* By means of prior study of available materials and through discussions with appropriate department heads, the observer should gain a general knowledge of the process flow, reporting relationships, and other pertinent information so as to obtain an overall view of the operations.

3. *Determine observation points.* To profitably observe the workers and to understand the task performed, key vantage points should be selected with the aid of the supervisor. Such posts should be relatively unobstrusive and still permit a clear view of the work. If possible, the sequence of observation points should follow the flow of work.

4. *Begin observation.* The actual observation should begin at the work station with the analyst visually studying the worker performing his job and carefully determining the overall nature and purpose of the job.

5. *Observe in depth.* Continued observations are made, through a complete work cycle if possible, with the analyst attempting to organize the pattern of work into a logical sequence. A successful analyst will be alert and attentive throughout the observation period. He should seek an understanding of the important elements of the job and the task performed to gain insight into the skills, abilities, and qualifications required.

6. *Conclude the observation.* After the observation has been completed, the analyst should immediately review the notes taken and fill in or expand on the various items noted. If areas are unclear or further elaboration is required, questions are noted for further clarification with the worker and/or supervisor.

For hourly rated or relatively routine clerical jobs, a skilled observer normally will be able to obtain sufficient information for practical job evaluations through the techniques described. For other salaried positions, particularly at the administrative and management levels, it is desirable that information on job content be obtained by means of a skilled interview. This technique is usually considered the most complete and accurate means of compiling data and gaining a thorough understanding of the job.

THE ROLE OF THE INTERVIEWER

Interviewing, for the purpose of this chapter, is defined as the process of obtaining information for job analysis by skilled, professional questioning of the people most directly involved with the job being analyzed. The interviewer is defined as the analyst charged with the responsibility of conducting the interview and, on the basis of the information obtained, analyzing and evaluating the position reviewed. While it is conceivable that the interviewer and the analyst could be different persons, as a practical matter—to ensure probing, analytical questions eliciting the response required for effective analyses—the interviewer and analyst are normally one person.

Selecting Interviewers. Since the interviewer's abilities largely determine the success of the interviews and the quality of the job evaluation program, interviewers must be selected with great care. Among some pertinent questions to be considered when staffing the organization for this purpose are:

1. Are people available within the company with the necessary skills and personal characteristics to be good interviewers?
2. From what departments will the interviewers be drawn?
3. What will be the effect on the operations losing such men?
4. Should experienced interviewers be employed?
5. What is the external job market situation for such people?
6. Who will conduct the training of interviewers, and what will it cost?
7. How will a job as interviewer-analyst fit into a career path?
8. How will the interviewers be received within the organization?

In addition to the organizational considerations involved in selecting interviewers, other criteria relating to personal traits and characteristics must also be considered. Although the specific requirements for an interviewer will vary from company to company, depending on the company's internal environment and management style, some requirements are shared by practically all companies, and these are discussed below.

1. *Communication Skills.* The ability to speak, write, and understand the language of the employee is absolutely essential. It is not necessary for the respondent to feel the interviewer is a "person like himself" but rather that the interviewer is a person who can "understand him"; thus the language of the interview must conform to a shared vocabulary, and the interviewer must show he is capable of understanding. The interviewer will deal with people of varied backgrounds, skills, and abilities, and yet he must have the varied communication skills required to intelligently discuss job content with all.

2. *Extensive Business Knowledge.* The interviewer must possess considerable knowledge of business and industry and of the varied operations and positions likely to be analyzed. He must have wide acquaintance with jobs in general so he may better understand any particular position being analyzed by comparing or contrasting it with other jobs. Imagine, for example, the varied knowledge and ability required to effectively interview and analyze such diverse positions as an accounting clerk, a physicist, a structural engineer, and a vice president of finance. He must, in short, be conversant in many

fields and disciplines. While such knowledge can be acquired through extensive experience, formal education in the business disciplines is desirable. Those receiving such formal training normally would also possess the broadening outlook and poise so essential for an effective interview.

3. *Analytical Abilities.* The information gathering interview and job evaluation require good judgment and an analytical mind. The interviewer must be able to probe, question, verify, and comprehend during the interview; to gain necessary facts and eliminate the unnecessary (or untruthful); to place all in its proper perspective; and then to make sound judgments based on the information obtained.

4. *Knowledge of Behavioral Science.* Any profession which requires considerable human interaction calls for an understanding of personality and behavior. Interviews to collect job data in particular require a mature understanding of human behavior, since an analytic rather than an impressionistic approach is emphasized. The quality of the interview and the type of interaction achieved depend strongly on the ability of the interviewer to motivate the respondent to participate in the interview and to communicate fully. The interviewer must develop rapport and gain cooperation, yet he must also guard against suspicions, hostility, or embarrassment.

5. *Objectivity.* Those who are objective and have the ability to think critically and independently are most likely to be successful interviewers. Simply stated, there is no room for preconceived notions, biases, or persons likely to give extreme opinions.

Other favorable personality traits include an even temperament, sincerity, integrity, and the ability to get along with others. Particular note should be made of this latter point. It is essential for an effective interview, and, for that matter, for a successful evaluation program, that those most closely associated with it be able to develop a rapport with the respondents and all levels of management.

An interviewer who is unable to obtain sufficient or accurate job information, or properly to evaluate the information obtained, undermines the reliability of the job evaluation program. One who creates hostility or suspicion, or who leaves poor impressions, severely damages the reputation of the entire wage and salary program and those who administer it, and can foster more serious employee relations problems. On the other hand, an interviewer who is a true professional will make substantial contributions to the company that extend well beyond the collection of data on job content.

Training Interviewers. Despite the complexity of interviewing and its importance to the job evaluation program, newly selected interviewers often begin their jobs without any previous formal training in this field. We feel strongly that new interviewers must be thoroughly trained—both in a formal training program and continually on the job.

The formal training program will vary according to the background and experience of the new interviewer and the particular requirements of the company concerned.

An effective course of study, conducted by a capable individual and supplemented by available readings, should cover, at a minimum, the following subjects:

1. Interviewing objectives.
2. Preparing for the interview.
3. Opening the interview.
4. Conducting the interview.
5. The art of questioning.
6. Observing the respondent.

7. Importance of objectivity.
8. Closing the interview.

These subjects will be elaborated on in subsequent portions of this chapter.

The interviewer-trainee must also gain exposure to the job evaluation technique utilized by the company to enable him to probe for information essential to evaluation. Obviously, if the interviewer also analyzes the job, then extensive study in job evaluation is mandatory as part of the training program.

A thorough and well-implemented study program of the areas indicated above will provide considerable *knowledge* about interviewing. However, basic knowledge alone does not make a good interviewer, because interviewing is a *skill* developed through considerable practice and experience.

As part of the formal training, various techniques can be employed to develop this skill. One such technique involves role playing, in which one member plays the part of the interviewer, another the part of a respondent, and others in the group serve as observers. At the conclusion of the role playing session, the group, led by the trainer, discusses the strengths and weaknesses of the interview. This technique is more readily used when a large number of interviewers are being trained.

Observation of actual interviews conducted by an experienced interviewer is also a useful and highly recommended technique for training interviewers. The new interviewer does not actively participate in the interview other than to take brief notes and to observe. The actual interviewer and the observer then analyze the interview after its conclusion. It is desirable, if the situation permits, to have the trainee observe interviews conducted by several different interviewers so as to gain from their diverse experience and varying techniques. In a more sophisticated training program, the trainer can use audiovisual aids to demonstrate the principles and techniques of interviewing and to provide actual interview examples, and the trainee can listen, watch himself in action, and analyze the conduct of the interview.

The length of the formal training program depends upon the varying background and skills of the new interviewer, the abilities of those conducting the training programs, and company requirements. It need not be of considerable length; however, the development of basic interviewing skills requires considerable practice.

With the completion of the formal training program, the second stage of the training process begins, with the interviewer refining his skills and ability to interact with others through actual experience. The interviewer who learns from his mistakes, builds on his experience, subjects himself to critical self-examination, and strives for improvement will acquire the skill and reputation of a professional interviewer.

THE INTERVIEW PROCESS

Let us turn our attention now to the interview process itself. In the sections that follow, we will consider, in sequence, the steps involved in carrying out an interview.

Preparing for the Interview. Adequate preparation is essential to a successful interview. Before a position can be intelligently reviewed, the interviewer must possess considerable industry, company, and job knowledge. He must be able to talk in a common language with the respondents and thus be familiar with the jargon and technical terms of the positions being reviewed. Some of this knowledge is attained through formal education but most is a result of experience and specific advance preparation.

To acquire this knowledge, it is recommended that the interviewer consult technical literature pertaining to industry processes and techniques, company history and financial data, company publications, including annual reports, product literature, and recruiting aids, and advertising materials. For specific jobs, he should study organization charts to review reporting relationships, job titles, and the interaction between line and staff departments. Consultations should be held with management and supervisory personnel prior to the interviews to obtain guidance on the current organization and specific data on the interpretation of job content. Job information may also be obtained from existing job descriptions for the positions being reviewed, similar positions in other areas of the company (or other companies), and other positions in the same department, which will provide the interviewer with an overall view of the various interactions of jobs. The interviewer should use caution in relying on existing position descriptions. They may introduce biases which could hinder factual information gathering.

Advance formulation of questions is also recommended in the preparation stage. An interview that has little or no continuity, or in which the interviewer searches aimlessly for his questions, is likely to be incomplete and perhaps even damaging. The interviewer who is well prepared with previously thought-out and carefully formulated questions is more likely to communicate effectively and obtain the full information required from the respondent.

The value of an on-site inspection, such as a tour of plant operations prior to the conduct of the analysis, is surprisingly debated, with one school of thought holding that such tours are needlessly time-consuming or tend to introduce a bias or at least reduce the detachment required for impartial analysis. Most people, however, believe that a "picture is worth a thousand words" and therefore that the actual viewing of the concerned operations prior to the interviews provides a clearer understanding of the total picture and the specifics of the processes. A skilled observer may identify aspects of the job that ordinarily would not be discovered in the course of the interview.

As part of his preparation, the interviewer must gain the close cooperation of the management most directly involved. It is not uncommon for interviewers or job analysts to be looked upon with some disdain or suspicion, and this is even more noticeable if they are outsiders. Unless the analyst gains the management's cooperation, his task is considerably more difficult and, in fact, could lead to incomplete information gathering or biased evaluation. As a first priority, the analyst should secure proper authorization for the study and should inform appropriate personnel in advance that the interviews are to take place. Further, they must understand and concur with the purposes and objectives of the study and the procedures to be followed.

One further point, significant and yet easily overlooked, concerning preparation for interviewing: A respondent's reaction to the interviewer (and thus the interview, the job evaluation program, and the company) can be strongly influenced by the physical appearance and manner of the interviewer and the degree to which the interviewer fulfills the role envisioned by the respondent. Matters such as the dress, personal appearance, and demeanor of the interviewer are notably important and demand careful attention and consideration prior to the interview.

Setting for the Interview. It is difficult to generalize on the proper setting for an interview because of the varying conditions encountered and differences in job levels. It is often quite desirable to secure information directly at the work place and thus actually see the work in progress, the files or records kept, and the machines or equipment operated. This permits details to be uncovered that might otherwise be overlooked and permits questions to be answered firsthand, perhaps even by demonstration.

On the other hand, even though such on-site discussions are desirable, they are distracting and preclude privacy. It is generally agreed that the interview is so important to the collection of job data for evaluation purposes that it deserves the undivided attention, to the extent practical, of both the interviewer and the respondent. Thus, unless interruptions are necessary or particularly helpful, interviews should be conducted under circumstances wherein distractions are kept to a minimum and sufficient privacy is afforded to facilitate freedom of interaction.

To gain the benefits of both an on-site visit and a private interview, it is quite common to use both methods to gather data. For most administrative and middle and upper management-level positions, this is academic, of course, since on-site inspections are generally of little value.

The office or room used for the interview should afford privacy and be pleasant and comfortable enough to put the parties at ease. As indicated, telephone calls or other interruptions should be eliminated or kept to a minimum, and for this reason, even though the respondent may have a private office, the interview should be scheduled in a room reserved for interviewing purposes.

The Opening. The first five to ten minutes of an interview are considered crucial to the success of the interview. During this period, the initial and most influential impressions are created and the prevailing climate of the interview and the rapport between the interviewer and respondent are established.

The necessity for rapport requires more emphasis. An interview is an act of personal communication, an exchange of information, and a sharing of perceptions. This series of interactions occurs to the maximum mutual advantage only when the respondent sees the interviewer as one who is sincerely interested and likely to understand and accept him and what he has to say. When such a basis has been established, conversation is freer and a more revealing and objective dialogue emerges.

As most everyone approaches an interview with a certain amount of tension, the interviewer should begin by putting the respondent at ease through a few minutes of small talk, commenting on something that may well be of mutual interest. The interviewer himself should be friendly and unhurried and should show genuine interest. Since the respondent is also usually somewhat apprehensive and not sure of his role and what is expected of him, the interviewer should introduce himself by name, explain whom he represents, the purpose of the interview, the interview's structure, and how the information obtained will be used. Beginning questions should be those the respondent can handle with ease and assurance.

With the proper opening, the setting is established for proceeding with an in-depth information-gathering interview.

Conducting the Interview. It must be recognized at the outset that because of the human factor in interviewing, people conduct, participate in, and react to interviews in countless different ways. This is not to suggest, however, that the subject of conducting interviews cannot be discussed, but rather to indicate that the methods and techniques of interviewing vary with individual situations.

Motivating the Respondent. While to explore the subject of motivation is beyond the scope of this chapter, its importance to the success of the interview must be emphasized strongly. In order to obtain complete information, the interviewer must motivate the respondent to communicate readily and fully. This means the burden is upon the interviewer to make the interview meaningful and rewarding to the respondent and to create an atmosphere of sincerity, understanding, and acceptance. Obviously the human relations skills of the interviewer, as emphasized in the selection process, are of particular importance if the respondent is to be properly and effectively motivated.

Techniques of Interviewing. The skillful interview is vastly different from a simple question-and-answer session. In-depth and complete job information is acquired by the skilled interviewer through the use of varied interviewing techniques, examples of which include:

1. *Implication.* Without actually asking a question directly, the interviewer "implies" the question. This can be accomplished in several ways—for example, making a brief comment such as "I see" or "Oh, yes"; repeating a portion of a previous statement, thus implying that additional information is sought; and nodding and using various facial expressions. The major value of an implied question when used effectively is that it encourages continued response with little or no thought interruption on the part of the respondent.

2. *Pause.* A brief pause on the part of the interviewer, used at the right time, prompts additional and often more revealing responses. It makes the respondent feel he should continue, and gives him the impression the interviewer wants him to continue and is interested in what is being said.

3. *Listening.* Not to be confused with the pause, listening is another important technique. When the interviewer is talking, he is not gaining information from the respondent. The vast majority, perhaps 75 percent or more, of the talking in the information-gathering interview should be done by the interviewee. But listening is not a passive thing. To listen intelligently and with comprehension, the good listener must pay close attention and remember what is said.

4. *Observation.* Unlike on-site inspections of processes, machinery, records, or files, such as were referred to earlier, observation in this context is the attention to detail and notably to the behavior of the interviewee, thus gaining facts by inference and impression.

5. *Probe.* Not a question or even a series of questions per se, the probe is a technique to stimulate additional and more revealing information. It is a carefully tailored in-depth question which seeks to translate an inadequate response to one that meets specific objectives.

6. *Artful Questioning.* While this may seem obvious, it cannot be taken for granted. Skilled interrogation requires carefully phrased questions and the proper use of gestures, tone of voice, and facial expressions to overcome resistance, encourage participation, and impel the person interviewed to reveal the information needed.

Formulating and Posing Questions. Not only is a skilled interview not a simple question-and-answer session, but the questions are not mere impulsive queries. The questions posed during a skilled interview are the product of careful forethought and attention to specific objectives. They should encourage participation and elicit the information needed.

The questions must be worded so as to be meaningful and appropriate. If they are irrelevant to the subject at hand, they can lead to skepticism or distrust. They must be posed in a context familiar to the respondent. To generate proper responses, questions must not be embarrassing or threatening, contain elements of bias, or lead the respondent to the "proper answer."

Not only should questions be well thought out and carefully worded, but the manner in which the questioning itself is handled by the interviewer is of significance. Listed below are several suggestions for proper questioning.

1. Ask only one question at a time.

2. The voice and manner used in asking questions may be as important as the question itself, so use them to advantage.

3. Remain flexible and take advantage of openings suggested by answers of the respondent.

4. Be completely objective so that interview biases do not influence the respondent.

5. Encourage the interviewee to do the talking.

Control of the Interview. A major task of the interviewer is to focus and control the interaction between the parties so as to meet the interview objectives. This requires careful attention to the organization of the interview and consciousness of the time element. The interview cannot proceed helter-skelter; instead, the interview should:

1. Be conducted in a logical and orderly manner. However, for a more stimulating session, every once in a while the sequence of questions may be changed, particularly if they have fallen into a repetitive pattern.

2. Ensure adequate coverage of each area. All important areas should be explored, but a new topic should be started only when the current one is completed.

3. Be properly balanced. Subject areas should be given an amount of time commensurate with their importance. Problems will result if 90 percent of the interview is devoted to 10 percent of the job content.

4. Penetrate into the most important job duties so as to ensure the full and complete understanding of the critical elements of the job.

5. Efficiently utilize the time available. Rushing an interview or conveying impatience to the respondent is certain to lead to interview failure. On the other hand, the element of time is, of course, important, and the skilled interviewer will tactfully guide the respondent away from irrelevant discussions, let him know when a question or a topic has been sufficiently answered, and generally control the pace of the interview. Control of the interview is the task of the interviewer, and how well it is controlled depends primarily on his skill. Interviewers often use prepared interview guides to ensure control and thorough coverage. Samples of such guides are provided at the end of the chapter.

Ending the Interview. It is interesting that many interviewers find it difficult to know how to end the interview. When the interviewer feels he has all the job information, he should ask the respondent if he has any questions to ask or additional information to add, and then the interview should be terminated. To the extent practical, the interview should be ended promptly, particularly if a predetermined time allotment has been specified.

To close the interview, a simple statement will suffice, such as, "Thank you for coming to talk with me today. I'm glad we had this chance to explore your job together." At this point the interviewer simply rises (maybe extends his hand for a handshake) and walks toward the door.

Immediately after the interview, the interviewer should try to relax and think about the pertinent facts of the interview, making further notes as appropriate. If consecutive interviews are scheduled, a few minutes between interviews is recommended for this purpose and to allow the interviewer an opportunity to organize himself for the next interview.

The interviewer's job is far from complete when the interview session is over. The information has been gathered for some specific purpose—in this case, for job evaluation—and, thus, the interviewer must carefully review and analyze what he has gathered and answer two critical questions: is the information complete, and is the information accurate?

The *completeness* of the information is strongly dependent upon such interviewer-controlled factors as: adequate preparation for the interview; organization of the interview; the use of carefully formulated and penetrating questions; and the interviewer's ability to conduct himself and the interview in such a manner as to obtain complete information.

Concerning the *accuracy* of the interview, there is, of course, the possibility that a person may unwittingly give wrong information or make statements which he thinks he must make for one reason or another, even if they are wrong. But again the interviewer is responsible for accuracy, and he must, therefore, be able to distinguish facts from inaccurate statements. The skilled interviewer will verify information through his manner of questioning and, on the basis of his experience, identify erroneous statements or inferences. However, to the extent that the information needs to be verified beyond the interview, or that questions remain unanswered, the interviewer should follow up by obtaining information from additional and, as practical, independent sources.

In conclusion, the interview as an information-gathering technique is not infallible and is subject to errors and biases. However, although these possibilities for inaccuracy exist, a skillfully conducted interview is still considered the best information-gathering technique available.

INTERVIEW GUIDE
(NONEXEMPT)

Date:_____

Position Title:_____Dept.:_____
Incumbent:_____

1. FUNCTION of position

2. PRINCIPAL ACTIVITIES, and to what or to whom they relate. Type, calculate, post, —what? Take dictation or answer phone for whom? Test what materials for what characteristics?

3. Where accuracy of your work is important, how is it checked?

4. What is most difficult or complicated about your job? What makes it so?

5. What kinds of problems or questions do you refer to your immediate superior?

6. What kinds of contacts do you have with others, and with whom?

7. Do you instruct or follow up on the work of anyone else?

8. Other comments.

9. *Approx. Analysis of Time*

INTERVIEW GUIDE
(LINE MANAGEMENT)

Date:_____

Position Title:_____Dept.:_____
Incumbent:_____

1. ACCOUNTABILITY OBJECTIVE
   Reports to
   Accountable for

2. PRODUCTS
   Kinds
   Gauges
   Patterns (#)
   Formulations (#)

Fabricated forms
To cust. specs?

3. OPERATIONS or processes

4. EQUIPMENT utilized
Receiving or shipping statistics, where applicable—cars, trucks, lcl, ltl

5. Who SCHEDULES:
Products
Opers. or machs.
Manpower
Variety of prods., patts., orders, scheduled/shift, day, week

6. SPECIFICATIONS & CONTROLS—within which operations are conducted

7. Most frequent CONTACTS—with whom—why

8. ORGANIZATION SUPERVISED
Total people
Salaried
Hourly
Crews
Fluctuations
Union
Seniority groups

9. PRINCIPAL ACTIVITIES—(what you *do*)
Assignments
Instruction
Follow-up
Discipline
Complaints
Grievances
Contract interp.
Policy interp.
Selection
Training
Perform. eval. & recog.
Investig. oper. problems
Shut downs
Expedite correction
Get help
Follow through
Schedules
Flow of material
Follow through
Test runs
New prods. or patts.
Qual. improv.
Cost reduction
Job classif.
Incentives
Methods
Reports
Other

10. Most important OPERATING JUDGMENTS AND ACTIONS within your authority

11. Important OPERATING RECOMMENDATIONS made, for approval by others

12. Approx. breakdown of time

13. Other

INTERVIEW GUIDE
(STAFF MANAGEMENT)

Date:_____

Position Title:_____ Dept.:_____

Incumbent:_____

1. ACCOUNTABILITY OBJECTIVE
   Reports to
   Accountable for

2. SCOPE OF POSITION'S CONCERN—products—processes—equipment—operations—materials—people or their activities. Get statistics.

3. NATURE OF SERVICES rendered—controls developed or exercised—etc. Get statistics.

4. PROJECT EXAMPLES

5. MOST FREQUENT CONTACTS—with whom—why
   Inside

   Outside

6. ORGANIZATION SUPERVISED
   Salaried

   Hourly

   Union

7. PRINCIPAL ACTIVITIES—(what you *do*)

8. Approximate breakdown of time

9. Other

Part 2

Job Measurement

chapter 7

Developing a Perspective
on Job Measurement

EDWARD B. SHILS *Chairman, Department of Industry, Wharton School of Finance and Commerce, University of Pennsylvania, Philadelphia, Pennsylvania*

Too many employees look at job evaluation as a rationalization designed to justify the prejudgment of an employer or department head. The literature is full of detailed "systems" which appear to be unnecessarily complex and sophisticated. A point system with 38 factors has been lauded by one author as being the acme of precision and objectivity. Specialists' obsession with detail can so cloud the issue that ordinary employees or union representatives may grow bitter and suspect manipulation of the system.

The objective of the employer who sets up a job evaluation system is to provide a consistent measure of job worth which can be understood by everyone who is involved. In addition, a rationalization program can help in job training, personnel selection and recruitment, safety, work simplification, and other important areas.

No plan is so perfect that it is free of a single defect either in its manufacture or its administration. Plans are not people-free; hence, they are subject to human error and to varying degrees of subjectivity. The challenge is to alert those who administer a job measurement plan and the employees who must live with it to the plan's limitations so they can understand and accept the plan as it exists. All must learn that when minor errors are disclosed, these do not necessarily destroy the validity of the plan. On the contrary, a systematic plan may have errors, but it is nevertheless more useful than the confusion and inequity which result from unilateral management action based on hunches or playing favorites.

From the inception of a plan through its administration and subsequent revisions, supervisors and employees must be involved. It should be their plan, not the company plan, and it must protect them from favoritism and from internal pay inequities.

While the goal of rationality sounds so much better than simply proceeding like Topsy, one could ask, "How rational can a pay structure be?" In an effort to impress the more sophisticated employee, companies are moving into areas of abstraction, mathematics, and other complex techniques which shock those job analysts trained during the "civil service" period.

Personnel administrators may be placing too great an emphasis on charts, curves, and statistics. Statistical techniques may identify the problems, but supporting data are often lacking. Problems usually come to light through "symptoms." Complaints such as "I can't attract the caliber of people I need" or "I'm afraid that I am about to lose some of my best people to my competitors" are early indications of deep trouble. Administrators often investigate, talk to a lot of people, and produce a hypothesis about what is wrong. After that, the style is to provide statistics to support a conclusion. It is much more important to diagnose the problem correctly. Generally, statistical analysis takes up a great deal of time without getting to the heart of the problem.

Instead of attempting to substantiate a diagnosis by retreating to the calculator and graph paper, why not start out first with the hard data, then diagnose the problem more systematically and use follow-up investigation only to confirm or refine the problem?

There is increasing evidence that parties to wage decisions are greatly concerned about internal wage structures. It appears that rational wage structures based on informal or formal comparisons of job content are used currently by larger companies and unions to simplify internal wage structures and eliminate, where possible, individual job rate problems.

An AMA management study in 1960 disclosed that 65 percent of all employees in 500 responding companies were covered by formal job evaluation plans.

As these plans are also recognized by unions and brought into collective bargaining, they are found to simplify internal wage structures, reduce grievances, and assist in resolving grievances when they do occur. In nonunion companies, job measurement techniques are applied unilaterally by management, but usually involve participation and acceptance by those affected.

JOB EVALUATION ISSUES RAISED BY UNIONS AND EMPLOYEES

Union efforts toward a more rational internal pay structure have aimed at establishing union wage scales by negotiation and collective bargaining; setting pay rates for particular jobs; and attempting to put a floor under wages through advocacy of minimum wage legislation. While industrial unions have tended to push for increases in the entire structure, craft unions have fought for increases in the few selective occupations with which their members were concerned. These differing approaches are not as significant as they once were because interjob differentials measured in percentage terms have decreased, and both industrial and craft unions have bargained for wage scales that eliminate formal wage differentials based on race or sex. Area differentials still remain, with craft unions seeking their continuation, while industrial unions in nationwide contracts seek to eliminate them.

The official union position on job evaluation, with only a few exceptions—e.g., the United Steelworkers of America—has been one of strong opposition.

The opposition has been theoretical rather than pragmatic. Most union officials do approve of job rationalization techniques when they are faced with the issue and determine that job measurement can be helpful to the union cause.

Unions might officially frown on management-engineered job evaluation plans, but union officials have long used the principles of simple ranking and job classification in negotiations. Moreover, unions have never opposed job evaluation as long as it is not the *sole* determinant of wages or used as a substitute for collective bargaining. When faced by a need for a common yardstick to resolve intraunion disputes on relative job content, unions welcomed job measurement techniques. If other criteria were available to ascertain relative job content then unions could and did ignore job evaluation.

Unions favor the principle that more difficult and responsible jobs should receive more pay than less difficult jobs. Union leaders admit privately that they used evaluation before it was discovered by management.

Workers appear to be more concerned with their relative pay than with absolute wages, and hence they welcome rationalization which corrects internal injustice. Union leaders may not support formal job evaluation systems, but they do approve of job descriptions when used on a more informal basis. Furthermore, job rates are more honored by unionists than personal rates; unions, too, believe in paying for the job rather than the man.

While management often shows a rigid posture with respect to job content as the controlling factor in determining wages, union leaders more realistically point to other factors which in today's industrial scene have a more direct influence on pay. Included are the shortage of workers in a certain skill, the traditional sequence of jobs in the job hierarchy, seasonality of employment, promotional sequence, etc.

When management and unions are in accord in the use of job evaluation in collective bargaining, should such plans be jointly developed and jointly administered?

The question of management rights becomes the central issue in administration. Every time new equipment is to be installed, the company might have to negotiate the impact of this equipment on the classification of men assigned to it. For example, the union often believes that the bigger the machine, the more skill and responsibility are involved in operating it. Management, on the other hand, sees the larger machine as generally more automatic and hence easier to handle. Without union constraints as in a joint plan, the company would simply "get on with the job assignments." Perhaps, at a later time, the union might grieve. The union obviously is in a weaker position in arbitration than it would be if the company had to negotiate the job classifications with the union before the new equipment could be installed.

Union reluctance to accept a company plan stems from its fear and traditional distrust of any kind of industrial or "human engineering." All too often, management's compensation specialists claim that their methods are scientific and therefore infallible. Union leaders and employees in nonunion establishments argue, however, that even the most scientific system requires numerous judgments. Some managements have followed the advice of their consultants or internal committees blindly and have laid themselves open to charges of closed-mindedness. A statistical or quantified answer can get a nonunionized manager off the hook in a way not available to a business agent who would be accused by his constituents of playing "sweetheart" with the company on a job allocation under the new system.

One of the weightiest criticisms of job evaluation is that it is so rigid that it cannot adjust to changes in the job or in the marketplace. Critics oversimplify what they see as the prime function of job evaluation: namely, to determine salaries. Clearer thinking on the part of these critics would help them understand that the principal function of job evaluation is to set up a hierarchy of jobs to help in solving the problems of wage structure—not to solve the problem of wage levels. A proper maintenance program is necessary to avoid slippage in the new system. Staff and line must work together on job audits to minimize fears and personal concerns of reviewed employees.

Employees and unions continue to be disturbed by changes in traditional job relationships resulting from job evaluations. As one psychologist said about morale, "It's not that the worker is right or wrong about an issue, it's what's in his mind that must be considered." If a company hopes to improve performance through the application of job measurement, the techniques and procedures should reduce conflict, not increase it.

How do workers feel about distinctions between two jobs which appear to the job analyst to have the same skill content? The job analyst may see the job demands as being the same, while the employee sees one job as a dead end and the other as a step toward promotion and upward mobility in the organization.

A similar puzzle may be found when two jobs have similar content but one is characteristic of many firms in the community while the other is found only in the firm under study. It could be contended that one should receive higher pay than the other, because displacement in it would result in the worker requiring considerable retraining in order to qualify for a new position in another firm.

These complaints by employees or the union can be solved without trauma if the job measurement system builds in compensable factors to take care of these requirements. Also, where the plant is organized, fears can be reduced by the collective bargaining pact.

Another prime objection to job evaluation is a fear that supply and demand will not be considered in pricing the jobs. Many local unions lack professional staff who understand that jobs are evaluated first and then a study is made of wage levels for each key position. The average wage of the entire job hierarchy must be considered in terms of supply and demand, and where the union is involved, there will always be the protection of collective bargaining to temper the structure and provide modest adjustments.

When employers and unions agree to bargain on key or anchor jobs, the resulting rate adjustments generally can be applied to the rest of the job hierarchy with mutuality and harmony. Fear is sometimes expressed by the union that job evaluation limits the area of collective bargaining. This may be true where unions wish to negotiate, let us say, $600 across the board for all classifications. This application distorts the relative compensable factor totals in the point and factor comparison systems. Repeated dosages of the same procedure will result in wage compression. However, when unions negotiate percentage increases which are applicable to all jobs in the hierarchy, then the proper internal equities are maintained.

Charges are often levied by unions and employees that management-initiated plans are unnecessarily cumbersome, hard to administer, and difficult to understand. Unions want to know why simpler plans like the classification and ranking systems cannot be used instead of the point or factor comparison systems. Unions point out that for years before management initiated the sophisticated plans, the ranking or classification approach had been employed by unions on an informal basis as part of collective bargaining. Demands for craft minima have had this basis.

Another major issue between unions and management is that unions press for national wage levels and want to get away from the constraints of area wage surveys. Many employers—concerned with local living costs—want to compare rates within the area in which their plants are located. Unions want to bargain rates within the industry in which they represent workers and look at wages as a national pattern, industry by industry. They tend to reject arguments that living costs vary.

Unions and employees in nonunion firms fear skill dilution. Job statements and formal job descriptions permit job evaluation to be employed in work planning and work improvement. For example, if the employer finds that eight employees are spending one hour each on the same responsibility, he might assign this work to one full-time employee. The deleted duty might require a skill higher on the average than those remaining in each employee's package of duties. The net result might be a reduction in classification or "points" for the job. There is no doubt that changing technology is bound to influence job content and could result in reorganization and job displacement. However, were there no wage rationalization programs, employers would still be interested in work improvement. As employers introduce new technologies, they will seek to fund these new capital costs by increased employee productivity. This could result in displacement or the need to retrain employees for transfer to other jobs.

The effects of technology on job structure have aroused much speculation. Will the new technologies result in massive downgrading of job content? Should job classifications be broadened? Will new job descriptions for machine operators more closely resemble those of supervisors or technicians? Will automated jobs generally be worth less than conventional jobs? These and similar questions about job structure represent a host of thorny problems demanding the attention of both management and unions.

Knowledgeable executives have turned their attention to these questions. Most executives believe that current methods of job pricing are inappropriate to new machine-tending jobs. They believe that job description format needs revising in the direction of more emphasis on mental activities and less on manual. The contention that automation leads to wholesale downgrading of jobs has not been supported by most of the executives.

Job evaluation has come a long way since the pioneering work of Lott and Benge in the mid-twenties. Today its installation is taken for granted, and it is widely applied to manual and clerical positions. While many programs are carelessly maintained, management and workers agree that job evaluation has proved itself at the nonsupervisory level.

Up the scale, however, the record of job evaluation is less reassuring. While many front-line supervisory jobs are covered by job evaluation plans, managerial, sales, and professional positions are seldom formally evaluated.

Why is it that a company which has a good job evaluation plan for the clerical staff does not have an equally valid plan for its managerial group? Some of the reasons for difficulty in applying job evaluation plans to managerial jobs are given below:

1. Higher-level jobs range more broadly in duties and responsibilities than do manual or clerical jobs. This worries executives—they do not see how a job evaluation plan can cope with this problem.

2. There is a widespread feeling that at the higher level, the man makes the job.

3. Higher-level jobs are politically sensitive, and unless strongly supported by top management, plans to evaluate these positions are not likely to be pressed by staff people.

4. Failures of the higher-level management job evaluation plans continue

to exert a restraining influence on their rate of adoption. Generally, the failures are due to an inept approach to the problem. The common mistake has been to stretch clerical or manual plans upward. This is a misdirected effort.

The evaluation of exempt jobs is still in its infancy as compared with job evaluation at the manual and clerical level. As a result, the base salaries of exempt employees have tended to increase more slowly than those in the manual and clerical classifications.

THE WAR LABOR BOARD IN WORLD WAR II AND JOB EVALUATION

American businessmen have long respected the goals and promises of efficiency. The writings of Frederick Taylor, the Gilbreths, Gantt, and others were well-known to the undergraduate business student of the 1930s. In those days the promises of industrial engineering elicited the same excitement in business students as do management science and operations research in the current crop of MBA candidates.

With the exception of the government (the Federal Classification Act of 1923), most employers knew more about industrial engineering in the thirties than about pay rationalization.

During World War II, the nation operated under price and wage control. Wage and salary boards were not overly permissive in permitting compensation increases even when they were negotiated by employers and unions. The main drive was to hold the line except for catching up with increases in the consumer price index.

However, the War Labor Board in World War II did relax the "freeze" to permit periodic merit increases under some type of previously installed job classification plan. The government recognized the justification for an employee moving up through his grade range on the basis of merit and length of time in the grade.

Upward pay adjustments were also allowed when the aim was elimination of internal inequities. When a systematic job measurement analysis showed an individual to be in a lower grade or pay status than he should have been compared with other employees, the government permitted the adjustment, if a rational job evaluation plan was in effect.

Also recognized as a criterion for upward pay adjustments was external inequity. The Bureau of Labor Statistics made available monthly data to each firm and to the labor economists at the War Labor Board which showed area or national hourly earnings in such specific crafts as tool and die makers, carpenters, welders, etc. The employer, or in the case of an organized firm, both the company and the union, would present a petition showing that a negotiated increase requiring upward adjustment for a given group of employees was necessary. If the BLS survey disclosed their wages to be less than the market, then such data were used to justify the raises in pay.

In order to correctly apply BLS market data or even private market survey data accumulated by a company or union, it was necessary to make certain that the data covered *comparable* job content. The government was not receptive to granting raises simply on the basis of comparative job titles which were not supported by comparisons of job content. Company officials who raised their own wages or the wages of others without authorization by the War Labor Board could be fined and sent to prison. Therefore, it was very important to present a rationalized plan showing proper job measurement to governmental representatives.

In World War II, millions of employees were working in defense industries and were "frozen" in their jobs. This meant that they could not leave to seek work elsewhere without notifying their draft boards. Those without dependents who changed jobs without permission were in danger of being drafted. Since these employees were often being held in jobs in which earnings were frozen as of a base rate, the pastures always looked greener elsewhere. Hence, employers, unions, and government were very happy to have a pay rationalization plan to justify wage levels.

Because there were not many pay plans prior to World War II, the War Manpower Commission developed the *Dictionary of Occupational Titles* early in the war. This compendium was of great value for all personnel-minded persons, since it provided 21,000 short job descriptions, each with a code number. These books were made available to unions and firms and soon became the basis for moving forward into further rationalized pay plans.

The United States Department of Labor has continued to publish the *DOT*, and it now contains many thousands of additional short job descriptions. It serves as a bible to all personnel men. When personnel directors or compensation specialists develop their own company custom-tailored pay plans, they are often not able to relate either a point total or a standard title to similar jobs in all companies. Therefore, when the job being analyzed in the company plan can be identified in the *U.S. Dictionary of Occupational Titles,* the dictionary title and code should be entered in the company's personnel records. This can be done, however, only when the job under analysis is in all significant respects identical with the job defined in the dictionary.

During the Korean War, prices and wages were again frozen as of a given base date. The U.S. Wage Stabilization Board and the U.S. Salary Stabilization Board were then set up to operate almost identically with government procedures employed during World War II. While workers in defense industries were not frozen in their jobs, their willingness to stay in defense work was predicated on both internal and external pay equity. The government once more honored the criteria it had set up in World War II for relaxing the pay freeze. It permitted many adjustments to firms with rationalized pay and classification plans. By this time, pay rationalization had arrived.

In a 1963 Bureau of Labor Statistics study of 99 companies employing more than 1,000 white-collar workers, it was found that the following percentages of the companies developed the structure of white-collar pay plans in these years: 1941–1945 (12 percent); 1946–1950 (33 percent); 1951–1955 (26 percent); 1956–1960 (22 percent); and 1961–1963 (7 percent). This survey is important because it shows that many of these firms continued to adopt plans even after the original reasons for them had vanished. A third of the firms, seeing the benefits in World War II to firms which had pay plans, constructed plans in the years just after World War II and were able to benefit from government recognition of their rationalized systems during the Korean War.

PRINCIPAL JOB EVALUATION SYSTEMS

Formal job evaluation grew out of management thinking, while union wage scales emerged from collective bargaining. Both systems aimed to measure job worth and could be used together to improve understanding of what one pays wages for.

Today, almost all job evaluation programs are based upon job content analysis, the basic document being the job description, which defines the job's scope, difficulty, and end result if the job is performed adequately. In the sections that follow, the principal evaluation systems based on job descriptions will be discussed. However, there are other evaluation processes that are based upon elements other than job content. They are not as widely used or as well understood, and it might be useful to review one of them before proceeding to the more traditional systems.

Elliott Jaques developed the time-span method to measure the level of work in a job and to serve as the basis of an equitable salary structure. The concepts and mechanics of his system are explained in his *Time-Span Handbook*.[1] Jaques measures jobs in terms of their time span of discretion, i.e., the longest span of directly applied time, continuous or intermittent, involved in the performance of a task under the incumbent's own discretion. This period ends when the task is reviewed by the superior. Equitable payment is defined as the common norm of payment held by individuals of the same time span, when asked confidentially what *they* would consider fair pay.

Like other major systems, the time span approach seeks to measure job content. This, in engineering terms, corresponds to weight. The principal difference between Jaques' system and other systems is that Jaques used the calendar as a criterion of weight, while the more traditional systems consider size and density. In effect, then, the time space of discretion starts out with its end result—a total value based upon opinions of people asked in confidence how much the job is worth. Then the process proceeds to search for time units which can be arranged in a scale to reproduce the end results identified at the outset.

The time span approach is an interesting development in the field of job evaluation, and research on it is continuing. However, most job evaluation systems today still rely on job description. The U.S. *Dictionary of Occupational Titles* shows that these can be short and still be valuable. Most of the larger companies provide a detailed and somewhat sophisticated job description. In the opinion of many union leaders, these are unnecessarily detailed. The emphasis in the job description should be on the job and not on the person who is or will be performing it. The objective is to have those factors noted in the job which clearly facilitate comparison with other jobs in the company or in the industry.

The four major methods of job evaluation in use among American companies and in the public service are job ranking, job classification, the point system, and the factor comparison system.

Job evaluation begins with job analysis. On a basis of the job analysis by a trained evaluator, job descriptions and job specifications (attributes needed to fulfill the demands of the job) are developed. On a basis of this job information, each job is rated or evaluated. Job values or ratings provided by job evaluation may then be translated into wage rates, or jobs may be grouped to provide a series of grades, with rates or rate ranges for each grade.

General supervision of the whole job evaluation program is usually assigned to the employee relations staff. It requires a special competence, and an experienced wage and salary administrator should be assigned to direct this project. Studies indicate that the wage and salary administration effort requires about 1.5 full-time staff specialists per 1,000 employees once the program has been put into operation by committees and consultants. In small firms, the necessary competence may be secured by using the part-time services of one staff member, supplemented from time to time by independent consultants.

Employees and unions frequently participate in the job evaluation program. Employees should play an important role on the committee that plans the development and installation of the system. Employees should also serve on

[1] Elliott Jaques, *Times-Span Handbook*, Heinemann Educational Books, Ltd., London, 1964.

the rating committees which apply the required procedures to individual jobs. Participation by employees at all levels builds confidence in the equity of the plan.

Which job evaluation system is appropriate for a specific company will depend substantially on the compensable factors in the organization. After jobs have been studied and job information obtained, a directed and conscious effort must be made to determine what the organization is paying for. Using available job information, a decision is reached on the compensable factor or factors which determine the relative worth of jobs. Factors selected will largely determine whether a simple (job ranking) or a complex (point) system plan is best suited to the needs of the firm or whether a ready-made plan should be used, with or without modification, or whether a custom-built plan is imperative. Also to be determined is whether organization, employee, and union values can all be dovetailed sufficiently to yield a workable plan.

To be useful in comparisons of jobs, factors should possess certain characteristics. Factors should be found in different amounts in the various jobs. An attribute found in equal amounts in every job would be a worthless contribution to job comparisons. When it is discovered that many compensable factors exist, the most important should be selected.

When factors are reduced in number, job evaluation becomes easier to accomplish. Research indicates that results are just as satisfactory with few factors as with many. When more than a single factor is selected, these should not overlap each other in meaning. Employer, union, and employee viewpoints ought to be reflected by the factors chosen.

In the early stages of constructing the job evaluation plan, the committee will be seeking the single factor which is applicable to all the jobs in the organization and which could answer the question, "What is the organization paying for?" If no one factor or set of factors applies to all the jobs in the organization, the problem becomes one of determining factors for *groups* of jobs and then determining whether jobs should be considered in clusters.

If the factor or factors apply to *all* jobs within the organization, then it is time to proceed further. A good example of a single important factor is *job difficulty*. Examples of several factors which are usually selected include skill, responsibility, effort, and working conditions. Factors must be selected with care and patience. In most instances, a long list of suggested factors may be reduced substantially without harming a plan. The number of factors and their nature will ultimately determine what plan to follow.

In the larger organizations, key jobs are charged with the wage-making forces. Since key jobs are related to nonkey jobs and to each other, economy of effort suggests employing key jobs rather than all jobs as a source of data for compensable factors. Furthermore, since key jobs provide a channel of relationships between job groups, they provide the valued information as to whether given compensable factors are useful for comparisons *within* and *between* job groups.

When the proponents of the new system of job measurement find early in the process that no single factor or set of factors covers adequately all of the jobs in the organization, it then becomes necessary to classify the jobs into *groups*. In a typical large organization these divisions might be as follows: supervisory jobs, executive positions, sales, clerical, shop, and engineering jobs. Within each of these larger groupings or *clusters*, smaller categories present themselves, such as inspection or maintenance in the factory jobs. Other clusters are found in departments, skill families, etc. Content comparisons are least subject to noncomparability in these narrow clusters, weaker in the broader clusters or functional groups, and weakest between the broadest clusters.

Present practice employs different compensable factors even in the narrow job clusters. The current philosophy is that job measurement should be adapted to broad job clusters or functional groups. It has been found that wages of jobs within the same cluster tend to move together. Comparisons are made with ease within a cluster because of greater proximity, tradition, and custom. Moreover, all employees are well informed about transfer and promotion possibilities within the sequences of the cluster.

In determining whether or not to study jobs in a cluster, the size of the overall organization must be considered. Where the organization is large enough to think in terms of clusters, experience will show that the earnings of employees in different clusters will not always move together in equal amounts. The influence of the market on white-collar jobs as compared with blue-collar jobs is a case in point. There appears to be considerable economic justification for using the cluster system in large organizations. It may be concluded also that jobs in the same cluster should have their own set of compensable factors.

Discussion of this point has highlighted the difficulties of employment of the *same* compensable factors with respect to *all* job clusters in a large company. What is recommended therefore is the use of separate plans for each broad functional group. Hence, the manufacturing plant could employ the factor comparison plan, wherein key jobs are well defined and universally understood, while the clerical group could utilize the job classification plan.

In a clerical cluster, using the job classification plan, the committee could determine that pay is geared largely to the educational content of the job—e.g., the length of the preparatory training period, the nature of problems confronting the employee on the job, the serious implication of error, the responsibility for handling confidential information, etc. In the blue-collar cluster, the factors considered in the factor comparison method are mental, skill, and physical requirements plus responsibility and working conditions. When the cluster system is to be employed, it is best to evaluate jobs in, say, the clerical cluster before starting the factory plan.

It should be borne in mind that careful and patient involvement with suggested factors is bound to result in their numerical reduction and in a general improvement and an increase in the understanding of the plan. For example, the National Electrical Manufacturers Association and the National Metal Trades Association (now the American Association of Industrial Management) plan for factory jobs (NMTA-NEMA) was first designed by a group of 25 experienced men who knew intimately the 50 key jobs which had been selected. After detailed review of the descriptions of the key jobs and a listing of job characteristics, requirements, conditions, etc., the committee came up with 90 job attributes or characteristics. Careful study reduced the 90 compensable factors to 11 by *eliminating* factors of equal amount in all jobs, factors which applied to people rather than to jobs, and factors that overlapped so that one measured the other.

A United States Labor Department study concluded that the factors of responsibility (for material or product, safety of others, equipment or process, cooperation with others, instruction of others, and public contacts), job knowledge, mental application, and dexterity and accuracy required were factors applicable to *all* jobs.

An insurance industry study in the fifties indicated that factors might be reduced simply to job importance and job difficulty. These two factors are in reality mirrors of effective demand and supply, the influence of which is generally hidden from view in performing internal job evaluation.

A responsible committee should make the final decision on which major plan to follow and whether the cluster system should be used.   Depending on the size of the company, management may consider retaining an outside consultant to help review the job descriptions and, with the committee, distill compensable factors from these descriptions.   Reality should be the goal at all times.   Analyzing the current wage and salary differentials among key jobs in the company is important, and reasons should be sought to explain the difference in wages in terms of the factors.   A poll of worker opinions is appropriate, since workers think of these pay relationships constantly.   Beware, however, of workers' focusing on people rather than jobs.

A final decision on the employment of compensable factors must relate to organizational objectives.   The internal wage structure should be geared to provide incentives leading to employee promotions and upward mobility.   Obtaining human resources to meet the goals of the company should be within the firm's cost capacity.

The choice of a job measurement method must also recognize that the organization and its goals may change.   Furthermore, its technology might prove to be very different in a few short years.   The choice of the factor comparison system based upon key jobs might induce a rigidity which could be dangerous over time to some firms.   The point system, on the other hand, will provide a vehicle for constant change without a necessity to restructure the entire system.

The use of a ready-made system, which is already employed by other companies, will make it easy to secure comparable data on job content.   When job titles are standardized among the firms using the system, which might belong to the same trade association, all personnel departments will benefit.   However, using a ready-made system in which the factors are not relevant to the organization is a waste of time and will cause trouble.

The system chosen must blend in with the size of the organization, clusters in the organization, and the characteristics of the workers.   In some plants or firms, there will be little objection to a sophisticated, complex set of procedures, while in other firms simplicity is the tradition.   The ranking and classification methods are relatively simple, since no attempt is made to obtain quantitative measures of job value.   These plans are generally described as the "nonquantitative" plans.   The factor comparison and point methods are rather complex and are referred to as "quantitative" plans because of their use of points or monetary units in totaling the values of each factor included in each job.

The classification plan has been used widely in federal, state, and local governmental agencies as well as in smaller companies in private industry.   Ranking is also popular with smaller companies, since it is relatively inexpensive to install.   However, most American companies that use job measurement techniques employ the quantitative plans.

This frequency of use may indicate that quantitative systems are well suited to many industrial companies, but it does not indicate that such systems are any better in the abstract than any other evaluation systems.   A 1948 study by David J. Chesler showed an average correlation of .94 between point, factor comparison, and ranking systems in use.   The Chesler analysis stimulated other investigations which produced the conclusion that less complex systems tend to lead to results which are just as good as those contributed by the sophisticated quantitative plans.   Many quantitative systems are finally converted to classification plans by ranging point spreads between jobs.   This leads to better administration in the pricing of jobs.

Job Ranking Method.   The ranking system of job evaluation is generally used in smaller units.   It is the simplest method of the four and the easiest to explain. Jobs in the organization are ranked from highest to lowest. The system's major disadvantage is that it is employed without actually securing job facts; hence, it becomes somewhat subjective. Staff specialists or supervisors who know the organization generally do the job, and often the results reflect their biases.

Rather than worry about several compensable factors, the job is ranked as a whole. This method results in different responses from each of the raters, who undoubtedly are influenced by the present pay of the job, the incumbent, or the prestige value of the job. It might be possible to instruct raters to follow certain compensable factors rather than to regard the job as a whole, but if this is done the plan would lose some of its basic simplicity.

Job descriptions in this plan are generally very brief and similar to the length of such descriptions in the *Dictionary of Occupational Titles* issued by the U.S. Labor Department. In the procedure, a job evaluation committee studies descriptions of the jobs to be evaluated. Each member then ranks the job with a numerical value, 1 being the highest-rated job, 2 the second highest, and so on. The average for each job is its new ranking.

In the ranking method, jobs are generally considered by department, which reduces the value of the method for large companies in which interdepartmental ratings are necessary. Raters generally set up a deck of cards for the department, and then use the card-sorting methods or the "paired comparison" method. The cards have the job title and description written on them. Each job is compared with every other job on which ratings are required. Then departmental rankings must be combined into interdepartmental rankings. It becomes a problem to do this. To secure the services of one person who knows the ins and outs of all departments is difficult, so a committee made up of department heads is often used. By collating the number of rankings in a department and in the total organization, grades could be established for the entire firm. If this were done, the ranking system would actually operate as a job classification system.

Job Classification Method. The job classification method involves defining a number of classes or grades and fitting jobs into the classes provided. The Federal Classification Act of 1923 was the pioneer in this respect. By developing this rationalized system early, the government was able to persist in its theory of being accountable for the pay of several million federal employees under Civil Service. There had to be a doctrine of internal equity for the government to document and justify its accountability under the law. In the federal government today, any employee may appeal to the Civil Service Commission or to the Controller General of the United States if he believes that his grade and pay are less than the level of duty performed under the Classification Act.

The need for a classification of positions by duties and the gearing of salaries thereto was recognized in the federal government over 130 years ago. On the insistence of a number of government clerks urging "equal pay for equal work" in 1838, the United States Senate was moved to pass a resolution instructing department heads to prepare a "classification of the clerks . . . in reference to the character of the labor to be performed, the care and responsibility imposed, the qualifications required, and the relative value to the public of the services of each class as compared with the others."[2]

It was in 1923 that the federal government finally prepared the comprehen-

[2] Sen. Res. 25th Cong., 2nd sess., March 5, 1838, reported in Mosher, Kingsley, and Stahl, *Public Personnel Administration*, 3d ed., Harper & Brothers, New York, 1950, p. 208.

sive program first demanded of it in 1838. Nevertheless, other governmental jurisdictions were in the field as early as 1912, when the City of Chicago adopted its first classification plan. This was followed by Pittsburgh (1915), New York City (1917), Detroit (1925), and Los Angeles and San Francisco in 1930 and 1931, respectively.

The classification movement in government fitted admirably into the idea of a merit system and also into the wider aims of the efficiency and economy program. Hiring requirements in the federal civil service were to stem from job descriptions and job specifications after 1923. New principles of centralized financial control also demanded classification if the full possibility of better government was to be realized. Uniform accounting required a uniform job terminology in place of the hodgepodge of nondescript and conflicting titles.

Significant improvements in pay scales and in other provisions of the Federal Classification Act took place in 1928, 1930, 1941, 1942, 1945, 1946, and 1948. Finally, the old act was completely replaced by the Classification Act of 1949. For the first time, it made a clear distinction between the establishment of job evaluation standards (a task assigned to the Civil Service Commission) and classification of individual positions (a function left to the departments and agencies, subject to the Commission's power of post-audit and power to correct misclassifications). It also eliminated the former occupational services by setting up just two schedules (clusters) of grades, one for crafts and protective and custodial jobs, and another, called the "general schedule" (consisting of 18 grades), for all other classes of employment.

The job classification method may be compared to a bookcase which includes a series of carefully labeled shelves. The vertical arrangement defines a number of classes or grades, each of which can then be considered as one of the shelves. The toughest job is to describe each class or grade so that it will be possible to fit any of the jobs in the organization into a proper niche or shelf. The written grade descriptions permit the rater to evaluate the particular job and then to fit it into the proper class.

This method has a strong advantage inasmuch as in most organizations employees tend mentally to classify jobs in a shelf order in the job hierarchy. Managers tend to be stimulated by thinking of jobs as belonging to classes, and thus the problems of wage and salary administration become simpler.

This method can also be described as predetermined grading. For example, in the federal service, Grade GS-6 includes:

> All classes of positions the duties of which are (1) to perform under general supervision, difficult and responsible work in office, business or fiscal administration, or comparable subordinate technical work in a professional, scientific or technical field requiring in either case (A) considerable training and supervisory or other experience, (B) broad working knowledge of a special or complex matter, procedure or practice, or of the principle of the profession, art, or science involved and (C) to a considerable extent the exercise of independent judgment; or (2) to perform other work of equal importance, difficulty and responsibility, and requiring comparable qualifications.[3]

A review of the grade system used in federal civil service will reveal that Grade GS-6 will differ from other grades above and below it according to subtle gradations in such factors as job difficulty, supervision received, and the degree to which the employee is permitted the freedom of exercising his own judgment without immediate review.

In private industry often this plan is set up into job series, such as the engi-

[3] 5 U.S. Code 5104(6).

neering series, sales series, etc. These have been referred to earlier in this chapter as "clusters." The number of classes or grades in each series need not necessarily be uniform as between the several series.

The classification method is used by many small firms, which find that it provides a less awesome approach to job evaluation and reduces resistance on the part of employees and the union.

One weakness in the system is the difficulty of writing good grade descriptions. Most of these grade descriptions are based on duties and responsibilities rather than on compensable factors. The grade description must be so general that it will permit the classification of many different types of jobs, some administrative and some technical, unless there are many series or clusters created.

When grade descriptions are written generally in terms of duties and responsibilities, it encourages supervisors and employees to aggrandize the description of their own duties in their job statements, which later are evaluated by job analysts, who compare them with job and grade descriptions before final classification. High-sounding terms and phrases are used. For example, one young lady stated in her job statement that she "performed preventative maintenance on her typewriter." A second secretary stated that she "coordinated her boss," etc.

Another weakness of this system is that many jobs have duties which tend to fall in a higher grade while there are other duties in the same job which would fall in a lower grade. This forces the rater to average out the duties, thus putting the entire job into one grade. This weakness is eliminated by the use of the quantitative systems, which provide a weight for each factor evaluated in a numerical or monetary way.

The classification method also would involve the use of committees and perhaps an outside consultant upon initial installation.

The "Point" System. The point system is the method most widely used at the present time. It is one of the two quantitative systems, the other being the factor comparison system. In the quantitative systems, separate judgments are made on each of the selected factors and hence numerical values are attached to each factor. In calculating the entire value of the job, the total for each of the factors is the total value of the job.

The point method is somewhat similar to the classification method because both systems involve comparing jobs indirectly with a written scale. In the classification system the grade scale is vertical, while in the point system the degrees of each factor are described horizontally. For a detailed description of the mechanics of point plans, see Chapter 9.

In a 1955 study, E. Lanham of the Bureau of National Affairs found that 70 percent of companies with more than 1,000 employees used point plans, and only 12 percent of these large companies used factor comparison methods. On the other hand, the same study revealed that 55 percent of small firms used point plans and 25 percent used factor comparison plans.

The point plan is sophisticated and expensive to install. However, a valuable result of its employment is the development of a job evaluation manual which consolidates the factor and degree definitions as well as point values. These yardsticks can be used for many years without changes, even though the jobs themselves may change as a result of new technology, job dilution, or modification in the allocation of responsibility. Once the manual is complete, job rating can be initiated. The scales in the manual are used to evaluate jobs.

The popularity of the point plan is attributed to its wide use by trade associations and consultants who work with large enterprises. The most widely used of all the standard or ready-made point plans is the one developed for factory jobs by the National Electrical Manufacturers Association and the National Metal Trades Association (now American Association of Industrial Management). The AAIM plan is described in detail in Chapter 12, section 12.3.

The major advantage of the point plan is the longevity and stability of the rating scales. Point plans may increase in accuracy and consistency with use. The use of graphic rating scales and checklists reduces rating error and limits the influence of bias.

In view of the fact that points for each job may vary from 100 to, say, 500, with many jobs carrying weights of 333, 334, 335, 336, 337, etc., many plans provide for the ultimate conversion into job classes. Arbitrary point ranges then have to be decided upon.

Point plans, however, may be difficult to develop without outside consultants and internal committee members who have the time to worry about the details of factor selection and definition. Degrees of each factor must be worked out and weights allocated to factors with minute care. A point plan takes time to install, involves considerable clerical work, and is not easy to explain to workers and to the union. It very definitely will require centralized administration and appears more appropriate for use by larger companies.

The Factor Comparison Method.   Under the factor comparison method of job evaluation, one finds job-to-job comparisons similar to those made in the ranking system used in small enterprises. This differs from the point and job classification methods, where jobs are compared with scales.

Generally, the same five factors are used in all factor comparison plans, namely: mental, skill, and physical requirements, responsibilities, and working conditions. This factor rigidity may limit the technique's usefulness for particular organizations. "Key" jobs, which have the five factors in varying proportions, are selected and then compared with all other jobs, one factor at a time. For a detailed discussion of how factor comparison methods work, see Chapter 10.

It is quite possible that the major advantage of the system, namely, its simplicity in using the current hourly pay for each key job and applying a monetary unit to price each factor, might also be its major disadvantage, inasmuch as the use of the monetary unit can result in bias and subjectivity.

Another possible weakness in this plan is that to utilize the key or anchor job concept the wage rate must first be correct in terms of both internal and external alignment. Since these are anchor jobs, their usefulness will depend upon the validity of the anchor points represented by these jobs. Jobs, however, change slowly and imperceptibly. If these were to continue to change over time without detection of changes or correction of the scale, users of the job comparison scale would be making decisions on the basis of warped anchor jobs.

A still further disadvantage, especially to a small company, is the numerous and complicated steps necessary to build the job comparison scale from the key jobs.

A LAST WORD JOB MEASUREMENT

The literature is full of data showing the superiority of custom-made plans over the ready-made systems. Numerous studies were made at Purdue in the post-World War II years in which the straight National Electrical Manufacturers Association (NEMA) plan, the NEMA plan with modifications, and a factor comparison plan were analyzed statistically. It was concluded that the

NEMA shop plan and the factor comparison plan in those firms where these plans were examined placed from 77.5 percent to 99 percent of the total weight on skill factors. In most of these installations, two or three factors carried almost the entire weight.

In experiments carried out at Purdue by Lawshe, it was found that an abbreviated scale of only four factors, namely, learning period, general schooling, working conditions, and job hazards, produced results superior to the National Electrical Manufacturers Association plan. The Purdue researchers made a profound contribution to the science of job measurement. It was inferred from the research that applicable compensable factors may vary from one enterprise to another and from one cluster to another; that a limited number of factors might still produce a sound system; and that there ought to be enough factors in the system to satisfy the wishes of the parties.

There appear to be growing feelings among unions, companies, and employees that plans are growing more workable over time. This belief could be a mark of their validity. Experience serves to mitigate union fears that a job measurement plan exposes employees to faulty judgments, factor overlap, and bias. Patton, in a 1960 American Management Association Management Report, disclosed that 93 percent of the unionized firms and 86 percent of the unorganized firms found their job evaluation programs to be "rather successful" to "highly successful" in range. Many unions definitely favor job evaluation but officially may continue to oppose it.

A good job evaluation plan must involve the harmonious cooperation of top management, supervisors, employees, and union. All should take part in the initial planning. No plan should be launched in which an employee is not permitted to write up a statement of his duties and responsibilities as he sees them and sign and date it on the form provided. Complete participation in the process facilitates acceptance when the grades or allocations are announced. Furthermore, each employee should have the right to appeal his classification to a committee of employees.

The use of an outside consultant permits managers and workers to be taken through the learning and planning process by the consultant, thereby avoiding traditional eyeball-to-eyeball conflicts. The heat between boss and worker is transferred to a third party, who acts as teacher and catalyst. Once the plan is initiated and the job evaluation manual completed, there will be less need to use the outside consultant, except perhaps to bring him in periodically to audit the maintenance and policing of the system. For example, where key or anchor jobs in a factor comparison system begin to change, the outside consultant can bring up these changes without emotional stress to the parties.

When the job measurement work is completed and a formal job evaluation plan is prepared, the major challenge is to correctly price the jobs in the hierarchy and come up with a total wage structure. All parties to the rationalized system have by now become conscious of the difference between payment for the job and the pay which current incumbents on jobs are drawing. At this point, much conflict will result unless the wages for the newly classified jobs reflect proper internal equity as well as comparability with jobs of the same nature in the external market. Here the skills of the wage and salary administrators as well as consultants can be tapped. The only one of the four systems described in this chapter which will not require the same degree of pricing detail is the factor comparison plan, in which current dollars are used instead of points, grades, or ranks in determining job relationships.

chapter 8

Achieving Internal Equity through Job Measurement

RICHARD E. WING *Director, Compensation, Corporate Compensation and Benefits Department, Eastman Kodak Company, Rochester, New York*

This is a peculiar decade in which to describe job measurement and equity and their relationship to the administration of wages and salaries. Ten years ago it was generally agreed that equity in compensation could be achieved through careful job measurement; the untested assumptions implicit in most wage and salary administration practices were accepted without question. D. W. Belcher's book of 1955 outlined rather well some existing methods of job evaluation.[1]

These systematic practices had hardly been put to work, however, when contemporary theorists began to question their theoretical underpinnings. In a 1969 *California Management Review* article, Belcher himself reviewed the implications of recent work in psychology, sociology, and management science for compensation administration and concluded that existing practices were based on "untested assumptions—assumptions about the relationship between money and motivation; assumptions about how employees perceive equity and how this compares with employer concepts of equity; and assumptions about the relationship between perceived equity and motivation."[2]

The practitioner responds, "Did I make all those assumptions? I thought I

[1] David W. Belcher, *Wage and Salary Administration*, Prentice-Hall, Inc., Englewood Cliffs, N.J., 1955.
[2] David W. Belcher, "The Changing Nature of Compensation Administration," *California Management Review*, vol. XI, no. 4, Summer, 1969, pp. 89 ff.

designed a pay system which organized a group of human judgments into a program that employees and management would accept. Our program is just beginning to be well understood. Now the researchers tell me it's all wrong."

The following material comes from the synthesis of ideas exchanged informally between compensation administrators in industry and government and consultants faced with the immediate task of designing and implementing workable pay programs. Research is always welcomed. It may ultimately place some of this practical work on a firmer base, and it may likely reject and replace parts of this work with better concepts. This is progress.

EQUITY DEFINED

What is equity? Are there many types? Internal, external? Perceptions of those who determine salaries? Perceptions of those whose salaries are determined?

Equity is a perceived sense of rewards balancing outputs—pay proportionate to achievement—a parent's praise and criticism balanced with a child's perception of his behavior compared with the rewards and behavior of a brother or sister. Some might accept the notion that equity relates closely to fairness, but fairness is equally hard to define. The philosopher might say that equity, like beauty, is in the eye of the beholder.

Certainly there are many perceptive points from which pay equity can be viewed or felt.

If the foregoing descriptions of equity are confusing, try then to present a solid, tested, acceptable definition to the many managers of a large organization employing a variety of staff and professional specialists. Current practice *assumes* that the more important individual perceptions of compensation equity are derived within the organization in which a person works. Perceptions of equity may be influenced more forcefully by factors close to the person's actual work environment. One can hypothesize that an individual may derive his equity perceptions from sources which may be ranked in descending order of importance somewhat as shown below:

1. Within the smallest work unit: department or task group
2. Within the next larger organization unit: department, laboratory, or division
3. Among peers doing similar work
4. Among peers doing dissimilar work
5. Within the plant
6. Within the union, within the profession, or among managers having similar responsibility
7. Between plants within the company
8. Within the company as a whole
9. With outside companies

Probably the order of importance varies according to the type of job an individual has—i.e., a salesman's perception would probably differ from a factory worker's. *Presumably,* the broader the exposure of the individual to practices outside an individual work unit, the greater the number of considerations leading to perceptions of equity or lack of equity.

Several conclusions are suggested by this analysis of equity perceptions:

1. Executive perceptions of equity may be derived from sources far different from those influencing the majority of people in the organization. For example, one executive expressed great concern because a staff man suggested a specific pay action for factory people at one location based on community prac-

tice but recommended the action be withheld from other locations under the administration of the executive. The executive's perception of equity encompassed all locations; the staff man rated the local situation as more important.

2. It is probable that individual concepts of compensation equity are strongly influenced by the existing reward system in an organization and the way the reward system is administered. Thus, an organization that works hard to develop sound job measurement practices, promotes on the basis of ability and achievement, and awards salary increases for observable results will probably create an environment in which internal equity is perceived by many. Management reinforces its desire for achievement by rewarding those who achieve. Conversely, every time a salary increase is awarded to a nonperformer, equity perception among employees may be damaged. Poor promotion decisions are even more discernible.

3. Perceptions of equity, or standards of work value, are so variable and changing among people, among professions, and among various organizations that a single organization must develop its own set of value standards and sustain those standards over a period of time if they are to have meaning and are to influence perceptions of equity. Thus, the organization should use caution in attacking or changing a long-established set of job relationships, regardless of the source of the equity perceptions which originally generated the relationships. In the long run, internal relationships between job values (internal equity) are far more important than external relationships with other companies (external equity). There are some high-morale, effective organizations which pay wages and salaries that are modest by comparison with other organizations having similar work. Frequently these organizations have given great care to developing firm standards of internal job measurement. Therefore, pay distinctions are generally perceived as internally equitable.

It has been suggested that equity, or inequity, exists as an individual perception and that these perceptions are influenced by a variety of factors. Actually, psychologists have developed a theory of equity and continue to explore the relationships of equity to motivation. J. S. Adams[3] defined inequity as follows:

> Inequity exists for Person whenever he perceives that the ratio of his *outcomes* to *inputs* and the ratio of Other's outcomes to Other's inputs are unequal. This may happen either (*a*) when he and Other are in a direct exchange relationship or (*b*) when both are in an exchange relationship with a third party and Person compares himself to Other.

The general observations previously made on the subject of equity are consistent with Adams' definition. However, it should be emphasized that when people weigh their *outcomes* and *inputs* relative to their job and the jobs of others, they will consider many nonfinancial elements as well as financial rewards. Traditional restraints imposed on compensation administration, however, confine its actions to evaluating jobs and determining only financial rewards. Hence, this chapter should technically be titled "Achieving *Pay* Equity through Job Measurement." The concerned manager should always consider the fact that individuals paid well for the job they are doing may still feel a sense of gross inequity from a variety of nonfinancial factors which overwhelm the pay rewards. Such factors include lack of recognition, failure to achieve

---

[3] J. S. Adams, "Toward an Understanding of Inequity," *Journal of Abnormal Psychology*, 67 (1963), pp. 422 ff.

promotion, and inherent job dissatisfaction as Person compares his education, achievements, and interests with those of others.

PURSUING EQUITY

Two extremely different approaches can be taken to establish job values in an organization:

1. Derive value and price concurrently from measures outside the organization: *market value approach.*

2. Develop internal standards of comparison and measure relative job values within the organization: *job evaluation approach.*

Market Value Approach.   The market value approach—using salary survey data to determine the price to be paid for various jobs—appears the easiest to pursue.   It is frequently the expedient approach for some public, nonprofit institutions—situations requiring acceptance by employees, taxpayers, and political leaders.   It is difficult to quarrel with salaries determined exclusively by market survey information.

For most business organizations, however, the market value approach is less desirable because it may invite comparison between jobs that are not truly comparable.   It tends to ignore internal considerations and can produce inequities noticed by employees and executives.   Wage and salary surveys—even among companies within the same industry—are of questionable value if used for anything more specific than an overall reference point from which to price a company's salary structure.   Casually acquired survey information is no substitute for solid analysis of the relationships among the jobs designed to meet specific company objectives.

For example, consider a small company with these activities: a development laboratory with a technical director; a marketing and distribution organization with a marketing director who also manages a small advertising department; a manufacturing organization consisting of two small plants under the direction of a manager of manufacturing; and a small finance and administrative unit under an administrative vice president.   All major units except finance and administration report directly to the president.

The salary administrator arms himself with organization charts and brief descriptions of the staff and managerial jobs in the company.   By phone and three-hour individual visits to a group of 12 or 15 companies, he collects salary information for jobs in the other companies that are about like those in his company.

At this point chaos develops.   If the administrator is a relatively inexperienced staff man working for the administrative vice president, he may never recognize the problems he is creating.   Neither will the vice president, who merely wants an answer superior to the seat-of-the-pants approach the company has followed for years.   After all, he has provided several weeks of valuable staff time for a market survey of salaries!   Who can argue with the marketplace?   The salary data are collected, averaged, and used to determine fair pay for most of the company's jobs.   To be sophisticated, ranges of merit pay are developed with a spread of about ± 20 percent around the survey averages for the various jobs.   A final professional touch smooths some of the data so that there are constant percentage differences between salary ranges for work in each activity—technical development, finance, sales, etc.   No one pays any attention to the relationships of pay between jobs in dissimilar activities; after all, these arbitrary relationships are established by the survey!

When the final results are presented to the key management group, the technical director and the manufacturing manager complain that the salaries are too low in their activities compared with the sales salaries, but they cannot dispute the survey data, and the salary program is put into effect.

There are several basic weaknesses in the market value approach as outlined in our example, the most important stemming from difficulties in job matching.

If differences in size and organizational structure of surveyed companies are not taken into account, jobs cannot be properly matched. Except for a few skilled trades, service jobs, and factory operator jobs, there are very few jobs that are well matched between companies, even though they may have the same titles and involve the same general duties. This lack of comparability is particularly true of staff, supervisory, and managerial jobs. Reporting relationships, organization characteristics, and management expectations for each job will vary; and in many instances, subtle but important job responsibilities are unknown to the staff people exchanging the salary information.

Sheer differences in size among companies can make job matching impossible. In our hypothetical illustration, the salary administrator encountered several companies with three levels of outside salesmen, at least three companies had four levels, and still others had two levels. Since his company had defined only two levels of sales jobs, the data collector ignored third- and fourth-level sales jobs in the survey companies. He encountered even more difficulty with the technical job comparisons. Several of the larger companies had five levels of development engineers. Once again the salary administrator had described only three levels within his company, so the data collector ignored data for levels of engineering work beyond three.

Because of organizational differences, he found reasonable matches for managerial jobs in only two or three companies. Unfortunately, no company's jobs were comparable across-the-board; some had jobs which matched reasonably well in sales, others in engineering, still others in manufacturing. Final survey data reflected variations in salary policy among companies as well as errors in job matching. The companies surveyed differed significantly in pay objectives, so that some paid high salaries, others low, and some intermediate salaries. The low-paying companies produced the best comparisons for some jobs and the high-paying companies the best comparisons for other jobs. The net result was a wide variation in economic influence reflected in the pay levels of the company conducting the survey.

The majority of employees whose pay was determined by the marketplace technique accepted the results. There were complaints from some, but these were written off as the usual gripes of a few malcontents. There would have been more serious complaints, but very few employees had enough information at first to judge the extent of the internal inequities. Presumably, it will be several years before a large number of people recognize the inequities. Perhaps by the time serious demotivation becomes apparent in several areas of the company, changes in organization and supervisory training sessions will be tried to improve staff effectiveness.

If the illustration seems overdrawn, do not reject it hastily. In all too many organizations, in both apparent and subtle ways, a diverse set of unrelated *outside* pay relationships are influencing *internal* pay decisions. These decisions stem sometimes from inept staff techniques but frequently from the diverse ways in which influential managers perceive outside pay.

Sound techniques exist for translating salary survey information into an internal salary structure. Such techniques avoid some of the pitfalls in the hypothetical case just illustrated. However, even if one assumes the data collected are sound and are a well-balanced representation of the marketplace, does it necessarily follow that internal decisions of relative job worth should be based on the average prevailing statistical accident in society?

Staff and managerial jobs typically vary from company to company. A sound salary program, therefore, demands careful analysis of jobs and their interrelationships based on the intrinsic value of the jobs to a specific company.

Job Evaluation Approach.   The objective of job evaluation is to develop a set of value standards for establishing the *relative* worth of each job to a specific organization.   Job evaluation is *not* intended to provide absolute answers in terms of current dollar values.   (The absolute assignment of dollar values based upon surveys and pricing decisions is a separate problem discussed in Parts 3 and 4.)   The job evaluation process can be designed to group jobs into clusters having similar internal worth.   The process can further develop a relationship between and among all clusters.   The net result is to establish an internal structure of jobs.   However, it is *not* essential to produce job clusters and assign them salary grade numbers; the process can be designed to produce continuous job values without forcing jobs into clusters.   A soundly conceived and administered job evaluation plan offers many advantages to any organization:

1. *It permits top management to influence the standards against which jobs are evaluated without getting involved in the detail of job description.* Since no set of standards will apply to jobs in all companies, management participation in the determination of these standards must be an integral part of the job evaluation plan.

After all jobs are evaluated, key jobs should be selected to illustrate the full spectrum of relative values established for each activity.   The key jobs for each major activity in an organization—e.g., finance, marketing, research, and administration—should be charted to present the relative values horizontally between the activities as well as vertically within each.   Executive management can carefully examine the relative job value relationships between and within activities in order to appraise the results of the evaluation process and to determine whether evaluation guidelines are producing desired end results.   This process can be repeated periodically to keep management up to date with the program.

2. *It serves as an aid to manpower management.*   The involvement of operating managers in the job evaluation process allows them to relate organization plans, job design, and manpower planning to their total objective.   Jobs are characterized; value-determining elements of jobs are delineated.   Selecting people with appropriate experience and abilities to meet job requirements becomes a more precise process.

3. *It can help improve employee perceptions of pay equity.*   With sound job evaluation, presumably employees will perceive that their pay is related fairly to the value of the work they are asked to do.

Weaknesses in application of job evaluation principles, however, may retard complete acceptance of job evaluation as an important management tool, particularly in medium- to large-size companies and as applied to exempt jobs. Such weaknesses may arise from:

1. *Overemphasis on technique.*   Some wage and salary staff personnel have taken a rather mediocre evaluation plan and presented it to managers as a scientific measuring device as reliable as a physicist's measurement of atomic weights.   Using carefully chosen adjectives and point evaluation scales, some people have attempted to define relative values with precision, in some cases with only limited knowledge of the jobs to which the evaluation techniques were applied.   Thoughtful managers tend to rebel against such "expert" staff

assistance, and they question the ability of a few staff people to judge the intrinsic value of jobs.

2. *Inappropriate use of evaluation plans.*   A few evaluation plans that have been highly successful in relating hourly and clerical job values have been extrapolated to professional, administrative, and executive jobs.   Few plans are equally effective throughout the entire range of job content from janitor to company president.   In the exempt salary area, the ranking technique has also contributed to poor acceptance of evaluation plans.   With the ranking technique every manager and staff person is immediately expert in evaluation. Each is free to develop his own rules of thumb, and each can choose any jobs he wants to justify his results.   Also, ranking plans may tend to encourage managers to develop and defend high job values in their activities.

3. *Poor analysis of jobs.*   All too frequently, job content has not been analyzed adequately.   Even with a good evaluation plan, poor job analysis will yield poor evaluation results.

4. *Staff failures.*   Good evaluation demands a breadth of perspective and a keen insight into the management process and into the nature of a wide variety of jobs in a company.   The ideal evaluation expert is the executive with the broadest company experience.   Such a person is always too burdened with responsibilities to spend hours each week carefully collecting data and analyzing job values.   In choosing wage and salary administrators to supervise the data gathering, analysis, and surveys and to guide the evaluation process, managers have not always selected people with sufficient breadth and perspective to devise, maintain, and improve an evaluation program.

Understanding some factors that impair the acceptance of job evaluation helps to define the conditions under which sound internal value relationships can be developed and maintained.

There is no single panacea.   The best evaluation plans can fail.   A staff with heavy authority and executive support can fail.   The development of sound internal job relationships within a company requires a full set of balanced conditions, much as a high-performance engine requires excellent materials, machining to close tolerances, and a precision balancing of the assembled pistons, connecting rods, and drive shaft.

The best evaluation work within an organization requires a self-imposed total discipline.   Managers must thoroughly understand and accept the objectives of internal evaluation.   They must impose the discipline upon themselves because of the favorable objectives they perceive and want to achieve.

CHOOSING AN EVALUATION PLAN

An evaluation plan should be relatively straightforward in design.   It should apply to a wide range of highly specialized managerial and staff jobs, or specifically to factory nonexempt jobs.   The plan should emphasize the major elements of job value and ignore the trivial or irrelevant.   Above all, the plan should be applied with sensitivity and understanding.   Most evaluation plans are improved if they are first applied to an array of key jobs which serve to calibrate the evaluation factors.

The plan should be carefully developed and thoroughly tested.   Frequently the experience of qualified consultants is helpful in developing and implementing a program.   The better consultants will thoroughly involve responsible management and appropriate staff people in the design and testing of a plan. No long-term useful result is achieved by having a consultant actually evaluate all jobs, review the results with a few key executives, install the plan, and leave. Such an approach fails to develop the staff involvement necessary for continued application of the plan: the person appointed by management to administer the program would be forced to apply the plan by rote, since he was not exposed to the subtle philosophy and experience on which the plan was based.

Job evaluation requires extensive use of disciplined human judgment. No existing plan applied by inexperienced staff people can produce creditable results. A major part of the disciplined judgment comes about by involvement in the design and testing of the plan. Some may feel that the existence of the judgmental element and the requirement of experience would indicate that evaluation plans are of little value. Are the tools of a skilled cabinetmaker poor or useless because an inexperienced workman fails in an attempt to build a complicated piece of furniture?

IMPLEMENTING THE PLAN

A member of the wage and salary staff should analyze jobs in considerable detail. He should discuss the jobs with incumbents, and, with their supervisors or managers, should identify and define the reporting relationships surrounding a job and define the broad purpose for which the job is intended. Value-determining factors within the job should be identified on the basis of the major duties and job responsibilities. A summary of the major features of the job should be committed to writing and submitted to the responsible manager for approval.

Job analysis has always been guided by one basic rule: *define and measure the job and not the individual.* This important guiding principle applies to all job levels. Perhaps it is worthwhile to add one other precaution in evaluating exempt jobs—namely, consider only those aspects of the job that are currently being performed and are currently delegated. Responsibilities that are expected to unfold at some future date should *not* be considered unless the manager is in the actual process of redesigning a job. Incumbents do influence jobs; evaluation decisions need not be permanent; and a job can be reevaluated if a significant increase or decrease in responsibility is reported.

Roles of Staff and Management. Proper evaluation of jobs should be the responsibility of line management, with each level of management accountable to the next level for evaluation results. However, there is a definite role for qualified staff to perform in the process. Their role should be recognized, supported, and utilized if equitable job values are to be attained. It is essential that managers avoid reaching agreement with subordinate members about job values through a casual discussion of factors and without a prior review by a competent staff person. Only by exercising considerable care in this regard can the impact of neutral and experienced staff analysis become meaningful.

Within a large organization a systematic approach to job evaluation provides the framework within which final approval or authorization of recommended job values can be delegated to various levels of management. It also provides a framework within which both central and decentralized staff work can be conducted with recognition, respect, and cooperation between staffs. The charters of responsibility for central and decentralized staff in the evaluation process should be clearly defined.

Review and Approval. Details of an appropriate review and approval process must be related to the size and complexity of an organization. Nevertheless, there are some general principles worthy of consideration.

The final authorization of job values should be delegated to some degree and should not be retained in total as a chief executive function. For example, in a large company having at least six broad levels of management, final authorization of job values might be delegated as shown in Table 1.

The generalized scheme shown in Table 1 suggests that no managers, except the top executive group, authorize job values for people reporting directly to them. The term "authorize" is used in the context of a final decision, with no further executive review.

Before authorization, there should be an approval and recommendation routing for all job value changes or for the introduction of new job values. This vital sequence helps guarantee independent staff analysis. A typical sequence of preliminary approval and recommendation could be as follows:

Approval		*Review* *and* *Approval*		*Review* *and* *Approval*		*Authorization*
Recommending Manager	→	Wage and salary Admin. Staff (Staff of Oper. Executive)	→	Wage and Salary Admin. Staff (Corporate)	→	Appropriate Level of Management

Suggested approval and authorization schemes vary widely, depending on the size of an organization and the degree of centralization. However, some principles are always applicable:

1. Managers should not authorize values for jobs reporting directly to them.

2. Final authorization of job values should be a line management responsibility.

3. Independent staff analysis will be guaranteed by the approval sequence if the sequence is followed rigorously.

4. Dissenting viewpoints should be reconciled at each step in the approval and authorization process.

5. Any changes made along the approval route should be communicated promptly to the originating manager. Variations in the staff approval plan may exclude one of the staff approvals but should not exclude both.

What are the benefits of following a systematic job evaluation program as outlined in this chapter?

1. Managers are completely involved in job design and evaluation judgments. They are then in the best position to relate organization plans and manpower development considerations to the total process of managing people.

TABLE 1   Proposed Delegation of Authority for Job Values

Level number	Job level	Authorization for
	Board of Directors	Top executives
6	Top Executives	All operating executives and fourth- level management jobs
5	Operating Executives	All third-level managements jobs and any corresponding level of staff jobs
4	Activity Managers	Two levels of management jobs and corresponding levels of staff jobs
3	Third-Level Management	All nonexempt jobs
2	Second-Level Management	
1	Foremen	

2. An orderly relationship of job values evolves. Key jobs can be abstracted and surveyed to price the entire structure of jobs.

3. Valid external comparisons can be made. Evaluation principles are useful in sampling representative jobs in outside companies and pinpointing their place in the internal salary structure.

4. Results may be supported by social science research:

(a) *Learning theory.* Individuals find reinforcement of a company's stated policy that pay is determined on the basis of work performed.

(b) *Training.* A systematic body of knowledge, as opposed to personal whims and hunches, can be transferred between executives and between and among responsible staff personnel.

(c) *Communications.* A well-defined approach lends itself to forthright communications to all whose pay is affected by evaluation decisions.

(d) *Credibility.* The application of common evaluation principles to all jobs from the chief executive to entry-level jobs for inexperienced people avoids gaps in understanding and communications. Similar messages flow up and down the organization levels. People gradually perceive the fact that achievement is the biggest factor in pay determination.

(e) *Motivation.* Many demotivating or negative attitudes among employees are avoided by good internal evaluation of jobs.

A well-delineated approach lends itself to future improvement and change in an orderly fashion as social research and experience suggest practical improvements.

At this point it should be obvious that developing and maintaining internal equity through job evaluation requires work—constant work on the part of many people, both management and staff. Is it worth all the time required? Cannot the process be simplified? Managers have heavy work loads. How can they be expected to spend so much time on job evaluation? Job evaluation should play an important role in the total management of human resources. If a company expects to manage these resources successfully, and if the cost of total compensation is considered, developing and maintaining a sound evaluation program are well worth both time and effort.

Job evaluation is not a science. Guiding, training, and sharpening judgmental processes cannot be done by a computer. Every effort should be made to keep the evaluation process as simple as possible. Nevertheless, there is no shortcut for the initial and recurring individual involvement that managers should give to the program.

Finding the time within a busy work schedule is perhaps really a question of being convinced that the problem is significant and that results achieved bring a favorable return to the manager and to the company.

BALANCING INTERNAL AND EXTERNAL EQUITY

After the internal job relationships have been established, and after the job structure has been priced in some policy relationship to prevailing wages and salaries, there are other important variables to identify, analyze, and control.

Specific to job evaluation is the problem of reconciling decisions about internal equity with pay competition from external sources. During the past ten years, managers responsible for specialized functions have been constantly plagued by the tension existing between internal equity of job values and outside pay competition. At one time or another an imbalance between supply and demand has created special pay problems for a variety of specialists, such as scientists and engineers, mathematicians, data processing personnel, machinists, technicians, and patent attorneys. The future will bring other tensions which tend to distort internal equity of job evaluation. To maintain job evaluation integrity, important administrative actions must be taken periodically. Even without the tensions created by imbalances between supply and demand for certain skills, dynamic dimensions for salary administration must be identified and directed by policy.

The dollar values assigned to the salary structure must be adjusted periodically and by a sufficient amount to maintain a prescribed policy relationship to some defined external pattern of pay. The failure to adjust the price of a salary structure adequately accounts for much of the tension many organizations consider to be unusual external market pressures. First one group of specialists and then another begins to complain about external pay relationships. A more insidious problem for job evaluation is this: if structure repricing is inadequate, a slow "slippage" or "creep" of job values takes place. Faced with the need to pay competitive salaries, managers react to external pressure by rationalizing higher job values for their people. The upgrading of jobs does not take place uniformly. Some managers are more aggressive than others in promoting the upgrading; some functions do not have personnel with the kinds of specialized backgrounds that make such personnel susceptible to external pressure. Nevertheless, such jobs and output may be just as significant to an organization as the jobs subject to external pay pressure.

Failure to maintain a constant price structure relative to a defined external pattern of pay will ultimately result in the total disruption of internal job relationships. Even with a properly maintained salary structure, there will be pressures to upgrade jobs without justification. The evaluation program should define the criteria for determining whether a job has changed in value. In establishing these criteria, one should recognize that many changes in a job may not contribute to an increase in its intrinsic value, but may represent changes in emphasis caused by differing business conditions. Reasonably firm standards for upgrading can be justified on the basis that a company moving the price of its wage and salary structure properly is providing increases in real income in the long term. Some of this increase in real income adequately recognizes minor growth in job content accruing to many jobs.

If an organization has a policy for updating its pay structure, and if it has reasonable criteria for upgrading jobs, unique market pressure on pay for some jobs is probably a real fact and not the result of aberrations in salary program management.

There is no one best solution to unusual outside pressure on a few jobs. Many purists, in their support of internal equity, argue that the proper solution is to retain the established values for such jobs (keep internal equity) while at the same time providing special salary ranges that meet external pay pressure. The objective behind this solution is to maintain proper job values and to accept a temporary internal pay inequity; if the unique external pay pressure subsides, the salary ranges can be brought into line with those for other jobs having similar value. This is the only general solution worthy of detailed comment. If the problem is *clearly* one of external salary pressure, this approach is certainly to be preferred over other solutions.

Unfortunately, it has been this writer's experience that there are relatively few *real* serious market aberrations. The extent to which these aberrations exist and can be identified is related to how generously an organization's overall salary structure is priced compared with those of outside companies. Often a manager of a special activity reports inadequate pay for some specialty, but a detailed review of the problem indicates something quite different from pay competition. At one time or another, these have been the findings of practicing salary administrators:

1. A manager is quoting some information that relates to the *highest* salaries available for the specialty.

2. The pay competition reflects greater intrinsic job opportunity in some other companies. For example, one would expect that the internal value of specialists in the field of industrial design (design devoted to appearance and customer appeal) might be greater in automotive companies than in companies manufacturing industrial machine tools.

3. The internal evaluation program of a company is too rigid. For example, many companies have complained about the special market pressure on data processing jobs. Some of these companies failed to analyze and appreciate the impact of some of the systems design jobs. In other instances, the organization did not require (or sense the need for) sophisticated data processing that was necessary to other companies. No doubt, the supervisor of a small data processing operation chartered to do little more than an extension of key punch and tabulating work has problems in attracting and retaining specialists in systems design and programming. However, this problem is not one that can be solved with special salary treatment; the problem instead represents a situation in which more intrinsic job opportunity exists in other establishments.

4. A manager rightly identifies special pay competition, but all of it comes from establishments that are not included in the organization's general appraisal of external salaries. It is quite possible that pay throughout the organization would appear low if the outside salary comparisons used for a policy reference in pricing the structure were the same as those used by the manager to prove that his specialists are underpaid. If the manager has a real problem in attracting and retaining people, he will take small comfort from being told that his specialists are as well paid on a relative basis as other people in the organization, including the manager himself.

It is always possible to find some evidence somewhere in society that practically any job is under- or overpaid. Pay administrators should resist reacting to salary competition that comes from companies or organizations that are not included in salary surveys influencing the price of a company's entire pay structure.

Considerable space has been devoted to the subject of maintaining internal equity in the face of seemingly inequitable external pay relationships. There is always some degree of conflict between internal and external pay equity. The position taken by most salary administrators is that internal relationships should be given *first* priority, and external pay relationships for certain jobs must be compromised on occasion.

chapter 9

Using the Point Method
to Measure Jobs

HENRY A. SARGENT   *Principal, Edward N. Hay & Associates, Philadelphia, Pennsylvania*

In a broad sense, the point method includes any method of job measurement (or job evaluation, which is the more common term) in which jobs are measured quantitatively in terms of abstract numbers (usually referred to as "points"), which determine pay relationships but do not show the pay amounts. Some such methods, however, possess additional characteristics, and these are discussed separately in Chapters 10 and 12. This chapter is concerned with the point method in its basic form, which may be described as follows:

1. The objective is to measure the *content* of each job (i.e., the requirements, responsibilities, and conditions which distinguish that job from others and determine its relative worth) and thus establish equitable pay *relationships* between all of the jobs under consideration.

2. The job is evaluated by *factors* (i.e., determinants of job content and relative worth) instead of as a whole.

3. Although different point evaluation systems use different factors and different numbers of factors, under a given point system each factor carries its own scale of point values.

4. Each job is measured independently by each factor scale, thus determining individual factor point values, the total of which constitutes that job's evaluation.

5. These measurements are based on the job's requirements, responsibilities, and conditions when occupied by a fully qualified incumbent performing at the normal rate, i.e., a rate which is neither abnormally high nor abnormally low, but acceptable. It follows that pay relationships determined by evalua-

tion are base-rate relationships and do not reflect pay for length of service, premium for superior performance, etc.

6. Evaluations, once established, remain unchanged as long as the jobs remain the same. From time to time, however, jobs change or are eliminated and new jobs are created, thus requiring reevaluation of changed jobs and evaluation of new jobs by the same criteria to preserve equitable relationships.

HOW POINT SYSTEMS WORK

The validity of the set of factors and factor scales used in a point evaluation system can be judged only by the validity of the job relationships resulting from their application. Consequently, factors are selected and weighted on the basis of past experience. Criteria for choosing factors typically include: (1) common sense combined with understanding of the jobs, (2) acceptability to interested parties (company line and staff, employees, and the union, where one is involved), (3) prevailing pay relationships in the company and the labor market, coupled with analysis of the reasons for deviating from existing patterns (such as where qualified personnel to fill certain jobs are scarce and in high demand, thus artificially inflating going rates), and (4) satisfactory experience with like factors and factor scales used in other companies with similar operations and jobs. More important than the specific factors and factor scales used, however, are the skill and consistency with which they are applied. Experience has shown that a questionable system properly administered produces much better results than a fine system which is poorly administered.

The Factors. The factors represent the significant requirements, responsibilities, circumstances, and conditions which determine the content of the particular jobs to be evaluated, and should be selected with the following considerations in mind:

1. *Acceptability* to the parties of interest (top, middle, and lower levels of management, the employees, and the union if it is involved), since the factors are the basis of the evaluations, and the objective is to establish equitable relationships which will be accepted with confidence.

2. *Applicability* to the group of jobs to be evaluated. Each factor should contribute to the evaluation of at least one job (and preferably more).

3. *Ratability*, i.e., jobs to be evaluated, should carry different degrees of the factors by which they are evaluated. It is useless and confusing to use a factor which applies equally to all jobs.

4. *Distinctive nature.* Each factor should represent a separate element of job content, without overlapping another. It follows that each factor must be defined clearly.

5. *Number of factors.* It might seem that the greater this number, the greater the refinement of evaluations. This may be true, but only up to an optimum number, beyond which the danger of overlapping increases and the evaluation process becomes more complex, thereby increasing time and cost of application and the likelihood of inconsistency, differences in judgment, and controversy. A balance must be struck, and opinion and practice vary widely as to the optimum number. In the majority of cases, between 10 and 15 factors are used.

6. *Ease and economy of administration* tend to vary inversely with the number of factors. Reduction can be carried too far, however. Where very few (hence, very broad) factors are used, it becomes difficult to define clearly and comprehensively the ground covered by each factor and, therefore, to assure

accurate and consistent application of factor scales. Resulting increases in time and cost of achieving a consensus of evaluators and management and of gaining employee and union acceptance may outweigh economies in administration.

Different sets of factors are ordinarily used in evaluating different types of jobs unless the evaluation system is to be applied to more than one job category. For example, factors for evaluating hourly paid factory jobs might include:

1. Requirements:
   Education
   Experience
   Mechanical ability
   Job complexity
   Physical skill and complexity
2. Responsibility for:
   Materials and equipment
   Effect on subsequent operations
   Alertness and attention to orders
   Teamwork
   Safety of others
3. Working conditions:
   Repetitiveness and monotony
   Physical requirements (position, strength)
   Surroundings
   Exposure to hazard

On the other hand, a somewhat different set of factors might be used to evaluate nonexempt office jobs:

1. Factors for responsibility for materials and equipment, safety of others, surroundings, and exposure to hazard might be dropped because they apply to all jobs in the same degree and are of minor importance.

2. Mechanical ability might be replaced by one or more factors reflecting technical competence, analytical ability, etc.

3. Responsibility factors might be added for monetary effect, contact with others, etc.

4. Factor scales would probably be different in that maximum point values would be lower or higher, reflecting differences in the effect of the factors in determining job content.

For evaluating supervisory, managerial, technical, and professional jobs, a still different set of factors might be used, the nature of which depends in part on how far up the organizational ladder the evaluation system is to be applied:

1. Factors for working conditions would be dropped (or, where used, their maximum point values would be quite low) because they would have little or no influence on job content.

2. Factors for job requirements would not include physical or manual skills (for the same reason), but would include factors for managerial, motivational, and persuasive skills; and scales would probably be carried to substantially higher point value maximums.

3. Responsibility factors would be completely different, covering such considerations as responsibility for planning, execution, control, effect on costs and/or profit, etc.; and factor scales would also be carried to substantially higher point value maximums.

In practice, some point evaluation systems use fewer factors than those referred to, combining two or more into one factor and identifying each factor appropriately. In other point systems, a larger number of factors is used, each of which is usually an element of one of the factors referred to and carries its own name.

Factor Weight. Experience has shown that except by rare coincidence each factor carries a different force (or weight) in determining job content. Consequently, each factor scale has a different point value, although the maximum for two or more factors seldom applies to the same job. Respective factor weights (or maximum point values) are usually determined through (1) pooled judgment of the relative importance of each factor as a determinant of job content, and (2) correlation of results of these judgments with prevailing relevant pay patterns.

Where few jobs are involved and little difficulty is expected in gaining acceptance, the procedure can be relatively simple. Typically, (1) each of several knowledgeable people ranks the factors according to their importance, judgments are compared, and a tentative consensus is reached; (2) after factor scales have been tentatively determined, a representative sample of jobs is tentatively evaluated and the evaluations are plotted against rates of pay. If the line of central tendency is smooth (whether straight or curved) and there are few—if any—divergent cases, and if there is an acceptable explanation for each such case, the tentative factor weightings and scales can be adopted. If not, they are reexamined (together with the tentative evaluations), sources of trouble are identified, and the procedure is repeated.

Where a large number of jobs is involved or acceptance poses more of a problem, the procedure may be more complex. The sample of jobs tentatively evaluated should be larger, and sophisticated mathematical analyses may be required to cope with the volume in reasonable time and at minimum cost. The essential nature of the work performed is the same, however.

Factor Scales. The upper end of each factor scale is usually the maximum point value reflecting the factor's weight. In some systems a higher point value is shown to accommodate future developments, but this has the disadvantage of inviting its unjustified use. The lower end of the scale is either zero points (sometimes designated as "base" to make it more acceptable) or a specific minimum number of points commensurate with factor weight.

Most jobs are evaluated between maximum and minimum, and the scales therefore include intermediate point values, each of which must be identified clearly to guide evaluators in determining accurately and consistently the number of points to be assigned to each job. In a well-conceived system this is done by incorporating in the scale, for each point value shown, both written definitions of that factor level and judiciously selected illustrative examples of jobs evaluated at that factor level.

Two types of scale may be used, either one of which is acceptable, but only one type may be used in a given point evaluation system:

1. In one type, point value progresses arithmetically (i.e., intervals between point values are equal), so that when total evaluation points are plotted against pay rates they result in a curved line.

2. In the other type, the progression is geometric (i.e., intervals increase by a fixed percentage), and the resulting line is straight.

There are wide differences between point evaluation systems as to the absolute level of maximum and minimum point values. In some cases maximum is in the general order of 10, and in others it is substantially higher (even in the general order of 100 or more). Such differences are of no consequence insofar as job relationships within the scope of the particular system are concerned, since, irrespective of their absolute level, the evaluations express only relationships between jobs.

Benchmark Jobs. Evaluations of a selected group of representative (benchmark) jobs supplement and clarify the intent of factor scales, establish a framework within which other jobs can be evaluated, provide the basis for forecasting the system's effect on existing pay relationships, and provide one of the elements needed to determine the pay scale by which the evaluation program is put into effect. Where an evaluation system is developed from scratch, time and cost are minimized by using such a sample of the jobs to be covered. To serve these purposes, the benchmark jobs must be:

1. *Noncontroversial* as to rates of pay and other significant factors, to assure acceptance.

2. *Definable,* thus excluding jobs with unclear and/or varying assignments, responsibilities, etc., to minimize opportunities for inconsistency, error, and controversy.

3. *Representative* of the jobs to be evaluated, i.e., including jobs at low, intermediate, and high levels in major functional areas.

Since the validity of benchmark evaluations and the pattern of job relationships which they establish are critically important, they should be examined from as many standpoints as possible to assure they are reasonable and acceptable to (1) the evaluators before releasing their evaluations, and (2) individuals responsible for the decision to adopt the system. Benchmark jobs and their evaluations should then be listed in the sequence of evaluation points. Such a list would help evaluators by highlighting questionable evaluations and keeping overall relationships in full view while the former are investigated and resolved. Where departmental management is involved in benchmark evaluations, a single list by total points for jobs in the particular department is adequate. For senior managers with interdepartmental perspective and executives responsible for approval of the system, a single list of all benchmark jobs by total points is appropriate, and its usefulness is enhanced by tabulating jobs in each major functional area in separate columns and placing jobs up and down the page at levels corresponding to total point values.

When there are benchmark jobs of the same character, as may be the case when a system is applied at several locations, job family tabulations—e.g., for crane operator, typist-clerk, machine shop foreman, plant manager, etc.—may be useful. These are most effective when they display the jobs and their respective evaluations under each factor and in total, arranged in the sequence of total points.

Evaluation Manual. Good practice requires that evaluation criteria be consolidated, recorded, and placed in the hands of personnel concerned with evaluation work. This material constitutes the company's evaluation manual for the system and is the basic evaluation tool.

A manual's length and degree of detail are determined by the needs of the situation. Where relatively few jobs are covered by the system, where few individuals are involved in the evaluation process, and where acceptance is not a major problem, the manual may consist of only a statement of the factors and factor scales, their definitions, and selected benchmark illustrations; additional criteria may be provided by the complete file of benchmark evaluations. In more complex situations, the manual may also incorporate: (1) detailed procedures, (2) statements of purposes for which evaluations are (and/or are not) to be used, and (3) a list of benchmark jobs, or even the descriptions and detailed evaluations of selected or all benchmark jobs.

Initial Evaluation of Nonbenchmark Jobs. Jobs are evaluated one at a time, usually by functional area to preserve perspective. Criteria are (1) the factors, factor scales, and their definitions, and (2) the factor-by-factor evaluations of benchmark jobs. As evaluations are established for nonbenchmark jobs, these supplement the basic criteria. Accuracy, consistency, and impartiality are achieved through familiarity with evaluation criteria and techniques, clear understanding of each job, mature and well-informed judgment, cross-checking of independent evaluations, and validation of relationships, such as by reference to lists of the type previously described. Descriptions, specifications, and factor-by-factor evaluations of benchmark and nonbenchmark jobs are referred to frequently; consequently these should be filed systematically and kept readily available.

Maintenance of the System. Once the system is installed, it must be maintained thereafter to preserve its integrity. This involves reevaluating changed jobs and evaluating new jobs to keep pace with inevitable changes in products, processes, organization structure, etc. Too often over the course of time there comes a tendency to neglect this crucially important work, as a result of which pay relationships get out of line and the program becomes less useful and acceptable. Many sound programs have been permitted to deteriorate until time-consuming and costly wholesale revision or complete replacement were required, at needless expense and with considerable loss in employee confidence. Management's commitment to maintenance of an evaluation program should be a prerequisite to its adoption.

New and changed jobs are evaluated by the same criteria as in an initial application, but these evaluations are also guided by the detailed evaluations of jobs already covered by the system. After the system has been in effect for a reasonable period, it is better understood by supervisors, managers, employees, and union representatives, and acceptance of new and changed evaluations is usually easier to gain. Jobs to be evaluated at a given time usually come singly or in small batches from different functional areas, tending to make the evaluation and approval process less time-consuming than when interdepartmental patterns are being established. Even so, thorough grounding in evaluation, clear understanding of each job, mature and well-informed judgment, and cross-checking of independent evaluations remain as basic requirements.

PERSONNEL INVOLVED AND THEIR ROLES

The equity of pay relationships, although it can be evaluated by established criteria, is finally a matter of judgment. Similarly, the appropriateness and effectiveness of the criteria depend on the soundness of judgment used in determining them. Seldom, if ever, is a single individual possessed of sufficient maturity, knowledge, perspective, and unquestionable impartiality to assure validity of his judgment alone in development and/or application of the criteria. Consequently, it is practically always essential that actions in each phase of the evaluation program be based on a consensus of several appropriately selected individuals. Different types of experience and different degrees of maturity and perspective are required in different phases, thus making it possible to vary participants from phase to phase. The participants and their roles in each phase are outlined in the following paragraphs.

Top management should sponsor the program from its inception to establish clearly that it is adopted as a matter of policy and constitutes an important tool of management. Top management should also assure that the system's design and projected effect on pay relationships are appropriate for the company and the jobs involved, and that it is implemented and maintained properly.

A standing group of senior executives, such as the corporate compensation committee or a senior evaluation committee created for the purpose, usually is assigned responsibility for evaluation activities. Where membership does not include a senior executive who is well grounded in evaluation, the nonvoting secretary usually is the company official in charge of the program and thoroughly qualified in the subject. The committee's role is to provide perspective, broad guidance, and control, and usually involves:

1. In the *development phase:* (a) assuring timely and economical design of a workable and economical system appropriate for the operations and jobs to be covered, (b) assuring reasonable equity of resulting pay relationships and probability of acceptance, and (c) approving the system for adoption or recommending its approval.

2. In the *initial application phase:* (a) assuring timely and economical evaluation of nonbenchmark jobs in accordance with established criteria and procedures, and (b) resolving differences not settled at a lower level.

3. In the *maintenance phase:* (a) assuring prompt and economical reevaluation of changed jobs and evaluation of new jobs in accordance with established criteria and procedures, (b) resolving differences not settled at a lower level, and (c) approving all changed and new evaluations.

In large companies some of these functions are frequently delegated to divisional committees or to a subordinate company official. In small companies it is not unusual for a single senior executive (preferably assisted by an evaluation specialist) to perform these functions. These senior executive groups (or individuals) are normally also concerned with determining or recommending pay scales and adjustment thereof, approving individual pay adjustments within rate ranges where this is discretionary with management, etc.

Company evaluation specialists are almost always involved in all phases of the program and combine internal knowledge and perspective with evaluation know-how. In most cases they are also involved in related activities, such as job description and specification writing, salary administration, etc. These activities should constitute their exclusive assignments unless the volume of work is so small that they can also carry other unrelated duties. Their place in the organization structure should be such as to assure their impartiality and independence of judgment. More often than not when an evaluation program is undertaken, the company lacks qualified specialists and they must either be hired or developed internally under an outside consultant. The latter course is usually preferable since acceptable candidates can ordinarily be found who are already well oriented internally and can be trained relatively quickly. The roles of company specialists usually involve:

1. In the *development phase,* under direction and guidance of the senior executives in charge of the program (and of the outside consultant, where used), performing detail work and participating in developing recommendations as to: (a) selecting and defining factors, (b) weighting of factors, (c) determining and defining factor scales, (d) selecting and evaluating benchmark jobs, and (e) keeping related records. Where union agreement is required, they may also participate in supporting and explaining the company's position.

2. In the *initial application phase,* under direction and guidance of the senior executives (and of the consultant, where used): (a) evaluating nonbenchmark jobs, (b) recommending these for approval, and (c) keeping related records. Where union acceptance is desirable or agreement is required, they also participate in explaining and supporting the company position.

3. In the *maintenance phase:* (a) reevaluating changed jobs and evaluating new jobs, (b) communicating these evaluations to managers in the organizational units involved, (c) recommending mutually agreed-upon evaluations for approval at a higher level, (d) reconciling differences with departmental

management where possible and referring unreconciled differences to a higher level, and (*e*) keeping related records.   Where union acceptance is customary or required, company specialists also explain and support the company's position.

Good practice requires that at least two specialists develop the evaluation of each job independently and that their evaluations be compared and reconciled before release outside the evaluation unit.   In the maintenance phase this is frequently accomplished by having a qualified specialist determine a proposed evaluation, which is reviewed and approved by the senior specialist.

Departmental management has an interest in the evaluations of jobs under its direction and is in a position to contribute valuable insight to determination of pay relationships in its particular area of responsibility.   On the other hand, it frequently lacks interdepartmental perspective and can be suspected of bias.   Consequently its role:

1. In the *development phase* usually consists of furnishing and clarifying facts, although upon occasion opinions may be called for.

2. In the *initial application phase* is usually about the same, although departmental opinions may be called for more often and carry more weight.

3. In the *maintenance phase* usually assumes a different character, in that departmental management has a definite voice in determining evaluations of new and changed jobs within its jurisdiction.   Departmental approval is normally required, and if there is disagreement with evaluation specialists, differences are referred to senior management for adjudication.   Good practice also requires that departmental management be charged with responsibility to notify evaluation specialists promptly when jobs within its jurisdiction are changed or eliminated and new jobs are created.

The outside consultant, when one is used, plays a widely varying role, depending on the degree of expertise possessed by company personnel.   If the company has competent evaluation specialists, the consultant's role may be limited to providing broad independent judgment relative to the appropriateness and adequacy of the program and its administration, resolving particularly troublesome problems, etc.   If qualified company personnel are lacking at the outset of a program, the consultant usually carries the major burden and trains company personnel as the work progresses.   In the latter case, typically:

1. In the *development phase,* the consultant's role, subject to approval of senior management, is (*a*) to determine whether a new system should be developed from scratch or whether a system used and tested elsewhere should be adopted (perhaps with modifications), and (*b*) to direct activities of assigned company personnel (and sometimes members of the consultant's staff as well) in designing the new system where one is to be developed, or selecting and evaluating benchmark jobs where an existing system is adopted. Although the amount of consultant time used in this phase may tend to decrease as company personnel become more proficient, the consultant usually continues in charge, presents the system to senior and top management, and in some situations plays an important part in gaining union acceptance.

2. In the *initial application phase,* the consultant's role is determined by the progress of company specialists in mastering evaluation principles and practice. It can vary from direction and participation in evaluation of nonbenchmark jobs to occasionally reviewing progress and evaluation patterns and resolving problem cases.   His involvement in this phase should decrease markedly as work moves toward completion, since company specialists are expected to become better and better qualified during the course of application.

3. In the *maintenance phase,* the consultant's role, if any, is usually one of occasional review and audit and contributing an outside view where appropriate.

Once the evaluation program is approved, the consultant usually plays an important role in applying evaluation results to compensation questions—determining pay scales, policies, and practices.

Union representatives are important participants if union acceptance is customary or required. Their function may include broad surveillance of pay relationships and amounts determined by management, pressure to change those with which employees or the union are dissatisfied, and direct participation in designing, applying, and maintaining the system. Typically, when the evaluation program is a contractual matter:

1. In the *development phase*, the union becomes involved after the company has developed a complete system and submits it as a proposal. Union representatives in this phase are usually either empowered to execute an agreement or responsible for negotiating an acceptable package and recommending its adoption. They make such counterproposals as they deem appropriate and negotiate with company representatives until agreement is reached. The package usually includes not only the evaluation system but also provisions governing its initial application and maintenance, the pay scale, etc.

2. In the *initial application phase*, union representatives familiar with the system (frequently below the contracting level) keep in touch with local union officials and members, investigate complaints, and confer as necessary with appropriate company personnel to protect union and employee interests.

3. In the *maintenance phase*, new and changed job descriptions and specifications (usually prepared by company specialists) are submitted through appropriate channels to designated local union officials for review and signature. They may negotiate changes or disagree and refer the case to agreed-upon procedures for resolution of differences.

Union participation restricts the company's freedom of action, may bring into play bias and inexperience in evaluation, and adds to the burden of developing, applying, and administering the program. It also provides advantages. Some union officials (such as staff representatives) are competent in the evaluation field through experience or training elsewhere, or become so as the system is developed and applied in the company. Some local union officials also become familiar with the system through experience when their tenure is long enough. Their participation provides an additional check on evaluation judgments and tends to assure policing in the maintenance phase. More importantly, union agreement on pay relationships and amounts, criteria for their determination, and provisions for resolution of differences provides an outlet for claims of inequity which otherwise could lead to major problems and serious cost consequences, and substantially enhances employee confidence and acceptance.

FEASIBILITY OF THE POINT METHOD

When a company is considering adopting a job evaluation program, the first step should be to analyze the purposes to be served and the conditions under which the program is to be applied. If the purpose is unilateral determination of internally equitable pay relationships for a small number of jobs, and if employee acceptance is not a problem, a simple and inexpensive system such as overall job ranking may be adequate. Such a system, however, may present difficulties in assuring consistent application in the maintenance phase. If a large number of jobs is to be evaluated unilaterally, a more systematic and detailed approach is needed to assure impartiality and consistency.

When employee and/or union acceptance is a major consideration, a systematic approach is necessary to enable management to demonstrate the validity of its position and defend it in the event of controversy.

When the job evaluation program is intended to determine the external competitiveness of the company's pay structure as well as its internal equity, a systematic approach is required. Furthermore, the system chosen must be compatible with systems used by other companies with which the company wants to make comparisons.

The point evaluation method meets the needs for determining internal equity and can be applied in whatever detail may be required, at commensurate cost. It is probably more widely used in industry and business than any other single method, particularly for evaluating blue-collar and white-collar jobs. It has also been used successfully in evaluating supervisory, managerial, technical, and professional jobs, usually through the adoption of systems developed by consultants (or adaptation of such systems), since development of an acceptable system is time-consuming and costly. There are a few point systems which are used widely enough to provide valid information on competitive pay levels, although characteristically their use is confined to a few types of industry.

The decision to adopt the point evaluation method and the determination of the particulars of the system should be based on the facts in the case, balancing advantages against disadvantages and taking into account available variations in application of the method. In selecting a specific system, it is useful to remember that although the details (number and names of factors, factor weights, and absolute point of values) of individual point evaluation systems may vary, they normally yield similar job relationships when they are competently administered.

The advantages of the point method may be summarized as follows:

1. Appraisal of the relative worth of each job from more than one standpoint (i.e., through independent measurement by different yardsticks, one for each factor) provides greater assurance of accuracy and consistency than a single appraisal of the job as a whole.

2. Since relationships are stated in numerical terms, direct comparisons between jobs are easily made and quickly understood.

3. Equitable evaluations in terms of points are readily translated into equitable pay scales, and the latter can be adjusted from time to time while preserving equitable pay relationships. Hence, the point method presents great advantages from the standpoint of long-term applicability.

4. Evaluations in terms of points make it possible to accommodate the need for either (a) fine distinctions between jobs by establishing an individual rate of pay for each number of total points, or (b) pay grades of any desired breadth by grouping jobs within specified point ranges.

5. Appropriate and clearly defined factors and factor scales for the type of jobs involved and an adequate framework of benchmark evaluations minimize the chance for error, inconsistency, bias, manipulation, differences in judgment, and controversy.

6. Skill, accuracy, and consistency in evaluation improve with the use of the system.

7. Experienced and well-informed evaluators (whether they represent the company, the employees, or the union) in most cases agree on evaluations or resolve differences quickly.

8. With proper initial application of the system, an adequate evaluation manual, and a systematic and accessible file of descriptions and evaluations for

all jobs covered by the system, means are provided for assuring its continuing integrity through effective maintenance.

9. Adequate coverage in union agreements (where applicable) of subjects essential to initial application and continuing maintenance facilitates employee acceptance and establishes criteria and procedures for resolving controversies.

10. Management, employee, and union acceptance is facilitated by the system's flexibility in such matters as selecting factors, determining and defining factor scales, and selecting and evaluating benchmark jobs.

The disadvantages of the point method may be summarized as follows:

1. Development of an acceptable point evaluation method from scratch is time-consuming and costly and requires expert guidance. Consequently, the company should consider carefully whether a tailor-made system is needed. In most cases, an existing system can be adopted or modified with commensurate savings.

2. The point method's seemingly arbitrary and complex use of a variety of factors, differing factor weights, abstract point values, pricing of evaluation points, etc., is confusing to individuals unacquainted with the subject (supervisors, managers, employees, and union representatives) and tends to arouse suspicion. Consequently, time, effort, patience, and perseverance are required to gain understanding and acceptance of the reasons for using such an approach and of the validity of results.

3. The point method entails the time and cost of competent evaluation specialists to assure validity, consistency, and impartiality of evaluations.

4. Considerable time and attention of senior management are required in the development and initial application phases to assure that the system and its results are appropriate, and to a lesser extent in the maintenance phase to assure proper administration, to resolve differences, to approve new and changed evaluations, and periodically to review and adjust pay scales. Departmental management time and attention are also required in the maintenance phase for review and approval of new and changed evaluations.

5. Considerable clerical time and expense are required in the continuing process of typing, filing, etc., of job descriptions and specifications, evaluation records, and other material involved in administration of the program.

chapter 10

Using Factor Methods to Measure Jobs

EUGENE J. BENGE   *Benge Associates, Pompano Beach, Florida*

The factor comparison system of job evaluation was originated in 1926 when the writer was employed by the Philadelphia Rapid Transit Company to install an hourly wage rate evaluation plan. At that time, a few large and well-known companies had set up job evaluation systems. Attempts to apply one of these—a point system—failed, largely because of the great diversity of jobs included and the wide range of abilities and training required.

During World War I, Dr. Walter Dill Scott had developed a "man-to-man" merit rating system in which officers being considered for promotion were compared with known officers as to various attributes. We adapted this idea to evaluate selected key jobs, and soon discovered that knowledgeable people, whether executives or union representatives, came up with virtually the same job evaluation once a key scale, with anchor points, had been established.

The system was later used and expanded by Samuel L. H. Burk and Edward N. Hay, and ultimately the three of us coauthored one of the early books on job evaluation (see the bibliography).

The key scale is one basic difference between a point system and the factor comparison system. Once this measuring stick has been set up, evaluation becomes a simple process. Moreover, this measuring scale can be used for many years thereafter. Judgments on a given job are made against the key scale, one factor at a time.

Before job evaluation can actually begin, it is necessary to:

1. Gain approval of the study by management or by management and the union, if there is to be union participation.

2. Appoint a chief job analyst, with the necessary assistants.

3. Appoint a job evaluation committee to program the initial study, construct the key scale, evaluate jobs, and develop a wage and salary administration plan. A minimum of five members is desirable.

4. Designate adequate space for housing the analyst and for meetings of the committee. A large blackboard, 4 by 8 feet, will prove helpful in committee deliberations.

5. Inform employees and supervisors of the purposes and procedures of the entire effort, through either a series of meetings or a detailed letter to employees.

THE FACTORS

Five basic factors should be considered in evaluating hourly jobs:
1. Mental requirements
2. Skill requirements
3. Physical requirements
4. Responsibilities
5. Working conditions

When supervisory, technical, or clerical jobs are being evaluated, these factors become:
1. Mental requirements
2. Skill requirements, wherein skill is largely equated with experience rather than with muscular coordination
3. Physical factors, a combination of physical requirements and working conditions
4. Responsibility for supervision
5. Other responsibilities

As ever-higher jobs are being evaluated, the meaning of the five factors will change. This situation is illustrated in Figure 1, which suggests varying content of the five factors at eight job levels.

Since the specific characteristics of the factors are not absolutes, each company's job evaluation committee should define the five factors' content to best suit the purposes of the company's job evaluation program. The following sections describe factor content as established by a committee that evaluated salaried jobs in a railroad.

Mental Requirements. This factor considers the intellectual and educational level required to do the job, including:
1. Education—general level
2. Additional specialized education
3. Solutions to complex problems
4. Goal setting
5. Level of mathematics used
6. Analyzing cost or statistical data
7. Writing reports
8. Public speaking and persuasive presentations
9. Creativity

Experience Required. This factor considers months or years on the same or lower types of jobs. Five skill levels are generally found; each level assumes facility or experience in lower levels:
1. Conceptual—converting conceptual to practical; forecasting consequences of economic, social, industry, and company trends
2. Administrative—planning, organizing, coordinating, and controlling

Figure 1. Changing scope of factors.

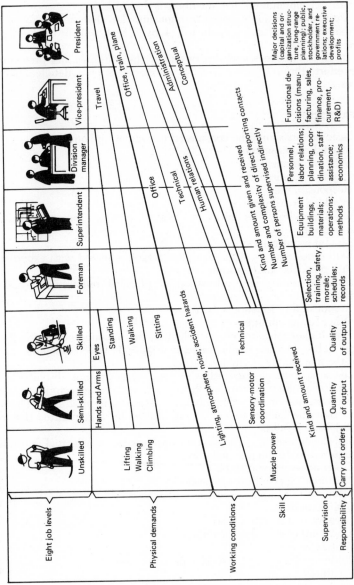

3. Supervisory—carrying out plans and procedures; telling who to do what, and when; seeing that work is done properly, and on time
4. Skill—coordinating muscular activities with specific job knowledge[1]
5. Muscular coordination, usually repetitive (as in machine operation)[2]

Physical Factors. This factor considers expenditure of muscular energy, as in walking, lifting, travel, etc. Also working conditions, including hazards.

Supervision. This factor considers the importance and complexity of supervision and/or counsel, both given and received.

Normally, it is possible to differentiate nine levels, as shown in Table 1.

Responsibilities. This factor considers the consequences if the employee makes a mistake in terms of:

1. Property or equipment—capital invested
2. Money, costs, or profits
3. Public contact
4. Methods, systems, procedures, or records
5. Safety of employees or public
6. Meeting emergencies

GUIDELINES FOR WRITING JOB SPECIFICATIONS

The job evaluation committee should instruct the job analysts on how job specifications should be prepared. Following are the instructions one committee developed:

1. Your primary interest is in the work as it is now being done.
2. Confine your attention to the job you are analyzing, and do not be influenced by the ability, or lack of it, of the employee on the job.
3. Avoid any preconception as to the importance of any job you are analyzing. Describe the job as you find it.
4. Use a single paragraph to express the duties which revolve around one phase of the work.
5. Use the active and not the passive voice: Do not say, "Typing is done by typist" but "Types reports."
6. Omit the subject of a sentence when the subject has been used once and is identical with the title of the job being described.

[1] May not be needed for present job, but may be desirable experience.
[2] *Ibid.*

TABLE 1   Supervisory Levels

Job level	Gives supervision	Receives supervision
1	Much	Little
2	Much	Some
3a	Much	Much
3b	Some	Little (gives counsel)
4	Some	Some
5a	Some	Much
5b	None*	Little (gives counsel)
6	None*	Some
7	None*	Much

* Has no subordinates.
3b may be more important than 3a.
5b may be more important than 5a.

7. Omit articles like *a, an,* and *the* where they are unnecessary to the meaning.

8. Do not use technical terms without explanation. The explanation may be made on the specification form or, if a somewhat lengthy explanation is required, use an attached paper.

9. Arrange the contents of the duties description in some logical order— e.g., in the sequence of a work cycle.

10. Where there are varied duties, list the important duties first.

11. State the duties as duties, not as qualifications. Do not say, "Should be able to operate machines," but "Operates machine."

12. State nothing but duties in the "Duties" section. Do not state requirements.

13. Avoid generalization. Specify exact activities incident to the task.

14. Indicate reporting line. For example, say, "Under supervision of (*position*), directs (*position*)."

15. Quantify wherever possible. State number of units, or percentage of total time devoted to a particular activity, or weights and distances involved.

16. Use action verbs to eliminate misunderstandings of the meaning or scope of the action described. At times, broad terms, such as *handles, supervises,* or *prepares,* can be used only when the terms are expanded and the action broken down.

17. There are three criteria for determining the accuracy of the specification:

(*a*) *Is it correct?* Does it express the correct activities, requirements, and conditions of work?

(*b*) *Is it comprehensive?* Does it cover all the important and normal duties of a job?

(*c*) *Is it specific?* Are the various items on the job specification so specific that they permit differential comparisons with other jobs?

Figure 2 presents a completed job specification, ready for use by the job evaluation committee.

PROCEDURE

After the organizing activities are completed, the job evaluation committee:

1. Selects and analyzes key jobs.
2. Constructs a key scale.
3. Evaluates nonkey jobs.
4. Evaluates key jobs.
5. Plots a scatter diagram.
6. Assigns jobs to grades.

Selecting and Analyzing Key Jobs. Much of the success of the program lies in the care with which the key jobs are selected and analyzed. These jobs provide the framework into which all other jobs are integrated.

It is common practice to select from 24 to 30 tentative key jobs. These should sample all levels of the organization vertically and all departments horizontally. Thus, if there were 10 major departments, it might be desirable to select recognized high, medium, and low jobs from each department. The jobs designated should be stable and representative of usual tasks in the industry. Any jobs whose current compensation is in dispute or for which there is a wide variation in rates should be excluded.

In addition, the purpose of the program should be fully explained to employees interviewed.

At the outset, it is desirable that the chief job analyst work painstakingly

Figure 2.   Job specification.

JOB SPECIFICATION

Date _3/10/71_

Job title _ASSISTANT CONTROLLER_   Dept. _CONTROLLER_   Employee(s) Interviewed _EDWARD VOIGT_

Duties (continue on other side if necessary) _UNDER SUPERVISION OF CONTROLLER, RECONCILES VARIOUS CONTROLS WITH SUBSIDIARY AND DETAIL RECORDS. ASSISTS IN PREPARATION OF FINANCIAL REPORTS FOR USE OF MANAGEMENT. ANALYZES GENERAL LEDGER ACCOUNTS TO VERIFY ACCURACY (PAYROLL, PENSION, SALES TAX RETURNS ETC) HELPS COMPILE ANNUAL FINANCIAL REPORT. OCCASIONALLY MAKES SPECIAL STUDIES AS ASSIGNED BY CONTROLLER._

Mental requirements	Skill requirements	Physical factors	Responsibilities	Supervision
_C-4_ Years education	Kind: _SCHEDULE AND COORDINATE CLERICAL EFFORT, DICTATION._	___ Sitting _95%_ ___ Standing _5%_ ___ Walking	Equipment _ADDING MACHINE_	Supervises _5_ Persons
_XX_ Add and Subtract _XX_ Multiply and divide _XX_ Fractions and decimals		_X_ Eyesight ___ Endurance	Materials	Analysis:
_XX_ Accounting ___ Shorthand ___ Grammar ___ Other.	Desirable prior experience: _ACCOUNTING BACKGROUND, SYSTEMATIZING_	___ Lifting	Records – _CLERICAL AND ACCOUNTING_	RECEIVES
Job instructions: _GRADUATE OF ACCOUNTING COURSE_	Time to develop average performance: _4-6 MOS._	Age: _30_ min. _60_ max. _X_ Indoor ___ Outdoor ___ Unlocalized	Methods – _SUGGESTS CHANGES_ Money _PREPARES CASH REQUISITION SLIPS_	Receives supervision from: _CONTROLLER_
___ Meet distractions ___ Meet emergencies ___ Stand monotony _X_ Make decisions _XX_ Analyze	Prerequisite jobs: _ACCOUNTANT_	_X_ Desk ___ Machine ___ Counter	Savings Public contact	Plans _WORK OF CLERKS_ Instructs _SUBORDINATES_
___ Patience ___ Tact _X_ Superior memory	___ Repetitive _X_ Varied Sensory training ___ Sight ___ Hearing _OPERATES ADDING MACHINE & CALCULATOR_	Illumination: _EXCELLENT_ Atmosphere: _EXCELLENT_ Hazards:	Confidential matters _PAYROLL, FINANCIAL STATEMENTS_ Other	Approves _STATIONERY REQUISITIONS_ Control devices: Highest job under: _CHIEF ACCOUNTANT_ ___ Written instructions _X_ Plans own time _WITH SUPERVISION BY CONTROLLER_

GIVES — Much Some None / RECEIVES — None Some Much:

	None	Some	Much
None	3	2	1
Some	6	⑤	4
Much	9	8	7

Symbols: Use X to indicate; XX to stress, P—preferred; R—required; or show amount or %

Prepared by _____ _J.R.B._ _____ Approved by _____ _T.W._ _____

with an analyst in preparing the first few job specifications. In this way the analyst learns how to translate his rough notes into concise statements on the specification.

We shall here carry through a simple example, using only 20 jobs to be evaluated, with 10 of them selected as tentative key jobs. Let us designate the 10 key jobs by letters:

A	F	K	P	The 10 under-
B	G	L	Q	lined jobs are
C	H	M	R	selected as
D	I	N	S	tentative key
E	J	O	T	jobs.

In the example we are following, we first analyze the 10 tentative key jobs and then prepare specifications for them. While the committee is studying these jobs to prepare the key scale, the analysts continue preparing nonkey specifications for evaluation by the committee.

Ranking Key Jobs. The first step in preparing the key scale is to rank the tentative key jobs in importance, one factor at a time.

Each member of the general committee is supplied with a set of specifications for the tentative key jobs. There are only 10 of these in our example, but normally there are at least 24 of them. It would be possible for each committee member to rank the specification forms themselves according to the mental requirements. However, this practice would require that each member have a work surface capable of providing room for 24 specifications.

Usually it is better to give each member a set of cards (3 by 2½ inches), one for each of the tentative key jobs. The committee member will have his 24 specifications in a three-ring binder and will make constant reference to them as he ranks the 24 cards in mental requirements.

Each committee member will also have a data sheet on which are listed the tentative key jobs in alphabetical order. When he has sorted the cards to his satisfaction, he will enter on the data sheet in the Mental Requirements column the rank order he has assigned to the 24 jobs.

The chief analyst will then summarize the mental rankings chosen by the five members on a large blackboard. The blackboard will show the 24 jobs listed alphabetically at the left; following that will be five columns, one column for each member of the committee. Each member records his rankings on his data sheet, and the rankings are then transferred to the blackboard. When all five members have recorded their rankings on the blackboard, it becomes possible to compare the mental rankings which each person has assigned to a given job with the rankings given it by the other four members of the committee.

Usually there will be considerable agreement, even at the outset. The objective of the blackboard work is to bring out the marked disagreements. These disagreements should be debated to clarify how each member has interpreted the mental requirements factor. As a result of the discussion, it is usual for committee members to wish to change some of their ranks. Each one should do this by reranking his cards and *not* merely by changing the numbers on the blackboard. After his cards are reranked, he should enter his final rankings on the data sheet.

The same process should be followed, a factor at a time, for the other four factors. This is a tedious task which usually requires about five hours of a committee's time.

After this step, the data sheets should be collected and summarized by averaging the five members' rankings as to each factor on each job. This averaging should be carried out to one decimal place only, and these figures in turn reranked from 1 to 24 in each factor.

The final ranks are considered the stable judgment of the committee. A final importance rank can be changed only if a majority of the committee votes that it should be changed and the entire committee reranks the factor or factors involved.

Table 2 shows the 10 key jobs as ranked by the committee in our simplified example.

Preparing the Key Scale. Since the tentative key jobs represent a good sample of all jobs, their present wage or salary rates presumably provide a good sampling of the pay scale.

If committee members evaluate in terms of dollars, experience shows that they may, consciously or otherwise, manipulate figures to achieve some fixed notion as to the monetary value of certain jobs. To defeat this possibility, we multiply present (or average) rates of the tentative key jobs by some arbitrary number, such as 1.7 or 2.3, to yield "units." Thus a job paying $200 per week might be allotted 340 units.

The next step in preparing the key scale is to distribute present unit values of each tentative key job horizontally over the five factors. Thus, if the first of the key jobs now receives 340 units, each member of the committee must ask himself how many of those units he would allocate to the mental requirements, to experience, to the physical factors, to supervision, and to other re-

TABLE 2   Importance Ranks Assigned by Committee

Job	MR	E/S	PF	S	R
C	1	2	9	1	2
D	8	9	2	9	8
F	3	4	8	4	3
H	2	1	7	2	1
J	6	6	5	6	5
L	5	5	6	5	6
N	4	3	10	3	4
O	9	8	3	8	9
Q	7	7	4	6	7
S	10	6	1	10	10

MR = Mental Requirements
E/S = Experience/Skill
PF = Physical Factors
S   = Supervision
R   = Responsibilities

sponsibilities.   Having made his decision about one job, he goes on to the next.

The votes of all members are then posted on the large blackboard and discussions about discrepancies ensue.   In this case it is possible for a member to change his entries on the board provided his figures always add up to the present unit value.   That is, if he takes five units off one factor, he must add that amount to one or more of the other factors of the same job.

When committee members are satisfied with the distribution shown on the blackboard, the figures are totaled, averaged, and checked mathematically.

Next, the units' rankings for each factor are determined *vertically*—e.g., the job receiving the largest number of units in the Mental Requirements column is ranked first and the job receiving the smallest number is ranked lowest.

The importance ranks are then compared with the units' ranks on a summary sheet in which the importance rank, units allocated, and units rank of each factor of each job are designated.   Table 3 shows the summary sheet for the jobs in our simplified example.

Inspection of the tabulation in Table 3 reveals that:

1. The importance ranks of jobs J and O in all five columns are poorer than the units' ranks (indicating that there were too many units for distribution, relative to the other eight jobs).

2. The five importance ranks of job F are consistently better than the units' ranks (indicating that we did not have enough units to distribute).

Hence jobs J, O, and F must be eliminated as key jobs.   Note that in job H, if six points were transferred from Supervision to Other Responsibilities, the units' ranks would then match the importance ranks for that job and for job C.   This transferring of units may be necessary with a number of jobs to bring about reconciliation of ranks.

Justification for this arbitrary balancing lies in the proven fact that the distributed units are not stable figures.   If the committee were to repeat the distributions a week later, many of the figures would change, which means that there is a large personal error in the units' allocations.

We have now *priced the ranks*, by:

TABLE 3   Summary of Importance Ranks Assigned Units

Units	Job	Mental			Experience			Physical Factors			Supervision			Other Responsibilities		
		IR	U	UR	IR	U	UR	IR	U	UR	IR	U	UR	IR	U	UR
331	C	1	91	1	2	76	2	9	7	8	1	61	2	2	96	1
132	D	8	32	9	9	21	10	2	19	25	9	21	9	8	39	9
222	F	3	60	6	4	50	5	8	6	9	4	40	5.5	3	66	6
323	H	2	77	2	1	78	1	7	11	7	2	66	-1	1	91	2
234	J	6	67	3.5	10	40	8	5	18	4.5	6	40	5.5	5	69	4.5
244	L	5	66	5	5	54	4	6	14	6	5	41	4	6	69	4.5
270	N	4	67	3.5	3	63	3	10	4	10	3	53	3	4	83	3
180	O	9	39	8	8	49	6.5	3	19	2.5	8	33	7	9	40	8
194	Q	7	48	7	7	38	9	4	18	4.5	6	32	8	7	58	7
140	S	10	22	10	10	49	6.5	1	22	1	10	20	10	10	27	10

IR = Importance Rank
U = Units Allocated
UR = Units' Rank

1. Eliminating jobs J, O, and F where the (fixed) importance ranks are consistently better, or poorer, than the (variable) units' ranks.

2. Transferring units within each job from one factor to another to achieve a correspondence of ranks.

The resulting tabulation is shown in Table 4.

When the figures in Table 4 are reranked from 1 to 7, they fall into perfect correspondence, as shown in Table 5.

Table 5 gives us a price, in units, for each factor of each of the seven final key jobs. In an actual installation we might expect to salvage 15 or 20 of an originally selected 24 to 30 tentative key jobs.

From Table 5 we can prepare a key scale, with seven "anchor points" in each factor column. Thus in the Mental Requirements column, job C would

TABLE 4   Seven Final Key Jobs

Units	Job	Mental			Experience			Physical Factors			Supervision			Other Responsibilities		
		IR	U	UR	IR	U	UR	IR	U	UR	IR	U	UR	IR	U	UR
331	C	1	91	1	2	76	2	9	7	8	1	61	1	2	96	2
132	D	8	32	9	9	21	10	2	19	2.5	9	21	9	8	39	9
323	H	2	77	2	1	78	1	7	11	7	2	60	2	1	97	1
244	L	5	66	5	5	54	4	6	14	6	5	41	4	6	69	4.5
270	N	4	67	3.5	3	63	3	10	4	10	3	53	3	4	83	3
194	Q	7	48	7	7	38	9	4	18	4.5	6	32	8	7	58	7
140	S	10	22	10	6	49	6.5	1	22	1	10	20	10	10	27	10

IR = Importance Rank
U = Units Allocated
UR = Units' Rank

TABLE 5   Final Key Jobs (Reranked)

Units	Job	Mental			Experience			Physical Factors			Supervision			Other Responsibilities		
		IR	U	UR	IR	U	UR	IR	U	UR	IR	U	UR	IR	U	UR
331	C	1	91	1	2	76	2	6	7	6	1	61	1	2	96	2
132	D	6	32	6	7	21	7	2	19	2	6	21	6	6	39	6
323	H	2	77	2	1	78	1	5	11	5	2	60	2	1	97	1
244	L	4	66	4	4	54	4	4	14	4	4	41	4	4	69	4
270	N	3	67	3	3	63	3	7	4	7	3	53	3	3	83	3
194	Q	5	48	5	6	38	6	3	18	3	5	32	5	5	58	5
140	S	7	22	7	5	49	5	1	22	1	7	20	7	7	27	7

IR = Importance Rank
U = Units Allocated
UR = Units' Rank

be shown at position 91, job H at 77, job N at 67, etc. Job titles, and not mere letters, would be inserted, as in Figure 3.

Evaluating Nonkey Jobs. The evaluation of nonkey jobs begins with the selection of six or more jobs from one department. Starting with the mental requirements factor, each member of the committee:

1. Ranks the *specifications* (or their small proxy cards) according to mental requirements.

2. Beginning with the highest in mental requirements, refers to the Mental Requirements column of the key scale to find a job there for which the mental requirements are approximately equal to those of the job under consideration. Sometimes the location falls between two jobs on the key scale.

3. Enters the units' value of the key scale level on the data sheet.

4. Proceeds similarly with the lowest job, entering its units' value on the data sheet.

5. Selects values for jobs between the highest and lowest, entering the values on a data sheet. The jobs have been subjected to *factor comparisons,* from which process the name of the system is derived.

6. Reranks the cards according to experience, using the same procedure to place the entries in the proper column of his data sheet, proceeding then to physical factors, supervision, and other responsibilities.

The "votes" of all members are then recorded on a blackboard, wide discrepancies ironed out, changes, if any, made on the data sheets, and data sheets turned in to the job analyst for summarization and averaging. The total units accorded a job constitute its evaluation.

Experience shows that it requires about half an hour for a job evaluation committee to cover one job. Thus, eight jobs might be thoroughly studied and evaluated in a four-hour sitting of the committee. Most committees believe that the importance of the subject with which they are dealing warrants this expenditure of time.

After a group of jobs has been evaluated, it is customary to enter their values in the scale. If the original key scale had 22 jobs, and 8 jobs of a certain department were evaluated against that scale, there would be a total of 30 jobs in each column of the key scale. So the process of adding jobs to the key scale continues until all nonkey jobs have been evaluated.

Figure 3.   Portions of a key scale.

Units	Mental	Skill	Physical	Responsibilities	Working Conditions	Units
201						201
200						200
181						181
180						180
179						179
178				Office manager		178
177						177
176						176
175						175
174						174
173						173
172	Office manager					172
171						171
170						170
169						169
168	Tax accountant			Tax accountant		168
167						167
166	Cost accountant	Estimator				166
165				Cost accountant		165
96		Multilith operator	Shipping clerk		Shipping clerk	96
95	Typist	Shipping clerk	Estimator			95
94				Shipping clerk		94
93					Estimator	93
92	Multilith operator					92
91				Multilith operator		91
90			Typist	Typist		90
89						89
88				File clerk		88
87			File clerk		Cost accountant	87
86					Typist	86
85					File clerk	85
84	File clerk		Office manager			84
83		File clerk				83
82			Cost accountant		Office manager	82
81			Tax accountant		Tax accountant	81
80						80

Evaluating the Original Key Jobs.   Employees holding key jobs could justifiably claim that their job rates were frozen into the system, for the assumption was made that their relative rates were about right.   The reconciliation process (importance ranks against units' ranks) has certainly substantiated considerable relativity.   However, it is well to evaluate the key jobs in the same manner as nonkey jobs.

To do this, remove the key jobs from the enlarged key scale, leaving only nonkey jobs to serve as a scale.   The key jobs themselves are then treated as a group, much as a departmental grouping was treated.   They are ranked in each factor, the highest and lowest ranks "pinned" to the nonkey scale being used, and intermediate jobs fitted in.   When all five factors have been assigned values, the values are added to get a total unit value for each key job.

The chances are high that the new unit values will not differ greatly from the originals.   Nonetheless, to ensure that the original key jobs are placed properly in the hierarchy for each factor, they must be reevaluated.   This step completes the evaluation proper.

Having total units' values for all jobs, we are in a position to:

1. Translate unit dollar values by means of a scatter diagram
2. Set up grades, by dividing the continuum of units into levels

APPLICATION OF JOB EVALUATION RESULTS

To convert units to money, a scatter diagram is plotted (see Figure 4) on graph paper, with money on the vertical axis and evaluation in units on the horizontal. A point is plotted for each job at the intersection of its two values, i.e., its present (or average) rate and its evaluated units. This procedure yields a path of dots runnning from the lower left to the upper right of the chart.

The wage (or salary) line is calculated by dividing the horizontal scale into six or more (seven, in this case) equal columns. The money values of the dots plotted in each column are averaged and this average value shown as an "X" in the center of each column. The line is drawn through these averages so that the distances above the drawn line approximately equal those below it. More refined mathematical methods are available.

The wage line provides the means for converting evaluated units (horizontal scale) to equivalent money value (vertical scale). For example, 500 units equal $130 and 600 units, $152.

Some companies pay the indicated job value, regardless of length of service; others use this value as a base rate for incentive pay. Usually, however, grades —having minimum and maximum rates—are established. In the next section we discuss two methods of setting up grades.

Grades. One way to establish grades is to divide the units into progressively larger fractions, as shown in Table 6.

Thus all jobs valued between 0 and 99 would be assigned to grade 1, and minimum and maximum rates selected for this grade, above and below the wage line.

A second way is to establish the pay grades *first*, determining how much overlap there will be, as shown in Tables 7 and 8.

Figure 4.   Scatter diagram.

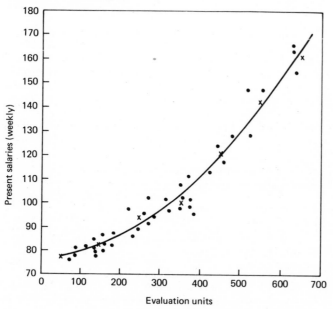

TABLE 6   Unit Values Assigned to Grades

Grade	Units
1	0–99
2	100–124
3	125–157
4	158–200
5	201–257
etc.	etc.

Plan A, shown in Table 7, is characteristic of static organizations; plan B, shown in Table 8, is typical of rapidly expanding organizations with high profits.

To determine the units' limits of grades, the middle area (in dollars) is first computed, as shown in Table 9.

The scatter diagram in Figure 4 relates these money values to job values, thereby allowing grade minimums and maximums to be established, as shown in Table 10.

TABLE 7   Plan A—Weekly; Slow Progression with Large Overlap of Grades

Grade	Min. step 1	Step 2	Step 3	Step 4	Max. step 5	Step increases 1 to 2	2 to 3	3 to 4	4 to 5
1	$ 80	$ 85	$ 90	$ 96	$102	$5	$5	$6	$6
2	85	90	96	102	109	5	6	6	7
3	90	96	102	109	116	6	6	7	7
4	96	102	109	116	124	6	7	7	8
5	102	109	116	124	132	7	7	8	8

Unit limits (minimum and maximum) of grades can be retained for many years, even though money values may change. The simplest way to effect a general salary (or wage) increase is to drop step 1 of each grade and add a step to the existing maximum. All (or most) employees then receive the next step rate above the present. In plan A, Table 7, this method would approximate a 6 percent payroll increase; in plan B, Table 8, an 8 percent increase.

Before a final application of findings is made, it is customary to make a survey of rates being paid elsewhere for comparable jobs. For low-level jobs,

TABLE 8   Plan B—Monthly; Rapid Progression with Less Overlap of Grades

Grades	Min. step 1	Step 2	Step 3	Step 4	Max. step 5	Step increases 1 to 2	2 to 3	3 to 4	4 to 5
1	$400	$430	$465	$ 505	$ 550	$30	$35	$40	$45
2	465	505	550	600	655	40	45	50	55
3	550	600	655	715	780	50	55	60	65
4	655	715	780	850	925	60	65	70	75
5	780	850	925	1,005	1,090	70	75	80	85

TABLE 9   Middle Range of Pay Grades

Grade	Plan A	Plan B
1	Up to $92	Up to $504
2	$93 to 98	$505 to 599
3	$99 to 105	$600 to 714
4	$106 to 112	$715 to 849
5	$113 to 119	$850 to 1004

this survey may cover the nearby community, but for technical and middle-management jobs a wide geographic area is usually necessary.

Payroll.   The effect of job evaluation on each employee must be worked out by filling out a summary sheet with the following column headings:

Department   Grade Minimum
Name of Employee   Grade Maximum
Job Title   Present Salary
Evaluated Units   Proposed Salary
Grade   Date Effective

TABLE 10   Grade Limits

Grade	Plan A	
	Minimum	Maximum
1	—	259 units
2	260 units	309 units
3	310 units	356 units
4	357 units	400 units
5	401 units	439 units

Usually jobs being paid below the minimum of their respective grades are immediately, or rapidly, brought up to the minimum.

Job rates above the maximum are not cut, but incumbents do not receive increases until the salary level catches up to them.

Employees within a grade are adjusted to the established step rates over a 12-month period, taking into account job performance.

Wage and Salary Administration.   Not infrequently, the job evaluation committee becomes a wage and salary committee.   Likewise, the chief job analyst may become wage and salary administrator.

The committee and the administrator develop policies on performance rating, salary increases, promotions, transfers, area rate surveys, reevaluations, evaluations of new jobs, etc.

As a result, the wage and salary plan becomes a valuable management procedure to control the complex problem of wages and salaries.

chapter 11

Goal-oriented Approaches to People and Job Measurement

CHARLES L. HUGHES   *Director of Corporate Industrial Relations, Texas Instruments Incorporated, Dallas, Texas 75222*

A number of trends are at work in industry which raise serious questions about the reliability and validity of measuring jobs for the purpose of placing a value on an individual's task.   Traditional job measurement makes certain assumptions derived from the bureaucratic theory of functional organization structure and stable job content.   In many contemporary organizations and probably in the majority of all organizations in the future, however, people will not be assigned to a finite set of tasks in a slowly changing organizational arrangement of people and jobs.

THE SHIFT FROM JOBS TO ROLES

The key word for the future is *temporary*.   Continually changing arrangement of roles performed and goals identified for achievement will characterize the organizational system.   Arrangements represented in classic organization charts composed of boxes circumscribing jobs with clear hierarchical linking along functional lines are being replaced by task forces organized around problems to be solved by groups of people in a temporary configuration of talents and skills. The organization chart will come to resemble a flow chart of project teams and individual tasks interconnected for maximum effectiveness and phased in time for the simultaneous accomplishment of identified business goals.

This trend toward organizing the effort of people around business objectives rather than functions will accelerate the management by objectives thrust and will penetrate below the management level to impact all organizational levels, including first-level nonsupervisory manufacturing and clerical operations. With this goal-oriented approach, the work environment will be characterized by:

1. Phasing out of the traditional superior-subordinate relationship.

2. An increased managerial time span for coaching people to comprehend, contribute, and orient themselves toward the attainment of meaningful and challenging goals. Conversely, because the organizational system and content of a person's responsibility repertoire are temporary, less time will be spent in judging and evaluating the worth of "a job."

3. Work groups—probably characterized as "teams"—will be composed to resolve the array of increasingly complex problems. This arrangement of people will stress interdependence of effort with interdisciplinary capabilities.

4. Work groups will be reorganized as problems are solved and goals are achieved, requiring maximum adaptability and flexibility of people.

Under these conditions there will be no identifiable thing called "a job" which can be measured except as a temporary condition existing for a moment in time.

At the present time, a job description for the purpose of job evaluation is typically a recitation of duties and responsibilities. This view of jobs tends to preclude the possibility of developing an organizational climate in which people can exercise their full range of skills and abilities in solving problems and achieving business goals. Under the goal-oriented system described above, however, we repeat, there will be no identifiable thing called "a job" which can be measured except as a temporary condition existing for a moment in time. This trend runs counter to the long-standing labor union interest in limiting the scope of an individual's activities. But it is on a converging course with the escalating concern with job enrichment for the purposes of motivation, productivity, and self-fulfillment.

The same conflict is present in management and executive job evaluation and compensation. Attempting to achieve survey comparability through detailed descriptions of jobs which are disappearing from the industrial scene is currently a problem because the classical functions of engineering, manufacturing, marketing, and the like, do not exist, particularly in the entrepreneur-oriented growth technology organization. As more organizations adopt a management by objectives style, the functional bureaucratic structure is being replaced by the project-oriented, free-form, goal-directed concept.

These shifts reflect the same change in values and structure that is occurring in society at large. Higher levels of education and increased geographic, economic, and social mobility are changing the values people place on work itself. As people become more intellectually committed to their organizations, they will also require more freedom to act, involvement in planning, and participation in structuring their work activities. This more humanistic and democratic value system is made necessary by competition and change, and is a requirement for growth and survival of organizations and individuals.

IMPLICATIONS FOR EVALUATION AND COMPENSATION

The position description as we know it today is obsolescent, if not already obsolete. It has questionable value as a compensation device and is of negligible value as a developmental tool. Measurement techniques will have to be integrated with the shifting organization structure and the business objectives of the enterprise. Jobs will be evaluated primarily in terms of their achievement of preset organizational goals.

Focus on Goals. Since the integrated work group will be prevalent, individual job evaluation will be replaced, or at least significantly supplemented, by evaluation of project groups and teams. The emphasis will be on project performance rather than position evaluation. Compensation will probably be determined for more organization members in two coordinated ways: (1) base salary related to the value of the skill attributes of the individual, and (2) bonus or incentive related to the balance sheet value of the team achievement. Incentive reward cycles will be phased with business cycles and not the calendar. The measurement of job value will be supplemented by measuring the value of the goal achieved. Compensation decisions will be made within the time frame of the project rather than the administrative cycle of the compensation people. Individuals will have an increasing range of alternatives from which to select the way in which they need, or prefer, to be paid on the basis of their family, tax, career, and life style situation. All of this will require significantly improved measures of individual and team contribution so that the earnings per share, value added, and other balance sheet criteria currently available for upper management can be translated into relevant criteria for other members of the organization.

Jobs should exist as part of the operational system for reaching business goals. The value of the business goals to members of society, both as customers and as shareholders, is integral to the free enterprise system. At the gross organizational levels these operate automatically. At the key executive level it is possible to perceive, measure, and administer the value of an individual's contribution to organizational effectiveness. The goal-oriented approach to people and job measurement requires equally reliable measures for all organization members—individually or in teams.

The Need for Change. For years, compensation specialists have been trying to educate operating managers on the importance of segregating the evaluations of jobs and people. The job evaluation is purported to be the standard against which the performance of people is subsequently measured. This view is necessary because job evaluation achieves a high degree of objective validity through the vigorous application of a systematic approach (the evaluation plan), and as such it is relatively unencumbered by the subjective and emotional considerations inherent in a performance review and appraisal situation. Job evaluation also uses common factors and thus lends itself to centralized (corporate) comparison and audit. Performance evaluation, on the other hand, involves judgments applied in fluid situations, by all members of the supervisory hierarchy, each using the criteria which he believes to be meaningful. The only concession the compensation technicians grant is in the case of top-level, single-occupancy jobs, where "the man makes the job."

Why have operating managers had so much difficulty over the years in perceiving this distinction? Perhaps the distinction between job and people valuations is an artificial one, promulgated by compensation technicians to safeguard the scientific chastity of their job evaluations from the arena of multi-criteria, multi-person judgments of people. Perhaps the two are, in fact, inseparable. It is interesting to note that Edward N. Hay & Associates began several years ago to encourage managers to make use of its guide chart factors—know-how, problem solving, and accountability—in evaluating people as well as jobs, thus gaining the advantages of common language and uniform approach. Maturity curve approaches, heretofore thought to be appropriate only for homogeneous groups (i.e., a small research laboratory), bypass individual job evaluation (on the assumption that job requirements are roughly equal) and determine base compensation according to degree level and years of pertinent experience.

MEASURING PEOPLE IN TERMS OF GOALS

The measurement of jobs and the measurement of people in terms of value to the organization will be dealt with together, since the two measures must be integrated to arrive at a total value. It is possible to adapt existing measurement techniques to this approach.

For example, the Hay guide chart system[1] is typically used to evaluate a job, and as long as the organizational arrangement is relatively stable, job content is finite, and the incumbent holds the same job assignment, it can be used in the standard approach. It is also possible to use the Hay guide chart system under conditions of chronic change, team orientation, and focus upon goal attainment. The know-how factor—specialized and management know-how and human relations skills—can be applied to the measurement of individual or team capabilities expressed in performance. The problem-solving aspect—thinking environment and challenge—can, in a like manner, be factored as part of the determination of the problem solving necessary to achieve individual and/or team goals. These two factors then constitute the people measurement, i.e., what skills and abilities the people bring to their roles. The Hay accountability factor, with its three dimensions of freedom to act, dollar magnitude of the end result of goal achievement, and the direct or indirect impact on results, can be used to measure both the value of the task and the resultant contribution.

In the future, it will become increasingly difficult to "capture" a job (even for a moment) unless job content is finite and the organizational structure is relatively stable. Instead, value measurements will be based on the skills and abilities that individuals and teams apply in resolving problems and carrying out predetermined tasks. Even with increasing specialization and complexity, these measurements, if structured properly, will be quite durable, since changes in the type and level of a person's contribution tend to be evolutionary.

The Hay guide charts, which appear in Chapter 12, Section 12.4, are well suited to such an approach. Individuals (and possibly teams) lend themselves to evaluation under the dimensions of know-how (specialized and managerial know-how) and problem solving (thinking environment plus challenge). Evaluations, as such, will avoid the academic separation of job and performance by merging the two into what is essentially a role definition. Although assignments will change frequently, roles will develop in an evolutionary manner and can therefore provide a valid tool for establishing base salaries along these lines:

1. Base salary level based on the sum of know-how and problem-solving content required for performance of the individual's characteristic role.

2. Base salary structure established at levels adequate to satisfy basic economic (maintenance/hygiene) needs.

3. At a given level, salaries will be normalized by eliminating or dramatically

---

[1] For a detailed discussion of the Hay Guide Chart-Profile Method of job evaluation and an explanation of the terms used—*know-how*, *problem-solving*, and *accountability*—see Sec. 12.4 of Chap. 12.

reducing "merit" pay opportunity. Single-rate structures for managers with equal amounts of the know-how and problem-solving factors may be a possibility.

4. Support (staff) jobs will receive relatively higher base salaries than operating jobs because know-how and problem solving (as compared with accountability) form a relatively greater part of total job content. By the same token, opportunity to contribute, and therefore to earn incentive awards, is relatively less variable.

5. Schedule adjustments will be administered on a group/calendar basis, irrespective of the business cycle based on economic and competitive labor market considerations.

Additional direct compensation will be provided in the form of bonuses and incentive awards. Contrary to the traditional "merit" increase, which was often determined with feeling-tone rather than objectivity, these awards will be based on the assessment of results against preestablished objectives. Again, the Hay guide charts may be used to implement this concept. The accountability factor, with its three dimensions (freedom to act, magnitude, and job impact), provides an excellent vehicle for measuring the opportunity of an individual or team to contribute to the financial success of the enterprise and for comparing resultant contribution against the opportunity (resources allocated) to accomplish the result.

Size and allocation of incentive award pools will be based on performance against plan with yardsticks suited to each organizational level. At the corporate level, appropriate yardsticks may be: (1) sales plus net income, (2) return on assets, (3) earnings per share, and/or (4) profit improvement.

At the group, division, or department level, the yardsticks should reflect the subunit's opportunity to contribute to total corporate goals. Therefore, since the total amount of accountability (calculated in points) in an organization subunit reflects the share of corporate human assets devoted to the accomplishment of objectives, the initial award allocation should be based on the ratio of each subunit's accountability points to total corporate accountability points. Award pool amounts will then be adjusted upward or downward according to the subunit's performance against the predetermined objectives. Suitable yardsticks may include improvement in return on assets, profit, share of market, and/or sales—whatever is relevant to the business.

Allocations to teams and individuals can be made by ranking teams according to relative contribution. Individual awards within a team may be equal, or, again, team members may be rank-ordered on the basis of contribution. Rankings can be combined at successively higher organizational levels, using benchmark teams or individuals for cross-unit comparisons. Specific criteria for measuring team members will be expressed in terms of individual team results versus objectives.

It is possible to use the goal-oriented approach to people and job measurement to relate managerial and real-time process to compensation. For example, this approach could be applied in the use of a special task force appointed to investigate locations for new plant sites and to coordinate the construction of new facilities at the site. The Hay guide chart technique could be used initially in the selection of task force members. People with specified levels of know-how and problem-solving capabilities would be drawn from the traditional functions, such as product line management, facilities engineering, market analysis, manpower utilization, and material procurement. As the work of the task force progressed, specialized teams would probably be appointed to work under the task force. Each team would be managed by one of the task force members. The task force's objectives for the new facility could then be developed in support of company goals, such as increased market penetration or reduced production costs.

The base salary of the task force members would be reviewed at the time specified by company policy. Changes in the base rate would be related to the capability level of the individual being reviewed. Bonus or incentive compensation would be paid to task force members when the new plant began operations if the initial operations achieved the objectives set by the task force. It is conceivable that this task force would then become the nucleus of a new task force or management team assigned to manage the new facility and develop the market area it serves.

ADVANTAGES OF GOAL-ORIENTED APPROACH

The goal-oriented approach outlined in the preceding pages can help an organization to:

1. Provide high leverage based on measurable operating results
2. Provide opportunity to earn compensation at superior levels
3. Relate compensation directly to performance
4. Maximize entrepreneurial achievement motivation at all organizational levels
5. Relate the award cycle to the business cycle and encourage sustained effort in achieving goals

Two additional characteristics of the goal-oriented approach can probably also be counted as advantages: (1) teams and individuals will have realistic compensation expectations, since they will have been able to monitor their progress against the predetermined goals, and (2) operating people will receive a relatively greater share of direct compensation in the form of incentive awards (as compared with support people) because of their proportionately greater opportunity to contribute.

In providing these benefits, the goal-oriented approach will focus measurement on two factors: (1) assessment of the human resources directed toward the objective, and (2) opportunity to affect organization financial performance. The first factor is used to determine individual base salary or wage, the second to determine the team bonus. The bonus or incentive may be allocated equally to the team members or differently based upon a rank order of their individual subgoals under the overall team goal.

The personnel and compensation experts' traditional intervening variable of job measurement is bypassed. Rather, the aim is to specify results required of people in order to achieve specific impact, and then to measure actual impact in terms of the results specified. This links overall organizational performance, measured in terms of financial effectiveness, more directly to teams and individuals. It creates for people an entrepreneurial situation parallel to— and directly derivative from—that of the organization. It will also tend to remove compensation experts from compensation decisions that derive from traditional job evaluation and place the system in the hands of the users, that is, the operating managers. This also achieves maximum internal consistency. At the same time, some of the mystique of traditional job evaluation is avoided and there can be a rise in the objectivity, simplicity, and effectiveness of compensation. Operating management will be responsible for the content of the system, and the personnel and compensation specialists will be responsible for the process itself.

In summary, a company wishing to implement a goal-oriented approach to people and job measurement should follow these guidelines:

1. Do not evaluate jobs—evaluate individual roles using know-how plus problem-solving.

2. Develop base salary structure, relating salary levels to total know-how and problem-solving points. Base salaries should not exceed 50 to 70 percent of the total direct compensation objective.

3. Evaluate team and individual accountabilities. Rank-order corporate, group, and division objectives to develop opportunity indexes.

4. Measure results in terms of opportunity to contribute and allocate the incentive award pool according to accountability points.

5. Adjust subunit pools and incentive awards on the basis of actual contribution.

6. Synchronize award determination and distribution with the business cycle of the subunit.

Compensation then orients efforts toward goals and becomes a true management system fully integrated with management by objectives, evaluation of organizational performance, determination of objectives, strategies, and tactical action programs.

chapter 12

Specific Job Evaluation Systems in Action

RAYMOND JACOBSON

D. H. EVEREST

FRANK M. LYNCH

CHARLES W. G. VAN HORN

12.1   White-collar Jobs in the Federal Civil Service

RAYMOND JACOBSON   *Director, Bureau of Policies and Standards, United States Civil Service Commission, Washington, D.C.*

The executive branch of the federal government is made up of about 65 departments and agencies. These range in size, in terms of the number of civilian employees, from the Department of Defense with more than 1.3 million employees to such very small but important agencies as the Federal Power Commission with less than 1,000 employees. The head of each executive department or agency is typically granted the authority to organize and direct the work of his agency, subject to such broad policy guidance as is laid down by the Congress or by the President. This authority always includes the authority to appoint and determine the compensation of the employees of the department. The power to appoint and determine the compensation of employees is limited by various laws which, generally speaking, provide very broad policy direction and provide for more specific direction and guidance to be exercised by the U. S. Civil Service Commission.

The total number of full-time civilian employees of the executive branch is about 2.7 million. Broadly speaking, from a job evaluation and compensation standpoint, these employees are handled in one of four different ways:

1. *Post Office Department employees* (approximately 750,000). Until 1970 these employees were classified into 20 grades on the basis of key job descriptions written into law. The Postal Reorganization Act of 1970 authorized the development of a new job evaluation and pay system through collective bargaining, but at the time of this writing the characteristics of the system had not yet taken shape.

2. *Blue-collar employees in all departments* (approximately 750,000, of which 80 percent work for the Department of Defense). These employees are paid under the Coordinated Federal Wage System, just now (1970) in the last stages of installation, under the direction of the Civil Service Commission. This system provides for the compensation of the employees in the manual-laboring and skilled trades and crafts occupations (including their supervisors) on the basis of a prevailing area hourly wage system, as determined by annual locality wage surveys. Job evaluation is performed essentially through a factor comparison system, based on job standards issued by the Civil Service Commission.

3. *White-collar employees in all departments* (approximately 1.2 million). The balance of this section will describe this particular subsystem in more detail. Basically, it covers clerical, administrative, technical, professional, and executive personnel, compensated on a nationwide uniform annual salary basis through comparison with national average private enterprise salary data gathered by the Bureau of Labor Statistics.

4. *Employees of various kinds paid under various special-purpose systems* (approximately 70,000). These include such relatively small but important special groups as the Foreign Service and the Public Health Service, paid on a "rank in man" concept; the physicians, dentists, and nurses in the Veterans Administration; employees of the Atomic Energy Commission, National Security Agency, Tennessee Valley Authority, etc. Each category has its own system of job evaluation and compensation, with some loose ties to the big white-collar system.

THE WHITE-COLLAR SYSTEM

The white-collar system has its legal basis in the Classification Act of 1949 as amended to date, although the basic job evaluation concepts of the system go back to the Classification Act of 1923. The title of the law provides a good hint of its basic concept, i.e., that positions are to be placed into *classes* so that all the positions in a single class are *substantially* identical with each other in their duties, responsibilities, and qualification requirements. Each class of positions is to be assigned to a particular *grade*, i.e., a zone of difficulty, responsibility, and qualifications. There are now 18 such grades, numbered in sequence from GS-1 to GS-18 (the highest). (The initials "GS" stand for "General Schedule.") The number of grades, their broadly written definitions, and the pay rate ranges for these grades are determined by the Congress.

The intent of the system is clear and easily understood. White-collar work of the very simplest and most routine nature (e.g., that of a messenger) should be assigned to classes at the GS-1 level, while the very most responsible, difficult, and important jobs (e.g., the director of a very important bureau such as the National Park Service or the Bureau of Labor Statistics) should be assigned to classes at the GS-18 level.[1] The responsibility for making this system work is divided between the President, the U.S. Civil Service Commission, and the heads of the departments and agencies:

1. *The President's* responsibility is primarily in the area of pay. He makes annual recommendations to the Congress on adjustments needed in the General Schedule pay rates. Such adjustments are designed to achieve comparability with private enterprise rates as determined by an annual survey of professional, administrative, technical, and clerical salaries made by the Bureau of Labor Statistics. The President discharges this responsibility by designating the Chairman of the Civil Service Commission and the Director, Office of Management and Budget, as his agents to jointly review the BLS report, to consult with agencies, unions, professional organizations, etc., and to make a report and recommendations to him.

2. *The U.S. Civil Service Commission* has a twofold responsibility. First, the Commission reviews pay and makes recommendations (jointly with Office of Management and Budget) as described above. Secondly, it provides leadership, guidance, and supervision over the job evaluation functions exercised by the departments and agencies of the executive branch. It is this second responsibility which is the primary subject of this section; so it is this which will be given a more expanded treatment below.

3. *The heads of departments and agencies* are responsible for ensuring that the individual positions held by the employees of the department or agency are described, evaluated, and classified in the appropriate grade and class, in accordance with the standards and instructions issued by the Civil Service Commission. It should be clearly understood that the authority to assign duties and responsibilities to individual positions is a line management authority exercised by the agency head or those subordinate supervisors to whom he delegates such authority. Likewise, the authority to decide the classification of an individual position or group of positions in a department is a line management authority, subject to certain checks and reviews.

Standard Development. In order to exercise its leadership and guidance function, the Civil Service Commission prepares and publishes an occupational handbook and position classification standards.

The occupational handbook is a set of definitions of occupational fields or *kinds of work* groupings as they are found in the federal service. There are now approximately 500 different occupations defined in the handbook and it is kept up to date as occupational content changes. They include occupations in such varied broad fields as clerical, social science, psychology, personnel and industrial relations, engineering, physical, biological, and medical sciences, law, accounting, fine and applied arts, supply and logistics, law enforcement and corrections, and general management. Each occupation is assigned a code number and an official title, as well as being given a short definition.

The position classification standards are a much more extensive set of documents. These standards comprise a description of the characteristics or criteria which distinguish one class of positions from another—i.e., what makes the

---

[1] There are also five executive grades paid at rates above GS-18, primarily for cabinet and subcabinet officers and members of boards and commissions. The jobs are almost all individually classified by statute and the job evaluation system described here, of course, does not apply.

difference between a GS-11 engineer and a GS-12 engineer. Each standard is developed through an individual, detailed study of a sample of the actual jobs of that kind in those federal agencies which are the principal employers of this kind of help. A draft of the standard is prepared, reviewed, and commented on by the using agencies and interested unions or professional organizations, and revised and published by the Commission. Once published, this standard then becomes the official guide which agency position classifiers use in deciding where individual jobs of that kind in their agency should be classified.

Since the standard is fundamental to the job evaluation process in the federal government, a brief explanation is needed. All standards (and therefore all job evaluations) are based on the analysis of jobs in terms of eight factors:

1. Nature and variety of work.
2. Nature of supervision received by incumbent.
3. Nature of available guidelines for performance of work.
4. Originality required.
5. Purpose and nature of person-to-person work relationships.
6. Nature and scope of recommendations, decisions, commitments, and conclusions.
7. Nature and extent of supervision exercised over work of other employees.
8. Qualifications required.[2]

Because of the great variety of occupations covered by this single job evaluation system, all eight factors are not necessarily considered to be of the same relative importance or weight in all occupations. Therefore, the standard for each occupation is developed by tailoring the general factors to the specific functions and characteristics of the occupation. This may involve treating certain factors in combination; possibly subdividing one or more factors; retitling factors to make them more meaningful to people in the occupation; etc.

When certain groups of related occupations contain functions which are common in terms of job-level characteristics, a single standard may be developed to deal with the grade-level evaluation of those functions in all the occupations affected. For example, a single *Guide for Evaluation of Basic and Applied Research Positions* has been published, thus making it unnecessary to treat research jobs in biology, physics, chemistry, etc., each in a separate standard. Similarly, general standards have been issued for all supervisory jobs, for clerical jobs, and for others.

The form of these standards also varies somewhat depending on the nature of the occupation and the degree to which it lends itself to various methods of treatment. Most standards are narrative in form, consisting of: (1) an introductory statement explaining the occupation and how it is distinguished from other occupations, how the standard eight factors are treated in the grade-level descriptions, etc.; and (2) a set of grade-level descriptions emphasizing those characteristics which distinguish one grade level from another in the occupation. However, some standards have been issued in tabular or chart form; others have established tables of numerical values which convert to grade levels; etc.

Regardless of format or specific content, the basic purpose of all standards is to provide sufficient guidance to agency operating personnel offices so that, given the same facts as to job content, two different agencies in widely separate geographical locations will evaluate these job facts to the same class and grade and be able to explain their evaluations to all interested parties.

---

[2] For a discussion of the eight factors, see section I, paragraph C, of *Introductory Material to Position Classification Standards*, U.S. Government Printing Office, 1970.

Agency Application of Standards.   With the extreme variation in size, variety of mission, and geographical dispersion of agencies, there is no one common pattern which all federal agencies use in job evaluation.   However, typical of most larger, geographically dispersed agencies is the following pattern:

1. The agency head's legal authority to classify jobs is delegated to his major line subordinates—e.g., bureau directors, commanding officers, etc.   The director of personnel of the agency is given the responsibility for providing training and technical leadership to the job evaluation process.

2. At the operational level, where the day-to-day evaluation decisions are made, the personnel officer is usually responsible for the actual decision in most instances.   Typically, the personnel officer in turn leans heavily on the judgment of the chief of his position classification office (which may go by various titles).

The process essentially is one by which a management official requests a review of a particular job because it is new or has changed significantly in content.   A position classifier reviews the job content with the employee (unless this is a new, vacant position) and with the immediate supervisor. Once an understanding as to the facts has been achieved, the classifier compares the job with the Civil Service Commission standards to determine the appropriate grade.   He may also use additional guidance material issued by higher headquarters within the agency, comparisons with similar positions within the agency, etc.   In making these analyses, the classifier is responsible for considering the management implications of the job content changes, effects on other jobs, organizational relationships, etc.

A more comprehensive type of total job evaluation review is usually done in most agencies through the medium of a regular (perhaps annual) review of all jobs in an organization.   This kind of survey program is typically scheduled on a regular, cyclic basis.   It involves a thorough briefing of the classifier in the current program and functions of the unit being studied, a review of organizational patterns, delegations of authority, flow of work, etc.   Sometimes, this kind of survey is done jointly with organizations and management specialists as part of a total management or operational audit.   The actual job evaluation process in this situation does not differ essentially from that in the individual case situation.   It is, however, broader in scope and therefore more likely to reveal significant problems or to enable the classifier to make major suggestions for improved work organization or job evaluation patterns.

The direct and immediate relationship of job evaluation decisions to pay is such that the evaluation process is highly charged and emotional.   Most agencies provide internal review procedures for disagreements to be resolved at a higher managerial level.   However, where an employee feels that his job has been improperly evaluated, he has, by law, a right of direct appeal to the Civil Service Commission.   These appeals are not particularly numerous and, in the majority of the cases, the Commission sustains the agency action.   However, the Commission does have final authority to classify any job on appeal, and, if it finds the agency to have incorrectly interpreted the standard, the Commission's decision must be put into effect by the agency.

Civil Service Commission Supervision.   In addition to its responsibility for guidance to agencies through standards development and its responsibility for final appellate action, the Civil Service Commission also has general responsibility for supervision of the job evaluation program.

This responsibility is exercised as part of a total personnel management evaluation program.   In this program, the Commission exercises surveillance over agency personnel management activities and programs to: (1) ensure that they meet regulatory and legal requirements, and (2) help agencies to make maximum effective use of their human resources by the application of modern personnel management methods.   The Commission's review of agency job evaluation activities, therefore, is thoroughly integrated with the total personnel management evaluation.   There has been greater emphasis in recent years on giving agency headquarters leadership and guidance in mounting more effective personnel management evaluation programs for their own subordinate bureaus, divisions, and field organizations.

If, in the course of these evaluations, it becomes clear that agency job evaluations are out of line with CSC standards, there is full authority to require agencies to take corrective action.   Such authority is used primarily to secure program management improvement, e.g., by establishing more effective training of job evaluation specialists, by requiring the institution of a regular job classification survey program, etc.   However, individual job classifications are corrected when necessary.

SUMMARY

This description has dealt with only one phase of the total job evaluation program of the federal government.   However, the white-collar job evaluation system is the largest of the various systems used in the federal government and is unique because of the wide range of situations with which it is designed to deal.

At the time of this writing (1970), the Civil Service Commission is making a sweeping review of all job evaluation *and* compensation systems in use.   The result of this review will probably be some legislative recommendations to the Congress in the winter of 1971–1972.   It is too early to forecast the outcome of this review, but it seems clear that significant changes will be recommended.

12.2   Steel Industry Plan

D. H. EVEREST   *Manager, Industrial Engineering, Western Steel Operations, United States Steel Corporation*

The job description and classification system for hourly rated production, maintenance, and nonconfidential clerical jobs currently used by most of the steel industry and the United Steelworkers of America (AFL-CIO) dates back to World War II.   The system was developed to eliminate intraplant wage rate inequities and to provide equal rates of pay for jobs that included essentially the same job content.

One of the primary goals was to develop a comprehensive system that would cover present and future processes, job technology, and skills so that it would serve over the long term to measure and maintain rate equity.

Formation of the Steel Workers Organizing Committee (SWOC) and recognition of the union in 1937 led to rate comparisons between plants and between companies which highlighted existing wage rate inequities.   In those early years, the vast majority of employee grievances involved wages. As adjustments were negotiated for one situation, additional problems were created for similar jobs at other locations.

The United Steelworkers of America (successors to SWOC in 1942) joined the companies in seeking a solution to the problem, and in 1944 the "Steel Wage Case"—involving the wage rates of approximately 400,000 employees of 86 steel companies—was brought before the National War Labor Board.

Twelve of the companies had already joined together to form a study group to review the problem, create a manual, and develop a system of classification in order to meet the defined objectives. That effort became known as the Cooperative Wage Study (CWS), and it finally grew to embrace almost all the companies in the steel industry in North America as well as many other companies and unions.

The National War Labor Board ruled on the case on November 25, 1944, and directed the parties to negotiate the elimination of existing intraplant wage rate inequities by:

1. Properly describing the content and duties of each job
2. Placing each job in its proper relationship with other jobs
3. Reducing the number of classifications to the smallest practical number by grouping those jobs having substantially equivalent content
4. Establishing hourly wage rates for the job classifications
5. Installing the newly developed hourly wage rates

To implement the Board's directive, United States Steel Corporation and the union formed a Joint Wage Rate Inequity Committee in February, 1945. The union and management were jointly responsible for developing an acceptable and workable job classification system. Elmer J. Maloy was committee chairman for the union and R. Conrad Cooper was committee chairman for the corporation; these two men proved to be statesmen in the field of labor relations as they guided their associates through those tedious years of development and implementation of the entire program. The basic concept of joint responsibility between union and management representatives in the creation and maintenance of the manual and the total classification system proved to be one of the cardinal points in the plan, and it remains intact even today.

As procedures were developed and the classification manual neared completion, the system was applied to 144 benchmark jobs and additionally to a broader cross section of jobs within the steel-producing companies of United States Steel Corporation. These applications yielded 2,345 "specimen examples," which provided the basic framework within which all jobs were to be classified. The next step was to describe and classify all the remaining jobs at each plant of the steel-producing companies of the corporation; about 25,000 jobs were covered at that time. Following the negotiation of the classifications under consideration at each plant location by local union-management committees, the Joint Committee negotiated a standard hourly wage scale, and new rates were installed in February, 1947.

Trade and craft jobs and assigned maintenance jobs were given special treatment, and special conventions were provided for testing, inspection, spell hand, and group leader jobs. Clerical and technical jobs, instructor and learner jobs, were held for later consideration, and classifications were finalized in 1948, 1949, and 1950.

In January, 1953, the numerous inequity agreements negotiated over the years by the union and United States Steel Corporation were consolidated and incorporated without change in substance into one document—the January 1, 1953, Job Description and Classification Manual. The 2,345 benchmark and specimen jobs were included in the manual, with the provision that descriptions and classifications of other jobs "shall be consistent with and properly related within the framework of the descriptions and classifications of the appropriate 'Benchmark' and 'Specimen Example' jobs. . . ."

During the 1950s essentially these same procedures were used to expand classification coverage throughout United States Steel Corporation to include jobs at many raw materials locations, steel fabricating and cement plants, and other nonsteel-producing divisions and subsidiaries.

Almost all of the large basic steel companies participated in the development of this classification system and its related procedures, and in 1947, after United States Steel Corporation and the United Steelworkers completed their negotiations, these other companies began to install the system. Since that time the system has been applied in many companies outside the steel industry in the United States and in other countries as well. A conservative estimate indicates that by 1970 more than 250,000 separate jobs and well over a million people were covered by the system.

In 1962, ten of the largest basic steel companies, known as the "coordinating committee steel companies" and the union revised the manual which replaced or supplemented individual company "Benchmark" or "Specimen Example" jobs. The revised document was known as the "January 1, 1963 Job Description and Classification Manual." Additional changes of a minor nature plus additional master job classifications for broader coverage were adopted by the parties during steel labor negotiations in 1971 which resulted in the "August 1, 1971 Job Description and Classification Manual."

The job classification program in the steel industry is considered the largest joint study and effort by management and a union in the history of American labor relations, and it has probably had the greatest economic impact. Both parties remain dedicated to keeping the system in effect and up to date. For example, the parties issued a new specimen example for the job of electronic repairman in 1958 as an addition to the 1953 manual, and in 1968 they issued six master job classifications supplemental to the 1963 manual for jobs associated with basic oxygen furnace operations—a recent development in steel-producing techniques. In 1971, new master job classifications for continuous casting operations were adopted and incorporated in the 1971 Manual along with other additional jobs to provide greater coverage for steel plant operations. It is anticipated that additional supplemental master job classifications will be issued for other new processes or operations as they are negotiated between the parties. In this manner union and management representatives are able to maintain the system as a useful and up-to-date tool even though jobs and processes change significantly over the years.

The Steel Industry Plan is now over 25 years old. It served to eliminate wage rate inequities at the time of its installation and it has survived as a means of developing wage rates for new jobs in the industry as well as for jobs that have changed. This accomplishment by representatives of both management and the union is without parallel in modern industrial history.

STRUCTURE OF THE SYSTEM

The system is based on the Job Description and Classification Manual and its full acceptance by the company and the union pursuant to the provisions of the basic labor agreements between the company and the union.

The Job Description and Classification Manual is the basic guide for classifying jobs and for determining their proper relationships for the purpose of establishing an equitable wage rate structure. It provides the instructions, explanatory language, master job classifications, and patterns for adequate job descriptions and proper application of the basic factors for classification of any new jobs that may be required. The manual also details procedures to maintain job descriptions and classifications in accordance with any change in job content.

The basic labor agreement establishes the standard hourly wage scale rate for each job class and provides for the application of the proper standard hourly wage scale rate to each employee who performs a particular job. As long as a job remains unchanged, its job class also remains unchanged; but standard hourly wage scale rates applied to all job classes can be adjusted as new labor agreements are negotiated.

Significant details concerning the functions and requirements of each job—i.e., the processes, equipment, and products with which it is concerned—are set forth in a job description. The job description provides the information necessary to classify the job; it is not to be construed as a detailed description of all the work requirements of the job.

Job classifications focus on the job itself rather than the individuals currently doing the job. These classifications are derived from a thorough analysis of the training, skill, responsibility, effort, and working conditions normally involved in performing the duties outlined in the job description. These job elements are subdivided into 12 basic factors in the manual, as outlined briefly in Figure 1. The classification of a particular job is determined by the rating in all of the basic factors, and the rating in each factor must be properly correlated within the framework of the master job classifications. Jobs are placed in the appropriate factor code level and assigned a corresponding numerical value in each factor by considering the specific requirements of the job, the factor instructions, the factor code level descriptions, and the master job classifications set forth in the manual. The master job classifications are illustrations of jobs that have been described and classified under the system, and, therefore, they provide an example of how to correlate the factor code levels or rating in each of the basic factors applicable to the job.

Each of the basic factors is divided into various levels which indicate codes for the numerical classification of the job requirement as it relates to that basic factor. Figure 2 illustrates the structure of basic factor number 10, physical effort. The other basic factors follow a similar format.

The final job class for a job is obtained from the sum of the numerical classification values assigned to the job in the 12 basic factors, using the closest whole number resulting therefrom. For example, if the decimal is 0.4 or less, it is dropped; if the decimal is 0.5 or more, the next higher whole number is the job class.

Job descriptions and classifications are prepared on a form similar to that shown in Figure 3.

The steel industry classification system places all hourly rated production, maintenance, and nonconfidential clerical jobs in one of 34 job classes, numbered consecutively from job class 1 to job class 34. The basic labor agreement negotiated between the company and the union specifies the standard hourly wage scale and provides an hourly wage rate for each job class.

HOW THE SYSTEM FUNCTIONS

The Job Description and Classification Manual sets forth general procedures and guidelines to be followed in the development of job descriptions and classifications. Implementation and administrative requirements related to the system are included in the individual basic labor agreements between the various steel companies and the union. Most of the labor agreement provisions

Figure 1.   The basic factors of job classification.

Basic factors	Maximum point value	Job requirement measured
1. Pre-employment training	1.0	The mentality required to absorb training and exercise judgment for the satisfactory performance of the job.
2. Employment Training and Experience	4.0	The time required to learn how to do the job, producing work of acceptable quality and of sufficient quantity to justify continued employment.
3. Mental Skill	3.5	The mental ability, job knowledge, judgment, and ingenuity required to visualize, reason through, and plan the details of a job without recourse to supervision.
4. Manual Skill	2.0	The physical or muscular ability and dexterity required in performing a given job, including the use of tools, machines, and equipment.
5. Responsibility for Materials	10.0	The obligation imposed either by authority or by the inherent nature of the job to prevent loss through damage to materials. Both care required and the probable monetary loss are considered.
6. Responsibility for Tools and Equipment	4.0	The obligation imposed on the workman for attention and care to prevent damage to tools and equipment with which he is actually working or which come under his control. Both care required and the probable cost of damage at any one time are considered.
7. Responsibility for Operations	6.5	The obligation imposed on the workman for utilizing capacity of equipment or process by maintenance of pace and machine speeds. This includes planning, instructing, and directing the work of others.
8. Responsibility for Safety of Others	2.0	The degree of care required by the nature of the job and the surroundings in which it is performed to avoid or prevent injuries to other persons.
9. Mental Effort	2.5	The mental or visual concentration and attention required by the job for the performance of work at normal pace.
10. Physical Effort	2.5	The muscular exertion required by the job when the employee is performing at a normal pace.
11. Surroundings	3.0	The general conditions under which the work is performed, other than hazard, and the extent to which these conditions make the job disagreeable.
12. Hazards	2.0	The probability and severity of injuries to which the workman is exposed, assuming that the workman is exercising reasonable care in observing safety regulations.

SOURCE: Adapted from *August 1, 1971, Job Description and Classification Manual.*

regarding job classification have been standardized—at least for the larger companies that participate in the coordinating committee and have adopted the system. This outline of how the system operates is based on the provisions included in the August 1, 1971 basic labor agreement for steel plant operations between United States Steel Corporation and the United Steelworkers of America. Most of the companies in the steel industry follow essentially the same pattern.

The agreement provides that the job description and classification for each job in effect on the date of the current agreement shall remain in effect unless

Figure 2.   Basic factor no. 10, physical effort.

Consider the muscular exertion required by the job when the employee is performing at a normal pace. Select that level which best describes the average degree of muscular exertion required throughout the turn.

Code	Job requirements	Numerical classification
A	Minimum physical exertion. Perform very light work such as sitting or standing for purposes of observations, and such work as very light assembly and adjustment. Plan and direct work. Weigh and record.	Base
B	Light physical exertion. Use light hand tools and handle fairly light materials manually. Operate crane-type controls, light valves. Operate truck or tractor. Sweep, clean up. Shovel light material.	0.3
C	Moderate physical exertion. Handle medium-weight materials. Use a variety of medium-sized hand tools for performing tradesman's work. Climb and work from ladders. Operate heavy controls and valves. Use light sledge.	0.8
D	Heavy physical exertion. Use heavy tools and handle heavy materials manually. Shovel heavy material. Use pick, heavy bars. Operate heavy pneumatic tools.	1.5
E	Extreme physical effort. Extremely heavy lifting, pushing or pulling.	2.5

SOURCE: *August 1, 1971, Job Description and Classification Manual.*

(1) management changes the job content to the extent of one full job class or more; (2) the job is terminated or not occupied during a period of one year; or (3) the job is changed by mutual agreement of officially designated representatives of the company and the union.

The August 1, 1971 Job Description and Classification Manual and the provisions of the basic labor agreement in effect are used to describe and classify all jobs established or changed after August 1, 1971.

The agreement also provides that a plant union committee on job classification consisting of three employees designated by the union shall be established at each plant.

When the company establishes a new job or changes the job content of an existing job to the extent of one full job class or more, a new job description and classification for the new or changed job are established in the following manner:

1. Management develops a job description and classification of the job in accordance with the provisions of the manual.

2. The proposed job description and classification are submitted to the plant union committee for approval, and the standard hourly wage scale rate for the job class is applied to the job.

Figure 3.   Master job description and classification (page 1).

MASTER JOB DESCRIPTION and CLASSIFICATION

Job No. __135__

DEPARTMENT __BAR MILLS__   JOB TITLE __SHEARMAN__

SUB DIVISION __ROLLING__   DATE __1-1-63__

MASTER JOB DESCRIPTION

PRIMARY FUNCTION:

Sets up and operates shear to cut product to specifications.

TOOLS AND EQUIPMENT:

Alligator or guillotine type power shears and controls, table rolls, measuring devices, knives, tongs, bars, hooks, wrenches, banding and marking equipment, etc.

MATERIALS:

Bars of various grades, sizes and sections.

SOURCE OF SUPERVISION:

Foreman

DIRECTION EXERCISED:

Shear Crew

WORKING PROCEDURE:

1. Obtains information concerning order specifications, rolling sequences, pieces, sizes, etc.

2. Sets up and adjusts shear to shear bars to specified length.

3. Changes shear knives.

4. Operates entry conveyor and table rolls controls to move bars from hot bed to gauges or shears and exit conveyor into cradle; aligns bars at shear.

5. Operates controls to trip shear to cut tests, crop ends and product.

6. Checks shear cut and determines need for knife changes.

7. Identifies product and prepares processing reports.

8. Directs others in banding material.

9. Hooks up and unhooks for crane.

10. Makes minor adjustments to shear.

The above statement reflects the general details considered necessary to describe the principal functions of the job identified, and shall not be construed as a detailed description of all of the work requirements that may be inherent in the job.

(Source: "January 1, 1963 Job Description and Classification Manual")

Figure 3.   Master job description (page 2).

MASTER JOB CLASSIFICATION

JOB TITLE_____BAR SHEARMAN_____ Job No._____135_____

Factor	Reason for Classification	Code	Classi-fication
1.	PRE-EMPLOYMENT TRAINING This job requires the mentality to learn to: Set up and operate shears requiring a variety of adjustments to cut product to specified length.	B	.3
2.	EMPLOYMENT TRAINING AND EXPERIENCE This job requires experience on this or related work of 7 to 12 months inclusive.	C	.8
3.	MENTAL SKILL Use considerable judgment in setting up and operating shear equipment to shear bars to specified length obtaining best yield.	D	2.2
4.	MANUAL SKILL Uses gauges and small hand tools to set up shearing equipment where the use of tools and gauges is simple and routine. Operates variable controls to move material and operate shear.	B	.5
5.	RESPONSIBILITY FOR MATERIAL Use close attention for part of turn to set up and operate shears to cut product to specification. Excess scrap resulting from too heavy cropping is variable but normally would not be more than 5% of turn. 5% x 150 tons x ($45 - $15) = $225.	C	1.2
6.	RESPONSIBILITY FOR TOOLS AND EQUIPMENT Moderate attention and care required to prevent damage to shear knives through improper setup.	C MED.	.7
7.	RESPONSIBILITY FOR OPERATIONS Responsible for continuity of operation of shear where the shear is limiting factor to mill production.	E	3.0
8.	RESPONSIBILITY FOR SAFETY OF OTHERS Ordinary care and attention required to prevent injury to others when operating shears where others are occasionally exposed. Changes knives with crew where individual acts may injure others. Occasional crane hooking.	B	.4
9.	MENTAL EFFORT Moderate mental or visual application required for performing shear operations, setups, and adjustments to shears.	C	1.0
10.	PHYSICAL EFFORT Light physical exertion is required to operate light controls, check lengths, check products and direct crew. Change and adjust shear knives.	B	.3
11.	SURROUNDINGS Heat in summer due to proximity of hot materials.	B	.4
12.	HAZARD Accident hazard moderate and probable injuries consist of mashed fingers, cuts and moderate burns.	B	.4

Job Class 11		Total 11.2

(Source: "January 1, 1963 Job Description and Classification Manual")

3. The plant union committee and management review and discuss the accuracy of the proposed job description and classification. If agreement is reached at this point, the issue is closed and the classification of the job is firmly established.

4. If management and the plant union committee are unable to agree, management installs the proposed classification and its associated standard hourly wage scale rate. The plant union committee may file a grievance alleging that the job is improperly described or classified, and the grievance may be processed through the grievance procedure, including arbitration, if necessary.

5. Once the job classification is settled by mutual agreement in the grievance procedure or by arbitration, that issue is closed and the job class for that job remains fixed until such time as the job is changed.

The agreement also is very explicit regarding wage rate inequity grievances. In effect, the agreement provides that once a rate is established by the parties, it remains very firmly fixed, since the agreement states:

> No basis shall exist for an employee, whether paid on an incentive or nonincentive basis, to allege that a wage-rate inequity exists and no complaint or grievance on behalf of an employee alleging a wage-rate inequity shall be initiated or processed during the term of this Agreement.[1]

The job classification procedure outlined above, although straightforward, is time-consuming. Management and union representatives have worked diligently over the years to keep the system intact, as well as workable, for use in solving wage rate problems.

One measure of the system's success is its results. In recent years, classifications for all but 1 or 2 percent of the new or changed jobs in the larger companies have been settled by the parties themselves prior to arbitration. This high rate of achievement is a tribute to both management and union representatives and indicates the effort put forth by both parties in maintaining the entire system throughout the years.

SALARIED JOBS

Within United States Steel Corporation a separate classification system (the C&T system) exists for nonexempt salaried jobs. Its origin dates back to the time of the Inequity Program for hourly paid employees; the "Manual for Job Classification of Clerical and Technical Jobs" is dated December 6, 1948.

The system embraces features similar to those of the hourly program, including joint management-union responsibility through a joint salary rate inequity committee, the development of the manual and negotiation of benchmark jobs, final negotiation of job descriptions and classifications at the local level, etc.

This method of job classification is based upon an analysis of the relative worth of jobs in terms of seven basic factors of job content:

1. Pre-employment training
2. Employment training and experience
3. Mental skill
4. Responsibility for performance
5. Responsibility for contacts
6. Working conditions
7. Responsibility for direction

In addition, a classification differential is provided to achieve specified rate

---

[1] Section 9-G, August 1, 1971 Basic Labor Agreement.

differences over the highest job directed, depending upon the number of people directed.

Using the clerical and technical manual, each job is analyzed on the basis of these factors and assigned to one of 16 salaried job classes. Employees are paid on the basis of the assigned job class for the job performed, in accordance with the provisions of the labor agreement for salaried employees negotiated between United States Steel Corporation and the United Steelworkers of America.

The C&T system, although developed for nonexempt salaried jobs associated with steel plant operations, has also been adopted by other industrial organizations and unions. The system has remained relatively unchanged since its original installation, and, like the hourly plan, it has served the parties well in eliminating salaried rate inequities and in maintaining proper salaried rate structures over the years.

BIBLIOGRAPHY

Agreement between United States Steel Corporation and the United Steelworkers of America—Production and Maintenance Employees, August 1, 1971, Pittsburgh, Pennsylvania.

Agreement between United States Steel Corporation and the United Steelworkers of America—Salaried Employees, August 1, 1971, Pittsburgh, Pennsylvania.

Job Description and Classification Manual for Hourly Rated Production, Maintenance and Non-Confidential Clerical Jobs, January 1, 1953, United Steelworkers of America-CIO and United States Steel Corporation.

Job Description and Classification Manual for Hourly Rated Production, Maintenance and Non-Confidential Clerical Jobs, January 1, 1963, United Steelworkers of America—AFL-CIO and Coordinating Committee Steel Companies.

Job Description and Classification Manual for Hourly Rated Production, Maintenance and Non-confidential Clerical Jobs, August 1, 1971, United Steelworkers of America —AFL-CIO and Coordinating Committee Steel Companies.

Salary Rate Inequities Agreement between Carnegie-Illinois Steel Corporation and the United Steelworkers or America—CIO, May 6, 1950, Pittsburgh, Pennsylvania.

12.3   American Association of Industrial Management

GLENN T. FISCHBACH   *Director of Engineering Services, American Association of Industrial Management, Melrose Park, Pennsylvania*

Fair wage and salary policies are essential to good industrial relations. If an organization were to formulate a statement of its industrial relations policies, it would probably conclude that compensation policy should be geared to achieve these two goals:

1. The general level of compensation should be consistent with the existing level for comparable jobs in the community or competitive hiring area.

2. Compensation for each job should be determined in relation to compensation for other jobs in the organization, with due regard for differences in knowledge and skill, responsibilities, and other factors significant to the general nature or type of jobs involved.

Achieving the first goal requires keeping informed through periodic compensation surveys of rates currently in effect and, even more important, determining whether the jobs surveyed are in fact comparable with the company's jobs. In many cases the survey may be misleading or of doubtful value because the jobs themselves are not comparable. For example, a tabulation showing average earnings for assemblers may be of little assistance to an individual company in checking its own rates because there are different classes of assembly work. Obviously a plant with simple, short-cycle, highly repetitive assembly is not particularly interested in what another plant pays assemblers who erect large machinery or complex equipment.

In many organizations the question of proper pay differentials between jobs does not get the attention it deserves. Inequalities in earnings on different jobs, due to lack of proper job classification and measurement, are often a source of dissatisfaction and a subject for repeated grievances or complaints. In fact, the establishment of proper pay differentials is an essential step in administering any compensation program, whether it involves payment in the form of salary, hourly wage, piecework, or other incentive. In some instances careful studies are made to determine accurate standards in terms of time and related expected results, but the rate of pay for achieving such results is literally "picked out of the air" without proper regard for the relative knowledge or skill, effort, responsibility, or other requirements necessary to do the job.

One of the reasons why pay differentials do not get enough attention is that management lacks knowledge for determining these differentials except on an arbitrary basis. Some managers may even feel that it makes no difference, since they pay whatever they have to pay in order to get a capable man for the job. This might be justified in an unusual situation, but as a regular practice it will inevitably create dissatisfaction. Soon there will be little relationship between pay and job requirements, and employees will either ask to be transferred to one of the "easy jobs" or will want to know why they cannot make as much on their jobs.

It is possible to take a great deal of guesswork out of determining pay relationships through a well-conceived job rating plan that: (1) defines job duties and responsibilities, and (2) analyzes and measures the requirements of each job in terms of factors significant to the employer, the employee, or both. This approach to job rating can:

1. Provide a means for arriving at the relationship between jobs, departmentally and interdepartmentally, on the basis of facts which can be defended in case of question.

2. Help prevent inequitable differences in pay levels for comparable work carried out by different departments.

3. Establish definite factors upon which compensation can be based, thus avoiding over- or underpayment of jobs with relation to one another.

4. Provide a basis for the adjustment of occupational pay rates that are definitely out of line.

5. Permit an accurate comparison of new jobs with similar jobs, or, if no similar jobs are available, furnish an accurate means of evaluating these new jobs, thus aiding in determining fair differentials.

6. Improve methods of selection, transfer, and promotion by pinpointing:

(a) Similar requirements of different jobs

(b) The hiring requirements of any particular job

7. Indicate hazards requiring consideration of physical fitness and safety instructions at the time of hiring.

8. Facilitate the making of pay rate surveys.

In providing these benefits, job rating can help management achieve an effectively administered, fair, and equitable wage and salary program.

THE AAIM RATING PLANS

The American Association of Industrial Management (formerly The National Metal Trades Association) believes that the use of job rating will promote good employer-employee relations in any organization. The data developed in the course of the rating process will provide a factual basis for discussion of pay differentials between jobs. Moreover, the adoption of a uniform job rating plan by a large number of companies, institutions, and organizations provides the basis for dependable, informative compensation surveys. Jobs of a generally comparable nature or type will have been classified according to the same criteria and using the same method.

Recognizing that manual and nonmanual jobs should be rated according to different sets of factors, the Association has for many years offered its member organizations two basic plans which are simple, thoroughly tested, and practical.

The AAIM plan for rating manual jobs considers 11 factors, with each factor subdivided into five degrees or steps. The factors and point values of each degree are shown in Table 1.

The rating plan for jobs of an essentially nonmanual type (clerical, technical, supervisory, etc.) considers nine factors in all cases, with two additional factors applied where supervision of others is involved. The factors and point values of each degree under this plan are shown in Table 2.

In both instances, the first step is to prepare an adequate description of job duties and responsibilities. If the description is properly written, the job can be readily identified by the incumbent or his supervisor from the description. In the case of manual jobs, the description is based primarily on personal observation of the work—including operations, materials, tools, equipment, methods, surroundings, and other distinguishing characteristics—as well as any necessary discussion with supervision as to the range of assignments. Descriptions of nonmanual jobs are derived from questionnaires submitted to incum-

TABLE 1   Points assigned to factors

Factors	1st Degree	2nd Degree	3rd Degree	4th Degree	5th Degree
Skill					
1. Education	14	28	42	56	70
2. Experience	22	44	66	88	110
3. Initiative and Ingenuity	14	28	42	56	70
Effort					
4. Physical Demand	10	20	30	40	50
5. Mental or Visual Demand	5	10	15	20	25
Responsibility					
6. Equipment or Process	5	10	15	20	25
7. Material or Product	5	10	15	20	25
8. Safety of Others	5	10	15	20	25
9. Work of Others	5	10	15	20	25
Job Conditions					
10. Working Conditions	10	20	30	40	50
11. Unavoidable Hazards	5	10	15	20	25

TABLE 2   Points Assigned to Factor Degrees and Range for Grades

Factors	1st Degree	2nd Degree	3rd Degree	4th Degree	5th Degree	6th Degree	7th Degree
Training							
1. Education	15	30	45	60	75	100	
2. Experience	20	40	60	80	100	125	150
Initiative							
3. Complexity of Duties	15	30	45	60	75	100	
4. Supervision Received	5	10	20	40	60		
Responsibility							
5. Errors	5	10	20	40	60	80	
6. Contacts with Others	5	10	20	40	60	80	
7. Confidential Data	5	10	15	20	25		
Job Conditions							
8. Mental or Visual Demand	5	10	15	20	25		
9. Working Conditions	5	10	15	20	25		
Supervision							
10. Character of Supervision	5	10	20	40	60	80	
11. Scope of Supervision	5	10	20	40	60	80	100

Score Range	Grades	Score Range	Grades
100 and under	1	311–340	9
101–130	2	341–370	10
131–160	3	371–400	11
161–190	4	401–430	12
191–220	5	431–460	13
221–250	6	461–490	14
251–280	7	491–520	15
281–310	8	521–550	16

bents and subsequently reviewed by their immediate supervisors to ensure agreement and completeness.

Once the supervisor has approved the description, the rater explains the various factors, their applications, and the degrees in each factor. Then the rater and supervisor jointly determine the degree of each factor that coincides with the duties performed and described. The degrees, corresponding point values, and explanations of the bases for the ratings are entered on the rating sheet, and the point totals and resulting grades are recorded. Departmental summary sheets are prepared for review to ensure consistency through comparison by factor.

Figures 4 to 7 are reductions of typical job descriptions and factor ratings, Figures 4 and 5 showing a job rated under the manual or "shop" plan and Figures 6 and 7 showing a job rated under the nonmanual plan.

The American Association of Industrial Management also installs executive rating for top and middle management positions under a plan which is corre-

Figure 4. Job rating specifications (shop).

JOB RATING SPECIFICATIONS (SHOP)	CODE NO. ___T-09___ DEPT ___Tool Room___ GRADE ___3___

JOB NAME___TOOL MAKER_____ CLASS _B_

JOB DESCRIPTION:

　　Lay out, construct, alter and repair a variety of tools; ordinary combination, blanking, piercing, drawing, bending and forming dies; box and stand type drill jigs; milling and other fixtures for general type of machining operations, and location and profile gauges, where design is available but involving ordinary development work as to mechanisms and details.

　　Visualize finished job, make necessary mathematical calculations, and select allowances for spring, shrinkage, lapping, grinding, scraping, fitting and finishing. Recognize and report for correction blueprint errors such as improper angles, radii, materials, etc., which would prevent economical production.

　　Perform difficult and exacting machine operations requiring a wide variety of setups and methods to maintain close tolerances; skilled bench work involving filing, scraping, grinding, lapping, fitting, assembling and adjusting to insure satisfactory performance. Make tool try-outs, detect faulty operation or defective material, and correct trouble.

TYPICAL PARTS:

REVISED	
BY	DATE

DATE_____

THE ABOVE DESCRIPTION COVERS THE MOST SIGNIFICANT DUTIES PERFORMED BUT DOES NOT EXCLUDE OTHER OCCASIONAL WORK ASSIGNMENTS NOT MENTIONED. THE INCLUSION OF WHICH WOULD BE IN CONFORMITY WITH THE FACTOR DEGREES ASSIGNED TO THIS JOB.

NMTA-18-A

Figure 5.   Job rating specifications (shop).

		CODE NO.	T-09

JOB RATING SPECIFICATIONS
(SHOP)

DEPT. _Tool Room_

GRADE _3_

JOB NAME _TOOL MAKER_   CLASS _B_   TOTAL POINTS _325_

FACTORS	SUBSTANTIATING DATA	DEG.	PTS.
EDUCATION	Requires the use of advanced shop mathematics, handbook formulas and trigonometry, together with complicated drawings or sketches, and a wide variety of precision adjustable measuring instruments. Thorough knowledge of machine shop practice, machine tool operations, principles of mechanics. Equivalent to complete, accredited apprenticeship.	4	56
EXPERIENCE	Over 3 and up to 4 years in the construction, alteration or repair of tools, dies and gauges.	4	88
INITIATIVE AND INGENUITY	Lay out, construct, alter and repair a variety of tools, dies, jigs, fixtures and gauges. Considerable judgment required to select allowances, work out mechanism details, perform ordinary development work, fit and assemble parts and mechanisms to close tolerances.	4	56
PHYSICAL DEMAND	Light physical effort in performing bench work or machine operations, equivalent to frequently lifting light weights. Occasionally lift or move average weight tools or machine attachments, rarely heavy.	2	20
MENTAL OR VISUAL DEMAND	Concentrate mental and visual attention closely in studying drawings, planning and laying out work, performing a wide variety of operations requiring close attention and a high degree of skill and accuracy.	4	20
RESPONSIBILITY FOR EQUIPMENT OR PROCESS *	Use various machine tools such as engine lathes, jig borers, universal milling machines and grinders, etc. Improper setup or operation may cause damage; seldom over $250.	3	15
RESPONSIBILITY FOR MATERIAL OR PRODUCT *	Improper construction, alteration or repair of tools, dies, jigs, fixtures or gauges may cause loss of time and material. Probable loss seldom over $200.	3	15
RESPONSIBILITY FOR SAFETY OF OTHERS	Numerous and varied temporary machine setups, e.g., work mounted on face plate of lathe, grinder, etc. Improperly fastened work may fly out or inattention in tool try-outs may cause lost-time injury to others.	3	15
RESPONSIBILITY FOR WORK OF OTHERS	Responsible only for own work.	1	5
WORKING CONDITIONS	Good working conditions. Use of machines involves some exposure to oil, dirt, chips, but with none present continuously to the extent of being disagreeable.	2	20
HAZARDS	Injuries, should they occur, may result in loss of time from loss of fingers, hand or eye injury, in the operation of machines, including making tool try-outs.	3	15
REMARKS	* Always stated in terms of 1935-1939 price levels to maintain a constant measurement. Current prices adjusted to that level by use of B.L.S. index. 1970 prices are 2.5 times the base figure.		

Figure 6.   Job rating specifications (clerical, technical, supervisory).

	CODE NO. __B-01__
JOB RATING SPECIFICATIONS (CLERICAL, TECHNICAL, SUPERVISORY)	DEPT. __Accounting__
	GRADE __15__

JOB NAME _____ COMPTROLLER _____ CLASS _____

JOB DESCRIPTION:

Responsible for establishing, coordinating and maintaining sound accounting practices and procedures, and for presenting complete factual reports and interpretations of results of operations to top management. In charge of general and cost accounting and billing functions, hourly and salaried payrolls, and general office services. Direct and coordinate the work through subordinate supervisors.

Supervise the preparation and issuance of all balance sheets, profit and loss statements and other statistical reports at regular intervals or as required for parent company and various subsidiaries.

Direct the compilation of all order, machine, parts, maintenance, repair and construction costs; the preparation of salaried or bi-weekly office and branch office and hourly shop payrolls; the submission of bills and statements to domestic and foreign customers. See that all books of accounts are audited periodically from an internal standpoint and assist independent outside auditors on annual audits. Approve purchase vouchers and contact vendors relative to incorrect pricing, accounting differences or other problems.

Initiate, install and administer improved accounting and clerical procedures; revise and modernize accounting instructions covering various general and branch office procedures. Contact company attorneys on various legal aspects or procedures and outside auditors on services rendered.

Perform the functions of Office Manager; purchase various office equipment after investigating requirements and equipment best suited. Direct the servicing of the General Office with stationery, printed forms; Addressograph, Multilith, Ditto and mail services. Plan and lay out work and see that assignments are made according to individual skill and ability for most efficient operation of the department. Instruct, direct, assist and advise subordinate supervisors and employees as to duties, methods, procedures, policies, rules and regulations. Maintain discipline, high morale and harmonious personnel relations, and take immediate action for violation of rules or other improper conduct. Secure employee cooperation, adjust primary grievances; pass on terminations, transfers and promotions; rate employees' performance periodically.

Prepare a variety of special reports and compile and furnish data and information as requested by operating management. Prepare annual departmental budget and administer operation during period covered. Co-sign checks on designated bank accounts for the parent company and subsidiaries. Serve as a member of the Budget and Management Advisory committees. Contact various subsidiary companies on numerous accounting and inventory problems, perform other miscellaneous duties, and consult with other executives and supervisors on problems incidental to operating a service department.

REVISED	
BY	DATE

DATE _____

THE ABOVE DESCRIPTION COVERS THE MOST SIGNIFICANT DUTIES PERFORMED BUT DOES NOT EXCLUDE OTHER OCCASIONAL WORK ASSIGNMENTS NOT MENTIONED. THE INCLUSION OF WHICH WOULD BE IN CONFORMITY WITH THE FACTOR DEGREES ASSIGNED TO THIS JOB.

NMTA-22-A

Figure 7.   Job rating specifications (clerical, technical, supervisory).

CODE NO.			B-01

JOB RATING SPECIFICATIONS
(CLERICAL, TECHNICAL, SUPERVISORY)

CODE NO. ____ B-01 ____

DEPT. ____ Accounting ____

GRADE ____ 15 ____

COMPTROLLER   CLASS ____ TOTAL POINTS ____ 500 ____

FACTORS	SUBSTANTIATING DATA	DEG.	PTS.
EDUCATION	Broad knowledge of general, cost and payroll accounting theory and practice, budgetary control, and finance. Familiar with business organization and administration, office management and economics, foreign exchange. Equivalent to college education in business administration.	4	60
EXPERIENCE	Over 7 and up to 8 years.	6	125
COMPLEXITY OF DUTIES	Wide variety of budgetary control, accounting and office management duties and responsibilities, involving general knowledge of related company policies and procedures. Duties require considerable judgment in devising new methods and procedures, modifying standard practices to meet new conditions, making decisions guided by precedent and based on company policies.	4	60
SUPERVISION RECEIVED	Under general direction of Treasurer as to policies and general objectives. Rarely refer specific problems to superior for other than policy decisions.	4	40
ERRORS	Probable errors in judgment or supervision may result in incorrect financial data, costs or inventory information. Considerable accuracy and responsibility involved.	4	40
CONTACTS WITH OTHERS	Contacts with various company officers, subsidiary companies and branches, requiring considerable tact and diplomacy to obtain results through influencing others.	4	40
CONFIDENTIAL DATA	Regularly work with confidential corporate financial data such as balance sheet, profit and loss statements, costs, etc. Disclosure may be detrimental to the company's interests.	4	20
MENTAL OR VISUAL DEMAND	Supervisory and contact duties involve normal mental and visual attention most of the time.	2	10
WORKING CONDITIONS	Usual office working conditions.	1	5
FOR SUPERVISORY POSITIONS ONLY			
CHARACTER OF SUPERVISION	General supervision of accounting, payroll, billing, and general office services, with responsibility for results in terms of costs, methods and personnel.	4	40
SCOPE OF SUPERVISION	Responsible for supervising 62 persons, including 9 subordinate supervisors.	5	60
REMARKS			

lated with the clerical, technical, and supervisory plan, but which measures those higher degrees of judgment and responsibility involved at the policy-making level. This completes an integrated program of measurement for all positions within an organization from top to bottom, assuring equitable treatment for all personnel.

ESTABLISHMENT OF WAGE AND SALARY STRUCTURES

The wage and salary structure should be calculated with the objective of distributing the available payroll money in a manner consistent with the grades established through the rating process. In other words, pay progress from grade to grade should be consistent, in terms of either money (straight-line structure) or percentages (curved-line structure), whether a single rate or a range is applied to each grade. The Association recommends the use of ranges overlapping approximately half a grade and a percentage progression, where AAIM rating plans are installed, but contractual obligations or other considerations may preclude this in some instances. Figure 8 illustrates graphically the

Figure 8.   Sample salary structure.

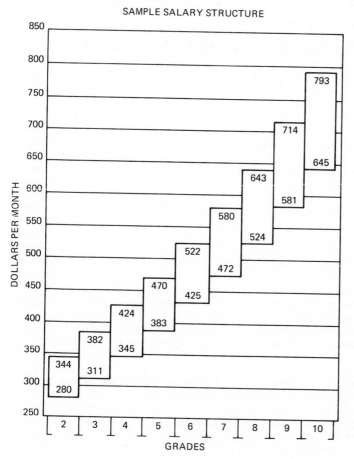

recommended type of structure. A wage structure would, of course, be in terms of hourly rates but structured similarly.

CONCLUSION

The American Association of Industrial Management job rating plans have been developed to consider factors of importance to both the employer and the employee. The plans are simple and understandable. Their soundness has been validated by more than 30 years of installations in manufacturing companies, banks and financial institutions, hospitals, universities, and town and city governments. Their broad coverage enables users to participate in meaningful surveys of wage and salary rates.

When used in conjunction with a sound employee appraisal program, these plans provide the basis for a fair and equitable compensation policy, which in turn is the keystone of good industrial relations.

12.4   The Hay Guide Chart-Profile Method

CHARLES W. G. VAN HORN *General Partner, Edward N. Hay & Associates, Philadelphia, Pennsylvania*

The Guide Chart-Profile Method was developed by Edward N. Hay & Associates to provide a systematic, easily administered approach to evaluating jobs at all levels in all organizations and to facilitate pay comparisons between companies. The method is based on Hay's long experience with business and government clients in the human resources area, and although initially designed as a job evaluation technique, its broader applications in job and organization analysis make it a useful management tool.

The method has evolved over a great number of years, relatively speaking, and incorporates the best features of earlier ways to measure job content. The process used prior to 1950 had many aspects of the factor comparison method. In addition, important new features built upon long experience and helpful and challenging exposure to a great variety of client personnel have resulted in refinements in the process which ensure a sound, universally applicable way of measuring relative job content.

Two principles are fundamental to the Guide Chart-Profile Method:

1. A thorough understanding of the content of the job to be measured
2. The direct comparison of one job with another job to determine relative value

Since it is difficult to compare and measure one whole job against another whole job, the comparison is made between aspects of job content which are present, though in varying degrees, in all jobs. These aspects which make up total job content are know-how, problem solving, and accountability. The sum of the measurements for know-how, problem solving, and accountability represents the value of the whole job. The three job elements are defined as follows:

1. *Know-how* is the sum total of all knowledge and skills, however, acquired, which are needed for satisfactory job performance.

2. *Problem solving* is the amount of original, self-starting thinking required by the job for analyzing, evaluating, creating, reasoning, and arriving at conclusions.

3. *Accountability* is the answerability for actions and for the consequences of those actions.

In measuring factory jobs, it is sometimes appropriate to consider additional job aspects—working conditions and physical effort. For simplicity in explaining the process, however, this chapter will talk only about know-how, problem solving, and accountability.

Basic to the entire process is a thorough understanding of the jobs, which is provided primarily through written job descriptions. The description should get at the essence of the job. Why does the job exist? What makes it tick? How does it affect end results? These important aspects are much more than a mere recital of what a man is supposed to do in a given job. A job description should be a perceptive critique of the external and internal conditions and objectives of the job, rather than a repetitive classified listing of generalities. Furthermore, at the management level a job description is more meaningful when it is examined with the help of the same kind of critique of the company, the corporate philosophy of management, the way management works, and the way the company's objectives get implemented.

At times, the accountability of the job seems to be the most difficult aspect to get clearly and definitively from the incumbent. What results is the job expected to produce? What is the degree of freedom to act encompassed by the job? What kind of effect does the job have on desired end results? This clarifying of a person's accountability in his job is an important by-product of the development of a salary standards program.

While the results of job measurement ultimately rest on direct comparison of one job with another, there is a series of steps in the measurement process which lead to the final comparison. An explanation of the development of these phases will help identify the process and its major elements and the concepts on which it is based.

The process begins with a small group of carefully selected benchmark job descriptions which represent the starting point. Evaluations of these jobs are based on multiple judgments about the relativity of the three aspects which make up each job and are expressed on an evaluation scale of numbers.

The numbering system used universally in the Hay process is a geometric scale with a ratio of approximately 15 percent between terms in the series. That is, the value of each aspect grows in 15 percent increments. For example, the terms in the series include 50, 57, 66, 76, 87, 100, and so on, up and down the scale. The selection of a geometric scale rather than an arithmetic scale is justified by empirical considerations and also by the fact that salary changes from jobs of low content to jobs of high content are geometric in character. For example, at the lower end of the scale, two jobs very close in content might have salaries of $100 and $120 a week, respectively, while at the higher end of the scale, two jobs fairly close together in content might be paid $1,000 and $1,200, respectively, but certainly not $1,000 and $1,020. Also, there seems to be a similarity between this characteristic of measurement and Weber's Law[1] in psychological measurements. Weber put it this way: "In

---

[1] See H. E. Garrett, *Great Experiments in Psychology*, Century Co., New York, 1930, pp. 268–274; and Edward N. Hay, "Characteristics of Factor Comparison Job Evaluation," *Personnel*, 1946, 22, pp. 370–375.

comparing objects we perceive not the actual difference between them but the ratio of this difference to the magnitude of the two objects compared."

That is to say, the observed difference between two objects is not absolute and independent of the objects themselves, but is relative to their size and is a constant fraction of one of them.

Multiple judgments on the job aspects are gained from three sources. The first lies in the use of a *committee* to evaluate jobs, where more than one person's judgment is brought to bear on the same subject. After the evaluation structure has been developed, the use of committees is often optional. The second source is procedural in nature and involves measurement of job content by several different means. One of these is *ranking and rating* for one aspect, and the usual practice was to rank and rate the benchmark jobs in terms of know-how content. Ranking is self-explanatory. Rating means establishing not only a rank order but also number intervals between the jobs. The general guideline used in rating jobs for know-how, for example, was this:

If, after a careful comparison of the know-how content of two jobs:

1. You can sense no difference, or first one job and then the other seems to have more know-how, there is no measurable difference and the know-how is the same.

2. You think you sense a difference, there is probably a *one*-step difference. A step is the smallest difference which can be sensed. It is the interval between two adjacent terms in the geometric series.

3. You are fairly sure you sense a difference, the magnitude is probably *two* steps.

4. You sense a difference clearly, almost without the careful study, there are probably *three* or *more* steps' difference. Differences of more than three steps can best be determined by comparing a chain of jobs where the differences between any two jobs do not exceed three steps.

To wrap up this measurement, the lowest know-how position is arbitrarily assigned a number in the geometric series. Having established this base, jobs with higher know-how have their step numbers (a simple arithmetic series 1, 2, 3, 4, and so on) converted appropriately to the other numbers in the geometric scale. For example, if 50 is chosen as the point value for the lowest know-how job in the benchmark sample, and the job with the next higher know-how is up one step, the value of the know-how of that job would be 57, which is the next value in the geometric series. Table 3 illustrates the relationship between the terms in the geometric series and the step values.

Profiling is a third independent measurement, entirely different in character from ranking and rating. In simple terms, a profile of a job is the proportion of know-how, problem solving, and accountability which make up the total job. It is a practical, business judgment. It is often fairly easy to recognize a job as being primarily a know-how job (e.g., typist) or an accountability job (e.g., president) or a heavy "think" job (e.g., creative research). These statements are qualitative profiling judgments. When evaluators go a step further and attach relative numerical values to these statements, saying that a given job appears to consist of X percent know-how, Y percent problem solving, and Z percent accountability, all adding to 100 percent, they are making a perceptive and useful profiling judgment.

Sometimes the agreed profile is the average of individual judgments of committee members, and in other cases it represents a reconciled judgment after open discussion.

The profile is probably the most valid and useful single judgment made about a job. There is a good reason for the general reliability of a profile, and

TABLE 3   Relationship between Geometric Scale and Step Value (Illustrative)

Geometric Scale	Step Values
50*	1
57	2
66	3
76	4
87	5
100	6
115	7
132	8
152	9
175	10
200	11
230	12
264	13

* The starting point for the scale is set arbitrarily. The scale can be started with any number in the series, since it is the ratio between the numbers that is important to the measurement, not their absolute value.

it is this: if a job is well understood, a reliable objective profiling judgment based on practical business grounds can be made by almost any thoughtful business person. It is not an esoteric matter.

Furthermore, profiles do not involve external comparisons with other jobs, and so they have an inherent, built-in tendency to be honest and objective as well as perceptive.

After pointing out the advantages and usefulness of profiling, we must also say that every so often a profile judgment goes off the beam. But again, this goes back to the *basic understanding* of the job under scrutiny. If thoughtful evaluators profile a given job all over the lot, then the chances are overwhelming that the job has been interpreted differently by the individual evaluators, or that this job is so vague that any one of several interpretations may be honestly made. The profile is a final test of the adequacy of the job description and analysis.

For a number of years, these steps represented the entire process used to produce relative evaluations for jobs. For example, if the ranking and rating judgment indicated 50 points of know-how for a job, and if the job's profile was 50 percent know-how, 25 percent problem solving, and 25 percent accountability, by simple arithmetic it is evident that problem solving and accountability would be 25 points each, and the total point value of the job would be 100. It will be observed that the profile is the device which establishes the relativity between the know-how scale of points and the problem solving and accountability scales.

Next in the evolution came the Guide Charts. The process described so far left a rather skimpy record of how the jobs were evaluated and why. Members of the committee knew, but it was difficult to explain this quickly to someone not interested in all the detailed measurements, and therefore very difficult to establish the credibility of the system used and the evaluation decisions based on it. At the suggestion and with the help of a few clients, the idea was developed of establishing a visual representation of the job evaluation results. This turned out to be three grids, or Guide Charts—one each for know-how, problem solving, and accountability. Thus, the first Guide Charts really reflected judgments and results reached through the means described above.

The grids themselves represented semantic measurements, and an important by-product of their development was increased insight into the meaning and measurement of know-how, problem solving, and accountability, because various amounts of these job content aspects had to be defined more precisely within the broad definitions already used in the evaluations. See Figures 9 to 11 for sample Guide Charts matching semantic expressions of the varying degrees of each job aspect with the geometric scales developed earlier. The numbers illustrated on the know-how chart shown in Figure 9 are steps, not points in the geometric scale. This intermediate notation is helpful in developing the network of point values as described in the application of the scale.

It was quickly recognized in early applications of the grid that the Guide Charts themselves provided another means of measurement—*slotting* jobs on the three Guide Charts. Also, the Guide charts became the vehicle through which all the different judgments were consolidated and tested for validity and consistency. The results of this consolidation are reflected in numerical values for all cells in the grids as well as in the meaningful and uniform progression from one cell to the others. At this point in the development of the charts, inconsistencies are highlighted, analyzed, and reconciled.

The semantics of the Guide Charts—the specific definitions of the varying degrees of the job elements—have been carefully worked out over a number of years and represent the best accommodation to cover all functions of business and other types of organizations. There were periods in their evolution where, through trial and error, attempts were made to change the wording—for example, to make the definitions better suited to engineering jobs or sales jobs—but it was found that such changes in wording made the definitions less appropriate for other kinds of jobs. The language on the Guide Charts illustrated in Figures 9 to 11 has been chosen with care so that it is appropriate to all kinds of functions. This is not to say that it is never altered to meet specific needs, because it is altered where indicated.

Today, as a result of long experience in a great number of varied situations, it is no longer necessary to create Guide Charts from scratch except in unusual or unique situations. Rather, Guide Charts are predesigned and used tentatively as a starting point. Jobs are evaluated by:

1. Gaining a thorough understanding of job content
2. Slotting jobs on each grid
3. Selecting an appropriate value in each cell on each grid. Ultimately, this determination rests upon direct comparison between the job under consideration and jobs that have been measured previously, using, for example, the "sensing factor" discussed earlier.
4. The point values for know-how, problem solving, and accountability for the job are added together to get total evaluation points. By calculating the percentages of know-how, problem solving, and accountability expressed in these number statements, a profile is developed which provides an independent check on the proper use of the Guide Charts.
5. After a number of jobs have been evaluated, e.g., 40 to 50, the results of the whole group are reviewed for obvious inconsistencies. This is known, somewhat facetiously, as "sore-thumbing." Where necessary, corrections are made. During this process the tentative Guide Charts themselves are tested for applicability to the given situation. Where indicated, appropriate adjustments are made to reflect facts about the jobs and the company.

While this process, once learned, is simple, there is no question about the need for careful coaching in the concepts and uses of the method. It is not a do-it-yourself technique.

Figure 9

Definition: Know-How is the sum total of every kind of skill, however acquired, required for acceptable job performance. This sum total which comprises the over-all "savvy" has 3 dimensions—the requirements for:

* Practical procedures, specialized techniques, and scientific disciplines.

** Know-How of integrating and harmonizing the diversified functions involved in managerial situations occurring in operating, supporting, and administrative fields. The Know-How may be exercised consultatively (about management) as well as executively and involves in some combination the areas of organizing, planning, executing, controlling and evaluating.

*** Active, practicing, face to face skills in the area of human relationships.

Illustrative
©
Hay Guide Chart for Evaluating
KNOW-HOW
Edward N. Hay & Associates
Phila., Penna.

Measuring Know-How: Know-How has both scope (variety) and depth (thoroughness). Thus, a job may require some knowledge about a lot of things, or a lot of knowledge about a few things. The total Know-How is the combination of scope and depth. This concept makes practical the comparison and weighing of the total Know-How content of different jobs in terms of: "How much knowledge about how many things."

Human Relations Skills

1. Basic: Ordinary courtesy and effectiveness in dealing with others.

2. Important: Understanding, influencing, and/or serving people are important, but not critical considerations.

3. Critical: Alternative or combined skills in understanding, selecting, developing and motivating people are important in the highest degree.

*** Human Relations Skills →	I. None or Minimal			II. Related			III. Diverse			IV. Broad			V.			
** Managerial Know-How	1.	2.	3.	1.	2.	3.	1.	2.	3.	1.	2.	3.	1.	2.	3.	
A. PRIMARY:	1	2	3	3												A
	2	3	4	4												
	3	4	5	5												
B. ELEMENTARY VOCATIONAL:	3			5												B
	4			6												
	5			7												
C. VOCATIONAL:	5															C
	6															
	7															
D. ADVANCED VOCATIONAL:	7															D
	8															
	9															
E. BASIC TECHNICAL-SPECIALIZED:																E
F. SEASONED TECHNICAL-SPECIALIZED:																F
G. TECHNICAL-SPECIALIZED MASTERY:																G
H. PROFESSIONAL MASTERY:																H

Practical Procedures
Specialized Techniques
Scientific Disciplines

Figure 10

Definition: Problem Solving is the original, "self-starting" thinking required by the job for analyzing, evaluating, creating, reasoning, arriving at and making conclusions. To the extent that thinking is circumscribed by standards, covered by precedents, or referred to others, Problem Solving is diminished, and the emphasis correspondingly is on Know-How.

Problem Solving has two dimensions:
* The environment in which the thinking takes place.
** The challenge presented by the thinking to be done.

Illustrative
©
Hay Guide Chart for Evaluating
PROBLEM SOLVING

Edward N. Hay & Associates
Phila., Penna.

Measuring Problem Solving: Problem Solving measures the intensity of the mental process which employs Know-How to: (1) identify, (2) define, and (3) resolve a problem. "You think with what you know." This is true of even the most creative work ... The raw material of any thinking is knowledge of facts, principles and means; ideas are put together from something already there. Therefore, Problem Solving is treated as a percentage utilization of Know-How.

Thinking Environment Thinking guided and circumscribed by:	** Thinking Challenge				
	1. Repetitive	2. Patterned	3. Interpolative	4. Adaptive	5. Uncharted
A. STRICT ROUTINE:						A
B. ROUTINE:						B
C. SEMI-ROUTINE:						C
D. STANDARDIZED:						D
E. CLEARLY DEFINED:						E
F. BROADLY DEFINED:						F
G. GENERALLY DEFINED:						G
H. ABSTRACTLY DEFINED:						H

Figure 11

Definition: Accountability is the answerability for an action and for the consequences of that action. It is the measured effect of the job on end results. It has three dimensions in the following order of importance:

* Freedom to Act—the degree of personal or procedural control and guidance, as defined in the left-hand column below.
** Job Impact on End Results—as defined at upper right.
*** Magnitude—indicated by the general dollar size of the area(s) most clearly or primarily affected by the job (on an annual basis)

Illustrative

Hay Guide Chart for Evaluating
©
ACCOUNTABILITY

Edward N. Hay & Associates
Phila., Penna.

Impact of Job on End Results

Remote: Informational, recording, or incidental services for use by others in relation to some important end result.

Contributory: Interpretive, advisory, or facilitating services, for use by others in taking action.

Shared: Participating with others (except own subordinates and superiors), within or outside the organizational unit, in taking action.

Primary: Controlling impact on end results, where shared accountability of others is subordinate.

*** Magnitude (annual basis)	(1) Very Small or Indeterminate $				(2) Small $				(3) Medium $				(4) Large $				(5) Very Large $				
*Freedom to Act ** Impact →	R	C	S	P	R	C	S	P	R	C	S	P	R	C	S	P	R	C	S	P	
A. PRESCRIBED:																					A
B. CONTROLLED:																					B
C. STANDARDIZED:																					C
D. GENERALLY REGULATED:																					D
E. DIRECTED:																					E
F. ORIENTED DIRECTION:																					F
G. BROAD GUIDANCE:																					G

With total points now available for a variety of jobs, a salary structure is established by plotting a scattergram of existing salaries on the vertical axis against point values on the horizontal axis. This leads ultimately to the establishment of a salary structure for the company with minimums, maximums, and midpoints.

One of the outstanding characteristics of the Guide Chart-Profile Method is the ease with which company salary structures developed as described here can be compared with external pay practices. A key to this comparison is called "correlation." It is not to be confused with the term *correlation* used in statistics.

The correlation process is simply the extension of the measurement process described previously to the measurement of job content in one company's job family (where numerical, or point, values are already established in that company) on the evaluation structure of another company. Thus, for example, a 1,000-point job in Company A might be equivalent to one of 500 points in Company B.

The result is an index, or ratio, which permits the translation of the numerical measurement of job content for a given job in one company to a numerical measurement of that same content in another company or to a numerical value on a common scale. It is not unlike physical conversions in science—pounds to kilograms, for example. One company, in this analogy, might measure job content in pounds, another company in kilograms, and a third company in stones. Appropriate conversion factors (like 1 kg = 2,205 pounds) permit a given content to be stated in either pounds, kilograms, or stones.

Correlation, as the term is used in Edward N. Hay compensation studies and programs, develops a *conversion* factor for a given company. Thus, when salary levels between companies are compared, the comparison is based upon salary levels for *like* job content in both, or all companies.

In the beginning there were eight companies involved, seven of which were compared with the eighth, whose scale represented the common yardstick. As our experience and data increased, there developed a standard or common scale to which all companies' points for a given job were reduced. The standard scale represents the collective judgments of seasoned consultants as well as of many executives in all fields of endeavor and is based on experience with a great variety of enterprises of all sizes—basic industries, scientific-oriented, marketing, service, nonprofit, governmental, etc. The standard scale always reflects real situations and not a sterile, mechanistic model.

The correlation ratio or conversion factor is a number statement of the relationship between the evaluation structure in one company and the standard evaluation structure. With the common structure as a link, it is easy to relate one company's evaluation structure to that of another company or group of companies. The ratio has no interpretive significance such as correlation has in statistical analysis.

In the early days of the development of the Guide Chart-Profile Method, each consultant freely chose the starting point on the know-how evaluation scale, and the problem solving and accountability scales were proportioned through the profile. Thus, if one company's program started at point value 25 and another company started at 50, this alone produced a ratio of 2 to 1. Further, since the evaluation scale is a relative, not absolute, measurement, the starting point is a valid free choice. We must go beyond this simple arithmetic relationship, however, to reflect certain nuances in different company characteristics.

The actual correlation usually is carried out by a team of two consultants who make the evaluative judgments on carefully selected jobs, often with personnel for the client company participating or observing. The results are analyzed graphically, as shown in Figure 12.

Graphic representation normalizes all the little variables which reflect the uniqueness of each enterprise. Committees from two companies, using identical Guide Charts, may interpret the charts in ways which reflect their individual folkways, biases, or basic characteristics and philosophies. Thus, one company may use tighter judgment on problem solving than another, or it may interpret the human relations choices in a slightly different manner. This is why the evaluation process in a company reflects, in a most interesting and unique way, how that company *values* various aspects of job content.

Figure 12.   Correlation graph.

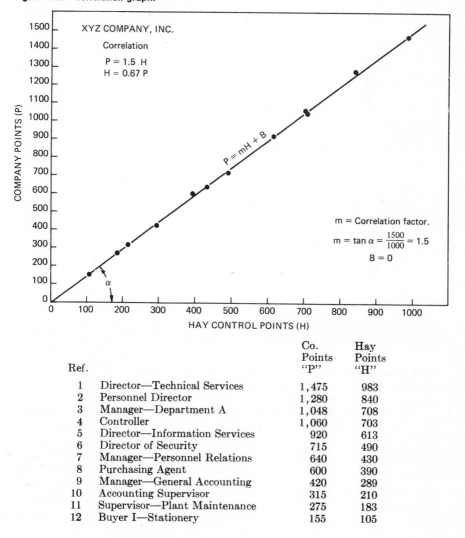

Ref.		Co. Points "P"	Hay Points "H"
1	Director—Technical Services	1,475	983
2	Personnel Director	1,280	840
3	Manager—Department A	1,048	708
4	Controller	1,060	703
5	Director—Information Services	920	613
6	Director of Security	715	490
7	Manager—Personnel Relations	640	430
8	Purchasing Agent	600	390
9	Manager—General Accounting	420	289
10	Accounting Supervisor	315	210
11	Supervisor—Plant Maintenance	275	183
12	Buyer I—Stationery	155	105

The following additional elements contribute to the consistency and validity of correlation results:

1. Comparison is based on evaluated job content—not job title or organizational level. It is not necessary (or usually possible) to find exact comparisons in the two structures under comparison. The Guide Charts are the means to deal with different characteristics or sizes in job content.

2. Continuing relationships with most of the clients provide a control for the continuing validity of client company data.

3. The larger clients often conduct independent surveys of their relationships to other selected companies which, on the whole, clearly substantiate our work.

It is important to recognize that the process used in the development of Guide Charts over the years is by its very nature thorough, detailed, and lengthy. However, most of this is circumvented by the use of tentative predesigned Guide Charts on which jobs are easily slotted, measured, and validated. Furthermore, these charts need possible revision only in cases of massive changes in company size, objectives, and character.

Another important characteristic is the ease with which individual external comparisons can be made with any group of companies whether or not these companies use the Guide Chart-Profile Method. For example, it is not necessary to get exact matches in jobs between companies. The Guide Charts provide the medium through which job differences can be reconciled and appropriate adjustments made to ensure true comparison based on relative job content.

As a procedure for establishing salary and hourly standards, the Guide Chart-Profile Method has several compelling advantages:

1. It is based on simple business concepts and principles that are easy to define and use.

2. It narrows matters of opinion to a minimum and brings sharp judgments to bear from more than one independent angle. It does not rely on single judgments, no matter how good they might be.

3. By providing a framework within which evaluation decisions must be made, it does away with endless committee discussions.

4. It forces disciplined and orderly thinking about job content, quickly highlighting vague, poorly conceived and designed jobs.

5. It provides a clear, understandable basis for interrelating all kinds of jobs at all levels—top executives, middle managers, hourly workers, day laborers, scientists, technical personnel, sales personnel, and professional people such as physicians and lawyers. It also takes into consideration the wide variety of conditions under which people work—conditions such as extreme heat, noise, isolation, danger, boredom, repetitiveness, and pressure of deadline.

The Hay method of job measurement has had its widest application in compensation. However, time and experience have proved its great value in several other important management areas:

1. *Organization analysis.* This is essentially the science of how a company's jobs and the job clusters known as sections, departments, and divisions are related to each other. The thoroughness and objectivity of the Hay method bring out the nature and extent of these relationships and help to reveal such things as work duplication, overlapping of authority, and accountability vacuums.

2. *Organization planning.* The long-range planning of many firms is unrealistic because no provision is made for the type of jobs that will have to be filled five or more years ahead. In a number of companies it is normal prac-

tice, when studying alternative forms of future organization structures, to provide a realistic basis for deciding among alternatives by evaluating the jobs that potentially exist in them.

3. *Manpower appraisal, planning, and development.* Hay has developed a method under which both jobs and the persons holding those jobs can be evaluated using the same Guide Chart terminology. With this measurement as a foundation, and with the aid of psychological appraisals, the employee's past and current performance record, and certain predictive techniques, we are able to forecast manpower requirements and potentials in the company's future. With these in hand, the company can then develop a program to train and develop people to fill those future jobs.

4. *Employee recruitment and selection.* When a company has evaluated the job it wishes to fill, it has taken a giant step toward getting the right man or woman for the job. The Hay method spells out the size of the job, its content, and its relationships within and outside the organization. This is important not only to the employer, but to the people who apply for the job.

5. *Employee motivation.* People work best when they know just what is expected of them, toward what objectives they are working, and what the rewards are for success in achieving these goals. The Hay method is directed at supplying such information. It defines the boundaries of the job, sets the compensation range for it, and (through the proper use of the job description) spells out the job's accountabilities.

6. *Corporate communications.* The Hay method gives a company a way to talk clearly about its jobs, for whatever reason such talking is needed. This is made possible by what the job evaluation produces: measurements, terms, and relationships serving as meaningful attributes that anyone can understand.

Part 3

Surveys

chapter 13

Achieving External Competitiveness through Survey Use

GEORGE E. MELLGARD   *Manager, Personnel, Pittsburgh Coke & Chemical Company, Pittsburgh, Pennsylvania*

In any economic system that permits an employee to choose his employer, every organization must compete for its employees either directly or indirectly with all other organizations. In order to compete, a company must first identify its rivals and then determine their nature and caliber. External competitiveness and internal equity are therefore the principal aims of management pay policy. Equity has been discussed at length in earlier chapters; our concern here is with the need to be competitive and the means by which a company can define just what is competitive for it. The compensation survey is the tool most frequently used by management to find out who is paying how much for what jobs. Labor unions, like management, are interested in comparative pay practices, since these may provide the justification for "more" in wages and fringe benefits.

COMPETITIVE FACTORS: MONEY VIS-À-VIS OTHER REWARDS

In the vast majority of cases, a survey of competitive factors is the first step in establishing or changing wage, salary, or benefit levels. Competitive compensation factors typically include: (1) cash—current or deferred, base or incentive pay, and (2) fringe benefits for personal and family security. Cash compensation and fringe benefits are competitive factors that can be measured in well-defined terms. Other factors which influence a company's ability to attract, retain, and motivate people—factors such as organization climate, management style, and opportunity for advancement—are not so easily measured or compared.

The relative influence of money as against intangible competitive factors varies according to job level. The higher the job, the broader its account-abilities and the more diverse the means of obtaining job satisfaction and a sense of accomplishment. In competing for managers, therefore, companies must keep in mind that money is only one of the factors that makes a job more or less attractive to them. Managers are also motivated by sheer job challenge, a belief in the value of the work they are doing, the drives for status and leadership responsibilities, and a competitive environment encouraging and facilitating achievement of specified end results.

Competition in the marketplace for higher-level people is based on com-pensation practice as well as on the intangibles mentioned above. At the lower levels, however, jobs are more narrowly defined, restricting the incum-bent's autonomy and opportunity to respond to challenges and to exercise lead-ership. Since the intangible factors have less impact on the job, money becomes proportionately more important in the competition for hourly and non-exempt people.

In addition, the marketplaces for managerial, clerical, and hourly people are substantially different in character and scope. Executive pay must be com-petitive nationwide. Clerical rates, on the other hand, vary from one locality to another and, hence, must be geared to the local going rate. The competi-tive market for hourly people varies according to whether or not a union is involved; in major unionized industries like steel and autos, the competitive market is industry-oriented and nationwide; smaller, nonunionized companies tend to compete for labor in a local market, the going rate of which would be influenced by the presence or absence of larger unionized companies.

Because the jobs are different in character and the marketplaces vary in scope, different approaches must be taken in determining competitiveness. At the lower levels, comparisons generally focus on job rates; at management levels, comparisons look to salary structures and trend lines. The objective of these comparisons is always to relate compensation to specified duties at the lower levels and to more broadly specified accountabilities at the higher levels.

At all levels, then, money—because it is measurable—is the universal yard-stick. Financial compensation, in the form of wages or salary and supplemen-tal benefits and services purchased for employees, is the most tangible bond between employer and employee. Money is the factor most commonly de-scribed and compared by the parties to the ultimate bargain, since the non-financial competitive factors of present environment and future opportunity are difficult to appraise.

Moreover, there are many ways to recognize and reward superior perform-ance, but there is no substitute for money (or other tangible rewards that can be easily measured in terms of money). The impact and value of these finan-cial motivators can be enhanced or destroyed, depending on how well they are administered. Thoughtful design, consistency of practice, dependability, and ethics play important roles in successful administration.

C. H. Greenewalt casts more light on the role of money vis-à-vis the intangibles:

> We should recognize the importance of financial rewards in balancing other types of incentive, and so ensuring able candidates for every field of endeavor. Personal prestige, for example, is more likely to accompany success in the sci-ences, in universities, or in the professions than in business. Were we not able to offset this by increased financial reward, I suspect that business would have much greater difficulty filling its ranks with able people.

If financial incentive is absent or greatly reduced, the number of candidates for top management positions will decrease since many men will have gone into vocations where the rewards seem more desirable. And the motives that remain seem less likely to produce the best in management for our business enterprises. Certainly the desire for power, or the desire for prestige, or admiration, are not characteristics that would be expected to lead to the kind of competence we need in business management.[1]

Base salary is the largest element in compensation. Furthermore, it is the pivot point for all compensation. All other forms—incentive compensation, profit sharing, deferred compensation, and fringe benefits such as insurance and pension plans—are to some extent related to base salaries. As one result, if the base structure is inequitable or noncompetitive, these secondary and dependent forms of compensation compound the anomaly.

Our chief concern here is motivational dollars—sensitive dollars above basic survival dollars which are tangible recognition of personal growth in a job and contribution to the organization. It is true that people are motivated by things other than money. But the obvious danger is that the employee who thinks that he is not being sufficiently rewarded in the material sense is apt to look elsewhere for more money.

STANDARDS OF COMPENSATION ADEQUACY

In making compensation choices, it is sometimes useful to conceive of general wage levels in geographic areas or industries or unions or companies, but it should not be supposed that such general wage structures actually exist, any more than a competitive price or a natural rate of interest really exists. Wage structures are intellectual constructs useful in thinking about wages and in arriving at decisions about them, but the spectrum of possible concepts and decisions is broad. Different industries, companies, and organizations seek different talents, and the levels of their compensation structures should reflect these variances. Some talents, moreover, are rarer than others. In making pricing decisions, a manager has one foot in general economic theory and the other in the highly practical considerations of labor-management relations and external supply and demand factors. The range of choices is considerable.

Although every wage rate is related to every other from a strictly statistical standpoint, some relationships are more significant than others. Suppose a window washer in Pittsburgh earns $2 per hour and a cotton picker in California, although paid by the hundredweight of cotton picked, averages $2 per hour. There is statistical equality, but one which is fortuitous and meaningless. Suppose, however, that printing pressmen employed by Pittsburgh and Chicago newspapers each receive $3.65 per hour. Here again is statistical equality but one which is important and meaningful. Similar examples may be drawn to illustrate many different types of relationships which influence the dimensions of wage structures—intraindustry, interindustry, rural-urban, between geographic areas, between occupations, between plants of a multiplant company, between large plants and small ones, between profitable companies and those less so—with every relationship having its own set of causes. Thus, a company may test the adequacy of its compensation practice in a wide variety of comparisons, but the question is, with what organizations are such comparisons appropriate?

[1] C. H. Greenewalt, "What Kind of Incentives?" a speech before the Illinois State Chamber of Commerce, 1951.

David W. Belcher[2] notes a number of standards employed by companies to determine whether their compensation is adequate to attract, retain, and motivate the people they need:

1. What other employers in the community and/or industry are paying
2. Union demands
3. Ease of recruitment
4. Labor turnover
5. Employee satisfaction levels
6. Product market competition
7. Profit prospects
8. Company prestige

Each of the standards or tests of compensation adequacy requires comparative knowledge of a labor market.

Pay comparisons can take a number of different forms. First, comparisons can be made in terms of relative wage/salary movements or in terms of absolute pay. Also, pay for similar jobs in different plants, industries, areas, or unions can be compared. Entire pay structures can be compared with each other, or comparisons can be made of a few key jobs in each structure. Also, comparisons may be made in terms of a gross concept of compensation costs which includes both cash and fringes, or cash and fringes may be compared separately. Although wages and fringes generally are bargained at the same time and are substituted for each other under some negotiating circumstances, basically they are subject to separate external comparisons.

Because employees understand and accept external comparison as an assurance of equity, external pay comparisons are to be valued. But a number of factors make it difficult to develop valid comparisons: problems of evaluating job content, established internal wage relationships, differences in stability of employment, corporate policies, prejudices, working conditions, variations in fringe benefits, and the financial conditions of the organizations involved. And even if these factors can be accounted for, variances from absolute external equity are inevitable as the applications of the data are modified through labor-management negotiations, bargaining between an applicant and the recruiter, or unilateral decisions of management. Other factors which influence how an organization uses competitive pay data include: the economic prospects for the economy as a whole, for the industry, and especially for the particular employer; the cost of living; technological innovation; the relative productivity of the employer and his competition; the standard of living of the workers involved; technical factors relating to specific jobs in the organization; the degree of unionization, internally and externally; historical relationships; standing differentials among firms, jobs, or areas; relative bargaining power of negotiators; ability to pay; and the present evaluations of the future of each of these factors in a dynamic system.

CONGLOMERATES' USE OF SURVEY DATA

Conglomerates face unique problems in the application of competitive pay data. Not only must they consider the multitude of factors mentioned above, but they must also develop compensation structures at the executive level which, if they do not facilitate, must at least permit transfer between divisions which may operate in entirely different industries. In the conglomerates, managerial compensation tends to follow industry patterns. Thus, there may be a different design for each component. At the same time, however, there is a

---

[2] David W. Belcher, *Wage and Salary Administration,* 2d ed., Prentice-Hall, Inc., Englewood Cliffs, N.J., 1962.

corporatewide need to motivate the executives and managers of the decentralized, autonomous units.

In lower organizational levels, conglomerates' compensation decisions generally are influenced by long-established pay patterns which may result in vast differences between divisions—differences reflecting plant locations, union-management relationships, management philosophies, differing industries, labor markets, and economic capacity. In any case, acceptance of the comparative wages criterion by a multiplant company should not imply establishment of uniform pay rates throughout all company plants. With decentralized operations and/or diversified products and/or markets within the same corporate structure, troublesome inconsistencies in pay structures might arise if compensation policies were not formulated which, while uniform in principle, would allow for variation and flexibility in administration.

BALANCING INTERNAL EQUITY AND EXTERNAL COMPETITIVENESS

Internal equity is best established by use of an evaluation or classification system to determine the relative value of all jobs by comparing the functional content of each job with that of other jobs in the organization. The end result is a hierarchy of jobs ranging from those requiring very little skill and responsibility to that of the semiprofessional tool and die maker or similar highly skilled trades; or, in the case of clerical, professional, and executive positions, ranging from that of office boy to that of chief executive officer. The objective of job evaluation is internal alignment.

A company usually conducts wage and salary surveys to compare its compensation practices with those of other organizations. The objective of surveys is to develop a competitive pay structure.

Used together, job evaluation and surveys equip a company with the information needed to develop a sound and consistent pay structure. Thus, the employee is assured he is being compensated on an equitable basis compared with both his colleagues and others in the area and industry, and the company is assured that its compensation cost is on a par with that of its competitors.

While both job evaluation and wage surveys attempt to achieve consistency in the wage structure, they use different criteria to evaluate consistency—i.e., internal versus external comparison. When internal and external comparisons yield conflicting results, the two must somehow be balanced to achieve a rate that reflects the job's value within the company as well as the going rate in the marketplace.

Some early pioneers in the field of job evaluation suggested that the prevailing community rate be incorporated into the job evaluation plan itself as a characteristic job factor. One may question, however, whether this does not defeat the basic purpose of job evaluation, i.e., *internal* consistency. Another extreme view is to focus primarily on market factors and use internal job evaluation only as a convenience for interpolation of survey results into the wage structure.

Experience seems to indicate that establishment of compromise rates in cases of conflict is probably the solution even in the face of a preference for evaluated rates. Internal consistency is more important than strict external competitiveness. The purpose of job evaluation is to provide a balanced pay structure within a particular plant or enterprise based on work which is typical of that plant or enterprise. Competitive practice is a general guide as to the adequacy of the whole pay structure—not necessarily of the pay for each individual job. It is essential that pay structures be flexible enough to bend when the need arises.

chapter 14

Conducting Surveys

GLENN L. ENGELKE *Corporate Personnel Director, Addressograph Multi-graph Corporation, Cleveland, Ohio*

Wage and salary administration is a basic function of personnel management. Although responsibilities assigned to the personnel function have increased in recent years, one of personnel's basic objectives remains unchanged: to develop pay policies and practices that will attract, retain, and motivate competent personnel. To achieve this objective, an organization will often rely on information it obtains from others in developing its compensation program.

Since there is a limitless amount of information available on compensation, it becomes important to be selective in the data that are used. Therefore, deciding the sources for data, determining the data to be requested from the sources, and interpreting the data are essential steps in establishing and maintaining a sound wage and salary program.

Few organizations today will decide what they will pay their employees independently of what other organizations are paying their personnel. Therefore, once a company has determined its internal job relationships, it will compare its pay practice with the rates currently paid to personnel in the same or similar classifications and in the same or similar industries. Such information will guide and influence the development of the company's pay plans.

The most common means of obtaining the desired compensation information is to survey the market. Competent personnel are required to design and carry out the survey so that the information obtained will be accurate as well as useful. Sound sampling techniques must be used to determine which companies and how many of them will be asked to participate, and questionnaires must be well designed and interviewers well trained to elicit reliable, valid data. In addition, the surveying company must gain the cooperation of respondents, and if a union is in the picture, its role must be considered carefully. Finally, the data gathered must be analyzed and interpreted with care.

SAMPLING

Persons assigned a responsibility in wage and salary administration appreciate the value of reliable outside pay data in making compensation recommendations and decisions. The data's value is enhanced if they can be expressed in objective terms, such as averages, percentages, ratios, or other mathematical expressions.

To facilitate understanding of reports based on sampling methods, it is appropriate to review some of the basic terms and concepts associated with sampling. The intent is not to cover the broad field of statistics, or even all of the statistical techniques useful in wage and salary administration, but to review only the statistical information which is relevant to sampling.

Sampling theory is the study of relationships that exist between an entire group and a sample drawn from that group. Sampling's application in wage and salary administration involves four basic concepts—population, sample, random sample, and stratified sample.

A sample is a group of individuals or objects usually selected to represent a much larger group, called the "population." If one were interested in the wages paid to electricians, the population would be defined to include all individuals performing the duties normally assigned to an electrician, regardless of job title. Conceivably, this population could be worldwide, and drawing a sample would be a difficult task. Usually one is interested in those in New York State or only those in New York City. Even so, attempting to obtain the wages of all electricians in New York City would represent a challenging assignment. Therefore, a smaller number of electricians would be selected as a sample representative of the total group.

In practice, a sample is almost never a perfect replica of the population, but there are ways of drawing a sample which may make it more representative of the population as defined. If a sample is drawn from the population as a whole without any regard for preselection, it is known as a "random sample." A random sample usually is defined as one where every element in the population has an equal and independent chance of being selected for the sample. Random sampling does not mean haphazard selection, but is based on some objective method of selection, such as every tenth person in the organization. If a population is known to comprise reasonably uniform elements or strata, precision can be improved by stratification. In a stratified sample, the population is first broken down into individual groups or strata and then a random sample is drawn from each stratum.

If some element or individual in the population is more likely to be chosen than other elements or individuals, the sample is said to be "biased." In most cases, an unbiased sample is desired. However, in some instances, a biased sample may by predetermination provide more meaningful data. A biased sample differs from a stratified sample because the stratified sample selects a sample size from each of the established strata, whereas a biased sample selects from the population in general without any reference to any breakdown of the population.

In practice, the wage and salary administrator will usually work with a stratified sample, since he will want to narrow the population from which he draws his sample to the companies, jobs, and pay practices that will provide useful information for his needs.

Often, in wage and salary administration, a first sample is selected—the specific firms in the area to be included in the survey; and then a subsample is selected—the specific jobs to be surveyed in the preselected sample.

Although the word *sample* is used loosely in everyday conversation, in strict technical terms it means a group from which generalizations, or inferences, can be made about the entire population. Sampling is the process which is used to ensure that the data collected are representative of the population. If a sample is truly representative, important conclusions about the population can be inferred from a study of the sample. Such an analysis is known as "statistical inference" or "inductive statistics." Since such analyses cannot be certain, probability often is introduced to indicate the degree to which the conclusions can be accepted.

However, determining the sample size or the information to be requested on a rigid mathematical basis may not provide the best results. Often a wage and salary administrator will know the organizations and the approximate number he should contact to obtain the information he wants. In such cases, his judgment may be of more value than a random statistical sampling. Here, he would be using biased sampling. As an example, a steel company in Pittsburgh may wish to determine whether the salaries being paid to its foremen are competitive. However, for the company to contact every steel company in the country or even in the city of Pittsburgh, while possible, would be impractical. Therefore, the company would have to determine the number of companies from which it must obtain data and then perhaps the minimum number of responses that it would consider acceptable for its purposes. If it were decided that 25 companies would make up the sample size, which 25 companies should they be? Should they be the largest 25? Or only those located in the Pittsburgh area? Should they include companies that are identified as leaders in compensation in the area, but not necessarily steel companies? A knowledgeable wage and salary administrator who has worked for a time in the Pittsburgh area probably would be able to name 25 companies that might provide the response best suited to answer the question about foremen's compensation.

From the above, it becomes obvious that sampling involves both judgmental and mathematical considerations. Judgment must be applied to define the broad parameters of the population from which the sample is drawn; the use of statistics ensures that the information obtained reflects actual practice and is truly representative of the entire population. Used together, judgment and statistics enable the wage and salary administrator to gather meaningful data which he can use with confidence.

Subjective Consideration in Sampling. Often, in obtaining wage and salary information, the sample will be defined by the type of information that is desired. For instance, a company may be seeking wage information about only one position—that of laboratory technician. There may be only a few companies in the company's area that employ technicians in research and development. Therefore, the company probably would contact all the companies. In other words, the entire population—all laboratory technicians in the area—would be included in the sample.

In most cases, however, the sample size and the specific companies and jobs to be included in the sample are not determined as readily. An arithmetic means of determining appropriate sample size is discussed in a later section. However, an appropriate sample size is not the only consideration in developing reliable data; the sample must also be truly representative of the population. As an example, a small manufacturer of screw machine products would be unwise to compare its wage rates with only the wage rates paid by large companies or by companies outside of its competitive area. The organization may wish to know what is being paid by large organizations and may even elect to compete on labor rates with large organizations; but where this is not the intent, the effort must be made to select a sample that is more representative of its own situation and circumstances. In other words, the organization should use a stratified sample rather than a random sample.

A frequently expressed watchword of wage and salary administration says, "You must compare apples with apples and not apples with oranges." The statement makes the case for sound sampling techniques. If an organization is to obtain useful, reliable information for comparative purposes, the companies and the information it receives from the companies must be directly comparable to the organization's own data, and the more so the better. However, since companies and jobs within companies are never exactly alike, someone will be required to determine whether the data that have been sent in by other companies should be accepted or not. Where there is doubt about the data being comparable, it is probably best not to include them rather than to try to adjust them, or interpret them, to make them acceptable for the sample.

Another related point is that whenever information is required, time, effort, and expense are involved in obtaining it. The amount of each of these factors involved is directly proportional to the accuracy and completeness of the information obtained. In the case of sampling, where the aim is to select from the population that which is representative of the whole, the quality and the value of the results will depend upon the time, effort, and expense devoted to selecting the sample.

Thus, if improved results can be expected by a biased or stratified selection of participating companies, resulting in a savings in time, effort, and cost, a biased or stratified sample should be used. The size of a sample does not necessarily guarantee good data or good results. It is the characteristics of the participating companies that will lead to good information on which meaningful comparisons can be based. What, then, are some of the general guidelines for selecting participants?

Industry versus Area Considerations. Organizations may seek information based upon a geographical definition—local, national, or even international. If salary information on typists is the concern, what is being paid locally is of far greater significance than what is being paid nationally. It may be interesting to compare local pay for typists with the national market; but if the objective is to decide what to pay a local typist, area rates should be used. For each position that exists, there is a labor market area. Therefore, when compensation information about a position is desired, the sample should be made up from companies from that area, whatever it may be.

Frequently, pay or pay practices may have unique characteristics within a certain industry which make it logical to select a sample only from organizations that are in the industry. An organization wishing information on compensation paid to metallurgical personnel in copper-producing organizations should draw its sample on an industry basis rather than on a geographical basis.

One basic question must be asked: What, specifically, is it the organization wishes to know? If the information it receives will be affected significantly by geographical or industry differences, sample members must be selected to include or exclude such differences.

Size of Organizations. Organization size, often measured by employees or sales figures, may influence compensation practice. Large organizations frequently pay above-average salaries and a range of benefits not found in most small organizations. However, there are always exceptions.

If size is an important factor, the sample should be designed according to what best meets the objectives of the survey. If direct comparability is desired, organizations of the same size should be selected. If general information of a broader sampling would be more appropriate, then the sample can be stratified so as to provide a distribution by whatever size is desired.

General versus Specific Information. If information is desired in a very limited area—e.g., the wages paid under an incentive plan in light assembly operations—then particular attention must be given to making certain that the sample includes only those organizations that have light assembly operations and that pay their personnel in the department through incentive pay plans.

If only general information is being sought, such as that pertaining to the periodic adjustment of pay structures, then a more general sample would be acceptable and provide reliable results. Obviously, the questionnaire should be designed to carry out the objectives of the survey, and care should be taken to make the questions clear and to leave no doubt as to what information is desired.

Participant Characteristics. Every organization is unique. Some organizations may be high-paying, some may be low-paying but provide substantial benefits, and others may pay about average rates and minimum benefits but provide stable employment. Knowledge of such characteristics can be useful to an organization in analyzing the results of a survey, or to all participants if it is an open survey in which all participants are known to each other. Judgments, evaluations, and interpretations can be most meaningful if based on an accurate view of a company's position on the information being presented. Knowledge of the peculiar characteristics of an organization, if of significance, may improve the value of the survey to the company conducting the survey.

Selection of Benchmark Jobs. In requesting information relative to pay, it is imperative that not only the sample size and the organizations sampled be appropriate, but also that proper jobs be selected to provide sound pay information in each organization. Jobs used within companies for internal comparison and outside the company in wage surveys are called "benchmark jobs." In deciding which jobs should be identified as benchmark jobs, consideration should be given to the following:

1. The job should be immediately recognizable, so that all those requested to provide information will not be confused about the job being surveyed.

2. Benchmark jobs should reflect the complete range of jobs, from low to high, from the easiest to the most difficult.

3. The jobs should be ones to which relatively large numbers of persons are assigned, so as to provide statistical accuracy.

4. There should be no shortages or surpluses of personnel on selected benchmark jobs which might influence the wage pattern.

5. The jobs should remain unchanged, relatively, so that they provide a good, stable basis for comparison, particularly if the jobs will be surveyed over a period of time.

6. The jobs should be good reference points as to level and responsibility, so that other jobs may be compared with them with confidence.

In brief, subjective judgment on sample size and sample selection adds another dimension to sound sampling which implements the mathematical approach. In the careful selection of specific companies and in the determination of benchmark jobs lies the potential success or failure of a survey. Adding subjective judgment to objective selection of the sample assures results that will be a sound basis for wage and salary decisions.

Mathematical Considerations in Sampling. Sampling, in wage and salary administration, is essential when it is impractical to survey every organization that exists. Therefore, a first concern is to determine how many companies must be included in a sample in order to assure reliable results. A second concern is to decide how many responses from organizations in the sample are necessary before meeting the needs of the survey. Basically, the size of a sample depends upon the variability of the data in the population being sampled and the desired precision of the results. As would be expected, greater variability in the data and greater precision in results require a larger sample size. The wage and salary administrator can elect one of two options: survey the entire population or, through sampling, tolerate some degree of error in the result while obtaining useful information.

While the mathematics and statistics involved in resolving these concerns of sample size and sample response can be formidable, guidelines can be provided which should prove helpful in determining sample size and evaluation of sample response. Figure 1 is such a guide.

The curves shown in Figure 1 are for populations ranging from 10 to 1,000. On the horizontal axis is a measure of precision. A ± 5 percent indicates a willingness to tolerate a ± 5 percent error in the results that are obtained by sampling. On the vertical axis is the percentage figure to be used in determining the sample size.

Using a hypothetical situation, assume that the total number of companies in the population is estimated to be 250. Assume further that a ± 5 percent precision is desired. To find the number of companies to be in the sample size, simply read up the ± 5 percent line until it intersects the 250 population curve. Then, reading across to the vertical, find the percentage figure to be used. In this case, it is 20 percent. Taking 20 percent of 250 gives 50 as the number of companies that should be in the sample. The input from the 50 companies should be representative of the data that would be provided by all 250 companies. The precision chosen determines the extent to which the sample is representative of the entire population.

The curves shown in Figure 1 may be expressed mathematically[1] as:

$$P = \frac{100}{1 + 0.00065 \times N \times a^2}$$

where P = percentage to survey
N = total number of companies
a = required precision

For example, if the total number of companies (N) is 500 and a ± 5 percent precision is required:

$$P = \frac{100}{1 + 0.00065 \times 500 \times (5)^2}$$
$$= \frac{100}{1 + 8.125}$$
$$= \frac{100}{9.125} = 10.96, \text{ or } 11\% \text{ approximately}$$
$$11\% \text{ of } 500 \text{ companies} = 55 \text{ companies}$$

[1] The material used in deriving the formula is based on the theory of "cluster sampling," which is reviewed in *Sampling Theory of Survey with Applications*, published jointly by the Indian Society of Agricultural Statistics, New Delhi, India, and the Iowa State University Press, Ames, Iowa, 1954. The constant of 0.00065 was based on empirical data from an analysis of a number of compensation surveys reviewed by the author.

Figure 1.   Sample size related to population.

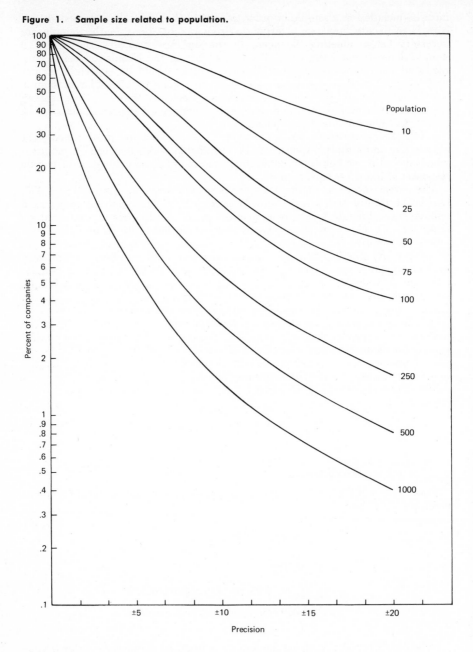

Thus, the formula indicates that where there are 500 companies in the population, and the desired precision is ± 5 percent, 11 percent of the population, or a total of 55 companies, would provide representative data for the 500 companies. The same result may be obtained directly from the graph shown as Figure 1.

It is worth noting that in the two illustrations using the graph, a population of 250 required a sample size of 50, whereas in the sample using the formula, a population of 500 required a sample size of 55. One might expect that if the population size were doubled, the sample size should be doubled. This is not the case. It does make the point that precision relies more on the absolute size of the sample than on a percentage relationship to population size.

Once the sample size is determined, a second concern of the wage and salary administrator is deciding the minimum number of responses that must be received for the data to be meaningful. For instance, if in a population of 500 a sample of 55 is indicated, how many companies should provide data on a given question to meet acceptance? Should it be half of the 55, say 28, or should it be more companies, or could it be fewer?

If it is assumed that, normally, 50 percent of the population should be able to respond to the question, then 50 percent of the respondents in the sample should respond to the question. However, occasionally less than the 50 percent expected will respond. If the minimum number of responses is not received, it may indicate that the question is not appropriate, i.e., a job being surveyed is not a benchmark job, or it was an inappropriate sample.

Figure 2 is a graph that indicates the minimum number of responses acceptable, assuming that a benchmark job is one which occurs in 50 percent of the population. It is based upon the mathematics of binomial sampling.[2] The horizontal axis indicates the number of companies in the sample. The vertical axis indicates the minimum percentage of responses required.

[2] If n is defined as sample size and k as number which respond, then k is related to n by the expression:

$$\sum_{x=0}^{k} \frac{n}{x!\,(n-x)!}\,(1/2)^n = 0.05$$

which constitutes the 95 percent one-sided confidence limit for a population fraction equal to ½.

Figure 2.   **Minimum response required for job inclusion.**

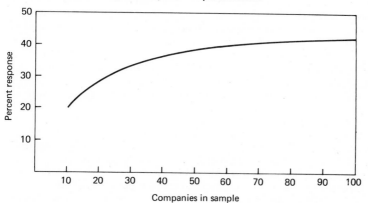

As an example, if there are 40 companies in the survey, read up from the number 40 on the graph until it intersects the curves, look to the vertical scale, obtaining a reading of 37 percent, and then take 37 percent of 40 to arrive at 14.8, or 15 companies.   Thus, if the sample comprises 40 companies, at least 15 replies must be received to each question asked in order to provide a reasonable response.

It is important to recognize that replies to a survey are not always equal. For example, suppose an organization is interested in obtaining wage rate information on 10 jobs from a sample of 40 companies.   The guideline suggests that at least 15 companies should respond to the request for information for each job.   If fewer than 15 respond, it is reasonable to assume that the results may not be acceptable.   Further, each of the 40 companies will respond differently on the 10 jobs.   Some companies will report on all 10 jobs; others will report on a majority, or about half, or only a few.   In addition, one company may report wage rates for 100 individuals on one job, whereas another may be able to report only five rates on the same job.   Oftentimes, the responses are weighted, where called for, to make them more meaningful and useful.

Just as care should be taken in deciding the proper sample size and the proper number of replies, it is equally important that the proper questions be asked so that the "proper" responses will be provided.   For example, the question of what companies pay for a specific job is different from the question of what the average pay is for all the individuals on that specific job.   Also, if a review of input reveals gross differences arising from error, the data should be rejected.

The objective approach to sampling, then, is of value for determining sample size and minimum acceptable responses.   Its primary purpose is to provide the wage and salary administrator with a useful method of defining the parameters involved in obtaining compensation information for management.

SELECTING AND TRAINING SURVEY INTERVIEWERS

The value of survey results depends to a large degree upon the selection of participants and the questions asked to obtain information.   Survey responses must be both accurate and complete, and to ensure that they are, the surveying organization must take great care to formulate questions that will elicit the desired information.

Some surveys, requiring limited information and therefore necessitating little or no explanation, are easily handled over the telephone or by mail.   Surveys which are more detailed, or which are being initiated with the intention of repeating them periodically, may require a more thorough or more personalized approach.   In such cases, personal interviews may be used to obtain the desired information.   The surveying organization arranges beforehand for a personal interview with the individual or individuals in participating companies best qualified to provide the survey data.   The questionnaire may be forwarded in advance of the scheduled interview to enable the respondent to review it, collect the data requested, and determine any questions he may have on items which are not clear to him.   Or an organization may choose to review the questionnaire personally with the participant to make certain that he understands the questions and the data that are to be provided.   In either approach, the accuracy and completeness of responses will depend as much on the success of communications between the surveying company representatives and participants' representatives as on the design of the survey questionnaire.

Therefore, the selection and training of survey interviewers are very important. A company may send one or two people to interview respondents, depending upon availability of qualified personnel, time constraints, and costs. Obviously, using two interviewers should result in a better understanding of the input from participating companies and the data that are provided. This is not necessarily so, but if questions arise, two persons are more likely to arrive at a correct interpretation of the data than just one person is.

Desirable qualifications for a survey interviewer include the following:

1. He should have a thorough knowledge of his own organization, particularly information relevant to the survey. Since a survey between organizations implies a direct exchange of comparable information, the one asking for data must be in a position to provide data on his organization. Sometimes this is accomplished by the surveying company providing a completed questionnaire of its data to the participants at the time of the interview. Or, the data can be furnished when the completed survey results are given to the participating companies.

2. It is also to be assumed that the interviewer will have a broad knowledge of wage and salary administration policies, practices, and procedures. For example, when a participant asks what is to be included in "average hourly rate," the representative from the surveying company must be able to respond directly and accurately, whether what is wanted is a rate that includes or excludes overtime, includes or excludes shift premium, cost of living, or other "adders," or whether the job rates reported should include day-work rates or incentive rates or both. He must be able to respond intelligently and correctly to any questions which may arise.

3. He should have a manner that is friendly and businesslike. He should be able to establish rapport quickly with a stranger; if he appears to be insincere, ill-informed, uncooperative, or negative in any way, the chances of obtaining reliable and useful information may be reduced. His impact should be that of a capable, competent individual seeking important information but not taking an undue amount of time in doing it. He should be perceptive so that he can identify areas which may be fuzzy or responses that are not completely clear or accurate and ask the right questions to get the right responses. He should also be willing to share or exchange additional data, if authorized, that may be of value to the participating company.

4. He should recognize that, since he is a representative of a company, his manner, dress, and deportment will leave an image not only of himself but of his organization.

In exceptional cases, it may be necessary to go outside the compensation department or even the personnel department to obtain individuals for the surveying team. In such instances, the above qualifications are still desirable, but the individuals must be trained to be as competent and as qualified as those experienced in the field.

One additional note which may apply to inexperienced surveying personnel, although it may apply to experienced personnel as well: i.e., when the interviewer does not know the answer to a respondent's question, he should admit it, and simply say, "I don't know, but I will obtain clarification on that question for you." He should not guess or try to "look good." If he does, he may inadvertently mislead or misinform the respondent.

Training of interviewers is necessary to ensure consistent handling of data gathered from respondents. In addition to assuring data reliability, training achieves several other objectives:

1. All interviewers understand the purpose of the survey, what is being asked for, and the ground rules under which it is being conducted.

2. In reviewing questionnaire details and the process to be used in completing the questionnaires, the interviewers will develop a common understanding of what to ask for, what is, or is not, acceptable in furnishing data, and where the difficult areas of the survey may be.

3. Training sessions often reveal weaknesses in the survey questionnaire which can be corrected, resulting in an improved questionnaire and more reliable responses.

4. Discussions between trainer and trainees about interviewing techniques—how to establish a friendly atmosphere, what to say about the surveying organization and its reasons for wanting data, etc.—will provide each individual with better insight and more ideas about how to approach and carry out his assignment. The result is that the group benefits from the individual thoughts of all those on the surveying team.

5. Quite often, individuals who conduct the survey interviews will also be responsible for tabulating and reporting the results, perhaps to provide the foundation for specific recommendations, future compensation planning, or policy administration. Individuals trained to obtain reliable data probably are the best ones to analyze the responses and prepare a summary of survey findings for the participants and, perhaps, for management review. Thus, training for interviewing not only ensures good input but also prepares the trainees to compile the results, probably resulting in a savings in time and costs.

Effective communication is the basis of obtaining reliable input. Since survey results depend so heavily on how well the questionnaire is designed and also, if personal interviews are used, on those asking and recording the data, it is well worth the time and effort to train people in questionnaire design and interview technique.

GAINING COOPERATION OF RESPONDENTS

Companies conduct wage and salary surveys to obtain reliable information about pay practices and policies. Survey data provide a sound basis for compensation comparisons. However, obtaining the essential data depends upon the cooperation of the companies selected for inclusion in the sample. Most companies are willing to respond to another's request for data, as long as the request is not unreasonable and does not violate company rules on the release of company data.

Most firms recognize the principle of reciprocity in exchanging wage and salary data. A company is willing to cooperate with another company to provide data when requested because one day it may be in a similar position seeking information and will want the assistance of other companies to obtain the data it requires.

A second reason most companies are willing to participate in a survey is that the surveying company usually is expected to compile the results of the survey and report the results to all the participants. Thus, a company can, by participating in a survey conducted by another organization, reap the benefits of the time, effort, and expense put forth by another company. It is able to obtain data with minimum involvement and cost.

One sure way to gain cooperation is to conduct a survey of interest to the participants. If the survey focuses on a subject of current concern, participation will be good. On the other hand, a survey which is not meaningful or useful to respondents may not receive wide support.

A survey will be considered meaningful by projected respondents if it encompasses companies in the same industry, companies regarded as peers in the same area, or companies that compete on some other basis. No organization believes that it can stand alone, impervious to what happens around it. So it is only natural that, when one organization is seeking information on a subject in which others are interested, they will be willing to participate—particularly if the other company is summarizing and reporting the results.

Another means of gaining cooperation is for the surveying organization to agree to gather certain additional information which is not necessary for its own survey but is of interest to respondents.

Finally, most people involved in wage and salary administration rely on outside data. Therefore, if a surveying company indicates that it will not only collect and summarize the data but will present charts, tables, or graphs that may be useful in interpreting the data and will provide the other organizations with guidelines on bases for their wage and salary planning or administration, companies will be cooperative because of the large return they receive for their relatively small input.

One cautionary note on the subject of surveys. Since the best way to obtain reliable data from other organizations is to conduct a survey, there is a danger of survey overload, i.e., surveys duplicating each other. A company should beware of gaining a reputation for "surveyitis"—always surveying what others are doing or thinking on every small item that occurs. Rather, it should conduct only those surveys which are important to its overall operations and which may be helpful to participating companies.

Another factor influencing a company's decision to participate is whether or not its identity will be revealed in the summary of survey results. Three common approaches to meeting participants' varying demands for anonymity are discussed in the following paragraphs.

First, the survey may be completely confidential, with only the surveying company known to all the participants and only the surveying company able to match data with the company that provided it. Each participating company in a confidential survey is identified in a manner that will enable it to identify its own input but that prevents it from identifying other participants with their input. It is common for companies using this approach to assign each participant a code number or letter. The surveying company should not assign numbers or letters alphabetically or in some other way that would permit another company to break the code. Another error to be avoided is to list company data that can be revealing, i.e., number of employees, annual sales volume, or other factors that can enable one company to identify another company.

A second approach is the open survey in which all participants are known to one another. In such cases, participants are willing to share data without a concern for anonymity or confidentiality. In open surveys, the surveying company openly lists all participants with their data input. Or it may protect the participants by assigning code numbers or letters to all companies and then sharing this information with them on a special sheet not a part of the survey. This provides every company with the identification of all the other companies in the survey but also prevents the identification of any participants should the survey itself get into the wrong hands, since the code sheet must be coupled with the survey to associate company with data.

A third approach is a compromise in which all participants are assigned code numbers regardless of whether they have requested anonymity or not. Those willing to share survey information are provided with a separate code key to the other companies that have agreed to disclose their names and data. All those wishing to remain anonymous are designated only by a code and receive only coded information.

Increasingly, companies that participate in special surveys, as opposed to larger general surveys, are tending toward open surveys. Often the output becomes meaningful only when associated with the company that provided it. Therefore, where the participants are known to one another and can rely on each other to treat both the input and the output on a confidential basis, there is a definite advantage in using the open survey. However, if any participants indicate a desire to remain anonymous, the request must be honored. To reveal a company name in association with data input is a serious violation of survey ethics and cannot be excused under any circumstances.

A point was made earlier in this chapter that the design of the survey questionnaire and the method of obtaining the data, whether by telephone, mail, or interview, were vital to the quality and usefulness of the output. The handling and reporting of data are equally important; each company's wishes must be respected as to its identification in the survey and its association with the data. A violation of a company's instruction in this area can jeopardize the future working relationship of the surveying company with all the other companies in the area or in the industry within which it operates.

UNION INVOLVEMENT IN SURVEYS

Normally, in wage negotiations for either hourly or salaried personnel, the union representatives may be expected to take one of two positions relative to sampling. They will either participate actively in the identification of participants to be invited into the survey and also the jobs and possibly the pay practices to be covered in the survey, or they may elect not to participate in any way but choose to question the data if, and when, they are presented in negotiations.

If a company does seek, and obtain, a union's participation in determining the sample—both as to organizations and the information to be requested—it must make certain that all input from other companies is treated in a completely confidential manner. If companies are to be identified to union representatives in an open survey procedure, then prior permission must be obtained from each participant to permit the showing of the data to union representatives, whether coded or uncoded.

Situations may exist where management and labor are open and able to work constructively to negotiate labor agreements. In such cases, it may prove beneficial to have union representatives offer suggestions about a sample, for consideration, which may be helpful in the negotiation process. However, it should be clearly understood that all data they see must be treated with complete confidence and that sound sampling principles will be observed. Further, it should be understood that the results will not be used in any way that would not be approved by the participating organizations. It would be common courtesy to advise each company entering the survey of the union's participation and to permit each company to make a choice as to whether it will provide the data requested, or whether it will decline to participate, or whether it will provide only partial data.

Obviously, if a union is not involved, the sample can be selected with objectives in mind that may not relate directly to labor relations. A broader scope of jobs, both union and nonunion, can be included without a concern about the union's reaction or interest.

In summary, where the labor-management relationship justifies union participation in the sampling process, care should be taken to protect the anonymity of the participants and their data so that this information will not be used in any way to the participants' disadvantage or to cause either wage or union problems with their work force. Further union participation in the sampling process normally will require some accommodation in the selection of participants and of the data input. This constraint may result in more limited responses and data. However, such accommodations have been worked out effectively in the past and have resulted in reliable information for management and labor review.

PROCEDURES FOR INTERPRETING SURVEY DATA

After the survey questions have been answered and the data returned to the surveying company, the next step is to analyze the data to obtain the information for which the survey was conducted.

Obviously, the interpretation of the data depends, to a considerable degree, upon the questions that were asked. If the questions required objective responses, such as average hourly rate, current cost-of-living allowance, salary, etc., then the results would be reported in equally objective terms.

Alternatively, the questions may have been of a more subjective nature, such as, "Do you think college hiring rates will go up next year? Please state your reasons for your opinion." Such a question requires the surveying company to analyze all the responses and then attempt to draw appropriate conclusions. The conclusion might be general, such as reporting that most of the companies surveyed believe college hiring rates will be higher next year. Or the company interpreting the results may attempt to report the data objectively, such as by indicating that 12 companies out of a total sample of 25 thought college hiring rates would be higher, 8 companies believed they would remain about the same as last year, 1 company predicted the rates would go down, and 4 companies had no opinion. Some generalized statement might follow summarizing the bases for opinions of the contributing companies. Interpreting subjective responses is difficult because the surveying company must understand the response, accurately reflect what was intended, company by company, and then also analyze the results from a total-input point of view.

To be of value, survey input must be accurate and must include all the data called for in the design of the study. However, since each organization is different in many ways from every other organization, survey data are subject to considerable variance. Therefore, the surveying company must ensure that what is reported is consistent with what was asked and that the report is truly representative of the facts. This may require judgment and decisions on what to include or exclude in a final summary of results. Occasionally, the surveying company may have to contact a surveyed company to clarify its data or, perhaps, to explain that some data received will not be included in the results because they were not comparable to what was asked for or received.

After all the decisions on data input have been made and the data are compiled, the data are ready for summary and presentation.

Results can be presented in a variety of ways, ranging from a simple tabulation of the input as received to a special survey report of the data. Such a report might include charts and tables and, perhaps, commentary about what the data indicated.

If data input are quantifiable, the output will be in the form of statistical interpretation, where terms like *mean, median,* and *standard deviation* assume importance. If the data responses are primarily qualitative, the interpretation is likely to be predominantly narrative, with some reference to numbers. However, the primary focus would be on trends, general conclusions, or explanations of what appears to be occurring in the area under study.

In interpreting results that are quantifiable, data processing equipment can be used to provide an almost infinite number of "cuts of data." Care should be taken, however, to remain objective, to seek only information that is useful, and not to attempt to overwhelm others with mathematical manipulations that may confuse rather than clarify. Various statistical techniques and their appropriate uses are covered in another section. However, it is worthwhile to recognize that the usefulness of data depends upon their accuracy and uniformity. People in data processing have a favorite expression, *GIGO*, which means "garbage in, garbage out." In other words, all of the sophisticated statistical techniques known cannot make bad data good or use them to lead to results which are indicative of the facts. It is far better to spend time on making certain that the survey sample is of the appropriate size and includes the proper companies for the type of information that is wanted, that the survey questionnaire has been designed so that accurate responses may be obtained, and that, if survey interviewers are used, they are well trained and good envoys of the company. If these factors have been given proper attention, then the collection of data will be easy, the errors in reporting of data will be minimized, and the interpretation of results will be a relatively easy task, resulting in reliable, valid, and useful data and a good survey.

chapter 15

Acquiring Competitive
Information from Surveys

HENRY C. RICKARD

J. A. ENGEL

L. EARL LEWIS

A company must periodically check the job market if it is to know how its own salary practice stands up to the competition. New perspectives must be sought constantly, not only to maintain a close feel for general price movements, but also to keep abreast of temporary price surges when demand exceeds supply in certain job specifications. Responding to pressures from many directions, the salary administrator is constantly adjusting his course, and he certainly needs a periodic navigational "fix."

Jobs, from clerical to corporate officers, call for varying kinds of salary surveys, ranging from a casual telephone check of one job to participation in broad-based surveys of the entire spectrum of jobs. Several kinds of surveys are available to the salary administrator. He may want primarily to use one, or to use several in combination. This chapter will examine some representative surveys:

15.1. Administrative Management Society survey
15.2. American Management Association survey
15.3. Bureau of Labor Statistics survey
15.4. Maturity curve surveys
15.5. Edward N. Hay & Associates annual compensation comparisons

15.1 Administrative Management Society

HENRY C. RICKARD   *Director, International Compensation Coordination, Edward N. Hay & Associates, Philadelphia, Pennsylvania*

Companies generally compete for clerical and other nonmanagerial personnel on a local or regional basis; and, as at all other levels, salaries must be competitive with the marketplace.

In some larger areas, salaries of clerical employees in a particular industry within the region (e.g., Connecticut banks) may be examined. Often a group of local companies will maintain an annual salary survey among themselves, and frequently companies undertake a "one-shot" survey of their competition.

A regional survey of broad scope and basic utility is the *Office Salaries Directory*, published by the Administrative Management Society of Willow Grove, Pennsylvania. The AMS has 168 chapters throughout the United States, Canada, and the West Indies. These chapters, in addition to collecting data for the international directory, develop supplemental local material. The 1969–1970 edition of the Directory presented data for 20 positions (13 clerical and 7 data processing) covering 621,000 employees in 7,314 companies in 132 cities. The remainder of this section will describe this survey.

AMS "OFFICE SALARIES DIRECTORY"

Companies participating in the AMS survey furnish data for only those jobs that substantially match any of the specific job descriptions submitted with the survey. (See Figure 1 on page 3-28 for job descriptions used in 1969–1970 in the AMS survey.) These 20 jobs are not intended to cover the entire clerical spectrum, but are considered to be both common and characteristic among all types and sizes of companies. The survey results are in two parts: (1) the Directory, which covers all cities and regions, and (2) the Local Supplement, which gives a detailed breakdown of local interest.

The Directory. This international survey shows the range of weekly salaries for the standard AMS jobs broken down into 128 localities and 7 large regions. A typical presentation is that of St. Louis, shown in Table 1.

Taking the data on Job I (typist-clerk), for instance, we find that there were 2,082 employees reported from 105 companies in the St. Louis area. Half of the people were paid in the range between the first and third quartiles, or, specifically, between $79 and $101 weekly. The average rate was $89 and the median was $89.

The highest and lowest reported salaries are not shown, since it is felt that the middle 50 percent of reported salaries is the best guide to the going salary rate.

In addition to the 128 local summaries (e.g., St. Louis), the Directory reports regional averages for the 20 jobs surveyed, as shown in Table 2.

The Directory also summarizes, by the same regional categories, such related data as: basic work week, overtime (daily and weekly), paid holidays, and union membership. (See Table 3.)

The Local Supplement. The local supplements give additional detail, such as

TABLE 1   Range of Weekly Salaries for Standard AMS Jobs—St. Louis

St. Louis Job category	Mail clerk—file clerk	General clerk B	General clerk A	Accounting clerk B	Accounting clerk A	Bookkeeping machine op.	Offset dupl. machine op.	Telephone switchboard op.	Typist-clerk	Stenographer B	Stenographer A	Secretary B	Secretary A	Key punch operator B	Key punch operator A	Tab. machine op. (intermediate)	Computer op. (intermediate)	Programmer B	Programmer A	Systems analyst (intermediate)
	A	B	C	D	E	F	G	H	I	J	K	L	M	N	O	P	Q	R	S	T
Average	80	90	107	97	130	95	103	95	89	92	102	106	124	91	96	104	120	161	174	179
First quartile	71	77	91	79	105	85	89	85	79	81	87	93	111	79	85	89	107	158	158	163
Median	75	87	107	91	128	93	99	95	89	89	101	103	123	89	95	107	128	163	178	178
Third quartile	89	103	123	111	158	105	119	103	101	107	115	117	138	103	105	117	138	173	188	198
No. companies	97	103	107	90	84	46	58	118	105	80	65	101	105	68	59	32	56	37	45	30
No. employees	1,199	2,447	1,456	601	488	129	132	332	2,082	699	737	1,226	788	536	342	126	263	282	202	85

TABLE 2 Regional Averages for Standard AMS Jobs

International and regional averages	A Mail clerk—file clerk	B General clerk B	C General clerk A	D Accounting clerk B	E Accounting clerk A	F Bookkeeping machine op.	G Offset dupl. machine op.	H Telephone switchboard op.	I Typist-clerk	J Stenographer B	K Stenographer A	L Secretary B	M Secretary A	N Key punch operator B	O Key punch operator A	P Tab. machine op. (intermediate)	Q Computer op. (intermediate)	R Programmer B	S Programmer A	T Systems analyst (intermediate)
Canada																				
1968	58	66	94	76	105	68	76	69	64	69	81	88	102	67	78	86	100	121	150	161
1969	61	68	97	80	110	74	77	73	68	72	86	92	107	73	83	91	109	130	155	159
Total U.S.																				
1968	74	83	101	94	117	86	96	88	82	88	100	105	122	85	95	106	117	143	174	183
1969	79	88	105	98	122	92	102	94	86	92	104	111	129	90	99	113	123	154	184	196
Eastern U.S.																				
1968	75	82	101	91	115	85	95	88	80	84	97	105	123	83	94	102	116	141	172	182
1969	79	90	107	98	121	94	102	94	85	90	102	112	133	89	98	112	123	157	186	196
E. Central U.S.																				
1968	74	83	100	95	116	91	98	90	83	91	103	108	124	84	98	110	120	144	176	184
1969	78	87	105	101	121	95	104	96	86	95	105	114	131	90	104	115	126	151	184	194
W. Central U.S.																				
1968	72	79	96	89	112	83	93	85	80	83	96	99	116	81	90	104	114	145	171	178
1969	76	84	101	93	119	89	98	89	84	89	98	104	122	86	94	108	119	154	180	197
Southern U.S.																				
1968	72	81	97	93	116	82	92	84	78	85	99	101	116	82	93	103	112	141	171	184
1969	76	85	102	94	121	87	96	89	82	91	102	104	121	85	95	105	119	146	179	191
Western U.S.																				
1968	80	93	106	101	125	94	105	96	89	98	109	115	128	97	106	114	124	148	179	192
1969	86	98	112	106	129	96	112	102	94	103	114	121	134	103	110	126	132	163	194	207

TABLE 3   Regional Totals

	Canada	United States					
		East	East Central	West Central	South	West	Total U.S.
Basic work week							
Less than 35	31	6	1	3	7	2	19
35	139	257	24	13	51	22	367
36¼	65	71	17	16	22	11	137
37½	260	333	125	139	214	122	933
38	11	18	10	19	13	11	71
39	17	49	24	43	41	32	189
40	93	832	747	880	973	636	4,068
Over 40	5	25	27	32	25	10	119
Other basic	3	15	6	15	3	4	43
No answer	673	42	7	4	13	5	71
Daily overtime							
8 hours one day	149	706	524	514	521	545	2,810
Regular number work hrs	243	301	104	97	117	89	708
Daily overtime not paid	190	521	294	479	610	183	2,087
No answer	715	120	66	74	114	38	412
Weekly overtime							
40 hours one week	100	1,080	767	906	1,091	633	4,477
Basic weekly hours	187	347	103	109	133	95	787
Other number hours	24	20	18	20	8	5	71
Weekly overtime not paid	198	79	39	76	76	68	338
No answer	788	122	61	53	54	54	344
Paid holidays—year							
None	1	2	2	4	3	2	13
Under six	0	12	19	30	208	22	291
Six	1	102	246	364	355	112	1,179
Seven	15	211	181	247	244	187	1,070
Eight	102	317	207	238	306	284	1,352
Nine	215	375	186	158	132	126	977
Ten	215	303	103	66	67	58	597
Eleven	41	171	14	24	15	29	253
Twelve	8	77	7	15	8	14	121
Over twelve	9	25	6	8	8	10	57
No answer	690	53	17	10	16	11	107
Union							
None	557	1,474	893	1,065	1,276	745	5,453
Part	40	98	62	57	46	65	328
All	27	31	19	25	24	34	133
No answer	673	45	14	17	16	11	103
AMS membership							
Member	1,069	903	486	709	733	481	3,312
Non-member	228	745	502	455	629	374	2,705
Total companies reported	1,297	1,648	988	1,164	1,362	855	6,017
No. of employee rates reported	87,248	167,517	97,997	91,447	103,264	736,675	533,900
Total clerical employees	184,084	692,023	311,182	253,668	306,910	302,498	1,866,281
Grand total employees	354,620	1,325,927	876,951	724,237	840,151	640,629	4,407,895

salaries paid by industry groups, vacation practice, information on various benefits, and, in particular, breakdowns of jobs in increments by salary rate—that is, how many employees are paid at each level. This is illustrated in Table 4, which shows, for instance, that 98 stenographers are paid between $100 and $104 weekly.

Apart from the general orientation obtained from the basic Directory, a local company makes its specific salary comparison by circling in red in Table 4

TABLE 4   Number of Office Employees by Job Rates

Weekly salary rate	Mail clerk—file clerk	General clerk B	General clerk A	Accounting clerk B	Accounting clerk A	Bookkeeping machine operator	Offset duplicating machine operator	Telephone switchboard operator	Typist-clerk	Stenographer	Secretary B	Secretary A	Key punch operator B	Key punch operator A	Tabulating machine operator	Computer operator B	Computer operator A	Total employees
Job code	A	B	C	D	E	F	G	H	I	J	K	L	M	N	O	P	Q	
Under 60	2																	2
60–64	1																	1
65–69	52	53		1					42				1	3				152
70–74	78	114	2			4			15	8	1		14					236
75–79	54	161	12	1		4		1	37	8	2		27					310
80–84	46	182	57	5		2	6	7	42	42		1	22		1			413
85–89	33	116	68	18	2	6	5	5	46	38	6	2	23	20	4			392
90–94	48	54	92	22	1	4	10	9	54	51	21	5	14	38	2			425
95–99	12	22	55	52	3	3	4	7	23	51	34	9	17	43	4			339
100–104	7	13	33	41	4	2	5	8	19	98	44	6	17	19	19			335
105–109	5	38	37	27	11	3	5	13	24	67	71	8	8	25	7	8		357
110–114	1	33	17	23	1	2	4	6	14	63	80	7	3	9	6	9		278
115–119	2	29	14	12	1	2	2	10	4	23	86	41	1	8	19	9		265
120–124	1	20	12	8	7	2	1	2	14	8	41	43	2	10	4	7		182
125–129	4	46	4	3	3		7	7	3	7	39	30	2	3	2	7		167
130–134	2	7	9	2	13		10	5	11		47	39	1	4	2	10	1	163
135–139		27	15	2	11	3		1	7	5	16	23	1	1	3	12	1	128

rates paid to each of its reported employees. The company can then observe how its rates compare with others in the community.

The AMS survey reports only nonsupervisory office workers. These persons do not usually move from city to city for better pay. It follows that a company is competing for clerical employees only with other firms in the same city or industrial area. Furthermore, since these workers are not bound by industry lines, the rates paid by all types of local business establish the market value for the community.

Figure 1.   Job titles and descriptions.

A   Mail Clerk—File Clerk
Circulates office mail, delivers messages and supplies. May process incoming or outgoing mail and operate related machines and perform other routine duties. Keeps correspondence, cards, invoices, receipts or other classified or indexed records filed systematically according to an established system. Locates and removes material upon request and keeps records of its disposition. May perform other clerical duties which are related.

B   General Clerk B
Performs clerical duties in accordance with established procedures requiring judgment in the selection and interpretation of data. Job requires a moderate amount of prior experience and considerable supervision.

C   General Clerk A
Performs complex and responsible clerical duties requiring independent analysis, exercise of judgment and a detailed knowledge of department or company policies and procedures related to work performed. Minimum supervision required.

D   Accounting Clerk B
Checks, verifies and posts journal vouchers, accounts payable vouchers or other

Figure 1.   Job titles and descriptions. (continued)

simple accounting data of a recurring or standardized nature, reconciles bank accounts, etc.

E   Accounting Clerk A

Keeps a complete set of accounting records in a small office with or without the use of an accounting machine, or handles one phase of accounting in a larger unit which requires the accounting training needed to determine proper accounting entries, prepare accounting reports, analyze accounting records to determine causes of results shown, etc.   May direct work of junior clerks or bookkeepers.   (However, excludes supervisors and persons at policy-making levels.)

F   Bookkeeping Machine Operator

Operates a bookkeeping machine to record business transactions of a recurring and standardized nature, where proper posting has been indicated or is readily identifiable.   May balance to control figures.

G   Offset Duplicating Machine Operator

Sets up and operates offset-type duplicating machines.   Cleans and adjusts equipment but does not make repairs.   May prepare own plates and operate auxiliary equipment, and may keep records of kind and amount of work done.

H   Telephone Switchboard Operator

Operates a single or multiple position PBX telephone switchboard.   May keep records of calls and toll charges, and may operate a paging system and perform duties of receptionist.

I   Typist-Clerk

Types letters, reports, tabulations, and other material in which setups and terms are generally clear and follow a standard pattern.   Performs clerical duties of moderate difficulty.   May prepare stencils or offset masters.

J   Stenographer B

Transcribes from dictating equipment, or records and transcribes shorthand dictation involving a normal range of business vocabulary.   May perform copy typing or clerical work of moderate difficulty incidental to primary stenographic duties.   May operate as a member of a centralized stenographic service.

K   Stenographer A

Performs advanced stenographic duties which require experience and exercise of judgment.   Transcribes from dictating equipment, or records and transcribes dictation of more than average difficulty which regularly includes technical or specialized vocabulary or frequently supplements transcription with the drafting of finished work from indicated sources, records, general instructions, etc.

L   Secretary B

Performs secretarial duties for a member of middle management.   General requirements are the same as for Secretary A (listed next), but limited to the area of responsibility of the principal.

M   Secretary A

Performs the complete secretarial job for a high level executive or a person responsible for a major functional or geographic operation.   Does work of a confidential nature and relieves principal of designated administrative details.   Requires initiative, judgment, knowledge of company practices, policy and organization.

N   Key Punch Operator B

Operates an alphabetical or numerical key punch machine to record pre-coded or readily usable data following generally standardized procedures.   May verify the work of others, using a verifying machine.

O   Key Punch Operator A

Operates an alphabetical or numerical key punch machine or verifier to record or verify complex or uncoded data working from source material which may not be arranged for key punching.   Selects appropriate number and kinds of cards.   Follows a pattern of operations generally standardized but frequently including rules, exceptions and special instructions which demand operator's close attention.   Frequently required to decipher illegible source documents and be able to assist in preparing new ones.

Fig. 1.   Job titles and descriptions. (continued)

P   Tabulating Machine Operator—Intermediate

Sets up, operates and wires a variety of punched card equipment, including tabulators and multipliers. Wires boards from diagrams prepared by others for routine jobs, uses prewired boards on complex or repetitive jobs. May locate and correct job difficulties and assist in training less experienced operators.

This work is performed under specific instructions and may include some wiring from diagrams. The work may involve tabulation of a repetitive accounting exercise, a small tabulating study, or parts of a longer and more complex report.

Q   Computer Operator—Intermediate

Operates computers utilizing established programs or programs under development. Selects proper tape, loads computer and manipulates control switches on console in accordance with established instructions. Observes lights on console, storage devices, etc., reporting any deviations from standards. Detects nature of errors or equipment failure and makes normal console adjustments. Maintains operating records such as machine performance and production reports.

R   Programmer B

Assists in the review of analysis of the preparation of the program instructions under direct supervision. Fairly competent to work on several phases of programming with only general direction but still requires some instruction for other phases. May prepare on his own the block diagrams and machine logic flow charts. Codes program instructions and prepares test data, testing and debugging programs. May also assist in the documentation of all procedures used through the system. Experience of trainee required for entry to this position classification.

S   Programmer A

With general supervision, analyzes and defines programs for electronic data processing equipment. Is generally competent in most phases of programming to work on his own, and only requires general guidance for the balance of the activities. Conducts analyses of sufficient detail of all defined systems specifications and develops all levels of block diagrams and machine logic flow charts, codes, prepares test data, tests and debugs programs. Revises and refines programs as required and documents all procedures used throughout the computer program when it is formally established. Evaluates and modifies existing programs to take into account changes in systems requirements. May give technical assistance to lower level classifications. Normally progresses from this classification to Senior or Lead Programmer.

T   Systems Analyst—Intermediate

Under close supervision, assists in devising computer system specifications and record layouts. Is qualified to work on several phases of systems analysis, but requires guidance and direction for other phases. Conducts studies and analyses of existing office procedures and prepares systems flow charts for existing and proposed operations. Under instruction prepares computer block diagram and may assist in the preparation of machine logic flow charting.

15.2   American Management Association

J. A. ENGEL   *Director, Executive Compensation Service, American Management Association, New York, New York*

The AMA's Executive Compensation Service has been furnishing information on compensation and related subjects for the past 20 years. From a modest beginning in 1950, when 250 companies participated, the Service has grown to the extent that approximately 8,000 companies in the United States and nearly 3,000 foreign firms now actively participate in ECS activities. ECS has offices in New York, Brussels, and São Paulo, Brazil. The Service provides industry with over 30,000 reports on compensation subjects each year.

OBJECTIVES OF ECS

This Service has recognized from the start that each company's management compensation problems are distinctly its own—that industry, size of company, competition, age and experience of individuals, and availability of qualified personnel are the primary influences on management compensation practices. The necessity for equitable position relationships within companies is of paramount importance; however, companies have found that it is impractical to isolate themselves from what others are doing. The aim of the Service has been to provide information that will enable individual companies to make sound comparative judgments.

Furthermore, the information that is available must be organized and put into readily usable form. The purpose of ECS is to provide an orderly basis for measuring a company's compensation practices against those of other companies of comparable size within their own industry as well as in industry in general. The Service is intended as a *guide* in establishing levels of pay and in improving other methods of compensation.

WHAT THE EXECUTIVE COMPENSATION SERVICE IS

ECS provides up-to-date facts on a continuing basis on how much and by what methods management personnel are paid. The Service covers positions from chief executive officer, down through first-line supervisors, including executive, staff, administrative, professional, sales, and supervisory personnel. Following is a listing of all of the Reports.

Domestic Compensation Service

1. Top Management Report
2. Statistical Supplement to Top Management Report
3. Middle Management Report
4. Administrative and Technical Report
5. Sales Personnel Report
6. Supervisory Management Report
7. Reports on Current and Deferred Incentive Compensation
8. Reports on Stock Purchase Plans
9. Reports on Salary Administration and Control
10. Reports on Benefits and Employment Contracts
11. Corporate Directorship Report

International Compensation Service

1. U. S. Expatriate Compensation Report plus International Divisions Report
2. United Kingdom Report
3. Federal Republic of Germany Report
4. Mexico Report
5. Brazil Report
6. Belgium Report
7. Netherlands Report

8. Switzerland Report
9. France Report
10. Argentina Report
11. Venezuela Report
12. Italy Report
13. Puerto Rico Report
14. Spain Report
15. Sweden Report
16. European Top Management Remuneration Report

The following sections describe the contents of six of the domestic reports.

Top Management Report.   For top management, ECS:

1. Reports average compensation of approximately 31,000 executives in 75 top positions in more than 3,800 companies.

2. Classifies companies in 53 different industries, each industry in a separate section. Summarizes each of the industry classifications in complete detail and presents overall summaries of major industrial groups.

3. Indicates the trend of sales and profits as a percent change from the previous year. Relates profits *after* taxes to sales. Shows average return on investment and relates all of these figures to the trends in compensation.

4. Reports compensation trends, related to sales and profits over the last *five-year* period in the industry sections, and summarizes trends in all industries since 1952.

5. Breaks down compensation into average salaries and average bonuses.

6. Shows five or more of the sales groups listed below for most industries:

ANNUAL SALES (IN MILLIONS)

Under $2	$50 to $100
$2 to $5	$100 to $200
$5 to $10	$200 to $500
$10 to $25	$500 to $1 billion
$25 to $50	Over $1 billion

7. Itemizes average annual sales, profits *after* taxes, average invested capital, and average number of employees for *each* industrial classification and *each* sales group.

8. Presents position descriptions for 21 typical top management positions found in the Report, with a chart showing typical organization relationships.

In addition, a comprehensive summary contains all-industry sales, profits, and compensation trends, sections relating compensation to responsibility, and the application of salary administration policies.

For small companies (under $10 million in sales), the Top Management Report provides compensation of executives in companies classified in 13 product categories plus an all-manufacturing summary. The compensation data are analyzed by company size based on sales volume in five groups at $2 million steps, from under $2 million to $8 to 10 million. In addition, average salaries and bonuses for eight top management positions are broken down by function.

For large companies (over $500 million in sales), the report classifies companies into five categories and analyzes their data by size based on sales volume. Also, the report shows relationship of salary to responsibility.

For divisional positions, comparison is made between compensation paid these positions and that paid similar positions in independent corporations.

Compensation is related to responsibility, and average salary and bonus are reported for eight top management positions by sales volume groups.

For Canadian companies, the report provides average compensation of some 3,000 executives in over 300 companies, either Canadian-owned or subsidiaries of United States companies.

Companies are classified into three categories and analyzed by size based on sales volume in up to seven groups. Average salaries and bonus payments are reported for 21 top management positions, with current-trend information, and comparisons are made of United States and Canadian compensation as a percentage of compensation in the United States.

The industries covered by the Top Management Report are listed below:

1. *Durable Goods Manufacturers*
   Aerospace
   Automobile and Truck
   Automotive Parts and Accessories
   Other Transportation Equipment
   Building Equipment
   Building Materials
   Electrical Equipment
   Electronics, Radio, and Television
   Fabricated Metal Products
   Furniture
   Glass and Allied Products
   Heavy Machinery
   Household Appliances
   Instruments and Allied Products
   Iron and Steel Foundries
   Iron and Steel Producers
   Light Machinery
   Non-ferrous Metals
   Office Machinery and Equipment
   Tools and Hardware
2. *Nondurable Goods Manufacturers*
   Bakery Products
   Beverages
   Chemicals
   Confectionery Products
   Cosmetics and Toilet Preparations
   Drugs and Medicines
   Food Products
   Grain Mill Products
   Leather and Leather Products
   Meat and Dairy Products
   Paper and Allied Products
   Printing
   Publishing
   Rubber
   Sugar
   Textiles—Apparel
   Textile Fabrics
   Tobacco
3. *Wholesale and Retail Trade*

      Department Stores
      Retail Chains—General Merchandise
      Retail Chains—Grocery and Drugs
      Wholesale Trade
4. *Utilities*
      Airlines
      Communications
      Gas and Electric
      Transportation
5. *Construction, Petroleum and Natural Gas, Finance, and Insurance*
      Banks and Trust Companies
      Finance Companies
      Insurance Carriers—General
      Life Insurance Companies

The management positions covered in the Report include:

Chief Executive Officer
Chief Operating Officer
Executive Vice President
Adminstrative Vice President
Long-range Planning Executive
Top Marketing Executive
Top Merchandising Executive
Top Manufacturing Executive
Top Financial Executive
Top Industrial Relations Executive
Top EDP Executive
Actuarial Executive
Advertising Executive
Agency Executive
Assistant to President
Auditors
Bond Department Executive
Branch Office Executive
Business Manager
Cashier
Circulation Executive
Claim Executive
Commercial Credit Officer
Commercial Executive
Construction Executive
Consumer Loan Officer
Controller and Comptroller
Credit Executive
Editorial Executive
Engineering Executive
Equipment Maintenance Executive
Estimating Executive
Exploration Executive
Freight Traffic Executive
General Management Executive
General Sales Executive
General Solicitor
Group Executive

Investment Executive
Job Superintendent
Legal Executive
Medical Executive
Mining Executive
Mortgage Department Executive
Operating Executive
Passenger Service Executive
Personnel Executive
Production Executive
Product Research Executive
Public Relations Executive
Publishers
Purchasing Executive
Traffic Executive
Rates Executive
Sales Executive
Secretary
Senior Customer Relations Officer
Senior Resident Counsel
Senior Trust Officer
Senior Vice President
Transmission Executive
Treasurer
Underwriting Executive

Middle Management Report. The Middle Management Report provides average percentages of exempt personnel on company payrolls, the trend of actual salaries, total payroll costs, adjustments in salaries and salary ranges, including general and merit increases, merit and promotional increase policies, communicating salary ranges, incentive compensation, and amounts budgeted for merit increases.

The report gives salaries for essentially all key positions between top policy-making jobs and first-line supervision, and breaks down each management position into job levels based on factors which influence compensation. The report makes possible direct comparisons between salaries in one company and amounts paid by other companies for similar responsibilities.

The report is based on the pay of more than 15,000 executives from 640 United States and Canadian companies in 73 fully described management functions, classified in more than 200 categories, from the smallest to the largest positions in each. In addition, the Canadian section provides comparisons with similar jobs in the United States.

The positions covered in the Middle Management Report include:
1. *Marketing*
    District Sales Executive
    Regional Sales Executive
    Government Sales Executive
    Product Planning Manager
    Sales Promotion Executive
    Export Sales Executive
    Marketing Research Executive
    Product or Brand Sales Executive
    Fleet Manager
    Advertising Manager

       Media Manager
       Trade Relations Executive
       Distribution Executive

2. *Manufacturing*
       Plant or Factory Manager
       Production Planning and Control Executive
       Quality Control Executive
       Reliability and Quality Assurance Executive
       Plant or Factory Superintendent
       Traffic Executive
       Manager of Materials
       Packaging Executive
       Purchasing Agent
       Warehouse Manager

3. *Financial and Legal*
       Banking and Cashiering Executive
       Corporate Insurance Administrator
       Top Tax Executive
       Contract Administration Manager
       Security Investments Director
       Credit and Collection Executive
       General Accounting Executive
       Cost Accounting Executive
       Plant or Works Accountant
       Electronic Data Processing Executive
       Systems and Procedures Executive
       Budgetary Control Executive
       General Auditor
       Chief Internal Auditor
       Office Management Executive
       General Attorney
       Patent Counsel
       Financial Analysis Executive
       Corporate Economist
       Long-range Planning Executive
       Operations Research Function

4. *Industrial and Public Relations*
       Employment Executive
       Employee Services Executive
       Employee Benefits Executive
       Labor Relations Executive
       Employee Training Executive
       Personnel Manager or Director
       Personnel Assistant
       Compensation Executive
       Management Development Executive
       Medical Director—Full-time
       Medical Director—Part-time
       Security Officer
       Safety Director
       Plant Personnel Executive
       Public Relations Manager
       Food Service Function

5. *Engineering and Research*
   Product Development Engineer
   Plant Maintenance Engineer
   Corporate Construction Engineer
   Chief Design Engineer
   Package Design Engineer
   Chief Industrial Engineer
   Plant Industrial Engineer
   Research and Development Executive
   Research Medical Director
   Process Research Executive
   Administrative Engineering Executive
   Installation Manager
   Service Manager

Administrative and Technical Positions Report.   The Administrative and Technical Positions Report is based on information supplied by 568 companies throughout the United States and Canada.

For each function surveyed, the report lists: a description of the activities covered, typical job titles, breakdown of positions into from three to six levels of skill and responsibility, current actual salaries, and salary range for each level of skill and responsibility, and further analysis of salary data by area of specialization.

The report also contains complete details on compensation trends, total payroll costs, frequency of salary payments, cost-of-living increases, incentive compensation, employment agreements, professional development programs, memberships in professional associations, salary administration, contract or temporary personnel, overtime payments, compensation differentials, and geographic location.

The positions covered in this report include:
1. *Administrative Field*
   Accountant
   Cost Accountant
   Credit Representative
   Tax Accountant
   Internal Auditor
   Budget Analyst
   Systems and Procedures Analyst
   Economic or Financial Analyst
   Attorney
   Patent Attorney
   Public Relations Representative
   Labor Relations Representative
   Job Analyst
   Employment Interviewer
   Technical Recruiter
   Personnel Assistant
   Industrial Physician
   Industrial Nurse
   Technical Librarian
   Publications Editor
   Buyer
   Value Analyst
   Administrative Assistant (Executive Secretary)

2. *Flight Occupations (Company-owned Aircraft Fleets)*
   Chief Pilot
   Captain
   Pilot
   Co-pilot
   Chief Mechanic
3. *Electronic Data Processing*
   Programmers
   Systems Analyst
   Supervisors
   Tape Librarian
   Scheduler
   Control Clerk
   Operators (Computers, Tabulating, Keypunch)
4. *Engineering Field*
   Mechanical Engineer
   Electrical and Electronics Engineer
   Chemical and Metallurgical Engineer
   Aeronautical Engineer
   Industrial Engineer
   Civil Engineer
   Ceramic Engineer
   Petroleum Engineer
   Mining Engineer
   Reliability Engineer
   Quality Control Engineer
   Safety Engineer
   Inside Sales Engineer
   Service Engineer
   Packaging Engineer
5. *Related Miscellaneous Technical Positions*
   Chief Draftsman
   Patent Draftsman
   Designer-Draftsman
   Designer
   Draftsman—Layout
   Draftsman—Detailer
   Specifications Writer
6. *Scientific Field*
   Chemist
   Microbiologist
   Biologist
   Mathematician
   Physicist
   Geologist (Mineral Deposits)
   Geologist (Petroleum)

Supervisory Management Compensation Report. The Supervisory Management Report provides, on a national and regional basis, an up-to-date, reliable source of information on salaries, salary ranges, and compensation practices for 55 categories of foremen and office supervisors, based on information furnished by 682 United States company locations. A special section reports data on supervisory positions in Canadian companies.

For each supervisory function surveyed, the report offers:

1. National and regional data on:
   - Current actual salaries and salary ranges for each level of skill and responsibility
   - Average rates of highest-paid employees supervised by each supervisory level
   - Average number of employees reporting to each supervisory level
2. A description of the activities supervised
3. Breakdown of the position into levels of skill and responsibility
4. Typical job titles

The report summarizes in detail recent compensation trends (in both the United States and Canada), salary range adjustments, merit increases and merit increase budgets, general increases, communicating salary ranges, differentials between supervisors' rates and those of employees supervised, working hours (factory and office), overtime pay practices, shift differentials, ratio of supervisory personnel to total employment, ratio of production employees to total employment, and training programs.

In addition, the report considers incentive compensation for supervisors, including detailed information and exhibits on:

1. Christmas bonuses
2. Year-end bonuses
3. Profit-sharing plans
4. Productivity plans
5. Management incentive plans
6. Supervisory incentive plans
7. Cost improvement and budgetary plans

The supervisory functions covered in this report include:

1. *Office Supervisors*
   Accounting and financial functions:
   Accounting and Bookkeeping—General
   Budgets—Statistics; Taxes—Auditing
   Cost Accounting; Inventory Control
   Payroll—Timekeeping
   Accounts Receivable—Payable
   Order Scheduling
   Order Handling—Billing; Credit
   Computer Equipment Operations
   Tabulating, Key Punch
   Office service functions:
   Office Administration; Clerical; Filing
   Typing—Stenography
   Mailing—Office Supplies
   Duplicating, Printing
   Telephone Switchboard (PBX)
   Other office supervisory functions:
   Production Planning and Control
   Purchasing; Traffic
2. *General Foremen*
   Production and Processing Functions
   Maintenance Functions; Service Functions
3. *Foremen*
   Production functions:
   Assembly—Light Bench
   Assembly—Heavy Bench

Assembly—Floor
Processing—Light Machine
Processing—Heavy Machine
Plating; Painting—Finishing; Packaging
Foundry, Core Room
Machine Shop—Production; Welding
Quality Control (Inspection, Testing)
Equipment Installation and Repair
Trades functions:
Maintenance and Construction—General
Carpentry, Masonry, Painting
Electrical Maintenance
Machine Shop—Maintenance
Pipefitting, Welding, Millwrighting
Tool, Die, and Gauge Making
Service functions:
Garage; Plant Protection
Power House, Boiler House
Equipment Operation; Yard Labor, Janitorial
Receiving, Shipping; Storeroom, Warehouse
Packing, Boxing, Crating
Material Handling, Trucking, Dispatching

SURVEY METHODS

Seven of the 11 reports in the domestic service deal primarily with salaries and bonuses paid to selected positions. These reports are Top and Middle Management, Administrative and Technical, Supervisory and Sales Personnel, the Corporate Directorship, and the Statistical Supplement to Top Management. Compensation data are obtained from over 6,000 companies in response to mailed survey questionnaires. Each questionnaire is carefully prepared to ensure that companies can match their positions to those for which compensation information is requested. The questionnaires range in complexity from a one-page Top Management Questionnaire, which is based on the use of functional titles such as "Top Marketing Executive," to a 50-page Administrative and Technical Positions Questionnaire, which is based on a classification guide that sets up predetermined responsibility levels.

Each year the companies invited to participate are carefully selected to secure a good cross section of all sizes in all industries covered. When replies are received, they are coded according to the requirements of the particular survey. Those replies in the control groups from which trend information is secured are matched with previous years' data. The data are then punched onto cards, and computer reports are run to develop both trend information and current-year compensation data. These tabulations are carefully studied and evalauted to be certain the data are typical, with unusual, extreme, and irregular information removed.

PRACTICAL APPLICATION OF SURVEY DATA

Generally speaking, the most usable and effective survey is one that is conducted by the company that intends to make decisions based on the results. In this situation, key factors such as comparability of participants in terms of company size, industry, and competition can be carefully controlled. Benchmark positions included in the survey can be selected to ensure a representative coverage of the total number of positions to be affected. What is perhaps most important is that the survey questionnaire can be designed to minimize the effect of differences between jobs with the same title. Finally, the standards of the analytical process can be kept on a high objective level.

As previously stated, ECS survey reports are intended as *guides* for establishing, maintaining, and administering compensation. While the various surveys are broad-based, they have benefited from the fact that each was the product of professionals in compensation administration.

15.3 Bureau of Labor Statistics

L. EARL LEWIS *Chief, Division of Occupational Wage Structures, Bureau of Labor Statistics, U.S. Department of Labor, Washington, D.C.*

The U.S. Department of Labor's Bureau of Labor Statistics conducts, each year, a large number of occupational wage surveys that are useful in wage and salary administration. They are of three major types: (1) *area wage surveys,* which provide data for occupations common to a wide variety of industries in the communities surveyed; (2) *industry wage surveys,* which provide data for occupations characteristic of the industry studied; and (3) the *National Survey of Professional, Administrative, Technical, and Clerical Pay.* Although differing in industrial, geographic, and occupational coverage, the three types of surveys form an integrated program of occupational wage surveys. A common set of survey methods, concepts, and definitions apply to each.

Survey findings are published in a variety of formats. First results are issued as press releases or advance tabulations that are available upon request from the Bureau of Labor Statistics, Washington, D.C. 20212, or from any of its regional offices.[1] Final reports are issued as sale bulletins and may be purchased from the Superintendent of Documents, U.S. Government Printing Office, Washington, D.C. 20402, or from the BLS regional offices. Many surveys are summarized in the Bureau's *Monthly Labor Review.*

[1] Addresses of the Bureau's eight regional offices are: *Atlanta, Georgia* 30309, Suite 540, 1371 Peachtree Street, N.E.; *Boston, Massachusetts* 02203, 1603-B Federal Office Building, Government Center; *Chicago, Illinois* 60604, 219 South Dearborn Street; *Dallas, Texas* 75202, 100 Commerce Street, Room 6B7; *Kansas City, Missouri* 64106, Federal Office Building, 911 Walnut Street, 10th Floor; *New York, New York* 10001, 341 Ninth Avenue; *Philadelphia, Pennsylvania* 19107, 406 Penn Square Building, 1317 Filbert Street; *San Francisco, California* 94102, 450 Golden Gate Avenue, Box 36017.

DESCRIPTION OF SURVEYS

Area Wage Surveys.   The Bureau's fiscal 1970 program of area wage surveys covered 168 localities, for which separate reports were (or will be) issued.[2] Eighty-five of these are the Standard Metropolitan Statistical Areas in the regular BLS program and were selected so that, with appropriate weighting, national and regional estimates for all SMSAs can be obtained.   The remainder of the areas were surveyed for other government agencies on a reimbursable basis and are a mixture of SMSAs and otherwise defined geographical locations; the occupational and industrial coverage of these surveys also differs slightly from that used in the Bureau's regular program.

All area wage surveys provide earnings information for a number of occupations common to a wide variety of industries and are intended to provide representation of the range of duties and responsibilities associated with white-collar, skilled maintenance trades, and other "indirect" manual jobs.   Measures of straight-time rates of pay that are provided include the mean, median, interquartile range, and full distribution of workers by narrow earnings classes. Data are provided for all industries covered by the survey, with separate tabulations, wherever practical, for major industry divisions.[3]

Area wage surveys are conducted annually, but in alternate years they also develop, separately for nonsupervisory office workers and for plant (nonoffice) workers, information on work schedules, shift operations, and pay differentials, and the incidence of paid holidays and paid vacation, health, insurance, and pension plans.

Industry Wage Surveys.   Approximately 50 manufacturing and 20 nonmanufacturing industries are covered by the Bureau's industry wage survey program. These industries were selected to give as broad a coverage of the nation's important industries as possible within the limits of available resources.   A majority of the selected industries are studied on a five-year cycle, but several comparatively low-wage industries are on a three-year cycle.[4]

Nearly all of the manufacturing, utilities, and mining industries are studied on a nationwide basis, with separate estimates for regions and areas of major concentration.   Surveys in trade, finance, and service industries usually are limited to selected metropolitan areas.

The occupations for which data are developed vary with each industry. They are selected as being characteristic of the particular industry and to provide representativeness of the range of rates, of methods of wage payment, and of men's and women's work activities.   Consideration in their selection is also given to the prevalence in the industry, the definiteness and clarity of their duties, and their importance as reference points in collective bargaining or in wage administration.

In addition to information on straight-time rates of pay for workers in the selected occupations, surveys in most industries also establish the frequency distribution of wages for broad employment groups, e.g., all production and related workers or all nonsupervisory workers.

[2] See appendix A for a listing of areas in the Bureau's fiscal 1970 program.

[3] The major industry divisions covered by the Bureau's regular area wage survey program include: (1) manufacturing; (2) transportation, communication, and other public utilities; (3) wholesale trade; (4) retail trade; (5) finance, insurance, and real estate; and (6) selected service industries.   The industrial coverage of other area wage surveys differs slightly.

[4] See appendix B for a listing of industries studied by BLS since 1965.

Weekly work schedules, shift operations and differentials, paid holiday and vacation practices, and health, insurance, and pension benefits are typically included in the information provided, along with the provisions made for other similar items, applicable to certain industries. The surveys also generally provide estimates of labor-management agreement coverage, proportions employed under incentive wage plans, and the extent to which establishments provide a single rate or a range of rates for individual job categories.

The BLS industry wage survey program includes annual studies of wage rates and scheduled hours of work (hours after which premium overtime is paid) for specified crafts (jobs), as provided in labor-management agreements in four industries: building construction, printing, local transit, and local trucking.   Information is also obtained on employer contributions to welfare and pension funds. Tabulations are provided for the United States and separately for selected cities. These surveys differ in a number of important respects from other occupational wage surveys conducted by the Bureau: (1) the wage rate data relate to the *minimum* (basic) rates of pay agreed upon through collective bargaining, and thus are not necessarily the actual rates paid to workers; (2) the information is obtained by mail from local unions or other union organizations, rather than by personal visits to individual employers; and (3) occupational definitions are not used in the data collection process.

In the spring of 1970, BLS initiated a series of occupational wage surveys in the public sector.   Providing information on the salaries of incumbents in selected occupations and data on the nature of supplementary wage benefits for various occupational groups, separate reports were issued for the following municipal governments by September 1971: Atlanta, Boston, Buffalo, Chicago, Hartford, Kansas City, Los Angeles, Louisville, New Orleans, New York City, and Philadelphia.

The PATC Survey.   The national survey of professional, administrative, technical, and clerical pay, conducted annually since 1959–1960, provides a fund of broadly based information on salary levels and distributions in private employment.   The 80 occupational-work levels currently studied include the following occupational categories: accountants, auditors, attorneys, buyers, job analysts, directors of personnel, chemists, engineers, engineering technicians, draftsmen, and a number of office clerical jobs. Definitions for these occupations provide for classification of employees according to various work levels based on duties, responsibilities, experience, and education.

Although reflecting duties and responsibilities in industry, the definitions were designed to be translatable to specific pay grades in the general schedule applying to Federal Classification Act employees. This survey, thus, provides information in a form suitable for use in comparing the compensation of salaried employees in the federal civil service with pay in private industry.

For each occupation, the survey provides average straight-time weekly or monthly, as well as annual, salaries. Salary distributions are also provided. The survey provides only national estimates for establishments within the scope of the survey.[5]   Data are tabulated for all establishments, establishments in metropolitan areas, and establishments employing 2,500 or more workers.

This survey does not develop information on supplementary wage provisions.

---

[5] Industry divisions covered by this survey include: (1) manufacturing; (2) transportation, communication, electric, gas, and sanitary services; (3) wholesale trade; (4) retail trade; (5) finance, insurance, and real estate; and (6) engineering and architectural services and commercially operated research, development, and testing laboratories.

SURVEY METHODS AND CONCEPTS

Data are obtained by the Bureau's representatives through personal interviews with officials of companies in the sample. Cooperation in these, as in all other surveys conducted by BLS, is on a voluntary basis. Individual data are kept strictly confidential. In the compilation of grouped data in all published reports, care is taken to avoid possible disclosure of an establishment's rates.

In the planning stage, consultations are held with appropriate management, labor, and government representatives to obtain views and recommendations related to scope, timing, selection and definition of survey items, and types of tabulations to be published. The industrial scope of each survey is identified in terms of the classification system provided in the *Standard Industrial Classification Manual*, prepared by the Bureau of the Budget. The scope may range from part of a four-digit code for an industry wage study to a uniform combination of broad industry divisions for the area wage studies.

The minimum size of establishment included in a particular survey is set at a point where the possible contribution of the excluded establishments is regarded as negligible for most of the occupations selected for study. Another practical reason for the adoption of size-of-establishment limitations is the difficulty of classifying workers in small establishments where they do not perform the specialized duties indicated in job definitions suitable for survey purposes.

The sampling design employed by the Bureau is almost always highly stratified. The sample is selected from a list of all known establishments that might possibly fall within the scope of the survey, which is compiled from information provided by regulatory governmental agencies (primarily state unemployment insurance agencies) supplemented, as required, by other sources such as trade directories and labor and management associations.

The sample for each survey is a probability sample, each establishment having a predetermined chance of selection. In order to secure maximum accuracy at a fixed level of cost (or a fixed level of accuracy at minimum cost), the sampling fraction used in the various strata ranges downward from all large establishments through progressively declining proportions of the establishments in each smaller size group, in accordance with the principles of optimum allocation. Thus, each sampled stratum will be represented in the sample by a number of establishments roughly proportionate to its share of the total employment. Although this procedure may appear at first to yield a sample biased by the overrepresentation of large firms, the method of estimation employed avoids the possibility of this bias by the assignment of proper weights to the sample establishments. The size of the sample in a particular survey depends on the number of establishments within the scope of the survey, the diversity and distribution of the occupations selected for study, the relative dispersion of earnings among establishments, and the degree of accuracy required. Estimates of variance based on data from previous surveys are used in determining the size of the sample needed.

All estimates are derived from the sample data. Estimated average earnings are weighted averages of individual earnings and are not computed on an establishment basis. The proportion of employees affected by any supplementary wage benefit provision is also estimated from the sample.

The types of occupations studied vary by each type of survey, as explained previously. Occupational classifications are defined in advance of the surveys. Because of the emphasis on interestablishment and interarea comparability of occupational content, the Bureau's job descriptions may differ significantly from those in use in individual establishments or those prepared for other purposes. They are typically brief and usually more generalized than those prepared by individual concerns. The primary objective of the descriptions is to identify the essential elements of skill, difficulty, and responsibility that establish the basic concept of the job.

It should be recognized that, although work arrangements in any one establishment may not correspond precisely to those described, those workers meeting the basic requirements established by the BLS definition are included. In general, workers are included in a classification if the duties as described are performed a major part of the time and the remainder is spent on related duties requiring similar or lesser skill and responsibility. However, in some instances, workers may regularly perform a combination of duties involving more than one occupation as described by BLS. In these situations, consideration for classification purposes is given to those elements of the job which are most important in determining its level for pay purposes.[6]

In applying these job descriptions, the Bureau's data collectors are instructed to exclude working supervisors, apprentices, learners, beginners, trainees, handicapped workers, and workers paid special rates for reasons of their part-time or probationary employment.

The measure of wages used by the Bureau in its occupational wage surveys relates to rates of pay for individual workers which exclude premium pay for overtime and for work on weekends, holidays, and late shifts. In the case of workers paid under piecework or other types of production incentive pay plans, an earned rate is obtained by dividing straight-time earnings for a time period by the corresponding hours worked. Production bonuses, commissions, and cost-of-living bonuses are included. Bonuses that depend on factors other than output are generally excluded.[7] Also, rates do not include tips or allowances for the value of meals, room, uniforms, etc.

Most of the surveys also develop information on the incidence of important supplementary wage benefits such as paid holidays, paid vacations, and health, insurance, and pension plans for which the employer pays at least part of the cost. These items are treated statistically on the basis that they are applicable to all workers in a designated category if a majority of such workers are eligible or can expect eventually to qualify for the benefit.

Job functions and factors in the establishment are carefully compared with those included in the Bureau's job definitions. A satisfactory completion of job matching permits acceptance of company-prepared reports where this procedure is preferred by the respondent. Generally, however, the Bureau's representative secures wage and salary information from payrolls or other records and data on the incidence of selected employer practices and supplementary benefits from company officials, company booklets, and labor-management agreements.

SURVEY USES AND LIMITATIONS

Data developed by the Bureau's occupational wage surveys have a variety of uses. Federal, state, and local governments use them in wage and salary ad-

---

[6] Thus, a worker would meet the basic concept of a stenographer classification if taking of dictation is a regular requirement of the job, even though a majority of time is spent on routine typing.

[7] Examples of such nonproduction payments are safety, attendance, year-end or Christmas bonuses, and cash distributions under profit-sharing plans.

ministration and in the formulation of public policy on wages. They are of value to federal and state mediation and conciliation services and to state unemployment compensation agencies in judging the suitability of job offers.

The data are also widely used in connection with private wage and salary determinations by employers or through the collective bargaining process. To the extent that wages are a factor, the data are also useful to employers in selecting locations for new facilities and in estimating costs for contract work.

Published reports for each area and industry surveyed by BLS provide occupational earnings information that may be useful to individual organizations for purposes of comparison and the determination of recent trends in pay levels. The Bureau's occupational wage surveys, however, are not designed to supply mechanical answers to questions of pay policy or administration.

Limitations on use of BLS surveys are imposed by the selection and definition of geographic units and industries for which estimates are developed, of occupations and associated items studied, and the periodicity and timing of the surveys. Depending upon his needs, the user may find it necessary to interpolate for occupations, industries, or areas missing from the program.

The averages developed by these surveys also have inherent limitations which should be carefully considered when they are used in pay administration. They are developed by grouping information from a large number of individual establishments which may differ considerably in their general pay levels and in their relative contributions to the aggregate data. Because of this, the published estimates do not necessarily reflect either the absolute or the relative occupational wage relationships found in most establishments. For example, employment in certain skilled maintenance crafts tends to be concentrated in the larger, higher-paying establishments, whereas employment in custodial and material-movement jobs is more widely distributed among establishments. In such a situation, the skill differential measure based on the survey averages will be greater than that maintained by most establishments. A similar condition often exists in the pay differences for men and women. Almost always, when occupational data are provided for both sexes, the survey average for men exceeds the average for women. Detailed studies by BLS indicate, however, that these differences are not indicative of differences within individual establishments. They result more from differences in the employment of the two sexes among establishments with different pay levels and from minor variations in duties.[8]

Year-to-year changes in averages for a specific occupation are not always accurate indicators of the movement of wage rates in the particular area or industry surveyed. They reflect not only the general changes in wage and salary rates, but also changes in the proportion of workers paid at different steps in the rate-range pay systems of individual establishments. During a period of a rapidly expanding employment, for example, pay rates of newly hired employees of companies with rate-range plans will have a depressing effect on the average. Also, large shifts of employment between relatively high- and low-paying companies can affect the BLS average. A decline in the BLS average would occur even though all companies retained their previous wage scales if the proportionate employment in the occupation shifted significantly from the high-paying companies to those paying less.

---

[8] In recognition of these survey limitations, BLS from time to time conducts detailed studies of occupational wage relationships and the pay differences for men and women. Results of these studies are available to the public.

Results of the BLS surveys are generally subject to sampling error. This error will not be uniform, since for most occupations the dispersion of earnings among establishments and the frequency of occurrence of the occupations differ. In general, the sample is designed so that the chances are nine out of ten that the published average does not differ by more than 5 percent from the average that would be obtained by enumeration of all establishments within scope of the survey. That error applies to the smallest breakdown published. Hence, the error present in broader groupings will be somewhat less.

The sampling error of the estimates related to the percentage of workers receiving a specific supplementary benefit (vacations, holidays, etc.) differs with the size of that percentage. However, the error is such that rankings of predominant practices almost always will appear in their true position. Small percentages may be subject to considerable error, but they will always remain in the same scale of magnitude.

Estimates of the number of workers in a given occupation are subject to considerable sampling error, as a result of the wide variation among establishments in the proportion of workers found in individual occupations. Hence, the estimated number of workers reported can be interpreted as only a rough measure of the relative importance of various occupations. This sampling error, however, does not materially affect the accuracy of the average earnings shown for the occupations.

Since some measure of subjective judgment enters into the classification of occupations and other items studied, there is some reporting variability in the results. A repetition of the survey in any establishment with different interviewers and respondents would undoubtedly produce slightly different results. However, when spread over a large number of establishments the differences, being random, would tend to balance out. Hence, analyses based on a small number of respondents must be used with care, even when all eligible establishments are studied.

APPENDIX A   BLS Area Wage Survey Program, Fiscal Year 1970

Area	Type of survey[1]	Reference date	Area	Type of survey[1]	Reference date
*Abilene, Tex.............	F	March, 1970	*Bakersfield, Calif..........	F	Feb., 1970
Akron, Ohio.............	I	July, 1970	Baltimore, Md............	I	Aug., 1969
*Alaska...................	F	July, 1969	*Baton Rouge, La..........	I	March, 1970
*Albany, Ga..............	I	Dec., 1969	*Battle Creek, Mich........	I	Apr., 1970
Albany-Schenectady-			Beaumont-Port Arthur-		
Troy, N.Y..............	I	Feb., 1970	Orange, Tex............	I	May, 1970
Albuquerque, N. Mex......	F	March, 1970	*Billings, Mont.............	I	March, 1970
*Alexandria, La...........	F	Jan., 1970	Binghamton (New York		
Allentown-Bethlehem-			State portion only)......	I	July, 1969
Easton, Pa.-N.J.........	F	May, 1970	Birmingham, Ala..........	I	March, 1970
*Alpena, Standish, and			Boise City, Idaho.........	I	Nov., 1969
Tawas City, Mich.......	I	May, 1970	Boston, Mass.............	I	Aug., 1969
*Amarillo, Tex............	F	June, 1970	*Bridgeport, Norwalk, and		
*Ann Arbor, Mich.........	F	Feb., 1970	Stamford, Conn........	F	Feb., 1970
*Aroostook, Penobscot,			Buffalo, N.Y.............	I	Oct., 1969
Washington, and Hancock			Burlington, Vt............	I	March, 1970
Counties, Me...........	F	Apr., 1970	Canton, Ohio............	F	May, 1970
*Ashville, N.C............	I	Feb., 1970	*Charleston, S.C...........	F	Sept., 1969
Atlanta, Ga..............	F	May, 1970	Charleston, W. Va........	F	Apr., 1970
*Atlantic City, N.J........	I	Dec., 1969	Charlotte, N.C............	F	March, 1970
*Augusta, Ga.-S.C.........	F	Feb., 1970	Chattanooga, Tenn.-Ga.....	I	Sept., 1969

See footnotes at end of table.

APPENDIX A   BLS Area Wage Survey Program, Fiscal Year 1970 (continued)

Area	Type of survey[1]	Reference date	Area	Type of survey[1]	Reference date
*Cheyenne, Wyo.	F	Apr., 1970	Los Angeles-Long Beach and Anaheim-Santa Ana-Garden Grove, Calif.	I	March, 1970
Chicago, Ill.	I	June, 1970	Louisville, Ky.-Ind.	F	Nov., 1969
*Christian County, Ky., and Montgomery County, Tenn.	I	March, 1970	*Lower Eastern Shore, Md.-Va.	I	Aug., 1969
Cincinnati, Ohio-Ky.-Ind.	I	Feb., 1970	Lubbock, Tex.	F	March, 1970
Cleveland, Ohio	I	Sept., 1969	*Lynchburg, Va.	F	Oct., 1969
*Colorado Springs, Colo.	F	Nov., 1969	*Macon, Ga.	I	Dec., 1969
*Columbia, S.C.	I	Feb., 1970	*Madison, Wis.	F	May, 1970
*Columbus, Ga.-Ala.	I	July, 1969	Manchester, N.H.	I	July, 1969
Columbus, Ohio	I	Oct., 1969	*Marquette, Sault Ste. Marie, and Escanaba, Mich.	I	May, 1970
*Crane, Ind.	F	Nov., 1969	Memphis, Tenn.-Ark.	F	Nov., 1969
Dallas, Tex.	I	Oct., 1969	Miami, Fla.	I	Nov., 1969
Davenport-Rock Island-Moline, Iowa-Ill.	F	Oct., 1969	*Middlesex, Monmouth, Ocean, and Somerset Counties, N.J.	F	Dec., 1969
Dayton, Ohio	I	Dec., 1969	Midland and Odessa, Tex.	F	Jan., 1970
*Decatur, Ill.	F	May, 1970	Milwaukee, Wis.	F	May, 1970
Denver, Colo.	F	Dec., 1969	Minneapolis-St. Paul, Minn.	F	Jan., 1970
Des Moines, Iowa	F	May, 1970	*Mobile, Ala., and Pensacola, Fla.	F	Aug., 1969
Detroit, Mich.	I	Feb., 1970	*Montgomery, Ala.	F	July, 1969
*Dothan, Ala.	I	Dec., 1969	Muskegon-Muskegon Heights, Mich.	F	June, 1970
*Duluth-Superior, Minn.-Wis.	F	June, 1970	*Nashville, Tenn.	F	Nov., 1969
*Durham, N.C.	I	Apr., 1970	Newark and Jersey City, N.J.	F	Jan., 1970
*El Paso, Tex.	F	Apr., 1970	New Haven, Conn.	F	Jan., 1970
*Eugene, Oreg.	F	Apr., 1970	*New London-Groton-Norwich, Conn.	I	Dec., 1969
*Fargo-Moorhead, N. Dak.-Minn.	F	March, 1970	New Orleans, La.	I	Jan., 1970
*Fayetteville, N.C.	I	Apr., 1970	New York, N.Y.	F	Apr., 1970
*Fitchburg-Leominster, Mass.	I	Aug., 1969	Norfolk-Portsmouth and Newport News-Hampton, Va.	F	Jan., 1970
*Fort Smith, Ark.-Okla.	I	Dec., 1969	*Ogden, Utah	F	Nov., 1969
Fort Worth, Tex.	I	Oct., 1969	Oklahoma City, Okla.	F	July, 1969
*Fresno, Calif.	I	May, 1970	Omaha, Nebr.-Iowa	F	Sept., 1969
*Great Falls, Mont.	I	March, 1970	*Orlando, Fla.	F	Sept., 1969
Green Bay, Wis.	I	July, 1969	*Oxnard-Ventura, Calif.	I	Nov., 1969
*Greensboro—Winston-Salem—High Point, N.C.	F	Oct., 1969	*Panama City, Fla.	I	Dec., 1969
Greenville, S.C.	I	May, 1970	Paterson-Clifton-Passaic, N.J.	F	June, 1970
*Harrisburg, Pa.	F	Dec., 1969	Philadelphia, Pa.-N.J.	F	Nov., 1969
*Hartford, Conn.	I	Dec., 1969	Phoenix, Ariz.	F	March, 1970
Houston, Tex.	I	Apr., 1970	*Pine Bluff, Ark.	I	July, 1969
*Huntsville, Ala.	I	Feb., 1970	Pittsburgh, Pa.	F	Jan., 1970
Indianapolis, Ind.	I	Oct., 1969	Portland, Me.	F	Nov., 1969
Jackson, Miss.	I	Jan., 1970	Portland, Oreg.-Wash.	F	May, 1970
*Jackson and Harrison Counties, Miss.	F	July, 1969	*Portsmouth, N.H.	F	Feb., 1970
Jacksonville, Fla.	I	Dec., 1969	Providence-Pawtucket-Warwick, R.I.-Mass.	I	May, 1970
Kansas City, Mo.-Kans.	I	Sept., 1969	Raleigh, N.C.	I	Aug., 1969
*Knoxville, Tenn.	F	Nov., 1969	*Reno, Nev.	F	March, 1970
*Laredo, Tex.	I	Feb., 1970			
*Las Vegas, Nev.	I	July, 1969			
Lawrence-Haverhill, Mass.-N.H.	F	June, 1970			
*Lexington, Ky.	F	Nov., 1969			
Little Rock-North Little Rock, Ark.	I	July, 1969			
*Lorain-Elyria, Ohio	I	Dec., 1969			

See footnotes at end of table.

APPENDIX A   BLS Area Wage Survey Program, Fiscal Year 1970 (continued)

Area	Type of survey[1]	Reference date	Area	Type of survey[1]	Reference date
Richmond, Va.............	F	March, 1970	*Springfield, Ill.............	I	Oct., 1969
Rochester, N.Y.			*Springfield-Chicopee-		
(office only)............	I	July, 1969	Holyoke, Mass.-Conn....	I	Oct., 1969
Rockford, Ill.............	F	May, 1970	*Stockton, Calif............	I	May, 1970
*Sacramento, Calif.........	I	Dec., 1969	Syracuse, N.Y..............	I	July, 1969
St. Louis, Mo.-Ill.........	I	March, 1970	*Tacoma, Wash............	I	Jan., 1970
*Salina, Kans..............	I	Feb., 1970	Tampa-St. Petersburg, Fla..	F	Aug., 1969
*Salinas-Monterey, Calif.....	I	May, 1970	Toledo, Ohio-Mich.........	I	Feb., 1970
Salt Lake City, Utah......	F	Nov., 1969	*Topeka, Kans.............	F	Oct., 1969
San Antonio, Tex..........	I	May, 1970	Trenton, N.J..............	I	Sept., 1969
San Bernardino-Riverside-			*Tucson, Ariz..............	F	March, 1970
Ontario, Calif..........	I	Dec., 1969	Utica-Rome, N.Y.........	I	July, 1969
San Diego, Calif..........	F	Nov., 1969	*Valdosta, Ga..............	I	July, 1969
San Francisco-Oakland,			*Vallejo-Napa, Calif.......	F	Sept., 1969
Calif.................	F	Oct., 1969	Washington, D.C.-Md.-Va..	F	Sept., 1969
San Jose, Calif............	F	Sept., 1969	Waterbury, Conn..........	F	March, 1970
*Santa Barbara, Calif......	I	Jan., 1970	Waterloo, Iowa...........	I	Jan., 1970
Savannah, Ga.............	F	May, 1970	Wichita, Kans.............	F	Apr., 1970
Scranton, Pa.............	I	July, 1969	*Wilkes-Barre–Hazleton,		
Seattle-Everett, Wash......	I	Jan., 1970	Pa....................	I	Feb., 1970
*Sherman-Denison, Tex.....	I	March, 1970	*Wilmington, Del.-N.J.-Md..	F	Nov., 1969
*Shreveport, La............	F	Apr., 1970	Worcester, Mass..........	F	May, 1970
Sioux Falls, S. Dak.......	I	Sept., 1969	York, Pa.................	F	Feb., 1970
South Bend, Ind...........	F	March, 1970	Youngstown-Warren, Ohio.	F	Nov., 1969
Spokane, Wash...........	F	June, 1970			

* Service Contract Act surveys are similar to those conducted under the Bureau's regular program but are more limited in industrial coverage, number of occupations studied, and types of supplementary benefits for which data are provided.

[1] The letter "F" designates a full survey of occupational earnings and establishment practices and supplementary wage provisions. The letter "I" designates an interim survey, limited to occupational earnings data.

APPENDIX B: BLS Industry Wage Survey Program, July, 1965–June, 1970

Industry	Date of last survey	Expected year of next survey
Part I. Regular Program Surveys		
Manufacturing		
Food and kindred products:		
Meat products............................	Jan., 1969	1974
Fluid milk...............................	Sept.–Oct., 1964	1970
Flour and other grain-mill products...........	Feb., 1967	1972
Candy and other confectionery products.......	Sept., 1965	1970
Tobacco manufactures:		
Cigarettes................................	July–Aug., 1965	1970
Cigars...................................	Mar., 1967	1972
Textile-mill products:		
Cotton and man-made fiber textiles..........	Sept., 1968	1971
Woolen and worsted textiles.................	Nov., 1966	1971
Hosiery (full-fashioned and seamless)........	Sept., 1967	1970
Dyeing and finishing textiles................	Winter, 1965–1966	1971

See footnotes at end of table.

APPENDIX B: BLS Industry Wage Survey Program, July, 1965–June, 1970 (continued)

Industry	Date of last survey	Expected year of next survey
Apparel:		
Men's and boys' suits and coats..............	Apr., 1970	1973
Men's and boys' shirts (except workshirts), collars, and neckwear.....................	Oct., 1968	1971
Work clothing.............................	Feb., 1968	1971
Women's and misses' dresses................	Aug., 1968	1971
Women's and misses' coats and suits..........	Aug., 1965	1970
Lumber and wood products:		
Sawmills and planing mills (South)............	Oct., 1969	1972
Sawmills and planing mills (West Coast).......	Oct., 1969	1974
Furniture and fixtures:		
Wood household furniture, except upholstered..	Oct., 1968	1971
Paper and allied products:		
Pulp, paper, and paperboard mills............	Oct., 1967	1972
Paperboard containers and boxes.............	Jan., 1970	1975
Printing, publishing, and allied industries:		
Newspaper printing[1].......................	July, 1969	1970
Book and job printing[1].....................	July, 1969	1970
Lithography[1].............................	July, 1969	1970
Chemicals and allied products:		
Industrial chemicals.......................	Nov., 1965	1970
Synthetic fibers...........................	Feb.–Apr., 1966	1971
Paints and varnishes.......................	Nov., 1965	1970
Fertilizers................................	Mar.–Apr., 1966	Not available
Petroleum refining and related industries:		
Petroleum refining........................	Dec., 1965	1970
Rubber and miscellaneous plastics products:		
Miscellaneous plastics products..............	Aug., 1969	1974
Leather and leather products:		
Leather tanning and finishing................	Jan., 1968	1973
Footwear.................................	Mar., 1968	1971
Stone, clay, and glass products:		
Glass and glassware, pressed or blown........	May, 1970	1975
Structural clay products....................	Sept., 1969	1974
Primary metal industries:		
Blast furnaces, steel works, and rolling mills....	Sept., 1967	1972
Iron and steel foundries.....................	Nov., 1967	1972
Nonferrous foundries.......................	June, 1970	1975
Fabricated metal products:		
Fabricated structural steel..................	Oct., 1969	1974
Machinery, except electrical..................	Fall, 1968	1970
Transportation equipment:		
Motor vehicles............................	Apr., 1969	1974
Motor vehicle parts........................	Apr., 1969	1974
Nonmanufacturing		
Mining:		
Bituminous coal...........................	Jan., 1967	1972
Crude petroleum and gas...................	Aug., 1967	1972
Contract construction:		
Building trades[1]...........................	July, 1969	1970

See footnotes at end of table.

APPENDIX B: BLS Industry Wage Survey Program, July, 1965–June, 1970 (continued)

Industry	Date of last survey	Expected year of next survey
Transportation, communication, electric, gas, and sanitary services:		
Local transit[1]	July, 1969	1970
Trucking[1]	July, 1969	1970
Communications	Late 1969	1970
Electric and gas utilities	Oct., 1967	1972
Retail trade:		
Auto dealer repair shops	Aug., 1969	1974
Finance, insurance, and real estate:		
Banks	Dec., 1969	1974
Life insurance	Oct.–Nov., 1966	1971
Contract cleaning services	July, 1968	1971
Services:		
Hotels	(See special	1975
Power laundries and dry cleaning	surveys	1971
Hospitals	below)	1972
Part II. Special Surveys[2]		
Eating and drinking places	Mar., 1970	Not available
Hospitals	Mar., 1969	Not available
Hotels and motels	Mar., 1970	Not available
Laundries and cleaning services	Apr., 1967 and Apr., 1968	Not available
Motion picture theaters	Apr., 1966	Not available
Nursing homes and related facilities	Oct., 1967 and Apr., 1968	Not available
Educational institutions	Oct., 1968 and Mar., 1969	Not available

[1] Annual survey of basic (minimum) wage rates and maximum schedules of hours at straight-time rates, as determined by collective bargaining between trade unions and employers.

[2] Special surveys are conducted by BLS, as required by the Wage and Hour and Public Contracts Divisions (WHPC) of the U.S. Department of Labor. Surveys of hotels, power laundries and dry cleaners, and hospitals (limited to selected localities) are included in the regular BLS program. The most recent surveys in these industries were made at WHPC requests and are nationwide in scope.

15.4   Maturity Curve Surveys

HENRY C. RICKARD   *Director, International Compensation Coordination, Edward N. Hay & Associates, Philadelphia, Pennsylvania*

It is traditional for engineers and scientists to compare salaries on the maturity curve or "age-wage" basis—that is, salary related to years since bachelor's degree. This kind of analysis characterizes most salary surveys conducted by the engineering societies.

It also is the approach utilized in the comprehensive survey of compensation paid to scientists and engineers engaged in research and development which the Battelle Memorial Institute conducts for the U.S. Atomic Energy Commission.

Representative of this traditional method is the biennial study by the Engineering Manpower Commission of the Engineers Joint Council (EJC). This in turn follows the maturity pattern of the first major survey which the EJC conducted of the engineering profession—the landmark report printed in 1946 entitled "The Engineering Profession in Transition."

Since this report clearly illustrates the basic concepts, the following three figures are taken from the 1946 EJC Report, although the further figures in this section are from current publications.

Typically, maturity curves consider salaries from two different aspects: (1) the educational level of the person; (2) the industry or field of his activity. These are often supplemented by additional analyses of company size and geographical region and, within each category, by detail charts showing for each year the upper and lower deciles and quartiles, the median, and the mean.

Figure 2 compares the compensation practice for professional engineers of differing education levels. Monthly salary rates for five levels of education (Doctor, Master, Bachelor, etc.) are plotted against experience level, which, for college graduates, is taken to be years since first degree. Similarly, Figure 3 (with two panels) compares these engineers' median earnings by occupational status.

Figure 4 compares annual composite medians of all engineers for five significant years (1929, 1932, 1934, 1939, and 1943) and shows that salaries went down from 1929 (the heavy dashed line) to 1934 but increased substantially from 1934 to 1939 and again from 1939 to 1943. This chart shows, for instance, that the median salary for a man 10 years out in 1934 was $2,200. This same median man five years later (in 1939), who was then 15 years out, was earning $3,700.

Figure 2. Comparison of median base monthly salary rates of professional engineers in each of five educational levels—by experience level in 1946.

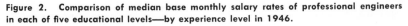

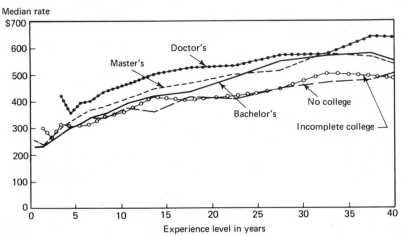

Figure 3.   Comparison of median base monthly salary rates of professional engineers in each of five educational levels—by occupational status in 1946.

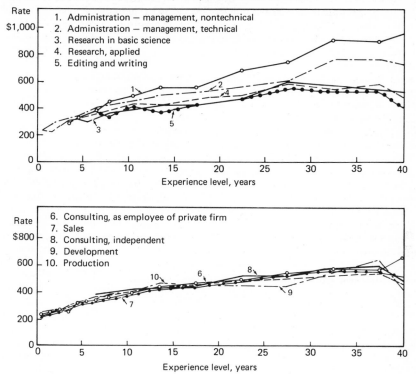

1. Administration — management, nontechnical
2. Administration — management, technical
3. Research in basic science
4. Research, applied
5. Editing and writing

6. Consulting, as employee of private firm
7. Sales
8. Consulting, independent
9. Development
10. Production

Figure 4.   Comparison of annual composite medians of all engineers for five significant years.

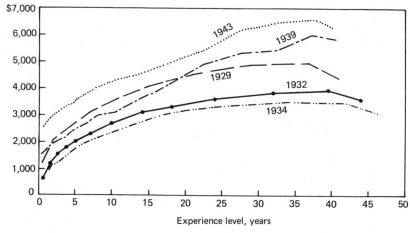

The Current Engineers Joint Council Surveys.   The EJC annual surveys continue in the basic tradition of the 1946 project.   The 1970 detailed report contains 136 pages, mostly of maturity charts by industry, geographical region, and size of company.   These are illustrated by the excerpts from *Engineer*, May–June, 1969, Figures 5 through 10, from the 1968 survey.   Information on the most recent reports is available from EJC, 345 E. 47th St., New York, N.Y. 10017.

Recent Trends of Earnings of Engineers.   Whereas median salaries dropped from 1929 to 1934 (see Figure 4), more recent trends have shown steady increases.   Figure 11 shows a comparison for the years 1953–1968.   In reading this chart, note that a "median-man" 10 years out of school in 1953 (C1) earned $6,200.   Fifteen years later, the equivalent median-man would have been 25 years out in 1968 and his earnings appear at $16,850.

The maturity curve analysis is intended to show overall levels and trends in engineering salaries without relation to measured job content except for the implication that a certain scholastic background and time factor probably correspond to an appropriate job level.   Where any individual's salary falls on the overall curves depends largely on his own innate capacity, his accumulated experiences, and the challenges in his job.   Certainly many young originators of important technical developments will not feel that an age-wage relationship should control their earnings.

Figure 5.   National norms: (a) supervisors and (b) nonsupervisors.

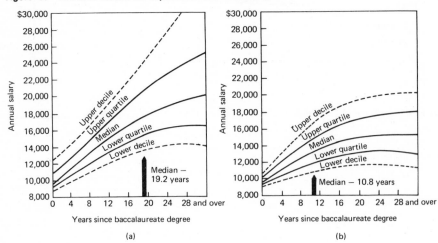

Years since baccalaureate degree

(a)   (b)

Figure 6.   Industry extremes: (a) aerospace and (b) state government.

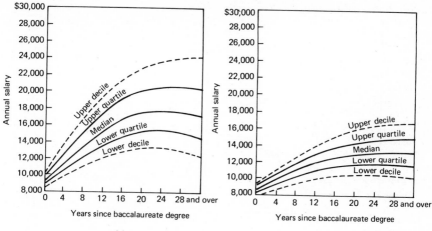

(a)

(b)

Figure 7.   Effect of degree.

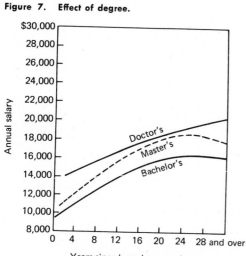

Years since baccalaureate degree

Figure 8.   Effect of location.

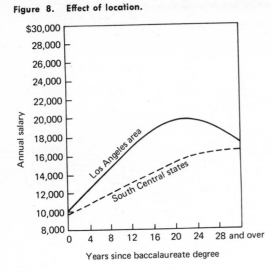

Years since baccalaureate degree

Figure 9.   Effect of employer size.

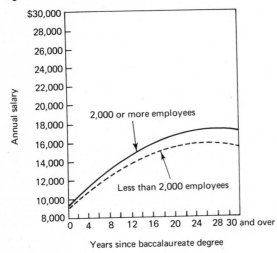

Years since baccalaureate degree

Figure 10.   Past surveys compared.

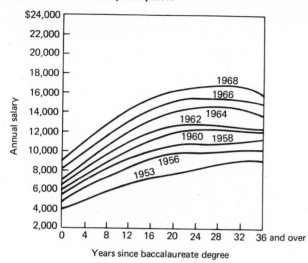

Figure 11. Trends in the earnings of engineering graduates, 1953–1968.

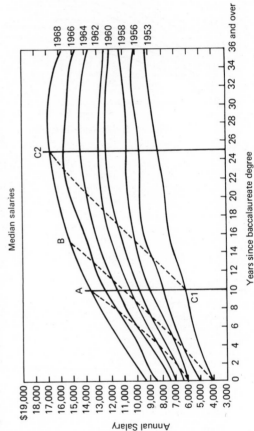

Table 1

Years since B.S.	0	1	2	3	4	5	6	7	8	9
Median ($) 1968	9,400	9,850	10,350	10,750	11,250	11,700	12,200	12,700	13,000	13,350
Avg. Annual % Increase 1966-68	6.0	7.5	7.5	6.5	7.5	6.5	7.0	6.0	6.0	5.5
Median ($) 1966	8,350	8,550	9,000	9,450	9,750	10,300	10,700	11,300	11,600	12,050
Avg. Annual % Increase 1964-66	7.0	6.0	5.5	5.5	4.5	4.0	3.5	4.0	4.0	4.5
Median ($) 1964	7,625	7,625	8,100	8,500	8,950	9,500	9,950	10,400	10,675	11,075
Avg. Annual % Increase 1962-64	4.0	4.0	4.5	3.0	3.5	4.5	5.0	5.0	4.5	4.5
Median ($) 1962	6,750	7,025	7,425	8,000	8,350	8,725	9,050	9,425	9,775	10,125
Avg. Annual % Increase 1960-62	3.5	2.0	2.0	3.5	3.5	4.0	3.5	3.0	2.5	2.5
Median ($) 1960	6,300	6,725	7,125	7,475	7,800	8,100	8,450	8,900	9,250	9,625
Avg. Annual % Increase 1958-60	4.0	5.0	5.0	5.0	5.5	4.5	4.5	5.0	5.0	5.0
Median ($) 1958	5,850	6,125	6,475	6,800	7,000	7,400	7,700	8,050	8,350	8,700
Avg. Annual % Increase 1956-58	8.0	5.5	6.5	6.0	5.0	5.5	5.0	5.0	5.0	5.0
Median ($) 1956	5,000	5,300	5,725	6,050	6,350	6,625	7,000	7,300	7,600	7,750
Avg. Annual % Increase 1953-56	7.5	7.5	7.5	8.5	8.0	7.5	8.0	10.0	10.0	9.0
Median ($) 1953	4,050	4,250	4,600	4,750	5,050	5,325	5,550	5,500	5,750	6,000
Total % Increase 1953-68	132	132	125	126	123	120	120	131	126	123

Table 2

Years since B.S.	10	15	20	25	30	35	40	Overall med. unadj.	Overall med. adj.*
Median ($) 1968	13,850	15,300	16,300	16,850	16,850	15,850	NA	15,000	13,900
Avg. Annual % Increase 1966-68	5.5	5.5	4.0	4.0	4.5	3.5	NA	9.5	8.0
Median ($) 1966	12,500	13,750	15,050	15,650	15,450	14,850	NA	12,500	11,850
Avg. Annual % Increase 1964-66	4.5	3.5	4.0	4.5	4.0	3.5	NA	5.0	6.5
Median ($) 1964	11,425	12,800	13,900	14,350	14,250	13,800	14,100	11,325	10,475
Avg. Annual % Increase 1962-64	4.5	3.5	4.5	5.5	6.0	5.0	6.5	4.5	2.0
Median ($) 1962	10,425	11,900	12,700	12,850	12,700	12,550	12,425	10,375	10,025
Avg. Annual % Increase 1960-62	3.0	4.0	2.5	2.0	1.5	1.5	1.0	4.0	2.0
Median ($) 1960	9,875	11,000	12,075	12,400	12,350	12,175	12,175	9,600	9,650
Avg. Annual % Increase 1958-60	4.0	5.0	5.5	7.5	6.5	4.5	6.0	4.5	4.5
Median ($) 1958	9,100	10,000	10,800	10,750	10,900	11,200	10,800	8,750	8,800
Avg. Annual % Increase 1956-58	8.0	3.5	5.0	4.5	3.5	5.0	5.0	6.5	5.0
Median ($) 1956	7,800	9,350	9,800	9,800	10,200	10,200	9,750	7,750	7,975
Avg. Annual % Increase 1953-56	8.0	8.0	8.0	5.0	5.0	3.5	2.5	6.0	7.5
Median ($) 1953	6,200	7,400	7,750	8,500	8,850	9,200	9,000	6,500	6,450
Total % Increase 1953-68	125	107	110	98	90	72	NA	131	115

NOTE: Above figures rounded to nearest $25 or .5%; nearest $50 since 1966. All percentages are compounded.
NA = Not Available. 35-year figure since 1966 covers 35 years and up.

Average yearly increases

	1953-56	1956-58	1958-60	1960-62	1962-64	1964-66	1966-68	Total increase 1953-68
Consumer Price Index	0.5	3.0	1.2	1.2	1.4	2.5	3.9	27.7
Gross Avg. Weekly Earnings of Prod. Workers in Mfg. Ind.	3.9	2.5	4.2	3.8	3.3	4.5	4.9	75.0

* Adjustments made for variation in length of experience.

3—59

15.5 The Hay Compensation Comparison

HENRY C. RICKARD   *Director, International Compensation Coordination, Edward N. Hay & Associates, Philadelphia, Pennsylvania*

The Hay Compensation Comparison is an analysis of salary dollars based on job size rather than job title or length of time since college degree. Concerned primarily with management jobs, the annual Hay survey updates and compares the salary practices of Hay clients whose jobs have been measured according to the universally applicable Hay scale.

Published in two basic U.S.A. editions, "Industrial" and "Financial," the survey encompasses all segments of industry, as well as banks, insurance companies, government units, educational institutions, nonprofit associations, and many other kinds of organizations. Hay offices in other countries maintain corresponding annual comparisons that include entirely local companies as well as foreign affiliates of large international corporations. Together these surveys constitute a worldwide index of salary practice which can be used by all participating companies regardless of industry, size and organization structure, and job functions.

The common standard of measurement derives from the Hay Guide Chart-Profile Method of job evaluation. As described in Section 12.4, each job is assigned certain point values based on the three critical aspects of job content —know-how, problem solving, and accountability—and the resultant total evaluation indicates the relative weight of each evaluated job in a company. Custom-fitted to each application, Guide Charts vary in overall point scope and in descriptive language, depending on company size, complexity, industry, etc. Moreover, companies operate under unique organizational influences, and different evaluation committees have different perspectives. Consequently, point values differ for each company; therefore, to permit comparisons, companies' point values are converted to the standard Hay scale by correlation. Points converted to the common scale are designated "Hay points" and expressed as H (for Hay) 200, H400, H600, etc.

Survey Input. The survey requires close collaboration between the consultant and the participants. In response to an annual questionnaire, each company provides detailed tabulations showing individual job titles and evaluation points, policy midpoints, actual base salaries, and total compensation payments. For each of these categories, dollars are plotted against the points of evaluated job content (Figure 12), and lines of central tendency are drawn through the dots (Figure 13). These lines are considered to represent the company's current practice. The annual Hay survey consolidates all such individual company lines and shows how each company relates to appropriate groups of other companies.

The Hay survey examines three aspects of cash compensation:

1. *Actual Base Salary Practice:* the central tendency of base salaries plotted against evaluation points. It shows what actually is happening (Figure 13).

2. *Policy Midpoint:* the salary structure or near-term goal against which base salaries are administered. It is a guide which may be official or unofficial (Figure 14).

3. *Total Cash Compensation:* the sum of base salaries plus supplemental cash (or equivalent) payments, such as sales commissions, discretionary bonuses, and incentive awards based on individual, division, or company performance, however determined.

The Report. On the basis of individual company scattergrams, lines of central tendency are read at standard Hay reference points (200, 400, 600, 1,000, 1,500, and 2,000 points) and charts are prepared which show high, low, average, median, and quartile lines. (See Figure 15.)

The Industrial Edition charts pay practices in the following categories:

Chart A. Base salaries—bonus and nonbonus companies
Chart B. , Total compensation—bonus and nonbonus companies
Chart C. Base salaries—bonus companies only
Chart D. Salaries—nonbonus companies only
Chart E. Total compensation—bonus companies only
Chart M. Policy midpoint—all companies

Figure 16 shows the relationship between the several lines examined in the industrial survey. As would be expected, the base salary of the bonus companies (line C) is lower than the base salary of the nonbonus companies (line D), but the difference is more than made up when bonus is considered (line E).

Figure 17 illustrates year-to-year comparisons and trends. The data shown here are for only line A (base salaries in bonus and nonbonus companies), but in the reports corresponding data are given for all lines.

Figure 18, a bar graph comparison, shows on a single display the relationship between *all* lines (Policy, Actual, and Total) of *all* participants at the key reference points. Actual base salary is defined by the shaded area, policy midpoint is indicated by a short vertical stroke, and extra compensation is shown by the unshaded extension. Companies are listed in the sequence of their actual base salary. The bar graph illustrates the differences between individual

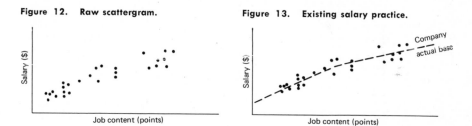

Figure 12.   Raw scattergram.

Figure 13.   Existing salary practice.

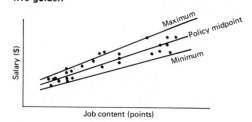

Figure 14.   Policy structure (administrative guide).

Figure 15. 1970 Hay Compensation Comparison: actual base salaries—bonus and nonbonus companies. (Edward N. Hay & Associates.) Quartiles Q3 and Q1 enclose middle 50% of company lines.

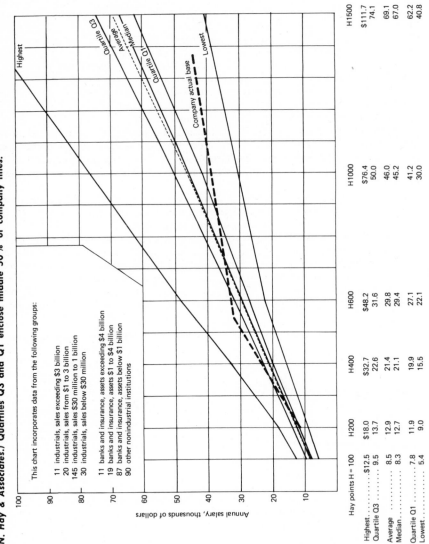

This chart incorporates data from the following groups:

11 industrials, sales exceeding $3 billion
20 industrials, sales from $1 to 3 billion
145 industrials, sales $30 million to 1 billion
30 industrials, sales below $30 million

11 banks and insurance, assets exceeding $4 billion
19 banks and insurance, assets $1 to $4 billion
87 banks and insurance, assets below $1 billion
90 other nonindustrial institutions

Hay points H = 100	H200	H400	H600	H1000	H1500
Highest.........$12.5	$18.0	$32.7	$48.2	$76.4	$111.7
Quartile Q3..... 9.5	13.7	22.6	31.6	50.0	74.1
Average 8.5	12.9	21.4	29.8	46.0	69.1
Median........ 8.3	12.7	21.1	29.4	45.2	67.0
Quartile Q1..... 7.8	11.9	19.9	27.1	41.2	62.2
Lowest......... 5.4	9.0	15.5	22.1	30.0	40.8

Figure 16. Comparison of chart average lines.

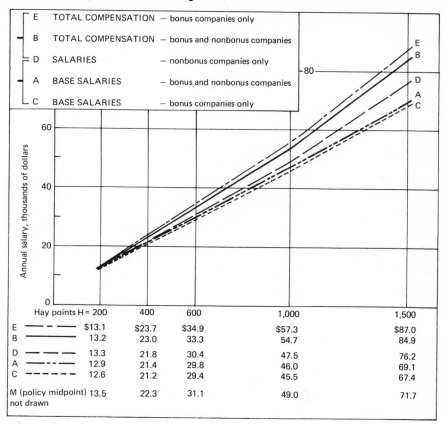

Hay points H =	200	400	600	1,000	1,500
E	$13.1	$23.7	$34.9	$57.3	$87.0
B	13.2	23.0	33.3	54.7	84.9
D	13.3	21.8	30.4	47.5	76.2
A	12.9	21.4	29.8	46.0	69.1
C	12.6	21.2	29.4	45.5	67.4
M (policy midpoint) not drawn	13.5	22.3	31.1	49.0	71.7

Legend:
- E TOTAL COMPENSATION — bonus companies only
- B TOTAL COMPENSATION — bonus and nonbonus companies
- D SALARIES — nonbonus companies only
- A BASE SALARIES — bonus and nonbonus companies
- C BASE SALARIES — bonus companies only

company practices. For instance, code 1 identifies a nonbonus company; its base salary intercept of $48,200 is the highest of all the companies at 600 points. However, code 3, a bonus-paying company, had a lower base of $40,900 but the higher total of $49,600. Further down the list, code 24 shows a base of only $34,100 and has the high total of $51,500.

Among the analyses of incentive compensation is a table that compares the amount of bonus paid at different point levels (Table 5 on page 3-66). This shows the wide variation that exists in bonus practices in industry. For instance, of the companies reporting bonus at H200, only 31 paid bonus in excess of 5 percent, whereas 80 companies paid less than 5 percent or none. On the other hand, at H1500 points, 82 companies paid over 5 percent bonus and only 10 companies paid less than 5 percent.

Using the Report.   This annual report provides each participant with:

1. A clear, graphic picture of its own internal salary relationships based on its individual scattergram

2. A comparison of its own compensation practice relative to all other participants or selected groups of participants (i.e., the competition)

3. Supporting tables and charts as guides in determining salary policy

Companies usually consider an adjustment in the formula for their salary

Figure 17.   Year-to-year trends.

Chart averages, 1969 versus 1970

The following tabulations compare 1969's average lines with 1970's as they appear on the printed charts.

Chart			H200	H400	H600	H1000	H1500
A	Base Salaries	1970	$12.9	$20.1	$29.8	$46.0	$69.1
	(000)	1969	12.1	21.4	27.8	43.5	64.9
		Diff.	$ .8	$ 1.3	$ 2.0	$ 2.5	$ 3.2
		%	6.6%	6.5%	7.2%	5.7%	4.9%

"Same company" increases (%), 1962–1970

Same-company averages consider, for each pair of years, those companies that appear in both years.

Chart			H200	H400	H600	H1000	H1500
A	Base Salaries	1970–1969	5.8%	6.0%	6.1%	6.1%	6.4%
		1969–1968	5.0%	4.7%	4.0%	6.2%	4.5%
		1968–1967	4.5%	4.6%	4.2%	4.7%	5.8%
		1967–1966	4.0%	5.2%	5.3%	4.1%	2.4%
		1966–1965	2.5%	2.7%	2.5%	1.6%	2.1%
		1965–1964	2.7%	3.2%	3.3%	1.6%	2.3%
		1964–1963	3.0%	2.7%	2.6%	2.1%	
		1963–1962	1.6%	2.4%	2.4%	0.8%	

policy at least once a year—it may not have to be changed every year, but at least it should be examined annually. This close analysis considers two factors.

How jobs compare internally with the existing policy structure.

1. It often happens that salaries are too low because administration has not used the money available in the existing policy structure. There is no point in constantly increasing the policy formula if the actual salaries are not kept in reasonable relationship to it.

2. Much of the usefulness of "policy" as an administrative tool is lost unless the policy midpoint stands in realistic relationship to actual base salaries, so that the policy structure line can provide the framework for relating merit increases to individual performance.

3. More adjustment may be called for at one end than at the other, and perhaps the character of the line should be modified by increasing (or decreasing) any bends or breaks that may be built into the policy structure.

4. The annual adjustment to the policy line should not necessarily be a percentage change in the formula but, rather, should be a new formula which will most appropriately locate the line in the pattern of the Hay charts.

How the company practice compares externally.   After considering the relative position of its own salary lines (base, policy, and total), and in the light of its compensation philosophy and economic status, the company establishes a new policy line as a near-term goal against which salaries will be administered for, say, the next year.

The Hay Compensation Comparison represents a continuing "end result" of

Figure 18.   Bar graph comparison at H600 points.

Company code	Policy	Actual	Total	0	$10M	$20M	$30M	$40M	$50M
1	48.1	48.2	48.2						
	38.4	44.4	44.4						
3	39.3	40.9	49.6						
	39.3	40.8	40.8						
	37.0	39.7	46.1						
	38.9	39.4	39.4						
	39.1	38.4	38.4						
	38.5	38.1	38.1						
	34.6	38.0	38.0						
	34.4	37.1	42.9						
	39.5	37.1	37.1						
	36.2	36.0	36.5						
	37.6	36.0	36.0						
	34.3	36.0	36.0						
	34.3	36.0	36.0						
	39.1	35.6	44.0						
	33.5	35.5	40.0						
	34.5	35.5	36.5						
	37.9	35.0	41.2						
	38.6	35.0	35.0						
	34.8	35.0	35.0						
	34.9	34.9	34.9						
	35.4	34.8	38.0						
	34.0	34.1	51.5						
	33.3	34.0	50.3						
	28.3	34.0	45.0						
	36.7	33.6	33.9						
	35.1	33.4	41.0						
	33.5	33.0	39.7						
	35.7	33.0	33.0						
	34.0	32.9	32.9						

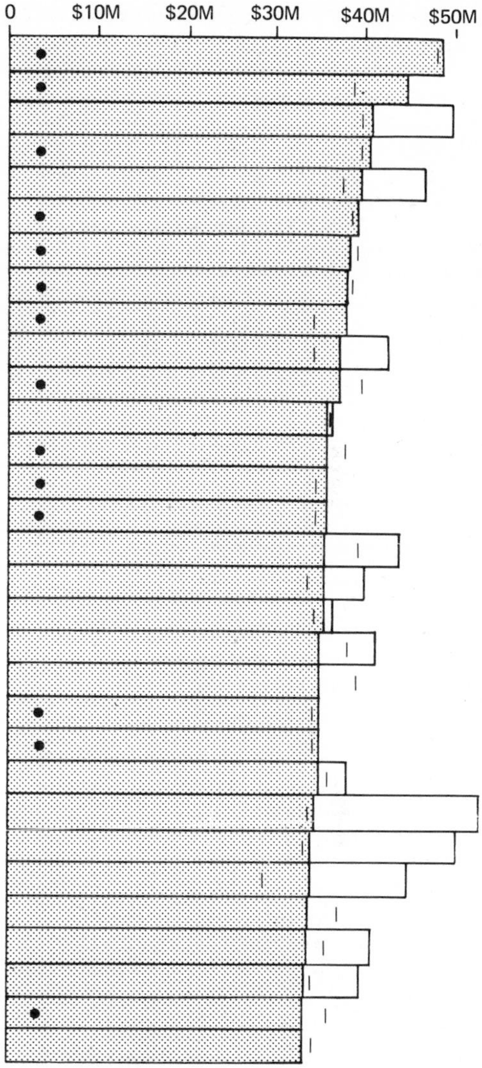

● = Non-bonus company

a painstaking analysis of jobs and of the environments in which they function. It is through the careful analysis by which job content is identified and related that the Hay evaluation procedures, including the annual surveys, acquire their unique validity.

TABLE 5   Amount of Bonus

Percentage range	H200		H400		H600		H1000		H1500	
	No. cos.	Average bonus	No. cos.	Average bonus	No. cos.	Average bonus	No. cos.	Average bonus	No. cos.	Average bonus
30% and up......	1	30.1%	4	37.3%	18	42.1%	47	45.3%	40	45.5%
20%–30%........	4	21.3%	22	24.0%	37	24.1%	29	24.2%	25	24.1%
10%–20%........	14	13.5%	48	14.1%	44	15.6%	22	14.9%	13	15.7%
5%–10%........	12	7.7%	22	7.2%	11	7.3%	2	6.5%	4	7.5%
1%–5%.........	26	2.7%	14	3.0%	6	2.2%	5	2.0%	2	1.5%
None this year at this level......	54	......	20	......	13	......	13	......	8	......
Line not at this level.........	19	......	0	......	1	......	12	......	39	......

chapter 16

Using Information Derived from Surveys

F. ELLIOTT AVERY   *Manager of Equal Opportunity, Southern California Edison Company, Rosemead, California*

Traditionally, wage and salary surveys are used to:

1. Determine the position of pay rates for various groups of jobs in relation to the labor market, which may be the local area, the region, the industry, or specific competitors for labor in the employing area.

2. Determine the competitive status of starting salaries.

3. Test the internal ranking (job evaluation) of various groups or jobs within the organization.

4. Check the adequacy of differentials between job levels in a promotional sequence.

5. Determine the need for, and the amount and form of, a general increase.

6. Develop a position and meet arguments in wage negotiations with union representatives.

THE DANGERS

Although surveys can provide valuable information needed to meet the purposes specified above, they should not be regarded uncritically. Many human and technical factors come into play which can undermine the usefulness of survey data and the conclusions and recommendations based on them. Knowing the potential sources of errors, however, can help us to avoid or overcome them.

Problems may arise if the data analysis is incomplete. For example, since it is easy to chart the company's pay rates against the rates obtained in the survey, the analyst may simply submit a chart rather than analyze the company's competitive position, together with other factors, and recommend a course of action. Or, data may be used improperly because the analyst does not understand the purposes of the survey. His work may be technically accurate but in pursuit of the wrong objective. For example, he may use interquartile ranges to test starting rates but fail to consider the length of time employees have been on their jobs.

There is also the danger that survey data may be put to inappropriate uses, which reduces their value and discredits the analyst—for example:

1. To force a conclusion on a department manager which he is reluctant to accept because of potential personnel problems or other overriding pressures

2. To provide bulk in a report

3. To prove a point which the analyst is unable to establish through more valid techniques, such as proper structuring of jobs or consistent internal ranking

4. To support what the analyst thinks is a consistent internal ranking, even though, for instance, substantial turnover or lack of interest in promotions in a given job series contradicts his conclusion

These "uses" may be considered unprofessional and cynical, but they do exist and should be recognized by those who make and analyze surveys and, more importantly, by those who make decisions on the basis of such analyses. These introductory remarks are not intended to discredit surveys but simply to encourage managers who use survey data to evaluate such information with sharp, critical judgment.

ENHANCING THE USEFULNESS OF SURVEY INFORMATION

Having identified the major sources of potential error in survey use, let us now take a look at how we can use surveys most effectively. Probably the most important factor is to know and understand your company's needs and objectives and, further, to *anticipate* these by having current data available when they are needed for decision making. Suppose, for example, that your organization is planning a reorganization which will require skills that do not currently exist in your organization. At the first hint of such a possibility, the analyst should ascertain where such skills are available and how much they will cost. If the jobs have never existed before, true hiring rates will have to be determined. If people with these skills are available only in other companies, data will be required to determine what starting and potential rates are necessary to hire these people from their current employment. And these data should be collected and analyzed and a recommendation provided before recruiting is to begin.

How well survey information is presented is another factor influencing its usefulness. The presentation must be geared to the operating style of the manager. Some managers read data better than charts. Some like the simplicity of averages. Some can tolerate, and even prefer, more complete, and therefore more complex, visual presentations.

Also, the important conclusions derived from the data should be summarized and appropriately emphasized at the beginning of any report. A chart alone is little better than raw data, but accompanied by conclusions and recommendations it can provide valuable input in decision making.

Care must also be taken that data obtained through surveys are based on companies and jobs comparable with your company and the jobs with which you are concerned. For example, data dominated by companies who must recruit and retain employees from a distant area should not be applied without question to a company whose employees can live nearby.

It is also necessary to examine the purpose of surveys, whether they are conducted by your organization or by outside agencies. The company, industry, or area mix for each job in the survey may have introduced biases which, if not detected, can create serious misunderstandings of the labor market.

At least one survey reports that approximately 5 percent of the total data are from contractor construction organizations. It neglects to state that these data from a high-pay industry are concentrated in five or six jobs—thus presenting some apparently amazing pay relationships.

Other questions should also be considered in evaluating a survey's usefulness for your organization:

1. Do the data come from organizations with which you compete in the labor market?

2. If more than one industry is represented, are the data broken down for each job within each industry?

3. Do measures of central tendency (such as the average, median, or mode) conceal too wide a distribution of rates or a bimodal frequency?

4. Are the respondents subject to the same type of employment pressures as is your organization? For example, if the survey is heavily populated with companies with a fluctuating labor force, it will not be a good guide for a company with a stable work force.

5. Do those conducting the survey have a vested interest in the result? If so, be wary and carefully test the data.

6. Are the data recent enough to be valid? Practically all data of bulk data surveys are published so late that in an inflationary situation they are obsolete by the time they are received. The time required to gather the information, shape it into a form suitable for publication, and actually print and distribute it means that bulk survey data will always be somewhat out of date. Moreover, the effect of this time lapse tends to become muddied. Different respondents report data valid on different dates, and the averaging process compounds the situation by blurring distinctions, thereby undermining survey reliability. In carefully controlled and reported data covering relatively few companies, this factor can be isolated and the data adjusted. In bulk surveys it is next to impossible.

WHEN TO ADJUST SURVEY DATA

In the nonsupervisory clerical and craft or production areas, jobs usually are sufficiently comparable so that the pay data need not be adjusted. However, in attempting to develop adequate comparisons for higher-level supervisory, technical, management, and staff positions, such comparability is difficult to secure. Therefore, it is necessary to base comparisons on jobs which, although similar, may vary in complexity and consequences from organization to organization.

Psychological research indicates that the average person cannot reliably discern differences of less than 15 percent. In the adjusted-data method of using salary survey data, it is assumed that the knowledge and discipline of the analyst permit him to discern differences as small as 7.5 percent. Thus, jobs can be ranked along the following scale based upon differences in scope, complexity, and consequences:

$$-30\% \qquad -15\% \qquad -7.5\% \qquad 0 \qquad +7.5\% \qquad +15\% \qquad +30\%$$

Positions which are determined to have equally offsetting characteristics, and therefore are of the same level, are rated equal and given a zero ranking. Similarly, if one job is considered to be close to a benchmark job but discernibly of a higher level, it would be rated +7.5 percent. Generally, to compare a survey position with another job that is more than 15 percent higher or lower is difficult and rather unreliable. However, differences of as much as 30 percent from the survey position can be determined by comparing through a series of jobs in various companies. If the difference between jobs is determined to be more than 30 percent, probably insufficient comparability exists for any meaningful comparison.

In using the data from the rankings, when a minus ranking is determined for a position in another organization, the salary level of the position is raised by that given percentage to bring it up to the level of the survey position. Thus, it is assumed that if the position in the other organizations is 7.5 percent below the survey position, your company would pay the salary of the other organization plus 7.5 percent if it wished to remain competitive with that organization. Conversely, a plus ranking would require reducing the actual salary down to the level of the survey position.

The formula used is:

$$\text{Adjusted Salary} = \frac{\text{the actual salary} \times 100}{\text{percent ranking} + 100\%}$$

For example, if the position in the other organization was paid \$950, and this position was 7.5 percent below the survey position, the following formula would apply:

$$\text{Adjusted Salary} = \frac{\$950 \,(100)}{-7.5\% + 100\%} = \frac{\$95,000}{92.5\%} = \$1,027$$

If the position in the other organization was 7.5 percent above the survey position, the formula would read as follows:

$$\text{Adjusted Salary} = \frac{\$950 \,(100)}{+7.5\% + 100\%} = \frac{\$95,000}{107.5\%} = \$884$$

Using this approach, data for similar jobs of different levels can be used to test the salary structure of the survey organization or to make other determinations when direct comparisons cannot be secured. This system also has the advantage of reducing an analyst's temptation to force a match of jobs of differing levels in order to get sufficient data on which to base his conclusions.

In the nonmanagement clerical, maintenance, and production areas, although the jobs usually are comparable, various surveys may indicate various pay relationships. These apparent inconsistencies most often can be attributed to variations in survey design:

1. There may be differences in the industry mix. One survey may have greater participation from high-paying organizations, and in another survey a greater proportion of the data may come from low-paying organizations.

2. The jobs may be of greater importance in one organization than in another. For instance, the rate of truck drivers in a transportation firm may vary from the rate of truck drivers used to distribute material between plants of a manufacturing organization.

3. The surveys may cover different geographical areas which have different rate patterns.

4. Companies with a fluctuating work force, where hiring and layoffs are relatively frequent, probably will have different rate relationships from those of organizations with stable employment.

5. If data are included on companies subject to special governmental regulations, some unusual patterns may appear.

6. The competence of those who have conducted the survey should be considered. There may be less emphasis placed upon job comparability than is required for an adequate survey.

If such inconsistencies are recognized, several alternatives are available. Generally, it is better to eliminate the data from a given survey or from that portion of a survey which appears inconsistent rather than to risk decisions being made upon the basis of inaccurate data.

Also, it should be emphasized that after the data are gathered and tested and a report is submitted for policy considerations, action other than that indicated by the analysis may result. After all, the salary levels in your company should be designed to attract and retain the kind of employees required by your company, not by any other organization.

Part 4

The Pay Structure

chapter 17

Determining Wage and Salary Policy

R. E. HOLLERBACH   *Director, Compensation and Personnel Development, Parke, Davis & Company, Detroit, Michigan*

Statements of wage and salary policy publicized by companies tend to be loosely formulated. The most commonly heard policy statements are these:

"We pay above-average rates"

or

"Our rates compare with the best."

This means that if a survey cites an average of $500 per month for a certain job, with lower and upper quartiles of $450 and $550 per month, the company is prepared to pay more than the quoted salary scale and, correspondingly, raises its ceiling well above $550. Rarely, if ever, does one hear that a company tends to maintain pay scales below the average or median pay scales reported in local or national industry surveys.

Despite the company's ambitious policy statements, its employees are likely to have an opposite view of company practice. When opinion surveys are conducted, the company is criticized with respect to wages and salaries more frequently than for other aspects of employment, such as working conditions or fringe benefits. More often than not employees rate the company's pay scales as "just average" or "inadequate." One of the main objectives of a sound wage and salary policy is reconciling these differences of opinion.

DESIGN AND ADMINISTRATION OF POLICIES

A company cannot hope to progress without effective employee efforts. Employees cannot obtain financial reward and job satisfaction unless the company achieves its objectives.

If pay takes a disproportionate share of profits, employees may be content with their gains temporarily, but the imbalance can lead to the failure of the company. Similarly, low pay rates allow higher company profits temporarily, but they do not attract or retain competent personnel. The result is performance mediocrity and its possible consequence, company instability and deterioration. Furthermore, pay must be defined for the employee and the company as the combined value of actual earnings plus benefit provisions.

The compensation executive must be adequately informed about employee viewpoints and company objectives before he can identify the route that will be mutually satisfactory and beneficial. He must recognize that the goals of employees are not constant or alike for all but differ from individual to individual and from group to group. To reach his objective, the executive has to analyze the nature of group formation and the influence this has on goals fixed according to individual and group needs. Generally speaking, company groups can be classified along the lines of performance tasks such as these:

1. Plant personnel, such as production labor, service labor, skilled trades, etc.
2. Clerical, stenographic, or semitechnical employees
3. Professional personnel engaged as technical and administrative employees
4. Management personnel who are first-line supervisors, middle managers, or top executives

Pay and pay structure plans cannot be limited to internal considerations alone. To ignore fluctuating economic and community factors is tantamount to developing a pay policy in a vacuum. In addition to identifying employee opinion, the compensation executive must be alert to the following external factors which have an impact on all pay policies and employee attitudes:

1. The availability of manpower in the marketplace
2. The current regional pay practices and policies of other companies at each location where the company operates
3. Regardless of geographical location, the prevailing policies and practices of other firms which seek the same types of employees

Employee viewpoints and industry practices must be reconciled with the conditions and problems management faces and which affect its attitudes and approach to pay and pay policies. Among these conditions, some of the most important are:

1. Differences in economic attitude and stability between a well-established firm and a relatively new firm
2. Company drive toward and opportunity for operational growth in sales volume and product diversification

NEEDS OF INDIVIDUAL EMPLOYEES AND EMPLOYEE GROUPS

The subject of employee needs, drives, and motivations is widely discussed today and accepted as a determinant in establishing pay structure and employee development programs. Although each employee is an individual in his own right with personal needs and ambitions, we can assume certain factors are universal and have a direct influence on attitudes toward pay policies.

Production, Maintenance, and Service Employees

This group is usually divided into three categories: general, semiskilled, and skilled workers.

The general group is sometimes referred to as "unskilled" because previous experience is not required, on-the-job training is either unnecessary or minimal, and the employee has little, if any, opportunity to exercise judgment in carrying out his job. Typical work assignments are janitorial services, routine material handling, and repetitive production line operations. This group consists of employees with limited service who have not yet been able to qualify for more skilled work, or employees with long service who are well satisfied to remain on these jobs. The short-service unskilled employee knows that any adverse business condition which necessitates a reduction in manpower is apt to affect him (or her) first. If he has dependents to support, a sharp curtailment of income is disastrous to him.

Pay policies for new employees in this group should give consideration to these items:

1. Employees have not developed skills which make it possible for them to gain other employment easily.

2. Employees have not been working long enough at a high enough level to have established personal financial security.

3. While a fair rate of pay is essential, income security is so significant that a benefit plan, such as a layoff allowance, is equally important.

Employees in this group who have been working for the company for a longer period of time but have not been able to qualify for more skilled work have additional and less concrete problems:

1. They, too, need a sense of economic security, but job frustration may be paramount. Because they have not been promoted, advancement is an issue.

2. Adequate pay, intensive in-plant training, and financial assistance for outside formal education all help to satisfy their ambitions and make them more upwardly mobile.

The long-service unskilled employee who is satisfied with his occupation has security through seniority but lacks interest in training for better positions. He will look for:

1. The highest possible rate of pay for his type of work

2. Paid time off provided through such benefits as extended vacations

3. Long-range security available in life insurance plans and retirement plans

The rate of pay in the unskilled group should be essentially the same for all employees, since their jobs offer limited opportunity to demonstrate individual skill. Rate increases based on length of service, adequate current income, security provisions, and training opportunities are the essentials of the compensation package.

Semiskilled employees utilize manual and/or intellectual processes and have some opportunity to control the flow of work; thus their effectiveness can be evaluated more easily. They handle responsible jobs, such as shipping, receiving, and stock control. They assemble units produced by less skilled employees into complex components or products. They operate production tools and equipment, and the techniques they use, through speed and efficiency, can result in greater or lesser output.

These employees share some of the need for security of their unskilled co-workers, but the reality of achievement has given a broader perspective to their needs.

1. Immediate income security is still important, but confidence and reliance on skill contribute to stronger personal security.

2. Skills have developed to the point where they may be in demand by other companies.

3. They can fill other less demanding jobs with ease so that the probability of unemployment is reduced for them.

Assuming that pay scales are equal to rates paid elsewhere, their personal interests lie in:

1. Rewards that recognize individual contribution and potential

2. Development programs to improve their skills or prepare them for better jobs, including supervisory positions

Pay scales and benefit programs for the semiskilled must take into account assessment of individual contribution and potential based on levels of productivity and/or quality of work. Differences in rates paid can be defended on a more objective basis, since performance expectations can be established. As long as base pay is reasonably competitive and offers some personal recognition, employee emphasis on training and development is apt to supersede the need for protection against unemployment.

The skilled group demonstrates some elements of professional knowledge and skill. For example, these employees are able to diagnose the reason for mechanical breakdown and to make an independent decision to institute corrective action which might even include fabrication of special parts. If assigned to production activity, they exercise critical, timely judgment about process continuation based on weighing variables such as temperature, viscosity, and appearance. Assembly of complex components into a working unit, and its testing, may be expected. Individual competence is apparent through high volume, high quality, low scrap rate, and the low frequency of rework required.

The skilled employees have reached the pinnacle, as success is measured in the hourly group. Because they can perform a variety of jobs, including the most complex, they enjoy the deep sense of security peculiar to people who are in high demand at most companies.

1. They do not fear lack of employment from any cause other than a general business recession.

2. They expect a high rate of pay combined with liberal benefits in all areas, such as hospital-medical plans, life insurance, vacations, and pensions.

3. They are willing to take the risks of a move from one company to another for more pay or better benefits.

Being the problem solvers of the hourly group and, frequently enough, the advisors to management as to the practicality of new or revised programs, this group enjoys an unusual feeling of personal satisfaction. Pay scales and pay structures must recognize their assets and must provide recognition for individual contribution while providing an income level high enough to attract and hold most of the competent employees. Job shopping is no problem, but their loyalties can easily be stimulated by a company wise enough to ensure that their personal desires to contribute creatively cannot be better satisfied by other companies.

Salaried Employees

This group is usually separated into two groups for pay administration:

1. Nonexempt salaried employees entitled to overtime premium pay by law.

2. Exempt salaried employees who are excluded from this legislation and do not typically receive overtime pay.

The Nonexempt Group. The nonexempt group includes clerical personnel engaged in maintenance of records and preparation of reports; typists, stenographers, and secretaries; and office machine operators (such as computer operators), draftsmen, etc.

Within this group, length of employment and varying degrees of job skill lead to categorization of these employees as beginners, intermediates, or seniors in these occupational groups.

The beginner group is heavily populated by chronologically young employees who are not more than a few years past high school graduation. They have the basic education required for higher-level positions, but because of their lack of experience they get the most routine assignments. They are predominantly female and typically do not aspire to a business career. Turnover will be high through rapid promotions or marriage. Because these employees rarely have to be concerned about dependents, they will change employers for a variety of reasons. Company policies should recognize that:

1. Long lunch hours and convenient shopping areas can take precedence over higher pay.

2. Frequent increases and higher pay will take precedence over the long-range security of retirement plans, life insurance, etc.

3. The opportunity to demonstrate individual competence by assignment to more difficult tasks is important.

The intermediate group consists of "graduates" from the beginner group. These employees have worked long enough to demonstrate their competence and dependability. They not only are expected to know company policies and procedures applicable to their job but have performed more complex tasks requiring individual judgment and have demonstrated their reliability through consistently accurate work.

In length of service these employees can vary from relatively short- to long-service employees, and those who quit, raise a family, and then reenter the business world. Employee needs will thus differ, and policies should recognize that:

1. Some are as interested in base pay, shopping convenience, etc., as is the beginner.

2. Immediate personal financial security available through benefits such as medical-surgical plans is as important as pay scales are to others.

3. Long-range security of retirement plans is also a major consideration for the older employee.

4. Training programs to sharpen skills and to qualify these employees for senior positions are essential.

The senior level of employees are those with highly valued knowledge gained through either long experience or specialized training.

Jobs for this group can be tailored to the individual so that experience and/or training can be utilized most effectively.

For the most part, these employees will be permanent members of the business world and are career-minded. They expect:

1. A pay structure which is flexible enough to reward distinguished performance

2. A broad range of benefits which provides current and long-range protection

3. Opportunity through training and/or educational assistance to develop professional skills so that they may qualify for jobs with exempt status

Deep loyalty to the company or to management members of the company is typical of these employees. However, since their skills are usually in high demand, they receive attractive offers from other companies. Job shopping can be minimized by pay scales which recognize superior skills and by benefits related to long service, such as extended salary continuance in the event of illness and extra weeks of vacation commensurate with years of service.

Exempt Professional Employees.   This group is stratified in much the same way as the nonexempt salaried group, according to beginning, intermediate, and senior levels.   Most of these employees are career-minded people who have expended considerable time, effort, and money at school to obtain expertise in their chosen fields.

Recent college graduates appear in this group as beginners who are highly educated but lack experience.   Movement to the intermediate group depends largely on demonstrated ability to blend theory with practical application in reaching solutions to problems in their fields.   Senior status is reserved for the most creative, original thinkers who can solve the most complicated problems, reach new and different workable solutions, provide leadership to the less skilled, and maintain current knowledge in their chosen professions.

These employees take competitive salary and benefit plans for granted because they can find employment readily at companies that offer adequate financial provisions.   Throughout their careers, a primary interest is an environment wherein they can function with a greater degree of independence and utilize their knowledge in the broadest, most uninhibited sense, that is, with considerable autonomy.

In addition to sound salary and basic benefit policies, they seek provisions for:

1. Financial assistance to permit study toward acquiring an advanced degree
2. Financial assistance for continuing education to keep up with current scientific developments, new business methods, legislation, and so on
3. The opportunity to attend conferences where recognized experts present papers on subjects of interest or where they can exchange viewpoints with their peers from other companies
4. Participation in the success of the company, resulting from their efforts, through special cash awards or stock ownership

The pay structure for these professional and administrative employees must be very flexible.   It must be sensitive to the subtle changes in job content—typical of this group—which become apparent as theoretical knowledge and practical skills are better integrated.   Employees then assume or receive more complex problems on a highly individualized basis.   Strict adherence to age, length of service, or similar norms will fail to recognize the employee who is on a "fast track" and may occasion the loss of his expertise to a more progressive company.

The Management Group.   This group consists of supervisors, middle managers, and top executives and represents a variety of skills and background. The nature of the company's product line is a determining factor in the weight that is given to background, experience, and education.   This is particularly true at the first level of supervision.   For example, the education and experience required to supervise employees engaged in routine, repetitive operations will differ significantly from the background and skills required for supervision of complicated processes; consequently, first-line supervision and middle-management positions may be held by either experienced employees who have been promoted from nonexempt jobs or relatively inexperienced employees who have specialized knowledge obtained through advanced education.

Supervisors have specialized needs, since they are in a new role and a new environment.   Being at the bottom of the management hierarchy, they feel the need to prove themselves to further their careers.   The recent graduate has the professional credentials but has not had the opportunity to demonstrate his skills. The supervisor who was promoted from the nonexempt ranks must supervise employees who were formerly his peers and is, in addition, competing with more experienced supervisors or highly educated younger people. In some ways his situation is analogous to the short-service, unskilled plant employee who is considered to have potential and has yet to demonstrate his capacity.

Policies should provide a grace or trial period during which these supervisors can assess for themselves their job satisfaction and return to their prior occupation without prejudice to their good standing in the company should they be inept as supervisors or should they find supervisory work distasteful. Similarly, the recent graduate should have the opportunity to transfer into nonsupervisory professional functions.

Pay policies should provide:

1. An adequate pay differential over the pay of subordinates for normal work periods as well as for extended work schedules and irregular shift assignments

2. Pay in recognition of supervisory skills which result in higher group efficiency and better product quality

3. Earnings comparable to the earnings of employees with similar competence, experience, and education who are assigned nonsupervisory functions

In addition to proper pay levels, comprehensive training programs are essential. They should be designed to help the supervisor improve in the art of managing people and to understand production standards and the techniques to be applied to meet quality and quantity requirements. Equally important are clearly established parameters of responsibility and exact definitions of accountability within which authority can be independently exercised.

Middle-management needs are essentially the same except that the newly appointed middle-management member is "farther out on the limb" and more in the spotlight. Success or failure can be pinpointed more exactly.

Middle management usually contains the most successful and best-paid employees promoted from the first-line supervisory group, and their earnings are usually adequate. However, policies which fail to reward the excellence of individual contribution through high base salary and supplemental programs can make these employees easy prey for executive search agencies, enticing advertising, and contacts made while attending business conferences.

Special inducements include the following:

1. Status symbols, such as a private office and a reserved parking space

2. Training and development programs designed to improve and broaden knowledge of other activities

3. Contingent compensation, such as bonus plans which dramatically improve earnings in any given year because they recognize unusual achievement

Top executives direct major functions and frequently are officers of the company. This select group has the opportunity to affect most directly the success of the company. They have had highly successful careers which usually result in a high income level.

As with the middle-management group, competitive salary structures, individualized salary increases, and status symbols are important, but "after tax" earnings take on greater significance.

Formalized salary structure and related benefits continue to be important at the top executive level, but maximum flexibility is also required. Programs should be designed to identify and reward individual achievement accurately and to permit variations suitable to personal needs. Some of the items to consider are:

1. Executive bonus awards directly related to achievement and substantial enough to provide real incentive

2. The option to defer awards to a point in time when the individual's income tax rate is lower, such as when he is retired

3. Perquisites such as a car at company expense, paid travel expenses for his wife, etc.

4. The right to select the type and size of benefits preferred from within the company's overall benefit package

The Sales Group. In addition to the foregoing, another large group of employees may have to be considered. Companies with their own distribution system may have sales employees in each of these exempt groups. While their needs are essentially the same, a significant difference lies in the method of their payment.

The highly individualized nature of a sales job leads many companies away from the base-salary method of compensation to plans wherein earnings are substantially or totally related to sales volume. Sales quotas and sales incentives are widely used for salesman compensation on the assumption that the typical "sales type" prefers it that way. Given a modest base salary or drawing account, the salesman supposedly views his earning potential as unlimited and subject only to his personal capability for success.

Whether this is in fact the case is debatable, as is the desirability of such a policy. The nature of the company's products, corporate actions, and the normal peaks and valleys in typical years are among the items that affect the salesman's ability to sell. Evaluation of these three influencing factors is essential in determining the appropriate compensation plan. Compensation executives should appreciate the fact that salesmen are members of the company and entitled to the same opportunities for development and those measures of security which are provided other employees.

EXTERNAL FORCES

The state of the job market and competitor employment practices at the local and national level condition employee attitudes and the wage and salary structure.

Peak Employment Periods

When companies are running at top capacity, employees at all levels of skill are difficult to recruit. Employees become aware of this, their expectations inflate accordingly, and the labor market becomes a "seller's market" in which employers bid against each other in their efforts to attract competent personnel.

There is a natural tendency to hold onto existing structures in the hope that "things will get better"—that is, revert to lower pay rates. For a short period of time, this procedure has merit. It avoids precipitous action which increases payroll costs. Payroll costs are difficult to reduce if the manpower shortage proves to be temporary. During pressures of this type maximum coordination is essential between the compensation executive and related departments of employment and manpower planning. If the shortage continues to the point where the number of open jobs is excessive and the forecasted long-range needs of the company are jeopardized, the compensation executive must institute changes in pay policy.

A number of options are available. Some of these are:

1. *Maintain parity.* In a rising economy, if productivity is improving and if profits are adequate, salary and hourly rate structures can move upward as

starting rates climb. Of all options, this modification is the easiest to administer because the earnings of all employees can be maintained in the proper relationship to the rates being paid new personnel.

2. *Modify increase policies.*   When employees are hired at a high starting rate, increases in pay can be made less frequently to avoid excessive costs. For example, if employees are eligible for an increase each six months, the policy can be changed to provide eligibility for an increase at nine-month intervals; twelve-month intervals between increases can be lengthened three to six months; etc.   In addition to or in lieu of extended time intervals, the size of increases can be reduced or the increases can be awarded on a highly selective basis.

3. *Reduce range spread.*   This method is particularly applicable if the spread from minimum to maximum of ranges was wide originally.   By raising the range minima without changing maxima, more attractive starting rates become available without a substantial increase in overall labor costs.   Employees may reach the maximum in a shorter period of time and the pay differential between new and long-service employees may be reduced, but the net effect on operating costs will not be altered significantly.

4. *Eliminate ranges.*   Traditional progressions within rate ranges based on length of service or merit may have to be abandoned.   While giving recognition to an individual employee via increases within a range is a highly desirable policy, it can become a prohibitive expense when starting rates are unreasonably high.   This is the least desirable option and should be utilized only when profit margins have been substantially reduced.

Shortage of Specialized Skills

When candidates for specific jobs requiring specialized skills become scarce and starting rates begin to rise, there is a tendency to abort good job evaluation practice.   On the surface there seems to be little hazard in artificially reclassifying these jobs upward so that a competitive rate range can be offered.   Unfortunately, this solution fails to consider two significant administrative problems almost sure to occur in due time:

1. When the supply of candidates becomes more adequate and when more realistic starting rates can be applied, it is virtually impossible to reduce the job from its artificial classification to a rate range in keeping with the true dimensions of the job.

2. Overrated jobs become "benchmarks" for management and are used to exert pressure for the reclassification of other jobs with equivalent responsibilities but not subject to the pressure of manpower shortage.

To avoid these situations, it is much more advisable to pay high in the properly evaluated rate range and, if necessary, to exceed maximum to prevent a skewed job evaluation system.

The compensation executive can usually exert better control of problems arising from a limited labor supply when the shortage applies to jobs which have been in existence for some time.   His position is much less tenable when the source of the problem originates from a new technology.

A case in point might be electronic data processing.   The advantages of the computer became obvious to many companies in a brief period of time.   The demand for programmers and operators soared overnight and their opportunity for higher earnings rose concurrently.   Pressures for larger salaries increased at a time when it was very difficult to get a "handle" on these jobs from a job evaluation point of view.

Under such circumstances, there are advantages to be gained by ignoring existing rate ranges and conventional evaluation techniques. In a new, untried field, the true dimensions of relevant jobs are rarely identifiable until the company and industry have lived with them for some time.

To avoid precedents which will be difficult to break when supply catches up with demand and when more logical job analysis is possible, a "special" range can be set as an expedient, tentative provision. This "special" range can ignore typical company rate structures and can be designed with a broad spread from minimum to maximum which might overlap two or three conventional ranges. By its extreme breadth, the special range affords the opportunity to attract and retain competent personnel while avoiding the misuse of the company's official structure.

Ultimately, a "job family" should emerge from this broad category. As pressures diminish and objective evaluation becomes possible, several levels of skill, responsibility, etc., will be identifiable. At this time, the "special" range can be abandoned and the appropriate number of job levels integrated into the regular rate structure.

Pay Practices of Competitors

At one time employers competing for the same employees were usually a few companies in the same small geographic area. A company on one side of a large city could ignore companies on the other side because employees tended to work close to their home site. As the work force became more mobile, competition for talent spread to include a 40- or 50-mile radius from the work site. At the present time it is not unusual to recruit on a national basis for certain skills. Competing for employees in the expanded horizon of the work force has affected not only pay rates but the hidden compensation offered through the benefit package. This total package has to be designed to provide favorable comparison with local industries and with national trends. A company at odds with local or national total compensation programs will have limited success in its recruiting efforts.

A company with different plant sites may have basic corporate policies to which it is committed, but these are subject to partial modifications in line with prevailing practices at any location. For example, increases on a merit basis may be corporate policy, but some localities or some employee groups will be allowed length-of-service adjustments in keeping with local practices. Six or seven holidays may be the corporate minimum, but 10 or 12 can be authorized for some areas.

Whatever the variation, it must be based on facts which can be clearly explained to the employee candidates who have become well-informed on compensation and benefits available at other companies.

To be able to show the advantages of company policy, the compensation executive cannot limit his attention to data generated from routine surveys of wages and salaries. In addition to comparisons of basic income he must know the following:

1. Frequency and size of increases

2. Reasons for granting increases: Are they based on service or merit? Are they related to the rise in cost of living? Are they across-the-board sharing in the company's improved productivity?

3. Ratio of employee benefits to individual earnings: What life insurance is provided at various income levels? What retirement income accrues for various years of service and earnings?

4. Continuation of earnings: What holidays are recognized? What are the vacation schedules? What is the income protection for illness or injury?

5. Funding of the benefit package: What is the employee's share in the cost of life insurance, medical coverage for self and dependents, retirement, etc.? Are supplemental provisions available at employee expense?

Taking all of these provisions into account, wage and salary policies can be designed to provide moderate earnings combined with liberal benefits, liberal earnings but moderate benefits, or any other variation.

CORPORATE CONCEPTS

Basic to the operation of almost every company is the need to make a profit. Nonprofit institutions exist but are in the minority, and even these usually try to earn enough to meet most of their expenses.

Because management wants to operate on a least-cost basis in every way, it has to develop techniques which assure that payroll dollars are expended in the most effective way. The degree of sophistication required in these techniques varies widely from company to company. Size and type of business, as well as growth opportunity, influence the variations in corporate attitudes toward pay and pay policies.

The well-established firm can very easily fall into a conservative approach to compensation. The company name is well known and attracts employees. Its years of success convey a sense of security to employees and employee candidates because adverse business conditions have been weathered successfully in the past. Stable employment exists because employees have accumulated too much service to leave for modest improvements in earnings.

The other side of this coin—the new candidates' viewpoint of the firm—cannot be overlooked in this atmosphere. Young, competent candidates can afford a few risks early in life, and consequently a "well-established firm" is not necessarily as meaningful to them as actual income. They may feel that promotional lines in older companies will be clogged with long-service candidates, thereby reducing the newer employees' opportunities. An additional obstacle may exist because policies and procedures are so deeply entrenched that creativity and innovation will be stifled.

Well-established companies, therefore, must modernize pay and benefit policies as assiduously as they do equipment and facilities for improved profit. One can stipulate that failure to do so will result in:

1. The loss of the most competent employees to more progressive firms
2. The inability to hire experienced or inexperienced replacements because their salary requirements exceed "par for the course" at the conservative firm
3. A drift toward mediocrity and the subsequent reduction in profit and growth

The new firm can err in the other direction just as easily. In its anxiety to "get up and go" it may:

1. Pay whatever a candidate asks just to get his talents.
2. Pay a cadre of employees far above market price to assure their retention.
3. Adjust salaries and wages too often and too liberally to indicate that it is a live-wire outfit.
4. Share profits with employees without due regard to the company's long-range financial needs.

In due time, the "new firm" establishes itself and stabilizes. More realistic pay structures and pay policies develop, but earlier freewheeling practices have resulted in exorbitant payroll costs which are not easily reduced. Employee resentments may grow as a result of the problems caused by the earlier freewheeling practices. Among these will be:

1. Employees at or above the maximum rate for their job due to the high starting salaries of the past

2. Limited room in the rate range for additional increases as a result of size and frequency of adjustments previously authorized

3. Indefensible differences in pay as new employees are hired at realistic pay rates

4. New-employee resentment because of a slower, more selective approach to rate increases

Growth opportunities of the company influence wage and salary policies in a number of ways.

The company satisfied with its current size may require different pay policies from those required by a rapidly growing company. Promotions result, in the main, from retirements, and many employees are likely to be on the same job for many years because there are no openings at higher echelons. In such situations, rate ranges sometimes are broader than normal and the rates paid can be higher than in other companies. For example, if a spread of 40 percent from minimum to maximum is typical for a given job level at most companies, spreads of 50 percent may appear at stabilized companies. While this provides a longer period of time during which increases can be given, it can lead to overpayment for a job and excessive cost. It only postpones the time when the employee must be told that he is at maximum.

The rapidly growing company lives more comfortably with narrow rate ranges because the employees who reach maximum have many opportunities for promotion to new functions. The company will maintain highly competitive starting rates to assure an adequate supply of qualified personnel and flexible increase policies designed to recognize and reward employees who can grow with the firm.

Rise or fall of profits tends to relax or constrict wage and salary policies. Any change in the way of doing business has an effect on employees and consequently on one of the largest single cost items of a company—its payroll. Despite employee attitudes or competitor practices the fundamental question facing the company is, How much should it cost to attract and retain the kind of employees we need?

In good times when high profits provide adequately for shareholder dividends and broad corporate programs, approval of liberal rate ranges and rate increase programs can be obtained more easily. Sharing the wealth with employees is less likely to be criticized because they are perceived as significant contributors to the company's unusual success. Despite the freedom of action implied for the compensation executive in devising a more liberal wage and salary policy, normal wage and salary levels should continue during high-profit periods. Dramatic increases in base wages and salaries which elevate them well beyond the acceptable level for normal-profit years should be avoided. Employee participation in the company's earnings is more logical when accomplished through special periodic payments which take the form of profit-sharing programs, Christmas bonuses, or similar plans. These are predicated on high profits and automatically disappear when profits fall.

When profits are below par, "tightening of the belt" in terms of wages and salaries is a natural tendency. At the same time pressure increases for greater production from every employee. Financial rewards for outstanding efforts may become so small they lose their significance as incentives. Manpower may be cut and normal wage and salary increase policies may be suspended during adverse business conditions even though top management recognizes that the recovery of the company may depend on the continuation of good compensation techniques. These nostrums should be avoided. If salaries and wages fall below a competitive level, the most capable employees will quit the company, leaving a preponderance of mediocrity to resolve the company's problems. Good replacement personnel will not be attracted to a low-paying company, with the result that recovery becomes impossible.

The success in maintaining an adequate compensation plan through good and bad times depends on utilizing well-designed, logically constructed procedures and controls. These provide the tools for top management to guard costs and to determine what funds will be available for increases.

CONCLUSION

The success of any technique or group of techniques at any one company does not ensure success at another company. To develop an effective program with compensation and benefits intelligently integrated, the compensation executive must appraise each technique carefully, determining its desirability for the company and its employees.

The basic ingredients of a sound wage and salary policy include provisions which recognize the need for a fair wage and the opportunity for employees to progress. Less apparent but equally important are the provisions for the employee's more personalized concerns and requirements. Wage and salary policies based upon pure statistical reference to competitive wages and salaries are conceived in the dark. Unless they give credence to ancillary programs such as training and development and assure the employee that he is a highly regarded member of the team, they will not be persuasive in the attraction of new employees to the company or in the retention of the company's current employees.

Leadership in the field of compensation will require executives who are willing to face the challenge of policies which go beyond routine statistical indexes and may be construed as idealistic. Undue emphasis on economic values without a humanistic approach will lead to an impoverished program. Industry practices, employee viewpoints, and the problems that management faces must be communicated coherently. The efficacy of a good compensation program depends on clear communication between those who administer it and those who are affected by it. The rationale of the plan—why it is designed as it is and what it consists of—must be communicated widely. Unless communication is open and uncomplicated, misunderstandings, confusion, and resentment follow.

chapter 18

Solving Technical Problems in Establishing the Pay Structure

DONALD R. THOMPSON *Vice President, Industrial Relations, Warner Gear/Warner Motive, Muncie, Indiana*

Determining wage and salary policy is one thing; setting up a practical and usable pay structure is quite another matter. After the basic policy questions have been resolved and when all the necessary information is at hand in terms of job evaluations and market rates, it is necessary to set up a system whereby real dollars of pay will be attached to real jobs that are occupied by real people. While many of the questions to be answered are essentially philosophical in nature, the philosophy that is applied may have to be quite pragmatic. That is, the basic requirement of the pay structure is that it work in practice. Failing this, all its theoretical soundness and inherent logic are useless. In fact, they are worse than useless, because they may mislead us into thinking we have a workable system when we do not.

The comments and suggestions offered in this chapter are not specifically applicable to hourly paid employees, although some of the general principles involved are the same. In particular, they do not apply to hourly paid employees represented by a union, where wage rates are negotiated and defined by a labor contract. (However, such jobs can be, and often are, evaluated to set rate differentials.) For the purposes of this discussion, we are dealing either with an organization where all employees are salaried, or with an organization where there is not a labor contract and management is free to use its best judgment in establishing pay rates for all employees in all jobs.

HOW MANY PAY STRUCTURES?

The first question to be answered is the basic one of how many pay structures are required. Ideally, one might say that the answer would be one pay structure. However, life is not always ideal, and there are situations which require the use of two or even several separate pay structures for different groups of employees or different groups of jobs.

While the possible situations are almost infinite in variety, some of the more frequent situations requiring multiple pay structures include geographical diversity—e.g., a company operating in widely scattered and differently priced labor markets; industry differences encountered among divisions of a conglomerate or in a company dealing in widely diverse kinds of business; cost-imposed differences caused by variations in marketing methods or other cost factors in different types of businesses; union-imposed differences, where the impact of negotiated labor rates is felt at certain parts of the structure more than at others; and market-imposed variations, caused by a particularly acute demand for certain types of skills.

Perhaps the most common example is the use of different structures for exempt and nonexempt jobs. The Fair Labor Standards Act (usually called the "Wage and Hour Law") requires the payment of overtime premiums to persons in nonexempt positions, but does not require such payments to those in exempt jobs. Unless the employer voluntarily chooses to make some sort of extra payment for overtime work in the exempt group, it may be desirable to apply a different salary policy in order to offset the overtime pay and to provide an earnings differential in favor of the higher jobs.

In addition to the above factors, which can be generally categorized as externally imposed, there may be internal reasons for using more than one structure, including basic philosophy. For example, in certain types of non-profit organizations, such as religious institutions, the organization may deliberately decide not to pay equitably in relation to evaluated job content for certain high-level positions.

In determining whether multiple salary policies and pay structures are appropriate, it is necessary first to identify job groupings which may require special treatment. These job groupings may be natural—i.e., the jobs may be closely related in terms of occupational characteristics and/or evaluation levels —or they may be artificial. For example, at a given point in time, all data processing jobs may be at a premium in the labor market—or just programmers may be in especially short supply. Such circumstances may confront us with the question whether we pay all data processing jobs above the normal policy, or whether we simply attach a premium to the pay rates for programmers.

Assuming a reliable job evaluation system, the best method of identifying job groups generally is through job evaluation. This point will be covered further in the discussion of salary grades and how to establish them.

USE OF SURVEYS

As a salary administrator you must be a confirmed skeptic in certain situations. One of these is the all-too-common case where a department head pleads with you for special treatment of his people and swears a blood oath that your company's current pay rates for these people are inadequate and that his best people are always leaving him for fantastically higher salaries with other employers. This may be true; but like the report of Mark Twain's death, it often turns out to be greatly exaggerated.

Without going into all the possible reasons for employee turnover (which may include the department head's own ineptness as a supervisor), it is obvious that we cannot justify a special salary structure just because one or a few people leave for higher salaries. We need to know whether they in fact went to similar jobs, or whether they succeeded in obtaining promotions for themselves. We must remember also that when we need somebody badly enough we will violate our normal salary policy to get him, and there is no reason to suspect that other employers would not do the same.

The best tool in such situations is a sufficient amount of reliable survey data. Aside from the general survey or surveys on which your overall salary policy is based, it is not only feasible but desirable in some instances to make special surveys. These need not be highly elaborate, but there are certain fundamental rules to be observed. First, make sure that the other companies contacted have jobs which are in fact comparable; and be sure to uncover, and make allowances for, special factors not applicable to your own company—e.g., family ownership, abnormally inflated earnings, or lack of a training program which compels them to go outside for all their key employees.

Second, make sure that you compare apples and apples. Never set out upon a salary survey without reliable job descriptions, and do not depend on a couple of quickie telephone calls and a vague generalized description of duties to determine whether you are talking about the same job. Certainly, do not rely upon job titles. As anyone who has ever dealt with a bank or an advertising agency can attest, a vice president is not always a vice president! Neither is the title Manager of Investment Services or Director of Advertising and Public Relations a reliable indication of what a job consists of or what an individual does.

As a general rule, standard surveys, such as those conducted by AMS (formerly NOMA) and the U.S. Department of Labor, are fairly reliable for lower-level, nonexempt positions. For routine clerical functions, job content tends to be pretty well standardized, although even a job title such as Typist or Key Punch Operator may not always denote a truly equivalent position. For most exempt positions, however, standard survey data are often misleading, at best, unless they are based on a common job evaluation method among participants, with correlation procedures to adjust for company differences (as in the Edward N. Hay & Associates Annual Compensation Comparison).

Where standard data are unavailable, insufficient, or unreliable, it is better to make your own special survey, focusing on the job or jobs with which you are particularly concerned. Because of manpower limitations, concern for objectivity, or requirements of confidentiality, you may wish to have an outside consultant make the survey for you—or you can do it yourself.

In conducting any survey, personal visits are better than written questionnaires; and written questionnaires are better than telephone calls. Take or send up-to-date written job descriptions; and obtain job descriptions, if possible, from the survey participants.

Many of these kinds of problems can be resolved, or at least minimized, by the simple Sergeant Joe Friday technique of "getting the facts." The alleged deficiencies of your own pay rates will often turn out to be minimal upon investigation of the actual circumstances.

DETERMINING AND DEFINING SPECIAL SITUATIONS

When your investigation does reveal a special situation requiring treatment separate or different from the majority of jobs in the organization, it becomes necessary to decide how far you are willing to go to alleviate the problem. Another way of putting this is to ask how willing you are to create problems in other areas—because that is almost certainly what special treatment for any small group will do.

Let us deal with a specific illustration—one which constitutes a fairly typical example.

Suppose you have a well-established formal program for job evaluation and salary administration. You have analyzed and evaluated all positions; you have secured reliable data for external comparisons; and you have set a midpoint salary policy with what is normally an adequate spread (say, 35 percent) from minimum to maximum. In simplified diagram form, your pay structure looks something like Figure 1.

With this structure, you have a salary range for any job incumbent, once the position has been evaluated. For example, let us say a certain job is evaluated at precisely 200 points. Applying the midpoint policy formula ($1.50P + $300), you get a salary midpoint of $600 per month. To get the minimum, you multiply by 0.85, and for the maximum by 1.15. Thus, the salary range for this job is $510 to $690 a month. The same procedure produces the salary minimum, midpoint, and maximum for any position, once it has been evaluated. Now, let us suppose that when you superimpose this structure on your scatter-gram of actual salaries (or vice versa), the result will look something like Figure 2.

Aside from the two special situations at 210 points and 245 points, the distribution shown in Figure 2 is about what you might expect to find. There are four red-circle rates (over the maximum) and 19 blue-circle rates (below minimum). This is normal, assuming that our policy midpoint line represents a good competitive level that is a short-term (one to two years) statement of where we want to be. We need to pay extra attention to those below minimum and move them up quickly into the range, but there is probably no need to hit the panic button.

We do need to analyze the two special situations with particular care, as they depart in marked fashion from the otherwise rather consistent pattern.

Figure 1.   Pay structure: policy midpoint with minimum and maximum lines.

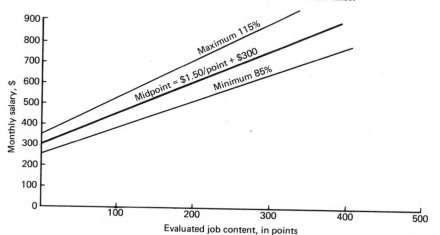

Figure 2.   Pay structure superimposed upon scattergram of actual practice.

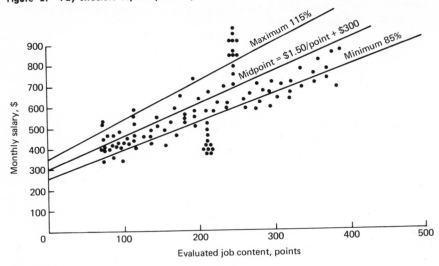

First, there is a grouping of jobs (or perhaps a number of incumbents in a job that occurs several times in the organization) at about the level of 210 evaluation points. Of 12 jobs so evaluated, only one is paid even within the salary range—and that one is well below midpoint; all the rest are below minimum—the majority are far below! We need to identify the jobs and the people and try to figure out why things are the way they are.

Have we perhaps (prior to formal job evaluation) historically seen these jobs as being much lower in the overall scheme of things than critical evaluation reveals them to be? If so, this could account for the low rates of pay associated with these positions.

Are the jobs correctly evaluated? Naturally, we must resist any temptation to "fudge" evaluations up or down just to accommodate existing aberrations in our pay practice; but this is a question that must be asked. There are indicators and clues. For instance, if the caliber of people we have in these jobs is consistently lower than we would like, and the really capable employees usually do not stay, this may confirm our suspicion that we did formerly underrate these jobs and pay less than was needed for the skills required and the responsibilities involved.

In this case, just from visual analysis of the scattergram we can rather safely assume that these jobs are not seriously overevaluated. The points would have to be cut nearly in half to get most of them within our proposed range! This is clearly not true of most jobs in the structure. We can conclude that we have not made it appear that the incumbents are underpaid by overrating the jobs.

Assuming, then, that the jobs are correctly evaluated, we clearly have a group of people who are grievously underpaid (1) in terms of our salary policy and (2) in comparison with most of the other employees. We need to begin immediately to take special action to correct this anomaly. Increases should be given more frequently than normal, and possibly in larger increments than usual, to move qualified employees into the proper salary range.

If there are in the group persons whose work performance is so poor that we cannot justify *any* increase, then they should be moved to lesser jobs or terminated.   With a competitive and equitable salary range, we can afford to have qualified people in these jobs.   That will surely turn out to be a better bargain for the company than the low salaries ever were!

Conceivably, there could be a peculiar job market imbalance which would cause certain positions to be so easily filled that a range below the normal structure could be used.   This is highly unlikely, however, and would probably not be a very smart thing to do even if we could get away with it for a while.

In the second special situation, we have a group of jobs, at about 245 points, whose incumbents are consistently paid well above the normal practice for the rest of the organization.   Of 15 jobs, 11 are paid above the maximum, four are within the range, and only one is below midpoint!

Again, we must determine whether the jobs have been properly evaluated. If they have been badly underrated, reevaluating them at a higher level would move the dots to the right on the scattergram, thus causing more of them to fall within the range.

Another question we should ask at this point is whether our ranges have sufficient spread.   While a 35 percent spread (maximum over minimum) is usually sufficient for most nonexempt positions, a 50 percent spread is nearly always better for exempt jobs.   This would cause our minimum and maximum lines to fall, respectively, at 80 percent and 120 percent of midpoint, instead of 85 percent and 115 percent.   Thus, in addition to encompassing more of the existing salary-job relationships, we can have more room to administer individual salaries within the ranges so as to reflect performance and any other valid factors affecting what should be paid to a particular employee.

We may want to start off with a 35 percent spread at the bottom end and gradually increase to a 50 percent spread at about the point where the exempt jobs begin, continuing the 50 percent spread on up from there.   This "fluted" or tapered range spread is preferable to one that changes abruptly from a narrower to a wider range, as illustrated in Figure 3.

A word of caution at this point: Do not assume that, because a little more spread may be good, a lot more is even better.   Ranges can be so wide that they become meaningless and even misleading.   As a rule of practice, it is safe to say that the maximum never needs to be more than 50 percent above the minimum, provided the midpoint has been set at a proper level.

Getting back to the second group of jobs in Figure 2, let us assume that we have satisfied ourselves the evaluations are correct.   We need next to uncover the reasons for this distortion.   We shall look not only at the jobs, but also at the people in them.   Do we have several cases of "superseniority," where the same people have been in the same jobs for many years?   If so, by yielding to the charitable impulse to grant some kind of salary increase every year, we may

Figure 3.   Increasing range spread.

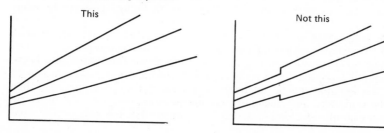

have succeeded in getting these employees to salary levels quite beyond anything their jobs would rationally justify.

Do we have overqualified persons in these positions? There is a constant temptation, one we all yield to at times, to ask for more than we really need—to hire an engineer when we need a technician; a designer instead of a draftsman; a bookkeeper rather than a clerk. If we have made this error, we shall inevitably have paid a premium to get and keep people with skills beyond those actually required. (Remember when a programmer had to be a college graduate with a major in mathematics?)

Are there personal reasons for some of the high salaries? Are they status-influenced? For example, secretaries to senior executives tend to be paid more than secretaries to middle managers, even when their jobs in fact may be less demanding.

Is there an historical basis? A department or function may in the past have been more important to the company than it is today.

A unit, or several specialized employees, may have been acquired by merger or otherwise. Their pay could reflect the organizational bias, as well as the pay practices, of the former company.

A "halo effect" may be the cause. In some life insurance companies, for example, anyone who is an actuary will be paid more—regardless of whether actuarial skills are required in his job. In a company where the General Counsel is exceptionally influential, attorneys will tend to command high salaries, irrespective of the actual need for legal know-how.

Having eliminated, or having made allowance for, any of these factors you have discerned (and any others that may be significant), you can still be left with a problem. This is where a special survey is likely to be useful.

Let us assume you are convinced, after careful investigation, that your policy salary levels for these jobs are at least 10 percent below the going rate in the marketplace for jobs you know are the same. What do you do?

Clearly, you have a number of choices. You can:

1. Ignore the situation and hope it will go away. (It will not, usually, unless the condition has already persisted for a long time and an overdue adjustment in the "people market" is ready to occur.

2. Artificially and arbitrarily inflate the evaluations to get a higher salary range. (Obviously, this will destroy the internal equity which is a primary objective of any good salary administration program. The harmful effects of such action will surely last far beyond your tenure in the job of salary administrator!)

3. Elevate the entire salary structure by 10 percent or more, so that the policy ranges will accommodate this group of jobs. (Even if your company could afford it, and you could sell them the idea, this would not be very smart, for many reasons too readily apparent to require mention.)

4. Recognize that you are dealing with a temporary market distortion, and simply elevate the salary ranges *for these jobs only* by a sufficient amount to make them competitive. (This is unfair, internally; but it does less violence to the structure than distorting the evaluations or changing the overall policy entirely. In time, the supply will catch up with the demand, and this particular problem will disappear. It will probably be replaced by another, equally vexing; but then, that is why companies need salary administrators.)

There may be other possibilities; but, of those listed, the fourth solution is the recommended approach. Simply add 10 percent (or 12 percent, or 15 percent, if it takes that much) to the midpoint salary for these jobs, and then compute the minimum and maximum in the usual fashion. If you have, referring to our example, decided to widen your ranges, that will help, too.

What you add may not always be quite as much as the competitive difference your investigation has disclosed. For one thing, people do not usually change jobs for 2 percent or 5 percent more money. Even 10 percent should not lure away most incumbents of exempt jobs, unless there are greater promotion or growth opportunities, or more exciting work—and you cannot fight that with money.

For another thing, there is often a leapfrog effect in this sort of action. If you, in company A, practice one-upmanship on company B, it is very likely that B will do it right back to you. You can easily get something like a gasoline price war going, with harmful results for all concerned. It is hoped that there are some valid reasons to stay with your company besides money. So long as you are in the ball park, you should be able to retain and motivate the people you want.

In considering raising the rates of special jobs, you may also be constrained by basic management philosophy. For example, if you are in a bank, you will probably never pay your investment people as well as many stockbrokers or investment houses will pay such personnel in prosperous times. Neither will you put them out on the street as fast when times get hard! Somewhere along the line, some of your people will just have to decide whether they want to work for a good bank, for adequate pay; or whether they want to opt for the higher rewards—and the greater risks—in a brokerage house. For another example, corporate attorneys (all of whom modestly confess to utter brilliance, outstanding legal acumen, and incredible work loads) never refer to the average net income of self-employed practicing lawyers. They cite instead the gross earnings of their more successful acquaintances in the larger big-city law firms. Moral: Do not be bluffed! Lose a Bernard Baruch or a Clarence Darrow occasionally, if it comes to that; but do not yield to every threat.

In summary: Make sure you have the jobs correctly evaluated. Get the true facts—not those urged upon you by someone with several axes to grind. Make a reasonable exception to your policy, if you are convinced it is justified. Then, stand your ground.

RANGES VERSUS GRADES

People who are uncomfortable with the concepts of job evaluation and salary administration (a category that includes most managers) always prefer salary grades to individual rate ranges based on specific job evaluations. There is something so solid and scientific-looking about the boxy-looking chart or the impressive tables! And it is so satisfying to be able to say confidently, "That's a Grade Seven job: minimum, $450; maximum, $600."

A fairly typical salary structure based on job grades is illustrated in Figure 4.

Beautiful, is it not? But will it work? How was it put together? Where did the numbers come from? Who decides which jobs go where? And why?

Actually, the structure in Figure 4, while purely illustrative and hypothetical in this context, can be very nearly duplicated in hundreds, perhaps thousands, of firms across the country. It illustrates most of the virtues claimed for such schemes and the faults found with them. A plan like it can be constructed by any still-wet-behind-the-ears personnel trainee, or any half-wit office manager, in a matter of minutes. And—more's the pity!—if presented with sharp graphics and a rousing sales pitch, it can usually be sold to management. ("Now that that's out of the way, we can get back to running the company!")

Orderly it is. Neat it is. (And neatness counts!) In fact, many of its brethren will not look so neat after they have been in use for a while. Like

Figure 4.   Salary grade structure.

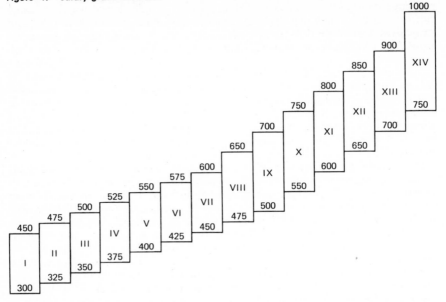

any salary structure, they will begin to show a bulge here and there; this happens to the best.

This structure, or its actual counterpart, was probably constructed partly by trial and error, partly by conjecture and fond hope. The bottom grade or two undoubtedly bear a close relationship to the actual market rates for entry-level jobs at the time the grades were set up. In some other portions of the structure, specific jobs will have been assigned salary levels that are solidly based on sound competitive data from surveys or other sources. For the lower half of the structure, the scheme very likely provides a reasonably good opportunity to pay salaries that will enable you to compete effectively in hiring a sufficient number of qualified workers.

The chief problem with such a structure, unless it is established on a basis different from most such systems, is likely to be internal rather than external. On what basis are specific jobs assigned to the various grades? How were the dollar ranges arrived at? What determines the spread from minimum to maximum? Is the value of each step up the ladder based on any defensible rationale? Of two jobs, one in grade V and one in grade II, how do you know the first is worth just that much more than the second—neither more nor less?

Looking at Figure 4 more closely, we begin to notice some things—and to have some suspicions. However sound may have been the choice of a $150 spread for grade I, what makes it also right for grades II through VII? If those are all right, why is it $175 for grade VIII and then $200 for grades IX through XIII?

It looks very much as if our salary expert had picked a $25 increment out of the air and then got hung up with it. Entranced by the precision and symmetry of it all, he proceeded blithely with this pattern until he realized that the spread should be greater. Then at grades VIII and X, he changed first the maximum and then the minimum, to go up by $50 increments instead. At the end, realizing he needed still more room, he let the maximum go up $100 in one step.

Yet, despite all this juggling of figures, we end up with a 50 percent spread for grade I and a 33⅓ percent spread for grade XIV—just about the exact opposite of what we probably ought to have!

Administrative simplicity is the chief virtue usually claimed for such structures. If you are satisfied with your ability (or your crystal ball) when it comes to assigning jobs to grades, such a system will probably serve you well— at least until you come up against managerial, professional, and specialized technical positions.

A camera, after all, is basically a simple device. Under ideal conditions, a plain box camera will make pictures as good as any. But conditions are seldom ideal. If your camera is to produce consistently good results under imperfect, changing, and even adverse conditions, it will require some very refined (and necessarily rather complex) components and accessories. Likewise, your techniques for salary administration, if they are to produce the results you need in the real world (imperfect as it is), will need some sophistication, which may involve complexities beyond the simplest approach available.

Now, is all this to condemn salary grade systems out of hand? By no means. Like box cameras, they have their uses and their place.

Where there are large numbers of relatively simple (i.e., routine clerical) positions which tend to group themselves naturally into clusters of jobs of approximately equal weight and value, such an approach does offer some simplicity and convenience. For an illustration, examine Figure 5, which shows the job evaluations in points taken from an actual company following an intensive study of a large sampling of positions. Note how a dozen or more clusters are readily identifiable. With close analysis of this scattergram, we can, by cut-and-fit methods, rather easily construct a system of job grades or classifications that would provide us with a sound basis for administering salaries.

Note, however, that this *should* be done by cut-and-fit. That is, the salary grades should fit the actual job groupings which naturally occur. The lines between job grades should be drawn *between* the clusters—never *through* them. Thus, the same pay will be available for positions which evaluation has shown to be similar in overall job content.

This exercise raises a couple of points—an observation and a question.

First, in order to create a really sound salary grade structure, you need to evaluate jobs. There is simply no other way to get the right relationships between jobs within the structure.

Second, if you have good evaluations, why bother with grades? Why blur the nice discrimination derived from the evaluation process by lumping all the jobs from, say, 100 to 120 points into a single grade and paying them all within the same range? If you can discern a quantitative difference of 20 percent when you analyze the jobs, why not let there be some difference (it will be less than 20 percent) in the rates of pay, in favor of the more important job?

As we saw earlier, it is simple enough, once jobs have been evaluated, to establish a formula whereby the range for any job can be easily and quickly computed when the evaluation points are known. Thus, the reputed advantage in administrative simplicity claimed for graded structures really does not amount to much. In most companies where there are large numbers of jobs, the midpoint, minimum, maximum, and position in range can be generated by a computer program and made available in quarterly or monthly printouts.

In summary, then, individual rate ranges are seen as preferable to grades.

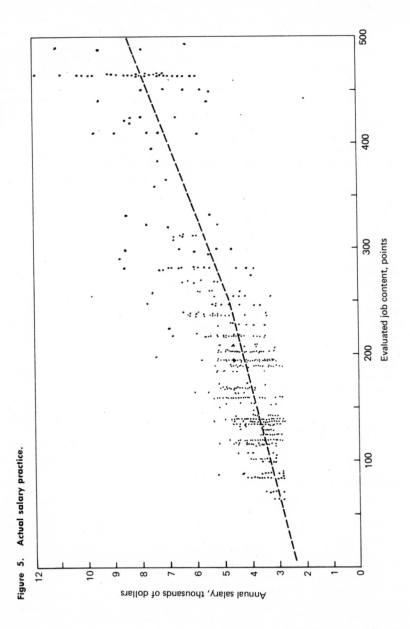

Figure 5.   Actual salary practice.

Where salary grades are used, great care must be taken to assign jobs to the proper grades—and job evaluation is the only really reliable basis for these assignments.

Relationships between Grades. If a graded structure is used, the size of the steps between the minimum of one grade and the minimum of the next is a matter of some import. Likewise, the relationship of one maximum to another is important—perhaps even more so. Like many other answers to questions in this business of salary administration, this one is probably going to have to be found empirically. The real test of what is right is what works best.

Points we need to consider include where the natural job clusters fall and what a normal promotional pattern might be within the structure. Indeed, the answer to the question, "What is a promotion?" may give us a clue as to what our increments ought to be between grades.

Also, we may want to ask, "What is a normal salary increase?" Naturally, the answer to this question will vary with the level involved, as we usually think in terms—at least roughly—of a percentage of current salary.

Putting these two points together, we will probably decide that a promotional increase should never be less than a normal merit increase. Usually, it should be more. Then, if one-grade promotions (e.g., from grade III to grade IV, or from grade IX to grade X) are a normal occurrence in our organization, we can rather readily conclude that the difference between one grade and the next should not be less than the amount of a minimum promotional increase at any given level. Certainly, it should be no less than the amount of a normal merit increase; and that is cutting it pretty fine!

Looking back at the salary grade structure depicted in Figure 4, we may suspect that too many grades, too close together, were used to cover the distance involved. We do not know this absolutely for sure; perhaps the pattern of jobs in a particular organization might justify the number and closeness of grades—even make it necessary and desirable. When we observe, however, that a promotion from grade VI to grade VII (halfway up the structure) would call for an increase of only $25 a month, we are inclined to wonder. That might be all right between grades I and II, but it certainly does not seem appropriate at higher levels.

As a general rule, differences very much below about 10 percent are suspect as being too small to be meaningful. At the other extreme, increments approaching 20 percent are likely to cause problems as being too large. Somewhere, then, between 8 percent and 15 percent you are likely to find the most workable arrangement. Remember that the increment does not have to be the same all the way up and down the structure. In fact, it should probably be smaller at the lower end and greater at the higher levels.

Also, you should remember that the maxima and the minima do not have to go up at the same rate. In fact, the increment between the maximum of one grade and that of the next should normally increase somewhat faster—i.e., in bigger dollar steps—than the increment between one minimum and the next. This is another way of saying that the spread should get wider as you go up the structure. That point is further discussed in the following section.

Range Spread. A frequent error in establishing the spread from top to bottom of a salary grade or rate range is the use of the same dollar spread for all jobs or for too many different levels of positions. There are at least two compelling and valid reasons for increasing the size (in dollars) of the spread as we move from lower to higher job levels.

The first reason is intensely practical. Since salary increases tend to be a function of current salary, it takes more dollars to cover an equal number of increases at the higher salary levels. Thus a spread of $150 will provide for six increases of $25 each, which may be fine at the lower levels. The same spread will accommodate only three adjustments of $50 each, which may be the appropriate increment when we are dealing with higher base salaries.

Leaving aside considerations of performance, and thinking only of the passage of time, we might expect that individuals would tend to stay longer in the better jobs than in the entry-level positions. We therefore need to provide more steps in the grade or room for at least an equal number of merit increases within a given salary range.

The second reason for widening the spread for higher-rated jobs is more philosophical, but it is just as important in practice. It has to do with the nature of jobs, how they are designed, and how people function in them.

Jobs at the lowest levels are very rigidly structured, and the incumbents in them tend to be closely supervised. The positions are so designed that there is little opportunity for individual thinking or independent action. Thus there is less chance for the quality of an individual incumbent's performance to make a significant difference in how much the job contributes to the achievement of the organization's total goals. To be more specific, whether we get mediocre or outstanding performance from one junior file clerk just does not change things that much. But the difference between barely satisfactory and really superb performance by a department head (who may be responsible for the work of 50 persons) or a key scientist can make a great deal of difference.

Since higher-level jobs permit more independent thought and action, there is a greater chance for the incumbent to vary the position's contribution by how well he does his work. To recognize and reward (and, it is hoped, to motivate) better performance, there should be more room in the range to administer the actual salaries of different incumbents in similarly rated jobs.

There is no theoretically based, absolutely scientific method of determining exactly how wide the range should be. Experience and practice, however, serve to establish some general guidelines and ground rules.

In the upper portions of the structure, it is safe to say that the spread (maximum over minimum) should not exceed 50 percent. With the possible exception of a very few positions at or near the chief executive level, this will produce a dollar spread which is quite adequate.

With a midpoint of $10,000 per annum, for example, we have a minimum of $8,000 and a maximum of $12,000; at the $20,000 level, the minimum is $16,000, the maximum $24,000. And at a midpoint of $30,000, the minimum becomes $24,000 and the maximum $36,000. Thus the same *percentage* spread of 50 percent of the minimum (20 percent above and 20 percent below the midpoint) produces *dollar* spreads of $4,000, $8,000, and $12,000 at these three levels.

At the bottom end of the salary structure, where we are dealing with entry-level, nonexempt jobs, a spread of 30 percent or 35 percent (maximum over minimum) is often quite adequate. We can gradually increase this to 50 percent at about the point where the exempt positions start and keep it at 50 percent from there on up. (See Figure 3 and the discussion of salary ranges at that point.)

Like most questions in this area of management, the matter of range spread has both philosophical overtones and intensely practical significance in its applications. But then, what good is any philosophy if it has no practical application?

Use of the Range or Grade Spread. Once we have a salary structure established, we still have a question or two to answer before we are ready to decide what should actually be paid to a real person in a real job.

Suppose we have salary grades. Who goes at the top and who at the bottom of the grade? How and why does a person progress from low to high—and when?

If we use individual ranges, how do we place a particular individual's salary within the range? What is the meaning of the midpoint? The minimum? The maximum?

In a graded structure, it is rather common practice to subdivide grades into steps or predetermined increments. These are normally used as the amounts of merit or automatic increases within grades, and they are also sometimes used to determine promotional increases.

Graded structures are most often administered on the assumption that everybody eventually gets to the top of his grade, if he keeps breathing long enough. Thus, whatever reasons are given, increases within a grade are really automatic. In the federal civil service, they are called "Ramspecks," after a former member of the Civil Service Commission; but whatever they are called, they are granted after specified periods of time, with little regard to the quality or quantity of work performed.

Many structures with individual rate ranges are in fact administered almost the same way. The easy thing to do is to give everybody a little something every year.

There is, however, a growing school of adherents to the doctrine of midpoint control. This approach is predicated upon the concept that the midpoint salary policy has been set at a proper competitive level, and thus it represents a fair and adequate rate of pay for the majority, who do about average work. Only those who do more and/or better work than the average, therefore, should be paid above the midpoint.

A refinement of the latter approach is illustrated by Figure 6. This particular illustration assumes a 50 percent range spread, but the same approach can be applied if the spread is less. The entire range is not intended to be available to everyone, in this scheme. Instead, it is divided into five equal zones, each associated with a level of performance. In effect, then, there are five smaller ranges, and five ceilings, depending on how an individual's performance is rated. Obviously, use of this approach requires a good performance appraisal program (see Part 5 for discussions of performance appraisal).

Whatever system you employ, you need to decide *beforehand* what your range means, or how your grades work. If you do not set up the rules before your structure is assailed, chaos will soon follow. Having a rationale and a program worked out in advance will not keep away all troubles, but it will give you some rules to work by.

DISRUPTIONS IN THE SALARY STRUCTURE

Some of the more frequently encountered problems have been alluded to—indeed, discussed at length—in the preceding sections. At this point, we can take up one or two other vexations that will surely visit themselves upon the unwary (or even the wary) salary administrator.

Several of the problems that manifest themselves are actually different versions of a single problem—salary compression. The major socioeconomic trend of the past 100 years in most of the civilized world (and especially in the U.S.A.) has been a leveling of social and economic differences. The difference between the top and bottom strata has, on the whole, been steadily reduced by a variety of devices, including steeply progressive income and inheritance taxes. The old adage that "the rich get richer, etc.," has been replaced by a situation approaching the exact opposite.

Figure 6.   Anatomy of a salary range: The range is a skeleton—flow of life is regulated by performance appraisal.

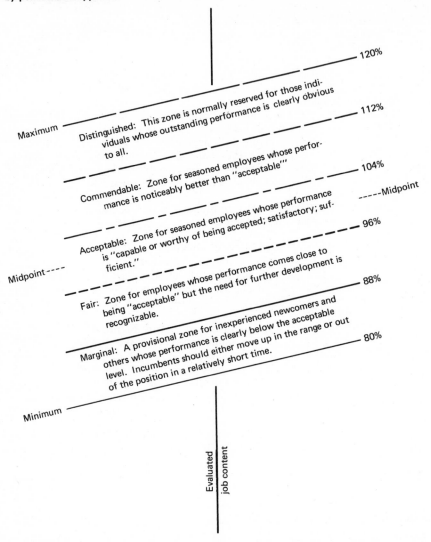

Please note that this phenomenon is not being condemned—merely observed. Certainly few of us would quarrel with the idea that a basic level of income somewhat above bare survival requirements ought to be available to anyone who is willing and able to work for a living.

From the salary administrator's viewpoint, the practical consequence is that the bottom of the structure keeps going up faster than the top; as a result, there is less and less room in between to recognize and reward different levels of job value. One large corporation, in the late 1960s, illustrated this point rather dramatically in its annual report to stockholders. The take-home pay of its chief executive officer, this firm pointed out, was equivalent to that of 11 and a fraction janitors. A generation earlier, the difference would probably have been on the order of 40 or 50 times, or more. We had better believe that top executives are motivated by something besides money!

To be more specific, let us say you are concerned with a salary structure that includes first-line foremen and other factory supervisory positions. You evaluate the jobs and place them where they belong with respect to the rest of your salaried jobs. Now, if your production workers are covered by negotiated wage rates, you are very likely to find that the highest average earnings of employees in the bargaining unit overlap a good portion of your foremen's salary range!

What you will do in this situation will vary, according to (1) how bad it is; (2) what options are open to you; and (3) what you can afford.

If the problem is created mainly by overtime earnings, you may select—as an increasing number of companies have—to make voluntary payments to foremen for overtime work, in order to maintain a differential. These may be at premium rates, at straight-time hourly equivalents, a fixed sum, or a percentage bonus. They may be paid with regular salary checks, monthly, quarterly, or in the form of an annual bonus. Obviously, it is an exception to your normal salary practice, but one necessitated and justified by factors over which you have no control.

Should you find that it is only the bottom one-fourth or one-third of your salary range that is rendered unusable, you really do not have much of a problem, assuming your range was wide enough (on the order of a 50 percent spread) to begin with. You simply forget about the bottom part of the range and work with what is left. At this level, where salaries are required to be competitive in only a local market and are strongly influenced by hourly wage rates, smaller increments of salary adjustment can be used than are acceptable at higher levels, and you can live with a somewhat narrower salary range.

On the other hand, if the problem is more severe (or when it is aggravated by a negotiated increase in hourly rates), you will have to make some compensating adjustments. It may be necessary to bend your salary policy line upward, making it start higher, with a flatter slope to the point where it joins up with the rest of your exempt structure. This is not particularly desirable, but you may be forced to do it. The alternative of elevating the entire salary structure by a percentage (*never* a dollar amount!) equivalent to the hourly wage increase is not usually open to us, if we want the company to stay in business.

A similar problem can be created by other factors. Suppose the federal minimum wage is raised to $4,160 a year. (Do not laugh; it could happen by the time this book is in print!) If your company's lowest salary rates are already far above this level, you may not feel the crunch immediately. But many companies will. Look back at Figure 1 and Figure 4. You can see that the effect of this increase (just draw a straight, level line across the chart at the $4,160 level) will be to cut off the lower portions of the salary ranges or grades for the lower-level jobs.

Now, what do you do? If you are forced to raise salaries for the lowest-rated jobs by 10 percent, do you raise all salaries 10 percent to maintain internal equity? Not likely. Do you simply raise those immediately affected and ignore the rest? This could result in having a wide variety of positions—some considerably more important than others—paid at the same rate or within the same range. That is neither fair nor really workable.

What most companies try to do in this situation is to adjust in progressively smaller increments up the line, letting the "ripple effect" disappear at a higher level. This is the same thing we talked about earlier, raising and flattening the lower portion of the salary policy line.

What we are doing if we use this technique is, of course, simply moving the compression effect up the line. Unless we can elevate the whole structure proportionately, some of the differentiation in salary that we would otherwise have just disappears.

As in the previous example, if the impact is minimal, you may be able simply to get along without the bottom portion of your salary ranges or grades at the lowest levels. If the job of a parking lot attendant, for example, is the only one affected, you do not need much of a range for that. It could almost be a single-rate job, anyway. So, anybody in it will have limited opportunities for salary increases. Many of the incumbents in these low-level positions, it is hoped, will be promoted into better jobs before the available head room is exhausted.

Other manifestations of this same basic problem are seen in the difficulties encountered in trying to fit newly hired college graduates into an existing salary structure. Again, these rates, in a highly competitive campus recruiting market, have risen faster than salaries generally. With holders of the Master of Business Administration degree, the problem is even more acute. Sometimes we just have to pay more than the early jobs are worth and hope that these glamor boys (and girls) will in fact live up to their advertising. If so, they will progress rapidly into positions that justify the salaries we have to pay them. If not, they will probably leave, anyway (most of them do in a few years).

chapter 19

Establishing the
Hourly Pay Structure

WILLIAM GOMBERG   *Wharton School of Finance and Commerce, University of Pennsylvania, Philadelphia, Pennsylvania*

WILLIAM ABOUD   *Wharton School of Finance and Commerce, University of Pennsylvania, Philadelphia, Pennsylvania*

It used to be that employers hired and paid employees to do a specific job; the link between what was made and what was paid for was deceptively simple. The growth of industry, the bureaucratization of the labor organization, the breakdown of manufacturing into myriad processes, and the addition to the organization of a complex distribution mechanism have increased the complexity of the relationship between what a worker is paid and what a product is worth.

The relationship has become so remote at times that some people have recommended a guaranteed annual income, an idea incorporated in the 1970 welfare proposals of President Nixon. Thus, money may be paid for a whole range of purposes with immediate production results at one pole and the welfare of the commonwealth at the other.

The assignment which we wish to cover, however, restricts itself to the hourly wage, the oldest method of paying people and now generally associated with blue-collar work.

We might also point out, however, that a number of large, progressive firms have abandoned the hourly wage for blue-collar workers and have instead put these workers on an annual salary—for example, IBM. In a sense, IBM has decided to treat blue-collar labor as a capital cost, paying for labor on the same basis it pays for capital equipment. Thus, payment is made irrespective of the degree of use of the instrument or the amount of its production.

This may be possible for organizations in rapidly growing industries, but for most manufacturers, labor is so important a cost in their product that they are loath to take this kind of risk.

FORMULATING WAGE POLICY

Any wage structure must flow from a policy, and this policy must be consistent despite the often conflicting demands of internal equity and external competitiveness. In terms of external competitiveness, the primary aim, of course, is to establish wage levels high enough to attract and retain the skills necessary to operate the business, but not so high that labor costs drive up production costs to the point where the company is unable to compete in the product marketplace. Depending on its specific situation, a company may formulate its wage policy to compete with:

1. Community wages. The company may choose to pay the going rate in the community or higher than the going rate or, if it can make economical use of marginal workers, lower than the going rate.

2. National rates, as in the railroad industry

3. Regional rates, as in the brewing industry

In defining the manpower marketplace in which it will compete, the company must consider how its workers and the labor market in general will react to its choice.

Some possible sources of information in determining wage policy are: (1) other existing wage agreements, (2) government regulations, (3) union-management agreements, and (4) union policies and influences, especially regarding which payment plans and means of administering them will be considered acceptable.

In addition to expressing a company's competitive pay position, wage policy must be committed to preventing the "accordion effect."

The accordion effect, or wage compression, comes about when increases are given in fixed monetary increments across the board. What happens is that when general wage increases are expressed in so many cents per hour, over a period of time the cents-per-hour settlements will narrow the gap between unskilled and highly skilled workers, thereby destroying the internal pay relationships. Figure 1 illustrates this phenomenon. To avoid the accordion effect and preserve existing relationships, wage increases may be expressed in percentages.

This phenomenon of compressing the wage rate has caused serious problems in the automotive industry, for both management and the union. Matters became so serious that the skilled workers were threatening to break away from the UAW and organize their own union. They were reconciled only when the UAW pledged to sign no agreement unless the skilled workers approved it as an independent voting unit.

DETERMINING ACTUAL WAGES

The problem of setting relative wages is subject to two contradictory forces:

1. *The equity sense of the job classification engineer.* The job classification engineer erects an internal value structure based upon a number of job variables applicable to the organization and then defines an equitable wage in accordance with the consistent treatment of these variables.

2. *The job market structure as viewed by the economist.* The economist is interested only in how many dollars the market is ready to pay for any wage. If tool and die workers are in excess supply, it will not trouble the economist

Figure 1.   The accordion effect.

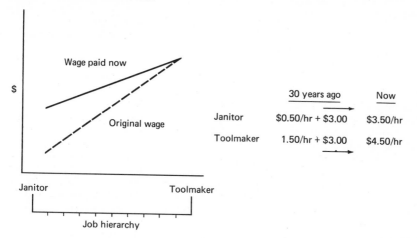

that foundry hands who are in short supply may be momentarily receiving a higher wage than toolmakers. Obviously, we have exaggerated for emphasis. But nevertheless, from the market point of view, the important consideration is what the market commands rather than what engineering rationality demands.

The employer very often finds himself torn between these two considerations. The net result is that we may define five kinds of equity:

1. The job evaluation rate based on relative job content
2. The comparative rate for the same job in other industries in the same area
3. The comparative rate for the same job in the same industry in the same area—the local industrial labor rate
4. The comparative rate for the same job in the same industry in other areas—the cosmopolitan industry labor market rate
5. The comparative rate for the same job in other industries in other areas—the cosmopolitan craft labor market rate

As an example, let us take a machinist and see the way the rate could vary. Suppose the rate for a machinist in the X automobile factory in Speedunk is $3.65, whereas the rate for a machinist in the Y textile machinery works in Speedunk is only $3.25. Again, the machinist's rate in the rival Z automobile factory in Speedunk is $3.75, whereas the machinist's rate in the M textile works in Podunk is $3.45. Thus, for the single job of machinist, we have several different rates, any one of which can be justified according to some concept of equity. Collective bargaining is the common method used to satisfy both labor and management that there has been equitable consideration of both the going rate for the job on the outside and its evaluated position in the internal job hierarchy.

External Considerations. Survey information can be helpful in establishing a fair and equitable measure for paying comparable wages for comparable work on the local level. A company may collect data by conducting its own survey, or it may wish to use data collected through:

1. The Bureau of Labor Statistics (Bureau of Labor Statistics Annual Regional Wage Data)
2. National and local trade associations set up to collect these types of data

(e.g., local survey groups, Chamber of Commerce, and/or other trade association groups)

3. Other government agencies, such as state labor departments

4. Research agencies, such as the National Industrial Conference Board

5. Union agreements and/or union surveys

Since the work content of jobs with the same title will vary considerably from company to company, it is best to build a survey around task groupings, or functions—for example, the paint shop or the machine shop—and compare similar jobs within the task groupings. (See Figure 2.)

In conducting a survey, management must first decide which task groupings or jobs are key occupations in its particular labor market. These jobs are also called "benchmark jobs" and are defined as jobs that have stable content and skill requirements (also educational, training, or apprenticeship requirements, etc.) wherever they are found in industry. Some examples of benchmark jobs are tool and die maker, electrician, and janitor. A benchmark job generally should represent a significant number of employees. All other jobs are slotted into an internal hierarchy between the top- and bottom-rated key jobs. Methods for doing this are discussed later.

The going rate for any particular job can now be found by collecting data on applicable jobs (task summaries) by one of the survey methods mentioned earlier. The spread between the top and bottom of the remaining rates gathered from the various employers can then be considered sound and tested and can become the maximum and minimum of a bracket for a particular job in your area.

A good rule of thumb is to utilize only the middle 50 percent of the reported data. Therefore, a large enough sample must be used. The final outcome must be an intelligible and well-balanced wage schedule which is related to a carefully defined job classification. To derive this kind of classification, it is necessary to consider those factors which could influence the data, such as the reported base rate and its method of calculation, working conditions, personnel policies, fringe benefits, seniority of workers and their efficiency, and how closely the job description fits the factory under observation. Job descriptions that do not match up at least 75 percent should not be used. (See Figure 3.)

After the data have been collected, they should be classified and organized for analysis and comparison with internal personnel data.

Brackets are then established (1) by a weighted-average method in which the maximum and minimum are a fixed percentage above and below the weighted average, respectively, (2) where the rates actually paid cluster, (3) where the minimum rates cluster if the reporting companies have a bracket system already, or (4) some combination of the above.

Figure 2. Task groupings.

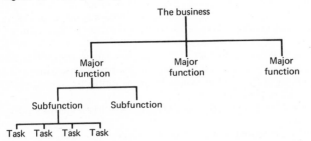

Figure 3.   Determining the going rate. Dots represent reported wages for Job A.

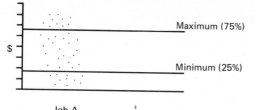

There are several precautions of which to be mindful in using the survey method to establish hourly job rates:

1. The data must come from the local labor market area.

2. Only key or benchmark jobs can be compared directly.

3. In evaluating the data, one must consider the number and type of reporting companies and the number of employees doing the job in each reporting company.

4. The survey rates should be compared with the local factory rates with caution, since job content varies within the job title.

Internal Considerations.   Job evaluation is a systematic method of appraising the value of each job in relation to other jobs in the organization.   When applied consistently, it orders jobs into a hierarchy according to their relative contribution and provides a mutually agreeable payment for each job commensurate with its agreed-upon position in the hierarchy, regardless of the individual performing that particular job.   The payment plan is based upon the theory that the more difficult the job, the more wage value the job comprises. It is important to recognize that jobs change over time, and that reevaluation may become necessary.

To evaluate jobs, the following steps must be taken:

1. Gather information about each job—identify the job, describe its duties and responsibilities, and specify the minimum qualifications necessary for a worker to hold the job.   Optimally, tasks are grouped into logical packages which become the jobs under consideration.

2. Decide which factors are important in distinguishing the relative value of a job in relation to any other job (i.e., the "compensable factors").   The compensable factors should be present in all jobs in varying amounts, they should be important in the performance of the job, and they should be mutually exclusive.

3. Impose a logical value system on the jobs that forces them into a hierarchy according to the degree of compensable factors they possess.   There are several widely used plans to determine the relative value of jobs—for example, the American Association of Industrial Management (formerly the National Metal Trades Association) plan, which considers 11 factors.   (See Chapter 12, Section 12.3, for a discussion of the AAIM system of job evaluation.)   Eugene Benge and his co-workers developed a factor comparison plan with as few as five factors, which is discussed in Chapter 10.   Other commonly used methods of job evaluation are ranking and job classification, covered fully in Chapter 7, and point systems, discussed in Chapter 9.

In determining relative job payments, other factors besides job evaluation will be influential:

1. Stability and duration of employment

2. Career aspects of the job, i.e., how high does the promotional sequence climb?

3. Market supply or demand for specific occupations

4. Traditional wage and factory social relationships

5. Working conditions, which are considered more important today than they used to be

6. Critical role of the job as a bottleneck

Influence of factors other than job evaluation is seen in many situations. For example, the increasing wage demands of sanitation workers in some cities have led to increased demands from teachers. Sanitation workers' wages were exceeding those of beginning teachers. The sanitation workers felt their demands were justified by the unpleasantness of their work and the critical need for the work to be done on time. It does not take long for a city to be buried in filth and threatened with disease when garbage remains uncollected. On the other hand, the results of a poor education for youngsters may not become apparent until years later when they are adults. Then again, teachers may look forward to a career as a principal or a superintendent. The sanitation worker is unlikely to go anywhere. In short, though a teacher must have at least four years of college, the sanitation workers insisted they were worth as much as beginning teachers because of the severity of their working conditions and the critical nature of the jobs they performed.

Another example of the influence of nonjob evaluation factors is in the building trades. Here, workers justify their high rates largely on the casual and seasonal nature of their employment. In addition, their union control over the size of the labor market through apprenticeship requirements enables them to take advantage of the law of supply and demand by restricting the supply of skilled workers.

PAYMENT

Payments of wages may be keyed to time alone or to expected production per time unit. The method for payment must be chosen early. Needs must be evaluated and the method that will work best for the establishment adopted. This is especially true in highly competitive enterprises where only a small difference in relative wages can destroy an otherwise advantageous market position.

Straight Time Payment. Wages may be keyed to time alone after a hierarchy of jobs within the plant has been established by job evaluation. The hierarchy may be developed simply by drawing a line from the top rate to the bottom rate and fitting all other jobs in between; alternatively, benchmark jobs can be picked and a trend line drawn on which to slot all the other jobs. (See Figure 4.)

The jobs may be covered by a single rate or a rate range.

Under a single-rate structure, each job or class of jobs in the hierarchy has one particular wage. Its advantages are that it is simple to understand and is cheaply and easily administered. It works well for highly repetitive jobs having few skill requirements. It has the further advantage of limiting the possibility of supervisors playing favorites among the workers.

The principal disadvantage of single rates is that individual differences are lost, especially in highly repetitive operations, so that outstanding performance cannot be recognized. Also, because of this characteristic, nonmonetary motivators become necessary to increase output.

An example of a single-rate structure is shown in Table 1. Note that the

Figure 4.   Establishing a trend line.

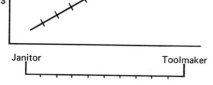

relationship from job to job is determined by a varying increment that slowly increases as the structure climbs to rate 14, then increases more rapidly until rate 20, when it slowly tapers off.   This is only one example, and increments can be designed to fit every kind of taste, purpose, and union pressure.

A *rate range structure* can be either open-ended, i.e., $3.15 to $3.85 per hour, for example, or in steps, i.e., $3.15, $3.25, $3.35, . . . $3.85 per hour.   It is usually built around an appropriate single rate, e.g., $3.50 ± 10 percent. The spread depends on company policy or collective bargaining, and it can be expressed as a fixed dollar amount or as a percentage.   Sometimes the bottom is what the job is allegedly worth.   Payments above that represent performance, longevity, or a combination of both.   Most often, however, the alleged value of the job is set at the midpoint.   Everyone on that job can get to the midpoint, but above that, performance, longevity, union rule, or some combination determines the amount of compensation over time.

Just as single rates are consistently related, so are the midpoints of rate ranges.   Movements within the range are governed by merit, seniority, or union rule, or some combination of all three.   Unless the administration of the system is very sophisticated, all workers within a given range will be at the top of the rate over time.   Furthermore, movement within the range is often subject to personal rate discrimination and is sensitive to differences in evaluators, supervisory or union, whose decisions as to work performance determine workers' wages.   (See Figure 5.)

Sometimes a probationary rate is used.   It is the minimum wage for a specific period of time after hiring or until work is satisfactory, after which time the incumbent receives the appropriate job rate.

Wage Incentive Payment.   The incentive wage system presents essentially the same problem as does the time work wage system, and that is, How do you determine a base wage?

Determining the base wage for the wage incentive payment plan involves the same steps and problems that have been examined for the basic wage of the straight time system.   Wage incentive payment plans in their application, however, do present certain problems.

First and foremost, if a union is in the picture, there is a subtle difference in philosophy of approach which if not explicitly expressed will be implicitly pursued.   The original philosophy behind the wage incentive plan when it was developed by management was somewhat the following: The base time wage represents the payment of a fair day's wage for a fair day's work.   Any excess work produced above this fair time standard is paid a bonus.   Thus, there is a subtle difference between the worker's involvement in the basic wage and the

TABLE 1   Single-rate Structure

Job or job class	Hourly pay	Percent increase between program steps
3	$2.435	
		1.8
4	2.48	
		1.4
5	2.515	
		1.8
6	2.56	
		2.1
7	2.615	
		1.9
8	2.665	
		1.9
9	2.715	
		1.8
10	2.765	
		2.5
11	2.835	
		2.5
12	2.905	
		3.1
13	2.995	
		3.0
14	3.085	
		2.9
15	3.175	
		4.4
16	3.315	
		5.0
17	3.48	
		6.2
18	3.695	
		3.8
19	3.835	
		5.2
20	4.035	
		3.8
21	4.19	
		3.8
22	4.35	
		2.8
23	4.47	
		3.8
24	4.64	
		2.6
25	4.76	

increment above the basic wage. This basic wage is paid to him as a matter of right; the increment above the basic wage, as a matter of performance.

This line of thinking will be rejected by the union. They will argue that wages can be paid either on the basis of the time that is spent or on the basis of the production that is achieved. If the choice is to pay workers in accordance with their productivity, then let the system be called "productivity wages"

Figure 5. The rate range.

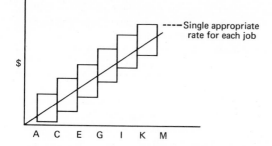

instead of a "wage incentive" payment plan. An implicit contract is entered into between the management and the worker, establishing a management obligation to furnish the opportunity for the workers to make a specified hourly wage at a normal working pace. The worker in turn obligates himself to meet the production standard that is set.

Although the details of wage incentive payment plans are as various as the engineering authorities who use them, most plans will fit into one of three basic categories. In discussing these categories, it is assumed that the basic time for the 100 percent point is the same for the three systems.

First, there is the system which pays a worker less per unit for each unit that he turns out above the 100 percent point. Thus, the worker receives less for the production above the 100 percent point than he does for the production below the 100 percent point. These plans will generally be rejected by the union. Or if the union is not in the picture, such a plan will probably serve as an excellent rallying point for any union that anticipates entering the plant.

In the second system, the worker receives more for production above the 100 percent point than for production up to 100 percent. These plans are to management's advantage when the overhead costs are heavy compared with the direct labor costs; the incremental cost of labor above the 100 percent point is more than compensated for by the savings in overhead. Usually, no union will object to this system. If there are any arguments, it will be over where the 100 percent production standard should be placed.

Then there is the straight piecework plan that pays a constant increment up to the 100 percent point and the same increment above the 100 percent point, and it is these plans that are most common.

In general, wage incentive plans are most useful in industries where individual workers exercise individual control over production speed. They do not make too much sense in factories where the worker tends an automatic process or where his speed is controlled by an assembly line. Here the worker's time is fixed by the speed of the line and the length of the work station.

Most of these plans are based upon standards which assume that a fully skilled operator is in the middle of working on a part with which he or she is familiar. If, as often happens in industries like the needle trades, runs of work change as often as two and three times a day, wide variation in performance over the entire work day is found. The reason for this may be time taken for learning a new part or, as the industry expression goes, time for getting your hand into the work.

It is not so much a matter of learning the work as it is a problem of regaining one's momentum as one shifts from old work to new work which, though done before, requires refamiliarization. In other words, the pace changes with every change of the psychological set.

Wage Increments. In addition to their basic wages—regardless of whether they are based on straight time or incentive methods—hourly workers generally receive extra compensation in circumstances specified below:

1. Overtime—usually time and one-half—paid for any hours worked beyond the standard day or week, and often double time on special holidays or Sunday

2. Late-shift differential—premium pay for hours worked on any shift other than the normal "day" shift

3. Call-back pay—guaranteed pay for a certain minimum number of hours if called back to work after completing a regularly assigned shift

4. Call-in pay—guaranteed pay for a certain minimum number of hours if called to work on a day one would not ordinarily work

5. Reporting pay—guaranteed pay for a certain minimum number of hours if the worker reports at the usual time but finds no work available

CONSIDERATIONS OTHER THAN BASIC WAGE

Fringe benefits—payments for old age retirement, sickness, holidays and vacations, etc.—have become important for blue-collar workers since World War II. The principal item to remember in assessing the wage impact of fringe benefits is that their cost must be calculated in increments to the basic hourly rate.

Also to be considered in figuring wage costs are governmental constraints. For one thing, there is the federal wage and hour law, which provides a basic minimum wage. Revisions of the Fair Labor Standards Act, the Davis-Bacon Act for the building trades, and the Public Contracts Law develop various formulas for the payment of prevailing wages for work done for the federal government. These are basics which have not appeared from nowhere but are the results of organized labor's lobbying activities in the national and state legislatures. They are nonetheless important because the provisions may have great impact on hourly wages in both union and nonunion situations.

Finally to be considered is union influence. Administration of a wage program does not call so much for the mastery of endless technique as it does for the ability to live with tension. This tension governs whether a plant is union or nonunion. It has been said that the union seems to influence the nonunion plant even more strongly than the union plant. Wage administrators in unionized plants know exactly what their plans are after they are through negotiating with the union. Administrators in nonunion plants have to be able to anticipate that their particular formula will keep the union outside, and it happens quite often that it costs more to keep unions out than to let them in.

BIBLIOGRAPHY

Belcher, David W.: *Wage and Salary Administration,* Prentice-Hall, Inc., Englewood Cliffs, N.J., 1962.
Benge, Eugene J., et al.: *Manual of Job Evaluation,* Harper & Brothers, New York, 1941.
Bullock, Paul: *Standards of Wage Determination,* Institute of Industrial Relations, U.C.L.A., Los Angeles, 1960.
Burtt, Everett J., Sr.: *Labor Markets, Unions, and Government Policies,* St. Martin's Press, New York, 1963.
Douty, H. M.: *Wages,* Institute of Industrial Relations, U.C.L.A., Los Angeles, 1951.

Douty, H. M.: *Wage Structures,* Institute of Industrial Relations, U.C.L.A., Los Angeles, 1954.

Goldner, William: *Hours of Work,* Institute of Industrial Relations, U.C.L.A., Berkeley, 1952.

Ireson, William G., and Eugene L. Grant, eds.: *Handbook of Industrial Engineering and Management,* Prentice-Hall, Inc., Englewood Cliffs, N.J., 1955.

Lott, M. R.: *Wage Scales and Job Evaluations,* Ronald Press, New York, 1926.

Perlman, Richard, ed.: *Wage Determination,* D. C. Heath, Boston, 1964.

chapter 20

Establishing the
Clerical Pay Structure

DENNIS S. KENNEDY   *Insurance Company of North America, Philadelphia, Pennsylvania*

H. PAUL ABBOTT   *Manager, Personnel and Administration, INA Corporation, Philadelphia, Pennsylvania*

The basic methodology used in establishing a clerical salary structure differs little from that of establishing hourly or professional salary structures. However, the nature of work performed by clerical employees requires that a slightly different mix of factors be considered in establishing the clerical pay structure. Often, therefore, the clerical pay structure will differ substantially from those established for hourly and professional employees.

THE CLERICAL JOB STRUCTURE

A clerical salary structure is the result of constructing a job structure through job evaluation and pricing this structure. Without a minimal job evaluation program, establishment of an equitable clerical salary structure is difficult, if not impossible. Without job evaluation the structure would be merely a reaction to the marketplace and individual managerial value judgments with inadequate concern for the harm resulting from internal salary inequities.

Job Classification. In small organizations each clerical job may be different enough from other jobs to warrant separate pricing of the jobs. However, most firms have discovered that their clerical jobs may be conveniently grouped into levels of responsibility, difficulty, or other job requirements. These levels are known as "job classifications." Job classification has become popular because grouping jobs into classes reduces the number of pay rates which must be used for administering clerical salaries.   This in turn reduces the administrative and economic burden of maintaining the salary structure.

Classifying jobs requires a decision as to the number of job classifications which will be established.   Past practices of the company, number and types of jobs, and types of salary increases which the company gives will influence the number of classes in the job structure.   For example, if the same job structure is extended to all levels of jobs—clerical, hourly, professional, etc.—the company will be required to construct more classes than will be necessary if the job structure applies only to the clerical jobs.   An excellent rule to follow is to have just enough job classes so that difficulty levels are easily distinguishable and all jobs in one level are relatively equal in difficulty.   Having too few classes means that one classification may be required to encompass several levels of difficulty and responsibility, whereas having too many classes makes it difficult to distinguish the jobs in one class from those in adjacent classes.   If the job structure is limited to clerical jobs, an organization should have from five to ten classifications.

Of the four prevalent job evaluation types, only the grade or classification type may be used to establish job classes as part of the evaluation process.   To classify jobs on the basis of the other three job evaluation systems—ranking, factor analysis, and point value—requires several steps after evaluation.   One classification method that may be applied to the remaining three evaluation methods requires that all the jobs be ranked and then divided into classes at those points where there is an obvious break in degree of difficulty.   For example, using a point value job evaluation system, a company may determine that although the possible point values that can be assigned to a job may range from 10 to 300, the jobs themselves may cluster around particular values.   Therefore, each of these clusters would become a separate job classification.   After the jobs have been thus classified, a description of each classification should be prepared in order to define accurately the difficulty level of the classification. Each job within the class should then be compared with the classification description in order to determine that the classification is appropriate to the job.

The factor analysis and point value methods of evaluation also permit the convenience of defining job classes in terms of money or point values, respectively.   Classification of jobs in this manner involves determining the number of classes desired and dividing this into the possible range of values in order to determine a quantitative measure for each job classification.   For instance, if the possible range of values in a point value job evaluation system is from zero to 100 and the company desires five job classes, then all jobs with point values from 1 to 20 will be in one class; from 21 to 40 points will define another class; and so on.   Best results are obtained through the construction of several tentative classification scales by varying the number of job classes from scale to scale. The company's jobs are then classified according to each scale, and the different scales are compared to determine which one most accurately places jobs into difficulty levels, makes the sharpest distinction between levels, and offers the desired number of promotion opportunities.

Although the above discussion assumes that each job class will have common intervals of quantitative value, it is possible to construct job classes with variable intervals.   However, a classification system using variable intervals is open to the criticism that the intervals were gerrymandered to force jobs into particular intervals.

Union Participation in Constructing the Job Structure.   A company with a unionized clerical force must consider union reaction in constructing its job structure. The actual method used to construct a job structure is similar in both union and nonunion situations, but in a union shop union pressure will make the process a bilateral one. The more closely the union can be drawn into the process of creating a job structure, the more readily will it accept that structure. In fact, joint development of a job structure may well prevent the issue of job structure from arising in a collective bargaining situation. If management does establish a job structure unilaterally, the issue will probably become a part of the collective bargaining process.

Although inclusion as an item for discussion during collective bargaining does not preclude establishment of an equitable job structure, the bargaining process often is an emotion-laden arena where the job structure cannot receive the reasoned consideration necessary to its establishment. As a result, inequities may easily be introduced into the structure. Therefore, the most reasonable course would be to obtain the union's view of the job structure before the issue becomes one for formal negotiation.

Legislation and the Job Structure. Recent social legislation on both federal and state levels has had a profound effect on the construction of job structures. The Equal Pay Act of 1963 and the Civil Rights Act of 1964, as amended, prohibit discrimination practices in a number of areas, including compensation. Both laws apply to firms engaged in interstate commerce, and their intent is that, within a company, equal pay must be available for persons in the same jobs. Specific application of these laws to the job structure means that jobs involving like duties and responsibilities must be evaluated similarly without discriminaton due to race, creed, age, or sex.

Maintaining the Job Structure. Once a job structure has been chosen, it is necessary to classify accurately all the employees who fall under the structure. Classification of employees should probably be left to clerical supervisors with assistance from the salary administrator. Once the structure has been installed and employees classified, periodic checks should be made to ensure that each employee's job classification is appropriate to the work he or she is doing. A job structure is valid and effective only so long as employees are properly classified. A great number of improperly classified employees severely limits the usefulness of the structure and may even cause a considerable morale problem.

ESTABLISHING SALARY LEVELS

Once the job structure has been agreed upon and established, it becomes necessary to place salary values on the jobs or job classes within the structure. For convenience, those factors which influence the levels at which a company places its salaries may be divided into four major areas: the clerical salary market, management philosophy, union influence, and legal considerations.

The Clerical Salary Market. Prevailing wages paid to the clerical population from which an organization wishes to draw its employees may be referred to as the "clerical salary market." Today, most companies are required to recruit their clerical employees from a pool of potential workers which, it would seem, is not growing as rapidly as is the demand for clerical employees. It is risky, therefore, for a company to assume that its clerical salary rates are competitive with the existing salary market unless it surveys the salary market at regular and frequent intervals.

A basic problem confronting any organization which is trying to measure the clerical salary market is the definition of its major competition for employees. An organization must accurately identify its salary market competition or it will establish ranges which are either not competitive with prevailing rates or which are uneconomical.   As there is no national clerical salary market, and as clerical pay scales vary significantly from location to location, an organization should survey the clerical salary market for each of its major locations.   In general, there is no industrial bias to clerical jobs, so a company must view all segments of the local business community as potential competitors for clerical employees.   Thus, the local clerical labor market is composed of those companies in close enough proximity to each other so that they must rely on the same general population for their clerical employees.

Transportation patterns will largely determine the size of the geographic area from which potential employees may be drawn.   In general, areas with adequate transportation facilities will permit the recruiting of employees from a broader area than would be possible in an area with an inadequate transportation system.   Other factors which will influence a company's ability to draw clerical employees to a particular location may include local wage taxes, the cost of transportation, parking facilities, and proximity to major shopping areas.

After defining the salary market competition, an organization must secure reliable data on pay levels.   Normally these data may be found in salary surveys such as are published by the Bureau of Labor Statistics and the Administrative Management Society.   Alternatively, a company may obtain the necessary information by conducting its own survey or it may use the results of a survey conducted by another company.   Where possible, a self-conducted survey would seem to be preferable.

A major advantage of the self-conducted survey is that the organization can limit participation to those firms it has identified as its major competitors for clerical employees.   Also, the company may limit the survey to those jobs in which it is interested.   Another advantage of the self-conducted survey is that for the surveyor, at least, the data provided by the survey are more easily interpreted since the survey has been designed to meet the company's needs.

There are situations in which conducting one's own clerical salary survey is not feasible.   If the organization has a very small clerical work force at a particular location, the number of employees affected might not justify the expense of a self-conducted survey.   Similarly, if the organization has a great number of locations, the sheer number of offices might make it impossible to conduct a survey at each location.   In these situations, use of salary surveys prepared by other organizations would seem to be indicated.   The use of someone else's survey does not, however, relieve the salary administrator of his responsibility for defining with whom the company is competing for clerical employees at each location.   This essential step is still required, but now the salary administrator must determine which available survey best describes the clerical salary market in which the company is competing.

There still may be cases where existing surveys are not adequate to meet the company's requirements.   At this point, the salary administrator must weigh the economic costs of conducting his own survey against the possible economic consequences of basing clerical salaries in one location on a salary survey which is not exactly descriptive of the local salary market.   It should be noted, while discussing readily available surveys, that these surveys are excellent sources of data for companies which conduct their own surveys.   They provide a ready check on the validity of the data a firm gets from its own surveys.

Once data on the salary market have been secured, they must be related to the company's job structure.   This is accomplished by evaluating, in the context of the company's job evaluation system, the jobs covered in the survey.   Jobs in the survey may then be placed in the various job classifications appropriate to the company, and the spread of salaries within each job classification can be resolved mathematically into such measures as means, modes, medians, and interquartile ranges. Although these statistical tools lend comprehension to an otherwise incomprehensible mass of raw data, the salary administrator, in conjunction with the company's management, must determine where in relation to the salary market, as indicated by a salary survey, the company is going to place its own clerical salaries.

Management Philosophy. Management's approach to salary administration will largely determine the relationship between the clerical salary market and the company's clerical salary levels. This approach could be called management's "salary philosophy." Management is primarily concerned with the expense aspect of clerical salaries. Thus, a clerical pay structure is seen as but another management tool to assist in allocating the company's financial resources. Specifically, a clerical pay structure must attract and retain the caliber of employee desired at a minimum expense level to the company. The expense aspect of salaries will influence the perspective from which management evaluates the many factors which determine clerical salary levels.

Major determinants of the response which management gives to salary market conditions are the present and the forecast financial positions of the company. Clerical salaries are one other item to be considered in determining the price to be charged for the company's product. Therefore, they will be influenced by the competitiveness of the product, for if the product's price may be readily increased as salary expenses increase, management will be less resistant to higher clerical salary levels. Similarly, if the company can absorb increases in clerical salary levels through increased productivity, salary levels will be generally higher.

Clerical salaries are also related to economic forecasts. If the company is in an expansive, growth period, its salary levels will be higher than they would be if its sales were declining. Similarly, the state of the nation's economy will affect the financial prospects of a company, and this in turn will influence salary levels within the company.

Management must also consider the availability of clerical employees which it desires to hire. Higher clerical salary levels will be required to compete in an area where the potential supply of clerical workers is not equal to the demand. In areas where there is a surplus of clerical workers, salary levels can be set at a lower rate. Although statistics are not a substitute for experience and personal sampling of the clerical labor force, the U.S. Department of Labor Manpower Administration publishes monthly reports on the unemployment rate within a number of urban areas. These figures will serve as a rough estimate of labor availability. However, as was mentioned before, the specific availability of clerical workers must be determined through experience.

The caliber of employee desired will also influence the level at which a company places its clerical salaries. If the organization is recruiting employees of better than average qualifications, it will be required to sustain higher salary levels than will be necessary if it is willing to accept employees with average or below-average capabilities. In fact, some companies have determined that for those lower-level clerical jobs which require little investment in training, a high turnover rate is more advantageous financially than are the higher salaries necessary to prevent rapid turnover.

A firm's personnel policies must also be considered when establishing clerical salaries. An organization cannot reasonably aspire to a reputation as a high-paying company without maintaining its salary scales at higher levels than those of its competitors. In fact, a company that desires such a reputation will reasonably be required to place its salary levels in line with the first quartile of its competitors' measured paid rates, which statistically places its paid rates above 75 percent of the paid rates of its competitors.   Similarly, a company which has the policy of competing with the going rate should establish its salary rates at or around the mean or median measurements of the competition's paid rates, which means that 50 percent of the paid rates are higher and 50 percent are lower.

The above is probably a representative sample of the factors which management must evaluate to establish clerical salary levels suited to the company's own situation.   The list is by no means complete or exclusive, although the factors presented above are probably more common than others.   At any particular time, changing social, political, and economic conditions will cause changes in the relative importance of one factor over another and may introduce new factors.   However, the salary levels ultimately established will be a direct result of management's interpretation of the factors it considers important.

Union Influences.   The unionization of significant numbers of clerical workers influences the levels of clerical salaries for both union and nonunion employers. Where penetration has been successful, the union may influence the job structure established in addition to bargaining with management on the appropriateness of salary levels.   With respect to clerical salaries, the most significant influence of a union is to make the establishment of salary levels a bilateral process between labor and management rather than the exclusive prerogative of management.   Nonunionized employers, on the other hand, will seek to discourage unionization of their employees by maintaining their clerical salary levels on a par with or higher than those paid to unionized workers.

As opposed to the management view of salaries as expense, the union views salaries as income.   As a result, the basic objective of all unions is the maintenance of wages at existing levels and increasing wage levels in the future. Thus, unions support and agitate for wage floors in the form of minimum wage laws.   They then use these statutes as justification for higher wage demands. It should be noted that most unions are not completely unmindful of the cost aspect of salaries.   The good ones are realistic enough to be concerned that excessive salary costs might erode the financial position of the company.   However, in the division of the company's resources between salaries and profits, the unions are present to give force to the employees' demand for a larger share of the company's earnings.

Salary levels established in unionized organizations are most often a compromise between union demands and management offers.   As has been seen in the section on management philosophy, the company evaluates a number of factors to determine the level at which salaries should be placed.   When dealing with a union, management must also determine what salary levels are appropriate, but here the objective is to determine the upper limits of clerical salaries that a company may sustain.   The salary administrator in the union situation may be asked to supply data on the local clerical salary market, but the issue is no longer primarily one of relating the company's clerical salaries to the external market.   Rather, it is one of relating union demands to the overall financial position of the company.   The union, on the other hand, will establish its demands on the basis of prevailing and minimum wages, the economic condition of the country, the profitability of the company's operations, settlements made by other unions, and the like.   A factor which must be considered by both union and management is the ability of either side to sustain a prolonged labor dispute.

Legal Considerations.   The levels at which a company places its clerical salaries are also regulated by the various levels of government.   In general, government influence on salary structures has the effect of establishing wage minimums. However, there have been instances where legislation has been designed to stabilize salaries.

The general effect over the past 30 years of federal action on salaries has been to raise progressively the wage floor while widening the number of companies subject to federal regulation of their pay practices. The Davis-Bacon Act of 1931 required certain government contractors to pay wages at prevailing rates, and the Copeland Act of 1934 prohibited contractors to the government from receiving kickbacks on the salaries paid their employees. The concept of a minimum wage was established by the Walsh-Healey Act of 1936, which authorizes the Secretary of Labor to fix the prevailing minimum wage for the employees of a number of government contractors. This piece of legislation also established the concept of a normal work week of 40 hours and a normal work day of 8 hours, with a requirement of premium pay for work performed in excess of the normal standards. The Fair Labor Standards Act of 1938 set minimum wages and established provisions for overtime pay for industries engaged in interstate commerce. Successive amendments to this law have set higher minimum wages while broadening the concept of interstate commerce to include more companies.

State laws governing wages and salaries are generally similar to federal laws. All states have enacted prevailing wage laws similar in intent to the federal statutes pertaining to government contractors. In addition, most states have legislated a form of minimum wage legislation, although these statutes are generally limited to the salaries paid to women and children.

The Stabilization Act of 1942 and the Defense Production Act of 1950 were enacted to stabilize the nation's economy, which was rapidly becoming inflationary as a result of World War II and the Korean conflict. The significance these statutes have for the present day lies in the techniques and principles developed in order to apply the laws to specific situations. Wage and salary survey techniques were refined; the concept of cost of living as it applied to wages was developed; and the development of job evaluation was speeded considerably. Although wage and price controls are interesting in the historical context, the government's past approach to stabilization of the economy in an inflationary period possibly could be applied to the country's current economic situation.

It is not the purpose of this chapter to give in-depth coverage to all of the legal considerations which influence clerical rate structures. Legal consideration is but one factor influencing the level at which clerical salaries are established. Although the salary administrator should be conversant with the legislation applying to salaries where his company is located, authoritative interpretation of specific statutes should be rendered by a qualified attorney. The salary administrator should discuss with the company's legal staff all matters which require legal interpretation.

Differentiating Clerical Supervisors from their Subordinates. The establishment of a clerical salary structure must consider the position of the clerical supervisor. This position is typically considered to be a part of management, yet it contains few management prerogatives. In general, the clerical supervisor is a recommender rather than a decider, but the position occupied by the supervisor is critical because this is where the company's business interests and the personal interests of the employees must be aligned.

A true clerical supervisor will be exempt from the legal requirements of the Fair Labor Standards Act. This exemption can cause serious inequities between supervisory and workers' salaries if a great deal of overtime is performed.

The 10 to 15 percent pay differential usually maintained between the supervisor and subordinate will be quickly erased if the subordinate receives premium overtime pay while the supervisor receives nothing. This is not a problem if overtime is not a normal, scheduled event, but if a clerical supervisor is expected to direct a staff which works overtime on a regular basis, the issue must be resolved or filling the supervisor's job will be that much more difficult.

The most common manner of maintaining salary differentials between supervisors and subordinates who are required regularly to work overtime is to establish a company policy of overtime pay for exempt first-level supervisors. Computation of such overtime is most frequently achieved through a formula of straight time or time and one-half. Other alternatives include payment of either a flat amount or a percentage of base salary. A company may also offer compensatory time off in lieu of overtime pay. Some companies utilize the amount of overtime put in by supervisors as a factor in determining annual salary bonuses.

The ultimate decision as to the method to be used in maintaining salary differentials between supervisor and subordinate salaries must of course be made by management after careful consideration of the company's situation. However, for ease of handling and psychological effect, probably the most effective means is to compensate supervisors through direct payment for overtime work. Special controls may be required in those situations where the clerical supervisor determines the amount of overtime worked, in order to prevent unnecessary overtime.

In a number of companies, the clerical work force may be structured so that there are no exempt employees specifically assigned to the task of supervising clerical workers. In these cases, work supervision generally is provided by an employee who performs the normal clerical duties of her unit but who is also responsibile for supervision of the work activities of her subordinates. This type of supervisor, sometimes better known as a "work leader," is normally not considered to be a part of the management team, and her supervisory activities are limited to giving work assignments, checking work quality, orientation, and the like. This type of supervisor has a minimal impact on personnel actions appropriate to her subordinates, such as employment, termination, salary increases, and promotions. The lack of management impact in this job requires that the work leader type of supervisor be regulated by the Fair Labor Standards Act, which means that she must be compensated at specified premium rates for overtime worked. Therefore, the differential between a nonexempt supervisor and her subordinates may be equitably maintained through the job structure, and the company will not be required to have a policy on overtime payment for exempt-level clerical supervisors.

INDIVIDUAL PAY RATES

Once management has established its job structure and determined at what levels the company will place its clerical salaries, it has the foundation of a clerical pay structure. However, it must now consider the manner in which the pay rates for individual jobs will be determined.

Fixed Rates. The easiest and most convenient method of determining individual pay rates would be to establish one rate for each job classification and pay everyone within that classification the same rate. Such a system is valid only in those jobs where there is little room for incentive or variation in individual production. Although there are undoubtedly some lower-level clerical jobs which have very little room for individual performance, most clerical jobs are such that the individual's manner of performing the job can exert a significant influence on the output of the job. Payment of fixed rates, therefore, would not seem to be applicable to most clerical jobs.

Salary Ranges. Paying employees for their on-the-job proficiency may be accomplished through the use of salary ranges. The salary range establishes a minimum and maximum salary which may be paid for a particular job or job classification. As an employee becomes more competent in his or her job, salary should increase from the minimum rate toward the maximum rate. The width of a salary range will depend upon the type, frequency, and amount of increases the company desires to give. Failure to establish a policy on increases at this point makes establishment of ranges hazardous, for they are not based on company policy and the ranges may be inadequate to meet the organization's needs when it finally does establish a policy on salary increases.

Automatic Increases. One of the most common methods of increasing salaries is taking action in scheduled amounts at predetermined intervals. This is simply a variation on the fixed-rate type of salary structure, with the end result that all the employees in a particular job classification with the same amount of tenure will have the same salary rate. The theory behind automatic increases is that the longer a person performs in a particular job, the more competent his performance will be. As with the fixed-rate salary structure, this type of increase should not apply to jobs in which individual initiative has a substantial impact; this factor would seem to limit its usefulness with respect to many clerical jobs. An element of merit may be introduced into the automatic progression system of increases by establishing provisions for the withholding of scheduled increases or the granting of increases before scheduled as the competence of the employee warrants. Where unions are distrustful of the ability of management to maintain an equitable merit system for increases, the company may be forced to institute a program for automatic increases.

Merit Increases. Relating an employee's job performance to his position on the salary range is possible through a merit increase system. To the extent that the job permits individual-performance differences and performance by an employee can be fairly and consistently measured, merit salary increases are probably the most sound. Most clerical jobs allow a sufficient amount of initiative and variation in performance to make the merit method the most appropriate means of granting salary increases.

A merit salary range will normally have three reference points. The first of these is the minimum, which is the lowest rate at which an employee should be paid. Next is the midpoint, which is the salary rate that should apply to the seasoned, competent worker. In using salary survey data, this is the point on the range which is used to relate a company's salary levels to the clerical salary market. The range maximum should designate the highest salary rate in the range, a rate reserved for outstanding performers. With the exclusive use of merit increases, employees of less than average competence should receive salaries below the midpoint values, whereas employees of better than average competence would be above the midpoint values. The basic purpose, of course, is to create an inverse ratio between turnover and high performance.

Combinations of Automatic and Merit Increases. The system of withholding increases or granting them early in accordance with job proficiency has already been mentioned as one method of combining automatic and merit increases. Another method is to give automatic increases to the lower levels of employees and merit increases to the upper levels. Another combination, which is probably the most popular, is to permit automatic increases until the range midpoint is reached and to require that increases beyond midpoint be based on merit.

This system is based on the premise that all employees should reach average competency within the context of the scheduled increases, but advancement beyond competency must be based on merit.

MATHEMATICAL RELATIONSHIPS BETWEEN SALARY LEVELS

The relationship between salary ranges must be established after evaluating the financial and personnel needs of the company and the needs of its employees.

A number of methods can be used to determine the amount of spread which should exist between the minimum and maximum of the range and how the ranges at one level should relate to the ranges at other job levels. The first is to have ranges with a constant money spread—which is not very equitable, because a particular dollar amount represents a greater percentage of lower-level salaries than of higher-level salaries. Another method is to have ranges with a constant percentage spread at all levels. This may be uneconomical because there are more jobs in a company at the lower clerical levels than at the higher levels. Also, the lower-level jobs have a higher promotion potential and thus would not require as great a range spread. Thus, the most economical course would seem to be a variable percentage or money spread, with the narrower range spreads in the lower-level job classifications. The extent of salary ranges is an issue the organization must resolve in the light of its own situation, but common practice would seem to indicate variable range spreads of 20 to 50 percent from the lowest to the highest job classifications.

Range spreads will be influenced by the number of job classes and the slope of the salary line. A salary structure may be established with wide ranges and no overlap between the ranges assigned to each job classification. However, this often has the effect of artificially pyramiding salaries to an uneconomical point. Reducing the range spread at each job level will also permit non-overlapping ranges, but the limited spread remaining in the ranges may not be adequate to sustain the types, amount, and frequency of increases the company desires to give.

Therefore, while a minimal amount of overlap between ranges is to be desired, most companies will find it impossible to eliminate range overlaps entirely. In fact, a reasonable amount of overlap may be desirable to assist the company in transferring employees. Also, the harshness of dividing the job structure into classes may be somewhat alleviated through overlapping ranges. However, too much overlap may cause employee discontent because workers in lower-level jobs may be paid at higher rates than employees in a higher classification. Thus, it would appear that although a certain amount of overlap between adjacent job class salary ranges is inevitable and even desirable, overlap should not be so great as to destroy the intent of the job structure, which is to differentiate between levels of difficulty.

ADJUSTING SALARY LEVELS

Although the clerical job structure in a stable organization will change very little over the years, salary levels for the various job classifications within the pay structure are more subject to change. Declining availability of labor or increased living costs will exert pressures on the existing ranges. Such pressures will be indicated by increasing turnover, declining productivity, and reduced employee morale. Every organization will vary with respect to the tolerances with which it will treat turnover, productivity, and morale problems; but when these issues can no longer be safely ignored, the company is required to adjust its ranges into a more competitive relationship with the existing clerical salary market.

Individual Placement within the New Range. Although the process of changing existing salary levels to a new relationship with the clerical salary market is almost identical with the method of establishing original salary levels, the act of changing a range from one salary level to another introduces a new issue—that of the relationship of an individual employee to the new salary level for his job.

There are a number of different methods of treating individual employees when their ranges change. The first of these is to do nothing but let the normal progress of salary increases bring the employee to his appropriate position in the new range. This method postpones the financial impact of a range change because individual salary actions will be spread over a period of time, but unless the company is blessed with very competent supervisors the individual employee may return too slowly to his appropriate position in the range. The theoretic justification for this method is that with increasing salary costs the company can demand greater levels of performance from its employees, so an individual's previous position in the range may not be justified in terms of the performance standards which go with the new salary range.

Another method would be to grant employees salary increases in the amount necessary to place the individual in the same relative position in the new range that he occupied in the old range. This procedure has the effect of making a range change felt immediately and in its entirety on the company's budget. In addition, such a practice does not allow the company to reassess its performance standards as it changes its ranges. This method is advantageous to the extent that the maintenance of an employee's position in the new range is not dependent on how conscientious his individual supervisor is. Also, this type of practice is more easily understood by employees, who often do not appreciate or agree with the concept of higher salary levels demanding higher performance standards.

General Increases. Many companies feel that there are economic factors which apply equally to all employees, and as a result they grant a general increase to every employee. Typically, this increase is a percentage of base pay usually equal to the cost-of-living increase as promulgated by the Bureau of Labor Statistics. Psychologically, this type of increase is satisfying to the employee, for he can readily see the justice in increasing his salary as the cost of living increases.

However, there are some major disadvantages to such increases which should be considered before the practice of granting general increases is instituted. First, the cost-of-living measurement scale, which is usually the Consumer Price Index, is not available in all locations. Second, the basic data for a CPI are related to the theoretical purchasing patterns of a factory worker with a family of four. Thus, the CPI, which is the only readily available measure of living costs, may not be appropriate. In addition, increased living costs do not directly affect the clerical salary market. Thus, by granting general increases the company may be making unnecessary and uneconomical investments in salaries. It is also possible for a cost-of-living change to be inadequate in meeting special competitive circumstances in the employment market.

SUMMARY

The clerical pay structure is a combination of the job structure and salary levels. The job structure is derived from the company's job evaluation system, while the salary levels assigned to the job structure are based on the salary market, management philosophy, union pressures, and government influence.

Once the clerical salary structure is established, consideration must be given to maintaining the differentials between clerical and supervisory salaries. This is particularly a problem when the clerical work force is expected to work a significant amount of overtime.

Determining pay rates for individual employees must also be accomplished after the salary structure is established. This is accomplished through the use of either fixed rates for individual jobs or salary ranges. Use of salary ranges requires that a decision be made as to whether progression through the range should be automatic or whether it should be on the basis of a merit system. A combination of both systems is also possible. The use of ranges requires that the mathematical relationship between the ranges for various job levels be defined.

A clerical salary structure must be periodically reviewed, for although the job structure is relatively stable, the salary levels frequently will require adjustment to maintain the desired relationship with the clerical salary market. Adjusting the salary ranges requires a determination as to how differences in an individual's relationship to the new and old ranges will be resolved.

BIBLIOGRAPHY

Belcher, David W.: *Wage and Salary Administration*, Prentice-Hall, Inc., Englewood Cliffs, N.J., 1955.

Beuttenmuller, Emil C.: "Maintaining Supervisory Earnings Differentials," *Compensation Review*, American Management Association, New York, 1969.

Lanham, Elizabeth: *Administration of Wages and Salaries*, Harper and Row, New York, 1963.

chapter 21

Establishing the Exempt and Management Pay Structure

CHESTER C. PAYNE   *Director, Corporate Compensation, The Dow Chemical Company, Midland, Michigan*

In previous chapters in this book we have talked about collecting the necessary data to understand jobs and the subsequent problems involved in measuring these jobs in relationship one to another. We have also discussed how to obtain and use information derived from surveys. In Chapters 17 through 20 we have talked about determining wage and salary policies which are necessary before a pay structure can be established, and the establishment of hourly and clerical structures. The present chapter continues the discussion of pay structures, but we switch our attention to the development of structures for exempt and management personnel.

FINDING OUT ABOUT YOUR PRESENT STRUCTURE

In the literal sense, not many of us are around when the pay structure is originally established. Almost all of us who face salary structure problems are now in a going institution and, therefore, are confronted with an existing structure. This structure may or may not be formalized. It may have resulted from considerable thought and effort, or it may have just evolved. But, if we are now paying people to perform certain jobs or functions, we do have some kind of structure. The first thing to do is to find out what it is.

In earlier chapters we have discussed how to collect data on job content and how to then place values on jobs. When we have evaluated the jobs, we can then compare these values with what we are paying people to see what our structure is now. A simple scattergram comparing these two variables will get us started.

Figure 1 shows such a scattergram. Each dot on the chart indicates the job value and the salary presently paid one incumbent. In a small organization all jobs can be placed on such a scattergram and a line of central tendency can be drawn. The line can be drawn merely by trial and error, or the data can be used for exact mathematical computations for those so inclined. Of course, the data may not show a straight line at all. It may be a curve or a jagged line, or it may even show little correlation between these two factors. The point is that it indicates our present pay practice.

In a large organization these data probably should be fed into a computer. The computer will summarize the data, give a formula for a straight line, or a curve if desired, and give a separate formula for each part of the data that may be compared with the formula for all of the data. This technique does not tell us what is right or wrong, but it does indicate what our pay practice is at the present time.

After making this determination we can then look into many other questions about structure. In particular, in this chapter we will emphasize problems which seem to be different in an exempt and management structure as compared with the clerical or hourly structures already covered.

Internal Comparisons. This same scattergram technique can help us considerably in making comparisons within our own organization. These comparisons have as their goal the attainment of internal equity between the many different kinds of people comprising an organization.

Probably two major comparisons should be made here. The first of these compares differences in organizational functions or in types of work being performed. Here we are concerned with whether the research people are being paid as well as or better than the marketing people, the accounting people, the manufacturing people, and so forth. Often, management will find they have been treating some functions better than others without even realizing it. They may, in fact, want to do so, but it should be done deliberately and not accidentally. In addition, people in the organization may tend to think that the real money is in a certain part of the business. As an example, perhaps people feel that the only function that management really tends to treat well is the

Figure 1.   Current pay practices.

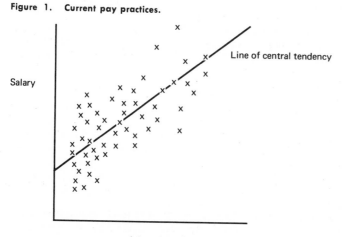

Salary

Line of central tendency

Job   values

marketing function. Thus, from a morale point of view, it is important that people know that internal comparisons are made, and that management is equally concerned about all parts of the organization.

The second major internal comparison that must be made is to look at different geographical locations in this regard. If an organization has multiple locations, it is important that management know what is being paid in Texas, Michigan, New York, California, and all stops in between. Again, if one location is being paid better than another for the same kind of work, it should be a deliberate management policy. As noted in our discussion of functions, members of the organization may feel that a certain geographic location is being paid better than are others. Therefore, it is very important that people know that such comparisons are made.

Maturity Comparisons. As we have been discussing scattergrams and structures in the exempt and management fields, we have talked about a comparison of dollars versus the size of the job. In the exempt area many organizations also take a look at a comparison of dollars versus some kind of maturity data. The maturity data usually take the form of either age or years since bachelor's degree.

As already stated, there are two fundamental reasons for any salary structure —to assure internal equity and to reach and maintain a proper position in the external marketplace. Many organizations have found it difficult to make market comparisons of exempt positions below the first supervisory level. This is because many individuals may have the same job title—e.g., salesmen, engineers, or accountants—but receive different salaries because over the years they have performed differently and progressed to different levels in the salary range for their jobs. Let us look at an example here to be sure we are aware of the problem. Suppose there are 100 salesmen in your organization and you want to compare their salaries with another organization using a job level comparison. You usually find that the other organization with which you want to compare yours has widely different practices from yours. You may have two job levels and they may have four levels covering the same kinds of people. Or, you may each have the same number of job levels, but you may have 10 percent of your salesmen in the top level and they may have 75 percent of theirs at this level. The organizational differences and the different practices in progressing exempt people through professional steps in a ladder often make it almost impossible to compare these kinds of people on the basis of job levels.

However, it would be easy for the two organizations in the example above to make a maturity comparison. Each could submit data to the other showing what they are paying their salesmen by age or by years since bachelor's degree. This may have little or no application in the internal administration of salaries in these two organizations, but it will certainly show to each how it stands with the other in this regard.

Some organizations also rely heavily on the maturity "structure" as a means of administering salaries internally. It is obviously just as easy to pay people by maturity data as it is by job level data.

The technique can be used throughout the organization and not just at the beginning technical level. It would seem to lose much of its value as people get older and as their positions start to differ widely.

SALARY RANGES

Now let us return to the salary structure made up of dollars versus job values. We have seen ways of determining a line of central tendency. Next, we must construct a minimum and a maximum line in order to provide what are usually called "salary ranges." Perhaps the first question is: How wide should our ranges be in such a structure? In other words, we know now what we pay on the average, and we need to decide what is the minimum and the maximum salary for each job level. This can be determined in many ways. One is by external survey—what are others doing? Another is to draw lines, as in Figure 2, which seem to follow our present practice. Another is just the application of good common sense.

As one example, we may decide that from our line of central tendency we will form merit ranges by going plus and minus 20 percent. One line would become the maximum that we intend to pay by job levels and the other the minimum. Or, we could use a different factor above the line from that below the line, for example, plus 25 percent and minus 20 percent.

Probably the only way to determine what is really needed is to try it out. External surveys should be helpful in getting in the right ball park, but conditions within an organization may dictate certain differences from competitive practice.

HOW MANY STRUCTURES?

Another question which should be raised continually is whether the same structure should be used throughout the organization. If the organization is entirely in one city and in one line of business, perhaps the answer is self-evident. On the other hand, if the organization operates in many locations and is widely diversified in kinds of activities or businesses, the answer is considerably more difficult. There are probably more reasons for adopting one unified structure in the exempt and managerial areas than in the clerical or hourly area. Exempt and managerial employees are comparatively mobile and are willing and perhaps even anxious to relocate in a better job or even in a similar job at more money. College recruiting for such people tends to be national in scope, and hiring rates tend to be uniform throughout the country. Many exempt and management personnel are in very short supply, and it is difficult or im-

Figure 2.   Establishing salary ranges.

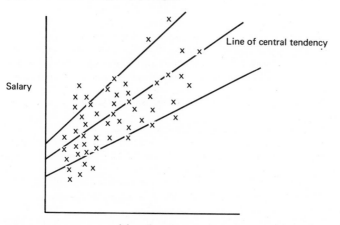

possible to pay them less money because they are in a certain geographical area or in a certain kind of business.

This problem, of course, gets considerably more difficult when expanded worldwide. Many types of organizations now have units in many different countries in the world. A further complicating factor is that a unit in Italy may employ people working there from Italy, England, Switzerland, the United States, and so forth, making the question of how many salary structures this organization should have in Italy an extremely complex problem.

To carry our example on, let us suppose that the organization is an American one which has expanded overseas. Perhaps 75 percent or more of the total members of the organization worldwide are Americans, but many other nationalities are increasing in number. In our example we have stated that this organization has moved into Italy. Perhaps there are 100 people in the Italian organization, composed of 80 Italians, 10 Americans, 5 Englishmen, 3 Swiss, and 2 Germans. What salary structure or structures should be used in this situation? It can almost be said that the problem defies solution! Probably at least two structures are absolutely necessary. If there are 80 Italians in this situation, it seems evident that their structure should be competitive in their home country—Italy. On the other hand, the Americans there have probably been sent by their organization to transfer American know-how into this situation. The chances are good that these people will feel strongly about the matter, and perhaps they will even demand that they be paid on an American salary basis.

It is not our intent at this point to explore these problems in further depth. Entire books are written on the complications involved. However, it is important that we recognize some of the difficulties in determining how many structures to have and where and how to use them.

BASE-RATE STRUCTURES AND TOTAL COMPENSATION STRUCTURES

Another major question for determination is whether the pay structure should show total compensation or base salary only. Once again, there seems to be no clear-cut, simple answer. If the organization involved has little or no payment other than base salary, then the question is little more than academic. However, if certain members of the exempt or management team receive significant monetary awards other than base salary, the question becomes highly important.

There seem to be ample reasons for a base-salary structure regardless of what else is decided upon. The reason here is that many of the external comparisons which need to be made to establish competitive position can best be made using base salary only. Regardless of how total compensation might compare competitively, it is probably important that the management of an organization know how its base-rate structure compares with base-rate structures of competitive organizations.

The real question, then, seems to be: Is a total-compensation structure helpful in addition to the base-rate structure? There are at least two ways to examine this. One question would ask whether a total-compensation structure is helpful internally. If so, then the question is answered. If not, a second question would ask whether a total-compensation comparison with other competitive organizations is either practical or helpful. This is considerably more difficult to answer than it might at first appear to be. If each organization involved paid people with only base rate and a cash bonus, such comparisons would obviously be practical and presumably helpful. However, this is almost never the case. Present tax laws either encourage or allow the establishment of many different compensation devices, some of which receive special tax treatment. In comparing total compensation, the problem is one of comparing the value of a cash bonus with deferred stock, or with stock options, or with dividend units, or with some other form of special compensation. Whether it is really practical to make such comparisons—and what is learned by them—is a complicated problem in itself.

PAY FOR PERFORMANCE

Earlier in this chapter we noted that exempt and managerial employees have greater opportunities than do lower-level employees to be creative and show initiative in their jobs. Because of this, salary ranges need to be wide enough to properly reflect differences in performance.

When structures are relatively narrow, as is true in the hourly and clerical areas, it is because it is harder to measure performance and, therefore, harder to pay for it. The narrower the structure, the more likely it is that most people will reach the maximum over a period of time. The difference may be that the top performers will reach the maximum in five years, an average performer in seven or eight years, and a below-average performer in 10 to 12 years. Obviously, management of an organization usually does not want this to happen, but it tends to happen nevertheless.

The exempt and managerial areas, as already noted, have wider ranges to enable us to better reward performance. However, there is one real hazard in this regard. The top performers in the lowest exempt and managerial jobs are regularly promoted to bigger jobs. Over a period of time many of the lower-level jobs will come to be filled by old-timers who have not really "cut the mustard." To some extent this is true throughout the salary structure, but it is truest at the lower level.

If we do not have some method of tying performance to pay within the salary range, we will find that all of our old-timers who have not really made good have moved to the top of their ranges. Wider merit ranges make it more important than ever that we find a way of properly relating our performance appraisal system to our pay practices.

The subject of performance appraisal is of paramount importance and is covered in Part 5 of this book. We must mention it here to emphasize its importance in properly paying people within our salary ranges.

If we believe that our organization should pay for performance, then we must plan how to bring this about. We have already noted the natural tendency to give average and below-average performers a regular raise until they reach the top of their range. We may want to set some rules which will limit how far such performers are allowed to go.

As an example, let us assume that the midpoint for job X is $1,000 per month, the minimum is $800 per month, and the maximum is $1,200 per month. Does this mean that all people, regardless of performance, can go to $1,200 a month, and that the only real difference is the time it takes to get there? In general, any performance appraisal system should be able to identify top performers, average performers, and below-average performers. One approach would be to say that the top performer can go to $1,200 a month, the average performer to $1,100 per month, and the below-average performer to $1,000 per month. Or, perhaps a system could be devised where available salary increases are influenced both by performance appraisal and by position within the salary range.

Regardless of the method used, the problems inherent in wider ranges because of wider differences in performance require that a better job be done in coordinating performance appraisal with position in the salary range.

SPECIAL PAY POLICIES

Obviously, the establishment of a pay structure itself does not require that all people within this structure be treated the same. On the contrary, there may be many good reasons for trying to individualize the compensation treatment of many people insofar as this is possible and practical.

This may be particularly true for tax reasons. The further up we go in the structure, the more difficult it is for our employees to realize appropriate after-tax income. For this reason, we may want to institute special pay policies which apply only above a certain level in the salary structure.

In addition, it may be desirable to allow employees to have something to say about how they are paid. As an example, some employees might prefer all of their income in current salary, while others might be interested in deferred compensation. This may be thought of as a "smorgasbord" of pay and benefits, with some employee participation in the planning of what best fits each situation. If this is done, it is necessary to place a dollar value on each specific policy or benefit to ensure internal equity.

There are significant problems in this approach which must be considered. Special handling of certain people can cause enmity and bitterness in an organization between functions, areas, and individuals. Therefore, any such special pay policies should be thoroughly investigated before implementation. If improperly used, they can demotivate an entire organization. If properly used, they can both motivate and reward employees individually.

SUPPLY AND DEMAND—THEIR EFFECT ON STRUCTURES

The salary structure attempts to say what one job is worth in comparison with another. The evaluation technique is concerned only with measuring job size. It treats all jobs as though supply and demand were in balance.

On the other hand, we know that supply and demand often are not in balance. There are always some jobs for which there are many qualified people. Each organization then must decide whether it wants to maintain internal equity and therefore pay more than the marketplace may really require. If a decision is made to pay only what the market requires, there are two ways to accomplish it. One is to say that for certain defined jobs the organization will go only so high in the salary structure. The second alternative is to fudge a little on the evaluation. Where the supply of people overbalances demand, certain jobs may be deliberately rated lower in the structure itself.

Probably a greater problem exists where the marketplace demands a higher salary level than internal equity would dictate. There are always some jobs for which there is a dearth of qualified people. Once again, there are two possible solutions to the problem. One is to deliberately pay either higher in the range or actually over the range for certain defined situations. The other choice is to fudge the job evaluation and place the job in the structure at a higher level than its true evaluation would indicate.

If the same jobs tended to be in either long or short supply over a long period of time, the situation would be well understood by all people concerned. In such a situation probably either of the two approaches could be used to accomplish the desired results with little to favor one over the other. However, the facts seem to be that a job that was in long supply a few years ago may indeed be in short supply today, and vice versa.

This would seem to indicate that we should not deliberately either inflate or deflate the true evaluation to solve the market problem. By not adjusting the evaluation, those who administer the program are constantly reminded of the fact that certain jobs are being paid low in the range and that certain others are being comparatively overpaid by internal standards. Thus, there is a regular automatic check on this problem, and a determination must be made as to whether the practice should continue. Where the job values are adjusted to satisfy either long or short supply, the whole problem may well be forgotten when the jobs involved change from over- to under-supply, or vice versa.

KEEPING THE STRUCTURE UP TO DATE

Earlier in this chapter we pointed out that we may end up with one exempt and management structure for the entire organization, or we may have two or more structures in different countries, businesses, and geographical areas. We also indicated that our structures need to be competitive and that surveys play a key role here. Once we have developed the structure, we must decide how to keep the structure up to date. How often should it be changed, and by how much? There is no one answer which fits all circumstances. I assume we would all agree that in times of rapid inflation keeping a structure up to date is vastly different from doing so in times of comparative stability of prices and wages. Under some conditions it may be desirable to revise a structure at least annually, and under other conditions every few years may be often enough.

If we ignore for a moment the vital factors of inflation and deflation, we are still faced with the question of how often our structure should be changed and by how much. There are two fundamental places to look for answers to these questions. One is the external marketplace and the second is within the organization itself. Let us first look at the external market conditions which tend to affect both the time to adjust the structure and the amount the structure needs to be changed.

One of these important external considerations is what is happening to the cost of living. Has there been a significant change in this regard since the structure itself was last changed? A second important consideration is the hiring rate necessary to add new people to the organization. Has this hiring rate been relatively stable, or has it changed in a significant manner since the last structure change? The third and perhaps most important external check is that which should be made regularly, with competition—whatever that is in the organization involved. Is our structure still a competitive one, or is it on the high or low side of competition? Has our position changed significantly since the last change in the structure?

Internally, there are probably two important comparisons which have a major bearing on this issue. One of these is the comparison of this structure with the hourly structure, the clerical structure, and any other internal structures. Is our structure in proper relationship to the others, or does something need to be done to properly relate it? Or, as is perhaps more often the case, are the other structures being changed in the near future, so that this structure must be changed in order to retain its proper relationship?

The second question internally pertains to how well the structure is really operating. This is probably more a seat-of-the-pants judgment than a scientific one. It is probably comparatively easy to know what structure is required in the hourly and clerical areas. It is much more difficult to determine what structure is needed to pay professional and managerial employees in widely different kinds of organizations and in many different geographical areas. A real expert in his field will develop a "feel" either that things are pretty good or that something is wrong. Developing and maintaining an exempt and managerial salary structure is probably as much of an art as it is a science!

One additional thought deserves serious consideration in this regard. If an organization is one in which there is no union, or threat of a union, then whether a structure is revised 3 percent per year or 6 percent every two years is probably purely academic. However, in many organizations today there are either unionized employees or the threat of unionized employees. Historically, union structures have been revised annually, and there seems to be no indication that this will be changed in the immediate future. Under such conditions, it may be wise to change the exempt and managerial structures at least as often as the union structure is changed, for purely psychological reasons.

Let us reiterate that no structure is good or bad except by external comparison. Regardless of all else, there is no substitute for good surveys done regularly. A structure which was competitive a few years ago may be sadly out of date today.

In making such surveys it is very easy to fall into a trap. Assume, for example, that a structure which was competitive a few years ago is now 6 percent low as determined by survey. If we assume that competition is going to raise structures next year, then at that time our structure may be about 10 percent low. Thus, management may authorize a 10 percent change in structure and feel that in so doing they have restored the competitive balance. As a matter of fact, raising the structure itself has been of little practical value unless the money is spent to ensure that average pay moves up with the structure.

Of course, the facts may be exactly the opposite. An organization which had a competitive structure a while ago may find that its structure is now 6 percent too high. So, it authorizes no change in structure this year but continues to authorize salary increases. If the amount of money being spent is as much as other companies are spending in a similar time, the results which the organization was trying to accomplish will not come about.

THE STRUCTURE AND ACTUAL PAY

This brings up the entire question of whether the structure should be different from that which is actually being paid. Some organizations calculate the line of central tendency, as described earlier in this chapter. Each year, then, their structure is what they are actually paying, and changes in the structure result automatically from salary increases given to their employees.

This can become a problem in external comparisons. Two organizations may compare structures and find they are similar. On the other hand, one organization may be paying at the midpoint of its structure while another organization is paying at the minimum of its structure. In this instance, their actual pay lines may be 20 percent apart even though the structures are almost identical. It is important that any organization analyze both its structure and the way it is actually paying its people, and that this be done in all external surveys.

In summary, a change in structure does not automatically accomplish anything with respect to how you are actually paying your people. If you are paying them too little, this can be corrected only by spending more money than your competition is spending in the time necessary to correct the situation. It will not be accomplished by a big raise in the structure itself and at the same time feeding in no more money than is being used by the competition.

COMPRESSION WITHIN THE STRUCTURE

Whenever people talk of exempt and managerial salary structures, it is almost inevitable that the term *compression* will be used. As the term is used in these areas, it implies that the bottom part of the structure has gone up faster than the top part and, therefore, that the structure has been compressed.

The trouble with most such discussions of compression is that nobody takes the time to define what it is. Or perhaps we should say that there is no definition which is uniformly accepted. Arguments can and do ensue (I have seen and participated in many) where there is no common definition of what the argument is all about. Let us point out the main problems in this area through the use of a relatively simple example.

Suppose that a number of years ago the average pay in our structure for job X was $500 per month and the average for job Y was $1,000 per month. Further, suppose that these same two jobs today have averages of $1,000 per month and $1,700 per month. The question is: Has there been compression in the relationship of these two jobs?

Those who believe that there has been compression point out that the ratio a few years ago was 2:1, and that the higher job today must have a value of $2,000 per month in order to maintain this relationship. Therefore, these people say, there has been compression, since the higher job is no longer being paid at twice the rate of the lower job. This argument automatically assumes that the way to determine compression is on a percentage basis!

On the other hand, it can just as easily be said that there is no compression, but rather that the higher-rated job has actually gained ground on the lower-rated one. This can be seen if we note that a few years ago the bigger job was paid $500 per month more than the smaller job and that now the comparison gives a plus $700. (For simplicity's sake the problem of taxes is being ignored at this point.) It is just as easy to decide that there has or has not been compression depending entirely upon the definition of the term.

The above example probably seems very elementary, and one which any grade school student can understand, but it is probably the heart of the whole problem when we come to adjusting salary structures. If for a moment we ignore external conditions and try to decide how our structure should be changed merely to provide internal equity, we are immediately into the question covered above. Does the top job need to go up $500 or $1,000 per month merely to maintain internal equity?

The important point here is not to get stuck on which of these choices is right. Obviously, many other factors, both internal and external, play a significant role when we are trying to arrive at any final decision. Over the years the writer has seen what seems like hundreds of people engaged in bitter discussions over the right decision here because each one has his own definition of compression.

COMMUNICATIONS

This chapter has been concerned with the mechanics and details of setting up and maintaining appropriate exempt and managerial salary structures. This is certainly a prerequisite for a successful salary program. However, a well-conceived and administered salary structure does not, by itself, guarantee a successful program. Perhaps the biggest single factor in the success or failure of the administration of any salary structure or structures is the communications necessary to get the job done. Presumably, a salary structure is ideal insofar as it maintains internal equity and a competitive relationship with the outside. At the same time it can fail miserably because nobody really understands it or has confidence in it.   Good communications may be more important and more difficult to accomplish than anything else discussed in this chapter.   The importance of this subject is emphasized by the fact that the concluding chapter in this book is devoted to its discussion.

IMPORTANCE OF THE EXEMPT AND MANAGEMENT PAY STRUCTURE

One concluding thought regarding exempt and management pay structures: A poorly conceived or administered exempt and management pay structure can do irreparable harm to an organization.   The future of any organization is probably largely determined by a relatively few people at the top.   If our structure is poorly designed or managed, and if because of this fact our top performers leave the organization, the results can be catastrophic.   If, on the other hand, our structure is well conceived and well managed, it can result in our exempt and management people being more highly motivated than is true of such people in other organizations.   If this results, our organization will have an advantage of incalculable value.

Part 5

Performance Appraisal

chapter 22

History and Theory
of Performance Appraisal

FRED E. SCHUSTER *Associate Professor of Management, and Assistant Dean, College of Business and Public Administration, Florida Atlantic University, Boca Raton, Florida*

Appraising the performance of individuals and of organizations is an inherent aspect of managing. Simply stated, it is impossible to make necessary decisions about individuals without measuring their performance in some manner. Hence, performance appraisal in a more or less formal sense is as old as the concept of management, and in an informal sense it is probably as old as mankind. Formal attempts at appraisal go back many centuries, and in this country rigorous scientific study of appraisal techniques and methods has a history of well over 50 years.

Over the years, there have been major shifts in the underlying assumptions of appraisal, its major purposes or objectives, and the uses to which it has been put, as well as considerable development and refinement of techniques. It is the purpose of this chapter to briefly summarize these developments to provide a perspective for evaluating the current status of performance appraisal.

Historically, appraisal has generally been used for administrative purposes, such as promotions and salary increases and for individual development and motivation. Other frequent uses of appraisal information have been employee selection and placement, manpower planning, and organization planning. Relative emphasis on these various uses of appraisal information has tended to shift over time. While the early applications of performance appraisal in this country emphasized administrative uses of appraisal (i.e., compensation and placement decisions), emphasis has more recently shifted toward a dual use of appraisal for administrative and developmental-motivational purposes. This shift in emphasis has been one basic cause of the considerable controversy over the last 20 years concerning the most effective approaches and techniques for appraisal.

In December, 1968, the author conducted a study of performance appraisal practices of *Fortune's* 500 largest industrial corporations. Of the 403 companies responding to the survey, 316 (or 78 percent) reported the use of some type of formal performance appraisal plan. When asked about the uses to which appraisals were put, these 316 companies responded as shown in Table 1.

These responses seem to confirm that the vast majority of companies today attempt to use performance appraisals simultaneously for *both* administrative and developmental-motivational purposes.

HIERARCHICAL VERSUS PARTICIPATIVE APPROACHES TO APPRAISAL

Until recently, all appraisal practices have been based on the implicit assumption that the superior is the person in the best position to judge the performance and behavior of his subordinate. Appraisals have thus emphasized the hierarchical relationship of superior and subordinate and have placed the superior in the position of "playing God" by passing judgment on his subordinate.

In this emphasis on passing judgment from above, the vast majority of earlier appraisal approaches have employed some form of trait rating. Basically, the trait-rating approach requires the superior to evaluate his subordinate, in some numerical or descriptive fashion, as to his possession of certain personality and behavior traits. Two types of forms typically used for trait appraisal are shown in Figures 1 and 2.

As can be seen, trait appraisals often bear a striking resemblance to grammar school report cards. In the 1950s, social science research revealed that this reliance on passing judgment from above may reduce the effectiveness of the appraisal process in achieving its motivation and development goals. For example, the work of Likert[1] and others at the Social Science Research Center has shown that hierarchical control may lead to lower motivation and may restrict rather than encourage individual development; on the other hand, these

[1] R. Likert, *New Patterns of Management,* McGraw-Hill Book Company, New York, 1961.

TABLE 1   Uses of Appraisals or Ratings in 316 Leading Industrial Corporations

	Responses	
Uses of appraisals	Number	Percent
1. Merit increases or bonuses	238	75.3%
2. Counseling the ratee	278	88.0
3. Planning training or development for the ratee	270	85.4
4. Considering the ratee for promotion	266	84.2
5. Considering retention or discharge	184	58.2
6. Motivating the ratee to achieve higher levels of performance	269	85.1
7. Improve company planning	178	56.3
8. Other	28	8.9
Total companies	316	

Figure 1.   Trait appraisal form.

Rate the employee in the following traits, using this scale: 3 — Excellent
2 — Acceptable
1 — Needs Development
0 — Not Observed

Appearance	_____	Ability to Learn	_____
Self-confidence	_____	Accuracy	_____
Ability to Express Self	_____	Meets Deadlines	_____
Alertness	_____	Health	_____
Ambition	_____	Enthusiasm	_____
Initiative	_____	Attitude & Acceptance of Responsibility	_____
Energy	_____	Use of Time	
Knowledge of Department	_____	Organizes Work to Get a Job Done	_____
Contacts with: Superiors	_____	Independence	_____
Peers	_____	Adaptable	_____
Customers	_____	Maturity	_____

OVERALL EVALUATION

All factors considered, my overall evaluation of this employee is (circle one):
1 — Outstanding
2 — A Good Man Who Should Do Well
3 — A Sound Man
4 — An Adequate But Limited Man
5 — Only Just Satisfactory

If reviewed, employee's reaction or comments

Reviewed with Employee by: _____   Date: _____

researchers assert that participative, supportive management tends to foster higher motivation and encourage development and personal growth.

Recent social science research findings indicate that a trend has been developing over the last several years in the field of manpower management away from traditional trait-oriented performance appraisal and toward a more positive motivation-oriented approach.   The origin of this new approach lies in the writings of such commentators as Peter Drucker[2] and Douglas McGregor,[3] who have suggested, on the basis of research findings such as Likert's, that a participative motivation-oriented approach to appraisal should lead to higher performance levels than the traditional trait-oriented approach.

Although research has revealed only recently that the hierarchical approach to appraisal conflicts with its developmental and motivational goals, the question of whether there might be such a conflict was raised early in the history of performance appraisal.   In a 1926 article, Arthur Kornhauser[4] presented the

[2] P. R. Drucker, *The Practice of Management*, Harper & Row, New York, 1954.

[3] D. McGregor, "An Uneasy Look at Performance Appraisal," *Harvard Business Review*, vol. 35, no. 3, May–June, 1957, pp. 89–94.

[4] Arthur W. Kornhauser, "What Are Rating Scales Good For?" *Journal of Personnel Research*, vol. 5, no. 5, September, 1926, pp. 189–193.

Figure 2. Employee performance review worksheet.

EMPLOYEE PERFORMANCE REVIEW WORKSHEET

Employee Name	Department	Rated By	Date

INSTRUCTIONS:

1. Check the block beside each factor which contains the closest description of the employee WITH REGARD TO THAT FACTOR ONLY.
2. Enter rating points (0, 1, 2, 3) for each factor in the far right column.
3. Add the points in each section and divide the results by the figure shown. Round fractions as follows: 0.5 to 1.4 = 1; 1.5 - 2.4 = 2; 2.5 - 3.0 = 3. Should you not rate a job on a particular factor, divide by the number of factors rated rather than the figure shown.
4. Enter the "Rating" on the rating card.

QUALITY

FACTORS	POOR – 0	FAIR – 1	GOOD – 2	EXCELLENT – 3	RATING POINTS
APPEARANCE OF WORK	☐ Work is generally sloppy and incomplete. Employee has little or no regard for appearance. Work must be redone often.	☐ Some work is sloppy and incomplete. Employee tries to do acceptable work but rework is required often enough to cause repeated reminders.	☐ Work is generally neat and complete. Employee has pride in his work. Rework seldom required.	☐ Work is exceptionally neat, well organized and complete. Employee has exceptional pride in his work. Rework rarely required.	☐
ACCURACY OF WORK	☐ Continuously makes errors. Makes no effort to check own work. Work must be checked 100% by others.	☐ Frequently makes errors. Checks own work fairly often. Work must be checked 50% of the time by others.	☐ Occasionally makes errors. Almost always checks own work for accuracy. Only spot checking required by others.	☐ Rarely makes errors. Always checks own work. Little or no checking required by others.	☐
SUPERVISION REQUIRED	☐ Constant direction required with little effect.	☐ High degree of direction required to maintain a minimum level of quality.	☐ Needs occasional direction to maintain a high level of quality.	☐ Rarely requires direction to maintain outstanding level of quality.	☐
				TOTAL POINTS	
				DIVIDED BY	3
				RATING	

Recommendations for improvement

☐ Has improved
☐ Little or no change
☐ Has regressed

Figure 2. Employee performance review worksheet—continued

QUANTITY

FACTORS	POOR – 0	FAIR – 1	GOOD – 2	EXCELLENT – 3	RATING POINTS
VOLUME	☐ Volume of work is below acceptable level.	☐ Volume of work meets minimum acceptable level.	☐ Volume of work meets that of average worker.	☐ Volume is exceptional; exceeding average requirements.	
UTILIZATION OF TIME	☐ Frequently wastes time between assignments.	☐ Occasionally wastes working time.	☐ Wastes very little of available working time.	☐ Utilizes working time to the fullest.	
ORGANIZATION OF WORK	☐ Work not organized; rarely meets deadlines.	☐ Work is partially organized; frequently misses deadlines.	☐ Work is well organized; occasionally misses deadlines.	☐ Work is exceptionally well organized; rarely misses deadlines.	
WORK PACE	☐ Works at slow pace; frequently stalls. Indicates laziness.	☐ Works at easy pace.	☐ Works steadily.	☐ Works at an energetic pace.	
SUPERVISION REQUIRED	☐ Constant direction required to obtain quantity produced.	☐ Frequent direction required to obtain quantity produced.	☐ Occasional direction required to obtain quantity produced.	☐ Rarely requires direction to obtain quantity produced.	
				TOTAL POINTS	
				DIVIDED BY	5
				RATING	

Recommendations for improvement

☐ Has improved
☐ Little or no change
☐ Has regressed

(CONTINUED ON REVERSE SIDE)

Figure 2. Employee performance review worksheet—continued

ALERTNESS

FACTORS	POOR – 0	FAIR – 1	GOOD – 2	EXCELLENT – 3	RATING POINTS
JOB KNOWLEDGE	☐ Grasp of job and scope very limited; requires considerable assistance and frequent instruction.	☐ Fair working knowledge of job; requires average assistance and instruction.	☐ Well informed on most phases of job; requires occasional assistance and instruction.	☐ Exceptionally well informed on all essentials of job; requires little or no instruction or assistance.	
ADAPTABILITY	☐ Can be used on routine tasks only; instructions must be repeated continually.	☐ Fairly adaptable to new tasks or changing conditions if properly prepared and instructed.	☐ Readily adaptable to new tasks or changing conditions with occasional assistance and supervision.	☐ Exceptionally adaptable to new tasks or changing conditions. Requires little or no help to adjust to new conditions.	
RESOURCE-FULNESS	☐ Unable to act independently in finding answers and solutions to problems; requires constant direction.	☐ Able to act independently on occasion in finding answers and solutions to problems; requires more than average direction.	☐ Able to act independently majority of the time in finding answers and solutions to problems; requires average direction.	☐ Acts independently in practically all cases in finding answers and solutions to problems; requires very little direction.	
JUDGMENT	☐ Decisions are usually unsound and not practical; no dependence can be placed on conclusions due to poor judgment.	☐ Decisions are usually sound and practical; exercises fair judgment in considering all factors and consequences before arriving at conclusions.	☐ Decisions are sound and practical in most cases; exercises good judgment in considering all factors and consequences before arriving at conclusions.	☐ Decisions are very sound and practical and well thought out. Judgment is always reliable.	
				TOTAL POINTS	
☐ Has improved	Recommendations for improvement			DIVIDED BY	4
☐ Little or no change				RATING	
☐ Has regressed					

Figure 2. Employee performance review worksheet—continued

CITIZENSHIP

FACTORS	POOR – 0	FAIR – 1	GOOD – 2	EXCELLENT – 3	RATING POINTS
WORK ATTITUDE	☐ Complete lack of interest in his job and company.	☐ Minor interest in his job and company.	☐ Some interest in his job and company.	☐ Very interested in his job and company.	
PEOPLE RELATIONSHIPS	☐ Does not get along well with others; not cooperative.	☐ Works fairly well with others; fairly cooperative.	☐ Works very well with others; fully cooperative.	☐ Works exceptionally well with others; goes out of way to cooperate.	
CRITICISMS & SUGGESTIONS	☐ Not responsive to criticisms or suggestions from supervision.	☐ Responds occasionally to criticisms or suggestions from supervision.	☐ Generally responds to criticism or suggestions from supervision.	☐ Always and enthusiastically responds to criticisms or suggestions from supervision.	
PUNCTUALITY (Including Early Quits)	☐ Continuously tardy (13 times or over during last 6 months)	☐ Frequently tardy (7 to 12 times during last 6 months)	☐ Occasionally tardy (3 to 6 times during last 6 months)	☐ Rarely tardy (2 times or less during last 6 months)	
ATTENDANCE	☐ Habitual absenteeism (7 occasions or over during last 6 months)	☐ Frequently absent (5 or 6 occasions during last 6 months)	☐ Occasional absenteeism (2 to 4 occasions during last 6 months)	☐ Rarely absent (1 occasion during last 6 months)	
☐ Has improved ☐ Little or no change ☐ Has regressed	Recommendations for improvement			TOTAL POINTS	
				DIVIDED BY	5
				RATING	

ADDITIONAL COMMENTS

5–9

classical arguments in favor of conventional, numerical rating scales but also set forth in the article a program for testing the usefulness of rating scales. To an amazing degree, he anticipated the recent criticisms of Likert, McGregor, and others. Kornhauser pointed out that the arguments in favor of rating scales were *a priori* and that scientific research would be required to determine whether there might be psychological factors that would limit the usefulness of such ratings. The effect of research reported by Likert, by Kay, Meyer, and French,[5] and by Meyer and Walker[6] has been to show that these psychological limiting factors do exist.

DEVELOPMENT OF PERFORMANCE APPRAISAL TECHNIQUES

Changes in the work environment over the last 20 years also have stimulated shifts in emphasis in performance appraisal. Whisler and Harper[7] have pointed out the following changes as being significant:

1. Shifts in the occupational structure toward higher skills
2. Development of automation
3. Increasing size of organizations
4. Growth of unionization among the hourly work force
5. Increase in staff activities
6. Greater specialization in roles of organization members, combined with increasing technical education
7. Changes in the philosophy of management from scientific management to human relations, and then to quantitative decision techniques and overall corporate planning

The movement toward greater decentralization and the creation of profit centers also have had a major influence on performance appraisal practices.

Both the recent social science research and the structural changes discussed above have had an impact on reorienting the emphasis of performance appraisal away from hierarchical judgment directed only toward controlling wages and salaries toward participation to stimulate motivation and development as well.

Research in the field of performance appraisal has reflected this shift in emphasis. Most research reported in the literature from the 1920s until the mid-1950s tended to stress the technical problems of appraisal, such as scaling techniques and the problem of obtaining objective appraisals.

Some of the earliest formal appraisal plans used in this country employed either open-ended essay appraisals or some form of adjective checklist. Because these approaches lacked both objectivity and precision, the attention paid to psychometrics in the early 1920s led to the development of graphic rating scales.[8] These scales also employed a list of traits, but in addition the rater was required to indicate his judgment of the amount of each trait possessed by the ratee by marking a point on a graphic scale (or continuum) provided. The major *technical* flaw of this approach was that, because of the "halo effect,"

[5] E. Kay, H. H. Meyer, and J. R. P. French, "Effects of Threat in a Performance Appraisal Interview," *Journal of Applied Psychology*, vol. 49, no. 5, October, 1965, pp. 311–317.

[6] H. H. Meyer and W. B. Walker, "A Study of Factors Relating to the Effectiveness of a Performance Appraisal Program," *Personnel Psychology*, Autumn, 1961, p. 291.

[7] Thomas L. Whisler and Shirley F. Harper (eds.), *Performance Appraisal: Research and Practice*, Holt, Rinehart and Winston, Inc., New York, 1962.

[8] M. Freyd, "The Graphic Rating Scale," *Journal of Educational Psychology*, 1923, vol. 14, pp. 83–102.

most ratings tended to congregate at either the high end or the low end of the scale.

Since the failure to obtain a distribution of ratings was then seen as the primary flaw of appraisals, attention shifted toward the development of methods to force a normal distribution of appraisals around the average or mean performance of all members of the work group. This led to the development of the forced-distribution technique.[9] Although this technique solved the technical distribution problem, it foundered on the logical objection of raters that many work groups do not reflect a normal distribution of individual performance.

Further technical refinements led to such approaches as the ranking[10] (ranking the members of a work group from best to worst in the order of their relative performance), paired-comparison[11] (a refinement of the ranking method which involves the systematic comparison of each member of a group with each of his peers in the group to produce the overall ranking), forced-choice[12] (a series of choices between pairs of equally positive and equally negative descriptive phrases), and critical-incident[13] (the systematic recording as they occur of actual instances of significantly good or significantly poor performance) techniques. Although these later approaches have been relatively successful in overcoming some of the technical obstacles to appraisal, none of them has been widely adopted, primarily because of various practical difficulties. For example, the critical-incident technique has been shown to be relatively objective and reliable, but it is also prohibitively expensive for many appraisal situations.

It should be noted also that all of these earlier approaches are hierarchical in nature—i.e., they rest firmly on the assumption that the superior is the individual most able to make an accurate appraisal.

Largely because of the many difficulties encountered with such rating programs, various researchers and management experts began in the 1950s to devise and to expound a number of novel approaches as alternatives to conventional ratings.

One of the important alternatives suggested was profit performance measurement. Under this approach, which was intended for evaluating the performance of profit center managers, a manager was to be judged almost solely on the basis of the profitability of the organization for which he was responsible. In a 1957 article, Joel Dean stated the philosophy of the approach this way: "Complex problems of measuring and weighting executives' contributions to profits are best solved by dividing the corporation into semiautonomous profit centers whose management is measured by the contributions his center makes to the corporation's overhead and profits."[14]

---

[9] J. Tiffin, "Merit Rating: Its Validity and Techniques," *Rating Employee and Supervisory Performance*, M. Joseph Dooher and Vivienne Marquis (eds.), American Management Association, New York, 1951.

[10] Edwin E. Ghiselli and Clarence W. Brown, *Personnel and Industrial Psychology*, (2d ed.), McGraw-Hill Book Company, New York, 1955, chap. 4.

[11] C. H. Lawshe, N. C. Kephart, and E. J. McCormick, "The Paired-Comparison Technique for Rating Performance of Industrial Employees," *Journal of Applied Psychology*, vol. 33, no. 1, February, 1949, pp. 69–77.

[12] Marion W. Richardson, "Forced-Choice Performance Reports: A Modern Merit-Rating Method," *Personnel*, vol. 26, no. 3, November, 1949, pp. 205–212.

[13] John C. Flanagan, "The Critical Incident Technique," *Psychological Bulletin*, vol. 51, no. 4, July, 1954, pp. 327–358.

[14] J. Dean, "Profit Performance Measurement of Division Managers," *The Controller*, September, 1957, p. 423.

MANAGEMENT BY OBJECTIVES

In a 1954 book, *The Practice of Management,* Peter Drucker proposed a new approach to performance appraisal, which he called "management by objectives and self-control." In the author's opinion, this remains one of the best statements of the concept itself and the rationale underlying it.

Since Drucker's term has been picked up by literally hundreds of other writers and has been redefined in many ways to suit individual views or purposes, it is perhaps important to establish clearly what Drucker meant and what he did not mean by the phrase. Drucker explains the rationale underlying his concept by saying,

> Business performance therefore requires that each job be directed toward the objectives of the whole business. And in particular each manager's job must be focused on the success of the whole. The performance that is expected of the manager must be derived from the performance goals of the business; his results must be measured by the contribution they make to the success of the enterprise.[15]

He went on to say,

> Some of the most effective managers I know . . . have each of their subordinates write a "manager's letter" twice a year. In this letter to his superior, each manager first defines the objective of his superior's job and of his own job as he sees them. He then sets down the performance standards which he believes are being applied to him. Next, he lists the things he must do himself to attain these goals—and the things within his own unit he considers the major obstacles. He lists the things his superior and the company do that help him and the things that hamper him. Finally, he outlines what he proposes to do during the next year to reach his goals. If his superior accepts this statement, the "manager's letter" becomes the charter under which the manager operates. . . . The greatest advantage of management by objectives is perhaps that it makes it possible for a manager to control his own performance. Self-control means stronger motivation: a desire to do the best rather than just enough to get by. It means higher performance goals and broader vision. Even if management by objectives were not necessary to give the enterprise the unity of direction and effort of a management team, it would be necessary to make possible management by self-control.[16]

A major turning point in the history of performance evaluation was Douglas McGregor's article, "An Uneasy Look at Performance Appraisal,"[17] which appeared in 1957. It seems safe to observe that no other article on the subject of performance appraisal, before or since, has created so much controversy.

McGregor was concerned in the article with the fact that most appraisal systems involved rating of traits and personal qualities. Because of the semantic problems this introduced, he felt such ratings were highly unreliable. Besides, this placed the manager in the untenable position of "playing God," which produced two main difficulties:

1. Managers were uncomfortable in this position and resisted making appraisals.

[15] P. R. Drucker, *The Practice of Management,* Harper & Row, New York, 1954, p. 121.

[16] *Ibid.,* pp. 129–131.

[17] D. McGregor, *op. cit.,* pp. 89–94.

2. It had a damaging effect on the motivation and development of the subordinate.

Although McGregor's criticism of trait rating was a bold new statement in this context, it was solidly supported by previous research in the social sciences, such as Likert's work in this area, which has already been mentioned. Other social scientists had been coming to similar conclusions, among them Ronald Taft,[18] who, in a 1955 article, surveyed the extensive literature of research into human judgment and concluded that few individuals are qualified to judge the traits and aptitudes of others. Taft, a psychologist, found that ability to judge is a personality trait, and that there are wide variations in the ability of individuals to judge the talents and aptitudes of other people. His research thus supports McGregor's conclusion that it is unrealistic and impractical to base performance evaluation on trait ratings by managers and supervisors, since these individuals will vary widely in their ability to make such ratings.

McGregor felt that Peter Drucker's concept of management by objectives offered an unusually promising framework within which to seek a solution to this problem, and he proposed a new approach to performance appraisal based upon assumptions consistent with Drucker's philosophy. He described his proposal as follows:

> This approach calls on the subordinate to establish short-term performance goals for himself. The superior enters the process actively only after the subordinate has (a) done a good deal of thinking about his job, (b) made a careful assessment of his own strengths and weaknesses, and (c) formulated some specific plan to accomplish his goals. The superior's role is to help the man relate his self-appraisal, his "targets," and his plan for the ensuing period to the realities of the organization. . . . At the conclusion of the six-month period, the subordinate makes his own appraisal of what he has accomplished relative to the targets he had set earlier. He substantiates it with factual data wherever possible. The "interview" is an examination by superior and subordinate together of the subordinate's self-appraisal, and it culminates in a resetting of targets for the next six months. Of course, the superior has veto power in each step of this process. . . . However, in practice, he rarely needs to exercise it.[19]

Another landmark article in the recent literature of performance appraisal is Kindall and Gatza's "Positive Program for Performance Appraisal."[20] In a sense, this article began where McGregor left off. Building on the philosophy stated by McGregor, these two authors proposed a specific, detailed plan for implementing a five-step performance appraisal program based on McGregor's assumptions:

> 1. The individual discusses his job description with his superior, and they agree on the content of his job and relative importance of his major duties—the things he is paid to do and is accountable for.
> 2. The individual establishes performance targets for each of his responsibilities for the forthcoming period.
> 3. He meets with his superior to discuss his target program.
> 4. Checkpoints are established for the evaluation of his progress; ways of measuring progress are selected.

[18] Ronald Taft, "The Ability to Judge People," *Psychological Bulletin*, vol. 52, no. 1, January, 1955, pp. 1–23.

[19] D. McGregor, *op. cit.*, p. 91.

[20] A. F. Kindall and J. Gatza, "Positive Program for Performance Appraisal," *Harvard Business Review*, vol. 41, no. 6, November–December, 1963, pp. 153–162.

5. The superior and subordinate meet at the end of the period to discuss the results of the subordinate's efforts to meet the targets he had previously established.[21]

A typical set of forms used for the management by objectives approach to appraisal is shown in Figure 3.   The forms used by different companies for this appraisal approach vary considerably, and some companies prefer to use only a blank sheet of paper.   It will also be noted that these forms emphasize an explicit relationship between the appraisal of performance against objectives and the determination of incentive bonus.   This direct tie between compensation and accomplishment of objectives is not uncommon; however, some companies make this tie less explicit and prefer to use appraisal data only as an input to a separate compensation decision process.

One of the first reports in the literature of a company's effort to apply the

[21] *Ibid.*, p. 155.

Figure 3.   Management by objectives form.

TARGETS FOR 1965

Submitted by: _____   Title: _____

Dept/Div: _____   Supervisor: _____

TARGET (Ranked Importance___ & Weight %___)		PERFORMANCE CRITERIA

Review Dates	PROGRESS & RESULTS
FINAL (January)	

Figure 3.   Management by objectives form——continued

BONUS CONSIDERATIONS

Briefly outline each target below. List most important first; the least, last.	Please describe results obtained on each target and, in view of all circumstances, give your opinion of their adequacy.
	Comments by: _____ (Name)

management by objectives approach to performance appraisal was contained in a series of articles by Meyer, Kay, and French.[22]   These articles report on the results of experimental research at General Electric regarding a positive approach to performance appraisal, such as that outlined by McGregor or Kindall and Gatza.   The approach at G.E., called "work planning and review," was a synthesis of McGregor's philosophy and the traditional need for administrative evaluations.   In a sense, the research program at G.E. tested and proved many of the aspects of McGregor's philosophy which had been stated as hypotheses.   It also validated the appraisal approach advocated by Kindall and

[22] H. H. Meyer, E. Kay, and J. R. P. French, "Split Roles in Performance Appraisal," *Harvard Business Review*, vol. 43, no. 1, January–February, 1965, pp. 123–129.

Figure 3.   Management by objectives form—continued

Summary appraisal   Bonus Percents by Grade and Performance

Summary appraisal	Salary grade							
	10	11	12	13	14	15	16	17
Unusually high level of accomplishment on all targets. ☐ →	20–22.5%	33–37.5%	46–52.5%	65–75%	65–75%	78–90%	91–105%	104–120%
More than reasonable. Results against all targets were slightly better than normal expectations. ☐ →	17–19%	28–32%	39–45%	55–64%	55–64%	66–77%	77–90%	88–103%
Reasonable, normal achievement for managerial personnel. Did well on all the more important targets. ☐ →	14–16%	23–27%	32–38%	45–54%	45–54%	54–65%	63–76%	72–87%
Adequate performance against targets. However, achievement on the most important target could have been better. ☐ →	11–13%	18–22%	25–31%	35–44%	35–44%	42–53%	49–62%	56–71%
Results against several important targets could have been better. ☐ →	7.5–10%	12.5–17%	17.5–24%	25–34%	25–34%	30–41%	35–48%	40–55%
Failed to achieve minimum acceptable level of performance on all important targets. ☐ →	0	0	0	0	0	0	0	0

Bonus percent recommended: _____

Gatza. The program included controlled research to compare the results of conventional appraisal with those of a work planning and review approach. The latter approach proved to be clearly superior for motivating and developing subordinates.

CURRENT PRACTICE IN PERFORMANCE APPRAISAL

Let us turn now to a discussion of current practice in performance appraisal. What appraisal techniques are being used at the present time by major American companies? Which employees have their performance appraised? What are the primary uses of appraisals? And, most importantly, what effect do the answers to the latter two questions have on the type of appraisal technique used in a particular company? The author's recent research study, cited in the bibliography, provided some answers to these questions.

Types of Plans. Table 2 shows the types of appraisal plans used by the companies surveyed. Somewhat surprisingly, 106 companies, or 34.9 percent, indicated they use only a management by objectives type of appraisal plan, and 75 companies, or 24.7 percent, indicated they use a management by objectives type plan (for a part of the work force or a part of the organization) in combination with another type of appraisal plan. Thus, 181 companies, or 59.6 percent, said that management by objectives serves as the basis of performance appraisal for at least a part of their work force. A total of 29 percent of the companies use some form of trait rating, and this was the only alternative besides management by objectives chosen by a significant number of companies. Each of the remaining alternatives was chosen by less than 6 percent of the companies. It thus seems clear that management by objectives is today by far the most common basis for performance appraisal in the largest industrial companies.

Of the companies having a management by objectives plan, 59.4 percent include all salaried employees in the plan, 17.9 percent include hourly employees, 70.8 percent include nonsupervisory salaried employees, 89.6 percent include first-level supervisors, and 97.2 percent include managers and executives. Thus, where management by objectives programs exist, they almost always apply to managers and executives, and they apply with diminishing frequency to other groups at progressively lower levels of the organization. In other words, the higher an individual is in the organization structure, the more likely he is to be included in a management by objectives program adopted by his company.

Uses of Appraisals. As seen in Table 3, the modal response (31.1 percent) of companies having a management by objectives approach to appraisal was that the principal purpose of the plan is the motivation of employees. Another 20.8 percent of these companies said the principal purpose of the appraisal program was the planning of training and development of employees.

Significantly, management by objectives is the only appraisal approach for which the modal primary use is motivation. Only 20 percent of the companies having a combination of management by objectives and some other appraisal

TABLE 2   **Appraisal Plans Used in 304 Leading Industrial Corporations***

	Responses	
Type of plan used	Number	Percent
1. Numerical or descriptive rating of only one general item, "How well does the ratee perform his job?"	16	5.3%
2. Numerical or graphic trait ratings	27	8.9%
3. Trait checklist	61	20.1%
4. Forced-choice system of rating	11	3.6%
5. Management by objectives	106	34.9%
6. Other	8	2.6%
7. Combination of (5) and another plan	75	24.7%
Total	304	100.0%

* Twelve of the 316 respondents did not specify type of plan used.

TABLE 3 Primary Use of Various Types of Appraisal Plans (Percent)

Type of plan	Not answered	Merit increases or bonuses	Counseling	Planning training or development	Primary use of appraisals Promotion	Retention and discharge	Motivation	Improve company planning	Other	Total
Overall performance.	25.0%	50.0%	0.0	12.5%	0.0	0.0	6.3%	6.3%	0.0	100.0%
Traits:										
Numerical.	14.8	25.9	29.6%	11.1	3.7%	0.0	14.8	0.0	0.0	100.0
Descriptive.	21.3	21.3	13.1	14.8	4.9	0.0	16.4	4.9	3.3%	100.0
Forced-choice.	45.5	9.1	0.0	9.1	9.1	18.2%	9.1	0.0	0.0	100.0
MBO only.	18.9	14.2	1.9	20.8	0.9	0.0	31.1	9.4	2.8	100.0
Other.	25.0	25.0	0.0	12.5	0.0	0.0	25.0	12.5	0.0	100.0
MBO plus another.	29.3	22.7	4.0	13.3	1.3	0.0	20.0	5.3	4.0	100.0
Total.	39.0%	17.4%	5.5%	12.2%	2.0%	0.5%	16.6%	5.0%	2.0%	100.0%

approach said that motivation was the primary goal of their appraisal program; and the modal response (22.7 percent) of this group was that the program was used primarily to determine merit increases or bonuses.

Thus, there appears to be a clear difference in viewpoint regarding the primary goal of performance appraisal between those companies using management by objectives alone and those companies using management by objectives in combination with other approaches.

The modal response of companies having most other types of appraisal programs was that the principal use of their programs is either counseling or merit increases and bonuses.

WHICH PERFORMANCE APPRAISAL PLAN IS BEST?

Taken together, these findings indicate clearly that the *tendency* of current practice is to adopt a management by objectives approach to performance appraisal when higher-level managerial, professional, and technical personnel are to be appraised or when the making of compensation decisions is seen as only one purpose of appraisal along with such other purposes as development or motivation. On the other hand, when compensation decisions are seen as the primary aim of performance appraisal, or when less skilled blue-collar and clerical employees are primarily concerned, companies are more likely to adopt some form of trait appraisal, most frequently trait checklists.

The question of how far down in an organization the management by objectives approach should be applied is probably one that can best be answered by a particular company on the basis of the requirements and constraints of the organization; the content of jobs at different levels; the skills, attitudes, and expectancies of individuals at different levels; and the management climate and the traditions of the organization. No blanket conclusion on this issue can be made from research data, although it has been noted that, to date, companies have most often applied management by objectives to top-level management jobs and have been progressively less inclined to apply management by objectives at each successively lower level in the organization. There may be some theoretical support for this decision, in terms of job content and the skills and expectations of individuals. There is, however, no specific research finding to suggest, overall, that management by objectives has been less successful at lower levels than at upper levels of organizations.

So far we have mentioned that two of the significant determinants of the most effective type of performance appraisal for a particular situation are the purposes for which the appraisals are intended and the expectations, abilities, and type of work performed by the individuals to be appraised.

Management Climate. Another important factor, often overlooked, is the management climate of the organization. To be effective, the type of appraisal plan adopted must be seen by all concerned as being consistent with the basic assumptions and style of management prevalent in the organization. Management by objectives as an approach to appraisal works best within a climate which emphasizes participation and a high degree of mutual trust and confidence within a framework of basic commitment to management by shared objectives and self-control. Within more traditional organizations, where management by direction and external control is emphasized and where mutual confidence is less prevalent, more hierarchical appraisal methods, such as trait ratings or forced-choice techniques, are likely to be seen as more consistent with the overall management climate and thus likely to be more effective.

Appraising Beginners and Experienced Personnel. Finally, another important factor determining the most effective type of appraisal in a specific situation is the maturity of the individual with regard to the particular job within which he is being appraised—*maturity* being defined as the length of time the individual has been in the job and the degree to which he has mastered the basic requirements of the job. Thus, the most effective appraisal technique for measuring the performance of someone experienced in a position may be quite different from the approach most effective in appraising the performance of a beginner.

For reasons that will be obvious, management by objectives is most effective when the individual being measured already has mastered the basic requirements of the job. Appraisal of an experienced person can focus on the degree to which his performance goes beyond basic job requirements and reflects his expansion of the job to fit his own potential. To the extent that this is not the case (i.e., to the extent that the focus of appraisal is on measuring the individual's progress along the learning curve toward basic mastery of the job), more directive and hierarchical appraisal techniques, such as trait ratings, ratings of performance characteristics, and ratings of overall performance, will perhaps be more appropriate. Thus, among the factors to be weighed in determining the appraisal approach to be used are the incumbent's length of time on the job, age, previous experience, and evaluated potential.

As has been indicated, there are a number of factors which may usefully be given explicit consideration in an attempt to determine the most effective appraisal approach for a particular situation. And information about what other companies have done in specific situations can perhaps provide some guidance. There are, however, so many interrelated factors to be considered that prescriptive formulas are not feasible. Unfortunately, appraisal remains an art rather than a science, and in the last analysis good judgment, assisted by knowledge of the practice and experience of other companies, remains the best guide to determination of the appraisal technique to be employed.

BIBLIOGRAPHY

Books

Argyris, C.: *Personality and Organization,* Harper & Row, New York, 1957.

Batten, J. D.: *Beyond Management by Objectives,* American Management Association, New York, 1966.

Blake, R. R., and J. S. Mouton: *The Managerial Grid,* Gulf Publishing, Houston, 1964.

Drucker, P. R.: *Managing for Results,* Harper & Row, New York, 1964.

Drucker, P. R.: *The Practice of Management,* Harper & Row, New York, 1954.

Foundation for Research on Human Behavior: *Performance Appraisals—Effects on Employees and Their Behavior,* Foundation for Research on Human Behavior, Ann Arbor, 1963.

Gellerman, S. W.: *Motivation and Productivity,* American Management Association, New York, 1963.

Ghiselli, Edwin E., and Clarence W. Brown: *Personnel and Industrial Psychology,* 2d ed., McGraw-Hill Book Company, New York, 1955, chap. 4.

Howell, Robert A.: *Management by Objectives—Should It Be Applied?* doctoral thesis, unpublished, Harvard University, 1966.

Hughes, C. L.: *Goal Setting,* American Management Association, New York, 1965.

Kellogg, M. S.: *What to Do About Performance Appraisal,* American Management Association, New York, 1965.

Likert, R.: *New Patterns of Management,* McGraw-Hill Book Company, New York, 1961.

Maslow, A. H.: *Motivation and Personality,* Harper & Row, New York, 1954.

McConkey, D. D.: *How to Manage by Results,* American Management Association, New York, 1965.

McGregor, D.: *The Human Side of Enterprise,* McGraw-Hill Book Company, New York, 1960.

Miller, Ernest C.: *Objectives and Standards,* American Management Association, New York, 1966.

Odiorne, G. S.: *Management by Objectives—A System of Management Leadership,* Pitman Publishing Corp., New York, 1965.

Schleh, E. C.: *Management by Results,* McGraw-Hill Book Company, New York, 1961.

Schuster, Frederick E.: *An Evaluation of the Management-by-Objectives Approach to Performance Appraisal,* unpublished doctoral dissertation, Graduate School of Business Administration, Harvard University, December, 1968.

Spriegel, William R., and E. W. Mumma: *Merit Rating of Supervisors and Executives* (Personnel Study No. 14), Bureau of Business Research, The University of Texas, Austin, 1961.

Valentine, R. F.: *Performance Objectives for Managers,* American Management Association, New York, 1965.

Whisler, Thomas L., and Shirley F. Harper (eds.): *Performance Appraisal: Research and Practice,* Holt, Rinehart and Winston, Inc., New York, 1962.

Articles

Blake, R. R., et al.: "Breakthrough in Organization Development," *Harvard Business Review,* vol. 42, no. 6, November–December, 1964, pp. 133–155.

Coleman, C. J.: "Avoiding the Pitfalls in Results-Oriented Appraisals," *Personnel,* November–December, 1965, pp. 24–33.

Dean, J.: "Profit Performance Measurement of Division Managers," *The Controller,* September, 1957, pp. 423–449.

Drucker, P. R.: "Managing for Business Effectiveness," *Harvard Business Review,* vol. 41, no. 3, May–June, 1963, pp. 53–60.

Flanagan, John C.: "The Critical Incident Technique," *Psychological Bulletin,* vol. 51, no. 4, July, 1954, pp. 327–358.

French, J. R. P., E. Kay, and H. H. Meyer: "Participation and the Appraisal System," *Human Relations,* vol. 19, no. 1, 1966, p. 3.

Freyd, M.: "The Graphic Rating Scale," *J. Educ. Psychol.,* 1923, vol. 14, pp. 83–102.

Granger, C. H.: "The Hierarchy of Objectives," *Harvard Business Review,* vol. 42, no. 3, May–June, 1964, pp. 63–74.

Hayden, Spencer J.: "Getting Better Results from Post-Appraisal Interviews," *Personnel,* vol. 31, no. 6, May, 1955, pp. 541–550.

Hoppock, Robert: "Ground Rules for Appraisal Interviewers," *Personnel,* vol. 38, no. 3, May–June, 1961, pp. 31–34.

Howell, Robert A.: "A Fresh Look at Management by Objectives," *Business Horizons,* Fall, 1967, pp. 51–58.

Kay, E., H. H. Meyer, and J. R. P. French: "Effects of Threat in a Performance Appraisal Interview," *Journal of Applied Psychology,* vol. 49, no. 5, October, 1965, pp. 311–317.

Kelly, Philip R.: "Reappraisal of Appraisals," *Harvard Business Review,* vol. 36, no. 3, May–June, 1958, pp. 59–68. Reprinted in Pigors, Myers, and Malm: *Readings in Personnel Administration,* rev. ed., McGraw-Hill Book Company, New York, 1959, pp. 368–384.

Kindall, A. F., and J. Gatza: "Positive Program for Peformance Appraisal," *Harvard Business Review,* vol. 41, no. 6, November–December, 1963, pp. 153–162.

Kornhauser, Arthur W.: "What Are Rating Scales Good For?" *Journal of Personnel Research,* vol. 5, no. 5, September, 1926, pp. 189–193.

Lawshe, C. H., N. C. Kephart, and E. J. McCormick: "The Paired-Comparison Technique for Rating Performance of Industrial Employees," *Journal of Applied Psychology,* vol. 33, no. 1, February, 1949, pp. 69–77.

Likert, R.: "Measuring Organizational Performance," *Harvard Business Review*, vol. 36, no. 2, March–April, 1958, pp. 41–50.

Likert, R.: "Motivational Approach to Management Development," *Harvard Business Review*, vol. 37, no. 4, July–August, 1959, pp. 75–82.

MacKinney, A. C.: "What Should Ratings Rate?" *Personnel*, vol. 37, no. 3, May–June, 1960, pp. 75–78.

Mahler, Walter R., and Guyot Frazier: "Appraisal of Executive Performance: The 'Achilles Heel' of Management Development," *Personnel*, vol. 31, no. 5, March, 1955, pp. 429–441.

Maier, Norman R. F.: "Three Types of Appraisal Interview," *The Appraisal Interview*, chap. I. Reprinted in *Personnel*, vol. 54, no. 5, March–April, 1958, pp. 27–40. Also reprinted in Pigors, Myers, and Malm: *Readings in Personnel Administration*, rev. ed., McGraw-Hill Book Company, New York, 1959, pp. 354–367.

Mayfield, Harold: "In Defense of Performance Appraisal," *Harvard Business Review*, vol. 38, no. 2, March–April, 1960, pp. 81–87.

McGregor, D.: "An Uneasy Look at Performance Appraisal," *Harvard Business Review*, vol. 35, no. 3, May–June, 1957, pp. 89–94.

Meyer, H. H., E. Kay, and J. R. P. French: "Split Roles in Performance Appraisal," *Harvard Business Review*, vol. 43, no. 1, January–February, 1965, pp. 123–129.

Meyer, H. H., and W. B. Walker: "A Study of Factors Relating to the Effectiveness of a Performance Appraisal Program," *Personnel Psychology*, Autumn, 1961, p. 291.

Neiman, Robert A.: "Measuring Supervisory Performance," *Personnel*, vol. 39, no. 1, January–February, 1962, pp. 39–44.

Patton, A.: "How to Appraise Executive Performance," *Harvard Business Review*, vol. 38, no. 1, January–February, 1960, pp. 63–70.

Richardson, Marion W.: "Forced-Choice Performance Reports: A Modern Merit-Rating Method," *Personnel*, vol. 26, no. 3, November, 1949, pp. 205–212.

Rowland, Virgil K.: "The Mechanics of Group Appraisal," *Personnel*, vol. 34, no. 6, May–June, 1958, pp. 36–43.

Schleh, E. Charles: "The Fallacy of Measuring Management," *Dun's Review*, November, 1963, pp. 49–113.

Spriegel, William R.: "New Findings on Appraisal: II. Company Practices in Appraising Managers," *Personnel*, vol. 39, no. 3, May–June, 1962, pp. 77–83.

Stolz, Robert K.: "Can Appraisal Interviews Be Made Effective?" *Personnel*, vol. 38, no. 2, March–April, 1961, pp. 32–37.

Taft, Ronald: "The Ability to Judge People," *Psychological Bulletin*, vol. 52, no. 1, January, 1955, pp. 1–23.

Tiffin, J.: "Merit Rating: Its Validity and Techniques," in *Rating Employee and Supervisory Performance*, M. Joseph Dooher and Vivienne Marquis (eds.), American Management Association, New York, 1951.

Tosi, H. L.: "Management Development and Management by Objectives—an Interrelationship," *Management of Personnel Quarterly*, Summer, 1965, pp. 21–27.

Vroom, Victor H.: "Some Personality Determinants of the Effects of Participation," *Journal of Abnormal and Social Psychology*, vol. 59, November, 1959, pp. 322–327.

Weiner, J. B.: "The Muddle in Management Motivation," *Dun's Review*, December, 1966, pp. 28–72.

Wikstrom, Walter S.: "Management by Objectives or Appraisal by Results," *The Conference Board Record*, July, 1966, pp. 27–31.

chapter 23

Appraising Hourly Performance

DR. BERNARD INGSTER   *Senior Principal, Edward N. Hay & Associates, Philadelphia, Pennsylvania*

Just as the hourly paid worker is slowly becoming an industrial anachronism, so are some of the long-established practices for appraising his performance. Hourly wages for lower-level jobs are being replaced by weekly salaries—although not as fast as it might seem. And new ways of considering performance appraisal and employee motivation are replacing the old.

Such changes have reawakened management interest in hourly appraisal systems now in use, the problems inherent in them, and some of the newer systems now emerging.

APPRAISAL TECHNIQUES

Typically, a worker who participates in a formal appraisal program will be reviewed after a 30- to 90-day probationary period and annually thereafter. The immediate supervisor records his opinion about personal worker habits such as attendance and cooperation, together with observations about the quality and quantity of personal production. Rating techniques used to establish the latter observations are diverse.[1]

Frequently, graphic ratings, showing performance standing along a relative scale from poor to excellent, are used. For example, the volume of work produced by a rough-grinder machine operator would be described on a con-

---

[1] Richard S. Barrett, *Performance Rating*, Science Research Associates, Chicago, 1966, pp. 58–59.

tinuous scale ranging from "fast setup time, uninterrupted operation" down to "long setup time between operations and frequent, lengthy delays for tool changes." The rating supervisor would mark the appropriate location along the line.

Other less common but well-known techniques include the following:

1. *Ranking* all employees in a particular unit in a hierarchy from best to worst

2. *Forced-choice comparisons* among either a set of individuals or sets of performance criteria. This is a difficult technique to use because it requires extensive research to determine what is good and poor performance for each operation. The research leads to a checklist which the supervisor marks and which is then analyzed against predetermined standards.

3. Descriptions of *critical incidents*—both of good and bad performance—during a specified period of work

4. *Work-sample tests*, which are brief, formal examinations of a worker's skill in doing a set of tasks—actually, a test of what he *can* do, not of what he *does* day to day

5. *Narrative descriptions* of overall performance

6. *Objective measures of productivity*, such as units produced per hour

Such evaluation techniques tend to be used among larger groups of people in large organizations. In the case of a very small organization, however, judgments about the quality of worker performance are usually made very informally.

USES OF PERFORMANCE APPRAISAL

Management's desire to appraise performance comes primarily from its concern with maintaining and improving a certain level of productivity. In the case of a foreman, for example, the greatest cost over which he has direct control generally is payroll—a cost directly reflecting the work of people. It is widely held that foremen can gain better cost control and their subordinates will perform more closely to established standards if workers: (1) understand clearly the objectives of the work they are doing; (2) regard the levels of desired output to be reasonable; and (3) are given accurate feedback about how they are doing.

A recent report from the famous Chicago Hawthorne Works of Western Electric Company[2] suggested additional reasons for using *hourly employee merit rating*—a term synonymous with *performance appraisal*. Western Electric believes that employees prefer knowing what the company thinks of them, and this need is fulfilled by the appraisal process. Further, supervisors are communicating with employees, giving them such information as where the company is going and what opportunity exists for them. In these discussions, employees learn of personal growth and development needs for present and future jobs, and supervisors discover employees' work aspirations.

At Hawthorne, supervisors may also get previously undisclosed information about the employee during the appraisal interview. This permits counseling, if

---

[2] "The Nature and Interpretation of Employee Merit Ratings," from a publication of the Training Department, Personnel Service Branch, Hawthorne Works, Western Electric Company, Chicago, *Performance Appraisal, Research and Practice*, ed. Thomas L. Whisler and Shirley F. Harper, Holt, Rinehart and Winston, New York, 1962, pp. 21–27.

appropriate, and allows for the strengthening of supervisor-subordinate inter-personal relationships. (At Hawthorne, employees are ranked in terms of whole-job performance—for example, a person is twelfth in a department of 25 press operators.)

Other uses for performance rating include wage and salary administration, promotion within a unit, transfer to another unit, layoff, and discharge and demotion.

KEY FACTORS FOR A SUCCESSFUL APPRAISAL PROGRAM

In companies where hourly performance appraisal is held to be an important contributor to overall corporate success, the appraisal programs generally share the characteristics discussed below.

Successful programs are acceptable to the people involved in them, and the acceptance seems to flow from the direct involvement of the participants in developing the system.[3] This includes top management, supervisors, the em-ployees who are rated, and, performing a special role to be explained later, the personnel specialist.

Successful programs have explicit statements of the rating purposes and objectives. Further, these objectives are clearly related to the performance measurement criteria used in the program. In some cases, employees are rated for purposes of financial reward. If so, the criteria should be appropriate for such findings. If the rating is aimed at personal development (or acquisition of new skills), the rated employee must be confident that other kinds of con-clusions will not be drawn from the appraisal. In general, participants must feel that the criteria are related to desired outcomes. If, for example, a worker understands the need for full, regular staffing of a high-speed, automated as-sembly line, then he can readily accept punctuality and attendance as important factors in evaluating his personal performance. Only what is truly important should be evaluated.

Successful programs ensure that the employee has a complete and current understanding of how the company feels about his efforts. Usually, hourly workers are appraised at intervals of six months or one year, the latter being the most common. Many managers believe that a really good supervisor lets an employee know day to day how he is doing.[4] In companies with this kind of open interpersonal climate, formal appraisal discussions may be reserved for the exceptional cases—for the employees whose performance has been out-standing or for the employee whose work has been less satisfactory than that observed during a previous review.

In companies with unions representing hourly workers, a successful appraisal program requires careful conceptualization of the union role. Unions should be in a position to challenge the evaluation *decision,* but they *should not* be placed in a position of passing on the performance of their own members. It is management's responsibility to determine what the level of performance is. It is the union's role to challenge the standards against which worker performance is measured, as well as to challenge the objectivity of the supervisor making the rating. In this sense, the union is the advocate for "due process."

Beyond these roles, however, the union should be viewed as a principal com-

[3] Barrett, *op. cit.,* pp. 134–140.

[4] Paul Pigors and Charles A. Myers, *Personnel Administration—A Point of View and a Method,* 5th ed., McGraw-Hill Book Company, New York, 1965, p. 393.

munications link with hourly workers. Management must not only ensure a continuous flow of information to the union about the appraisal plan, but management must ensure significant involvement of the union in each stage of the plan's development and use.

Unions may not want, officially, to be a party to the design of the rating procedure, but by including unions on their (the union's) terms, management can gain important insight into what would or would not be acceptable to a particular group of employees. If unions are not involved in these ways, management's efforts to implement a merit review program will be so riddled with obstruction and grievance claiming that the anticipated values of performance appraisal will never be realized.

The personnel department is frequently the fountainhead for the development and maintenance of the successful program. It is the repository for the applicable, key research on work-related motivational questions. Personnel specialists usually convince top management of the practical usefulness of appraisal programs, and they organize the total effort required to launch the activity. The personnel department administers the program, including the development of appropriate forms and instructions. They pay particular attention to reducing the burden of extensive written detail. But most importantly, for the achievement of a truly successful effort, the personnel specialist ensures that *raters are trained* to a level of full competence in working with all aspects of the program.

The rater must be well informed about the people and functions he is evaluating. He must know, understand, and agree to the appropriateness of the standards against which the rating is being made. (As described earlier, standards may be a comparison of one person's performance with that of others, or the comparison of a given performance with a job standard, or, in rare circumstances, the comparison of performance with an absolute standard.) The rater must conduct the review in a businesslike manner, exercising care that the worker perceives the experience as being a *mutual* examination of *commonly held* performance goals. Such interviews are held in private to protect the employee from any embarrassment in case the discussions must deal with poor performance. The interview must be unhurried, to demonstrate that the matters being discussed are, in fact, important.

In the situations described above, it was assumed that the immediate line supervisor administered the review. In most companies that is the procedure. There has been limited experience using an "objective, outside" rater who is not involved in the ongoing operations of the unit but collects data from the unit for measuring individual performance. This rater, particularly skilled in interpersonal communication, then conducts the appraisal interview.

THREATS TO PROGRAM SUCCESS

Raters who are unable to perform competently, of course, pose a serious threat to the success of an hourly performance appraisal program. And there are other factors that are equally jeopardizing. These can be divided among *internal* factors—that is, weaknesses inherent in the design or conceptual basis of the program—and *external* factors—those arising from challenges to the basic premise of merit rating. Let us take up the latter first.

External Factors: The Union. While an appropriate role for unions in developing rating programs has been described, it should be emphasized that unions almost universally do not support or encourage the establishment of such programs. Unions are particularly opposed to the use of performance appraisal for making administrative decisions about promotions, layoffs, or wage increases.[5] Long and serious work stoppages have occurred when companies have tried to use performance records to decide who keeps working when the company has a layoff to trim costs. Unions contend that seniority—the only objective measure easily identifiable—is the most equitable criterion for a layoff. Unions also contend that more experienced (i.e., high-seniority) workers will give the company the needed high production at quality levels because they are so familiar with the job to be done. Unions say long service means better work. (Not unlike the basis for choosing powerful committee memberships and chairmen in the U.S. Congress, one might add.)

Unions usually charge management with the responsibility for detecting worker incompetence close to the time of hire, not after several years under an employee merit rating program. They urge management to focus on "reasonable and uniform standards of work load," not on the "subjective opinions" of supervisors as they appear in performance reviews. Unions may accept recognition of variability in worker performance under an individual incentive plan— if the union is integrally related to the development of work standards. But they resist the application of performance appraisal criteria for the multiple purposes suggested earlier in the chapter.

External Factors: Race Sensitivity. A new "external" factor challenging traditional merit rating techniques is the growth in racial and ethnic awareness over the past 10 years. More and more racial prejudice is presumed if a white supervisor gives a black subordinate a less than satisfactory performance rating. Even more difficult is the issue of using performance records for promotion or layoff. There is a controversial but growing practice in considering racial balance in allocating new job opportunities or laying off workers—without regard to traditional criteria of seniority, skill, and performance.

The potential for and occurrence of racial clashes on such issues are well known, but national policy still tends to support some structured and protected job opportunity for minority group members in order to accelerate their full and equal entry into jobs and industries where access had historically been restricted. This challenge to formal merit rating occurs in nonunion as well as union environments, and contemporary managements are becoming increasingly sensitive to the demand for equity, objectivity, and supervisory skill in the administration of performance appraisal programs.

Internal Factors: Developing Equitable Performance Criteria. Weaknesses in the design of appraisal programs often grow out of the difficulty of establishing measurement criteria to be used. For example, if the objective of a program is to maintain and improve a given level of productivity, the questions must be asked: Is the employee who is being rated actually *able* to improve his performance? If the worker is held to an established quantity of output, does he fully control the equipment he operates—its maintenance, the supplies, and the raw materials introduced into the process? Or does he suffer from "opportunity bias"[6] in his performance rating?

Opportunity bias is illustrated by two production punch press operators, side by side, working with similar dies but using machines which have significantly different operating characteristics. One machine may be easily affected by temperature shifts that make it difficult to hold specified tolerances. Manage-

---

[5] Joseph Tiffin and Ernest T. McCormick, "Industrial Merit Rating," *Performance Appraisal, Research and Practice,* ed. Thomas L. Whisler and Shirley F. Harper, Holt, Rinehart and Winston, New York, 1962, pp. 4–7.

[6] Barrett, *op. cit.,* p. 55.

ment might need to rotate employees so that machine differences are equalized, not an uncommon annoyance in plants with standard-hour individual incentive plans.   Or to cite another common situation: two workers operating similar paper mills might have significant differences in output depending upon the characteristics of the pulp mixture each has been given by upper levels of management.   One mill operator might need to work very much harder and with much greater skill than the other just to stay close to production standards.   It is because of the great difficulty of choosing sound and appropriate criteria for individual hourly worker performance rating that many plans do not adequately tie together the measure used and the goal desired.

Internal Factors: Consistency in Ratings.   Another major challenge to merit rating program administration is maintaining consistency and controlling variability of the ratings.   The rating of "excellent" performance by the day shift supervisor of a particular department may not be at all comparable with the "excellent" rating awarded by the night shift supervisor in the same department.

Or consistency can be overdone.   For example, a supervisor concerned about his own appraisal may be reluctant to show low ratings for his workers.   He is, after all, supposed to train and develop their competence, and their failure too clearly reflects on him.   And, too, there are supervisors who are so concerned about "keeping peace" with their subordinates that they systematically avoid discussions of deficiencies.

The importance of rater training has already been stressed, but it should be pointed out here that even effectively trained raters may not be able to measure various facets of performance consistently and reliably.   Over a period of time, both the rater and the person being rated—and the job being done—undergo changes which might undercut the reliability of a measurement.[7]   This points up again the importance of the *relevance* of measurement criteria.   Rigid standards that do not appear to be influenced by changes in the work environment may seem to be reliable.   However, such standards may soon fail to measure what is really important in performance.

Internal Factors: Periodic Revision.   The last problem with appraisal plans to be discussed here is the need for periodically revising the program just to overcome the boredom of supervisors and employees using the same rating scales and talking about the same things year after year.   Since many hourly workers stay in the same jobs for many years, there is a tendency for job performance to stabilize at an individual-worker level.   No significant gain in performance will be observed after about two or three years of using a particular score or technique of rating.[8]   The plateau can be raised, however, by reexamining and, most likely, revising the program—particularly by including the workers being rated in the planning stage.

A NEW DEPARTURE: RESULTS-ORIENTED APPRAISAL

If it is becoming more common to treat hourly workers like salaried workers (a practice long established at IBM and growing in acceptance at companies like Texas Instruments and Motorola),[9] then it is reasonable to search for techniques for appraising hourly performance that have been most successful with salaried groups.   The most powerful new management tool for improving white-

[7] *Ibid.,* pp. 18–20.

[8] *Ibid.,* p. 124.

[9] James MacGregor, "Some Prosper by Yanking Time Clock, Easing Employee Rules," *Wall Street Journal,* May 22, 1970, p. 1.

collar performance—primarily at the professional, supervisory, and managerial levels—is the results-oriented appraisal, which focuses clearly on the end results to be achieved through a job. The strong motivational pull results from the fact that the worker is looking forward toward achievement rather than merely backward at accomplishment.

The vast majority of hourly merit rating programs are "after the fact" appraisals. Very few programs force hourly employees to look ahead to yet uncharted achievement. If the specific objectives of work are clearly stated, if there is worker agreement on the definition of what is "satisfactory" accomplishment, and if there is agreement on how accomplishment is to be measured, then performance appraisal becomes self-appraisal, admittedly the best motivational insight for personal growth and development. None of the appraisal techniques described earlier in this chapter have this quality in their designs.

Most of the traditional hourly merit rating programs stressed individual effort in relation to a highly fragmented aspect of work—they were concerned with standardized, piece-part production efforts which give workers little control over the end results of their work. Under these circumstances, the usual suggestion plans to improve production methods were largely ineffective.

Not until management radically reorganizes lower-level jobs and job functions is it possible to even consider the use of the most modern personal development appraisal systems. Not surprisingly, where these reorganizations have been carried out, productivity improvements far outdistanced any other form of hourly work incentive currently in use. Further, one element for performance success in these reorganizations is also found in the successful traditional merit rating programs—the concept of *participation* in the planning and implementation of the activity.

One very popular "new" form of work organization is known as the *Scanlon Plan*, which in fact is not a single plan but a philosophy of employee participation with various forms of attendant work practices. In such plans, management and employees jointly consider goals, problems, and activity programs. There is usually a committee system including departmental production committees and overall screening or steering committees. All effort is geared toward: first, determining the current capabilities of a unit; second, agreeing on new levels of output needed for growth; third, agreeing on methods to achieve the higher productivity; and fourth, agreeing on an equitable distribution of the financial gains realized by the effort. The power of this strategy has been convincingly described in an article by Fred G. Lesieur, former president of the local union that cooperated in the first complete Scanlon Plan installation.[10] In each company reported on:

1. Workers took a broader view of the company's problems.
2. Management achieved higher quality of production.
3. Indirect service groups—tool rooms, maintenance, etc.—strongly supported direct labor operations.
4. Automation was achieved without conflict over possible loss of jobs.
5. Company profits exceeded the growth pattern of competitive forces. Most companies would hope that their merit rating program could deliver similar results.

It should be emphasized again that a results-oriented management philosophy can be applied to these lower-level jobs only because *individual job functions* have been reorganized into larger, more complex jobs through the participation

---

[10] Fred G. Lesieur and Elbridge S. Puckett, "The Scanlon Plan Has Proved Itself," *Harvard Business Review*, September–October, 1969, pp. 109–118.

process.   These larger, combined functions are similar to the complex job content of professional or supervisory jobs.

On the transistor production lines of Texas Instruments, for example, the production flow has been divided into segments which encompass closely related, individual job functions in the line.   These segments have become cooperative units of work in which individual production operators now concern themselves equally with the work performed at every step of the process in their unit.   They no longer think only about doing their individual little part of the job correctly—fitting a small part into a larger whole.   Each worker in the unit is part of a *team* which is responsible for the productivity and quality of the whole unit.   Within these larger units of work, results-oriented philosophies can be applied because the job content is great enough to allow decision-making power and individual responsibility to be exercised meaningfully. Instead of describing accountability for end results in *individual* terms—as would be the case for management jobs—every member of the unit is accountable in a shared way for acceptable production.

This effort has not only resulted in large boosts in productivity but has also reduced irritating personnel problems.   In many ways, the Texas Instruments program is an important development and extension of the Scanlon philosophy. It comes to grips very basically with the boredom and low motivation of workers doing highly repetitive tasks on machines which control *them*.[11]

In these highly routine production line situations, management is well advised to use traditional performance appraisal techniques on the machines rather than on the man—the potential for productivity gains will be higher.   But if the jobs of hourly workers can be expanded, if the opportunity to assume responsibility and develop accountability can be designed into their jobs—then performance appraisal can lead to the impressive improvements in hourly productivity that are actively sought in the American economy.

[11] Two interesting case studies in non-American companies are described in John R. P. French, "Effects of Participation and Goal Setting in Performance," *Performance Appraisals, Effect on Employees and Their Performance*, ed. Alvin F. Zander, The Foundation for Research on Human Behavior, Ann Arbor, Michigan, 1963, pp. 19–41.

chapter 24

Appraising Performance
of Clerical Personnel

R. C. ALBRIGHT   *The American Bankers Association, Washington, D.C.*

A good performance appraisal system for clerical workers is effective to the extent that it shows each employee what results are expected of him—and follows through by telling him how well he has achieved those results. It helps each employee to improve his performance on the job and assists him in his long-range development. Secondary benefits to the organization include the identification of training needs and potential talent.

CRITERIA FOR SUCCESS

A clerical performance appraisal program can be successful only if it is implemented by those closest to the performance situation, the line supervisors. Since they will be responsible for carrying out the program, they should be involved in its initial development.

Line supervisors should participate in designing the appraisal form to be used in the program and in defining the terms to be used in evaluating performance. What do *average, excellent,* and *below standard* mean? Since words of this type do not necessarily have the same meaning for everyone, clarity of use and a common understanding of terms, especially those that are unique to the industry, assume significance. *Honesty,* for example, may have one meaning in evaluating a clerk-typist and quite another meaning when applied to a bank teller.

A supervisor must understand the value of the program to himself and to his subordinates if he is to be committed to it. Proper training will help develop this commitment as well as teach him how to do his part successfully.

A supervisor who is inadequately trained is likely to fall into appraisal traps, thus seriously undermining the entire program.

A common problem often related to inadequate training is the tendency of a supervisor to be too generous in appraising, creating what is often called the *halo effect*. For example, the supervisor may give an employee he likes a higher rating than is truly justified, or the supervisor may be blind to certain weaknesses in his employees because he also has these weaknesses. There is the danger that the poorly trained supervisor will place too much emphasis on an employee's past record and not enough on his current achievements, or that he will tend to give higher appraisals to the employee who does not complain or have too many bright ideas than to the one who pesters but also gets the job done.

A second problem common to appraisal programs carried out by poorly trained supervisors is the *horns effect*. The supervisor may give appraisal ratings that are unjustifiably low because he sets his standards too high. The employee who does not do the job as well as the supervisor, who in turn remembers how well he himself did it, may be rated lower than those who do work that is unfamiliar to the same supervisor; and the maverick or noncomformist may get a lower rating simply because he is different. There is also a tendency on the part of the uninformed supervisor to give lower appraisal ratings to employees on a weak team and higher appraisal ratings to those on a winning team, regardless of individual performance. Allied to this is the danger of overemphasizing *one incident* in evaluating an individual's performance: a recent mistake by an employee may cause the supervisor to forget months of good work.

What has to be remembered here is that one incident is only a small part of what the employee has been doing. Unfortunately, the tendency is to overlook how he performs the rest of his daily routine. Thus, one of the major purposes in formalizing an appraisal system is to compel the supervisor to consider the *entire job performance* of the employee rather than just one aspect of it.

THE APPRAISAL PROCESS

Alternative Systems. Stripped to essentials, the various approaches to the clerical staff can be characterized in terms of the appraisal forms used. Some of these approaches are discussed below.

1. *The graphic scale*, as shown in Figure 1, is widely used because it is simply constructed and easy for the line supervisor to handle. The graphic scale has serious limitations, however, in the assumption that all factors have equal weight and that this is true in all jobs. Obviously, the importance of the different factors will vary with the results expected from the person on the job. Even though the section for subjective comments allows the supervisor to consider unique requirements of each job, the fact that these factors are given equal weight prevents graphic ratings, by themselves, from being useful in consistently obtaining accurate appraisals for large numbers of employees.

2. *The nonpoint scale*, shown in Figure 2, is a variation of the graphic scale form. It defines more fully the factors used in the rating form, and it allows for written comments by the rater.

3. *The checklist* shown in Figure 3 is easy to complete and also provides a place for written comments.

4. *The narrative form* shown in Figure 4 allows the supervisor to gear his appraisal to the specific job under consideration, but it does not require the use of the same criteria by all supervisors, and therefore appraisal methods

Figure 1.   Graphic rating scale.

Clerical Performance Rating

Entry date _____ Date of birth _____ Name _____

Division/Dept. _____ Present position _____

Instructions: Read carefully each of the factor descriptions and the explanations of each of the ratings. Judge the employee on the basis of the work now being done. Consider each factor separately; do not let your rating of one factor influence your rating of another factor. Rate each factor by circling the appropriate number.

In certain instances you might want to explain your rating. While you are not required to write an explanation, you are expected to be able to discuss any rating if called upon to do so.

* * * * * * * * * * * * * * * * *

Explanation of ratings:

   1 — Superior: Outstanding, on a par with the very best.
   2 — Above average: Very satisfactory, well above minimum standards.
   3 — Average: Satisfactory.
   4 — Below average: Marginally satisfactory at best. Needs improvement in this factor.
   5 — Low: A serious handicap to job performance.

ABILITY TO LEARN: Consider how quickly employee learns (ability to retain instruction and information).
   1   2   3   4   5   Comments: _____
_____

INITIATIVE: Consider ingenuity (self-reliance and resourcefulness; ability to know what needs to be done).
   1   2   3   4   5   Comments: _____
_____

JOB ATTITUDE: Consider the interest and enthusiasm shown (attitude toward the bank and supervision).
   1   2   3   4   5   Comments: _____
_____

KNOWLEDGE OF JOB: Consider the knowledge of job and related work.
   1   2   3   4   5   Comments: _____
_____

INDUSTRY: Consider responsibility to duties (ability to apply time and energy).
   1   2   3   4   5   Comments: _____
_____

QUALITY OF WORK: Consider accuracy of work regardless of volume (ability to perform work efficiently).
   1   2   3   4   5   Comments: _____
_____

QUANTITY OF PRODUCTION: Consider the volume of work produced (ability to produce results).
   1   2   3   4   5   Comments: _____
_____

COOPERATION: Consider ability and willingness to work in harmony with and for others.
   1   2   3   4   5   Comments: _____
_____

PERSONALITY: Consider ability to get along with fellow workers (personal conduct, courtesy, tact, friendliness).
   1   2   3   4   5   Comments: _____
_____

APPEARANCE: Consider neatness, personal dress, and personal habits.
   1   2   3   4   5   Comments: _____
_____

Figure 1.   Graphic rating scale—continued

Summary and Conclusion

A.   Considering overall job performance, this employee is evaluated:

1	2	3	4	5
Outstanding	Above average	Average	Below average	Unsatisfactory

Write a brief paragraph giving an overall summary of the employee's job performance. _____

_____

_____

_____

_____

_____

B.   Does this employee have further potential beyond the next step? _____ If yes, for what position? _____

C.   Is there any other work regardless of department or division for which you feel this employee would be qualified? _____

_____

D.   What are the employee's most serious limitations? _____

_____

E.   What can or should we do to help the employee improve where weaknesses are indicated and to prepare him for advancement? _____

_____

F.   What can or should the employee do to improve or prepare for advancement? _____

_____

G.   Has the employee taken any academic subjects this past year? _____ Please specify _____

Accounting (name of course) _____ Stenography (name of course) _____

Finance (name of course) _____ Other (name of course) _____

Law (name of course) _____

H.   Are there any limiting factors such as health, habits, or character that influence this rating? _____ If yes, explain: _____

_____

I.   Number of days absent since January 1st _____ Tardy _____

Rated by _____   _____   Approved by _____   _____

Initials   Date   Initials   Date

· * * * * * * * * * * * * * * * * ·

J.   Summary of review with employee, including employee's reaction. Use quotations to summarize his reactions when possible.

_____

_____

_____

_____

_____

Discussed with employee by _____   _____

Initials   Date

Figure 2. Nonpoint rating scale.

Performance and Merit Evaluation

Date _____19 _____

Name_____Office _____ Dept. _____

Position (designate concisely, such as teller, stenographer, etc.) _____

Is this employee's job properly described in the job description? Yes ☐   No ☐

Suggestions for Completion of Report

Read carefully the phrases describing qualities. Then on the basis of the person's actual performance on the job, place a check (✓) mark above the degree which most nearly describes the person's performance on that factor.

    A check mark to the right indicates he does not quite measure up to specification.

    A check mark in the center indicates specification adequately covers employee.

    A check mark to the left indicates superiority to specification.

Base your judgments upon the entire period covered and not upon isolated incidents alone. Be objective.

Rate on each factor separately. Do not allow judgment on one factor to influence judgment on other factors.

Amount of work					
Consider number of assignments completed and volume of output in relation to nature and conditions of the work performed. Disregard quality of work. Explanation	Extraordinary volume of work completed.	Consistently turns out a good volume of work.	Amount of work completed is satisfactory but not unusual.	Output barely acceptable.	Amount of work entirely inadequate.

Quality of work					
Consider thoroughness, accuracy, and orderliness of completed job. Disregard amount of work handled. Explanation	Unusually high-grade work is consistently performed. Quality is exceptional in all respects.	Quality is of high grade, but not exceptional.	Work is reasonably complete, accurate, and presentable.	Quality occasionally is unsatisfactory.	Work usually lacking in thoroughness, accuracy, or neatness.

Dependability					
Consider the manner in which worker applies himself to his work, if he does jobs on time, and the amount of supervision required to get the desired results. Explanation	Justifies utmost confidence. A minimum of supervision required.	Applies himself well but occasionally needs direction and supervision.	Fairly reliable and conscientious. Normal supervision required.	Cannot always be relied upon to get desired results without considerable supervision.	Entirely undependable. Needs constant supervision.

Judgment					
Consider the wisdom of his decisions in the absence of detailed instructions and judgment in unusual situations, where discretion is allowed. Explanation	Thinks quickly and logically in all situations. Judgment can always be depended upon.	Judgment usually of a high degree.	Judgment adequate in normal situations only.	Makes frequent errors in judgment. Works best with detailed instructions.	Judgment entirely undependable

Ability to learn					
Consider his mental ability in mastering new routine, grasping explanations, and his ability to retain this knowledge. Explanation	Brilliant and keen mind coupled with eagerness to learn.	Quick to grasp new ideas and methods.	Learns satisfactorily.	Learns by excessive repetition. Needs guidance.	Slow in learning even simple procedures. Needs constant guidance.

Attitude					
Consider attitude toward job and bank. Explanation	Enthusiastic about type of work; booster of bank.	Happy on job; favorable attitude toward bank.	Seems to be satisfied with job and bank.	Shows little interest in either job or bank.	Disgruntled on job; critical of bank.

Cooperation					
Consider extent to which employee works harmoniously and effectively with fellow employees, supervisors, and others with whom he comes in contact. Explanation	Exceptionally successful in working with and assisting others.	Quick to volunteer to work with and assist others.	Generally works well with and assists others.	Cooperation must be solicited. Seldom volunteers to work with or assist others.	Fails to cooperate. Unwilling to work with or assist others.

Capacity and ambition for future growth					
Review all the factors previously considered and judge employee's capacity and ambition for future advancement both in his present department or branch and in the organization. Explanation	Outstanding candidate for future development. Given opportunity, could be expected to go far in the organization.	Capable of developing beyond present level of work.	Has probably reached most suitable job or level of work.	Barely capable of handling present level of work.	Entirely out of place in present job. Should be moved to simpler work or dismissed.

Figure 2. Nonpoint rating scale—continued

Personal statement — to be filled out by employee in ink in own handwriting.

Full
name _____

Address _____ Phone _____

Marital   Name of
status _____ spouse _____

Children:
Name _____ Age _____

Name _____ Age _____

Name _____ Age _____

Name _____ Age _____

Person to be notified in case of emergency:

Name _____

Address _____ Phone _____

List your outside activities such as:

Educational courses
Home study _____
Civic activities
_____
_____

Business
development
record
Mos. ending
_____

Green slips
Cust. _____

Prosp. _____

Interviews
_____

Sales
No. _____

Amt. $ _____

Attendance
record

Abs. _____

Tardy _____

Personal characteristics	Superior	Above average	Average	Below average	Unsatisfactory
Grooming					
Manner of speech					
Tactfulness					
Self-confidence					

Executive characteristics	Superior	Above average	Average	Below average	Unsatisfactory
Initiative					
Ability to organize work					
Ability to develop others					
Ability to delegate work					

Comments

What outstanding qualities will aid his advancement? _____
_____

What qualities or physical handicaps, if not corrected, will hinder his future development? _____
_____

Give any other pertinent facts which should be known concerning this employee _____
_____
_____

This performance rating was discussed with employee _____ By _____

Rated by _____ Reviewed by _____
            (Department head)   (Officer in charge)

This space for use of personnel division only _____
_____

Figure 3.   Checklist.

Final Personnel Appraisal

Name _____ Date _____

Division _____ Job title _____

1. Transferred _____ To _____
   Date   Division

2. Left employ of bank _____ Reason _____
                                          Date

3. Do you recommend reemployment? _____ If not, why? _____

A. What was his performance?   Unsatisfactory _____ Satisfactory _____ Superior _____
   Comment:

B. To what extent did he give indication of future development?
   None _____ Little _____ Moderate _____ Substantial _____
   Comment:

C. Had you any indication that he might become unsuited for bank work? _____
   Comment:

The following checklist of traits is provided to help you confirm your conclusions above. It is assumed that the person was *satisfactory* in these traits unless you indicate by check mark any of them in which he *was unsatisfactory* or *superior*.

Unsatisfactory	Trait	Superior
_____	First impression	_____
_____	Ability to learn	_____
_____	Speed	_____
_____	Accuracy	_____
_____	Dependability	_____
_____	Ability to get on with others	_____
_____	Initiative	_____
_____	Cooperation	_____

_____
Supervisor

_____
Division manager

_____
Operating officer

Figure 4.   Narrative rating form.

<u>Employee appraisal</u>

Name _____ Position _____ Anniversary _____

Date of employment _____ Years in present position _____ Transfer _____

Office _____ Previous position _____ Promotion _____

Reports to _____   Merit _____

                                                                      Other _____

Attendance   ☐ Satisfactory   ☐ Marginal   ☐ Unsatisfactory

Performance, results, and methods — Give production figures (be specific).

1. What has this person accomplished in measurable results since last appraisal?
   (Consider quantity and quality of work.)

2. How does this person go about getting his/her work done?

3. How well does this person work with people?

4. List outstanding personal qualifications or characteristics that help or hinder
   this person.

5. Recommended action to improve performance in present position.

The performance and personal qualification sections of this appraisal have been
discussed with the employee by:

Name _____ Position _____ Date _____

Approved _____

Figure 4.   Narrative rating form—continued

6. Current status (check one):

☐ Immediately
   promotable

This person is doing outstanding work in present position and can fill immediately a specific position in a higher salary range with only casual training.

☐ Promotable

Same as above except systematic and extended training would be necessary, or promotion would not be in best interest of bank.

☐ Satisfactory

This person is supplying what can be reasonably expected, but could not be considered beyond the present assignment in the near foreseeable future.

☐ Questionable

This person's performance in present position is not completely satisfactory. He may be able to improve.

☐ Unsatisfactory

Performance not acceptable in present position, and has not been able to improve under guidance. Management action (transfer, demotion, separation) is indicated.

7. Do you recommend a salary increase? _____ If so, in what amount $ _____

Proposed effective date _____

Supervisor _____

Officer in
charge _____

Date _____

CONTROL
_____
Personnel department

_____
Committee

_____
Payroll section

_____
Department notification

_____
Employee notification

_____
Personnel file

Note: Return this report promptly to the personnel department.

and factors may vary too widely. The form in Figure 4 also includes a simple variation of the forced-choice method.

5. *The forced-choice form* shown in Figure 5 allows a narrative discussion of job accountabilities and objectives as well as a forced-choice appraisal of performance and work traits. One unique feature of this particular form is that it makes provision for updating accountabilities by extracting them from the person's job description and including them in the appraisal form each time it is sent to the line supervisor.

Difficulties can be encountered in the use of these forms. The narrative format, for example, can leave too much freedom for the rater who writes well and too little opportunity for expression by the nonverbal supervisor. A recent cartoon showed an employee talking to his supervisor: "The word 'lousy' is a bit general. Specifically, sir, what do you think of my work?" Examples that are even worse are the following excerpts from Army Officer Fitness Reports:

> "Deep down, he's shallow."
> "Exceptionally well qualified, since he has committed no major blunders."
> "Never makes the same mistake twice but seems to have made them all once."

Many specialists in the field feel that forced choice (Figure 5) is the most effective method of obtaining objective appraisals from the line supervisor. The forced-choice form is difficult and time-consuming to construct, and supervisors tend to resist its use because they do not like to be forced to make a choice in their appraisal of any employee. Thus, many forced-choice forms provide space for written comments where the supervisor can qualify his forced choices on the form. Despite these difficulties, many feel that of all the techniques available, a well-constructed forced-choice performance appraisal form can greatly assist the clerical supervisor to make reasonably objective appraisals of his subordinates.

Performance Standards. Generally speaking, there are three standards against which individual performance in clerical positions can be appraised:

1. In relation to other people in the same category of jobs
2. In terms of the work standards set for the job
3. In terms of absolute job-skill standards, such as the number of words typed per minute, number of units assembled per hour, or number of errors committed in a specific period of time

These work standards can be developed according to tangible factors—for example, What kind of record the individual has in productivity? and so forth. Or they can be developed according to judgmental factors—for example, How well does the individual plan, organize, direct, and control?

Clerical personnel are most often appraised in terms of job standards based on tangible factors, since judgmental factors are not apt to be as important a part of their jobs. Appraisals using job standards are also more versatile than comparisons with others on the same job or absolute standards, as shown in Table 1.

Changes in modern technology require periodic review of established job standards. Incorrect standards can seriously damage the effectiveness of any appraisal program.

Appraisal Participants. Experience and tradition have long suggested the line supervisor as the appraiser. Some feel, however, that at times it is appropriate for others to become involved, including:

1. *Supervisor's supervisor.* By involving two persons, it is hoped that a more objective analysis of the subordinate's work can be obtained. Unfortunately, persons in higher positions do not always know the actual work performance of an employee who is several steps down the ladder in the hierarchy.

TABLE 1 Comparison of Standards Used on Performance Appraisal

Standards can be used in:	Job standards	Other people in similar work	Absolute standards
Salary and wage administration.......	Yes	No	No
Promotion within unit..............	Yes	Yes	No
Transfer to another unit............	Yes	Yes	Yes
Layoff..........................	Yes	Yes	No
Discharge for cause................	Yes	No	No
Administrative control..............	Yes	Yes	Yes
Performance counseling.............	Yes	Yes	Yes
Research.........................	Yes	Yes	Yes

Comment

Job standards: Generally the best— require clear understanding of what can be expected.

Other people in similar work: Easy to use, especially if there are enough people on one job to rank them.

Absolute standards: Limited because absolute standards are available for only a few jobs.

2. *Peers.* At the clerical level, appraisal by an employee's peers might be very difficult to implement. However, those advocating this type of appraisal claim it adds a new dimension that can facilitate objectivity if the peer group has sufficient interaction and stability over a long period of time.

3. *Subordinates.* Having his subordinates appraise an individual is again an attempt to obtain objective appraisal. The major drawback is that subordinates usually see only a part of what their supervisors do.

4. *Self.* More recent efforts to improve appraisals have included the request that a subordinate rate himself. At best, this provides another perspective on the individual's work.

In spite of the arguments put forth in favor of involving the individual himself, his peers, his subordinates, and others, it is still generally agreed that the major responsibility for the appraisal should rest with the person most familiar with the individual's work—his immediate line supervisor. Others who may be less directly involved—either by providing a general framework for the appraisal or by using information generated in the appraisal—are discussed below.

The Manpower Planning and Development Specialist. Appraisal systems can, among other things, provide information for manpower planning and development which is directly useful in determining future training and development needs of both the individual and the entire organization. The manpower planning aspect of performance appraisal can be especially important at the clerical level, since this area usually involves a large number of employees. At current-day training costs, such planning is critical to the ultimate profitability of an organization. A well-trained staff that is motivated to develop itself further is an invaluable competitive asset.

The Wage and Salary Administrator. Today's salaries and benefits represent as much as half of the annual operating cost of an organization. Effectively rewarding an employee requires the ability to identify the degree of performance with appropriate salary increases. This is particularly true at the

Figure 5.   Forced-choice form.

Performance Review

Employee _____   Date _____

Position _____   Department _____

_____   _____

_____   _____

Purpose   When completed, this performance appraisal form will serve as a guide for the review of a staff member's job performance and salary.

- -

The immediate supervisor should review the current job description and make the primary rating with the senior officer's approval. The performance and salary review forms should be filled out in ink and forwarded in a sealed envelope to the Personnel Department by the return date indicated on the salary review form. These forms will be processed for appropriate review and approval and returned to the department head.

A full and frank discussion with an employee concerning his salary and performance is strongly urged since it is felt that, if conducted sincerely and wisely, it will contribute toward a better relationship between the staff member and his immediate supervisor, senior officer, and the bank. The form should then be returned to the Personnel Department for filing in the staff employee's personnel folder.

1. Utilizing the key outlined on the following page, rate the level of performance of each accountability and work trait on the basis of work done during the past year. Try not to let your appraisal of one accountability or work trait influence your rating of another accountability or work trait. Do not try to consult or recall prior ratings. You will be more objective if you forget them. One individual rarely merits identical ratings in every accountability or work trait. Be selective! Make independent decisions on each rating.

2. Consider Current Overall Performance without undue emphasis on recent or infrequent occurrences.

3. Under Other Comments you may explain, if you wish, individual ratings and / or make recommendations for a promotion, transfer, or further training needs.

4. Any recent major Change in Accountabilities should be recorded on the last page for future review.

5. The rater(s) should sign this form at the bottom of the last page.

Figure 5.   **Forced-choice form—continued**

KEY:

1 — Outstanding, exceptionally high level (top 5%)
2 — Superior, exceeds the expected level (next 10%)
3 — At expected level (middle 70%)

4 — Below expected level (next 10%)
5 — At marginal level (bottom 5%)

1.   ACCOUNTABILITIES (as listed in approved job description)   Performance

Figure 5.   Forced-choice form—continued

JOB OBJECTIVES   Performance

II. WORK TRAITS (Please continue to use key to describe
                           performance.)   Performance

Attitude —	Willingness to adjust to changes: Degree of interest and enthusiasm — . . . .
Communication —	Ability to convey ideas and plans Written — . . . . Oral — . . . .
Cooperation —	Ability to work with and through others including: Supervisor — . . . . Peers — . . . . Subordinates — . . . . Government officials, educators, bankers, etc. — . . . .
Delegation —	Ability to effectively assign work to others — . . . .
Development —	Ability to develope attitudes, knowledge, and skills in: Self — . . . . Subordinates —. . . . .
Organization —	Ability to effectively organize time and effort on Work assignments — . . . .
Forward planning —	Ability to plan ahead in order to meet changing needs of banking industry —
Judgment —	Ability to arrive consistently at a sound decision(s) — . . . .
Volume of work —	Ability to produce expected results in a given time — . . . .

III. CURRENT OVERALL PERFORMANCE

Having rated each accountability and work trait, please indicate what the employee's overall
performance is in his present position.

1. ☐ Performs at an outstanding level (5% could be here)
2. ☐ Performs at a superior level (10% could be here)
3. ☐ Performs at expected level (70% should be here)
4. ☐ Performs at below expected level (10% could be here)
5. ☐ Performs at marginal level (5% could be here)

Figure 5.   Forced-choice form—continued

IV. OTHER COMMENTS (i.e., long-range potential, readiness for immediate or future advancement, career
development recommendations)

4 ☐ Potential should not be evaluated at this time
3 ☐ Not promotable to a higher level of responsibility
2 ☐ Promotable but needs further development
1 ☐ Ready for immediate advancement

REMARKS:

V. CHANGE IN ACCOUNTABILITIES (Please list any recent major changes in the employee's accountabilities
that you feel should be reviewed in the future by the Evaluation Committee.)

IMMEDIATE SUPERVISOR   SENIOR OFFICER

Date _____

clerical level, in which salary increases are often looked upon as the only real measure of performance.

The wage and salary administrator provides the framework that can guide the line supervisor in making salary recommendations. This framework will inform the supervisor how his subordinates' salaries stand in relation to salaries for comparable jobs in other companies. The supervisor is also informed of the grades of the subordinates' jobs and the ranges of their salaries within the organization. In addition, the wage and salary administrator can alert the line supervisor and the organization to possible violations of the law, such as the Equal Pay Act.

The Personnel Specialist. Today's personnel specialist expends a great deal of time and energy in gathering information and developing data on personnel activities to guide management in making personnel-related decisions. Appraisals are necessary, as well as beneficial, to this function. They can provide an inventory of persons qualified for greater responsibilities and promotions, and of persons whose performance has been below par or unacceptable, which may lead to termination and the need for a replacement. Thus, appraisal information can help in career planning and in the proper placement of talents and abilities as they are demonstrated by individual employees.

Appraisal Frequency. How often clerical performance should be appraised depends on the objectives and needs as well as the administrative capabilities of your own organization. The *annual* performance appraisal is probably the easiest to administer, but many feel this occurs too infrequently and is not apt to motivate employees sufficiently.

Semiannual appraisals are more difficult to administer since they involve additional paper work; moreover, supervisors must be motivated to rate their employees more frequently. Many people feel, nonetheless, that semiannual appraisals are desirable, arguing that more frequent dialogue between supervisor and subordinate is vital to the proper motivation of the subordinate.

Quarterly appraisals can truly be an administrative burden. On the other hand, if the forms used are simple and supervisors have been properly trained and motivated, the appraisals can serve as an excellent communication vehicle regardless of the size of your organization.

Other factors that should be considered in determining the interval between appraisals include:

1. *Length of service.* Many firms feel it is logical to appraise more frequently in the first few years and then to taper off in the latter part of an employee's career. To some, however, such a policy is entirely unacceptable on psychological and administrative grounds. They feel it would be extremely difficult to motivate an employee to perform his job well if he is appraised only once every few years.

2. *Nature of position.* How easily a clerical position can be evaluated depends on the complexity of the job and the skills required. Jobs that can be appraised with ease should be appraised more frequently.

3. *Size of organization.* Size considerations can certainly help determine the frequency of appraisals. Obviously, paper work can become a major problem. (Wernher Von Braun, the famous scientist, pointed out that the United States faced only two major problems in conquering space—gravity and paper work.)

4. *Number of employees by category.* It is easier to carry out a performance appraisal when the same job is held by a number of people. Therefore, the more people there are in the same job, the more frequently their performance can be appraised.

THE APPRAISAL INTERVIEW

The crux of any appraisal system is the discussion held between the supervisor and his subordinate regarding the subordinate's performance. It is in this interview that the supervisor, as the person best qualified to appraise the employee, can provide direct feedback about the appraisal.

A real danger here is that a well-designed appraisal form can totally lose its effectiveness if the supervisor does not know how to use it properly and then discuss it meaningfully with the subordinate. Evidence today suggests, unfortunately, that too many supervisors conduct such interviews poorly—so poorly, in fact, that many managers feel that the appraisal interview should be either discontinued entirely or carried on only by professional counselors. Without the appraisal interview, however, there really would not be any appraisal program. Furthermore, subordinates have clearly indicated a desire to discuss their performance with their own supervisor in order to:

1. Find out where they stand.
2. Get recognition for good performance.
3. Learn how they can improve on the present job.
4. Find out how they fit into the "big picture."
5. Learn where they are not performing satisfactorily.

An appraisal program is in effect a medium of communication between supervisor and subordinate, and the appraisal interview is potentially the most effective way of implementing such a program. This is particularly true of personnel at the clerical level. Often the appraisal interview is their only opportunity to learn how they are doing. If this is true, then why do supervisors resist conducting appraisal interviews? Here are some thoughts expressed by supervisors themselves:

1. "No time—the work comes first."
2. "Dislike criticizing people."
3. "It's unnecessary and unimportant."
4. "Not interested in doing it."
5. "Fear of having an argument with the employee."
6. "Afraid of inability to conduct the interview."
7. "Don't like the feeling of embarrassment."
8. "Dislike being judge and jury."
9. "No one ever helped me—it's a cold, cruel world."
10. "Afraid that any compliments offered will result in a request for a salary increase."

These comments would seem to indicate that this resistance can be attributed to a lack of understanding of the purpose of an appraisal interview and a lack of training in effectively conducting one.

Perhaps the first thing to do is to identify what an appraisal interview should *not* be. This may help in understanding why the interviews often fail. They are *not*:

1. An attempt to turn the supervisor into an amateur psychoanalyst or social worker
2. An attempt to manipulate an employee
3. An effort to remake or remold adult personalities
4. A substitute for day-to-day coaching and counseling
5. An effort to discipline or threaten
6. A cure-all for all supervisory problems

After all, a person who is 30 years old has spent more than 250,000 hours of his lifetime developing his behavior patterns. A 10-minute, a 30-minute, or a one-hour appraisal interview is not going to change his work habits substantially.

As we indicated before, standards of job performance are developed to help measure the results expected on the job. The appraisal of an employee's performance is the next step in measuring how well he is doing that job. Once the program's objectives have been determined, they must be communicated to the supervisor so that he will be able to conduct an appraisal interview which meets those objectives. He then needs to be trained in the techniques of conducting an appraisal interview, including the preparation necessary for the interview, the environment in which the interview should be conducted, and the manner of conveying his appraisal to his subordinate.

In preparing for the appraisal interview, the supervisor should review the appraisal form's objectives and familiarize himself thoroughly with the employee's background. In addition, the supervisor should consider the subjects that will be covered in the interview—specific incidents that will be discussed and broad questions that will be asked to encourage conversation.

The interview should be conducted in privacy with no interruptions. The supervisor should strive to create an informal atmosphere and convey his willingness to listen to the subordinate. In any event, the supervisor should avoid being dogmatic or, if the subordinate disagrees with what he is saying, becoming defensive.

Before turning to the actual performance appraisal itself, the supervisor should explain the purpose of the appraisal to the subordinate. Then he can evaluate the employee's performance on the job, stressing his strong points and pointing out possibilities for improvements in weak areas. In no case should the appraisal become an evaluation of the employee's personality. At the end of the interview, the supervisor should summarize his and the employee's comments and indicate to the employee that the supervisor is always available for future discussions.

The character of the feedback during an appraisal interview is critical to the employee's acceptance of his supervisor's appraisal. Not only should the supervisor discuss the employee's entire performance in an appraisal interview, but he should also *show* the employee the completed appraisal form. Often a supervisor conducts a fairly good interview and the employee thinks he is performing the job satisfactorily; then the supervisor writes something entirely different on the appraisal form. This is why many employees place no faith in an appraisal program.

Honesty and frankness on the supervisor's part are vital to the success of an appraisal interview. A supervisor who is well trained and motivated by management will recognize the importance of candor. Although authority for developing an appraisal program lies with management, the responsibility for carrying it out lies with supervisors, and they cannot discharge the responsibility successfully if they are unwilling or unable to discuss job performance honestly with their subordinates.

CONCLUSIONS

There are no pat formulas for performance appraisal interviews or forms. They have only one consistent pattern—change! Yesterday's methods are not being used today, and more research and validation are critically needed. There is still far too much pseudoprofessional expertise being practiced by ill-equipped supervisors. However, major steps have been taken toward implementing an effective appraisal program if we see to it that supervisors and subordinates know what the appraisal program's goals are, see that an appraisal program which achieves its goals will also be of benefit to them, and work in an environment that encourages open dialogue between the supervisor and his subordinate.

chapter 25

Appraising Executive Performance

H. L. JUDD *Director of Personnel, United States Gypsum Company, Chicago, Illinois*

Appraising employee performance is probably as old as business itself. Any businessman will tell you that some employees perform better than others. If some employees perform better than others and the difference is noticeable, then why a formal performance appraisal program?

A systematic approach to executive performance appraisal can provide many benefits. It can help upgrade performances, identify those persons capable of promotion, and improve total company results by motivating executives to achieve topflight performance. Moreover, a systematic approach facilitates objectivity in the appraisal process.

Over the years, our company—United States Gypsum Company—has used many performance appraisal systems. We believe that our current program is vastly superior to any other system we have used, but we also recognize the possibility that a few years hence we will find even better ways of appraising and motivating executives.

This chapter will describe the performance appraisal system we use through-out our company—at all levels and in all functions for all exempt salaried employees. This approach, which we believe has been successful in its application to our company, may be termed an accountability management program. Thus, it is a good deal more than just a method or system for appraising executive performance. The primary value of the program lies in its effectiveness as a management technique for accomplishing results. It stresses the importance of setting objectives for each person consistent with the accountabilities of his position. Planning objectives aimed at achieving corporate goals and assigning them to appropriate managers helps channel the managers' efforts into the most productive areas.

More specifically, the program exists for the following purposes:

1. To establish realistic, clear, and challenging objectives for each executive, administrative, and professional employee in relation to specific accountabilities of his position

2. To help each employee to use his full capabilities in his present position and assist him in preparing for greater responsibilities

3. To facilitate effective salary administration

Appraisal of each employee's performance in accomplishing these accountabilities and objectives is a vital part—but nonetheless only a part—of the total program.

SETTING PERFORMANCE OBJECTIVES

Management's essential role is to establish and maintain long-range corporate goals which are translated into annual goals or objectives. These company goals are further translated into functional, divisional, or departmental objectives for specific divisions and departments, so that each executive and major department head knows what is expected of him over the next 12-month period. And he, in turn, translates his (department) objectives into more specific objectives for each of his immediate subordinates, and so on down the management ladder until all salaried exempt positions have been assigned annual objectives in line with the accountabilities of their positions. This is the first and primary step in the program. It takes planning and effort to work out individual position objectives, but the reward for the effort is substantial in terms of motivation, accomplishment, and personnel development. A significant by-product of the program is its application to effective salary administration.

Integrated Company Goals.   The superior must play the key role in establishing objectives for two reasons:

1. To assure that positions reporting to him have integrated, harmonizing objectives

2. To assure that objectives are not only realistic but also challenging enough to stretch the abilities of the subordinate

Corporate goals are identical with the objectives of the chief executive, while objectives of functional department heads are basically a distribution of broad assignments which comprise and serve to accomplish the objectives of the chief executive. It is obvious that the vice president, marketing, should not plan to create markets which cannot be fed by operating or which cannot be economically serviced by traffic. Likewise, manufacturing should not plan the installation of new equipment to increase production if engineering cannot design such equipment or if marketing cannot justify increased production. Each functional department head, then, despite his own personal qualifications, cannot establish his own objectives except as they relate to (or are compatible with) those of his superior, and this is true down to first-line supervisors.

For some employees in some work environments the pressure to complete or exceed all objectives may be so great that they will tend to set easily attainable goals. On the other hand, some people may set their sights too high. The best method to level the load and assure that each employee's targets are fair and challenging is to have the superior play the key role in setting them.

Personal Goals.   There is, however, more to a man's worth than doing those things which his position and his boss require him to do. There is, in addition, the vital element of the man himself: what he brings to the job—his own ideas, foresight, creativity, and drive and, in fact, his own personal objectives. These unique personal characteristics are a significant source of corporate vitality.

To unite management-imposed objectives and the individual's personal or self-imposed objectives into an integrated plan, and further, to assure the individual's acceptance of objectives assigned him, it is necessary for superior and subordinate to meet at the beginning of each year to develop a mutually agreed-upon program of objectives for the subordinate. These objectives should be determined on the basis of:

1. Total corporate goals
2. Functional component goals
3. Immediate section goals
4. The incumbent's personal, self-imposed goals

The objectives should be defined in terms of the individual's position account-abilities. They might be stated in the form of specific and quantitative results, such as profitability, share of the market, reduced costs, and product improvement, or they might be in less tangible areas of managerial accomplishment such as improved public relations. The important point is that they be specific, realistic, and attainable but, at the same time, challenging and measurable.

APPRAISING PERFORMANCE AGAINST OBJECTIVES

Once objectives have been set, it becomes the superior's responsibility to ascertain the degree of progress and success being achieved, to identify the causes of inadequate achievement and suggest solutions, and to keep the incumbent oriented toward those objectives.

Frequent Evaluation. Unlike appraisals of employee characteristics, performance against objectives cannot be evaluated adequately on an annual basis. The basic purpose of the program is to assure that appropriate goals are set and *attained:* an after-the-fact evaluation will not achieve this purpose. If below-par performance is to be corrected, the individual must be informed by his superior that he is not performing up to expectation, and this should be done early enough to permit the man to improve and reach his objective, or, if necessary, to revise the objectives as conditions during the year may warrant.

Regular evaluations of progress, *at least semiannually,* are a proper requirement for the following reasons:

1. They permit current evaluation (and, if need be, modification) of performance.

2. They provide adequate time for improvement.

3. They permit revision and addition of objectives during the year as conditions warrant.

4. For purposes of salary administration, they permit action to be taken on current performance.

Counsel on Progress. We recommend that the superior counsel his subordinates on their performance as often as seems necessary from the quality of their performance. As a minimum, however, we feel all should be counseled twice a year.

Counseling is necessary for two reasons:

1. To provide advice and assistance to the subordinate to improve his performance and help him achieve his goals

2. To aid the superior in gaining understanding and insight into each subordinate's problems and the reasons for demonstrated performance—good or bad

PERFORMANCE APPRAISAL IN SALARY ADMINISTRATION

In a program such as this, effective salary administration is a necessary service, as salaries serve as a basic incentive toward accomplishment of accountabilities and objectives.

A salary administration program generally develops salary ranges for all positions, within which each incumbent may be paid according to his merit or performance level. Each range is divided into four or five equal parts or sub-ranges. An individual's position in the range is determined by his level of performance as appraised by his superior. For example, an employee whose performance has been appraised as outstanding by his superior during the year qualifies for a salary increase commensurate with that performance, within the limits set by company salary policy.

The important point to be made here is that *salary action will be related to actual job performance.*

ACCOUNTABILITY MANAGEMENT AT WORK

United States Gypsum Company has developed an accountability management worksheet to facilitate consistent and appropriate performance appraisals. The worksheet is shown in Figure 1, and in the sections below we discuss how it is used.

Part I. Accountabilities. The position's accountabilities—that is, the results it is expected to accomplish—have been defined in a position analysis, and unless changes actually have been made, these accountabilities should be transferred verbatim from the position analysis to the worksheet and numbered consecutively.

Part II. Objectives. Working alone, the executive and his superior each examine each accountability in part I to determine what objectives they separately feel must be planned in order to get satisfactory results in that accountability. Each man prepares a draft of each objective, identifying it with a specific accountability. When this is done, superior and subordinate meet prior to January 15 to mutually agree upon objectives for the next 12-month period.

These objectives should be in line with company objectives and clearly defined in terms of budget figures, percentages (increase or decrease), cost standards, yields, margins, volumes, time schedules, or whatever concrete criteria may be feasible. There will, of course, be certain objectives that do not lend themselves to quantitative description, and these will need to be defined and set forth in qualitative terms.

Part III. Standards of Measurement. Having developed the list of objectives, the incumbent and the superior, during this meeting, identify standards of measurement—i.e., sources of information on which appraisals will be based—which will ensure an objective analysis of the incumbent's performance as well as provide him with his own guidelines for action.

Wherever possible, it is most desirable to develop quantitative standards (e.g., information derived from the "Quarterly Labor Condition Letter," the "Monthly Sales Report," etc.). Obviously, the progress and results for certain objectives cannot always be measured by using statistical data.

Once these standards of measurement have been decided upon, the purpose of the initial meeting has been completed and parts I, II, and III of the worksheet can be typed in triplicate, with one copy each for the executive and his superior and an original to be sent for approval to the next higher level of management.

Figure 1.   Accountability management worksheet.

Accountability management worksheet

Name of employee:	Position title:	Time in position: _____Year(s) _____ Months
Plant, district, office:	Department:	Reports to (title):

PURPOSE OF THE PROGRAM: "Accountability Management" is a results oriented management method designed to serve three primary purposes.

1. To establish realistic, clear and challenging objectives for each employee in relation to specific accountabilities of the position, the sum total of which blends into the functional or location objectives and ultimately the Company's objectives.

2. To assist each employee to utilize his capabilities in his present position and assist him in preparing for greater responsibilities.

3. To serve as the foundation of a soundly administered program of salary administration based on achievement, providing incentive, and making possible true merit reward.

SPECIFIC OBJECTIVES OF THE PROGRAM:

1. To define the expected end results for each position.

2. To establish realistic standards of measurement to assure an objective evaluation of progress and results in relation to objectives of the position.

3. To stimulate employee's performance.

4. To assist placing of employees in positions in accordance with their ability; uncover exceptional talent and aid in the development of competent personnel to carry out Company objectives.

5. To aid in compensating employees for superior performance by relating measured performance to salary levels.

NOTE: Be certain you have reviewed and fully understand the material presented in the "Accountability Management Manual" before entering any information in this worksheet.

Figure 1. Accountability management worksheet—continued

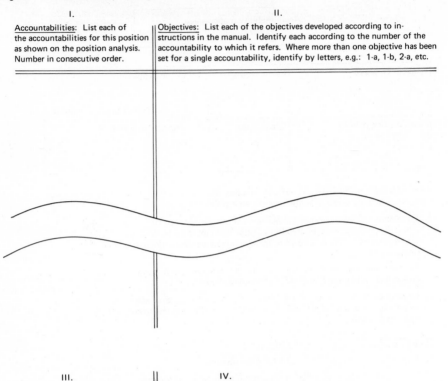

I.

Accountabilities: List each of the accountabilities for this position as shown on the position analysis. Number in consecutive order.

II.

Objectives: List each of the objectives developed according to instructions in the manual. Identify each according to the number of the accountability to which it refers. Where more than one objective has been set for a single accountability, identify by letters, e.g.: 1-a, 1-b, 2-a, etc.

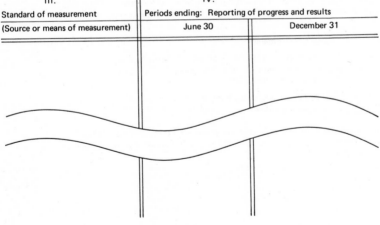

III.

Standard of measurement

(Source or means of measurement)

IV.

Periods ending: Reporting of progress and results

June 30

December 31

Figure 1.   Accountability management worksheet—continued

V. Other important performance: Prior to completing the summary performance evaluation (section VI), list and describe below specific instances of critical performance not covered by objectives. Indicate period in which performance occurred.

VI. Summary performance evaluation: In this section you are to apply your judgment in evaluation of the incumbent's performance according to the materials in this worksheet. Do not be concerned with character traits or qualities — but with results only.

Interim   Annual

☐   ☐ ←— Outstanding: Exceptional — Clearly unique — far above others at his position level. Includes 2 to 4 percent of all salaried-exempt employees.

☐   ☐ ←— Superior: Clearly and substantially above required performance. Includes 10 to 15 percent of all salaried-exempt employees.

☐   ☐ ←— Competent: At or somewhat above required performance. Similar to most others. Encompasses "good" to "very good" performance. Includes 60 to 75 percent of all salaried-exempt employees.

☐   ☐ ←— Adequate: Acceptable but below most others in performance — fair. Includes 10 to 15 percent of all salaried-exempt employees.

☐   ☐ ←— Problem area: Unacceptable. Failure to meet minimum standards. Management action necessary. Includes 2 to 4 percent of all salaried-exempt personnel.

Part IV. Reporting of Results. The two columns in part IV are for the superior's recording of the incumbent's actual performance in each period. Comment should also be made as needed to qualify or clarify the record.

Recording performance, like setting objectives, should be as factual and objective as possible. For example, this statement tells very little: "Did a good job of increasing sales in his district." This statement is much better: "Increased sales in his district 3 percent over prior period as compared with objective of 2 percent increase." Comments such as: "Severe competitive price-cutting in his district during quarter" and "Opportunity ran 15 percent behind January 1 projection" add further dimension to the evaluation.

Part V. Other Important Performance. It is recognized that all important performance by an individual over a 12-month period probably will not be the result of preset objectives, and, in fact, that some performance may not be directly related to those objectives. And yet, a meaningful evaluation of performance must take these important incidents, whether favorable or unfavorable, into consideration. Part V is available for the recording of important performance which cannot be adequately evaluated in terms of objectives accomplished.

Part VI. Summary Performance Evaluation (Ratings). This final section of the worksheet is the rating chart for the superior's appraisal of the incumbent's overall performance level in terms of results achieved.

Up to this point the manager has not had to rate the incumbent on his performance but only to record his progress and results. Now the manager must perform the most difficult step in the appraisal procedure—applying personal value judgment to performance.

Because there is no way to apply a purely mathematical yardstick to an individual's total performance, evaluation must remain the task of the superior. Throughout history leaders have been appraising their subordinates, and traditionally on a highly subjective basis. The rating the superior will assign to his subordinate in part VI of the worksheet is also a subjective rating, but if based on accurately recorded performance measured against challenging objectives, it can be a fair and realistic appraisal of total performance.

This summary performance evaluation is made on the total annual accomplishment of each employee following the completion of the December 31 column of part IV of the worksheet.

An annual report of summary performance evaluations (Figure 2) is then prepared by each plant, district, or department manager and submitted to the manager's superior for approval and forwarding to the corporate personnel department.

IMPORTANT CONSIDERATIONS IN PERFORMANCE APPRAISAL

Keep in mind that in this exercise the manager is appraising performance only —results. He is not at this time appraising appearance, attitude, ability to get along with others, or any other personal quality or characteristic. This is a work-centered evaluation of achievement.

Before assigning the rating for the period, the manager should analyze and evaluate each objective in terms of three dimensions:

1. The importance or impact of each objective on the overall job. Some objectives will be of primary importance—without them, the position would not exist—while others may be of only secondary importance or of a supporting nature.

2. The level of difficulty or challenge in the objective. Some objectives will

Figure 2. Annual report of summary performance evaluations.

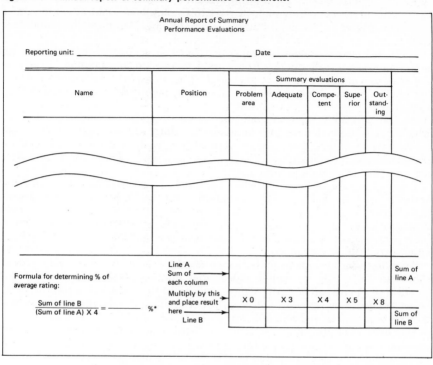

Unit Performance vs. Percentage of Average Ratings

It is recommended that managers compare the average rating of their people with the total performance of their unit or department.

The calculations on the reverse side enable managers to make such a comparison. The result of the calculation represents the percentage deviation from a standard weighted distribution of ratings as recommended.

The following ranges serve as a basis for comparing the calculated percentage rating to unit performance. (Unit performance evaluated in terms of generally accepted measurements of such performance as determined and employed by senior managers in rating over-all performance of units reporting to them).

If unit performance is:	The percentage of average may be:
Outstanding	110–120%
Superior	105–110%
Competent	95–105%
Adequate	90–95%
Problem area	Under 90%

require a special output by the individual to accomplish them, while others are routine in nature. How difficult were this subordinate's objectives to attain?

3. The degree of accomplishment. Was the objective partially completed? Fully completed? Exceeded? To what degree?

With this analysis done, the superior is now in a position to evaluate total performance on a scale ranging from "problem area" to "outstanding." Because the scale is somewhat novel, it may be helpful to explore the rationale which led to its design. First, however, let us look at the scale as reproduced in Figure 3.

As you will note, there are only five steps or grades in the scale, each of which is represented by a key term—*outstanding*, etc.—a description to the right of the term, and a space on a vertical bar graph to the left. Ratings are recorded by simply finding the key term and description which most accurately describe the individual's performance.

Percentages are indicated in the performance rating descriptions and the vertical bar is divided unevenly to conform with the statistical concept of normal distribution. This concept tells us that the distribution of any given trait in a population, if plotted on a graph, will yield a bell-shaped curve. Thus, most people will exhibit an average amount of the trait; only a few will exhibit either very little or very much.

Applying this concept to performance appraisal in terms of the rating scale shown in Figure 3, we would expect that most salaried exempt employees would turn in *competent* performances. Only 20 to 30 percent would be rated either *adequate* or *superior*, and even fewer would fall into the extreme categories—*outstanding* and *problem area*.

One method of obtaining a satisfactory distribution of ratings is to force them into the desired curve. Using this approach a manager is told that a certain number must be rated as outstanding, a certain number as superior, and so on. The problem with this approach is that unless the rater is evaluating an exceptionally large group, the forced distribution will likely contribute to error and distortion rather than correct them. If, for example, you have only two people

Figure 3.   Performance appraisal scale.

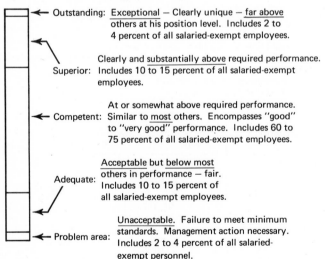

under you, it is obvious that you cannot distribute them according to a normal distribution curve—they may both be outstanding or they may both be unacceptable. At the same time, for any individual within a group, the chances remain 2 to 1 that he will be in the competent group, while the odds will be 25 to 1 against his being either outstanding or unacceptable.

The rating scale in the worksheet has been devised to *imply* the normal distribution by its form and by its language. The division of the vertical bar graph has been made in such a way as to remind the rater that most people will be rated *competent*, etc. Percentage figures included in the descriptions are for the same purpose—*to remind the rater*—and are not to be taken literally but to be used with judgment. In using judgment, it is recommended that our managers compare the average rating of their people with the total performance of their unit or department. For example, if the overall performance of a plant or sales district is considered something less than superior, a finding that the average rating of its people was superior would not be consistent. If such is the case, the need for a more realistic determination of individual ratings would be indicated.

chapter 26

Appraising Performance
for Individual Development

R. L. FORD *Manager, Manpower Planning & Development, Kennecott Copper Corporation, New York, New York*

In the last decade or so, there has been a tremendous resurgence of management interest in executive performance appraisal systems. Part of this renewed interest can be traced to Peter Drucker's theory of management by objectives, first put forth in the fifties and later given practical application in business by consultants, academicians, and industrial managers.[1]

Today management by objectives or variations of it find wide acceptance in industrial circles, and the underlying concept is used in a variety of executive appraisal and management programs. Because of the various systems going under the name, it is almost impossible to get any meaningful evaluation of management by objectives techniques on an industrywide basis; one can obtain data only by in-depth study of one or more programs or, in certain instances, by studying the features common to a number of plans. Certainly it is safe to say that experience has been mixed and that management by objectives is by no means a panacea for the maladies common to older executive appraisal approaches. About the only general observation that can be made—and for this management by objectives is entitled to accolades—is that the technique has been responsible for the tremendous decline in the use of trait-oriented rating systems.

---

[1] Peter F. Drucker, *The Practice of Management*, Harper & Brothers, New York, 1954.

APPRAISAL PURPOSE

There are many reasons for undertaking executive appraisal programs, most of which can be grouped under two broad headings:

1. *Administrative:*   To guide personnel decisions on such matters as salary, executive incentive award, the grant of stock options, promotions, transfers, and manpower planning.

2. *Developmental:*   To act as a motivator for improved performance, individual, organizational, or both.

A third purpose of appraisal programs might be designated information or feedback, but since feedback is an integral part of the administrative and developmental purposes, it will not be considered independently.

Whether any single executive appraisal system can serve both sets of purposes is a matter that is frequently debated.   However, this is a secondary problem.   The much more crucial question is whether the executive appraisal program, per se, can serve either the administrative or the developmental purpose.

Appraisal is a process of evaluation—an act of making a judgment as to the value of something or someone—in this instance, the value of executive performance.   In the strict sense of this definition, the appraisal program would seem to come closest to meeting the requirements of the set of purposes designated "administrative."   Base compensation and extra-compensatory reward decisions are, or should be, related in large measure to the value of individual executive performance.   Promotion, transfer, and manpower planning are also related to performance evaluation, although to a different dimension—the dimension of expected performance under the requirements of a different position, at a different point in time, and in a different environment.

With reference to the fulfillment of the developmental purposes, appraisal, as defined, is a somewhat remote mechanism.   Whether the appraisal is based on the attainment of objectives or some other system makes little difference.   Appraisal is a limited process—the process of making a value judgment.   Either it must be naively assumed that imparting that value judgment to the appraisee will serve as the stimulus to redirect that individual's energies and efforts toward work-oriented performance improvement, or it must be recognized that appraisal is only a minor contributor to the developmental process.

Performance is the product of a dynamic interaction between individual and situation variables.   Under the best conditions, the appraisal process and subsequent informational feedback may help to improve understanding of these forces.   But it seems likely that factors extending far beyond the appraisal process must be operative to effect performance improvement.

A TOTAL MANAGEMENT APPROACH

It follows that in order to facilitate individual and organizational development, what is needed is a systematic, broad-based, integrated approach to management.   Appraisal may be an important part of that approach, but it is by no means the whole; rather, systematic management makes possible effective executive appraisal, which then completes the circle by making a valuable contribution to the total management system.

Of course, I recognize that in many organizations management by objectives has supplied the means for a systematic and integrated approach to management of the business.   However, this is not always the case.   Moreover, other organizations have successfully developed a total approach, suitable to developmental purposes, without using management by objectives.

The point is, then, that managers should focus on developing an integrated approach to managing the business, not on a specific technique. Techniques will come and go, and although they may contribute to managerial competence over the short haul, they are only means to an end—the effective organization of human behavior to attain enterprise goals and to serve enterprise purposes.

Management by objectives, although broader in scope than most appraisal systems, is really a technique. As such, it can be judged only in terms of its effectiveness in serving organizational needs. In many instances, management by objectives has come closer than any other system yet devised to achieving an integrated management approach; in other cases, it has flopped.

The development of an integrated approach requires considerable effort, the commitment of all key managers, purposeful strategic planning at the top of the organization, probably some organizational realignment and a restructuring of traditional managerial control systems, and perhaps a vague vision of change in leadership style, involving behavioral changes at all executive levels.

Thus, even though management by objectives represents a significant step forward, it is probably not the whole answer. Douglas McGregor used the term *cosmology* to describe the overall view.[2] The term is appropriate, for a managerial cosmology is indicated.

Obviously, the scope of a global approach to management is too extensive to be detailed in the framework of this writing. But a broad overview can be undertaken, with emphasis on aspects of the management process particularly related to individual development and to appraisal as a subsystem of the whole process. The reader is cautioned in advance that the treatment is far from complete.

Before proceeding to that examination, however, a cursory look at motivation theory is essential to an understanding of the ensuing material.

MOTIVATION THEORY

Abraham Maslow has contributed significantly to our understanding of motivation[3] with the development of his need hierarchy theorem.[4] Dr. Maslow arranged human needs in pyramidal fashion, ascending from lowest to highest. At the base of the pyramid and designated "Level 1" he placed man's *physiological* needs. Incorporated in this set of needs are food, shelter, clothing, and rest.

Level 2 included the need for *security* or *protection from deprivation*. These second-level needs do not arise until man possesses something of value. Then he acts to preserve his entitlement to it. At Level 3 Dr. Maslow placed man's *social* needs: the need for identification, the need for a sense of belonging, the need for association with others, and the need for giving and receiving love.

At Level 4 man's *ego* needs come into play. These include the need for recognition, status, and respect. The highest-level human need was represented by Maslow at Level 5: the need for *self-actualization, self-realization,* or *self-fulfillment.* These terms cover man's need for full utilization of his innate capacity, for development of personal competence, for acquisition of increased

---

[2] Douglas McGregor, in *The Professional Manager* (eds. C. McGregor and W. G. Bennis), McGraw-Hill Book Company, New York, 1967.

[3] In using the term *motivation,* my feeling is that motivation is not something which is done to someone, but rather an innate quality of the individual.

[4] Abraham Maslow, *The Need Hierarchy: Management and the Behavioral Sciences,* Allyn and Bacon, Boston, 1968.

skill and knowledge, for use of creative and innovative ability, and for rendering service to others.

Maslow contended that until the needs at each level are satisfied, human beings are not motivated by the needs at the next higher level. However, once the needs at Level 1 are satisfied, they no longer offer any motivational impact; the needs at Level 2 would then be motivators. In this sense, there is a cyclical character to man's needs.[5] On the other hand, Maslow feels that motivation toward higher needs is semipermanent in character and that these needs will continue to motivate man even after he has experienced some fulfillment of them.

Insofar as the corporate executive is concerned, the lower-level needs are not likely to provide motivation. The potentialities lie largely in the range of Levels 4 and 5.

Studies by David McClelland lend weight to Maslow's work.[6] McClelland found the need for achievement to be considerably higher in business executives than in other professionals (lawyers, doctors, and professors). Other significant research findings by McClelland were that persons with high achievement needs enjoyed situations in which they had responsibility for problem solution, and that high achievement needs were also associated with the desire to set goals and to set them midway between low-risk and high-risk levels. He found that the achievement-oriented individual also exhibited a strong desire for feedback pertaining to job performance.

Herzberg, Mausner, and Snyderman, in studies carried out primarily with middle managers, found that achievement, recognition, the nature of work, responsibility, and advancement (in that order) led to feelings of satisfaction in the work situation.[7]

Certainly there appears to be support for the importance of higher-order needs as motivators of executive performance. With respect to Level 5 needs —self-realization, etc.—rewards for performing close to the limits of personal capability are largely intrinsic to the individual. To date, business and industry have not used intrinsic rewards effectively. When intrinsic rewards have been realized, it has generally been by accident rather than by design. Extrinsic rewards—i.e., compensation, stock option, incentive bonus, benefits, etc.—meet certain important needs, but beyond a given level they are just so much gravy and do not satisfy the highest-level needs. The task is not to cease providing extrinsic reward, but to develop a management system which will provide intrinsic rewards as well.

Certain other characteristics of motivation are important to bear in mind as we attempt to structure an overall approach to management. Motivation is in large measure an emotional force. Man himself is an inextricable combination of rational and emotional forces, but in situations involving contact with those in a position to exercise power the emotional content is particularly strong. If an executive perceives that he is threatened, he is not going to be motivated in the direction of the attainment of enterprise objectives, though he may be motivated in different directions. It matters little whether or not his perception

---

[5] For example, place an American corporate president on a deserted island for a period of time, and his concern will be satisfying his physiological needs rather than using his full capabilities.

[6] David C. McClelland, *The Achieving Society*, D. Van Nostrand Company, Inc., Princeton, N.J., 1961.

[7] F. Herzberg, B. Mausner, and B. Snyderman, *The Motivation to Work*, John Wiley & Sons, Inc., New York, 1967.

is accurate, for emotional response is a condition of perceived, not objective, reality.

As was discussed above, an appraisal program can facilitate individual development and truly motivate people only if it is supported and reinforced by an appropriate total management process. Broadly speaking, the total process includes organizational climate, structure, and purpose, the place of individuals in the organization and the type of goals they are expected to achieve, the communication and control systems characteristic of the organization, etc. These elements comprise the management process and determine how effectively performance appraisal, as a piece of the whole, can serve individual development purposes.

THE MANAGEMENT PROCESS

Management Climate. Although *management climate* is not a very precise term, almost everyone in the organization recognizes the existence of an overall set of conditions that tend to characterize the work environment. Attitudes of individual management members might be worlds apart, but still there is a pervading management climate that is not necessarily associated with the views of any particular manager. Seldom is this management climate expressed in any written document. In fact, the climate is most often recognized by the actions and deeds of management members. This collective representation of management deeds has tremendous impact upon the members of the organization. It is worthwhile, then, to look at a few important conditions that must be deliberately cultivated if individual and organizational growth is to be maximized.

Perhaps the most important of these conditions is *mutual trust*—trust that is felt in the interpersonal relationships between individual executives and their subordinates and in the more impersonal relationship between the management group and employees. In part, this means that the organization must develop a reputation for treating employees with equity and fairness. But it means far more than that. It means the willingness to deal with people in a manner which is protective of their dignity and security; it means establishing an atmosphere that has the quality of assurance and that encourages reliance.

Trust has a great bearing on an individual's willingness to commit himself to the attainment of enterprise objectives and to engage in a meaningful dialogue on those objectives. Dialogue, in turn, is a base for understanding responsibility and performance expectations. Likewise, trust is an important and necessary ingredient of the creative and innovative exercise of capability. Finally, trust is an important aspect of an individual's willingness to accept change and, perhaps more significantly, of his willingness to change his personal behavior.

Mutuality of trust is, in part, brought about by example. It is also brought about by encouragement of meaningful relationships and by expression of empathy and warmth in interpersonal dealings. Research evidence indicates that trust develops more readily when there is opportunity for relevant personal interaction, and also that subordinates are more likely to trust their managers when it is known that the latter can control the situation at the next managerial level.

Closely allied to trust, and certainly dependent on an atmosphere of mutual trust, is *openness in communications.* Open communication means encouraging a free flow of information and allowing each individual free access to information and data relevant to the performance of his organizational responsibilities. In decision making, open communication means encouraging a candid exploration of facts, attitudes, feelings, and interrelationships critical to the evaluation of the situation, problem, or decision under discussion. It means the freedom to bring disagreements into open discussion.

In a bureaucracy, information flows only in accord with the lines on the formal organization chart. Not only does this hamper the ability to get the job accomplished within a reasonable time framework, it also hampers the exchange of ideas from one managerial level to another and across functional or operational lines.

Openness of communication in interpersonal relationships facilitates understanding of constraints that might be operative in the accomplishment of a task, project, or target. If the individual responsible for the achievement of a target can communicate his problems openly, alternative courses of action can often be found. If a subordinate can appreciate the constraints that his manager is facing, what may seem to be arbitrary action or behavior on the manager's part is more readily understood. As business is increasingly faced with problems demanding interdisciplinary attention, openness of interpersonal communication becomes increasingly important in the effectiveness of the group process.

Management climate that truly facilitates personal and organizational growth must also be *humanistic*—that is, the atmosphere must be characterized by basic consideration for the worth of the individual employee.

A management that develops a humanistic climate, in which mutual trust and open communication are encouraged, has taken a giant step toward gaining the individual's identification with the "establishment." Such a climate facilitates individual recognition and helps to promote feelings of positive self-image and self-esteem. It is a climate which supports the individual in his search for self-realization, thus providing a fertile environment for positively motivated behavior.

Organizational Considerations. The organization structure must be designed to accomplish enterprise objectives. Organization design, therefore, requires careful consideration of the constraints which may hamper achievement of those objectives. Authority must be allocated to minimize the effect of the constraints, and responsibility must be distributed among individual positions so that the combination of responsibilities in any one job is not so unusual that it would be impossible to fill the job. These and related considerations are fairly traditional management problems and do not warrant further elaboration at this point.

A factor frequently neglected, however, is that changes in organization structure inevitably require changes in attitudes and behavior. It cannot be assumed that organizational changes will automatically elicit appropriate behavioral changes. Nor is it sufficient to issue a new organization manual setting forth the purpose of the change. The change, for instance, from a functionally aligned organization to a matrix-type organization structure requires a major change in attitude and behavioral patterns throughout the organization. Gaining acceptance of and commitment to the new mode of operation is a major undertaking. Achieving success in this undertaking is essentially a task of securing emotional, as opposed to just rational, acceptance of the change.

A matrix-type organization, for example, will be successful only to the extent that attitudes of collaboration and teaming can be successfully introduced into the organization and made a part of the competence of organizational members. Extensive effort is necessary to achieve these results. Intra- and intergroup "gut-level" dialogue is an essential prerequisite. Disagreements must be allowed to come to the surface, and problem-solving competence of individuals and groups must be greatly enhanced. "Win-win" attitudes, as opposed to traditional "win-lose" attitudes, must be encouraged. The corporate reward systems must be utilized to support desired behavioral change. While the introduction of change is a subject of its own, the important point to note here is that deliberate change processes must be built into the effective practice of management.

Still another consideration that is oftentimes overlooked in organizational design is the question of organizing to facilitate management development. A few recommendations are pertinent in this regard.

1. *Build challenge into the job.* Ensure that the range of responsibility is broad enough to sustain interest, require attention, and offer the opportunity to be innovative in the use of problem-solving ability. Whenever possible, design the position so as to offer final decision-making responsibility even though the realm of the decision making may be relatively narrow.

2. *Design jobs around natural managerial control points.* These may be profit centers, project centers, cost centers, product lines, geographical units, knowledge areas, etc. These are points where relatively independent objective performance indices can be found and where feedback opportunity is maximized.

3. *Reduce number of management tiers.* Generally speaking, the more echelons existent, the less opportunity there is for meaningful discrimination of responsibility and exercise of appropriate decision making. A concomitant gain in clarity of understanding and communication is also likely to be experienced in flat organization structures.

A particular line-staff problem in connection with management effectiveness is also worthy of consideration at this point. It is essential that the line manager exercise leadership in sponsoring the development of his subordinates. The staff role in this relationship must be consultative and advisory. The staff can and should be expected to supply methodological expertise as needed. Also, the staff should be involved in overall executive manpower planning and in establishing interunit criteria for ensuring that corporate purpose is served. But staff intrusion in the manager-subordinate relation, unless by line invitation, should be strongly discouraged. There are strong indications that management by objectives programs, for instance, are far more effective when they are carried out by line managers and staff intervention is infrequent.

Future organization design will require less hierarchy and more flexibility. Organizational subsystems and the decision-making processes within those subsystems will have to be studied carefully. Given a growth in knowledge consistent with or exceeding the pace of the past two decades, those in entry management posts may be the only individuals possessing the specialized skill required in certain technical or functional areas. Decision making within the subsystems will depend on the competence of these individuals. Under these circumstances, higher-level authority can ill afford to second-guess junior counterparts. Within a defined sphere of influence, the lower-level subsystem will have to have final decision-making authority. The higher-order subsystem will be concerned with different responsibilities, such as strategic planning and resource allocation, in which competency is a product of successful experience and broad capability.

There is already a need to define management responsibility in broader terms. Responsibility must be thought of in terms of long-range results as opposed to specific tasks or activities. Reversing the practice of position descriptions establishing limits of authority, emphasis will be placed on defining freedom to act within broad intersystem relationships.

Enterprise Purpose, Plans, and Objective.   Although many corporations have operated and continue to operate without a statement of enterprise purpose, to do so is somewhat like launching a moon rocket without any navigational reference points.   Not only does a statement of enterprise purpose set forth the broad boundaries of the business, it helps to prevent waste of money, time, and effort in the pursuit of endeavors outside the scope of those boundaries. Additionally, purpose normally provides an indication of growth and profit expectations.

The statement of enterprise purpose also sets forth the basic value systems guiding the progress of the corporation.   The overall intent of relations with stockholders, employees, customers, and the public should be set forth.   These statements provide a base for continually testing the degree to which enterprise purposes are being met.   Properly designed, the statement of purpose is the first in a series of appraisal systems in the business.

The efficacy of the modern corporation is highly dependent on the strength and quality of its strategic planning processes.   In a world where change is constant, strategic planning is not only an essential of organizational growth, but a necessity of organizational survival.

Sound strategic planning begins with projections of the environment in which the corporation expects to be doing business some years hence, taking into account the probable effect of the projected situation on likely areas of corporate involvement.   Planning also requires projections of corporate resources: capital, knowledge, raw materials, market and distribution skill, and executive and manpower availability.   It considers the internal and external constraints likely to impinge on corporate progress.   Then it seeks to identify the opportunities particularly appropriate for the corporation and to develop alternative courses of action by which the corporation might take advantage of those opportunities.   Finally, the strategic planning process identifies the major assumptions used in its analysis to permit periodic review of the strategic plan.

The product of the strategic planning process is the identification of essential corporate objectives, generally spanning a five-year term and broken down year by year.   While these objectives are specific, they are generally broad in scope. They encompass financial results, as well as all other functional, operational, technical, marketing, and manpower results deemed essential to the accomplishment of the ends set forth by the strategic plan and essential to progress in terms of the enterprise purpose.

While the component elements of the strategic plan may flow upward through the organization, the corporate objectives generally flow downward.

If goal setting is to be taken seriously by others in the organization, strategic planning and the establishment of objectives for the corporate whole must be pursued diligently at the top of the organization.

Individual Goal Setting.   Individual goal setting is essentially an upward-flowing process.   The individual management member, however, is guided by the broad objectives of the unit of which he is a part.   He is also guided by the broad responsibility areas of his particular position.

The concepts underlying the goal-setting process are relatively simple, but in practice they often prove difficult to attain.   A typical goal-setting process might include:

1. A discussion between manager and subordinate to clarify understanding of responsibility and priority among responsibilities.   At this session, the broad objectives of the unit are outlined and, preferably, distributed in written form. A date is set for goal submission.

2. The tentative set of goals is normally submitted in advance of a subsequent

discussion session to permit review and comparison with goals submitted by other peer-group members.

3. In the second discussion between manager and subordinate, goal modification, if indicated, is discussed. Measurement criteria for goal attainment are selected. Questions relating to clarity, specificity, and target dates are resolved. Both parties retain copies of the commitment document arising from this discussion.

4. Follow-up progress discussions are held periodically on an agreed-upon schedule.

Most goal-setting programs suggest the preparation of at least three types of goals: (1) operational or functional goals, relating to the attainment of the broader organizational objectives; (2) relationship goals, dealing with improved interpersonal relations; and (3) self-development goals, dealing with personal improvement.

Newer approaches to goal setting often involve group processes. Group sessions facilitate common understanding of responsibility and performance expectations and provide for coordination of intragroup goals. At progress and accomplishment review sessions the subtle exertion of peer-group pressure often leads to more realistic reporting and better planning for future goal attainment.

Feedback. The most appropriate and effective periodic feedback occurs when the subordinate executive is given the responsibility for initiating progress report discussions and at the end of the goal period is given the responsibility for final accomplishment reporting.

Progress reports can be verbal or written. Final accomplishment reports normally are in writing. Verbal reports necessitate face-to-face meeting. Written reports can be submitted and then discussed, but the preferred procedure is to have the written report brought to a discussion session without requiring prior submission. This procedure enhances the opportunity for dialogue.

Self-reporting is probably best for the individual's self-image and self-esteem. It is also consistent with the desire of the individual, in most cases, to maintain a measure of control over the situation. Further, it provides the opportunity for the astute manager to identify areas of discussion which are likely to evoke defensive reactions and to gauge his comment accordingly.

It is the managing executive's responsibility to indicate any area of disagreement with the subordinate's progress or accomplishment report. Problems in this regard are minimized if care has been exercised in the goal-setting session to ensure that goal, timing of achievement, and measurement criteria have been stated explicitly and are understood and accepted by both manager and subordinate.

Management Control Systems. Not infrequently the inadequacy of existing management control systems is encountered and brought to light by the goal-setting process. Poor control systems are particularly evident when measurement indices are difficult to find. The problem may relate to inadequacy in organizational design or it may be confined to the control systems area. While all responsibility or goal areas are not quantifiable, greater quantification is possible in most positions than is usually realized.

Wherever possible, adequate information should be made available to the incumbent of a position to enable him to take remedial action to bring out-of-control situations back into line. Yet, few management control systems make provisions for the individual to have the necessary information to initiate prompt corrective action. Often the management control system supplies a multitude of data that are irrelevant to the effective control of the work, or there is a complete absence of data.

The problem requires considerable attention. Most management members are interested in doing a good job and can contribute significantly to the design of an appropriate informational feedback system relating to their own area of responsibility. Yet, they are seldom consulted in this regard, and control systems are designed by people upstairs or by staff groups who assume that control must be exerted from the top down. Motivational theory does not support this view; the most effective controls are those that allow for self-regulation and permit self-adjustment.

Further, there is a tendency to build control systems around the achievement of the corporate financial plan. Achieving of financial goals is only one dimension of a total job and oftentimes a dimension that is less meaningful to the individual manager than sales, quality control, marketing, production, technical, or manpower considerations. Accomplishment of the financial plan is more often than not a consequence of actions taken in these areas, not vice versa.

If individuals are to be expected to perform effectively, they must have access to relevant reports when they need them. Emphasis should be on self-control as opposed to imposed control. Feeding back control data to the person responsible for performance, with expectation that he will use the data to regulate or improve his performance, can inspire confidence and achieve results more effectively than admonition from above.

Administrative Considerations. Progress and accomplishment reports, and any evaluation comments in relation thereto, are tools for the effective management of business. They should be left in the hands of the line manager to enable that manager to plan an effective approach in working with the subordinate on a day-to-day basis. At an appropriate point in time, for instance, the supervising manager may plan to work with the subordinate manager on scheduling techniques, aid the subordinate in gaining improved understanding of a new technical process, or provide assistance in the development of a more realistic budget, forecast, or estimate.

The accomplishment report is thus used as an action plan for providing learning to the subordinate. It identifies the areas in which his developmental experience should be concentrated during the period immediately ahead. Guidance and counseling are everyday activities, not something that occurs at set, periodic intervals.

The accomplishment report is not likely to serve most personnel needs very adequately, in any event. Some organizations attempt to force the service of personnel needs by insisting that the supervising manager apply appraisal data on a normal distribution curve or other statistical basis. This policy is self-defeating, for it leads to the manipulation of these reports, consciously or unconsciously, to justify salary adjustment actions.

A well-designed salary administration plan is not dependent on precise performance discrimination for effective maintenance. Broad performance discrimination is all that is required. The most effective performers should be granted increases more frequently than others in the organization. A moderately effective group might be moved along at a lesser rate with a greater time interval between adjustments. The plodders, but people the organization desires to retain, might be moved along at a still slower pace, in terms of both percentage of adjustment and timing. Proven ineffectuals should be encouraged to leave and should not receive salary increases. Maintaining an up-to-date structure, an effective distribution within the salary grade, and an appropriately arrived-at salary increase fund will normally suffice to maintain an equitable salary administration program. This is not to imply that salary adjustments should not be related to performance. It merely means that salary administration decisions cannot be made on a basis that tries to refine a judgmental process into an exact science.

Executive incentive award decisions follow a similar pattern. Provided overall corporate profit performance justifies incentive payout, the variables become: (1) divisional performance against expectations; (2) unit performance against expectations; and, finally, (3) individual performance against expectations. Once again, gross performance discriminations are normally all that are required for award determination purposes. Instead of having a time payout variable, performance discrimination is made and applied against variable dollar payout.

Executive replacement planning requires an approach that extends considerably beyond current performance results. Performance evaluation is only one element in an effective program. Other elements of replacement planning revert back to the strategic planning process, the examination of constraints, the projections of the organization structure into the future, and projections of position specifications into that same future. Analysis of performance in terms of functional and operational competence, leadership style, interpersonal capability, and consideration of individual personal objectives enters into executive replacement. Much of this information is not available in typical appraisal reports and accordingly must be developed by different means. Absence of appraisal data poses minor constraints in this regard, but certainly these are not insurmountable.

SUMMARY

Performance appraisal is a by-product of an effective approach to the management of human effort. Since the basic managerial job is to organize human resources to achieve enterprise purposes, emphasis should be placed on the design of a totally integrated, systematic approach to management. Given such an approach, management can effectively utilize individual or group goal-setting methodology. The existence, however, of a goal-setting program and an appraisal system based thereon is not, in itself, a guarantee of managerial effectiveness.

Effective management has many components. The design of a systematic approach involves making certain assumptions about the nature of human endeavor and, in particular, about human motivation. On the basis of the findings of others, it has been suggested in this chapter that motivation is an innate characteristic of human beings. Management can create conditions to channel this motivation in the direction of organization objectives. To do so requires recognition of individual needs and a measure of compatibility between individual and organizational objectives.

An integrated approach to management requires attention to the totality of the process. The character of the management climate, the structure of enterprise purpose and strategic plans, the establishment of organization objectives, the effectiveness of organization, the design of control systems, and the effective use of rewards all require attention. A limited examination of each area points to a few of the considerations warranting further attention if the attempt to manage successfully is to yield results.

chapter 27

Appraising Performance
for Incentive Purposes

RONALD G. FOSTER   *Vice President, Marketing, Worthington Pump International, Mountainside, New Jersey*

In ancient Rome, spectators appraised the performance of combatants with a turn of the thumb—when it was raised upward, the incentive payoff was life, and the consequences of the downward turn have been well documented.

In the modern business world, hitting the incentive jackpot may not be a life-or-death matter, but the ego and financial enhancement at stake can be a very effective executive motivator.

Over the past two decades increasing numbers of companies have embraced various types of incentive compensation plans in the hope of sparking their key management members to raised levels of performance and, in turn, of improving corporate results.

One AMA study in the late sixties showed incentive compensation plans in use by 45 percent of United States commercial and industrial firms, and *Business Management* in its February, 1970, issue recorded 78 of *Fortune's* top 100 industrials using incentive award plans. The motivational promise of such plans has indeed taken hold on the United States business scene.

On the other hand, the amazing growth curve of incentive-plan use in industry has been unable to mask the disenchantment of many former believers. In a growing number of companies a search is under way for means of discarding or replacing incentive programs which, despite the promise, have proven heavy in cost and light in motivation. Search for the answer to why some plans suffer an early flameout while others burn more brightly with time, and a lengthy list of reasons is certain to turn up. On close examination, however, the common denominator, *performance appraisal*—its use or misuse, its application or misapplication, its simplicity or sophistication—will surface repeatedly as the primary factor in the success or failure of an incentive plan.

Any employee, from the president to the sweeper, relishes a bonus, but emotions vary from disinterest to disappointment, from doubt to distrust, when bonus rewards begin fluctuating with no apparent relation to the individual's efforts and achievements. From the payout side of the ledger, most boards of directors are not unwilling to reserve a generous percentage of profits for incentive-plan payouts, but when results are not forthcoming, serious misgivings arise.

Basically an incentive plan proposes to propel the corporation forward to the achievement of certain goals by motivating executives to achieve subgoals or derivative individual goals related directly to their functional duties. In this sense, an incentive plan should effect a merger of an individual's self-interest and corporate interests. By stretching for a sizable bonus reward that can increase greatly his material well-being, the executive will be accomplishing significant results which, when combined with those of his peers, will, it is hoped, add up to the accomplishment of corporate goals.

This goal-setting approach provides the basis for appraising performance, corporate and individual, and greatly enhances the chances for successful use of an incentive plan by forging a link between achievement and reward which can be more readily understood, objectively administered, and of greater motivational value than other more traditional performance appraisal systems.

PERFORMANCE APPRAISAL METHODS IN INCENTIVE PLANS

To appreciate some of the difficulties of appraising performance in incentive plans and the effects on motivation which may result from these difficulties, let us examine some approaches that have been tried.

As with many new devices dropped in top management circles, many of the first incentive-plan proposals were undertaken conservatively with a one-toe-in-the-water approach. Typically, a board of directors was asked to allocate a certain percentage of profit dollars to reward the achievements of a select group of management after acceptable levels of stockholders' equity, return on capital, etc., were met. After the auditors left and the board of directors was satisfied that the listed requirements had been met, the president was awarded a bonus plus a sum for distribution on a discretionary basis to his select group of managers.

Such a system does have merit. It promotes, to some degree, a feeling of teamwork and perhaps a certain *esprit de corps* among the chosen few. But the inequities fault the system. First of all, rewards are after the fact—profit sharing, not incentive. Few know whether bonuses will be paid, or how much, or to whom and why. Conspicuously absent is the motivational-pull factor—the demanding conscience throughout the year to do more, to accomplish specific results in order to reap the bonus carrot. Additionally, more often than not the president parcels out bonus rewards using a general performance rating system with coverall labels such as "outstanding," "good," and "average"; this method often undermines fairness in relating bonuses to actual performance.

Such an appraisal system is full of pitfalls—most conspicuously, the halo effect.

Perhaps the engineering manager who worked late every night but accomplished little was rewarded heavily in relation to the sales manager who was rarely visible but produced significant volume results in a tight market.

Additionally, there is a tendency toward leveling evaluations, often based on the executive's estimate of his own performance. "Anyone who works for me has to be above average in performance" translated means "I'm above average, ergo. . . , etc.," which of course may or may not be true, but it is doubtful that his subordinates all perform at the same level.

Somewhat related to this appraisal trap is blind obedience to the bell-shaped-curve lore, where the evaluating executive proceeds with some preset appraisal guide, such as that 80 percent of the incentive group must be average, 10 percent above, and 10 percent below, and forces his evaluations accordingly.

In an effort to avoid the subjectivity defects of such appraisal systems, some companies took refuge in a purely mechanical system which related the accomplishment of corporate goals directly to the participant's salary. For example, if the corporate goal of 15 percent return on assets was met, participants would receive a bonus of 10 percent of current salary; a 16 percent return on assets yielded a bonus of 20 percent of current salary; and so on, up to a maximum bonus of perhaps 50 percent. Such an incentive plan avoids the possible inequities of subjective individual performance appraisal with an "all win or all lose" team approach, but in so doing it eliminates the individual motivational pull entirely.

More than one company has seen some of their best-performing executives head for greener pastures when year-end results yielded no bonus awards because others on the team rested their oars.

Other incentive plans, in searching for a meaningful link between performance and payout, resorted to the once popular trait appraisal system frequently used in determining base-salary increases. This device purported to measure performance by rating the individual in terms of a checklist of personal traits such as drive, energy, personality, analytical ability, etc.

Unfortunately, many of these personal characteristics frequently had little bearing on the functions the individual was supposed to perform and often bore no relation to actual results.

As we have seen, however, despite the failure of these various performance appraisal systems to squarely match performance with payout, the use of incentive plans in industry continued to grow. Perhaps one of the reasons was that managements had initially established one link between performance and incentive payments in setting corporate performance goals and felt that what they needed now was a method of also tying individual performance goals to incentive payments.

The aid that the much maligned incentive systems needed emerged gradually during the sixties as persistent managements began borrowing techniques from fields such as organizational planning and long-range planning and developing a business management system widely called "management by objectives."

In most corporations it had become standard practice not only to establish certain financial goals for the year ahead, but also to prepare business plans reflecting the corporate goals several years in advance. The central idea in the management by objectives technique was to develop specific functional objectives for each executive which, when combined, would enable the corporation to achieve its goals. Individual performance, in turn, would be measured simply by determining whether these preset objectives were attained, or the degree of their attainment.

Incorporating the new management by objectives system into existing incentive plans as the performance-measuring device appealed to plan administrators and participants alike. On the surface, it promised to come the closest to equating actual performance results with incentive awards. Furthermore, it could be easily explained and accepted as a rational and equitable system for bonus payments, it facilitated objective rather than subjective or discretionary judgments, and it provided clear justification for the incentive plan's very existence—to accomplish the business goals of the corporation.

ONE APPROACH

That the benefits described above can result from the proper incorporation of the management by objectives system into incentive plans has now been demonstrated by many firms.   But, as all practitioners have discovered, there are many hazards that must be guarded against, and considerable time, effort, and thought must be expended on the road to truly successful application.

Establishing Individual Objectives.   The process of establishing individual objectives can be divided into six key steps:

1. *Review the organization's business plans both for the short term (current year) and for the long term.*   Most progressive companies today have built into their business as standard operating procedure not only a budget and operating plan for the coming year, but also a longer-range plan showing the direction they wish to take over the next three, five, or perhaps ten years.   Obviously, the individual objectives set must be in harmony with these plans or the organization can be torn apart with individuals hotly pursuing goals north, east, and west when the corporate goals lie south.

2. *Review the individual's current position in the organization.*   What functions is he held accountable for?   A sales manager typically is held accountable for achieving certain volume goals, but it is pretty difficult, if not unfair, to set product profitability objectives for him if the price-setting authority rests with others in the organization.

3. *Separate the principal functions an individual is accountable for into specific objectives.*   This should be done, of course, in the context of the company's short- and long-range business plan.   Thus, an engineering manager accountable in broad terminology for planning and developing new products might have these two very specific objectives among others in the coming year:

   a. Complete the design of new product X and release for manufacture 5/1/72.

   b. Complete research program on product Y by 12/1/72.

Note that the first objective relates to the current year's business plan, while the second objective may relate to the company's longer-range plan of introducing product Y in 1975.

4. *Determine what means of measurement can best be used to determine accomplishment of the objective.* Finite measures such as ratios, raw data, and target dates are commonly used wherever appropriate.

> "Increase number of dealers from 700 to 800." (Goal for sales manager)
> "Reduce accounts receivable by 15 percent." (Goal for comptroller)
> "Complete initial production run of product X by 7/15/72." (Goal for manufacturing manager)

Many important objectives, such as those concerned with development of subordinates, can hardly be measured in quantitative terms.   Yet the difficulty of applying yardsticks to such objectives should not preclude their inclusion. Even for objectives such as management development certain nonfinite measures can be agreed to, such as expanding the responsibilities of subordinates, rotating special job assignments, attendance at training seminars, etc.

5. *Determine what standards of performance will be applied.*   What should be considered good, commendable, or outstanding achievement?   Here again is

an obvious negotiable judgment area.   But if this judgment is going to be made at the year end, is it not far more desirable to reach agreement at the outset? Now the sales manager knows in advance that attaining the forecasted sales volume will be appraised as "good" performance, and that to reach the "outstanding" label he must stretch to attain a preset figure—20 percent beyond budget.

6. *Weight each stated objective.*   Individual objectives vary in importance. Some may be of modest priority, others of top priority.   Accomplishment of the objectives should be weighted accordingly.   This can be done in a number of different ways (one method is illustrated in Table 1); but regardless of the method used, such weighting should provide a clear understanding for the participant of the relative emphasis his boss will apply to each objective in the year-end appraisal process.

Structuring Objectives in Incentive Compensation Plans.   One of the initial considerations in the design of any incentive system is who shall participate and why.   This may involve a number of considerations which will not be detailed here.   For purposes of our sample objectives-setting matrix, however, we will assume that our incentive plan covers those whose direct impact on corporate results is easily discernible and approximates the 1 to 2 percent of total employees generally recommended by consultants in the compensation field.

Additionally, we will assume that our sample corporation has the relatively common organization structure illustrated in Figure 1.

Next, let us assume that the incentive plan will embrace the incumbents of the positions shown in the organization: corporate president (and key staff officers), division general managers, and their functional department heads.

As a further step, let us assume that corporate and divisional goals have been set—usually a mix of financial and individual objectives.   Now the division general manager, with his respective short- and long-range business plans prepared and approved, establishes the following *individual* objectives with his sales manager:

1. Achieve budgeted sales volume of $30 million
2. Increase number of dealers from 700 to 800
3. Establish fourth field sales region in Southwest
4. Achieve 20 percent increase in dealer parts stocking program
5. Recruit and train three new salesmen

To each of these objectives a measurement, performance standard, and weighting factor are now applied, as shown in Table 1.

Having completed the individual objective-setting process, complete with preset measures of performance, standards of performance, and weighted factors, a scoring matrix similar to that in Figure 2 can now be devised.

Figure 1.   Organization chart.

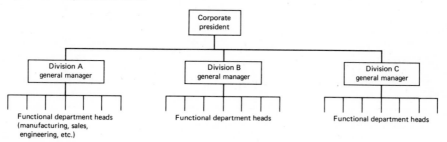

TABLE 1 Individual Objectives

Objective	Measurement(s)	Performance standard	Weight factor
#1.......	Dollar volume	Budget = Good 110% Budget = Commendable 120% Budget = Outstanding	3 (Top priority)
#2.......	Number of dealers	750 = Good 800 = Commendable 850 = Outstanding	3 (Top priority)
#3.......	Field office leased Field office staffed Target date 7/1/72	Qualitative judgment { Good Commendable Outstanding	2 (Significant priority)
#4.......	Percent increase over prior year	+10% = Good +20% = Commendable +30% = Outstanding	3 (Top priority)
#5.......	Number of men Caliber of men Effectiveness of training Target date of 9/1/72	Qualitative judgment { Good Commendable Outstanding	1 (Modest priority)

In the year-end performance appraisal, the calculations might be as shown in Table 2.

Dividing the total weight factors (12) into the total weighted value (120) yields an achievement value of 10 points, or commendable performance of individual objectives.

The achievement value scale range 1–15 in Figure 2 and the sales manager's performance score of 10 are merely a convenient mathematical system which would be tailored to fit whatever bonus limitations a company decides upon in designing the incentive system. For instance, an achievement value of 15 points could equal a bonus of 60 percent of salary; 10 points would equal 40 percent of salary; 5 points would equal 20 percent of salary; etc., provided *individual* performance was the sole measurement to be used in calculating bonus awards.

Between the extremes of basing incentive payments exclusively on corporate performance and basing them on individual performance there is a happy medium which combines these performance measurements.

Combining Corporate, Divisional, and Individual Goals. Just as incentive plans

Figure 2. Scoring matrix for individual goals.

Achievement value	1	2	3	4	5 (Good)	6	7	8	9	10 (Commendable)	11	12	13	14	15 (Outstanding)	Weight factor	Weighted value
1. Dollar volume					Budg.					+10%					+20%	3	
2. Number of dealers					750					800					850	3	
3. Fourth sales region					Qualitative judgment											2	
4. Dealer parts stock					+10%					+20%					+30%	3	
5. Three new salesmen					Qualitative judgment											1	

TABLE 2   Individual Performance against Objectives

Objective	Actual performance	Achievement value		Weight		Weighted value
#1.	+10%	10	×	3	=	30
#2.	750	5	×	3	=	15
#3.	Commendable	10	×	2	=	20
#4.	+30%	15	×	3	=	45
#5.	Commendable	10	×	1	=	10
		Totals		12		120

fail to motivate individual executives if the appraisal is based solely on group performance (the "all win—all lose" approach), so do they fall short of their end purpose of achieving division goals and, in turn, corporate goals if the appraisal considers only individual performance.

Accordingly, most successful approaches to incentive plan design combine appraisals of corporate performance, divisional or group performance, and individual performance. This blending of individual, divisional, and corporate goals makes incentive systems work from the participant's point of view as well as from the shareholders'. Incentive rewards should accrue to the executive for his performance both as an individual *and* as a team player.

Normally, corporate and divisional goals will include specific financial objectives which, when integrated with individual objectives, might resemble the incentive matrix shown in Figure 3.

Now our sales manager has all the rules of the incentive plan before him. He knows in advance that his bonus will be predicated partially on his degree of performance against individual objectives (40 percent), partially on the performance of himself and his division counterparts as a team (40 percent), and partially on the performance of all executive participants in the larger team effort to accomplish corporate objectives (20 percent).

Figure 3.   Total scoring matrix: corporate, division, and individual goals.

Achievement value	1	2	3	4	Good 5	6	7	8	9	Commendable 10	11	12	13	14	Outstanding 15	% of incentive factor	Net achievement value
I. Corporate performance																	
A. Earnings/share					$4.00					$4.50					$5.00	20%	
II. Division performance																	
A. Profit (before federal income tax)					$6.0 million					$7.0 million					$8.0 million	20%	
B. Income/sales ratio					10%					11%					12%	10%	
C. Return on assets					8.5%					9.0%					9.5%	10%	
III. Individual performance					Net score from individual objectives matrix											40%	
											Total net achievement value						

Sample scoring for our subject sales manager in the combination performance appraisal might turn out as shown in Table 3.

INCENTIVE PERFORMANCE VERSUS REGULAR PERFORMANCE

As we have just seen, one of the basic differences in appraising performance for incentive bonus payments as distinguished from appraisal for base-salary increases is the reward combination based on team achievement in addition to individual achievement.   Another, but perhaps more subtle, difference should be the stretch factor.   "Do your job—that's all we ask" is not enough; "Reach beyond the norm" should be the premise upon which goals are set and performance is appraised.

"Getting the goods out the door" is not enough for the manufacturing executive; he should also be bending his efforts toward cost reduction, automated production methods, or supervisory improvement programs in order to reap the incentive harvest.

Nor can the executive expecting a bonus be content with a passive position as a member of the team.   He must be motivated toward synergism in his peer relationships to achieve group, divisional, or corporate objectives.

JUST A BEGINNING

The preceding examples are indicative of only one approach in appraising performance for incentive purposes, and the mechanical-matrix models are intended to serve the reader in helping him visualize the concepts involved rather than to suggest that some magic formula lurks behind the success of an incentive plan.

Appraising performance for incentive-plan purposes is a difficult, demanding process.   Fortunately, advances through experimentation with various performance measurement systems have brought us well beyond the Roman "turn of the thumb" approach to the current management by objectives technique.   In the final analysis, however, this technique, like others, is no substitute for judgment; on the contrary, it demands sound, unbiased reasoning and courage in every phase of its application.

Setting meaningful goals, measurements, and performance standards requires a penetrating analysis of all the complexities of the business environment and

TABLE 3   Total-performance Scoring

Measurement	Actual performance	Achievement value		Percentage factor		Net
I. Corporate Performance:						
A. Earnings/Share.......	$4.50	10	×	20%	=	2.0
II. Division Performance:						
A. Profit................	$6.0MM	5	×	20%	=	1.0
B. Income/Sales Ratio.....	12%	15	×	10%	=	1.5
C. Return on Assets.......	8.5%	5	×	10%	=	.5
III. Individual Performance:						
A. Individual Objectives						
Matrix...............	....	10	×	40%	=	4.0
Total net achievement value.						9.0

the current and hoped-for future position of the corporation therein, its products, its markets, its competition, its image, and its people.

Robert Townsend points out in his book, *Up the Organization*, that when he headed Avis it took him and his top associates six months to settle on one corporate objective.

Picking your measurements is no simple matter, either. Surely, you want to become "the most profitable enterprise in the industry." Are you going to measure this on net income alone, or on return on assets, income/sales ratio, earnings per share, or some mix of these common balance sheet indices?

If executives are really going to be motivated to stretch their team performance, where should the performance/payout standards like "good," "commendable," and "outstanding" be fixed? If financial measurements are used, perhaps starting with the budget forecast at the "good" level might be reasonable, but then what degree above that base figure should be considered "commendable" or "outstanding"—10 percent? Twenty percent?

Each management must make these determinations based on the characteristics and environment of its own business. Perhaps the market is shrinking, and just repeating the performance of the previous year would be an outstanding achievement and should be rewarded accordingly. Conversely, if the market expands 30 percent in a given year, a volume increase of the same magnitude hardly spells outstanding performance.

While an earnest effort should be made to set objectives which will have constant validity throughout the year, recognition should be given to significant business events which might require some infrequent adjustments as the year progresses. Thus, most practitioners suggest periodic reviews of these preset objectives throughout the year so that performance progress may be monitored and any needed revisions made.

The art of fixing individual objectives for incentive purposes is an equally difficult task and requires considerable executive courage in negotiating objectives, measurements, and performance standards with a subordinate.

Ever present in this negotiation process are personality tones pressuring for lower target standards for ease of accomplishment and high rewards, or, conversely, the rose-colored-glasses approach, where the standards are set so high that they become truly beyond reach.

Yet, despite these inherent difficulties in applying the management by objectives approach to incentive plans, it comes closer to the fundamental goal of equating performance and reward than any appraisal system yet evolved. As some companies have discovered, the expenditure of time and effort required to make it work is often the best investment they have ever made.

Part 6

Noncash Compensation

chapter 28

Relating Noncash Benefits to the Total Compensation Package

WILLIAM T. RYAN   *Senior Consultant, Edward N. Hay & Associates, San Francisco, California*

Prior to World War II, the compensation package of employees in manufacturing industries consisted mainly of cash, paycheck items—wages, salaries, and financial incentives or bonuses.   Noncash benefits in most situations were limited to those provided through employer paternalism and generally were applicable only to salaried employees.

Today, from 25 to 35 percent of the total compensation package is represented by noncash benefits, which include such items as social security, workmen's compensation, pensions, group insurance, supplementary unemployment benefits (SUB), time off with pay, and compensation not paid currently—deferred bonuses and the economic gain from stock options.   This growing list of items and the substantial business cost it represents are causing problems, misconceptions, and concern in many companies.   To illustrate:

1. There is considerable doubt that the noncash benefit part of the compensation package is contributing very much toward helping the employer to attract, retain, and motivate high-caliber personnel.

2. It is recognized that certain benefits do not meet the needs or desires of some employee groups to whom they are provided; in some instances they may even produce negative results, such as encouraging malingering and absenteeism or the early retirement of skilled employees who are in short supply and are badly needed.

3. There is a general and serious lack of understanding of benefit plans by the employees to whom they apply, by their families, and also by management.

These problems have been attributed, to a considerable degree, to practices that have been followed in establishing the noncash benefit program. In some companies, the program has "just grown," with additions and changes being made piecemeal. In others, many of the benefits negotiated for union-represented employees have simply been extended to salaried and other non-union groups without serious consideration being given to their appropriateness and possible impact. During the 1950s, as a result of the experiences of World War II and the Korean War, when wages and salaries were subject to government controls, it was generally accepted that the latter groups should receive compensation improvements equal at least to those that were negotiated for the company's union-represented employees. Some companies felt that the most effective and equitable approach was to pass on to their nonunion employees practically anything and everything that labor contract negotiations produced for union-represented groups. Salaried employees thereupon became subject to collective, mass treatment, with little room for recognition of their different needs and expectations or of individual performance and contributions to the company's welfare and growth.

In efforts to improve upon the situation described, companies today are recognizing that, for effective results, separate total-compensation packages are needed for different groups of employees. Each of these packages must be made up of cash and noncash elements, properly related, which specifically meet the needs and desires of employees in the group and also the needs of the company. In the typical manufacturing company, employees are divided for compensation purposes into six major groups—union hourly, nonunion hourly, nonexempt salaried, exempt, executive, and overseas—each of which should receive different total-compensation packages. In some instances, there might be subgroups of employees within major groups, and, for each of these, separate total-compensation packages would be applicable. Care must be taken to ensure that each package incorporates the company's compensation philosophy, is compatible with the packages of other groups of employees, and is effectively integrated with statutory benefit programs.

The following discussion covers some of the factors and problems involved in establishing and maintaining total-compensation packages for each of these six groups. It is contemplated throughout that each package would comprise logically integrated elements that would satisfy the needs and expectations of employees in the group and help the company to attract, retain, and motivate high-caliber employees at a total cost for each package no higher than that incurred by competing companies. Whether these aims are realized, and whether the growing list of complex noncash benefits are effectively related to the total-compensation package, will depend largely on the capabilities of the company staff responsible for developing and administering the program.

Recently, many companies of all sizes have centralized staff responsibilities for compensation and benefits under one division in the corporate industrial relations department. In the form of organization that appears to be most effective, the manager of this division reports to the corporate vice president, industrial relations. The division provides expert advice and assistance to management in the development and implementation of compensation policies and programs. Reporting to the manager of the division are professionals with know-how and experience in the fields of direct compensation, noncash benefits, the computerization of personnel and compensation data, personnel and compensation research, and the communication of compensation programs to affected employees. Through organization and staffing in this manner, the total approach to compensation can become workable, economical, and effective.

UNION HOURLY

It is of extreme importance for a company to obtain union contracts which will enable it to operate each of its plants or production lines on a competitive and profitable basis. Whether a company's operations are confined to one industry or whether they fall in several different industries, steps must be taken to guarantee that labor costs and productivity compare favorably with those of competitive industry companies. Accomplishing this objective is not easy, because pay, hours, and work practices vary, not only between industries but also according to contract conditions with different unions in the same industry. The compensation package, of course, is a major factor in this picture.

In certain industries, such as autos, basic steel, and containers, where costly-pattern compensation packages have been developed over the years through negotiations with large international unions, it has been difficult to avoid extending the same package to subsidiaries or divisions engaged in different lines of business. However, with profit margins narrowing and a growing number of companies operating in several different industries, it is likely that in the future companies will aim toward providing each operating unit with a compensation package appropriate to its industry.

The proliferation of noncash benefits has produced many bargaining-table problems for management. Pressure to add, change, or improve items comes from employees, local and international union officers, and even outside sources, e.g., insurance companies and their agents. In any negotiations held on the West Coast today, it can be expected that the list of union demands will include coverage for dental care, prescription drugs, and group auto insurance. Psychiatric coverage is popular in Detroit and certain large industrial communities in the East. Occasionally, "nonnegotiable" demands are made, covering first-of-a-kind items like sabbatical vacations and vacation bonuses. The list seems endless, yet it is still growing.

New benefit additions sometimes have resulted from a negotiating practice that was quite common in the past, under which the contracting parties would allocate a portion of the annual cost package, say, 6 cents, to fringes, with union representatives having nearly full discretion for determining the specific items to which the new money should be applied.

It is not surprising that negotiated benefits often produce disappointing results from the standpoint of the company. In one industry, the "improved" accident and sickness insurance plan provides for the payment of weekly indemnity benefits for a maximum of 104 weeks per disability for employees having two or more years of service. Over the past year, weekly benefits paid to the typical disabled employee have ranged from 75 to 82 percent of net take-home pay (average gross weekly pay less withholding for income and social security taxes). This high benefit level, which makes working economically unsound for some employees, has encouraged substantial overutilization and produced costs for the employer far in excess of normal experience.

The SUB plan in another industry can produce equally unsound results under certain conditions. It provides for an eligible worker to receive up to 95 percent of his take-home pay during a layoff for anywhere from six months to a full year, depending on seniority. Thus, for not working at all, he may receive only 5 percent less than for working 40 hours a week. Some of the newer, popular benefits may also fall in the unsound category, e.g., a good portion of the prescription drug plans, which are cumbersome and costly to administer.

Outlined below are some suggested steps that can or should be taken to establish and maintain a noncash benefit program for union-represented employees that effectively meets the needs of both the employees and the company:

1. Company officials must be made aware of the significance of the noncash program—that, for example, if the company's total employment cost for union hourly employees averages $5 per hour, possibly $1.50 of this cost goes to pay statutory benefits and those resulting from company-union negotiations. If the bargaining unit comprises 5,000 employees, the benefit program will cost about $15 million a year.

2. The total-compensation package should be analyzed to determine:

(a) Whether the noncash benefits, including statutory items, are in balance and are effectively integrated with the direct-compensation elements

(b) Whether the elements individually and as a whole are logical and meet the important needs and desires of employees and their families

(c) Whether any of the noncash benefits or cash elements are producing unsatisfactory or negative results, and whether any are incurring inordinately high costs

(d) Whether the noncash benefits compare favorably with the industry pattern for the area, if one exists

If this analysis reveals that the total-compensation package is not accomplishing company objectives, or that certain elements of the program are not meeting the needs and desires of employees, or that program costs are too high in relation to competition, then short- and long-range plans should be laid out and steps should immediately be taken to make necessary corrections and improvements. The alibis and palliatives that have discouraged and retarded constructive action in a great many companies, such as "It can't be done with this union," "Let's wait until after the union election," or "Disruption and loss of production are bound to result," should not be permitted to stall or prevent activation of a vital program of this nature. Experience has shown that surprisingly favorable results can be achieved in negotiations if problems are properly identified and a carefully planned and reasonable program is pursued vigorously.

3. The company's labor relations staff must be comprised of professionals who are experienced and knowledgeable in all aspects of direct compensation and noncash benefits as they relate to worker groups at operating locations. This staff should receive continuous support from corporate benefit plan specialists and economists, as well as from outside consultants, in order to keep abreast of developments in this rapidly changing field. Many companies today would be well advised to emulate the international unions in the area of providing their principals and negotiators with the support of competent staff specialists.

4. Procedures and machinery must be established for the effective communication of the essentials of the total-compensation and benefit program to worker groups. This is a highly complex, continuing program and it can be carried out effectively only if trained, experienced specialists are assigned to the job. Best results are usually obtained if an outside consulting firm is retained to assist the company's specialists and operating heads in both the development and the implementation of the program.

NONUNION HOURLY

In the situation under discussion, nonunion hourly groups of employees are frequently found both at plants where the main body of hourly paid employees are represented by a union, and at operating locations where none of the employees have been unionized.

At a plant location where a union has bargaining rights for production and maintenance employees, the excluded hourly employees usually occupy such positions as laboratory analyst, research technician, recorder, and production clerk. Since this group is susceptible to union organization and could have been included in the bargaining unit all along, many companies extend to the group the full package of cash pay and benefit items that are negotiated for the union-represented production and maintenance employees.

At plant locations where hourly employees are not represented by a union, management should establish in each instance a total-compensation package that effectively meets the needs and desires of employees and that is in keeping with industry and competitive practices. Lacking union policing and pressures, the natural tendency might be to neglect or delay making periodic improvements needed to keep this compensation package in tune with changing conditions. However, it is vital that the company ensure that all elements of the package are kept on a modern and properly integrated basis.

NONEXEMPT SALARIED

In many large manufacturing companies, nonexempt salaried employees can be divided into three groups—i.e., unionized employees located at plants, nonunionized employees located at plants, and employees located in headquarters, administration, and sales offices.

Unionization of plant nonexempt salaried employees has been attributed in a number of instances to compensation and personnel policies that left much to be desired. It has been frequently stated that past neglect of these employees by management "forced" them to unionize for protective reasons. Following unionization, management has generally found it necessary in contract negotiations to provide the group with a greatly improved package of direct-compensation and noncash-benefit items, patterned to a high degree after the package applying to plant production and maintenance workers. A number of large companies who have had this experience with white-collar unionization at some of their plant locations have elected to extend to other plants and even to headquarters, administration, and sales offices some or all of the compensation and benefit items negotiated for the unionized group. Whenever improvements in salary rates, cost-of-living supplements, holidays, or vacations, for example, are negotiated for the union-represented white-collar group at the plants, they are automatically passed on to these nonunion, nonexempt salaried employees.

One does not have to be a behavioral scientist to recognize the weaknesses of this practice and its negative effects on the nonexempt salaried work force. The purpose of the total-compensation package is to assist management in its efforts to attract and retain *high-caliber personnel* and *to motivate them*. High-caliber individuals occupying nonexempt salaried positions cannot be expected to be satisfied with across-the-board, general adjustments in pay or with noncash benefits that are geared primarily to the needs of production and maintenance employees. Such a compensation package and policy would have little inherent motivational value for the salaried worker.

Today's most successful compensation programs recognize that the white-collar worker is independent and prefers individual to group treatment. These programs no longer provide general salary increases of, say, 5 percent per year plus merit increases totaling from 1 to 2 percent of covered payroll. While a sum equaling 6 to 7 percent of payroll may still be expended, increases are based on individual performance and may amount to as much as 10 to 12 percent of individual salaries. The guiding principle of this system is that individual performance determines who shall receive increases in salary as well as the size and frequency of the increases that are given. Of equal importance, all employees are informed that performance is the major factor considered in this determination. Unsatisfactory performers receive no increases and are encouraged to leave. Average performers are encouraged under the system to improve their performance and thereby qualify for greater rewards. The same concept is applied in determining promotion increases.

In the programs of these more progressive companies, noncash benefits are adapted, to the highest degree possible, to the needs and desires of the high-caliber, high-performance group. This means establishing noncash benefit plans separate from those for the company's unionized employees. For example, options for receiving benefits under the pension plan might be more flexible; a deferred profit-sharing plan might provide for full vesting after three to five years of participation; new forms of survivor benefits might be available for employee election; a thrift or profit-sharing plan might offer the employee the opportunity to acquire shares of the company's stock or mutual funds, or to obtain tax-sheltered investment earnings under a voluntary-contribution provision of such plan; or partial withdrawals from individual accounts in a thrift or profit-sharing plan might be permitted to meet emergency needs or educational expenses. There would be little point in including in the package such benefits as sabbatical vacations and supplemental unemployment benefits, which appeal mainly to employees in the low-performance group. The high performers, who are anxious to move ahead in the company, are not interested in "make-work" or "time-off" benefits of this type.

Each year, the salary range structure should be adjusted to reflect changes in competitive rates, the cost of living, and other economic conditions. The other elements of the total-compensation package for nonexempt salaried employees should be thoroughly reviewed and updated at intervals of from two to three years, and employees of the company should understand that this activity is carried out according to a definite time schedule. In these periodic reviews, past experience is appraised, trends and developments are examined, employee suggestions are evaluated, and an exhaustive study is made to determine if and how the plan should be changed. Under this procedure, it is possible to maintain a sound balance and relationship between all elements of the total-compensation package for the group. Piecemeal "improvements" between these review dates should not be permitted; nor should the review be related in any way to labor contract negotiation. The review should be carried out independently, with the sole purpose of developing an effective compensation package for the nonexempt salaried group. Most labor negotiators have outgrown their old fears that anything management might do for salaried employees could weaken their bargaining position.

EXEMPT

For purposes of this discussion, exempt employees are those who occupy supervisory, administrative, professional, and outside sales positions, excluding those falling in the executive group.

The following paragraphs discuss some of the conditions, problems, and items which should be considered in developing and administering a total-compensation package for the group of individuals upon whom the future growth and success of the company are heavily dependent. Included are those of maturity and experience, those who have been identified as having a high degree of potential for early advancement to top management positions, and new employees who are in various stages of training and development. It is essential that the elements of this package be carefully structured to meet the particular needs and desires of this group; that the package itself be competitive with the compensation packages of other employers in the same industry; that individual performance and achievements be given recognition and be adequately rewarded; that the details of the package be effectively communicated to employees; and that the package be maintained on a sound and current basis. In the same manner as outlined in the preceding section covering nonexempt salaried employees, the salary structure should be adjusted each year to reflect changes in competitive and economic factors. Also, all elements of the package should be thoroughly updated at intervals of from two to three years.

Supervisory Group.   Supervisory employees are responsible for planning, directing, and coordinating the performance of work that is done by others. An effective total-compensation package for supervisors should satisfy the needs and desires of the entire group of employees who have been assigned and devote their full time to these responsibilities. If the unique situation of the supervisory group is not recognized, the supervisory compensation package usually will fail to accomplish its intended objectives. The classic illustration of this failure is many companies' inept handling of the foreman issue. While lip service has been given to the theory that foremen are an integral part of management, many of these employees are subject to archaic compensation programs that are unsound and unsuitable for individuals who are part of a company's supervisory group. For example, large numbers are paid the same single salary rate, without regard to differences in individual performance and achievements; many are eligible for overtime pay and receive vacations and other benefits as provided in the union contract covering production and maintenance workers; and some receive less cash pay than the workers they supervise.

It is vitally important that each supervisor understand thoroughly the principles and objectives of company compensation policy, that he be intimately familiar with all of the elements of his own compensation package, and that he be qualified to effectively administer the compensation package(s) applying to those he supervises.

It should be expected that questions will arise concerning the relative value of the company-paid portion of the total-compensation packages that apply to different groups of employees, e.g., the package negotiated for union-represented employees versus the one in effect for supervisory employees. An accurate comparison of base compensation payments, including premiums and incentives, can be made by simply examining the figures reported on W-2 withholding statements. But there exists no similarly straightforward method for comparing the value of noncash benefit items. Many companies attempt a comparison based on costs incurred in providing such items. This method has serious weaknesses, first, because it assumes that different benefit items which cost the same are of equal value to employees, and, second, because it disregards the fact that the cost of providing group insurance, pensions, and certain other benefits varies significantly, depending upon the ages, sex, and length of service of employees, funding policies, and investment experience.

A preferable method of assigning value to noncash benefits is the situation-oriented one, which bases the comparison on what the employee would actually be entitled to receive under each of the packages in the situations of disability, retirement, termination, layoff, etc. Even though an individual item in one package, say, the SUB plan, might by itself appear to be a superior benefit in the situation of unemployment, there might be items in another package, such as severance pay and a profit-sharing account, which would come into play in that situation and perhaps be even more beneficial to the employee. With the information made available through this type of analysis for all of the situations to which compensation and noncash benefit items are directed or may be applied, it is possible to draw a sound conclusion as to the overall relative worth of the two programs. Figure 1 illustrates the application of the situation-oriented method in comparing the value of cash payments and several noncash benefit items to a supervisor and an individual under the hourly worker program.

Administrative Group. This group includes many staff employees who are in a position to make valuable contributions to the company's success in the form of innovations and new ideas. Usually the needs and desires of the members of this group are the same as those of the supervisory group, and, accordingly, a single total-compensation package is suitable for both. In many instances, however, the true worth of the capabilities and potential of these individuals is not given proper recognition in company position classification and salary adjustment programs. Any arbitrarily established ceilings which preclude such recognition should be removed and, in addition, procedures should be established to ensure that staff positions will be reclassified upward as incumbents gain proficiency and are assigned heavier and more complex responsibilities. It is vital that these employees be eligible for reclassification adjustments in recognition of position growth, and also that they receive earned performance increases.

Professional Group. The professional group in manufacturing companies includes such employees as engineers, scientists, and lawyers. Usually, all elements of the total-compensation package developed for supervisory and administrative employees are extended to this group. Some companies, however, use the maturity curve method rather than traditional job evaluation and salary range techniques in administering professional salaries. Others argue that the maturity curve method places too much weight on such items as the attained age of the individual or his years of experience since graduation, and insufficient weight on the individual's performance and attainments on his job; further, that it leads to the granting of uniform or escalator-type salary increases and operates to produce uniform rates for large groups of employees, all of which promotes complacency.

Plans which have met with success in a number of companies use the two systems in combination. Positions occupied by professionals are classified into the standard grading structure, using job evaluation methods, and incumbents are eligible to receive performance, professional-growth, and promotional adjustments under the company's normal salary administration policy for other groups of exempt employees. Maturity curve techniques are then used in making interdepartmental comparisons and in determining whether the general level of professional salaries is in proper alignment with outside companies. The objective is to encourage a high degree of initiative and creative thinking on the part of these employees.

Outside Sales Group. A fairly large percentage of the individuals who become outside salesmen as young men continue in that position for their entire business career. While a few may be promoted to sales management or administrative positions and occasionally into other departments of the company, the majority seem to prefer a career in selling. If these desires are not considered

Figure 1.   Situation-oriented compensation comparison.

Cash Payments

Employee works all year

	Hourly worker	Supervisor
Base rate	$8,070	$11,400
Shift premium	150	—
Holiday premium	200	—
Sunday premium	290	—
Scheduled overtime	180	—
Vacation premium or bonus	160	—
	$9,050	$11,400
Less employee contributions to:		
Pension plan	—	120
Profit-sharing/savings plan	—	240
Major medical	—	40
Net	$9,050	$11,000

Supervisor Ahead by 22%

Selected Benefit Situations

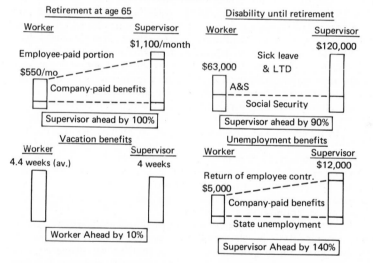

in developing the exempt compensation package, the company may lose some of its senior salesmen, or the morale and efficiency of these individuals may be impaired.   It is essential that the company's compensation package meet competitive conditions and provide this group with continuing opportunities to increase their cash earnings and to build equity through retirement, profit-sharing, and group insurance plans.

Incentive Plans for Exempt Employees.   Although seldom used effectively because of misconceptions, incentive plans have tremendous motivational potential.   Properly designed and administered, such plans can stimulate creative thinking as well as superior efforts and accomplishments.   A company cannot afford, however, to "experiment" in this area by "trying out" plans that may be working satisfactorily in other companies or industries. Each company's own situation, its management philosophy, and its total-compensation package must be studied and given recognition in designing an appropriate incentive program.

Experience has shown that once a company decides it is ready to adopt incentives, the program should be made applicable to *all* exempt employees on the same date. If the opportunity to earn additional pay is sound for one department or division, it is impossible to explain logically to employees of other departments or divisions why they should be denied the same opportunity. Whether one plan is appropriate for the entire exempt group or whether separate plans would be more effective for, say, outside salesmen or supervisory employees, are questions which each company must resolve for itself. For a fuller treatment of sales and management incentives, see Part 7, Chapters 36 and 37.

This is a complex, highly specialized area of compensation, and any company considering an incentive program should engage the services of a qualified consulting firm to provide technical advice and assistance, not only in the design and installation of the program, but also on a continuing basis to ensure that it is properly maintained and administered.

EXECUTIVE

Peering into the future to determine conditions and trends that will likely prevail in 5, 10, or 15 years is a prerequisite to the development and maintenance of an effective compensation package for the executive employees of a company. A model compensation package that effectively motivated executives of a basic steel company 30 years ago, or one that produced outstanding results in a major chemical company throughout the 1950s and 1960s, or even some of the more modern packages may have little to offer today as a guide to a company that is developing or updating its executive compensation package.

Today's compensation package must, of course, satisfy current needs and desires of executive employees. These needs and desires, however, will not remain constant; in all likelihood, they are subject to greater change than at any time in recent history. The characteristics—age, interests, attitudes, and goals—of the "new generation" executive offer convincing proof that no company can safely assume its present compensation package, however effective it may have been in the past, will fill the bill in the future.

In shaping their total-compensation packages to meet these changing conditions and requirements, companies are finding that greater flexibility is a vital necessity, and further, that it is becoming more difficult to maintain a good interrelationship among all of the elements that comprise these packages. For example, with the increasing proportion of younger men on the executive work force, many large manufacturing companies are amending their noncash benefit plans to make early retirement more attractive for executives. The pension plan may provide for an unreduced pension at age 60, plus a supplemental payment to age 65 when Social Security commences; provision may be made for outstanding stock options to be exercisable for, say, a three-year period following early retirement; the full amount of group life insurance protection may be continued to age 65 and thereafter may taper down to one-half or one-quarter of that amount over a six- to ten-year period; and comprehensive health plan benefits for the executive and his dependents may be continued for the remainder of their lives.

Of equal importance is the compensation package's attractiveness to "new generation" executives. Under the provisions of the Tax Reform Act of 1969, most executives will find it advantageous to receive the major portion of their total compensation in base salary and year-end profit-based bonuses, paid currently. As a general rule, deferring this type of compensation until after termination or retirement should be less attractive. The base salary, alone, paid to executives should be in line with the prevailing level of competitive-industry salaries and should represent a full reward for the attainment of profitable performance. The bonus should represent an additional reward, payable only for years when profits of the company exceed a fair return on stockholders' investment, with each individual executive's award being geared to his personal contributions toward the earning of such profits. Thus established, these two elements provide a sound base for projecting and developing the noncash elements of a balanced executive compensation program.

Stock options, both qualified and nonqualified, still afford the executive one of his most promising opportunities for building an estate. Only outstanding executives should be considered for this benefit. Small grants at intervals of from one to two years have been found preferable to one-shot grants of sizable amounts.

In the area of health and disability, more firms are recognizing that they can obtain Volkswagen mileage from payroll dollars spent in broadening their existing coverages for executives and their families. A comprehensive, basic hospital-surgical-medical plan, with physicians' charges paid on a reasonable and customary basis, is an essential today; inclusion of convalescent and custodial care under a superimposed major medical plan is becoming more common; benefit items such as group long-term disability (LTD) are being steadily improved; and diagnostic and preventive services, long overdue, are on the horizon for general adoption.

Along with Social Security, private retirement programs are being updated periodically to provide long-service executives with retirement income at age 65 ranging from 40 to 70 percent of their final five-year-average salary. A trend is developing to provide for adjustments in pensions after retirement, through the purchase of variable annuities, or a formula which gears adjustments to movements in the cost-of-living or wage rate index, or an automatic annual increase factor, such as 2 or 3 percent.

Supplemental retirement plans of the thrift or profit-sharing type can appeal to both the older and the younger groups of executives in a company. Employer contributions to these plans are usually invested in company stock which, on distribution, may be subject to extremely favorable tax treatment. Many of these plans permit participants to contribute voluntarily to the trust a sizable percentage of their salaries and to designate the type of fund or funds in which such contributions are to be invested, e.g., government securities, fixed-income corporate securities, or common stocks. This additional opportunity to accumulate tax-sheltered income is, of course, of particular interest to executives.

Indicative of the trend toward greater individualization of executive compensation is the attention being devoted to a restructuring of company death-benefits programs. In manufacturing companies, benefits payable upon the death of an executive may range from two times to ten times his total annual cash compensation—usually base salary plus bonus. These payments arise usually from group life, accidental death and dismemberment, and travel accident insurance coverages and from retirement plans and profit-sharing funds. In practice, they invariably provide either too much or too little. It has been estimated that in one out of four death claims, the proceeds are paid to someone other than the employee's spouse or children. A growing number of companies are taking steps to increase the effectiveness of this benefit by offering alternative programs from which executives can select the one that best fits their individual situations and needs. These alternatives, such as a "survivor benefit," may be provided under either a group insurance or a pension plan. In the interest of putting these benefits to the best possible use, beneficiary designations for each plan should be reviewed and updated at least once a year, and executives should be encouraged to give active attention to tax and estate planning. If necessary, the company should assist executives in obtaining competent professional advice from outside lawyers, accountants, insurance advisors, and trust officers.

Traditional time off with pay benefits for executives are being reappraised critically. Such items as extended or twice-a-year vacations to reduce stress or distress, or tapering-off work schedules extending over, say, a five-year period leading to normal retirement date, are incompatible with and do not relate effectively to other elements of an executive compensation package that is directed toward creation and maintenance of a dynamic and demanding environment. In reshaping policies covering these benefits, the "positive" is being accentuated. For example, instead of encouraging executives to relax or slow down at age 55 or 60 in preparation for retirement at age 65, everyone now is urged to think and act in terms of sustained, high-quality performance and contributions to the company's success and growth right up to the date of his retirement. Under today's modernized compensation program, attractive early-retirement benefits are available for those executives who are unable or who may not wish to continue working under these conditions until they reach age 65.

If administered selectively rather than on a blanket basis, perquisites can be used effectively to recognize, reward, and motivate executives. Admission to the executive dining room, like the assignment of the title of "vice president," connotes status and prestige for the individual, and a company should exploit to the fullest the incentive potential of this element of its executive compensation package.

A company's top management and board of directors should expect to devote more time and attention in the future to executive compensation. The cash and noncash elements of the executive package have become more complex, and the conditions affecting successful administration of this package are more susceptible to change than in the case of the compensation packages that apply to other groups of employees.

OVERSEAS EMPLOYEES

Conditions affecting international remuneration and its related problems are changing rapidly. Whereas United States employees sent abroad a few years ago were provided with a compensation package intended to establish them as overseas residents, today's practice is to regard such employees as mobile managers alternating between domestic and foreign assignments. Overseas employees are covered by the same compensation package as other employees, with certain temporary increments to offset the effect of any significant differences in taxation, cost of living, housing, or education of children.

For third-country nationals, the value of the compensation package should equal that prevailing in the host country or in the home country of the individual, whichever is higher. At the executive level, it should be equal to that provided to counterpart United States expatriates. Increasingly, pension benefits for this group are provided through an offshore trust arrangement.

For local nationals, the compensation package should be designed to satisfy the laws and customs of each country and to meet the needs and expectations of local employees.

Because of the complexity of international remuneration, most companies rely on outside consulting specialists to assist them in establishing and maintaining effective total-compensation packages for their overseas employees.

NONCASH BENEFITS FOR OTHER GROUPS

Many manufacturing companies are taking steps to improve the compensation packages that apply to their already retired employees and to their outside (nonemployee) directors.

Retirees. Retired employees receive widely varying benefits under programs financed in whole or in part by company contributions. For some, Social Security constitutes the entire package—a monthly benefit payment and Medicare insurance benefits. At the other extreme, the retirement package may include, in addition to Social Security, substantial annuity payments from both a pension and a profit-sharing plan, deferred compensation payments, major medical coverage as a supplement to Medicare, continued comprehensive health care coverage for dependents not eligible for Medicare, and a substantial amount of group life insurance.

Many companies have voluntarily bargained with unions on benefits for retirees. In a few of these instances, agreement has been reached to extend to bargaining-unit retirees the same improvements in pensions and group insurance benefits negotiated for active employees. During 1969, the National Labor Relations Board, in an unfair labor practice case, found that retirees are "employees" within the meaning of the National Labor Relations Act, that benefits of retirees are included within wages, hours, and other conditions of employment, and that employers must bargain over changes in such benefits.

Generally, improvements for retired salaried employees, usually made at intervals of from three to five years, have provided for increases in monthly pensions, extension of new health care insurance benefits to both retirees and their dependents, and company reimbursement of Medicare Part B premiums for the retiree and spouse if age 65 or over.

The cost of making improvements in benefits for retirees can vary greatly among companies, because of the ratio of retirees to active employees, the accumulated years of employee service preceding retirement, and the variety and type of benefits provided in the package. For this reason, many improvement programs for this group have been approached with caution.

Outside Directors. There has been a gradual trend among manufacturing companies to increase the number of outside directors and to decrease the number of inside directors. At the same time, corporations are becoming steadily more complex, and a heavier burden is being placed on members of the board of directors. Many companies are now evaluating the structure and composition of their boards with the aim of correcting any existing problems of over-age or ineffective directors. These studies are revealing the need for a better approach to compensation for outside directors.

In past years, when outside directors were often large stockholders of the company or officials of banks with which the company did business, the compensation of outside directors represented little more than a reimbursement of expenses incurred in attending meetings. While director compensation has been improved somewhat over the past decade, it is generally recognized that many members of this important group are still grossly underpaid for the responsibilities they assume and the contributions they make to the success of the enterprise. Outside directors today are typically paid an annual retainer ranging from $2,000 to $10,000, plus a fee of from $100 to $300 for each meeting attended. In addition, they are reimbursed for traveling expenses. In scattered instances, they are given an opportunity to participate under company benefit programs such as group life, travel accident, and major medical insurance. A growing number of companies are adopting policies which require the mandatory retirement of outside directors at ages ranging from 68 to 72 and which provide for attractive post-retirement benefits in the form of deferred compensation and continued coverage under group insurance programs.

For the future, companies should point toward the establishment of a total compensation package for their outside directors that recognizes the expanded functions and responsibilities of the board and provides a suitable incentive and reward for effective performance.

chapter 29

Types of
Noncash Compensation

GINO P. GIUSTI *Employee Relations Manager, Texas Gulf Sulphur Company, New York, New York*

Many employees think of noncash compensation as of secondary importance, but, at times, this form of compensation may be an employee's sole source of income—for example, when an employee is disabled, whether on or off the job, when he is out of work, and when he is retired.

In the early 1900s, both government and business began to develop noncash benefits to assist needy workers. Workmen's compensation, for example, was first established in Wisconsin and New York in 1911 to provide state-sponsored insurance benefits for employees injured on the job. Unemployment compensation first went into effect in Wisconsin in 1934. One of the first group insurance plans was written for business in 1912. In that year Montgomery Ward obtained insurance through the Equitable Life Assurance Society of the United States to provide its employees with life insurance, survivorship annuity, medical care, and short-term disability benefits.

The depression of the 1930s had a significant impact upon noncash compensation, leading to passage of the Social Security Act of 1935. This Act provided retirement income, widow's income, death benefits, and limited medical benefits.

During the first half of the twentieth century, both business and government established a myriad of noncash compensation programs. Some of the programs were accelerated by wartime wage freezes and by increases in income tax rates. Many of the noncash compensation programs are discussed below under four general headings: (1) legally required governmental programs; (2) employer-sponsored group insurance programs; (3) deferred compensation plans; and (4) other benefits.

LEGALLY REQUIRED GOVERNMENTAL PROGRAMS

Workmen's Compensation. The nineteenth century saw a major growth of industrialization in the United States. With the employment of more people in factories and mines, the problem of assisting disabled employees in the event of occupational accident and disease became more apparent.

Prior to the advent of workmen's compensation laws, when an employee was injured on the job his only recourse was to sue the employer. To collect any damages, the worker had to prove that the employer was negligent. Such a suit involved substantial costs, and it was difficult for the worker to prove negligence. The purpose of the workmen's compensation laws was to remove these hardships from the injured worker.

The impetus for workmen's compensation laws came from the federal government. In 1908 a federal act was passed which provided benefits for civil service employees injured on the job, regardless of who was at fault and without the costs and delays of legal procedures. This federal statute provided an impetus to the various states, and by 1920 all but six states had adopted employer liability or workmen's compensation laws. Presently, all of the states have workmen's compensation statutes covering some portion of the employers within their jurisdiction.

The advantage of workmen's compensation is that persons injured on the job are assured of receiving prompt payments for such injuries regardless of who was responsible. Under these laws, the employer pays the entire cost of all occupational injuries; the dollar amount of the employer's liability, however, is limited by the same laws.

The state workmen's compensation laws differ. In some states the employer has the option of accepting or rejecting the coverage. If he rejects the coverage, the employer is much more vulnerable to the employee's lawsuit. Some states require the employer to obtain insurance to protect the risk; some states allow the employer to carry his own risk and be "self-insured"; some states give the employer a choice of obtaining insurance or of being self-insured. As mentioned previously, the cost of workmen's compensation is borne by the employer.

The benefits provided through workmen's compensation include medical care costs, disability income extending for various time periods, and lump-sum payments for special injuries, dismemberment, or death.

There is a wide range in the benefits paid under the medical care provisions of workmen's compensation. In some state jurisdictions, all medical costs incurred as a result of an occupational injury are paid; in other states, only limited benefits are provided for medical care.

Workmen's compensation also provides disability benefits. Most of these benefits are limited. For example, an employee may receive a certain percentage of his normal weekly wage up to some maximum. This benefit may be paid for the duration of the disability or, in many states, may be paid for a period of up to 500 weeks. In some states, there is also a dollar maximum which limits the amount that can be paid out to any one recipient.

For disabilities due to dismemberment or loss of sight, schedules of benefits assigning dollar amounts for various injuries are provided. These benefits may be paid either weekly or in a lump-sum payment.

Death benefits are payable to the survivors of occupational accident victims in most states. The maximum amounts payable vary from one state to another.

Unemployment Compensation. As was the case with workmen's compensation, the impetus for the state unemployment compensation programs came from a federal statute, namely, the Social Security Act of 1935. The federal government wanted to encourage individual states to help unemployed persons maintain some purchasing power. To pay for this program, all employers with four or more employees had a 3 percent federal tax levied on their payrolls. If a state enacted an approved state unemployment compensation system, the federal tax was offset up to 90 percent by contributions to the state tax. Partly as a result of this federal action, all states have instituted some form of unemployment compensation program. In all but a few states the total cost of unemployment compensation is borne by the employer. The cost to each employer may vary depending upon his experience.

The state laws regarding unemployment compensation lack uniformity. Hence, the benefits and their duration vary considerably. Lower-income workers generally receive a larger percentage of their previous earnings than workers with higher incomes. The benefit period usually extends to 26 weeks. Normally, eligibility for unemployment compensation is restricted to employees who have worked a minimum number of weeks and earned a minimum amount during that period.

While unemployment compensation provides unemployed workers with a formal governmental plan of payments, there are many other formal and informal private plans in use. Such private plans may include severance allowances or supplemental unemployment benefits, commonly referred to as SUB plans. A SUB plan provides for company supplements to unemployment compensation, while a severance allowance generally provides for a lump-sum payment at termination.

Social Security. By far the most involved and most changeable program within the noncash compensation area is Social Security as established by the Social Security Act of 1935. Although it is legally required and all employers must adhere to its guidelines, Social Security must be viewed as an integral part of the employee benefit package, with particular impact in the areas of: (1) retirement benefits; (2) disability benefits; and (3) survivorship or beneficiary benefits.

Not only its impact but also its cost make Social Security an important consideration in the noncash package. Employer and employee pay identical Social Security taxes. In 1970 this was equal to 4.8 percent of the first $7,800 of earnings; in 1971 the percentage to be paid by each was increased to 5.2 percent.

Originally, the primary objective of the Social Security Act was to provide covered employees with a retirement income related to pre-retirement earnings. Over the years, however, the Act has been modified to encompass more than just retirement benefits.

In 1956, the Act was modified to provide disability benefits, provided the disabled wage earner was at least 50 years of age. In 1960, the age requirement was eliminated altogether. In 1958 eligible dependents were included to help determine the amount of benefits to be paid to disabled employees. The Act was liberalized in 1961 to permit all workers to receive reduced retirement benefits at age 62, thus making early retirement more attractive.

The Act was further amended in 1965 to provide Medicare for those employees over age 65 and otherwise eligible to participate in the Social Security program. Advocates of an all-inclusive cradle-to-grave approach to Social Security are making progress toward this end, as each change to the Act either adds to the value of the Social Security benefit or covers additional categories of workers.

One of the major employer costs in the noncash compensation area is the pension or retirement plan. Prior to World War II, a standard rule of thumb in development of pension plans was to provide about 30 percent of pre-retirement pay as a retirement benefit. During the two decades that followed World War II, the 30 percent level has been raised to about 50 or 60 percent. Most private retirement plans integrate the benefits provided by social security with their private plan benefits so that the two retirement benefits combined provide a 50 to 60 percent level of retirement income.

EMPLOYER-SPONSORED GROUP INSURANCE PROGRAMS

Group insurance is insurance issued in the form of a master policy to the employer and provides insurance coverage to employees. All the premiums for the policy are paid through the employer, although individual employees may contribute to the cost of the group insurance.

There must be a minimum number of employees to form a group. In the states that have a statutory minimum, 10 employees is a usual requirement. In most contributory plans (those in which employees contribute to the premium) at least 75 percent of those eligible must participate in the plan before the insurance can become effective in that company.

Insurance amounts must be determined according to criteria which prevent either the employer or the employee from choosing the amount. Such criteria may be salary, length of service, occupation, age, or family status.

Group Life Insurance. Group life insurance may take several forms. Typical plans include basic life insurance, accidental death provisions, traveler's accidental death insurance, and widows' pensions. The latter three, however, are generally supplemental to the basic life insurance plan of an employer.

Generally, only active, full-time employees are eligible for group life insurance. A waiting period is usually applied to new employees before they become eligible for insurance. Most companies specify a waiting period ranging from one to six months of active employment before such benefits become effective.

In some cases a time period is specified during which an employee must decide to apply for coverage. If he decides to obtain coverage after the eligibility period expires, he may be required to provide evidence of insurability— that is, he may be required to pass a physical examination.

The magnitude of benefits provided under group life insurance is determined in several different manners: the amount of the death benefit may be a flat sum or it may be determined on the basis of the employee's salary, position with the company, or length of service.

When a company provides a flat sum for a death benefit, the employee's beneficiary receives the same dollar amount at the time of death regardless of the employee's pay, position, or length of service. For example, all the employees of a company may be eligible to have life insurance equal to $5,000.

Probably the approach used most commonly is to base the amount of life insurance upon the salary received by an individual employee. For example, the death benefit may be equivalent to two times the man's annual earnings up to a maximum dollar limit.

In some cases, the amount of life insurance is based upon the employee's position with the company. For example, foremen may have life insurance coverage in the amount of $10,000 and production workers coverage of $7,000.

Another method used is to base the amount of life insurance upon the employee's length of service with the company. As the years of service increase, the amount of life insurance also increases. This method provides more death benefits for older employees, with the result that premiums for life insurance become more and more expensive, especially if the employer's turnover is low.

Group life insurance plans generally have a maximum dollar limit for individual coverage. The limits are established according to the insurer's underwriting standards and in conformance with the maximums specified in the insurance statutes of various states. Presently, common maximums range from $100,000 to $200,000.

Usually, group life insurance plans have a conversion privilege which can be used when an employee terminates. When an employee leaves a company, his coverage under that company's group insurance plan is generally maintained for 31 days. During that time the employee is entitled to convert his life insurance coverage to an individual plan. An individual policy is issued to him without evidence of insurability and the premium is based upon his attained age. Generally, the premium on the individual policy is higher than that under the group policy because the administrative costs for an individual policy are higher and the pooled-risk effect is lost when the individual is outside the group.

Group life insurance premiums may be paid solely by the employer, solely by the employee, or by the employer and employee jointly. There are increasing pressures for employers to carry the entire cost of employee benefits, and life insurance is no exception.

Group life insurance is generally purchased as *yearly renewable term insurance*. The protection offered by this plan expires each year but is automatically renewed without requiring evidence of insurability. The annual premium, however, may be adjusted from year to year in accordance with the experience of the group. If more benefits are paid than had been anticipated, the premium will be increased.

Another form of group life insurance is termed *wholesale*. In this plan, each employee applies for, and receives, an individual policy from the insurance company, there being no master policy issued to the employer, as in the case of yearly renewable term insurance. Wholesale insurance is used for groups in which as few as 10 lives are insured. The terms of the plan, however, are uniform and are determined by the employer.

As mentioned earlier, a life insurance plan may be supplemented by other death or disability benefits. Many companies have a basic life insurance plan which includes an additional benefit in the event of accidental death. The formula for determining the amount of accidental death benefit may be the same as or may vary from that used for determining the basic amount of life insurance.

Also, many companies provide an accidental death, dismemberment, and disability policy separate from the basic group life insurance plan. In those instances, the premiums are more frequently paid by the employee.

Some companies also provide payments to the beneficiary of an employee when death is incurred while traveling on company business. Again, the amount of this benefit, the employees who are eligible, and who pays the premiums vary from group to group. Generally, however, the cost of travel accident insurance is paid by the company, and the amount of the death benefit may vary from about $30,000 to a maximum of $300,000.

Some companies also offer a widow's pension. The amount of this benefit is in some cases based upon the employee's age, service, years of marriage, age of dependents, or some combination of these factors. Some companies also provide noninsured death benefits. These plans may be handled formally or informally and the benefit amounts vary. Eligibility for noninsured death benefits is most frequently based upon length of service with the company.

Group Health Insurance.   Group health plans provide reimbursement to individuals, in whole or in part, for expenses incurred for various medical services. Some of the plans apply to specific medical expenses, such as hospitalization and surgery, while other plans provide much broader coverage.   Generally, a qualified group must consist of 10 or more employees.

Group health insurance is an outgrowth of group life insurance and group disability insurance.   The principal features of health insurance originated in the 1930s.   Up through 1950, benefits were generally limited to hospital confinement and surgery.   Since that time, however, this form of insurance has developed into much wider coverage.

As with group life insurance, premiums for group health insurance may be paid by the employer alone, the employee alone, or jointly.   The premium is usually determined by the experience of similar groups during the first contract year.   After the first year, the premiums may be adjusted in accordance with the experience of the newly insured group.   The cost of health insurance is affected by the insured's sex, age, family status, earnings, and local costs of medical services.

The major provision under the health insurance plans is the payment, in whole or part, of the medical expenses incurred by the employees and their dependents.   The major categories of coverage under health care include hospitalization, surgery, major medical, and dental care.

Hospitalization.   Most hospitalization plans deal separately with expenses for room and board and expenses for other hospital services—e.g., laboratory work.   Under some plans, there is a fixed dollar benefit payable for each day of confinement.   Most plans, however, pay the actual charges up to a certain maximum.   In some cases, the maximum may be the hospital's actual charge for a semiprivate room.   The duration of these benefits may extend from a 70-day maximum to a 365-day maximum; in some plans, there may be a dollar maximum rather than a specified period of time.   Normally, a dollar maximum is applied to the other hospital services mentioned above.

Surgery.   Surgical expense insurance reimburses the employee for charges made by physicians for various surgical procedures.   Benefit amounts are usually specified in a schedule which lists the more common operations and the maximum dollar benefit which can be applied to each operation.   Some surgical plans provide benefits equal to the fee actually charged, provided that the fee is reasonable and customary.   Some benefits, such as maternity, may pay a fixed sum regardless of the actual charges.

Major Medical.   As noted above, hospital and surgical insurance may not cover full costs.   Also, other medical costs, such as for drugs and nursing home care, are not included in the hospital and surgical portions of health insurance. All of these medical expenses, generally after a certain deductible amount paid by the employee, are usually included in a major medical insurance plan.   The specific aim of major medical plans is to provide substantial benefits where medical expenses are large because of the duration or severity of the case. Some companies have a comprehensive medical expense plan instead of the hospital-surgical-major medical plan.

Where the major medical plan is supplementary to hospital and surgical plans, there is usually a benefit coverage gap between the basic hospital and surgical plans and the major medical plan.   This benefit coverage gap is called a "corridor" and represents the sum (generally about $100) to be paid by the employee before payments are made by the major medical plan.

Both major medical plans and comprehensive plans have a coinsurance feature.   The coinsurance feature requires the insured (employee) to pay a certain portion of the medical costs. Usually, the employee must pay 10 to 25 percent of the total medical costs, and the employer pays the rest. Another feature common to both types of plans is a clause which limits duplication of benefits which might occur if the employee is eligible for medical benefits through other sources.

Most of the major medical plans have a maximum benefit ranging from about $5,000 to $25,000; many of the plans have a $10,000 maximum. The maximums may apply to a single claim or they may be lifetime maximums.

Dental Care. A new area of coverage which is becoming more common is dental insurance. In the past, dental expenses were reimbursed under the major medical plan and were limited to treatment required as the result of an accident. Recently, however, some dental plans have been put into effect which provide benefits for a wide range of dental expenses. Such coverage frequently has a maximum benefit allowance which could range from $1,000 to $2,500 per year and contains limits or coinsurance features for orthodontia and similar procedures.

Short-term Disability Benefits. Employers and employees were concerned not only about the payment of medical expenses incurred by an employee, but also about the loss of income, particularly when an employee is disabled by an occupational injury or disease. Therefore, plans were developed to provide short-term disability income benefits during such periods, and these plans can be considered as part of the employer's health care program.

Disability benefits are frequently based upon the employee's earnings and may extend for varying periods, generally depending upon years of service. A seven-day waiting period is usually required in cases where the disability is due to illness; no waiting period is usually required where disabilities result from accidents.

Short-term disability insurance premiums are based upon the amount and duration of the benefits. The makeup of the insured group in terms of age and sex, as well as the degree to which the work is hazardous, will also affect the cost of this insurance. Some employers pay the entire cost of this insurance; in other companies, the employees contribute to the cost of this insurance.

A growing number of companies are starting to assure their employees full pay during short periods of illness, whereas short-term disability insurance provides only a portion of normal pay. These full-pay, short-term sick-leave plans have been most common for salaried employees.

The duration of paid sick-leave benefits varies considerably, ranging from only a few days to several months. In some plans, sick leave accumulates and may be carried over into the next year. Some plans require a waiting period before benefits become effective; others do not.

Paid sick leave is normally not provided in cases of occupational injuries or diseases, since such cases fall under workmen's compensation laws. The plans used by some employers, however, supplement the legally required payments.

Four states have enacted disability benefit laws which provide some portion of income lost due to disability from a nonoccupational illness or injury (not covered by workmen's compensation laws). In some states—New York, for example—sick benefits paid by the employer may be offset against other short-term disability benefits. Statutory disability benefits generally extend to about 26 weeks and normally are paid for jointly by the employer and the employee.

Long-term Disability or Income Replacement Plan. Protection against loss of wages is a concern of all employees. Plans designed to remove this concern include: guaranteed annual wage, supplemental unemployment benefit, sick pay, and disability pension.

An emerging vehicle of protection against loss of income is long-term disability (LTD) coverage. Prior to the development of the LTD plan, most companies had various forms of sick-leave or accident and sickness plans but little in the way of income protection for prolonged, involuntary absences due to sickness or accidents. Compulsory benefits, such as social security and workmen's compensation, bridged some of the loss between full and zero salary.

Private plans other than LTD are also called upon to keep disabled employees financially independent of welfare, but these plans are of short duration. Many group life insurance plans, for instance, contain total and permanent disability provisions which will pay monthly installments. Normally, however, such payments are made for five years only. This still leaves a gap in long-range plans for the disabled employee.

A typical LTD plan covers the employee to age 65 or retirement and provides 50 to 70 percent of pay after an established waiting period has elapsed. The waiting period coincides with the period during which short-term disability benefits are paid. Most LTD plans include Social Security and any other statutory disability benefit as part of the 50 to 70 percent of salary.

LTD plans are either insured plans or self-insured (pay-as-you-go) plans or funded through a pension plan. Certain cost advantages are inherent in each approach, and the employer will, of course, need to investigate which method of funding best meets the needs of his particular company and its overall benefit program for employees.

The 1956 amendments to the Social Security Act permit disabled employees to receive full Social Security benefits as early as age 50. Also, many private pension plans have provisions to make at least a part of the employee's credited pension available before age 65 if the employee is totally and permanently disabled.

Pension Plan. Pension plans have made great strides since the 1920s, when only salaried personnel received any benefit at retirement and even that benefit was paid under very informal arrangements. During the depression years of the 1930s, there was a shift to the secure, but more expensive, insured plans.

World War II aided the growth of pension plans as employers, faced with a tight labor market, began to supplement direct wages with benefits. Payments to pension funds are viewed by the Internal Revenue Service as legitimate business expenses and, in effect, cost the employer only a small part of each dollar paid to the pension recipients. This is so because the return on the investment in the pension fund normally accumulates over the years, and the interest, dividends, and capital appreciation are nontaxable to the employer.

One of the most important influences on pension and other benefit plans was the National Labor Relations Board ruling in the *Inland Steel* case in 1948. The NLRB held that employee welfare plans were valid subjects for collective bargaining even though they were more complex in nature than wages or work rules. Labor took quick advantage of this new ruling, and the pension drive was on. In 1949, strikes in which pensions or other welfare plans were the key issues accounted for 26.4 percent of all strike idleness during the year.

Pensions may be funded through *insured plans* or *noninsured plans*. The most common form of the insured plan is the deferred group annuity, in which annuities are purchased for individual employees under a group arrangement. Under the insured plan, the insurance company provides complete services from administration to investment, and the pension benefit is guaranteed by the insurance company. As would be expected, because of the services and guarantee provided, the insured plans are generally more costly than the noninsured plans. However, the major reason for the difference in the cost between insured and noninsured plans is the greater investment flexibility of noninsured plans.

A noninsured plan is generally funded by a trust agreement between the sponsoring company (employer) and a trust company. The trustee oversees the investment of funds but obtains instructions from the sponsoring company as to when to make pension payments or how much need be placed in the fund for pension purposes. The fund is free to invest in equities, with the result that, during inflationary periods, payments into the fund may be reduced significantly or pension benefits may be increased.

In response to the swing of pension funds to noninsured plans, insurance companies developed two new programs: *deposit administration* and *immediate participation guarantee*. Both of these programs are very similar to a non-insured trust fund.

The trend in retirement benefits can best be summed up by saying that they will be larger in the future. Generally, pensions are tied to compensation and service; therefore, as compensation increases as a result of inflation, so do pensions. Also, plans are being rewritten with increases in benefit formulas.

DEFERRED COMPENSATION PLANS

Employer group insurance programs, discussed above, are examples of income received in a form other than current salary. Another class of such benefits is referred to as "deferred compensation"—that is, the award is made currently but payment is deferred to a later date.

These awards usually are stock or cash and may, in some instances, require the employee to purchase the award. Types of deferred compensation usually requiring purchase by the employee include: (1) employee savings plans, (2) stock purchase plans, and (3) stock options. Some awards that do not require purchase by the employee include: (1) stock bonuses, (2) phantom stock plans, (3) profit-sharing plans, and (4) deferred cash compensation.

Deferred plans were desired by employees because of their tax advantages and because employees hoped the award would appreciate significantly between the time of the grant and the time it is paid to the employee. However, the Tax Reform Act of 1969 may well bring about a shift in management compensation from capital gains and other forms of deferred remuneration to current compensation in the form of cash bonuses.

Most major companies are using at least one of the deferred compensation plans described below.

Employee Savings Plans. In an employee savings plan, or thrift plan, a participant voluntarily contributes a certain percentage of his salary and, generally, the company matches all or part of the employee's contributions. These contributions are placed in a trust and invested for deferred distribution. Many of the plans are open to all employees in the company after they have been on the payroll for some specified period of time. Generally, the plans limit the proportion of salary that an employee is permitted to save; 6 percent seems to be most common. The company's contributions are typically one-half of the employee's contributions.

The trust is established to invest the employee and employer contributions. In some plans the employee can direct the trust to invest his savings in equities or fixed investments, while in others all company contributions are invested in the employer's stock.

Employees like a savings plan because they receive the employer contributions and they hope for appreciation of their investment. A major problem with all stock plans is a possible drop in the value of the stock. Another problem is that some employees may invest when they cannot afford to do so. To the extent that an employee can afford to save, the savings plan does encourage thrift by using payroll deductions as a basis for systematic savings.

Stock Purchase Plans. A stock purchase plan is one wherein an employer provides the mechanism for an employee to purchase the company's stock on a regular basis. Generally, the purchase is made through a stock brokerage firm selected by the employer. All transactions are between the employee and the brokerage firm, except that the employee authorizes the company to withhold a certain amount from his salary and to send that amount to the brokerage firm for the employee. The employer generally pays the brokerage commissions and the administrative costs but makes no contributions toward the actual purchase of stock. The brokerage firm maintains all the stock records of each employee in the plan, including the accounting of partial-share ownership.

Some managements theorize that employees who are also stockholders tend to do better jobs and to understand the company's problems better. However, the depressing effect of a decrease in the value of the company's stock, if it should occur, may more than offset these advantages.

Stock Options. A stock option gives an employee the privilege of purchasing shares of the company's stock at future dates at the price prevailing at the time the option was granted. In the event the price of the stock rises, the employee will find it profitable to exercise the option; or, should the stock decline, the employee may elect not to exercise his option. Most companies limit stock options to a small number of key executives whose decisions are important to the success of the company.

There are two basic kinds of stock options: *qualified,* which are permitted a tax-favored treatment, and *nonqualified.* To qualify for tax-favored treatment, the plan must abide by Internal Revenue Service rules on options and be approved by the company's stockholders. In 1964 the IRS rules were considerably tightened, thereby lessening the financial attractiveness of stock options as a compensation vehicle. Under the new regulations, the price of qualified options must be equal to the market price on the date the option is granted; no price discount is allowed. In order to qualify for capital gains tax treatment the employee must hold the exercised stock for a period of three years instead of the six months previously required. Further, he must exercise the option within five years from the grant instead of ten years, which means less time for capital appreciation.

A qualified option is one of the few compensation elements that permit an employee to obtain capital gains income while he is still active with the company. However, with the advent of the 1969 Tax Reform Act, beginning in 1972 the taxes on earned income are limited to 50 percent and the maximum capital gains rate (after the first $50,000 of long-term capital gains) is increased to 35 percent. These changes, combined with the three-year holding period stipulated in the 1964 law, make qualified options less attractive as a source of capital gains income.

In short, a qualified stock option plan creates no income to the employee when the option is granted or when the option is exercised, but it can generate capital gains income when the employee sells the stock.

A nonqualified stock option plan is subject to fewer restrictions than a qualified plan. In a nonqualified plan, the option may be priced below market value, the time between grant and exercise dates may be longer than five years, and more recent lower-priced options may be exercised even if earlier, higher-priced options are still outstanding.   However, a nonqualified option is not eligible for capital gains treatment, and, when exercised, the option creates immediate taxable income to the employee.

Stock Bonus.   A stock bonus plan, like most compensation plans, may have many variations.   In its simplest form, an employee may be awarded a certain number of shares of stock in recognition of his valuable service to the company. If the award is immediately available to the employee, it is also immediately taxable; however, some plans do not give the employee the stock until a later date, thereby deferring the tax burden.

The stock bonus seeks to give the employee a greater stake in the company's progress and to enchance his motivation to increase the company's earnings and the value of the stock.   To the extent that executives are not forced to sell the stock in order to pay income taxes on the award, the grant makes it possible for them to make an investment which would have been impossible otherwise. Quite often, a stock bonus plan is complemented by a cash award plan.   Cash awards are another form of compensation and are generally geared to results. They are valuable to younger key employees in assisting them in providing for some of their immediate needs; they are also useful to the higher-paid executives in assisting them in paying the taxes on the stock awards.

Phantom Stock Plans.   A phantom or shadow stock plan is a long-term compensation plan involving use of a company's stock as a measurement for compensation.   This type of plan puts an officer or key employee in the shoes of a stockholder and provides him with an incentive to increase both the current dividend rate and the market value of the stock without having to put up any of his own money.   Stock units, or theoretical shares of stock in the company, are assigned each individual participant as an incentive bonus award.   Generally, when a dividend is declared on the company's common stock, the individual receives the same dividend in cash for each phantom share he has been given, or the amount of the dividend is accrued until his retirement, termination, or death.   Also deferred for payment is the increased value in the company's stock from award date to payout date.   Generally, such plans require that the participants agree to continue in the employ of the company for some exact period, such as five years, and that they be available for consultation and refrain from competing with the company during the period of deferred payment.

Profit-sharing Plans.   Some companies utilize profit sharing as one of their deferred compensation plans.   Under such a plan, the company may place a certain percentage of profits in a trust for payment to eligible employees. Awards may be declared regularly, if company earnings permit.   Usually, the maximum annual award, both to any individual employee and to the trust in total, is established in the plan.   The funds are invested by the trust for the benefit of the awarded employees.

Since the employee generally does not receive any of the fund until retirement, the award is not immediately taxable to the employee.   In addition, the profit-sharing trust is exempt from all federal income taxes and the employer is permitted to deduct his contributions into the plan on a current basis.

A profit-sharing plan is very similar to an employee savings plan, except that the employer generally contributes all of the funds needed in the profit-sharing plan.

Deferred Cash Compensation.   Continuous efforts by companies to recruit and retain top management personnel have resulted in the increasing use of nonqualified deferred cash compensation plans.   One of the prime reasons for adopting such a plan is that it acts as a holding device on the participant, since the ultimate payments are generally subject to the individual's continued service with the company. In addition, the payments are usually contingent upon consulting and noncompetitive provisions.

Deferred compensation plans typically provide for future payment to an executive or key employee in consideration of services rendered or to be rendered prior to the start of the future payments. The obligation may arise as a result of an individual contract with an executive or key employee or a plan for a group of employees. Another form of contract commonly used contains a provision, separate from the compensation clause, under which the executive, as part of his employment contract, is engaged for a specified annual sum to furnish consultative and advisory services for a period of years following termination of his active employment.

One of the primary objectives is to defer the compensation, and, therefore, the payment of income taxes, to a time when it is expected the executive will be in a lower income tax bracket and therefore will be able to retain a greater share of the benefits than if such payments were made currently.

OTHER BENEFITS

The more imaginative compensation managers of corporations realize that executives may be better rewarded by adjusting compensation to the executives' needs. This does not necessarily increase the compensation cost to the company. For instance, if a certain executive purchases additional life insurance with his after-tax income, would it not be better for the company to switch some current salary dollars to the purchase of the life insurance? It would cost the corporation no more money and the executive would have more money available for other uses.

In determining to what degree a company can provide such benefits to executives, one needs detailed information as to exactly how its executives, as a group and as individuals, spend their income. With this information in hand, the compensation manager can determine the appropriate compensation mix for each executive. New plans and services may be needed in a corporation to satisfy the demands of each executive—for example, personal life insurance, automobile insurance, homeowners insurance, and personal liability insurance, professional services in areas such as financial, tax, and estate planning, club memberships, transportation, regular physical examinations, etc.

If the corporation is substituting a custom benefit for current salary, then it is important that the benefit not become taxable income to the employee; otherwise, there may be no benefit in making the substitution. However, if the corporation, in addition to the payment of current salary, provides custom benefits, then the employee may be ahead after paying the tax.

Some benefits serve as status symbols and aid in motivating certain executives. Such items may be original art in one's office, or the availability of a preferred parking space, or the use of corporate aircraft. Many of the status symbols provide no additional monetary compensation to the executive; however, there is personal satisfaction.

chapter 30

Costs of Noncash Compensation

KENNETH H. ROSS *President, Huggins & Company, Inc., Philadelphia, Pennsylvania*

ROBERT H. SELLES *Huggins & Company, Inc., Philadelphia, Pennsylvania*

A retrospective glance at the post-World War II trend in noncash compensation costs relative to total payroll reveals that fringe benefits are no longer a small, insignificant appendage to the wage and salary structure (see Table 1). As recently as 1929 the only legally required payments were workmen's compensation and government employees' retirement. Vacations and paid holidays were usually limited to office workers, with the one-week vacation common and paid holidays considerably fewer than today. There were no old age and survivors insurance and unemployment compensation programs. The United States Chamber of Commerce estimates that if allowance for time not worked, including vacations, holidays, and sick leave, is included in noncash compensation, then fringe benefits as a percentage of total compensation nationwide increased from 3 percent in 1929 to 24 percent in 1969.

CHANGES IN ATTITUDES AND CONDITIONS

This phenomenal rate of growth has been the product of changing social attitudes and economic conditions. For the past quarter-century the economy of the United States has been identified with expanding industrialization, a rising national income in terms of real dollars, and an inflationary trend in prices and wages. Yesterday's luxuries tend to become today's demands. In this environment there has been a gradual extension of government-sponsored programs such as old-age, survivors, and disability insurance, unemployment insurance, workmen's compensation, state disability laws, and, more recently, health insurance and medical care for the aged.

Along with these developments in governmental programs there has been considerable growth in private programs of life and health insurance and pensions. World War II brought with it the excess profits tax and price and wage controls. However, the National War Labor Board did not prohibit increased employer contributions to employee benefit plans. Wage supplements of this type became a popular subject of labor-management discussions. Any doubts that group insurance and other benefits were within the scope of collective bargaining were removed in 1949, when the Supreme Court upheld the National Labor Relations Board ruling that the right of labor to bargain collectively over wages, hours, or other conditions of employment included bargaining over retirement and insurance plans. Soon thereafter, the Korean War brought about reintroduction of wage and price controls and renewed emphasis on employee benefits as against wage increases.

Beginning in 1942 (or even earlier for some plans), the Internal Revenue Code offered substantial tax-saving inducements to employers and employees to create "qualified" pension and profit-sharing plans. The principal tax advantages are threefold: (1) the employer's contributions to a plan are, within limits, deductible as a business expense of the employer during the taxable year in which paid; (2) the employer's contributions, although made in return for the employee's services, are, within limits, not taxable as gross income of the employee in the taxable year when paid by the employer but are taxable when received by the employee, that is, normally, after his retirement; (3) the income of a qualified "pension trust" or "profit-sharing trust" established by an employer and maintained by contributions of the employer, or of the employees, or both, is exempt from income taxation. These exemptions, together with the current high rate of tax on personal and corporate income, have stimulated the growth of "qualified" pension and profit-sharing plans.

Thus, wage and tax laws have had a significant impact on the development of supplementary compensation and have contributed to the fact that employer contributions toward the cost of employee life insurance, health insurance, and pension plans have increased substantially as a percentage of payroll during the past 20 years. (Refer to line 1 b. in Table 1.)

COMPETITION RESULTING IN INCREASING FRINGE BENEFITS

Ours is a society of rapid social and technological change, which in recent years has seen the development of new industries, new skills, and a better-educated and generally very mobile work force. The relative shortage of specialized technical and managerial personnel has resulted in competition, not only in direct compensation of employees but also in fringe benefits. This shortage has been an additional factor in the rise in popularity of employee benefit plans over the last few decades.

Present indications point to extension of existing arrangements, not merely to keep abreast of inflationary trends, but to increase benefits—and costs—in real terms. We have witnessed a continuous development of new coverages and increased benefit limits in group life and health insurance. During the 1960s great strides were made in coverage against loss of time or disability. In addition, there has been considerable interest in survivor-income benefits, dental and vision care, nursing home care, provision for prescription drugs, educational and tuition-refund programs, thrift plans, and stock option and bonus

TABLE 1   Comparison of 1949–69 Employee Benefits for 146 Companies

Item	1949	1951	1953	1955	1957	1959	1961	1963	1965	1967	1969
All industries (146 companies)											
1. As percent of payroll, total	17.9	20.5	21.3	22.9	24.5	25.6	27.0	28.2	28.0	30.2	31.7
a. Legally required payments (employer's share only)	2.5	3.1	2.9	3.0	3.2	3.7	4.2	4.7	4.3	5.1	5.4
b. Pension and other agreed-upon payments (employer's share only)	6.5	6.5	7.2	8.1	8.5	9.1	9.3	9.6	9.9	10.3	10.9
c. Paid rest periods, lunch periods, etc.	1.7	1.8	2.2	2.2	2.4	2.3	2.5	2.6	2.5	3.0	3.1
d. Payments for time not worked	5.8	7.2	7.3	7.7	8.5	8.7	9.2	9.5	9.5	10.0	10.6
e. Profit-sharing payments, bonuses, etc.	1.4	1.9	1.7	1.9	1.9	1.8	1.8	1.8	1.8	1.8	1.7
2. As cents per payroll hour	27.0	34.8	40.2	47.1	54.9	62.7	71.1	80.0	86.5	102.1	120.1
3. As dollars per year per employee	547	715	829	978	1,134	1,289	1,468	1,660	1,802	2,107	2,498
All manufacturing (67 companies)											
1. As percent of payroll, total	15.4	17.9	19.2	21.1	23.0	24.2	25.9	27.1	27.4	30.2	31.9
a. Legally required payments (employer's share only)	2.8	3.3	3.1	3.3	3.6	4.1	4.7	5.2	4.8	5.5	5.8
b. Pension and other agreed-upon payments (employer's share only)	4.1	4.9	5.6	6.5	7.1	7.8	8.0	8.3	9.0	9.8	10.5
c. Paid rest periods, lunch periods, etc.	2.0	2.1	2.7	2.9	2.9	2.8	3.1	3.2	3.2	3.6	3.6
d. Payments for time not worked	5.2	5.8	6.1	6.5	7.4	7.7	8.4	8.6	8.8	9.6	10.2
e. Profit-sharing payments, bonuses, etc.	1.3	1.8	1.7	1.9	2.0	1.8	1.7	1.8	1.6	1.7	1.8
2. As cents per payroll hour	23.8	30.7	36.2	43.4	51.8	60.1	68.2	75.6	83.0	97.8	115.8
3. As dollars per year per employee	483	644	768	916	1,078	1,220	1,415	1,591	1,766	2,058	2,448
All nonmanufacturing (79 companies)											
1. As percent of payroll, total	19.8	22.6	23.0	24.3	25.6	26.7	27.9	29.1	28.5	30.3	31.6
a. Legally required payments (employer's share only)	2.4	3.0	2.7	2.7	2.9	3.3	3.8	4.4	4.0	4.7	5.0
b. Pension and other agreed-upon payments (employer's share only)	8.3	7.7	8.4	9.3	9.6	10.1	10.3	10.5	10.6	10.8	11.2
c. Paid rest periods, lunch periods, etc.	1.4	1.5	1.8	1.7	1.9	2.0	2.0	2.1	2.0	2.6	2.8
d. Payments for time not worked	6.2	8.4	8.3	8.7	9.4	9.5	9.9	10.2	10.0	10.4	11.0
e. Profit-sharing payments, bonuses, etc.	1.5	2.0	1.8	1.9	1.8	1.8	1.9	1.9	1.9	1.8	1.6
2. As cents per payroll hour	29.5	38.0	43.5	50.0	57.4	64.8	73.5	83.5	89.2	105.5	123.6
3. As dollars per year per employee	597	771	877	1,027	1,178	1,342	1,511	1,714	1,831	2,147	2,537

SOURCE: Chamber of Commerce of the United States, "Employee Benefits 1969."

plans. Other fringe benefits provided by a number of organizations for all or certain classes of employees now include moving and travel allowances, company-paid or -subsidized cafeterias, housing, conventions, entertainment, membership in trade and professional organizations, club membership, automobiles, parking, company products, credit cards, legal services, investment counsel, estate planning, malpractice and other liability insurance, and time off for military or jury duty.

FEDERAL GOVERNMENTAL CONTROL OF PRIVATE PLANS

Increasingly, the federal government is reaching out for methods of controlling and limiting private employee benefit plans. While its initial influence on pension and profit-sharing plans was through qualification for tax credit, a definite trend is developing toward requiring certain benefit provisions before qualification is granted. Although still in the planning stage, there are constant efforts to have compulsory vesting of employer-financed benefits after 10 years and to collect reinsurance premiums to guarantee payment of benefits in full. Recently issued regulations on integration of private plan benefits with Social Security are complex and restrictive and indicate an apparent effort to make social security play an increasing role in providing retirement benefits at the expense of private pension plans.

A similar trend is noticeable with respect to health insurance. Constant pressure is exerted by some groups to have the Medicare program extended to all persons covered under Social Security rather than to cover only those 65 and over. Any such change would reduce the coverage under private health insurance plans and, in the opinion of many observers, increase the cost to the employer.

COST EFFECTS OF PROGRAM DESIGN: GENERAL CONSIDERATIONS

There are wide differences of opinion regarding just what constitutes fringe benefits and how their cost should be computed. Some employers consider workmen's compensation, suggestion awards and shift differentials, overtime premium pay, and similar items fringe benefits. Others do not regard total payroll as the correct base in computing fringe benefits, but would use straight-time pay for time actually worked. In a 1969 Chamber of Commerce study sampling 1,115 companies from all sectors of the economy, fringe benefits, including an allowance for time paid but not worked, amounted to 27.9 percent of cash payroll. However, if the computation base is changed to "straight-time pay for time worked," this percentage is increased to 34.1 percent; if overtime premium pay, shift differentials, holiday pay, production bonuses, and other miscellaneous payroll items are considered fringe benefits, the percentage becomes 42.8 percent.

Also note that, as a result of rising wage rates, fringe benefits as cents per payroll hour and as annual dollars per employee increase far more rapidly than as a percentage of payroll.

Cost Variations by Region and Industry Groups. Table 2 indicates industry and geographic variations in the cost of fringe benefits as percentages of annual payroll. These tables must be interpreted with caution. In addition to the general level of benefits provided, the age-sex-salary-service distribution of employees of a particular company will determine cost. Companies with identical benefit packages may experience substantially different costs as a result of variations in characteristics of the groups of employees involved. Also, certain

TABLE 2   Employee Benefits as Percent of Payroll, by Region and Industry Groups, 1969

Industry group	Total, all regions*	North- east*	East North Central*	South- east*	West*
Total, all industries..........................	27.9	29.1	28.5	25.7	27.0
Total, all manufacturing.....................	27.0	28.6	27.1	24.2	25.9
Manufacture of:					
Food, beverages & tobacco................	30.3	33.8	32.0	26.7	28.4
Textile products & apparel................	22.2	25.7	**	17.7	**
Pulp, paper, lumber & furniture............	23.9	26.3	23.9	22.6	22.7
Printing & publishing......................	25.6	25.6	28.6	20.7	24.9
Chemicals & allied products...............	32.2	33.9	33.9	29.0	25.1
Petroleum industry.......................	32.4	**	**	32.0	32.9
Rubber, leather & plastic products..........	27.1	24.5	27.3	**	**
Stone, clay & glass products................	27.4	30.3	26.1	19.6	30.6
Primary metal industries...................	29.9	31.0	29.3	30.5	27.7
Fabricated metal products (excluding machinery & transportation equipment)......	24.6	27.0	23.6	20.4	25.1
Machinery (excluding electrical.............	26.8	27.6	27.2	21.4	25.2
Electrical machinery, equipment & supplies...	26.5	29.2	26.7	18.1	23.8
Transportation equipment..................	28.5	29.4	28.2	22.5	33.1
Instruments & miscellaneous manufacturing industries.............................	25.9	27.6	25.4	27.0	21.5
Total, all nonmanufacturing..................	29.3	30.0	32.3	27.2	28.1
Public utilities (electric, gas, water, telephone, etc.).................................	30.3	32.1	30.1	28.6	30.5
Department stores.........................	23.1	23.0	21.9	18.9	26.5
Trade (wholesale & other retail).............	21.7	25.3	23.2	18.7	20.7
Banks, finance & trust companies...........	33.9	37.8	34.0	30.8	31.4
Insurance companies......................	30.3	32.9	29.3	28.2	30.1
Miscellaneous industries (mining, transportation, research, warehousing, etc.)..........	25.1	26.8	25.3	22.9	23.6
Number of companies......................	1,115	336	341	196	242

* States in each region are:
  Northeast: Connecticut, Maine, Massachusetts, New Hampshire, New Jersey, New York, Pennsylvania, Rhode Island, and Vermont.
  East North Central: Illinois, Indiana, Michigan, Ohio, and Wisconsin.
  Southeast: Alabama, Arkansas, Delaware, District of Columbia, Florida, Georgia, Kentucky, Louisiana, Maryland, Mississippi, North Carolina, Oklahoma, South Carolina, Tennessee, Texas, Virginia, and West Virginia.
  West: Alaska, Arizona, California, Colorado, Hawaii, Idaho, Iowa, Kansas, Minnesota, Missouri, Montana, Nebraska, Nevada, New Mexico, North Dakota, Oregon, South Dakota, Utah, Washington, and Wyoming.
** Fewer than three companies reporting.
SOURCE: Chamber of Commerce of the United States, "Employee Benefits—1969."

costs, such as those for employee pension plans, may, within limits, be varied from year to year depending on the rate and level of funding.

To the extent that noncash compensation is designed to improve the efficiency of employees by relieving them, to some degree, of concern over what might happen to their families in the event of their illness, retirement, or death and to help in attracting and holding capable employees in a competitive labor market, it is necessary to be able to pinpoint the cost of specific benefits aimed at specific individuals or groups to facilitate sound decision making in this area. Benefits must be related to costs, while costs are very much a function of plan design.

Use of "Waiting Periods" for Cost Control.   To a limited degree the existence of an employee benefit plan which provides some form of compensation against the loss of income through illness, accident, retirement, or death will have a favorable effect on employee morale and on the organization's ability to attract and retain qualified personnel. The rate of employee turnover is usually a function of attained age and length of service and is usually highest among newly-hired, younger employees. A considerable amount of administrative effort can be avoided by the introduction of a "waiting period" before the employee becomes eligible to participate in these plans. Such waiting periods, if employed, may vary from a few months to a number of years, depending on the plan involved. For instance, it is not unusual to have a requirement of three or more years of service or the attainment of a certain minimum age, such as 30 or 35, for eligibility in a pension plan. On the other hand, group life and medical insurance plans usually will have waiting periods of less than six months.

Funding Medium for Employee Benefit Plans. Any employee benefit plan may be insured by the employer or by an outside service or insurance organization. The choice will depend in part on tax considerations, but also on the employer's ability to absorb possible fluctuations in annual cost, including substantial claims in any one year. An outside organization is usually better equipped to provide impartial claims administration and necessary legal, investment, and administrative services and, most important, is in a better position to absorb large deviations from expected claims. Special considerations applicable to pension plans are discussed later.

COST EFFECT OF PROGRAM DESIGN: PENSION PLANS

Since pension plans constitute the most costly fringe benefit for most employers, careful plan design is of great importance in this area. In the case of union-negotiated plans the bargaining is frequently conducted on a "cents-per-hour" basis so that the cost comes first and the benefits are determined later. However, nonunion pension plans have an infinite variety of possible provisions and it is important for an employer to have some knowledge of the effect of these on costs.

Social Security Integration. One of the chief concerns of pension plan designers is to avoid duplicating Social Security benefits. Pensions may be integrated with Social Security benefits in a nondiscriminatory fashion so that the total retirement income, including Social Security benefits, bears a reasonable relationship to actual earnings prior to retirement for all classes of employees. What this relationship should be is itself a question requiring a decision not only on the level of benefits to be provided, but also on how benefits should be allocated between long-service and short-service employees, between those retiring from active service and those retiring after having terminated service, and between newly-hired employees and employees who were in service prior to the introduction of the plan.

As previously mentioned, an employer desiring to recognize the substantial benefits and costs of Social Security in designing his pension plan is confronted with complex and restrictive rules. Even though compliance with these rules becomes increasingly burdensome, the cost of Social Security to an employer (5.2 percent of the first $7,800 of each employee's earnings in 1971 and scheduled to increase to 6.05 percent by 1986) is sufficiently great that a private plan is virtually forced to provide relatively lower benefits on the first $7,800, or less, of annual earnings than on earnings in excess of the chosen limit. Furthermore, the maximum of $7,800 will be increased to $9,000 in 1972.

Normal Retirement Age. The determination of the normal retirement age has a major bearing on the ultimate cost of a pension program, since a change of a single year in the normal retirement age may make a difference of as much as 10 percent in cost. The question will arise as to whether such retirement age is to be mandatory. The effect on the company's operations of the loss of key personnel through mandatory retirement must be measured against the possible advantage of creating advancement opportunities for younger employees. The same type of question must be resolved with regard to the company's attitude on the subject of early retirement with or without a reduction in benefits.

Employee Contributions. Primarily because of tax considerations, most pension benefits in the United States are funded by employer contributions. Employee contributions come from after-tax dollars, whereas employers receive tax credit for their contributions. In Canada, where employee contributions to registered plans are tax deductible within certain limits, the majority of pension plans are contributory and employee contributions usually amount to 5 percent of earnings.

Although employee contributions will automatically reduce an employer's burden in providing a given level of pension benefits, they usually have the disadvantage of being fully refundable—invariably with interest—on termination of service before retirement. Furthermore, they add significantly to the costs of administering a pension plan, since each employee's contributions must be accounted for individually.

Vesting. The employer's sense of responsibility to employees terminating service prior to retirement also has a significant impact on cost. It is not unusual to give the employee a partial or fully vested right to contributions made by the employer on his behalf, provided that certain minimum age and service requirements are met. Conversely, the absence of a vested interest may also involve an indirect cost, e.g., labor immobility, the retention of less desirable employees, and difficulty in acquiring new talent. If turnover of employees is heavy, a provision for liberal vesting will be expensive, adding possibly 30 percent or more to pension costs. On the other hand, a liberal vesting provision could have virtually no additional costs if turnover is light.

Under contributory pension plans where liberal vesting is provided on termination of service, a high proportion of employees prefer a cash withdrawal to a pension deferred until retirement, even if this means forfeiture of any vested rights to accumulated employer contributions. Under these circumstances, liberal vesting provisions can be included in the plan at a less significant increase in cost. Forfeiture of vested rights is often incorporated in contributory plans to achieve the aim for which the plan was established—i.e., to encourage the accumulation of funds to provide a pension—and fortfeiture provisions are justified on the basis that the employer's interest in the welfare of a terminating employee after his retirement should be no greater than the interest shown by the employee himself.

Funding Medium. The choice of funding medium is significant from the viewpoint of benefit costs. Funds may be accumulated under a trusteed plan where the administrator is responsible for managing the invested assets, and benefits are paid directly from the fund. Any mortality risk is, therefore, borne by the fund and, indirectly, by the employer. On the other hand, funds may be deposited with an insurer under a variety of pension contracts, including individual policies. Under some of these arrangements the insurer merely plays the role of investment medium, with or without the insurer's guarantee to underwrite mortality and investment losses. Investment performance may be based on the overall performance of the insurer's invested assets or may be based on the performance of a separate account, consisting of pooled assets of similar plans. The latter arrangement often gives the employer the option to choose a blend of various types of securities, consisting primarily of bonds, mortgages, and stocks.

In the late sixties interest rates increased considerably, undoubtedly in response to a rising tide of inflation and the expectation of continued future inflation. Under these circumstances, employers questioned to what extent the relatively high yield on investments should be used to reduce employer cost of traditionally fixed benefits under a pension plan and to what extent investment performance should be reflected in upgrading pension benefits to offset the erosion of purchasing power of such benefits. A number of equity-linked products and cost-of-living-related annuities have been developed to add to the wide array of options available to the employer in deciding on the design which will meet the objectives of his pension plan.

Administration. A pension plan should preferably be designed to minimize the amount of record keeping and to maintain investment flexibility sufficient to optimize the investment return consistent with safety of capital. At the same time, the plan should allow the employer some latitude in determining the rate at which funds are accumulated in the light of current business conditions and within the limits prescribed by income tax rules and regulations.

The degree of flexibility in these areas will depend on the funding medium selected by the employer as well as the actuarial cost method. The latter determines the rate at which funds are accumulated to build up the assets required to cover liabilities incurred on account of pension credits for past, current, and future service. Such investment and funding flexibility does not detract from the fact that a pension program is essentially a long-term commitment for which the ultimate cost is determined by plan design, investment return, mortality, administrative expenses, and the characteristics of the employee group, regardless of the amount allocated to the program in any particular fiscal year. The amount contributed in any one year under a qualified plan affects the employer's tax liability for that year, his required contributions for future years, and also the investment performance of the accumulated fund.

COST EFFECTS OF PROGRAM DESIGN: MEDICAL INSURANCE

In recent years we have witnessed rapid increases in the cost of various medical services. This has been due in part to inflation in the cost of goods and services, but it is also a reflection of the introduction of more advanced medical techniques and more intense utilization of medical facilities.

The need for some type of prepaid medical services plan is now as great as ever before. During the last few decades, hospital- or doctor-sponsored and insured medical plans have been expanded widely. In addition, public demand is growing for coverage against all losses, including those of a minor nature which would normally not have a disastrous effect on the individual's budget. To control costs and prevent undue utilization of medical facilities, it has been found desirable to involve the employee in the cost of medical benefits. Such participation may take the form of deductible amounts and limited coinsurance. These features avoid the administrative cost of handling small claims, reduce the frequency of claims, and allow available resources to be channeled to areas of greater need, including coverage for costly procedures or long-term chronic conditions.

Open-ended liability under these plans may be avoided by imposing benefit-year or lifetime-maximum benefits, the latter often with a provision for gradual reinstatement. There are usually also provisions requiring notification and proof of claim within a certain reasonable time after a claim has been incurred.

Duplication of coverage under more than one policy has been found to increase claims frequency and should be avoided by a "coordination of benefits" provision.

COST EFFECTS OF PROGRAM DESIGN: DISABILITY INSURANCE

There are other benefits, such as short-term or long-term disability plans, where the size of the benefit has an effect on claims frequency. As benefits increase in relation to income, both claims frequency and duration will also generally increase. Reduction in the waiting period before benefits commence will have a similar result. It is interesting to note, for instance, that a long-term disability plan with a relatively long waiting period superimposed on a short-term disability plan which provides benefits during that period costs considerably more than a similar long-term disability plan which is not so superimposed.

The criteria for determining disability and the continuation of disability are largely subjective matters influenced by the attitudes of both the company and the employee. Nonetheless, these criteria play an important role in determining the cost of the program and the success of rehabilitating the disabled employee. In order to maintain some incentive to return to work, disability benefits paid to the employee must be somewhat less than take-home pay after various payroll deductions, and must be reduced by any other disability benefits payable under other salary continuance programs, workmen's compensation, Social Security benefits, and any other benefits to which the employer contributes. The importance of sound administration and claims control is brought out by the fact that there is a high degree of correlation between disability claims costs and swings in the economic cycle, which indicates the possibility that disability insurance tends to be transformed into unemployment insurance. To prevent a plan from also being converted to a retirement program, disability benefits as such should cease at retirement age. At that time, the pension plan should provide the retirement benefits, which ideally would include credit for the period of disability and hence represent a "full" pension.

COST EFFECTS OF PROGRAM DESIGN: GROUP LIFE INSURANCE

One of the oldest forms of supplementary compensation is group life insurance. The traditional form is one-year term insurance, without cash or loan values, and without the requirement of evidence of insurability on individual risks. In order to obtain an average cross section of mortality risks, the individual is required to join the plan within a certain time of becoming eligible, provided he is then actively at work, and the amount of insurance is usually determined by a fixed schedule, generally salary-related. If the employee wishes to join after the date when he becomes eligible, evidence of good health is required. Furthermore, successful operation of a group life plan requires the participation of a minimum number of eligible employees, often set at 75 percent. Employee contributions, if any, must be small enough to attract even the younger employees, with the balance paid by the employer, to prevent a situation in which some employees would prefer to buy individual insurance at lower rates, thus increasing the average cost for the remaining employees. This in turn would give rise to further dropouts, raising the average cost for remaining employees still further. An "assessment spiral" of this type would destroy the basis for a group life plan.

Inclusion of Pensioners. Costs are increased substantially by the inclusion of pensioners under a group life plan. Recognition should be given to the fact that the need for insurance is generally less after retirement, and benefit amounts should be graded down at or after retirement in order to lessen the impact on the premium rate, which is generally determined each year as a rate per thousand dollars of insurance in force.

There are a number of alternative methods of providing pensioners' insurance. Pensioners may be excluded from the term insurance portion of the plan entirely and the cost of future benefits may be provided by the employer at retirement through a single lump-sum premium. Whole-life insurance purchased in this manner does not result in taxable income for the employee provided such insurance has no cash value. One other approach is to use employees' contributions during their working years to purchase amounts of permanent life insurance, which will remain in force after retirement without further payment of premiums. The employer could then buy term insurance by paying for the difference between the amount of insurance to which the employee is entitled under the terms of the policy and the actual amount of paid-up insurance purchased by the employee.

Disability Benefits under Group Life Plans. One final comment on the effect of plan design on the cost of a group life insurance program concerns the inclusion of disability benefits. Before long-term disability plans gained wide acceptance, it was customary to provide for a monthly disability income under group life policies. This was achieved by providing that upon total and permanent disability the face value of the group life certificate, or a portion thereof, would become payable in fixed periodic installments. Upon recovery, the unpaid balance would then be reinstated as term insurance. This benefit has proved to be costly and less flexible than those provided by current long-term disability plans with benefits related to earnings and integrated with other benefits. Modern policies usually provide for a one-year or, more commonly, a long-term waiver of premium without any changes in the scheduled amount of insurance, sometimes with reduced benefits after retirement.

RELATIONSHIP BETWEEN WAGE ADJUSTMENTS AND FRINGE COSTS

Designing a supplementary compensation program acceptable to both employer and employees requires careful consideration of a large variety of alternative benefits. Limited resources must be directed into areas where they will be most effective in achieving specific objectives. Many benefits are salary-related. Any revision of salary scales, therefore, involves a change in the cost of noncash compensation beyond the immediate effect on cash payrolls. In the interest of proper financial planning and cost control, the employer must be aware of projected benefit costs and of the effect on accrued and future liabilities arising from current plan revisions and extensions.

chapter 31

Stock Options

DONALD R. SIMPSON   *Director, Noncash Compensation Services, Edward N. Hay & Associates, Philadelphia, Pennsylvania*

In the broadest sense, stock options are rights to purchase securities under certain prescribed conditions.   In this broad context, both employees and nonemployees may receive options, and the options granted may or may not be freely transferable.   This chapter, however, is concerned only with options granted on a discretionary basis to executives as employees of a company. These options have been the subject of considerable attention by the lawmakers over the years, and the laws have been changed a number of times.   Currently, executives may be granted two types of options:

1. *Qualified options* are typically five-year options granted at 100 percent of market price.   Exercised stock must be held three years to qualify appreciation for long-term capital gains treatment.

2. *Nonqualified or nonstatutory options* are not subject to special rules as to option price or holding period.   But neither are they eligible for special tax treatment.   Appreciation at time of exercise is ordinary income to the optionee and deductible to the company.

In addition to qualified and nonqualified options, restricted stock options were granted from 1950 until they were disallowed by changes in the tax laws in 1964.   Typically these were 10-year options granted at 95 percent of market price, subject to very favorable tax treatment.   Although restricted options may no longer be granted, many granted before 1964 are still in effect today and therefore must be included in any discussion of stock options.

A comparison of the major features of these three types of options, based on 1970 tax laws, is shown in Table 1.

TABLE 1   Comparison of Stock Option Types

Item	Restricted	Qualified	Nonqualified
Plan needed.........	Yes	Yes	No
Stockholder approval needed	No	Yes	No
Maximum years of plan	None	10 years	None
Employee status needed for grant	Yes	Yes	No
Continuous employment status needed	Yes (until 3 months before exercise)	Yes (until 3 months before exercise)	No
Discrimination permitted	Yes	Yes	Yes
Maximum term of option	10 years, if granted after 6/21/54	5 years	None (typical, 10 or 15 years)
Option price.........	Minimum, 85% of market value	Minimum, 100% of market value	None
Maximum stock......	None	None	None
Ineligible employees..	Owners of 10% of stock, unless option was at 110% of market value, option was granted after 1954, and option was not for more than five years	Owners of 5% of stock (10%, for very small companies)	None
Time limits on exercise	None	1 year	None
Holding period for capital gains treatment	2 years from grant, 6 months after exercise	3 years after exercise	NA
Tax on exercise......	None, if price is 95% or more; if 85–95%, ordinary income for difference between price and market value	None, except for tax preference income (which can develop tax if total preference income is over $30,000)	All appreciation as ordinary income
Company tax deduction	Any amount taxed to employee as ordinary income (i.e., normally only any tax for 85–95% discount)	None (unless stock is sold within 3 years, then any amount taxed as ordinary income	Amount taxed to employees as ordinary income

HISTORY OF STOCK OPTIONS, 1920 TO THE PRESENT

Prior to 1950. Until 1945, there were no specific regulations concerning stock options. Stock options were rarely granted to employees, and in the few cases in which they were, a distinction was generally made between "proprietary" and "nonproprietary" options. Proprietary options involved no income to the recipient at time of exercise, and any profits upon sale were treated under long-term capital gains rules, assuming the stock was held for the minimum period specified by the law. Nonproprietary options created income to the recipient upon exercise, taxable at ordinary income rates. Thus, proprietary options were roughly equivalent to today's restricted and qualified options, and nonproprietary to nonqualified options.

In 1945, the Internal Revenue Service took a position that all options were in fact compensation, in effect eliminating the special treatment formerly allowed for proprietary options. This position was later sustained in the courts, which led to the enactment of special legislation as part of the Revenue Act of 1950.

1950–1964 Restricted Stock Options. The 1950 tax law, as reinforced by the refinements of the Internal Revenue Code of 1954, established clearly for the first time a major incentive device for the entrepreneurially minded executive—the restricted stock option. Option price could be as low as 85 percent of market price, although full paper profits realized on exercise were taxed as long-term capital gains only if the option price was 95 percent. or more of market at time of issue. If the option price was below 95 percent, the difference between option price and market price at time of issue was treated as ordinary income when the option was exercised. Thus, the effect of the proprietary-option concept was effectively included in the law, with the added benefit of complete freedom to dispose of stock after a nominal six-month holding period, with profits treated at long-term capital gains rates.

The newness of the law establishing restricted options, and the potentialities for windfall profits, encouraged some unsophisticated managements to grant options unwisely, to the inordinate enrichment of "in" groups and the detriment of the stockholders. Many options were far too large for the circumstances and were really granted without full evaluation of the optionee's potential for future contribution to the company.

Also, the significant increases in overall market levels encouraged executives to seek option opportunities as a quick way to get rich. This attitude was reinforced by the fact that once a large option was exercised, the company had no further real hold on the executive, since the appreciation on the stock would qualify for long-term capital gains treatment after only six months. Often the executive was actually encouraged to change jobs, so that he could realize his option profits without negative reaction from his employer.

On the other hand, restricted stock options did offer what was then really the only practical means by which an executive not already wealthy could build up a significant equity position in company stock or build an estate. Virtually all other means required the executive to invest from current income, thereby reducing his standard of living.

1964 Tax Law Changes. Nevertheless, by 1964 significant pressures had developed from those who felt that the potential for windfall profits from the restricted options was too great, and that the abuses outweighed the incentive values.

Probably most compelling in the minds of advocates of more restrictive laws was the rapid growth of options. In a study of the use of options by 298 companies from 1951 to 1958,[1] the American Management Association found a threefold increase in the number of companies granting stock options, as shown in Table 2.

In response to these concerns, the 1964 tax law changes prohibited the granting of restricted options in the future (although already granted options would still receive the tax advantages to which they were entitled under the old law),

---

[1] George F. Washington and V. Henry Rothschild, *Compensating the Corporate Executive,* The Ronald Press Company, New York, 1962, p. 569.

TABLE 2   Stock Option Use, 1951—1958

Year	Percentage of Companies
1951–1954	11.6%
1955	12.9
1956	25.4
1957	27.1
1958	32.9

and a new tax-favored option was created—the qualified option. However, the qualified option was significantly less advantageous in most major respects:

1. The option could be issued only at market, not at a discount.

2. The option expired after five years rather than ten years.

3. The stock obtained by exercise of an option had to be held three years in order to qualify appreciation (at time of exercise) for long-term capital gains treatment, instead of six months.

4. An option could not be exercised if an earlier option at a higher price, either restricted or qualified, was still outstanding.

Short range, the most drastic of the changes—however well meant by the legislators to control abuses—was the specification that an option could not be exercised until all earlier options at higher prices had either lapsed or been exercised. The impact of this restriction was multifaceted. Since virtually all restricted options were for a 10-year period, any qualified options (limited to a five-year term by the new law) granted at lower prices during the years 1964–1969 were likely to be unexercisable—i.e., they would lapse before the higher-priced restricted options lapsed. For the balance of the 1960s, therefore, this provision eliminated stock options as a useful tool for any company which had issued options in the early 1960s and then had encountered adverse circumstances. Thus, many companies were deprived of a significant medium-term management incentive at the very time they needed such incentives most to achieve turnarounds.

For the 1970s, of course, the problem is not nearly as severe, since the executive needs only to wait out the five-year period for a high-price option and then exercise his lower-price option. However, by the 1970s, other limitations on the values of stock options had more than offset any gains achieved from a complete cycling of five-year options without the burden of 10-year options at higher prices.

Long range, the most drastic restriction was the requirement that stock be held three years in order to qualify for capital gains treatment. As Arch Patton points out in a *Harvard Business Review* article (September–October, 1970), it seems unfair to require the executive who is building a business to hold stock for three years when the trader in the market is required to hold stock only six months. In any case, the risk and expense problems created by this provision have been compounded by two other developments in the late 1960s, namely, the dramatic increase in the cost of money and the major bear market in 1969–1970. The combination of these factors has forced many executives into the agonizing decision of whether to be "disloyal" and sell the optioned stock (with remaining profits being treated as ordinary income) or to hold the stock and risk major losses if stock prices fall below the original option price. Unfortunately, most often the "loyal and faithful" executive who retained his stock in the bear market suffered serious financial consequences—the exact opposite of the intent of the company in granting options in the first place.

At the time the 1964 restrictions were enacted, many felt that options were doomed. After the passage of the 1964 law, AMA conducted a survey among companies having stock option plans to find whether any were thinking of cancelling their plans in view of the new law. Of 344 companies which responded to the survey, only one indicated it was abandoning its plan.[2]

Moreover, contrary to the gloomy predictions of 1964, more recent studies indicate increased use of stock options. In a 1969 survey, AMA found that of

[2] American Management Association, *Executive Compensation Service: Reports on Stock Purchase Plans*, AMA, Inc., New York, 1969, p. 8.

100 large industrial companies, 88 had qualified stock option plans.[3]   One consultant in a survey of 100 leading industrial corporations found that 92 granted options in one form or another.[4]   Another consultant, in a survey of 530 large companies with average sales of $883 million, found that nearly 80 percent used stock options as a compensation device.[5]

An Edward N. Hay & Associates survey, based on data current in late 1968, showed that 54 of 89 companies, or slightly over 60 percent, had option plans. Actually, these figures are slightly misleading, since the survey also showed a sharp difference in practice between industrial and financial companies, as shown in Table 3.   An interesting side note is that the three financial companies which reported option plans were all banks (three of 13 banks) and that none of the three stock insurance companies surveyed reported the use of options.

Thus, until the enactment of the 1969 tax law a clear trend was developing: virtually all companies whose stock is freely traded would eventually adopt option plans.   The few exceptions to this pattern were companies whose stock prices were either static or consistently going down.   Obviously, a stock option is of little value (or can even be of negative value, as discussed later in this chapter) if the stock is unlikely to increase in price.

1969 Tax Law Changes.   The 1969 tax law changes added two further limitations on potential option profits which can be significant.

Paper profits at the time of exercise are classified as "tax preference" income —i.e., items of income from tax shelters.   Since the law specifies that tax preference income beyond a certain limit will be taxed at a special rate of 10 percent, the inclusion of paper profits increases the optionee's potential tax burden. (The limit on untaxed tax preference income is figured as the sum of the individual's regular taxes for the year plus $30,000.)

Further, the 1969 changes established, for 1971 and thereafter, special ceilings on income definable as "earned income"—mostly wages, salaries, and bonuses.   For 1971, the earned income tax rate ceiling is 60 percent, and for 1972 and thereafter, the ceiling is scheduled to be 50 percent.   However, any tax preference income which exceeds $30,000 (without the extra credit for taxes) is deducted, dollar for dollar, from the amount otherwise covered by the ceiling.

Thus, paper profits can—in the extreme situation in which all such profits are tax preference income (e.g., for an executive earning $200,000 per year or more)—add a tax equal to 30 percent of profits (10 percent for tax preference directly, and 20 percent from the loss of earned income credits) under a scheduled ceiling of 70 percent for other ordinary income.   And to add further pain

[3] *Ibid.*
[4] "Stock Options Fall into Disfavor," *Business Week,* Dec. 27, 1969, p. 36.
[5] *Ibid.*

TABLE 3   Use of Stock Options: Industrial versus Financial Companies

	Industrial companies		Financial companies	
	Number	% of total	Number	% of total
Use options..............	51	80%	3	20%
Do not use options.........	12	20	13	80
	63	100%	16	100%

to such an individual, the extra taxes do not change his cost basis for the stock, so that no credit can be gained when the stock is eventually sold.

The maximum tax on long-term capital gains was increased for amounts over $50,000 in any year. The new maximums are 29.5 percent for 1970, 32.5 percent for 1971, and 35 percent for 1972 and thereafter. At the time he sells the stock, therefore, the executive may be subject to an increased capital gains tax (35 percent versus the former 25 percent), and, in addition, he can pay up to an extra 30 percent again on half of the profits as tax preference income, a net of 15 percent.

Thus, the very high-bracket executive, or the one who plans poorly, or the one whose financial affairs do not allow effective planning, can end up paying a total tax of 80 percent of his profits!

The extreme, however, should be a very unusual situation, since virtually all executives should be able to develop some credits from the various deductibles —which are, even in today's inflated economy, still fairly substantial ($30,000 to $50,000 or more). Thus, the real effect of the laws ranges from zero additional tax to around 30 percent additional tax, from calculations using actual cases of typical executives.

Nevertheless, the potential impacts of these new tax considerations, coupled with the fact that the typical executive has little time, skills, or interest in effective financial planning, have caused most companies to reevaluate their stock option plans. The obvious choice for many companies is the nonqualified option, which has two attractive advantages:

1. The wording of the tax law changes seems to classify profits from non-qualified options as earned income, i.e., qualifying for the 50 percent ceiling —and data so far available from "informed sources" seem to confirm this interpretation. If so, the very high-bracket taxpayer is obviously better off—a tax of only 50 percent, cleaned up immediately, versus a potential tax of as much as 80 percent, involving financing and risk problems.

2. The company can get no deduction from profits derived from a qualified option, whereas a deduction is available for the profits of a nonqualified option. Thus, the company can recover part (almost half, in the typical case) of what many consider the real cost of the option, i.e., the loss in assets from selling optioned stock at a price lower than the market on the day of the "sale" (exercise). Or, in another context, the company can get a windfall deduction— a tax credit, without expenditure of cash, chargeable against P & L for the option profits.

In our opinion, however, a major factor is the loss of freedom in tax deferral for the recipient of a nonqualified option. In this type of option, tax is due immediately on exercise—and the company must withhold for estimated taxes. In contrast, tax can be deferred under a qualified option (except for tax preference impacts) until the stock is sold, and, if the stock is sold immediately, the consequences are the same as for a nonqualified option. Thus, the recipient of a qualified option has the choice, at time of exercise, of giving the option a nonqualified status or continuing on with the tax deferral to a more advantageous time. (However, an executive who pays tax preference taxes, and then sells in a subsequent year but before the end of the three-year holding period required for long-term capital gains treatment, can wind up paying extra taxes, i.e., there is in fact extra risk with a qualified option.)

SPECIFIC CONSIDERATIONS ON USE OF OPTIONS

Who Gets Options and Who Should Get Options? Qualified or nonqualified options may be—and usually are—given on a highly selective basis to key officers and executives. Actual practice varies widely from company to company, depending upon size, past use of options, current stock price prospects, and management philosophy. Despite the opportunities for being selective and encouragement to be selective from the laws themselves, however, many companies do not use discrimination. These companies often determine option amounts solely on the basis of salary levels and exclude only marginal employees. For companies which do apply eligibility criteria, only the following seem to be common to all:[6]

1. Future, as well as present, key executives and officers are generally eligible.

2. Employee members of the stock option committee are generally excluded, although in some companies committee members may be granted options by action of the rest of the board of directors, the chairman of the board, or the president.

3. In some companies, executives over 60 or 65 are ineligible, and several plans specify the cancellation of exercise rights when the executive reaches normal retirement age.

4. Under several plans, the executive must earn a minimum salary, typically $10,000 to $15,000 a year, to be eligible to receive an option.

According to a 1970 Conference Board report[7] (based on 1967 data), all the top men in the 179 manufacturing companies surveyed were likely to receive a qualified stock option. At the next three levels—key managers, middle management, and first-line supervisors—there was considerable variation in the percentage of managers who were likely to receive stock options. Half of the plans excluded middle management entirely. In the balance, options were often confined to a few of the first-line supervisors and middle managers heading major departments or operating units.

This study determined that the "organizational level tapped by the plan is an important determinant of the proportion of key managers likely to receive options. . . . The further down into the organization the plan goes, the more likely it is that upper middle management executives, as a group, will be granted options, with individual considerations becoming less important."[8]

In the study, each cooperating company was asked for the 1966 salary of the lowest-paid employee granted a qualified stock option up to the time of inquiry (spring, 1967). Only 10 percent of the manufacturers granted options to employees earning less than $10,000 a year. On the other hand, only 15 percent restricted the plan to executives earning $25,000 or more.

In another study of 168 companies in 1967,[9] only 1.7 percent granted qualified stock options to employees earning less than $10,000, 44.6 percent granted them to employees earning between $10,000 and $15,000, and 31 percent granted them to employees earning from $15,000 to $20,000.

The 1969 Edward N. Hay & Associates Survey of Noncash Compensation confirmed that most companies do not specify eligibility criteria; rather, they use broad-plan definitions (typically the format preferred by the SEC—namely, "officers, executives and key employees"). Of the 61 companies that responded to a question on the lowest salary level generally eligible for options, 13 re-

[6] American Management Association, *Executive Compensation Service: Reports on Stock Purchase Plans*, AMA, Inc., New York, 1969, p. 20.

[7] Harland Fox, "Qualified Stock Options for Executives," *The Conference Board Report*, no. 505, 1970, p. 10.

[8] *Ibid.*, p. 12.

[9] American Management Association, *Executive Compensation Service: Reports on Stock Purchase Plans*, AMA, Inc., New York, 1969, pp. 20–21.

ported that employees earning under 15,000 a year (in 1968) could be eligible, and another 17 reported the lowest level generally eligible as between $15,000 and $20,000 a year.

In recent years, a trend has developed among newer, smaller companies (e.g., in the computer industry) of granting options extensively to all supervisors and key technical personnel, as an inducement to employment and also to some degree as a substitute for other forms of compensation—even salary. In a period of expansion and particularly bull market conditions, this format proved to be highly successful in attracting and motivating the specialists needed by such companies.

How Large Should Options Be?   As is the case with option eligibility, option amounts vary widely from token options to 10 or 12 times annual compensation. (Stock purchase plan options are typically modest—under 5 percent of annual compensation rate—to avoid problems of discrimination.)

The tendency is for option amounts, as a percentage of annual earnings, to vary with position level. Thus, if the options granted to a company president total five or six times his compensation, the options granted to the lowest eligible executive would tend to be in the order of 2.5 times the annual compensation rate. Option sizes also tend to vary by frequency of options or past history.

In a "first time" plan, option amounts tend to be much higher than in subsequent plans. Companies which grant options regularly (annually or every two or three years) tend to award smaller options to individuals—although cumulative amounts may be larger—than companies which grant options every four or five years in an irregular pattern.

The 1970 Conference Board study,[10] including 12 executives, showed that over half of the options were for amounts less than the annual compensation rate, and 20 percent were in amounts 200 percent of the annual compensation rate or more—slightly over one-third of the options were 100 percent but less than 200 percent of the annual compensation rate. However, this group appears to include a number of optionees earning less than $20,000 who received the smaller options.

Option plans often specify a maximum option or total of optioned shares which may be given to any one optionee; a 1969 AMA study[11] found that about 50 percent of the plans surveyed specified such a maximum. However, these maximums typically provide a round figure—10,000 or 25,000 shares—or else a percentage of the total authorized, e.g., 4 percent, which may or may not be a really limiting factor in terms of compensation multiples. For example, the limitation may be three or four times the total compensation of the top eligible officer, or may be 10 or 12 times his compensation, or higher. Thus, most limitation formulas appear to be more window dressing for stockholders than real, thoughtful guidelines for option grants.

In our opinion, arbitrary limitations are at best an unnecessary negative in a plan and often tend to distort the true benefits of a plan. Often, the maximum places an inequitable limit on the benefits for the chief executive and other executives vital to the company's success. Moreover, a limit can encourage options of this amount, even though they are not warranted.

We feel that parameters should certainly be established, but as part of a

[10] Harland Fox, "Qualified Stock Options for Executives," *The Conference Board Report*, no. 505, 1970, p. 23.

[11] American Management Association, *Executive Compensation Service: Reports on Stock Purchase Plans*, AMA, Inc., New York, 1969, pp. 20–21.

total option plan geared specifically to the company—not by simply adopting arbitrary criteria which may or may not be appropriate.

Purposes and Uses of Options.   Questions of eligibility and of size and frequency of option grants must be decided in terms of the specific purposes the company intends options to serve.   Some of these purposes, and the policies which normally follow from them, are discussed below.

Incentive Pull.   Options can indeed provide a major "incentive pull" for an executive optionee to improve and maintain the market value of the company's stock.   However, the incentive is a true incentive only if the optionee can make a real impact on end results and if end results are reflected in the stock price.   Earnings, after all, are only one of many factors influencing the market value of stock.   Further, the long-range best interests of the company are not always served by focusing on short-range improvements in the market value of the company's stock.

Thus, from this viewpoint, stock options should be granted only to those few people who:

- Occupy positions that provide a real and significant opportunity to influence the market value of the stock.
- Can be expected to exercise responsibly the opportunity afforded by their position to serve the very best total interests of the company.

However, in this context, it should be borne in mind that the executive will be motivated only by options in amounts—singly or cumulatively—which present opportunity for substantial profits.   On the other hand, there can be significant *negative* motivational impact from large option amounts which prove to be unprofitable, since an executive granted an option will usually automatically assume a dramatic profit—and be sorely disappointed by "losing" the expected profit.

Also, it should be noted that in a company which has a record of erratic performance in the market or where the prospects for significant increase in the near-term future are small, an option will have little initial motivational value even for the most sophisticated (financially) executive—the motivation will come only from actual price increases.

Finally, in granting options, the motivational factors relating to the past cannot be ignored.   Often one of the most troublesome problems presented in the operation of an option plan is the situation in which a predecessor has made substantial profits from options (usually under more liberal tax laws), but the successor is faced with a cycle of declining prices (coupled with more restrictive tax laws).   And attempts to compensate for past options by granting higher current option amounts often backfire—either by compounding the "loss" from an unprofitable option or, worse, by involving the individual in financing problems beyond his depth, to the detriment of his on-the-job performance.

Ownership Interest.   Traditionally, a major purpose of option plans has been to provide the equivalent of an ownership interest which will increase motivation—and efficiency—thereby more than offsetting any eventual dilution.   Occasionally (or possibly often) options are granted in lieu of salary or other compensation, so that salary or bonus levels can be lower.   This approach is often used by young companies with great expectations—for example, many computer companies which were created in the 1960s.   The advantages are that compensation costs can be kept low while the company is developing, while, at the same time, executives and key technicians have an opportunity to realize tremendous financial rewards if they make a go of the company.

Tax Advantages.   Many evaluate options in terms of efficiency—that is, net cost to the company per after-tax dollar received by the executive.   Generally, efficiency increases are realized from options only when granted to executives in the 40 to 50 percent tax bracket (which means income of more than $35,000).

Proponents of this view usually consider options as an alternative to cash bonuses. To weigh the efficiency of the two devices, the company's net cost of a cash bonus is compared with the net cost of granting an option which will yield equivalent after-tax profits to the executive. Since qualified options do not represent a tax-deductible cost for the company and cash bonuses do, the cash bonus usually is less expensive and therefore more efficient.

A key assumption in this viewpoint is that the cost of an option and its ultimate financed worth can be calculated, and that it can therefore be used as an alternative to cash for those whose tax bracket makes this profitable.

Such an approach is particularly intriguing to the "figure-minded" executive. However, there are certain potential problems in this approach:

1. The assumption that the option's cost to the company and value to the recipient can be calculated is at best debatable. It is true that a sophisticated investor in the stock market is often willing to place a value on warrants, puts, or calls. However, it should be remembered that all trading in this area consists of two participants—one who feels the price is a bargain (so he buys) and one who feels the price is too high (so he sells). In terms of corporate option plans, the price must be at least fair in the minds of both parties, but strong pressures exist to express prices as a bargain to *both.*

Also, it is safe to say that very few corporation executives, even among financial companies, are sophisticated investors. Thus, they probably lack the understanding to figure the worth of the option or its effects on their tax position. It is not that such financial matters are beyond the capabilities of the average executive, but rather that he is unable to devote the time and effort needed to develop that understanding.

2. Stock market prices are affected by a number of factors, most of which are only vaguely related to the performance of the company itself. Each year prices of blue-chip companies may vary 50 or 100 percent, and cyclical variations may drastically affect prices—even blue chips can fare badly in bear markets. If prices go down, and the option becomes worthless, or even appears to be worthless, there is a strong possibility of "buyer's remorse," particularly in an unsophisticated investor, who is not accustomed to, or emotionally conditioned to, speculations.

In a typical stock ownership situation, losses are personal problems. However, in a corporate situation, losses of an earned bonus can become a corporate problem, rightly or wrongly—and pressures can develop for "something else" to offset the losses. And, regardless of other factors, an executive who is upset about personal financial losses is very likely to be less effective in the company's interests than one whose financial affairs are secure.

3. The assumption that there could be a real choice between a bonus or stock options may be fallacious, particularly in terms of a supplemental plan providing substantial cash bonuses equivalent to option profits developed by some executives in dynamic companies. At best, such an approach would require drastic attitudinal changes by most boards and by most stockholder representatives. We would suspect that a pattern which would routinely allow executives of typical companies to double or triple earnings in years when things are going well (because business is good for everybody) would simply be unacceptable to most boards and to most stockholder groups—and in fact would be inviting stockholder lawsuits.

Status Symbols. In any plan it should be recognized that options are a status symbol, tangible recognition of in-group status. On the positive side, therefore, options can be useful for recognizing the "comer" who cannot be otherwise rewarded by salary or bonus without distorting the company's salary and incentive plans or for the "loyal and faithful" executive who has reached a plateau (temporary or permanent). On the other hand, the lack of an option can be a major disappointment to a plateaued executive.

Extra Bonus. In many situations, it is considered desirable, expedient, or necessary to provide extra compensation to an executive or a group of executives. When such compensation would be subject to criticism if paid directly and so reported on a proxy statement, or if internal relationships would be disturbed by extra cash compensation, a stock option can serve quite usefully as an acceptable, respectable "extra bonus."

In this context, either qualified or nonqualified options can be used. Often the executive owns enough stock to make him ineligible for a qualified option, or the executive clearly intends to sell the option immediately after exercise (giving due attention to the "insider trading" rules of the SEC which require that any short-term trading profits—defined as purchases and sales within a six-month period—realized by an officer are returnable to the company).

From the company standpoint, the extra bonus can be additionally desirable if the option is nonqualified, because of the tax deduction obtainable without outlay of cash against the P & L, provided reported earnings are not adversely affected. However, in granting extra bonuses through stock options, due consideration should be given to dilution aspects, as discussed below.

Dilution Aspects of Stock Options. No discussion of options would be complete without a critical examination of the impact of options on stockholders' equity.

From a pragmatic point of view—without attempting philosophical justifications—most stockholders and directors are not concerned about dilution when stock prices rise substantially during the option period—particularly if earnings also increase in substantial degrees. However, as many executives have discovered to their sorrow, stock prices do not always rise as hoped—and in fact may rise only 25 percent or so during an option period.

When the price rise is nominal, the optionee faces a difficult decision. Should he exercise the option and take the risk that a relatively small dip in prices will not only wipe out his paper profits but also cause a loss in his investment, or should he exercise his option and sell immediately for the short-term profit at ordinary income tax rates, or should he forego exercising the option? His choice among these alternatives will depend on three major factors: (1) his ability to finance the option, (2) the attitude of his company toward short-term sale, and (3) his own relative sophistication in financial matters. Often, however, the decision will also depend upon his willingness to ask—many executives will forego option profits rather than risk criticism for exploring the possible reactions to short-term selling.

If his solution—voluntary or otherwise—is to not exercise the option, there is bound to be a negative motivation from the resulting paper losses, even for a highly paid executive. If the solution is to hold the stock and risk the downturn, there is at best a limited motivation and a very real possibility of a negative motivation from later loss. And if his solution is to buy and sell for short-term profits, there is normally at least a degree of guilt feelings or concern about implications of disloyalty.

Thus, regardless of the choice, options on stock that is not appreciating rapidly can leave a real negative impact on the optionee. Recognizing this, more and more companies are encouraging executives to sell and realize the short-term gains. While this may be a solution to the motivation problems, it also leads to increased earnings requirements which, if not met, can dilute stockholder equity.

From the company standpoint, any exercise of options results in an expensive dilution of earnings. For example, assume a $20 option price, an increase of 25 percent to $25, and an earnings of $2.50 (a conservative PE ratio of 10). If 100,000 shares are exercised at a profit of $5, the total paper profit is $500,000 —but the earnings requirements of the company are increased by $250,000 after tax. Thus, for the typical company in the 48 percent tax bracket, the paper profit is equal to the before-tax profits which must be earned for the stock if the current PE ratio, or stockholders' equity, is to be maintained. Thus, the company could pay a bonus equal to the paper profit at an after-tax cost which would be amortized by savings in earnings requirements in only one year! Further, even if the stock goes up 50 percent—$10 per share—such represents only two years' earnings requirements! The picture is brighter, however, for the company with a PE ratio higher than 10.

Use of "Phantom Stock" for Options. Because of the potential problems outlined above, some companies are now adding a new dimension to stock option plans—phantom options. These are options for artificial or hypothetical shares, with no shares actually being purchased. A payment is made by the company at the time of exercise, equal to the paper profit (or occasionally a multiple of the paper profit, such as 150 percent). The payment may be in cash, stock, or any combination thereof. The amount of the payment is ordinary income to the recipient and probably qualifies as earned income under the 1969 Tax Reform Act. In general, a phantom option offers the advantages of the non-qualified option without the disadvantages of dilution and the requirement to sell actual stock.

Further, some companies are offering tandem options which permit choices as to which option is exercised, depending on circumstances at the time the expiration date of the option approaches. Tandem options can be qualified, nonqualified, phantom, or various combinations thereof. Such choices can be particularly useful in maximizing employee appreciation—and profit— from options, by permitting the deferral of any decision until the best possible informed judgment can be made.

THE FUTURE OF OPTIONS

While the tax law changes in 1969 and 1964 have drastically reduced the value of stock options, we believe the options still have a place in a company's total compensation package and still can be quite useful. Our feelings are based on four factors:

1. The negative impact of the 1969 law comes only for paper profits which exceed $30,000 in any one year, and even then would affect significantly only the executive whose salary runs well above $100,000 per year and whose total income is so great that he is unable to spread his tax preference income.

2. Cash alone is not sufficient to motivate most high-level executives—thus, other compensation devices will always be needed.

3. The 1969 tax law removed or diminished in value sharply a number of other tax shelter and tax-advantaged devices, thereby making the remaining devices more valuable, whatever their degree.

4. There is no alternative means of providing the executive with very substantial amounts of money—no alternative, that is, which is acceptable to the individual, the stockholder, the financial community, and other employees.

Thus, rather than spelling the end of options—or at least the end of qualified options—we would see the 1969 laws as reinforcing the 1964 law changes and impacting on the way in which option plans are administered.

We think that in the future the trend will be to grant smaller options and more frequently, and that tandem options will become the norm rather than the exception. The smaller option amounts will lessen the potential penalties from tax preference rules, and the more frequent options will allow a degree of dollar averaging to minimize risks of negative motivation from unprofitable options.

Also, we believe that more attention will be paid to the place of options in the company's total compensation package and that greater attempts will be made to integrate options with other programs. In this area, greater concerns about costs will also encourage companies to consider buyouts of marginally profitable options, rather than allowing the issue of stock which will increase earnings requirements.

chapter 32

Employee Contracts

LAWRENCE WM. MUTH   *Director, Corporate Economic Research and Statistical Reporting, Johnson & Johnson, New Brunswick, New Jersey*

Employee contracts are receiving an increasing amount of attention in industrial relations circles. In some instances, this is undoubtedly the result of publicity given recent changes at the top executive level of the business world. In other instances, interest may have been stimulated by reference to the use of employee contracts in the published accounts of corporate mergers. Although more and more personnel executives are seeking information on contracts, they are finding little, if any, background in the literature of industrial relations.

To overcome this apparent gap, the author conducted a survey of employee contract practices of 100 major United States corporations during the spring of 1970. These 100 organizations included banks, insurance companies, retail concerns, and manufacturing concerns.

In preparing a questionnaire for the study, it was decided to separate executive employment contracts from field sales employment contracts. Separating the two categories allows a distinction to be made between normal circumstances and those instances where a company has sales representatives who, because of personal contacts and attachments, might have significant impact on a company's volume. In these latter instances, companies may use such contracts as a protective device.

It was also determined that it would be desirable to distinguish between employment contracts and what are commonly called "security" or "patent agreements." Trade and professional associations, including The Conference Board and the Executive Compensation Service of the American Management Association, have conducted surveys on the use of security and patent agreements and have apparently satisfied the need for information on this topic. Furthermore, these kinds of agreements are generally restricted to protecting knowledge gained or inventions produced while in the employ of a company. While these kinds of agreements may, on occasion, relate to employment contracts, they generally contain no commitment on the part of the company to retain the employee for a specified period of time, nor is there any commitment on the part of the employee to perform prescribed functions or assume responsibility for specific activities.

For the purposes of this survey, security and patent agreements are not considered to be employment contracts. This study is confined to those contracts containing special provisions which go beyond the items covered in normal employer-employee situations. Specifically, an employment contract is considered to contain an agreement covering an individual's duties and the functional area for which he is responsible. It also spells out the compensation the individual is to receive and the various items which it covers, such as salary, bonus, or stock agreements. Regulations and restrictions are sometimes incorporated into the contract to help define in more precise language the relationship between the company and the individual. The period of time during which the contract is to be in effect is included in the agreement as well as the procedure to be followed in amending, terminating, or extending it.

FREQUENCY OF USE

Table 1 shows the response to the survey. The spirit of cooperation so often found in personnel executives is clearly evidenced by the 78 percent who responded to the letter requesting their participation and by the 75 percent who completed the questionnaire and, in many instances, submitted additional background information. This additional information gave substance to the raw data by detailing circumstances under which certain action might be taken. In cases where company policy precluded employment contracts, unusual circumstances—e.g., acquisition of another concern—might create the need for action beyond the limits of the normal employment policy.

This is not intended to imply that employment contracts are used only in instances of company acquisitions or mergers. As a matter of fact, only six of the company executives who reported that their companies used employment contracts made any mention of their use in such events.

Employment contracts are also useful and desirable in other situations—in recruiting certain high-level executives or for handling the employment of an executive for a terminal position. In addition, they are sometimes used to handle the employment of an executive with special talent or experience for a short-term job.

Only six of the 75 respondents, or 8 percent, indicated that their organizations use employment contracts for members of their sales force. A greater proportion of those surveyed, however, indicated that they use such contracts with certain key executives. Twenty of the 75 respondents mentioned that

TABLE 1   Total Use of Employment Contracts

							Participants using employment contracts for			
	Surveyed		Response		Participated		Salesmen		Executives	
	Number	%	Number	%	Number	%	Number	%	Number	%
Total............	100	100	78	78	75	75	6	8	20	27

employment contracts were used for some of these individuals. The 20 affirmative responses included those instances where the responding executive made clear that the only contracts currently in effect applied to executives obtained in mergers or acquisitions. The 20 participants using contracts for executives all indicated that their use was quite limited. This is, of course, no surprise, since by their very definition employee contracts are restricted to those instances where the agreement covers some aspect of employment or remuneration beyond normal policy.

An interesting sidelight can be drawn from the data by separating the results into manufacturing and nonmanufacturing concerns, as shown in Table 2. The ratio of participants to those requested to participate is high for both the manufacturing concerns and the nonmanufacturing concerns. This high percentage of participation is an indication not only of the common interest in this subject, but also of the fact that the need for information on employment contracts transcends commercial classification. The figures alone indicate the frequency of contract use; and the reasons for using them—discussed below—give substance to the raw data.

ADVANTAGES TO THE COMPANY

In discussing advantages gained by the company from employment contracts, the overwhelming majority of respondents pointed out that they were an instrument which permitted the company and the employee to agree in writing on the precise details of what the employee is expected to accomplish. By putting the agreement into writing, misunderstandings and misinterpretations can be eliminated or at least substantially reduced. It was generally felt that avoiding such problems with individuals whose talents and knowledge can play an important role in the future of the company is worth the effort involved in preparing such a contract. It also emphasizes the need for both parties to pay careful attention to all aspects of the contract and to agree on the meaning of what is put in writing.

Another advantage to which several of the company executives referred can be broadly classified as holding power, that is, assurance that the special talents, knowledge, or ability of the individual covered by the contract will continue to be available to the company. In a few instances, this holding power has a built-in procedure for continuation into the employee's retirement years. This latter approach is a variation of deferred-income programs often used to maintain some relationship with key employees who retire. However, since this study is concerned only with the use of employment contracts for active employees, the procedure of offering a program of deferred income which would be in effect only after an employee retired was not considered.

TABLE 2   Manufacturing versus Nonmanufacturing Use of Employment Contracts

							Participants using employment contracts for			
							Salesmen		Executives	
	Surveyed		Response		Participated					
	Number	%	Number	%	Number	%	Number	%	Number	%
Manufacturing...	78	100	62	79	59	76	4	6	18	29
Nonmanufacturing	22	100	16	73	16	73	2	13	2	13

Company executives also feel that the use of an employment contract makes the employee more aware of the fact that something out of the ordinary is being made available to him.   This is not meant to imply that the contract should be used as a status symbol, but rather that unusual items have been agreed upon and this agreement is put in writing.   This is borne out time and again in the responses of the companies using employment contracts. Phrases such as "used only for the highest-level executives," "used only in exceptional cases," and "used only to meet special situations" indicate that the individuals covered by such contracts are indeed being treated in a manner that differs from normal policy.

On the other hand, some executives took the contrary view, expressing the feeling that an individual who felt it necessary to ask for an employment contract was showing a lack of confidence in the organization hiring him.   Such an attitude did not—in the opinion of those personnel executives—seem to be a sound basis upon which to build a good employer-employee relationship. In fact, one such executive expressed himself strongly on this point by saying that if an employment contract were requested, he would feel this sufficient cause to rule out the applicant as a potential employee.

ADVANTAGES TO THE INDIVIDUAL

Several of the respondents stated that the primary advantage of such contracts to an employee was the increased sense of security resulting from putting the agreement into writing.

Personnel executives indicated that the formality of spelling out the agreement not only reminded the employee of his commitment to the company but also defined the company's obligation concerning his remuneration and in a fashion sufficiently precise to eliminate questions during the life of the contract.

This reminder of the employee's personal commitment does not reflect an undesirable employer-employee relationship.   Rather, it appears to be an indication of the value attached to having a mutually agreed-upon area of responsibility put into writing to avoid future misunderstandings.

SUMMARY AND CONCLUSIONS

The scope of participation in the survey seems deserving of mention.   Banks, insurance companies, retail concerns, and manufacturing organizations all showed their interest in this subject by responding to the questionnaire.   In fact, each of the categories of commerce included in the makeup of the survey is represented in the responses.   What may perhaps be an even more significant indicator of the interest in this subject was the number of instances in which the participants included in their response a request for a copy of the survey results.   This was true in spite of the fact that the letter requesting their participation stated that "a copy of the completed results will be furnished to each participating company."

Employment contracts are of considerable interest to personnel executives. This interest may stem from any of the following reasons:

1. These contracts are sometimes made public when executive changes take place at the top levels of some of our major corporations.

2. Contracts can be useful in the consummation of a merger or an acquisition.

3. Contracts may be a desirable part of a company philosophy concerning its relationship to key executives.

These expressions of interest do not reflect a high incidence of the use of such contracts, since the survey shows they are used infrequently and by only a minority of the participating companies. It does, however, seem appropriate to conclude that they reflect a continuing desire on the part of the personnel executives to remain alert to anything related to personnel activities that may be of value to their company.

This thought was perhaps best expressed by one of the responding executives who commented that he was anxious to see the results of the survey to help him decide on whether to recommend their use in his company.

It would be inappropriate to conclude this study without attempting to put the restricted use of employment contracts into proper perspective. The fact that the companies using such contracts restrict them to only a few key executives should not be considered an indictment of employment contracts. This would be almost as grave an error as concluding that since company officials numerically represent such a small proportion of a company's total employee count, it follows that company officials are not too significant in the scheme of things.

What seems to be a more reasonable conclusion is that employment contracts serve a useful purpose in certain specific circumstances. These circumstances will vary from company to company, but the use of such contracts indicates that some unusual or extraordinary action was deemed appropriate. Their use, therefore, seems to be another manifestation of management's ability to face up to unusual situations and, through the exercise of judgment required to direct the progress of an organization, find some acceptable solution.

Part 7

Incentives

chapter 33

Relating Incentives to the Total Compensation Package

TIMOTHY P. HAWORTH   *General Partner, Edward N. Hay & Associates, Philadelphia, Pennsylvania*

The total compensation package is a many-splendored, multifaceted thing of almost infinite variety and complexity. It is extremely rare to find two institutions or organizations with precisely the same ingredients in the total package, mixed in identical relationships of degree and kind. New ingredients are constantly being introduced, old ones are falling by the wayside, fads come and go, and tax laws change and make formerly attractive programs less or more so. It is a dynamic, shifting, changing field. Essentially, the total compensation package comprises four major ingredients:

1. *A basic, regular commitment* in terms of annual, monthly, semimonthly, biweekly, or weekly salary or daily or hourly wage rate.

2. *Security and benefit programs,* such as life insurance, health insurance, retirement or pension plans, disability income programs, and savings and thrift plans

3. *Perquisites and working conditions,* such as paid vacations, holidays, recreation facilities, cafeterias and special dining facilities, air conditioning, uniforms, company cars, office furnishings, and so forth

4. *Incentives,* in the form of additional compensation, commissions, bonus plans, piecework, standard hours, prizes, contests, safety awards, suggestion systems, profit sharing, stock options, etc.

Surrounding this patchwork of ingredients are behavioral, environmental factors—deliberate or accidental—that often merge or are in conflict with parts of the compensation package: management style, a spirit of public service, pace and challenge, boldness and zest, a stuffy or formal atmosphere, enthusiasm and fun, contagious creativity, positive or negative conflict, and tension.

Together, all of these components add up to the total compensation package in the broadest sense, if compensation can be considered psychic as well as economic—and, indeed, it is often difficult to separate the two. Each economic facet has intrinsic value, but also carries with it extrinsic values in the form of status or recognition or symbolic accomplishment. Many men strive to become millionaires—but they strive not only for each of those million dollars but even more for the status, the visible accomplishment of having won their place in that exclusive club.

Into the warp of salary and the woof of benefits can be woven intricate patterns of special programs to make a total fabric. Most such fabrics are partly thoughtful design, partly happenstance, and partly anachronistic inheritance. Where, in this total scheme of things, do incentives appropriately fit? What kind? How much? To what degree?

Incentives Defined. For the purposes of this discussion, "incentives" are variable rewards granted according to variations in achievement of specific results. Before-the-fact knowledge of the rules of the game is essential if there is to be real incentive pull. By way of contrast, many "bonus" plans are simply after-the-fact devices to reward achievement that happens to have occurred. "Incentive" plans are designed to play a causal role, as well as to reward the effect.

PREREQUISITES FOR EFFECTIVE INCENTIVES

There are, certainly, many situations in which fluctuating incentive awards are inappropriate as part of the compensation package. Certain prerequisites must be met for incentives to be appropriate at all. Furthermore, the degree to which these prerequisites are met gives useful clues regarding the weight that incentives can have in the total mix. Among these are:

1. *Adequate, competitive floors* in basic commitment (salary or wage) and security areas (benefits), on top of which incentives can produce variable income. Incentive awards must fluctuate according to results accomplished if they are to have real pull. But their fluctuation must not jeopardize an individual's basic livelihood. He is taking a risk—he is shooting crap—but not with his bread, butter, and mortgage money.

2. *Significant individual or group impact* on important results. The situation must be one in which working harder or smarter or more creatively or more accurately really makes a difference in results. It is pointless to pay incentives to an hourly worker on a belt-paced operation of a go, no-go nature. It is equally pointless to dangle incentives in front of an executive in a situation where external factors are determinative.

3. *Measurable results.* Individual or group situations in which the goals are quantifiable, objective, and clearly demonstrable lend themselves most easily to incentive forms of compensation. Qualitative, intangible results are more difficult to measure with objectivity and accuracy and require more sophisticated approaches in an atmosphere of mutual trust.

4. *Reasonable time spans.* These are important in terms of measuring the accomplishment against which incentives will be paid, and the shorter the time span, the better. Results which will not be known or measurable for more than a year are difficult to tie to fluctuating incentive payments and require a

certain kind of person to be effective. Most of us need to eat the elephant a bite at a time.

5. *Management commitment* to the program. This is vital to its success. It means commitment to the cost and time necessary to administer it properly, and these must be carefully assessed before embarking on an incentive program: there are many situations in which the potential gains just are not worth the cost and effort involved. It also means a commitment in terms of integrity to the spirit as well as the letter of the program: having the guts to stick with it when the payout falls off, and the honor to cough up when results go through the ceiling.

6. *A salubrious climate* in which striving toward individual and group excellence is encouraged and applauded. Climates can be changed and manipulated to significant degrees, but adverse peer (or superior) pressure must be faced when it exists, because it can defeat the finest incentive program.

Given the presence of these prerequisites to a degree adequate to justify incentives as part of the total compensation package, how much weight should be given this part of the program relative to the others? What should be the mix of base to bonus to benefits?

Generally speaking, modern business management tends to say incentives should be given the maximum possible weight in the mix of compensation ingredients consistent with the degree to which the prerequisites exist and apply. And you will find that they exist and apply in different degrees in different mixes in different parts of the same organization: they will be different at different levels, in different divisions, in different types of functional jobs, and in different geographical locations.

This implies, of course, that incentives can and should be selectively applied throughout the organization rather than imposed lock, stock, and barrel on all of it. If hourly incentives are appropriate, use them. But using them at the hourly level need not compel you to use them for the sales force, nor should using incentives for the sales force require a parallel application in manufacturing. Where appropriate, use them. Where less appropriate, minimize their impact, or do not use them at all.

Selective application of incentives within the same organization does, however, carry with it one major guiding principle: there should be equity of total compensation opportunity among incentive and nonincentive positions of equal status and weight. This can be achieved with integrity by balancing the incentive position's opportunity for greater gain and a concomitant risk of greater loss against the comparative security of straight salary for the nonincentive position.

The steadily increasing interest in incentives as an important part of the total compensation package is primarily due to improvements in the design of such programs as well as to heightened awareness of the benefits to be derived from them. Factors which should influence the design of an incentive program and which, in turn, are influenced by an effective incentive plan are discussed in the following sections.

INCENTIVES AND COMMUNICATIONS

Incentive compensation affords a rare and precious vehicle of tangible, nonverbal communication in an institutional environment. Individuals often get confused signals regarding the purpose of their assignments, the real intention of management, and what is considered critically important in their job. Managements (and managers) have a way of saying one thing and meaning another ("Quality is of number one importance," "The customer is always right," "Service is our business," "How many did you ship today?"). A lot of lip service is given to a lot of things, and it is not always easy to discover what the name of the game really is.

All too frequently, compensation programs are either quite unrelated to or actually in conflict with the real name of the game. When seniority and length of service are given more emphasis than performance and results in determining salary increases, the message finally trickles through even the thickest skull that the name of the game is survival, and keep a low silhouette. When mediocrity survives with impunity, when conformity to the lowest common production denominator is condoned if not encouraged, the name of the game is anything but productivity. When gracious, elderly gentlemen are retained in high office after they have run out of gas, the name of the game is clearly, "Be gracious rather than be effective."

Incentives make it possible for an institution to put its money where its mouth is, and having done so, the company does not have to shoot off the latter quite as much in order to pay off the former according to the real name of the game. When significant incentives are tied directly to critical-result accomplishment, a little verbal doubletalk for nicety's sake is not really confusing or misleading. One can be sympathetic and generous as well as genuinely helpful in a situation of failure without being confusing: "Gosh, Joe, it's a shame you didn't make that quota last month, and I know it wasn't your fault at all—let's see what we can do to make sure you really sock it this month so you can win that incentive award."

If this works with hourly people and salesmen, it is even more effective in the echelons of top management. No board of directors wants to tell its chief executive officer he failed. Quite the contrary: after a poor year for the company, the board will sympathize with him, tell him it was not his fault—"We all know housing starts were off, money was tight, the surtax was imposed at just the wrong time for us, and that catastrophic six-month strike was a courageous stand on principle (no check-off and no union shop)." At the same time, if there is an incentive plan that regretfully has no payoff after such a year, the real message will get through to the top management involved while the board is saying all these nice, friendly, supportive things.

What is the name of the game, for each particular job at this particular point in time? Is it productivity—more units per man-hour or machine-hour or both? Is it volume of sales for the salesman, or improvement in volume against a three-year rolling average? Or product mix? Or sales volume while controlling or reducing advertising expenditures? Or return on investment? Or return on capital employed? Or earnings per share? Or increase in market value of stock to put us in a better position for acquisitions?

What are we really paying the occupant of this position for? What are the critical makes-or-breaks of the job? If he were an outside contractor and we were negotiating on a fixed-fee, lump-sum payment, what would be his commitment? Define it and tie his incentive compensation to it, and you have really communicated.

No other part of the total compensation package can facilitate communications in quite the same way, although salary administration can walk down the same road with less impact. Furthermore, if incentive payments are made frequently (weekly, monthly, quarterly, or semiannually), the program carries with it the built-in requirement for regular communications. Every time an incentive payment is made, effective communication has occurred. You have to pay each employee regularly, and having to sit down and compute the amount of his incentive award forces review and communications on a regular basis.

Targets, goals, and results established as criteria for measuring incentive award amounts also provide the great blessing of being able to communicate in a diagnostic and remedial way about situations rather than people. One can talk about the results a person's job is designed to accomplish and how to improve them, rather than talk about the person himself and what is wrong with him as an individual.

Effective incentive plans demand clear definition of results to be achieved. They require measurement and periodic reporting. They build in a desire for remedial improvement and utilization of all helpful services to do so. Thus, they are the essence of effective communication, if handled properly, to a degree impossible in most other components of the total compensation package.

INCENTIVES AND MANAGEMENT DISCIPLINES

It should go without saying that it is futile to attempt to manage toward an unknown end, but that situation obtains more often than most of us would like to admit. Try to define the absolute purpose or purposes, the basic reason for being of a hospital, or a university, or a commercial bank, or a business enterprise. Why does it exist? What is it trying to do? What results is it trying to accomplish? What is success, and what is failure?

As soon as one attempts to move beyond immediate, simplistic, tactical targets, one gets into trouble. Yet how can one organize and structure the institution without clearly understanding its purpose? How can individual, or functional, or subunit objectives be identified without knowing the total result they collectively are to achieve?

An effective incentive program requires planning, in total and in part. It requires forecasting and budgeting. It requires definition of strategy and of tactics, of purpose and of process. It requires measurement and reporting, reviewing and auditing. But if these critical aspects of effective management are currently primitive or inadequate, the incentive plan can, itself, serve as the catalyst that causes the act of real management to occur, and to occur in time to be effective.

Generally, incentives are inappropriate unless sound management disciplines and processes are already in effect. Certainly this is the ideal situation, but waiting for that millennium may postpone indefinitely a device which can cause it to arrive much sooner. Clearly, it is operating backwards to manage soundly a company, a department, a plant, or a subordinate just in order to be able to administer the incentive plan. But if that is the result, thank heavens something made us do the management job we should have been doing anyway! The tail may be wagging the dog, but if a wagging dog is the desired result, three cheers for the tail!

An incentive plan that offers opportunity for rewards large enough to be motivational and that is rationally communicated to each participant can result in a groundswell demand from the participants themselves for sound management disciplines. What am I supposed to be trying to produce? How fast? How good? With what tools and assists? How much is enough, and how much is sensational? How did I do yesterday? Last month? Last quarter? How am I doing today?

The act of designing, implementing, and administering a sound incentive compensation plan forces this discipline on management—demands a process which should have occurred anyway. The executive-contract analogy is a sound one and a highly productive exercise. Consider each participant in the incentive plan an independent contractor, and outline the basic elements of the contract. What is he to do, to provide, develop, make, contribute? At what level of quality? Within what time period? What is it worth to the enterprise? Is it worth more or less if it is better or worse, if it is supplied faster or more slowly, or if it is bigger or smaller?

The thoughtful use of a good salary administration program can achieve some demand for excellence in management, but a well-designed incentive program on top of it can greatly enhance the impetus in that direction. Moreover, the absence of effective management and management systems is better spotlighted through an incentive plan than through salary administration.

INCENTIVES AND MOTIVATION

Variable economic opportunity based on individual or group accomplishment can play a profound role in personal motivation. Money, or a money equivalent, is itself significant. As a symbol of achievement, however, it has deep motivational penetration. Most people respond constructively to legitimate and exciting challenge. Confronted with a target (which they accept as valid, preferably because they participated in establishing it), they shoot at it.

One of the more astounding aspects of American life is the way grown men respond to artificially structured competitive games. The United Fund drive, where we divide solicitors into teams, attend report lunches where we stand up and announce results, with every $10,000 moving that ball down the football field depicted behind the speakers' table—the sales contest in a life insurance company—class competition in fund drives among alumni of Old Siwash—amazingly, these devices are effective.

Knowing what is expected of you, and what you expect of yourself, is a critical part of motivation. Incentives provide that information and provide visible, tangible rewards in recognition of achievement.

Furthermore, incentives tend to speak to the psyche of more and more of the younger members of today's work force. There is increasing interest in individual fulfillment, self-realization, and maximizing one's potential. There is an impatience with junior roles for juniors, a demand for responsibility with a real chance to have impact, limited only by competence and capacity.

Incentives provide that opportunity far better than any other form of compensation. Moving up in a salary range requires ability, no doubt, but it also requires plain old survival and the passage of time. On the other hand, an incentive plan says simply, "This is what accomplishing these results is worth: if you do it, you'll get it; if you do more, you'll get more; and if you do less, you'll get less—but you have the same crack at it that everyone else in this job has, regardless of age, or length of service, or time in the job."

Unquestionably, incentive compensation can be a significant motivator in and of itself. More importantly, it can be used in a supportive way in relation to other motivators in the behavioral, environmental arenas. People may be willing to work longer or harder or more carefully because there is a crisis (a hurricane destroyed the telephone lines) or because they know their work is critical to a project's success (the quality of equipment on a LEM is of obvious importance), but it also is supportive and comforting to know you are getting paid commensurately with the way you rise to the challenge or the crisis.

Thus, it is probable that more mileage is obtainable in terms of improved results through incentive compensation than through other components of the total package. The basic security programs—pension, group insurance, and so forth—are necessary and desirable, but they are difficult to utilize for improved results and to identify with such outcome. Improved fringe benefits may well provide greater peace of mind and thereby release an individual from private concerns to concentrate more effectively on the task at hand, but beyond that, they provide little incentive pull.

This fact should be kept in mind when designing fringe programs. When plans are designed as multiples of total compensation (base plus incentive payments) rather than as multiples of base rates or salaries only, there is a double reward for the high incentive producer. Such a person not only receives the incentive payment itself, but he also increases his life insurance or his retirement benefit through his own efforts.

It may be that incentive payouts should also be considered when criteria are established in such areas as vacations. Most vacations are determined by length of service rather than by results contributed by the individual. Frequently, also, vacation and holiday pay is computed at the base or salary rate rather than on average total earnings; this approach is less costly in dollar outlay but fails to take advantage of some of the pull from the incentive part of the compensation package. There is also room for consideration of the possible use of incentives as a criterion in earning holidays beyond the minimum normally provided.

A well-structured and administered base-salary program can, indeed, have some impact on motivation when the frequency and amount of salary increases vary appreciably according to individual performance. A salary increase is, however, a permanent thing: once granted, it is rescinded only rarely. Most managers prefer to discharge a person rather than cut his salary, and the higher one climbs the company totem pole, the truer this is.

Because of their permanent impact, salary increases tend to be based on fairly long-range judgments of performance, both in retrospect and in prospect. One's track record is examined over a period exceeding the most recent year, and one's probable future sustained performance level is also considered. There is motivational pull in this, but it is long-range by nature rather than immediate. Incentives recognize current achievement and the payoff is prompt, unconditioned by other considerations. But it is not permanent at all. To get the same incentive award again next year, or next month, or tomorrow, one must produce comparable results.

INCENTIVES AND COST CONTROL

The basic analytical process necessary to determine whether an incentive program is worth the effort is, in itself, a highly useful exercise in cost control. Once the decision is made in favor of the incentive plan, the opportunity is at hand for ongoing, regularly recurring, and effective cost control.

Giving a heavy weight to incentives in the mix of base to benefits to bonus in the total compensation package is prudent and conservative financial management. Essentially, it makes compensation costs variable, according to productivity and results, rather than fixed. The shift is particularly significant at the salaried level in the organization; direct labor is usually considered a variable cost already.

Obviously, the real cost of a penny-an-hour wage increase varies depending on where it is applied. For example, an increase in the incentive rate may well cost less than the direct outlay if it spurs increased productivity while utilizing the same space, equipment, overhead, and time. But for an equivalent direct outlay for more time off with pay (holidays, vacations, or shorter work weeks), the real cost is more than just the actual layout of cash; it is also the profit lost through lost production while maintaining the same overhead, selling expense, and so forth.

Application of this concept of real cost is even more dramatic in its implications at the salaried or sales level, and the higher in the organization you go, the more significant it is. The compensation of the chief executive officer and his immediate staff is not usually a variable cost—it is overhead—except when incentives are paid strictly according to greater results for the corporation or institution: if greater results are not realized, the incentive award is not paid. This is not true of base salary, and is true of benefits only when they are expressed as multiples of total compensation rather than as base salaries.

It is an interesting aspect of typical American industrial experience that greater, more intensive, and more consistent thought has gone into the development of hourly incentives and their costs than has been true of the development of incentives at the salaried level. This is true not only in cost aspects. It is true in the management aspects—the stress on layout, work processes, equipment and mechanization versus labor costs, and the justification of capital expenditures. It is also true in the psychological and motivational aspects, the what-makes-Johnny-run considerations. Yet almost every aspect of the design, implementation, and administration of an effective hourly program has its counterpart at the salaried level.

Much can be learned and usefully applied at other levels in the enterprise by understanding the basic considerations of hourly incentives. If you are considering a sales incentive plan or a management incentive plan, we urge your careful reading of Chapter 35 on hourly incentives and the application of many of the same concepts of analysis that are well defined in it.

Everyone seems to understand and accept the proposition that management is prudent and conservative when it pays its hourly employees on the basis of piecework or its sales force on straight commissions. In each payment there is a quid for each quo, and you cannot argue about that. In fact, this approach has been considered so callous, so materialistic, and so ruthless that it has done much to create the image of the pragmatic businessman in our society.

Yet many enterprises which feel that incentives are prudent and ruthless at the hourly level fear being considered profligate and extravagant if they apply incentives at the management or professional levels (e.g., some regulated or semi-regulated companies and savings banks). Yet they are quite comfortable in hiring outside contractors to build a new building or plant on a fixed-fee basis and feel themselves both clever and prudent when they add penalty clauses and incentive premiums for failing to meet or beating completion deadlines. And a university or nonprofit institution feels it to be sound and responsible management to retain an outside fund-raising firm at a flat fee of 10 percent of the amount of contributions resulting from a campaign yet somehow considers it recklessly irresponsible to think of giving its executives or professionals the opportunity for similar incentive awards tied to measured, accomplished results.

In each case, the whole trick lies in defining and measuring the results demanded and in appropriately tying rewards to that measurement. It is no simple trick, sometimes; yet accepting the impossibility of defining and measuring results is almost the same as accepting the impossibility of managing at all. Once results are defined and made measurable, however, the task becomes one of record keeping and providing information in time to be of value; that is the essence of effective cost control, and sound incentive plans require it.

INCENTIVES AND TALENT INVENTORIES

It has been said that the famous General Motors incentive plan has more than justified its weight in costs by providing an accurate, ongoing inventory of talent throughout the organization.   A well-structured plan paints a clear picture of accomplishment for each participant.   Over the years the consistently successful, high-producing "comer" will have blazed his way across the compensation sky and left a trail of incentive awards that is unmistakable in its meaning.

The very existence of an incentive plan necessitates continual review and appraisal of individual and group accomplishment.   Every plan must be kept up to date and revised to reflect changing times, shifting targets, and unanticipated challenges.   If changes are handled effectively, the winners who are consistent in their accomplishment can be traced with ease: the fruits are there for all to see, and they cannot help knowing them.

As an ongoing record of individual competence, incentive payoffs have the major virtue of reflecting reality in critical areas of real value to the enterprise, rather than subjectively imagined or appreciated character attributes which may or may not have meaning.   They indicate the degree to which what a person did was considered to be of importance, in tangible witness whereof the enterprise paid him X amount of cold cash dollars.   Over a period of time, they index the degree to which a person *actually was* effective, regardless of whether or not a lot of people thought he *could* or *would* be effective.

The validity and accuracy of that record depend, of course, on the validity and accuracy of the incentive plan itself—how suitably its rewards are tied to results.   If the plan is valid and kept current, the resulting footprints in the golden sands of time are a far more reliable inventory of talent than a long string of performance appraisal forms in an individual's personal file.

True, these footprints identify the winners and the comers, but what about the also-rans who ran extremely well?   What about the square pegs in the round holes?   Some men are born great, some achieve greatness, and some have greatness thrust upon them.   What about those who failed to achieve greatness, but could have done so under the right circumstances?   What about those who could have handled greatness thrust upon them but it was not?

It is in these cases that performance appraisals can be a valuable management tool.   Matched with the presence or absence of achieved results over a period of time, appraisals can help identify areas in which an individual needs development, or they can help find the position in which he can show his greatness.   There is nothing wrong with square pegs, unless they are placed in round holes.

Thus, incentives and incentive payments relate to the total compensation package by providing a unit of measure of accomplishment which can be used reliably to validate the level of the total and to judge whether it really was worth it.   And that same unit of measure, as a record over a period of time, can be a most valuable assist in the processes of management development, of management inventories, of selection for promotions, and of structuring a team to man a new facility.

INCENTIVES AND MANAGEMENT STYLES

A difficult and frustrating aspect of managing an enterprise of size and substance is the massive momentum it builds over a period of time and its consequent resistance to change. On the grand scale, it is the first heartbreak of every newly-elected President of the United States: how to change this massive thing around, how to get it going in even a slightly different direction, how to have major attitudinal or policy changes penetrate layer upon layer of bureaucracy until they finally make a visible difference where the action really is. Perhaps the classic illustration (in reverse) of this phenomenon is the historic capacity of the Chinese gently but effectively to absorb and neutralize every foreign conqueror.

Every executive has this problem. Every enterprise has this problem. Every institution has this problem: how to manage change, how to create a structure with sufficient flexibility to permit it to change, to adapt, to bend, before it breaks under its own weight or runs madly off a cliff, impelled by its own momentum.

As times change and managements change, how does one cause the institution and its people to change accordingly? How does one change the Post Office? How does one change the Penn Central Railroad? How does one change academia?

Every management team develops its own management style to achieve its goals and accomplish change, and each is a little different from every other. Yet no management wants to place undue constraints on key subordinates, and each recognizes the need for if not the desirability of various styles in various parts of the organization. There is no one best way to run a production facility, or a sales district, or a commercial bank.

Moreover, most institutions and enterprises are not simple monoliths. The typical organization has a basic hard core which is the traditional guts of the business—its essential stock in trade—and on which its major claim to fame rests. This it knows very well indeed—it is the master, or at least one of the masters, in the field. But in addition to that core, it usually has one or several new ventures in fields a little or a lot less well known to it; new developments thrust upon it through changing technologies or circumstances; new businesses acquired or entered in order to diversify, to balance seasonal cycles, or simply to employ idle capital. It therefore finds itself managing simultaneously that which it knows quite well and that which it finds substantially unknown, either because it happens to be unfamiliar with it or because it is thrusting out on the frontiers of knowledge.

Obviously, the various parts of such an organization will require very difference management styles. The traditional, well-known part of the enterprise may respond successfully to a command style and structure—a neat, symmetrical pyramid with well-defined chains of command moving along clearly charted pathways. Other parts may require a creative, dynamic style and structure—a matrix of intermeshing assignments and groups, each having substantial autonomy but moving toward a common end. And all the parts— despite the different management methods required to run them—must exist compatibly within the same total framework.

Within that complex, shifting, dynamic environment, a thoughtfully designed incentive program can at once assure an underlying uniformity of management style throughout all parts and levels while maintaining adequate flexibility to permit different parts and different levels to adopt the style that suits their unique needs at any point in time. The uniform style is made explicit through the mechanics of the incentive program, requiring: (1) mutually established purposes—the name of the game (e.g., the high jump); (2) mutually accepted measuring instruments (e.g., feet and inches); (3) mutually agreeable standards of accomplishment (e.g., seven feet is terrific, six feet is outstanding, and five feet is good); (4) before-the-fact commitment to reward each level appropriately (e.g., the gold medal, and so forth).

Working within the framework provided by this overall, uniform style, the various parts and levels have freedom to choose the terms in which their approach will be defined. Flexibility is therefore assured by permitting the use of different processes by which the results are defined and the differing nature of the results identified as suitable; various processes by which the measuring instrument is selected and its nature defined; and various processes for establishing standards to assure adequate acceptance by and challenge to the individual, commensurate with acceptable contribution to the overall results of the total enterprise.

Thus, in their most effective and sophisticated applications, incentives can be the basic vehicle for communicating and implementing management style—can, indeed, be the steady pulsebeat of it—without putting any executive or any part of the organization in a managerial straitjacket.

SUMMARY

In summary, the total compensation package has two essential foundation stones: first, the basic, regular commitment of salary or wage; and second, the essential security programs usually described as "fringe benefits." These are the musts—and they must be pitched at an adequate level to be competitive in the marketplace and also to provide a thoroughly satisfactory standard of basic living. The level at which they are pitched and the manner in which they are administered can have substantial impact on the morale, enthusiasm, and dedication of the people involved in the enterprise or institution.

Above these foundation stones can be erected a structure of incentives and perquisites which can determine the tone, the quality, and the common thrust of the total organization. Incentives particularly lend themselves to motivating people and communicating with them, to promoting management disciplines, to generating timely cost control information, to identifying current and potential talent, and to articulating a basic management style which can also accommodate variations to suit the needs and personalities of individual managers and their areas of responsibility.

Incentives are not, of course, a panacea. They are not a substitute for effective management, although they can shore up mediocre management for a surprisingly long period of time. Moreover, there are many circumstances in which incentives are inappropriate and result only in throwing money down a rathole.

But when the circumstances are ripe and the climate salubrious, they offer almost infinite opportunity as a device of integrity and equity to draw from each his best and to reward it; and, in concert, to accomplish the best for the total enterprise or institution, which will also be rewarded in its own way, in its own time.

chapter 34

Designing Incentives for Hourly Personnel

H. W. LIEBER *Assistant Manager, Industrial Engineering, Western Electric Company, New York, New York*

FREDERIC L. TAYLOR *Department Chief, Industrial Engineering Research, Western Electric Company, New York, New York*

A direct incentive system, properly designed and administered, can increase productivity and help reduce unit cost, yet there are as many instances of failure or partial failure as there are successes. Why? The answer lies both in the decision process and in the commitment of the management involved, for it is clear that a successful wage incentive system is a mark of successful management. The decision process consists of first designing the system and then evaluating the effects of its installation by simulation. The commitment is management's long-term obligation to pay the real cost of system mainte-nance (often hidden in the early stages) and to administer the system with frankness and integrity.

MANAGEMENT DECISION PROCESS

In deciding whether to install a wage incentive program, management must consider the company's existing wage practices, labor productivity, and current labor costs as well as the cost of administering an incentive plan. These fac-tors must be evaluated by personnel knowledgeable about the company's basic goals and reasons for existence, its weaknesses, and its strengths. Such knowl-edge is certainly available within the management structure of the company.

But equally important is knowledge of wage incentives. Incentive system knowledge does not come solely from reading material nor from special training courses, nor is it gained in our colleges or universities. It comes from experience in the installation, maintenance, and administration of wage incentive systems. Such knowledge may be internal in the company, but if not, it is essential that it be available when incentives are being designed. Many good consulting organizations can provide the needed expertise. With the knowledge pool established, the decision process collects facts for evaluation.

Current Wage Practice. For an incentive plan to be truly motivational, the hourly rate structure underlying it must be based on equitable relationships among the hourly jobs. This equity may be achieved through job evaluation, which defines the relative worth of the jobs to the company. At the minimum, both the company and the employee must be reasonably convinced that rate differentials are fair.

Further, the company must examine the value of its employees in terms of wages and the caliber of employees these wages attract. A wage incentive system will increase take-home pay, which in turn affects employee turnover, the desire for employment, and, ultimately, the character of employment.

Productivity. Since present and future productivity levels have a profound effect on unit costs, they must be considered carefully in deciding on incentives. This is probably the most important aspect of the decision process and certainly the most difficult, since no statistical test can determine whether productivity estimates are accurate.

To determine productivity levels, a measuring stick (standard) is required. There are two basic techniques for standard development: predetermined time standards and performance-rated standards.

Predetermined time standards are based on tables of established time values for all basic body motions or combinations of these. These time values are preestablished and are rated for consistent productivity level. Training in application rules allows the user to determine standard or "should take" rate structures through his knowledge of the motion pattern and frequencies.

Performance-rated standards are established on the spot, using such techniques as time study and work sampling. The trained user actually times the operation (either statistically or with a stopwatch), classifies the sequences, rates the operator's skill and effort, and calculates the rate.

Although these measuring techniques overlap in areas of use and many people feel they are in conflict, there is no real disagreement. Performance-rated techniques must be employed to obtain standard times for those forms of work that predetermined times cannot measure. For instance, most allowances and machine control elements other than the operating characteristics of the machine, such as speeds and feeds, must be determined by using the performance-rated technique. On the other hand, performance-rated techniques may, over a period of time, develop into a time standard as time values are accumulated for a variety of parts or operations.

It is recommended that predetermined times be chosen as the basic measuring technique with performance rating as a supplement. Well-known and widely accepted predetermined time systems are available commercially.

Benchmark operations—e.g., an entire department or operations scattered throughout the company—are selected to simulate productivity change. Operations chosen to be benchmarks should be representative of the company in terms of employees, working conditions, methods, tooling, material handling, repetitiveness, and job cycle. These operations are measured by trained applicators who make reasonable judgments on operation standardization and methods improvements. Normal allowances are determined and a standard rate is calculated. The resulting benchmark rates, carefully determined and based on high task evaluations, represent the productivity levels expected from wage incentive use. The change in productivity level represents the average increase in production due to standardization of methods, work flow, tools and fixtures, operation skill and effort, etc., all of which is the direct effect of wage incentive system installation.[1]

Savings resulting from increased productivity can be calculated in accordance with normal company procedures. At this time, however, they are only paper savings, not necessarily real, since factors of management-employee relations and/or company policy and procedure may significantly affect real savings. For instance, increased sales may in itself be undesirable; rather, a reduction in unit cost without production increase may be the goal. Under these circumstances, company policy on layoff or termination, turnover, reduction in employee morale, and benefits will all have a significant effect on how soon and to what degree paper savings are realized.

Regardless of possible qualifications, calculations of production increase and unit cost reduction are extremely important in management's decision process. More important than a dollar change, these paper savings represent a potential level of plant efficiency in all factors of operating—a barometer of efficiency indicative of an alert, up-to-date, modern management team. This level is obtainable through hard work and commitment, and one means of attaining it is through wage incentives.

Costs. There are as many opinions and variations on how to evaluate incentive plan costs as there are accounting methods and equipment replacement procedures. The simplest way to view the problem is to imagine the incentive plan as an equipment replacement problem. Consider a machine which costs more to run and maintain but far outproduces the previous machine. The running cost increases per machine but is reduced per unit produced. Is this an increase cost, a savings, or both? Further, if total production levels are fixed (due to fixed sales), along with other fixed expenses such as overhead and burden, then the new machine may be the only source of potential savings.

There are two fundamental costs associated with wage incentives (other than system design cost): labor costs, and maintenance and administration costs.

Labor Costs. The most obvious wage incentive cost occurs in the increased take-home pay of the employees. It is equally obvious that the type of wage incentive plan—how it is designed—will also affect employee take-home pay. Much has been written on the various early plans (e.g., Bedeaux, Haynes, Garret, and Rowan plans), and today there are hundreds of variations. But it is rare indeed that today's modern wage incentive plans do anything more or less than pay employees on a one-to-one basis *the net company labor savings due to increased productivity.* (The point at which payments are started will be discussed later.)

Employee participation in savings is a negotiable question between management and union, but management should not consider a plan that does not offer its employees the entire financial gain for increased productivity. Plans that offer sliding scales or partial participation in labor savings are unrealistic today. On the other hand, suggestions that employees participate in overhead and burden savings are equally unrealistic. The direct labor cost then (on a

---

[1] Opponents of wage incentives point out that methods can be improved and standardized without going to the final step of wage incentives. Proponents claim that wage incentives force the preceding economy steps and their constant maintenance.

one-to-one basis) will remain constant on a per-unit basis both before and after wage incentive installation. For instance, if an efficient operator produces one unit in one hour and takes home $2 (base rate) and while under incentives produces 1.2 units in the same time frame, the take-home pay must be $2.40.[2] Many incentive plan experts will not accept this commitment, but the authors consider it a fundamental principle of sound incentive plan design. Management should relate increased operator take-home pay to unit cost as shown in Table 1. In this example, both labor and material costs are fixed expenses on a per-unit basis, reflecting management's decision to provide labor savings under incentives to the operator on a straight-line basis. Under these conditions there are no direct labor savings. In fact, as noted in the preceding example, labor costs actually represent a larger percentage of unit cost after incentives.

Maintenance and Administration Costs. A functional wage incentive plan requires administration that is sound and maintenance that is preventive. Management must figure the costs involved in maintaining the plan and be willing to commit the money to do it properly. However, many companies have unknowingly undermined the plan by either failing to consider administrative costs or attempting to economize where it is not possible.

A policy and procedure manual outlining the incentive plan must be written. The administrators of the plan must enforce the stated policies without variation. The manual should be reviewed periodically, although changes in wage incentive policy should be kept to a minimum. Management should estimate the cost associated with administration and later, when the plan is functional, not overeconomize on this important aspect of the plan. Management must be committed to maintaining the incentive rate structure and to auditing both the administration and the maintenance procedures.

The costs of standardizing tools, fixtures, process and work flow, and methods are all preliminary costs involved in establishing an effective rate structure. Each time an operation is reexamined, such standardizing steps must be taken. Once the operation is standardized and effective, a time standard is developed. A rule of thumb is to assume that each rate will require reexamination at least once a year. Further, on the average it will require from four to six hours of standardization and rate analysis for each minute of operation cycle time up to and including a five-minute cycle. As the cycle time increases (less repetition), the analysis procedure becomes less critical and accordingly is not as

---

[2] The example assumes that the entire increased output is attributed to increased operator skill and effort with all other process variables remaining constant. The improved performance is representative of a good operator becoming highly efficient.

TABLE 1   Unit Costs before and after Incentives

	Before incentives	After incentives
Productivity.....	100/hr.	150/hr.
Cost/Unit:		
Labor.........	$0.20	$0.20
Material.......	0.65	0.65
A.O.E.*........	0.15	0.10
Unit cost......	$1.00	$0.95

* All other expenses (burden, overhead, etc.).

expensive, relatively.   Maintenance cost of rate structures can be estimated if total rate structures and cycle times are known.

Each rate structure should be audited at least once every two years, and management must estimate the costs involved. The auditing procedure (to be discussed in detail later) does not have to cover 100 percent of the costs. Rather, it is similar to the sampling inspection procedure.

DESIGNING THE PLAN

In designing a wage incentive plan, the first consideration is whether individual or group incentives will be used. Then questions of structure must be decided—e.g., the scope of the plan, at what productivity level bonuses will begin, special allowances, etc.

Individual or Group Incentives? In an individual incentive system, each operator has a rate structure, including all allowances, with which actual productivity is compared and the bonus calculated. The bonus or its related operator efficiency is converted to actual hours worked versus standard hours allowed, and the calculated efficiency is determined for a predetermined time period, preferably daily.

It is apparent that individual incentives maximize employee efficiency; employees have been known to operate at 150 percent of high task standard rates. The outstanding operator's maximum bonus is limited only by his own productivity. The poor operator is recognized immediately and corrective action can be taken. It is not uncommon for the second-shift operator to slide into the chair while the first-shift operator slides out, all without missing a single beat in the producton line. Individual incentive operators often skip or minimize their personal delays; many will produce for a few minutes of their lunch period and start again early. On machine operations, operators will make all kinds of attempts to increase machine speed, even to the point where waste or quality or machine maintenance becomes a problem. The material handler responsible for supplying incentive operators is constantly harassed by them. Poor-quality tools, fixtures, or materials which hurt performance are simply not tolerated. In short, individual incentives create highly efficient operators.

Since individual incentives maximize efficiency, they appear to be the best choice. In some cases they are, but this depends almost entirely on the willingness of management to suffer the high administrative and maintenance costs of this type of plan. Individual incentives maximize the number of rate structures and therefore maximize the problems and costs of rate maintenance.

Rate erosion, errors in calculations, and operator-introduced method improvements become major problems in this plan. Because the standards used to establish the rates do not represent an exact answer, and because to some degree they depend on the theory of large numbers for accuracy, it is possible for two operators not to have the same relative standard. This may not be apparent to management, but it is obvious to the people doing the work. Furthermore, accounting and inventory systems are complex, since individual operations must be summarized daily. All of these factors add up to increased maintenance and administration cost for individual wage incentives.

The group incentive plan has become popular in recent years because it is less costly to administer and maintain than individual incentives. The principle of the plan is the same as that of individual incentives—to pay operators for increased skill and effort. As the name implies, groups of operators produce against a rate structure. Under the group incentive plan, group size and makeup become very important considerations. For the most efficient operation a community of interest must exist and each member of the group must be able to measure his contribution, as well as that of other members of the group, to overall group results.

Groups that become too large and too diverse tend to lose their effectiveness. It is difficult to estimate the optimum size of a group, as this will depend to a great degree on the complexity and variety of operations. For example, a machine group operating on a three-shift basis, where the process is a continuous operation producing a limited variety of product codes, could reach 400 to 500 people and still operate effectively as a group. Opposed to this are homogeneous groups as small as 15 to 30 operators.

Compared with individual incentives, group incentives allow for simple counting and crediting procedures, since pay points can be established where completed units leave the group. Payroll and accounting effort is also reduced since output credit is calculated for the group rather than for each operator, with the bonus being a group bonus divided among the operators rather than a different bonus for each operator.

Perhaps the single most important detriment to group incentives is that the group effect tends to reduce the desire of the outstanding performer to produce at his highest efficiency. Although there is a tendency for the group to increase the efficiency of a poor operator (especially if the group is compatible and pulling together), this tendency is nothing like the spotlighting of poor operators under individual incentives, which results in the average efficiency of individuals rising to a higher level than the average on group incentives.

The choice between the two types of incentive plans is a difficult one. Although individual incentives gain higher efficiency, they also cost more than group incentives. One seldom-recognized and little-discussed factor which often indirectly affects the choice between individual and group incentives is the caliber of shop supervision. When front-line supervision is poor, the balance seems to shift toward individual incentives, mainly because this type of system requires minimum supervisory leadership qualities.

Plan Structure. In the early days of wage incentive plans, rates were established on a piece rate basis in which a specific amount was earned for each unit produced. This method had a great advantage in that it was easy for the operator to keep track of his earnings. Later, as the necessity for guaranteed base rates was recognized and widely accepted, earnings were calculated in terms of bonus earned over and above the normal guaranteed base rate. No longer could the operator multiply the units produced by a standard dollar figure and determine his earnings for the time period. The guaranteed base rate in terms of dollars per hour was not synonymous with the piecework rate of dollars per unit. The operator, in addition to knowing the rate, needed to know the actual hours worked to calculate the bonus. The process became more involved as operators were shifted from job to job. When base-rate structures changed as a result of hourly increases, all incentive rates had to be recalculated. Administration of the piecework plan became quite expensive.

It was natural, then, for the operator to think in terms of pieces per hour. Knowing this figure, it was easy to calculate whether a bonus had been earned, but calculating the amount of bonus was quite difficult. For instance, if the standard required 100 units per hour and the operator produced 125, the operator had difficulty figuring the bonus in terms of dollars. It is obvious that an incentive plan designed so the operator cannot easily calculate the bonus earned is a plan doomed to failure. Thus, management was forced to supply instant, on-the-spot calculating of earnings and bonuses for the operator.

In designing an incentive plan, it is important to recognize that people want to know where they stand, how much they have produced, and how much money they have earned. A yardstick is useless if it cannot be readily used to measure. The overall emphasis in the design of the plan is simplicity. The plan, with all its ramifications, must be understood by its administrators, the shop supervision, and, most of all, the people to whom it applies.

Participation Point. The key question involved in the design of incentives is: "When should the operator start to participate in bonus earnings?" The point in efficiency rise at which this bonus starts will have a profound effect on unit cost, on employee morale, and, in fact, on whether the plan will succeed. This point is called the "participation point," since anything short of this point is paid at the regular base rate or daywork rate. It is indeed difficult to determine at what point in the rise of shop efficiency the employees should participate in increased earnings. It is fairly obvious that a shop operating at 40 percent efficiency (40 percent of high task) cannot be paid 250 percent of present base rates when the shop reaches the high task efficiency of 100 percent. Here the shop efficiency is so low to start with that the payment to reach 100 percent is not reasonable. On the other hand, it is unfair for management to expect a 250 percent increase in productivity without increases in employee take-home pay. At some point in the rise in efficiency the operators must begin to participate in bonuses—but what is the correct point? If placed too high, the plan will fail; if too low, the company will give away its rightful profits.

The first fact to recognize is that it is unrealistic to blame employees for shop efficiencies of 40 percent (high task). Under average conditions, employees working without outside stimulus (such as incentive plans) will average from 65 to 70 percent efficiency. This efficiency is a measure of the operator's skill and effort level. It is not necessarily a measure of shop efficiency, since such factors as methods, work flow, interruptions, etc., have a very real effect on overall shop efficiency. For instance, even though two operators perform the same function and work with equally high effort and skill, it is entirely possible that differences in methods can result in vastly different productivities. In short, shop efficiency and operator efficiency are not necessarily synonymous.

It is apparent that a wage incentive plan must not be predicated on poor methods and work flow. Rather, standards must be based on well-engineered shop operations, making it desirable to standardize operations before incentive installation. This includes the training necessary to obtain this goal. Unfortunately, it is almost always impossible to fully standardize the shop before installing incentives. But the plan design must be based on an effective shop, which will range from 65 to 70 percent efficiency without incentives. The difference between present efficiency and incentive plan entrance efficiency is due to engineering analysis and implementation of management's efforts, and is strictly a management gain. No part of this gain should be involved in the incentive plan.

There are incentive plans with participation points that start at 80 percent or 87 percent or even 100 percent. With the large number of incentive plans in use today it is probably safe to say that participation points range from 70 to 100 percent. Some plans allow for bumps in participation points whereby the bonus is reached immediately upon reaching the point. For instance, with a 25 percent bump bonus plan at 100 percent, the operator earns base pay to 100 percent, 25 percent bonus at 100 percent, and more than 25 percent bonus as 100 percent is exceeded. Many early incentive plans varied the incentive bonus so the operator got something less than a straight one-to-one ratio of bonus earned to units produced. The authors believe both the bump participation plan and plans that pay less than a one-to-one bonus ratio are unrealistic today, and accordingly they do not recommend their consideration.

It is reasonable at this time to ask why incentive plans have such a wide variety of participation points. Part of the answer is similar to the answer to why base rates vary for the same operation in different companies. Yet this is not the whole answer. A company cannot establish the participation point simply to maximize gains, for if it does, the plan may fail and nothing be gained. If an employee's average efficiency was 60 percent, and he had worked at this level for years, would he be interested in an incentive plan that offered participation, say, at 90 percent? It is unlikely that he would, for to gain any bonus he would first have to increase his efficiency by 50 percent.

The highest participation point must be reasonably close to the "good" level of operator skill and effort prior to incentive installation. The average level is 65 to 70 percent, while the "good" level is approximately 80 percent. In these terms, then, the highest participation point is 25 percent below 100 percent (high task level), and anything less depends on management philosophy.

There is one other qualification which must be considered in choosing the incentive participation point, and this is the method of allowances. All plans add to the rate structures allowances for nonstandard variations. The result of allowance calculation influences the selection of participation points. For instance, some plans use a minimum participation point (87 percent) but provide allowance for fatigue, coordination, personal time, etc., while other incentive plans participate at 80 percent but minimize allowances.

To simplify the selection of participation points, the authors recommend that only three be considered: 15, 20, and 25 percent. These points are representative of 87, 83, and 80 percent efficiency as measured against high task (incentive-level) standards. When the operators reach the point selected, they start participating in incentive earnings or bonuses and continue to participate on a one-to-one basis. If a low task standard is used (approximately 15 to 25 percent less demanding) and is not factored to a high task level, then the participation point should be 100 percent with the same earning potential as the 15, 20, and 25 percent participation points for high task standards.

The authors are familiar with incentive plans that use an unfactored low task standard and provide participation points starting at 80 percent. In reality these plans start bonuses when operators reach about 66 percent of high task level, for the low task level is about 83 percent of high task ($0.83 \div 1.25 = 0.66$). There is only one justification for payment of bonus starting at operator efficiency of 66 percent (high task), and that is management's unwillingness or inability to raise operator efficiency to a good average day work level before the installation of incentives. The usual shop supervisory techniques for motivating employees will not be sufficient to gain an effective efficiency level prior to incentive installation. In fact, the job of gaining an adequate efficiency level may be so costly that management will allow the incentive plan to take over part of the shop supervisor's job. The authors do not recommend this approach to incentive installation or design, since incentives cannot provide a lasting crutch for poor supervision.

Incentive Coverage. An incentive plan will not be effective unless most operators participate in the plan and in the bonus. The aim of both management and employees is to maximize incentive coverage, but unfortunately not all work is measurable—or measurable to the point of confidence. Management should resist attempts to measure work that can be measured only vaguely, even though management wants this work included in the incentive program.   The employee prefers work that is measured vaguely (because of the obvious opportunities to beat the standard).   The result is great pressure on the administrators of the plan to include all employees in the coverage.

There are additional inducements for management to increase incentive coverage.   For instance, the material handler provides supplies to incentive operators, and both the operators and management want supplies delivered on time and in a manner not to inhibit production.   Obviously, the material handler must participate to the point where, at least, he exerts enough extra effort to prevent interruptions in the process.   But how do you measure and standardize the material handler, or the layout operator, or the maintenance man?   The effort and cost to measure these assignments and obtain accurate frequencies, much less maintain the standard, can be completely prohibitive.   Yet if the incentive plan is to be a success, almost all of these indirect labor jobs which affect productivity, waste, quality, or downtime must participate in potential incentive earnings.

In both individual and group incentive plans, the difficult-to-measure functions participate in average group earnings.   On individual incentives, the material handler is paid the average earnings of the group he services.   With group incentives, special calculation is not needed, since it is already available. While the material handler participates in average earnings and is therefore covered in the incentive plan, management must make sure that the assignment is loaded properly so the material handler cannot loaf and still earn a bonus.   This information is gained by measuring the assignment by a statistical sampling technique known as "ratio delay" or, more recently, "work sampling."

Management should aim for incentive coverage of 100 percent, but realistically something less may be accepted.   This coverage varies, but two guides are provided in determining coverage:

1. Do not provide direct incentive application when the standards cannot reflect minor changes in motion pattern, work flow, and job standardization.   If the standards cannot reflect these, then creeping changes will erode the rate and make it useless.

2. Do provide incentive coverage for operations (other than those directly measurable) which affect the efficiency of direct incentive operations, but provide this coverage on a group average basis and periodically measure work loads by working sampling.

Machine Operations.   An operator working on a manually controlled assignment employing super skill and effort can obtain 144 percent efficiency, or a bonus of about 65 percent, depending on the incentive plan participating point. But what if this same operator works on a machine which controls the output? An operator then cannot increase output, has little chance of demonstrating superior skill and effort, and has no chance of increasing earnings.

The problem is further complicated when operations that are only partially machine-controlled are considered, or operations, such as conveyor line assignments, in which the operator's work assignment is paced to some extent by circumstances beyond his control.

It is clear that operators who are machine-controlled must have incentive coverage, and the system and its policies must be designed to include them.[3]

---

[3] It should be noted that incentive plans may not be used in companies whose operations are highly automated or machine-controlled.   Although incentives tend to reduce downtime and setup times and the operators keep the operation effective, other motivational systems have achieved the same ends.   The question is one of cost effectiveness for the industry involved.

Furthermore, operator performance on machine operations must be measured, and the assignments, in terms of number of machines, attention time, etc,. loaded to maximize effectiveness.

Allowances. Provision must be made in the design of the incentive plan to introduce new operators into the plan and to allow for improvement time. Generally, this means training periods that place new employees outside incentive coverage until they have mastered the skills of the assignment. In group incentives the introduction of a new employee will affect group earnings until the new operator learns the assignment. The same is true to a lesser extent in individual incentives, as a new employee will adversely affect earnings of average-earning operators (such as material handlers), or even act as a production detriment on a progression line conveyor assembly.

New employees should initially be excluded from the plan. Training periods should be established by roughly classifying operations into typical training periods (such as four weeks, six weeks, etc.). The new operators are paid at base rate while learning the assignment. When the training period is completed, operators are introduced into the incentive plan provided they attain a minimum specified efficiency.

When an experienced operator is forced into a new assignment, an allowance for learning is required. Here the operator has already learned all the skills necessary to perform the operation, and obviously he must not be penalized during this learning period by reverting to base rate. A solution to this problem is to pay the operator the average bonus earned on the old job for a period of time while he is learning the new assignment, or to allow for a diminishing rate over a specified period until standard is reached.

The theory of a learning allowance is more than just the problem of introducing experienced employees into new rate structures. Consider the question of job cycle length or lapse. An operation with one-minute cycles is quickly learned, but how long will it take an operator to learn an assignment whose cycle is four hours? Or on job shop assignments, can operators be expected to operate at 100 percent skill and effort when each job is different and the lapse before repeating an assignment may be a matter of weeks?

The solution to these problems is an external allowance for start-up learning time on top of normal-rate structures. This allowance is external simply because it is subject to change, while the normal rate must be maintained. Learning curves are available for most industries or can be designed specifically for the company's needs.

The following list of miscellaneous allowances usually established and maintained through work sampling must be considered in every rate structure. The allowance itself must be external and in addition to the normal rate:

1. Fatigue—excessively fatiguing assignments
2. Interruptions—supervisory discussions or waiting for work
3. Personal time for personal needs and recovery
4. Mechanical breakdown
5. Poor (material) supplies
6. Line balancing—inability to exactly match loads on each operator when the production on one governs the other's production
7. Setup, repairs, material handling, and layout

Each of these possible allowances must be considered, yet each does not have to be measured, maintained, and designed as part of the basic rate structure. Where this is too expensive, a nonstandard allowance can be considered external to the wage incentive plan and the actual time involved allowed either at average earnings or at base-rate pay. Whatever is decided here must become policy (in writing) and understood by all involved.

INSTALLING THE PLAN

Obviously, it is important that the union (if there is one) be fully informed about the wage incentive plan. In fact, the plan will become a negotiable item to be clarified and made part of the management-union contract. This phase of communications is seldom overlooked; on the other hand, it is only rarely that the plan is adequately explained to operators and supervisors. Successful installation of a wage incentive plan also requires standardization of processes, development of reporting procedures, and training.

Communications. It is recommended that each operator and supervisor be candidly informed of the advantages and possible difficulties of the incentive plan. The people involved must be made a part of the thought process which developed the plan and must be committed to its success. Often, hourly employees misunderstand management's real goal in installing an incentive plan. Fears of sweatshops and rate cutting must be dispelled, and the only way to do this is through demonstrated management integrity. Furthermore, cheating on incentives must be frankly discussed with the people. Safeguards against cheating, rate cutting, etc., must be employed, and both the need and the penalty must be understood. As stated before, a feeling of team effort by management and the operators must be established.

In time the management-employee relationship will evolve into constant pressure by the employee to loosen the rate structure and incentive policy, while management will strive to hold its position. There is no proof that grievances increase with incentives, but the type of grievance changes. This type of conflict must be discussed with employees prior to incentive installation, and management's commitment to maintain the system and to enforce its policies must be made clear.

Process Standardization. Before incentive rate structures are developed, a real attempt should be made to standardize the various ingredients in the process. For instance:

1. *Material flow:* Material movement and quality should be reexamined according to industrial engineering techniques.

2. *Tools and equipment:* Maintenance of tools and equipment should be reevaluated to effect good condition.

3. *Methods:* Each operator's motion pattern should be examined for improvement. Trained rate setters are well-versed in the standard motion economy principles. The process of establishing standards or rate structures is mechanical in nature and need not be discussed here. Management should expect rate development to follow the normal procedure. To ensure that rates are reliable, management must insist that only trained personnel establish rates; an attempt to economize in this area can have disastrous results later on. Many fine consulting firms provide personnel trained to perform this function.

4. *Documentation:* Of vital importance, regardless of who establishes the standards or rate structure, is the complete documentation of all conditions on which the rate is based. Unless such documentation is available, it will be impossible at some later date to determine if any changes in conditions have occurred, and rate grievances will be difficult, if not impossible, to solve. Many practitioners use Polaroid cameras to take photographs of the work place in order to support the written documentation.

Incentive Plan Reports. A new system requires new reporting procedures. The wage incentive plan will require new or better control and reporting procedures on inventory (both beginning and ending and partially completed units), quality, waste or scrap, and time. These data are used in incentive reports on efficiency, standard cost, and employee earnings.

Training.   Operators introduced into new methods or changes in the process must be trained.   There are two main techniques for conducting this training:

1. *Vestibule training.*   This is a form of off-the-job training in popular use. The new operator or one requiring a refresher course is removed from the job and assigned to training for a time frame.   During this period, the operator practices the various skills required to perform effectively.

2. *Audiovisual aids.*   This form of on-the-job training uses both audio and visual aids to teach the operator order of assemblies and motion patterns. Coupled with left- and right-hand charts, this training procedure has done much to reduce learning or start-up time.

MANAGEMENT COMMITMENT

It hardly seems necessary to discuss the need for management commitment to a wage incentive system.   Yet, even if the system itself is sound, without a commitment on the part of management it is doomed to failure.   Specifically, this commitment must be demonstrated in the areas of system administration, maintenance, and auditing.

Administration.   As previously mentioned, management must define the proposed wage incentive system in written policies and procedures.   This wage incentive manual must be thorough and simple to understand.   Obviously, it must not conflict with the union contract, but it should spell out exactly how the system will be administered.   There is no easy way to do this—just plain hard work and constant review are necessary.   The manual must be complete prior to incentive installation or it is apt to be overlooked.

Furthermore, management must be completely committed to the policies and practices stated in this manual, although this should not restrict revision or improvement.   This commitment is most important from top management, but it is also a commitment of the entire company.   If the wage incentive policy states that wage incentive rates will not be changed except in cases of clerical error or method changes, then top management must insist that these conditions be met to justify rate changes.   If the wage incentive policy states that rates will be established using certain standard techniques, then management must not abort the techniques by negotiating rates.   It is a two-way street.   If policies are to be enforced with integrity by management, then management must not allow the policies to be bent by employee or union pressure.

It is obvious that a company's labor relations organization plays a major role in the management commitment to wage incentives.   Although the authors recognize that compromise is essential to labor-management agreements, it is important to realize that a successful incentive plan can be undermined, unknowingly, in negotiated agreements.   The important point here is that in negotiating, the labor relations group should be especially careful in what it gives away in wage incentives.

Top management's intentions in committing to wage incentives must be clear to middle and first-line supervision.   If shop foremen and system maintenance personnel do not understand or do not believe in the success of the system, then it will surely fail.   Management must understand that every pressure on these people is to abort the system.   Shop foremen look better with high earnings.   Who ever heard of a union grievance on loose rates?   If high earnings are a result of high efficiencies, then the shop foreman has done a fine job and should look good.   But what if efficiency is average with high earnings?   Obviously something is wrong.   The major commitment of management is a commitment *not to let this happen!*   And happen it will, for erosion of incentive rate structures is inevitable at a rate of from 1 to 5 percent a year.

Maintenance. One of the most important phases of any successful wage incentive system, but one that is too frequently neglected or given only minor attention, is that of maintenance. The most precise and carefully introduced plan can soon deteriorate if continuous attention is not focused on updating the wage incentive standards and making certain that such standards are not being misapplied.

Incentive maintenance is not an easy task, and people assigned to it must be thoroughly trained in all aspects of the system and completely knowledgeable on the details of the rate structure. These people must know of the art of methods improvement and, most important, they must know of the management commitment. Their assignment is to keep the rate structure as pure as possible. All the pressures push these people toward taking the easy path, especially if their decisions are mainly judgmental. Management must fill this gap—and fill it in an effective, time-proven manner. An auditing procedure must be established.

Auditing. Information concerning major changes in product or methods is usually available early enough and in sufficient detail to enable the industrial engineering organization to determine the effect on existing wage incentive rates. On the other hand, minor changes resulting from changes in frequencies or operator-initiated shortcuts often go unnoticed or are deemed unimportant. Any one such change may not materially affect the rate, but the accumulation of many changes over time can have a devastating effect. Problems also arise when wage incentive rates are mistakenly applied to operations not covered by the rate.

To avoid such erosions to the wage incentive system, management should install an auditing or review program. A program of wage incentive auditing includes a number of important items and is designed to detect:

1. Engineering and/or product changes
2. Changes in manufacture
3. Creeping changes, often operator-initiated
4. Misapplications of predetermined times
5. Inconsistent time study methods
6. Incorrect allowances
7. Obsolete and misused wage incentive standards
8. Errors in recording time charges
9. Poor attitudes of industrial engineers
10. Poor attitudes of foremen

Before any auditing program is established, management must decide several important questions, such as the organization to be responsible for auditing, the coverage desired, and the level of management to receive the formal audit reports.

Auditing Responsibility. The organization charged with the responsibility for auditing should, to the fullest extent practicable, report to a third- or fourth-level manager sufficiently separated from the actual establishment of the wage incentive rates to ensure an unbiased, impartial disclosure of the findings. The reason for this should be evident. It is wishful thinking to ask, and expect, the supervisor responsible for establishing and maintaining the wage incentive program to audit his own work and report deviations from sound wage incentive practices to his superiors. If the company is a multiplant organization, an ideal arrangement is to have the primary responsibility for auditing invested in an organization reporting to the headquarters staff, with perhaps a secondary or supplementary auditing organization at each of the factory locations. The company size, number of plant locations, variety of product, and similar considerations will influence the decision whether all auditing will be conducted by the headquarters organization or whether such activity should be supplemented by local auditing.

In any event, the organization charged with auditing should be staffed with topflight, competent industrial engineers possessing broad experience in all types of wage incentive rates and all phases of work measurement, including the application of predetermined time systems, time study, work sampling, and similar techniques.

Audit Coverage. With regard to the audit coverage desired, consideration must be given to such factors as whether individual or group incentives are employed, the number of groups involved, how frequently new products are introduced and old ones replaced, the frequency and magnitude of changes in methods, and the budget which can reasonably be allocated to auditing. A good rule of thumb is to develop a staff capable of auditing wage incentive jobs or groups once every two years.

Reporting. Any auditing program, to be meaningful, must be more than a disclosure of deviations from sound rates and practices. Unless prompt corrective action is taken on the audit findings, the program is but an exercise. To ensure that such corrective action will be taken, the report of the audit findings should be forwarded to the plant manager, with copies to the manager or director of the shop involved, the manager or director of industrial engineering, and the chief industrial engineer. Other interested organizations may also be included on the routing sheet, particularly if the findings include comments on their contributions to the wage incentive system.

Follow-up. An important facet of any auditing program is a follow-up system. After a reasonable period following the completion of an audit, a follow-up review should be made to determine the corrective action taken with regard to each of the specific findings of the audit. A follow-up report should be issued and forwarded to the same distribution list as was the original report.

CONCLUSION

The authors have discussed criteria for designing a successful wage incentive plan which are both straightforward and simple. The plan must provide for labor savings as bonuses to employees on a straight-line basis. Participation points in incentive earnings start at 80, 83, or 87 percent, and coverage is maximized. The plan is rigidly administered and maintained through auditing procedures.

The encouragement of this type of approach in designing incentives removes attention from the wide variety of incentive plans with various participation points and sliding bonus earnings as depicted in most works on this subject. If examination of these plans is desired, the reader is directed to the bibliography.

BIBLIOGRAPHY

Louden, J. K.: *Wage Incentives,* John Wiley & Sons, Inc., New York, and Chapman and Hall, Limited, London, 1944.

Lytle, G. W.: *Wage Incentive Methods,* rev. ed., The Ronald Press Company, New York, 1942.

Maynard, H. B.: *Industrial Engineering Handbook,* 3d ed., McGraw-Hill Book Company, New York, 1971.

chapter 35

Designing Incentives
for Sales Personnel

F. L. FLETCHER   *Managing Partner, F. L. Fletcher & Associates, Philadelphia, Pennsylvania*

EDWIN D. MEADE   *Principal, Edward N. Hay & Associates, Philadelphia, Pennsylvania*

As is true of every other aspect of industrial life, the sales function has changed as much since World War II as it did in the entire preceding century. And the rate of change continues to accelerate. Geometrical growth of new products and services, rapid expansion of national firms into international markets, the growing trend toward diversification through either internal development or acquisition and merger, the widespread use of computers and other sophisticated information systems—all of these have required companies to develop new ways of doing business and the sales function to develop new ways to conduct the sales operation.

The most obvious result is that sales has become marketing. Where once salesmen operated almost totally independently, today they work in concert with advertising, promotion, marketing research, or, in highly technical industries, with research people, scientists, etc. Where once the salesman was the key factor in making a sale, today sales accountabilities are spread among a number of functions. And where once it was appropriate to tie sales pay to sales volume, usually through a straight commission system, today the dispersion of accountabilities and the growing emphasis on sales service and sophisticated technical know-how must be reflected in the sales pay system.

What must also be reflected in the sales pay system is that, despite the fantastic technological development we have seen since the early 1950s, no way so far has been found to mechanize the buy-sell transaction. Sales is still a very human undertaking, and motivation is a crucial factor in the success of the undertaking.

The concern of this chapter is how to motivate salesmen—specifically, how cash and noncash incentives can help achieve marketing goals. The assumption underlying our discussion of incentives is that the total pay system must be geared to the specific nature of the sales/marketing operation. Does the company sell to retail or industrial markets? To what degree is marketing support a factor in sales? What proportion of the salesman's accountability is service rather than sales? Does the sales job require special technical know-how, and at what level of sophistication? These are the factors which must be dealt with in figuring marketing costs and the proportion of the total marketing budget that should be allocated to sales compensation, and all of them are related to the one critical question: Where do the accountabilities lie? If the company manufactures consumer packaged products and advertises heavily in the mass media, a proportionately greater share of the marketing budget should be allocated to advertising than would be the case if the company sold capital equipment to industry. Similar reasoning is applicable in determining the mix of the salesman's compensation. The greater the support he receives from allied marketing functions—the larger the role they play in sales—the greater should be the salary portion of his compensation. And similarly, if an important part of his job is servicing his accounts and providing technical information—that is, nonselling jobs—his total compensation should not be tied solely to sales volume. Rather, the degree of his impact on sales volume should be reflected in the mix of his compensation package—in the ratio of salary to incentives.

Another factor which must be considered in developing a pay plan is competitive practice. If a competitor pays a salesman total compensation of $13,000 in increments of $10,500 salary and $2,500 incentive for 100 percent quota accomplishment of $400,000 in sales, another company in the same market will have to pay its salesmen within a relative range if it wishes to retain an effective sales force. As a rule, smaller companies with less well-known products tend to pay their salesmen at somewhat higher rates than larger companies whose products have broader acceptance. The greater investment of large companies in recruiting and training is part of the reason for this; and in most cases the large companies are willing to spot their smaller competitors a slight differential in salesmen's pay. The slightly lower pay usually is offset by certain other features, such as corporate prestige, cars, trips, meetings, management training, and long-range opportunities for promotion.

In the sections that follow, we discuss cash and noncash incentives as one aspect of total sales compensation within the framework of the larger marketing operation. In addition, sample incentive plans are described.

CASH INCENTIVE PLANS

Should payout be based on total sales volume dollars, since the company must achieve certain volume levels to survive, or should the varying profit margins of product lines be taken into account in setting standards of rewards, or should some combination be used? Should a quota be set for a total dollar sales or should there be several quotas set for major product lines? Should weighted incentives be used to emphasize particularly desirable product lines?

Quota Systems. The principal problem in using a quota system is setting the quotas that provide all salesmen with an equitable incentive opportunity.

Quotas can be based on the company's overall sales forecast broken down to individual salesmen. Or they can be set by the salesman and his manager on the basis of sales forecasts for his specific territory. A combination of these approaches generally yields the soundest quota estimates.

Companies use various techniques to reduce the possibility of inequities arising from the established quota system. One common method is to figure the quota as the average of the preceding year's actual sales and the coming year's sales forecast, and then to cut in a moderate incentive at some point under quota—e.g., at 80 or 90 percent.

In cases where market variables make it difficult to set individual quotas, a group quota is set for each sales district. The group incentive pot is then distributed among individuals on the basis of performance appraisal.

Nonquota Approaches.   In some cases, a pure sales dollar quota system is not appropriate to a company's marketing program. For example, management may want salesmen to concentrate on a few long-cycle, large-dollar-volume orders or on opening up new accounts. Or the business may be highly technical, with salesmen relying heavily on assistance from company specialists, or customer service may be the salesmen's most important accountability.

In such cases, performance appraisal is the alternative to the quota as a means of measuring and rewarding performance. The appraisal system must be based on the accountabilities developed in a carefully written job description.   These major accountabilities should be measurable by some semi-quantitative standards and avoid—as far as possible—the realm of purely personal judgments.

Occasionally, more specialized concepts are used in constructing sales incentive plans. One approach is based on the company's recovering the direct costs associated with the salesman—salary, car, etc.—through the use of a formula which triggers the incentive plan into action. For example, if $20 of sales volume is required to produce $1 of profit, and the salesman's salary is $12,000 and his allied costs are $5,000, he must produce $340,000 (20 × $17,000) before the company recovers the cost of having him on the payroll; beyond this $340,000 break-even, the salesman can begin to earn incentive payments.

Determining Incentive Payout.   In most quota systems, incentive amounts are figured according to dollar sales volume over quota. In cases where price fluctuations significantly affect dollar volume, however, the quota can be stated in units.

Incentive rewards may be stated as a percentage of dollar sales over quota or, more frequently, as a percentage of salary—i.e., beat the quota by 10 percent and the reward is 10 percent of salary. The latter approach more strongly emphasizes the salary element of total compensation and rewards the better-paid and presumably better salesmen at a higher rate.

SPECIFIC DESIGN QUESTIONS FOR CASH INCENTIVES

The pure-commission salesman sells today to eat tomorrow, and quite naturally will place his day-to-day interests ahead of the longer-range interests of the company. In companies with long-range growth aspirations, the marketing objectives of the company may require the salesman to carry out programs that interfere with his current ability to earn incentives—e.g., introducing a new product or making a special survey of his district, etc.

The company therefore must design the sales job to include these accountabilities and then develop a sales compensation program which will provide the salesman with sufficient base salary to discharge these responsibilities without jeopardizing his financial position. Companies tend to forget that base salary entitles them to acceptable performance of all the accountabilities of the job.

Developing Performance Standards. The problem is to determine what is acceptable performance, and then, what is adequate pay for that performance. Setting this standard is the thorniest problem in the development of an incentive plan, since it also represents the approximate point at which the salesman begins to earn incentives. The standard may be set by formula or by appraisal or by some combination; but no matter how it is set, it is unlikely to satisfy everyone. Nonetheless, both company and sales force will generally live with some degree of inequity in order to obtain the mutual benefits of an incentive plan.

Split Sales Credits. Another continuing problem, particularly for companies with multidivision or multiplant customers, is split account credits for sales orders. When the order is placed in New York, the material is delivered for consumption in Texas, and there is a testing laboratory in the Midwest—and each place is called on by a different salesman—how is the order credited against quota?

There are two approaches: (1) the sales manager acts as judge in each individual case and makes the allocation of credit; or (2) credit can be allocated according to an arbitrary formula which will sometimes result in inequities. In both approaches about the same number of people will be unhappy in the same degree. However, the second approach saves valuable time by using clear-cut ground rules. Also, dissatisfaction is directed against a procedure rather than against an individual.

Windfalls and Disasters. Another major problem is the possibility—in a constantly changing market environment—that the salesman's incentive earnings can be influenced dramatically by circumstances beyond his control. The chances of this happening are greater, of course, in a formula plan than under a plan based on performance appraisal. In a formula plan, the impact of disaster is reduced when: (1) the base salary is equitable and competitive; and (2) the incentive cuts in at some figure less than actual quota. To protect against windfall, the formula can have a sharply reduced payoff beyond some figure such as 120 percent over quota. The reasoning is that performance of better than 20 percent over quota—when quota is equivalent to acceptable performance—is usually the result of a windfall or a faulty quota, and that such performance should not be rewarded to any significant degree. Some plans have fixed ceilings. There is a considerable body of opinion, however, which holds that a fixed limit to opportunity can have a negative psychological effect, even though attainment of the ceiling is highly improbable.

House Accounts. Large, important accounts which, because of managerial relationships, are not controlled by the salesman can cause another problem, since these usually are not credited to quota. In most instances, however, the salesman is required to make service calls on these accounts. In such cases, a salesman must be reminded that the job accountabilities, rewarded by base salary, require this activity. In addition, usually a senior salesman with a high base salary is deployed to cover these special important accounts.

Inclusion of Marketing Staff. The question of whether marketing specialists who work closely with the field sales force should be eligible to participate in the sales incentive plan can provoke lively discussion. Some companies arbitrarily limit the plan to the field sales force and reward closely allied groups by more frequent merit increases or faster opportunities for promotion. Other companies include the specialists in the plan if a majority of their time is spent in the field working with salesmen and the common objective is to increase sales volume. Product managers, whose major accountabilities are planning, profitability, and product line management, usually are excluded from sales incentive plans.

New-product Introduction. The development and market introduction of new or modified products is usually a key objective of most growth-oriented companies. A substantial portion of this task generally falls to field salesmen as part of their continuing relationship with customers and prospects. The time devoted to this task can restrict opportunities in regular sales efforts and reduce the potential for incentive earnings. However, this activity is of prime importance to the long-range growth objectives of any company. There are two approaches to this problem. The first is to consider this activity as part of the basic job accountabilities rewarded by salary, and the second is to create a special incentive program, running separately but concurrently with the regular program, as a one-time reward for performance in new-product introduction. There is no overwhelming majority for either approach.

Price Changes. In the current economy, price changes—principally on the up side—are a way of life. In certain commodities, such changes substantially affect results against a quota measured in dollars, leading to higher incentive earnings for the same performance. When significant price changes occur, the quota should be adjusted commensurately. What is significant is a judgment for each company; however, a change of 5 to 10 percent normally should be reflected in a quota change.

Timing of Incentive Payments. Another consideration in structuring a sales incentive plan is what is the most effective period of time for payment of incentives. Many companies, whose sales cycles are relatively short and repetitive, pay incentives monthly to spur the salesmen to continuous effort. However, some companies feel that monthly payments are so small they lack impact, and therefore they pay incentives quarterly. Where orders are in larger dollar amounts and require more time to develop, companies use either a semiannual or annual payout cycle. Companies favoring the six-month period feel that waiting a year for the reward dampens motivation; in addition, the six-month period allows quotas to be set semiannually, thereby facilitating greater precision in quota-setting. Some companies consider the six-month period a discrete unit; others make partial payment on the first six months with an annual adjustment. Companies using the annual period generally have a sales pattern of a small number of large orders with a long gestation period and a hard core of large, important customers whose volume business accounts for a large proportion of total sales volume.

Transfers. A sales incentive plan may sometimes complicate the switching of salesmen from one territory to another. The problem is not as difficult as it appears on the surface. The stickiest situation is when a salesman in a well-developed territory with good incentive earnings is shifted to a weak territory in order to build it up. If he continues to be paid according to the incentive plan, he will suffer a severe loss of income. The usual procedure therefore is to guarantee the salesman his last year's full income as protection while he develops the poor territory.

Relationships between Base Salary and Incentive. The proper relationship of incentive to base salary, as discussed earlier, is a matter for thorough analysis. The salesman is no longer the only factor in the sales equation. Rather, advertising and promotion, technical services, marketing services, etc., are critical support elements in the development of quality volume business in a highly competitive environment. How important this support is in obtaining sales should be reflected in the degree of incentive opportunity built into the incentive plan. The more critical this support, the less the impact of the salesman, resulting in smaller incentive opportunity and larger base salary as a proportion of total compensation.

SAMPLE CASES OF CASH INCENTIVE PLANS

Now that we have considered some of the theoretical issues involved in developing sales incentives, it may be helpful to take a look at some plans actually in use.

Company A. The company develops, manufactures, and sells nationally a product line of commodity and specialty chemicals. The company has been in business for a number of years with a slow, steady growth pattern, and emphasis is placed on improving current products rather than developing radically new products. The sales force comprises about 60 salesmen, reporting to five district managers. Salesmen are given technical training and are supported by product managers and technical specialists for the major product lines. Geographical distribution of customers strongly influences the product lines handled by individual salesmen. Sales volume varies widely from salesman to salesman, with extremes from $500,000 in specialty chemicals up to $5 million in commodity products.

The incentive plan is deceptively simple, the key element being the sophisticated know-how and experience of the sales administration. The plan is as follows:

1. A judgment is made, based on history and forecast, as to the minimum sales volume the individual salesman should achieve to justify his base salary. This judgment is minimum quota.

2. A judgment is made on the highest sales volume that the individual could achieve if everything fell into his lap, excluding windfalls.

3. A judgment is made as to the salary that would be paid the salesman if the high volume were his normal volume.

CALCULATION

Actual base salary	$14,000	Minimum volume	$1,000,000
Estimated base salary	17,000	Maximum volume	1,400,000
Incentive increment	3,000	Volume increment	400,000

Thus, for $400,000 additional sales, the salesman would receive an award of $3,000, and awards for volume between $1,000,000 and $1,400,000 would be prorated on the basis of this relationship.

4. Individual contracts are developed yearly for the salesmen and the end results are analyzed to ensure relative equity between salesmen in terms of total compensation.

5. An additional amount equal to about 25 percent of the incentive opportunity is available for a performance appraisal award based on important sales accountabilities that cannot be measured fairly by sales volume.

Company B. This company's sales are highly concentrated in a very small group of large industrial customers. This condition will exist in the foreseeable future. Market planning is heavily involved in forecasting the future growth of these customers on an individual basis. The salesman is assigned a group of customers—each one of which has an individual sales quota. The incentive is 1 percent of sales over each individual quota. The base-salary accountabilities emphasize the elements of service required to maintain or increase share of business with these key accounts.

Company C. This company is a medium-sized company with aggressive growth aspirations in what might be broadly categorized as the electronics industry. Currently, the company has some salesmen, but a majority of the sales volume is developed by manufacturer's representatives. The company's intentions are to create a company-employed sales force and to eliminate (except in a few areas) the manufacturer's representative apparatus. Ambitious growth plans are linked to aggressive new-product development. There are four major product lines. As a first step, the company has developed a base-salary structure for salesmen that is internally equitable and externally competitive. The incentive plan offers an additional opportunity of up to 30 percent of base salary depending on performance.

This is how the plan works: Quotas are set semiannually for each of the four major product lines, and incentive awards are paid every six months. In each of the individual product lines, 80 percent of the quota must be achieved before the incentive plan goes into effect. The rise in the incentive earnings curve is moderate from 80 to 100 percent, increases sharply from 100 to 120 percent, and decreases rapidly over 120 percent of quota. If 100 percent of the quota for each product line is achieved (rather than 80 percent), the incentive curve is boosted sharply upward. In addition, there is a performance appraisal incentive opportunity of 25 percent maximum to reward the sales service accountabilities of the sales job. The estimated incentive cost to the company for an overall sales performance 10 percent over quota would be about 1.5 percent of incremental sales over quota, yielding a good incentive to the sales force and a good return to the company.

Company D. This company takes a somewhat unusual approach to measuring sales performance for incentive purposes. The changing nature of the competitive marketplace makes it almost impossible to set meaningful volume quotas; however, the salesman can to a degree influence the price to the customer and the cost to the company. Moreover, the company's accounting system can calculate gross profit margins on each order, identified by individual salesmen. Therefore, the company adopted a formula by which the salesman must first achieve a gross profit margin return equal to his base salary plus $20,000 (a round figure) of closely allied sales expenses. Once the salesman has recovered his costs to the company, he shares in a percentage of the additional gross profits. A problem in this type of plan is to assure that salesmen of equal ability have territory assignments of equal potential, so that richness of the territory does not reward one salesman unjustly compared with his peer salesmen.

Company E. This case is a rather common example of an incentive plan designed to forestall the consequences of a poorly set quota. Incentives start on the first sales dollar and run at a moderate rate until quota is reached. The incentive rate is sharply increased until 120 or 129 percent of quota is reached, and then it is sharply reduced to eliminate windfall situations. Usually when this incentive approach is used, base salaries fall in a lower segment of the salary range.

Company F. This type of plan is directed at rewarding the profit quality of sales volume over quota. All sales over quota receive volume incentive reward, and there is also an opportunity for additional award based on the gross profit margin of the sale. For example, sales over quota with a gross profit margin under 25 percent receive only the volume reward, but sales over quota with a gross profit margin over 25 percent receive additional awards which vary with the size of the profit margin.

Company G. A traditional approach to sales incentives is the draw and commission arrangement. For example, the salesman receives a $500 monthly draw and a 5 percent commission on all sales. The commission earnings are charged against the draw, with the salesman paying his own expenses.

The current trend is away from this type of plan. The salesman tends to see himself as an entrepreneur rather than a company representative, and he sells on a day-to-day basis rather than in terms of long-range company objectives. Moreover, in some cases, the salesman can earn more than the company president. However, in a hazy market environment, this approach gives the company close control over sales costs.

Company H. When sales are made through distributors rather than directly to the end user, a combined quota and appraisal plan is generally used. This is used because a pure quota plan will not measure and reward effectively a number of the important accountabilities of the salesman's job—i.e., acquiring and maintaining quality distribution in his assigned area, working with and training distributor personnel, calling on end users to stimulate sales volume for his distributors, etc. These accountabilities usually can be measured in terms of the end results achieved, thereby providing the foundation for performance-based incentive awards. The quota portion of the incentive can be based on any of the approaches discussed earlier, whichever is most appropriate.

Company I. In selling a highly technical product, orders typically are large and few in number with a long time period between original inquiry and delivery, and accountabilities are shared among salesmen. In these situations, the incentive plan must be based on measured performance of all the salesman's job accountabilities, although it is sometimes possible to inject an element of quota as a trigger point for the incentive plan.

The following case illustrates such an approach. This company's marketing environment is characterized by a limited number of competitive suppliers as well as customers. The size of the market is known, and each supplier's share of total market can be estimated. In this case, the company ruled that the incentive plan would not take effect unless a 30 percent minimum (reset annually) market share was achieved (the trigger). Base salaries were considered to be internally equitable and externally competitive. The maximum incentive was set at about 30 percent of base salary, which could be reached only by distinguished performance. The formula allotted each salesman a maximum of 1,000 points for incentive purposes. The number of salesmen × 1,000 points ÷ ⅓ of the salary payroll = value per point. In this case, the value was about $5 per point. A maximum of 500 of the 1,000 possible points was allowed for volume performance beyond the 30 percent market penetration. Points for volume penetration were awarded by region, and the regional pot was distributed among salesmen on the basis of sales management's judgments as to each individual's contribution to the penetration achievement in the year. The remaining 500 points were awarded according to performance of major job accountabilities, each of which was assigned points. Performance necessary to earn these points was determined on an individual basis, with the standards of measurement agreed upon in advance. Accountabilities such as the following were used:

1. Market intelligence to indicate the probable pricing strategy of competitors.

2. Technical intelligence to indicate how the company could use its engineering know-how to strengthen its bid.

3. Control of contract relations with customers to avoid possible renegotiation charges which could increase costs over the life of the contract.

NONCASH SALES INCENTIVES

Noncash incentive programs have been used widely by industrial and financial companies for several decades. Since the early 1960s their popularity has grown as companies have recognized their unique advantages for certain incentive purposes. Although financial reward is the motivation behind virtually all work, cash prizes for incentives often represent more of the same and not much more in terms of total earnings. Extra cash is sometimes looked upon as pocket money by salesmen, with no family motivation. Cash is not as promotable as merchandise or travel. It does not have the same commemorative or status value. It cannot be pointed to with pride (many salesmen would not wish to admit that an extra $25, $50, or $100 is that important to them). Because of withholdings for taxes and other deductions, cash prize winners do not even get what they win! Finally, purchases made with cash prizes are usually at retail and in after-tax dollars.

Prizes and travel, on the other hand, tend to overcome many of these disadvantages. They are something extra—not just more of the same. Prizes and travel usually involve the family and an extra measure of motivation. Prizes and travel are promotable through colorful catalogs, travel folders, posters, and mailing pieces. They have great commemorative and status value: they can be pointed to with pride as visual symbols of achievement. Although prizes and trips may be taxable as income, the reporting responsibility rests on the winner, and usually there is no withholding by the sponsor. Finally, purchases provided by noncash incentives are nearer to wholesale cost and tax liability is at the "fair market value," usually interpreted as wholesale.

Noncash incentive programs may involve distributors, jobbers, dealers, route salesmen, and the company's marketing staff as well as salesmen, and they can be aimed at a variety of sales objectives, including: (1) increased sales volume; (2) introduction of new products or services; (3) moving slow items and reducing inventories; (4) opening new sales territories; (5) attracting new customers; and (6) emphasizing special products.

Generally a noncash incentive program is designed to achieve one specific goal within a limited time span. The goal is broken down into some measurable performance standard, and performance awards are stated in points or stamps or some other unit which can be converted into merchandise prizes. Or awards may be all-expense-paid vacations.

General Considerations in Developing a Noncash Incentive Program.   Cash incentive plans are usually geared to overall management objectives in sales and marketing; the one-time noncash incentive program, on the other hand, is usually aimed at important subobjectives which may be viewed as discrete units in progress toward the more general goals—for example, an insurance company may want to increase its policy renewal rate, or an auto dealer may want to clear out slow-moving inventory. In determining whether a noncash incentive program is appropriate to its specific needs, a company must consider these questions:

1. Can a simple and clearly determined objective be established, specifying exactly what is intended to be accomplished and to what extent?

2. Is this objective reasonable? Can it be accomplished by individuals (or groups)?

3. Is the objective measurable? Can the individual (or group) performance required by the incentive program be measured through existing record keeping systems?

4. Can the participants be clearly designated—and can other individuals, related by activity, be included so as to achieve a united effort toward the objective?

5. On the assumption that the objective can be reached or exceeded, what is its accomplishment worth (in payout) to the company in total or per individual for measured increments of performance?

6. Can a budget be calculated and allocated in an amount sufficient to stimulate and reward participants?

7. Is there an appropriate theme and promotional plan to introduce and support the program over its life cycle?

8. Does the plan have top management support?

Once a company decides to embark on a noncash incentive program, it must develop a plan for promoting the program, involving the following steps:

1. Develop a campaign theme which is consistent with company requirements and objectives.

2. Provide advance information to all persons involved in the operation and supervision of the program. Meet with them in advance, advise them of the plans, demonstrate the promotional material, and enlist their support.

3. Plan a dynamic kickoff. Use all possible resources for announcement. Personal letters, advance teasers, company papers, magazines, bulletin boards, posters, payroll envelopes, displays, etc., should be exploited to disseminate information about the program.

4. Maintain promotional pressure by a continuous flow of communications both at the office and to participants' homes, providing a regular report on the progress of the competition.

5. Provide for official registration, principally to assure that eligible persons are aware of the program and its objectives, rules, and award opportunities. Through the issue of a registration certificate, pledge card, or some other type of form, the incentive program also takes on a more official character.

6. Plan an exciting finish for the program—for example, a meeting at which management can express its appreciation to all participants, honors can be distributed, and special awards made to top performers.

Fundamentally, an incentive stimulates individual or group accomplishment by offering a reward for performing a specific unit of action. Determination of the unit of action is essential to program planning, since it provides the means for realistically evaluating the potential returns of the program and for establishing a budget—i.e., for each 1 percent you exceed your sales quota, you receive X incentive. While there is no absolute standard to determine the value of the incentive or the costs of such programs, a general rule of thumb is about 8 to 10 percent of sales salary as a maximum reward, and a cost ranging from 30 to 80 percent of the resulting profit or saving. These guidelines do not in any way represent mandatory maximums or minimums. There may be many sound reasons for changing this suggested scale.

Illustrative Examples. Some examples of noncash incentive programs are given on the following page.

Sales/Volume—Insurance Office

Program................ To increase policy applications and sell more insur-
ance, and to increase policy renewal rate above
average
Time................... Three-month program—repeated three times a year
Participants........... Office sales force of 21
Unit of action/Awards.... For each policy application obtained, 300 stamps
For each $100 of annual premium sales, 500 stamps
For each contractual renewal, 500 stamps
Bonus................. For each fourth application obtained, 600 stamps
Promotion............. Letters with catalogs to homes, bulletins, mailers
to homes, weekly meetings

Sales/Volume—An Insurance Company

Program................ To increase sale of profit-sharing contracts
Time................... One year
Participants........... 72 salesmen
Unit of action/Awards.... For each $1,000 of new policy sales, 1,000 stamps
For each new profit-sharing contract, 3,600 stamps
Bonus................. Top performance award each month to salesman
with highest volume, 3,600 stamps
Promotion............. Campaign with announcements, mailers, bulletins,
catalog, and saver book distribution

Sales/Volume—A Local Automobile Dealer

Program................ To increase sales volume and upgrade purchases, to
increase accessory sales, and to clear out slow-
moving models
Time................... 60 days
Participants........... 8 floor salesmen
Unit of action/Awards.... For each $1,000 of sales volume, 5,000 stamps
For each $10 of accessory sales, 150 stamps
For each air conditioner (model xx), 3,000 stamps
For each car (model xx), 2,000 stamps
Bonus................. For top-volume salesmen (each month), 5,000
stamps
Promotion............. Sales progress chart, bulletins, meetings

Sales/New Dealers—Greeting Card Manufacturer

Program................ To increase card sales to present dealers and to
recruit new dealers
Time................... One year
Participants........... All present dealers
Unit of action/Awards.... To dealers for:
Each $10 order over monthly quota, 100 stamps
Each new dealer recommended, 100 stamps
Each new dealer, if appointed, 1,200 stamps
Each $10 purchase made by newly appointed
dealer within the first 90 days, 100 stamps
Promotion............. Bulletins to all dealers, enclosures in monthly
statements, repeated mailings

Sales/Demonstration—A Construction-machine Distributor

Program................ To increase demonstrations to qualified prospects
Time................... Three months
Participants........... 14 dealer salesmen

Unit of action/Awards.... For each complete demonstration of the "Load-master" unit to a prospect on the list of qualified prospects:
For each demonstration, 5,000 stamps
For each sale resulting from a demonstration, 20,000 stamps

Bonus................. For each third demonstration, 2,000 stamps
For each third sale, a travel award*

Promotion.............. Letters, bulletins, phone calls, meetings, and catalog distribution
* Destination and size of trip to be set relative to value of sales.

Sales/Dealer Loader—A Candy Manufacturing Company

Program................ To increase sales of candy, tobacco, and accessories
Time................... One year
Participants............ Five salesmen, 90 retail dealers
Unit of action/Awards.... To salesmen for:
Each $100 over candy quota, 1,000 stamps
Each $100 over tobacco quota, 1,200 stamps
Each $50 over accessory quota, 300 stamps
To retail dealer for purchases: between 100 and 600 stamps per box, carton, or gross, the amount variable with the item
Stamps delivered with orders

Bonus................. Monthly top-performance bonus to salesman who has greatest dollar volume over his quota, 1,200 stamps

Promotion.............. Contest award chart, meetings, catalogs. For retail dealer—bulletins, packing slips, and invoice stuffers

Sales/Referral—A Local Bank

Program................ To increase deposits and obtain new customers
Time................... Three months to one year
Participants............ Tellers, secretaries, clerks, bookkeepers
Unit of action/Awards.... For each new account (over $100), 500 stamps
For each $100 of additional deposit registered, 100 stamps (up to $1,000)
For each $100 of auto loans handled, 500 stamps
For a new-deposit referral, 500 stamps (awards given only when a new-deposit referral card filled out by employee is turned in by new depositor)

Promotion.............. Bulletins and notices, letters to employees' homes, weekly meetings, catalogs

The author of this section wishes to thank the Sperry and Hutchinson Company for its assistance in preparing the noncash incentive section.

CONCLUSION

There are several basic approaches to the construction of sales incentive plans, with an almost infinite number of possible modifications, variations, and combinations. Given this wide range of possibilities, the key is to thoroughly study your marketing objectives, carefully analyze the design possibilities in order to construct a plan that best fits your own situation, and closely monitor the results.

chapter 36

Designing Incentives for Management Personnel

WILLIAM F. DINSMORE *General Partner, Edward N. Hay & Associates, Philadelphia, Pennsylvania*

The purpose of this chapter is to discuss issues and principles of designing management incentive plans. Intelligent design of an incentive plan requires thoughtful and informed consideration of whether and why to develop such a plan. It is appropriate, therefore, to address these questions briefly as a preface to discussing design choices.

Incentive compensation plans are quite common in American industry. Of 206 companies participating in the industrial edition of the 1970 Edward N. Hay & Associates compensation comparison, 66 percent had some form of managerial incentives. NICB data for 1969 give a similar picture: 69 percent of the manufacturers and 54 percent of retailers surveyed reported using management incentive plans.

As these figures indicate, managerial incentives are used in a substantial majority of industrial companies. Hay data, confirmed by other sources, indicate a growing trend toward managerial incentives in recent years, and there is no evidence to suggest this trend will be reversed or even slowed. As a matter of fact, changes in federal tax legislation in 1969 seem to have given new impetus to the trend. The maximum tax rate of 50 percent on income paid for services, coupled with increased taxes on capital gains income, should enhance the attractiveness of cash compensation and probably will increase interest in incentive compensation.

In addition to considering the prevalence of incentive systems, one should also consider how a bonus or incentive program may affect total cash compensation. Figure 1, based on the 1970 Hay Compensation Comparison for

Industrial Companies, compares the pay practices of companies which pay only salaries with those of companies which pay salaries plus a bonus or incentive. The lower line represents average total compensation in nonincentive companies, which is salary alone. The higher line represents average total pay in incentive-paying companies, which comprises salary plus incentives. Clearly, the incentive-paying companies pay considerably more than the nonincentive companies, particularly at higher management levels.

This is a fact of great importance to nonincentive companies. Incentive and nonincentive companies compete in the job market for the same people. Nonincentive companies do not compete solely with other nonincentive companies. To the extent that compensation influences an executive's choice of one company over another, the incentive-paying company has an advantage over the nonincentive company. The executive does not offer a discount to the nonincentive company because it pays salaries only.

Although we recognize that compensation is only one of a number of factors in corporate competition for people, we know also that relative compensation position is important to a company's competitive strength in the manpower market. The nonincentive company, existing in a market in which a majority of companies pay incentives, has three choices. It can decide that it can attract and retain the amounts and kinds of people it requires with compensation significantly below that of a number of other companies. This is reasonable and feasible under a number of circumstances. Or it can decide to match, through salaries, what incentive companies accomplish through a combination of salaries and incentive awards. This is much less frequently reasonable or desirable.

Figure 1.   Average total compensation in bonus and nonbonus industrial companies.

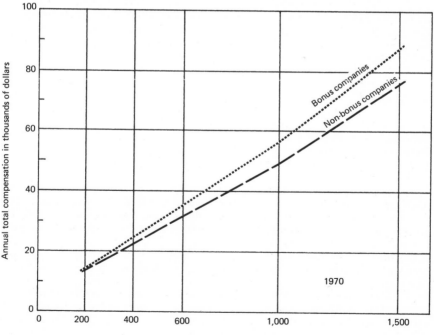

The third choice is incentives. If a nonincentive company feels a need to increase significantly its general level of compensation, it will likely be more prudent for it to accomplish this by providing incremental income through a well-designed incentive plan than by substantially increasing its salaries. It is likely to be more prudent for it economically because of the greater variability inherent in incentives. It is also likely to be more effective motivationally. At least, there is an opportunity that it will be, given effective design and administration.

A well-designed and administered incentive plan is based genuinely on performance, particularly individual performance. Performance objectives are established before the fact, performance is measured against the objectives after the fact, and awards are distributed on the basis of performance. Participants know this, observe it, and understand the relationship between particular awards and particular performance. This is what distinguishes effective incentive plans from "bonus" plans, in which money changes hands in varying amounts for reasons which are sometimes obscure to the recipients. Bonus plans not explicitly based on performance may contribute to a general feeling of goodwill, but more often the bonuses come to be taken for granted as delayed salary. Moreover, they usually do not have an effect on corporate results that is evident enough or measurable enough to justify the cost involved.

The prevalence of incentive compensation and the generally higher levels of compensation in incentive companies are reasons for a nonincentive company to consider incentive compensation. But they are essentially defensive reasons. The objective of achieving greater motivational effectiveness of compensation is a positive reason. It is also the only reason which would make the undertaking worthwhile.

If an incentive plan is initiated for defense reasons alone, it will be a lot more trouble than it is worth. It will also be costly, with more money paid for no improvement in results. Undertaken for positive reasons, properly understood, properly designed, and with a sustained commitment to making it work, incentive compensation is indeed worthy of consideration by companies which pay salaries only. Let us turn now to considerations involved in making incentive compensation an effective process.

CONSIDERATIONS OF SCOPE

In the next section, we will discuss criteria for selecting participants in a management incentive plan. But eligibility criteria have to be formulated within some general notions of how inclusive or exclusive a plan is to be. Some issues of principle and practice are of value to consider at this point.

Obvious questions to be raised are: If incentive compensation can be an effective motivational and compensation process, can it not be equally effective at all levels? Should we not discuss in this chapter incentives in general, rather than managerial incentives? At least, should not our definition of "managerial" for this purpose be very comprehensive, more or less synonymous with "exempt personnel"?

The Difficulty of Specifying Goals. The answer to these questions is by no means a categorical "no." As discussed earlier, however, an incentive plan is based on measuring performance against predetermined goals and granting awards commensurate with the performance achievement. While setting performance standards in terms of specified goals may be feasible in concept and certainly would be desirable in practice at lower levels in an organization, it is nevertheless true that the farther down in the organization one goes, the harder this is to accomplish.   It is this practical difficulty in setting goals and measuring performance which is the primary reason for restricting the scope of management incentive plans.

The fewer the people involved, the more significant the jobs involved, the more feasible is the process.   Even though the advantages which may be claimed for incentive compensation would, in principle, apply at all levels, as a practical matter it is highly desirable to limit the scope of incentive compensation until and unless performance measurement is sufficiently perfected to permit wide extension.

The Risk Aspect.   Another consideration argues for limiting the scope of incentive plans.   A major purpose of incentive compensation is to encourage entrepreneurial spirit and orientation.   Entrepreneurs take risks.   In incentive compensation, risks attach to individual performance, over which the individual presumably has considerable control, and to corporate performance, over which he has much less control.   If his influence on performance is negligible, he really is not in a position to be entrepreneurial.   As regards corporate performance, this is increasingly the case the further down one is in an organization.   Risk-taking implies also financial ability to withstand risks which eventuate adversely.   In this respect, too, the further down in an organization one is, the less he has this ability.   Hence, the entrepreneurial purpose of incentive compensation is a reason for limiting its scope.

International Participation.   Another factor to consider in determining incentive scope is whether companies which have international operations should include their international managers.   United States companies today typically exclude overseas personnel, except possibly United States expatriates.   This practice, however, is at variance with the idea of being truly an international company.

Recently, there have been indications of a trend away from this exclusion and toward inclusion of managers of any nationality, in any location.   Quite obviously, in such companies, eligibility criteria (which are discussed in the next section) must be independent of factors influenced by national and cultural differences.   Salary, for example, clearly is not a usable criterion.   Job content, however, where jobs are measured on the same bases worldwide, would be a particularly useful criterion of eligibility in international incentive plans.

In practice, few companies have incentive plans which apply broadly to, say, exempt personnel, or even to a majority of them—domestic or international.   Companies that are satisfied with the effectiveness of incentive compensation apply it to a very limited segment of the exempt population.   Edward N. Hay & Associates' data indicate that incentive compensation typically begins with jobs having salaries around $20,000 per year, or, for international personnel, jobs of commensurate value.   This cutoff point seems consistent with the considerations just reviewed.

CRITERIA FOR ELIGIBILITY

Having defined the general scope of an incentive plan, a company must develop criteria for determining specific eligibility.   To be most useful, the criteria should indicate a position's importance to the company—its opportunity to influence overall company results.   These may range from very general to very specific; the most common means for identifying people eligible for award consideration include the following:

1. Wholly discretionary eligibility

2. Salary level
3. Organization level
4. Job evaluation

In my judgment, job evaluation is the most useful criterion of eligibility, with salary level the second choice. The following sections explain why.

Wholly Discretionary Eligibility. Eligibility based on an individual's or committee's personal judgments will not lead to an effective or equitable incentive plan. In fact, wholly discretionary eligibility is virtually unworkable except in a pure bonus plan. Because eligibility would be based on a "feel" for jobs and men rather than specific criteria, it would require a great administrative undertaking to identify all degrees of worthiness throughout all levels of an organization and somehow select the most worthy from among this heterogeneous assortment of performances and opportunities. It is not a realistic option for dealing with the issue of eligibility in a genuine incentive plan.

Salary Level. As compared with wholly discretionary eligibility, salary level offers some rationale for defining eligibility. It is not without deficiencies, however. Salary reflects a number of considerations not related directly to a position's importance—for example, past performance, length of service, and favorable or adverse management prejudices. It is not, therefore, a wholly objective or neutral criterion for determining who shall be in and who shall be out of an incentive plan.

In another respect, salaries do not correlate by any means perfectly with importance of positions, where "importance" means relative opportunity to affect company results. Jobs are designed to achieve different kinds of purposes. Some jobs exist, for example, to provide specialized knowledge and develop recommendations for someone who decides whether or not to do something. The salary for such a job must be commensurate with the expertise required to do the job. The salary may be as high as or higher than the salary for another job in which the knowledge requirement is less but the responsibility for results (and, hence, importance) is greater.

Organization Level. It is possible to define eligibility in terms of organization level—e.g., all people reporting to division general managers. This sounds very logical and very workable, but it is neither. If the purpose of eligibility criteria for incentive compensation is, as it must be, to assure equity of opportunity, organization level as the criterion is unsatisfactory.

The principal reason is that a job's importance is determined more by the size of its division than by its place on the organization chart. A third-level manufacturing job in a large division may be a significantly larger job, for example, than the second-level manufacturing job in a small division. To exclude the former job while including the latter would be inequitable.

Job Evaluation. Any method of job evaluation makes some measurement of the relative importance of jobs. Since the reason for specifying eligibility criteria is to develop means for determining position importance, job evaluation is a logical criterion for incentive eligibility. By its very nature, it avoids the distortion inherent in salary levels and organization levels. It focuses on job content alone, discounting the nonjob-content influences on salaries and taking account of organization levels only as they are an actual aspect of job content. Moreover, job evaluation is particularly apt for international incentive plans in that it acts through national and cultural idiosyncrasies to arrive at a supranational measure of job importance.

The Principle of Arbitrariness. There is no criterion which is without difficulties and deficiencies. Any criterion will exclude some jobs from incentive eligibility which someone feels should be included, and vice versa. In this connection, a word should be said in support of what may be called *the prin-*

ciple of arbitrariness. That is, no matter what criteria are used to draw a line between eligibles and noneligibles, there is something essentially arbitrary in how and where that line is drawn. But rather than fret about it and feel a need to apologize for it, it should be recognized that arbitrariness in this regard is inescapable. One's judgment, therefore, about alternative criteria should accept the fact that all are arbitrary to some degree, and it should focus on what each does to limit arbitrariness.

SALARY STRUCTURE AND PRACTICE

In developing an incentive plan, a company must examine its base-salary structure and administration practice to ensure that they provide the sound foundation necessary for incentives to be fair and effective.

The first step is to consider internal relationships and, where pay relationships do not reflect job relationships, to make the changes necessary to achieve equity. Incentive compensation should not be added to a salary structure with significant inequities, for to do so would simply compound the inequities.

Additionally, a company must consider the competitiveness of its total compensation (salary plus projected incentive payments). There is not, however, a precise point at which a company is competitive and below and above which it is either uncompetitive or supercompetitive. Rather, a judgment must be made as to the general level of compensation a company needs to maintain to accomplish its objectives and fulfill its notions of how it wishes to pay people.

This general level of compensation may be accomplished with differing mixes of salaries and incentive payments. The same level of total compensation may be paid as low base salary and high incentive, or vice versa. Which is right? Which is better for a particular company? There are no objective answers to these questions; the answers are essentially choices of management philosophy and style. There are, however, some things to be considered in reasoning about the choices for a particular company.

First of all, there is the factual matter of the difference in salary practices between companies which pay only salaries and companies which pay salary plus incentive or bonus. Figure 2, based on Edward N. Hay & Associates data for 1970, shows that, on the average, salary-only companies pay higher salaries than salary-plus companies. This is not surprising. If anything is surprising it is that the difference is not greater in favor of salary-only companies. The small difference between the two indicates that salary-plus companies by and large pay competitive salaries, with incentive or bonus payments being clearly additional compensation. But the individual salary-plus company, even if it accepts the principle of setting its salaries at competitive. levels, still has to decide *how* competitive it wants to be, for any salary which is at least average in terms of prevailing pay practices is, by definition, competitive.

Incentive-paying companies may take vastly different positions on how competitive their salary structure will be. Two companies come particularly to mind because they are both very large and successful and very far apart in their views as to the proper competitive level for salaries in an incentive-paying company. One keeps its salary structure at the average of industry in general and pays very substantial incentive awards when performance warrants. The other company keeps its salary structure in line with the upper 20 percent of United States industrial salary practice and also pays very substantial incentive awards when performance justifies. The first company's philosophy of reward is that salaries should be adequate but on the modest side, and incentive opportunity should be large in proportion to salary. The second company feels the same way about incentive opportunity, but feels that performance judg-

Figure 2.   Average base salaries in bonus and nonbonus industrial companies.

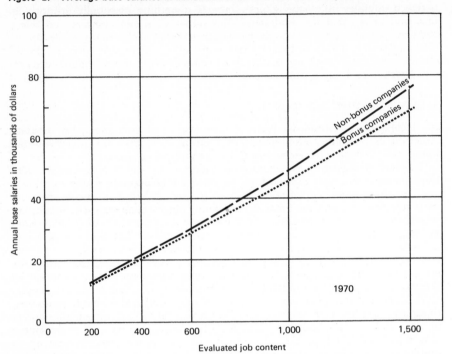

ments will be made much more rigorously if base salaries are quite high rather than only average.   The company reasons that since everyone knows that salaries are competitively high, everyone will be more willing to mete out and accept stricter judgment of performance, and that, further, they can be tough in their judgments without fear of interfering drastically with a person's standard of living.

Is one company right and the other wrong?   Clearly, it is impossible to say that, particularly since both companies have good records of success.

All that can be said by way of guidance to a particular company is that it must have or formulate its own philosophy on the point illustrated by the two companies: How competitive should salaries be?   It must then decide how high it is willing for total compensation to be under various conditions of performance.   From these two determinations it has made the basic decisions as to the overall magnitude of its (cash) compensation plan and the mix of salaries and incentive payments.

DETERMINATION OF AGGREGATE INCENTIVE AWARDS

An important requirement of incentive plans is the development of some means for determining (and limiting) the aggregate of incentive awards in any one year.   Some criteria or devices are needed to guide management in fulfilling its obligations to both shareholders and incentive plan participants.

The Formula-oriented Approach.   Most companies use a formula to create an incentive fund.   Formulas are used to:

1. Measure corporate achievement in the current year

2. Yield a fund large enough to reward incentive plan participants adequately in the current year, considering individual and perhaps divisional achievement, in addition to corporate achievement

3. Safeguard shareholders' interests by assuring a reasonable return on their equity before any incentive compensation is paid to management, and stipulating above this level a fair allocation of earnings between stockholders and management

Developing a formula to accomplish these purposes is an empirical rather than a scientific exercise. That is, the formula is simply a mechanical means of producing an amount of money, as determined by the company's ideas as to where its total compensation level should be, to distribute among a specified number of people. Because company policies on compensation levels and number of participants are basic to incentive plan design, a formula cannot be developed until after these determinations have been made.

Examples of formulas for incentive funds are numerous and readily available in proxy statements, sometimes in companies' annual reports, and in various publications on compensation. Formulas vary in detail but are quite similar in basic principle. Typically there is some sort of threshold of corporate earnings. Incentive awards may not be paid until the threshold is reached, and incremental earnings above the threshold accrue to the incentive fund—are divided between shareholders and management—at a specified rate. The threshold is defined as a percentage of net worth, capital employed, shareholders' equity, or some other measure of corporate performance. Selecting the measure to be used requires a judgment as to what best reflects the totality of what management has to work with in producing earnings. This judgment may vary somewhat by industry and does vary a great deal by managers' preference and opinions.

A typical incentive fund formula is shown in Table 1. In this example after-tax earnings are used. Either pre-tax or after-tax earnings can be used. In either case, the amount available for the incentive fund would be essentially the same under most circumstances, if the figures in (2) and (4) were adjusted appropriately. The critical issue is whether the company wants to include or exclude taxes in the formula measurement of management's performance.

A Goal-oriented Approach. In our work with incentive plans at Edward N. Hay & Associates over the last several years, we have been moving away from using formulas for incentive funds. Our experience has led us to feel that such formulas do not effectively reflect corporate achievement in the current year. It is very difficult, and it may be impossible, to develop a formula that will do this objectively over a long period of time. If a formula is constructed in general enough terms to cover the broad range of circumstances a corpora-

TABLE 1   Incentive Fund Formula

1. Net earnings, after taxes.................	$5,000,000
2. Subtract 6% of shareholders' equity ($30,000,000), i.e., threshold............	1,800,000
3. Earnings in excess of threshold............	$3,200,000
4. Available for incentive fund:	
5% of first $1,000,000 of (3)............	$ 50,000
6% of balance of (3)...................	132,000
	$ 182,000

tion encounters over the years, it cannot be sensitive enough to the particular circumstances of individual years to be a useful measure of short-term corporate performance. We also believe that the effectiveness of incentive plans depends significantly on the clarity of incentive goals. Because a formula tends to state goals in imprecise terms, we feel that it can undermine the motivational strength of an incentive plan.

The alternative we have found effective is to have corporate goals stated each year. They may be expressed as targets for earnings per share or in some other form. The purpose is to specify goals, in terms which are communicated easily, in relation to perceived opportunities for the current year. We think this arrangement serves the first of the three purposes—to measure current corporate achievement—better than does a formula.

The second stated purpose of a formula is to provide a fund of sufficient size to reward participants appropriately, considering the several aspects of performance which determine awards in a given year. In the kind of alternative which we have found effective, the aggregate of awards in a given year is the sum of individual awards earned by corporate, individual, and divisional performance, if the latter is involved in the plan. With a formula, a fund is created which may or may not be distributed in its entirety; under the non-formula arrangement, the amount to be distributed is automatically determined by awards received.

The third of the stated purposes for a formula is to assure protection of shareholders' interests—to prevent a disproportionate allocation of earnings to incentive plan participants. This, of course, a formula does directly, assuming its elements are soundly conceived. However, it is wholly a matter of judgment as to what in the terms of a formula is a reasonable allocation of earnings between shareholders and participants. A formula has an apparent precision in this regard, but the precision is more apparent than real.

Another means of protecting stockholders' interests in determining aggregate incentive award is to specify what is reasonable *total* compensation in terms of competitive pay levels. Thus, with base salaries constant, the incentive portion is varied to reflect performance, and the two combined yield total compensation in line with competitive practice.

Because this approach provides a control on total compensation as well as incentive awards, it really affords stockholders greater protection than the apparently more explicit protection provided through a typical formula. Moreover, this means of determining aggregate incentive award is totally consistent with typical corporate practice in establishing salary levels in that in both cases the assurance to shareholders is based on their confidence in management's good judgment.

None of this is to argue against using an incentive fund formula if that is a company's preference. It is rather to make the point that a formula is not the only way to satisfy the purposes for which it is usually established.

ALLOCATION OF INCENTIVE AWARDS

We have discussed the general scope of an incentive plan, eligibility criteria, and aggregate amount of incentive awards. Once a company has dealt with these issues in designing a specific plan, it must determine how to allocate incentive awards among the eligible participants. Common sense tells us that the president is likely to get a larger incentive award than a plant manager. But what criteria may be built into the incentive plan for judging or determining what magnitude of difference is appropriate between the awards for these two positions?

For purposes of this discussion, let us assume that performance of all participants is equal. We will discuss performance at some length a bit later on, and disregarding it here will simplify our discussion.

What we are seeking in the matter of allocation is a distribution which reflects the relative contributions, or opportunities for contribution, among the jobs involved. The three criteria of job opportunity most often used are:

1. Actual salaries
2. Midpoint salaries of ranges or grades
3. Evaluated measurements of job content

Actual Salary. Actual salaries of participants can be used in two ways to determine incentive awards, both of which force an arbitrary judgment as to the relative importance of the jobs included in the incentive program. One way is for each participant to receive that percentage share of the total of incentive awards which his salary is of total salaries of participants. The other way is to decide that awards will be, say, 25 percent at stated salaries, 30 percent at the next higher group of salaries, and so forth.

Actual salary, used in either of these ways, is not a very satisfactory basis for allocating awards. As mentioned earlier in discussing eligibility criteria, salaries reflect a number of considerations besides relative importance of jobs and value of contributions of individuals. In even the most soundly administered salary plans there will be a number of salary inequities at any point in time. By basing incentive awards on salaries, a company not only loses an opportunity to use incentive awards to moderate salary inequities but also compounds the inequities.

Midpoint Salaries. Midpoint salaries of ranges or grades are a much more acceptable basis than actual salaries for determining awards. They avoid the basic inequity problem involved in the use of actual salaries. As with actual salary, however, it is still necessary to decide what percentage of incentive award will apply at each salary range or grade.

Evaluated Job Content. Evaluated measurements of job content avoid the inequity problem involved in using base salaries. They also provide an objective measure of the job's relative importance, thus precluding the need, which exists with both actual and midpoint salaries, to make what is inherently an arbitrary determination of the percentage award to apply at each salary or salary level. These relationships based on job evaluation can be, and should be, carried over directly to the determination of appropriate incentive award relationships among jobs.

In using job evaluations to determine incentive relationships, one can utilize either the measurement of the total job or that part of the total measurement which deals with job importance. At Edward N. Hay & Associates, we speak of the latter as accountability—that is, what the job is responsible for accomplishing as opposed to the managerial and technical skills required to fill it— and it is this measurement which we use in developing incentive plans. We think accountability is inherently the most logical of the several evaluation criteria because it measures relative opportunities of jobs to affect company results. These relative opportunities, as modified by performance, are fundamentally what incentive plans seek to reward.

PERFORMANCE

The significant characteristic of incentive plans, as distinguished from bonus plans, is emphasis on performance. Bonus plans involve some manner of after-the-fact judgment of performance, on the basis of which payments are made or withheld or made smaller or larger. Incentive plans, as the term is used in this chapter, involve before-the-fact commitments about performance and after-the-fact measurement of performance against these commitments. Payments are made or withheld, or made smaller or larger, on the basis of performance, as with bonus plans. But there is an important difference. The relationship between performance and reward is specified beforehand and after the fact; it is communicated and understood by all participants. The incentive plan is therefore a system of communication as well as a system of compensation.

In designing an incentive plan, assuming that the emphasis on performance is properly understood and accepted, there are several kinds of questions about performance which need to be decided. They are:

1. What elements of performance are to be incorporated in the plan? Corporate? Individual? Divisional? One? All three? Others?

2. If more than one of these elements of performance is included, what should be the relative weights of individual elements?

3. How should objectives be expressed for whatever elements are included, and how should performance be measured?

Elements of Performance.   As with other design issues of incentive compensation plans, there is no automatic answer to the question of what elements of performance should be included. Nor is there any universal answer applicable to all situations and companies. There are some principles, or guides to reasoning, by which the choices can be approached logically.

The beginning point is to consider the purpose for which an incentive plan is being created. That purpose, almost certainly, is to help improve performance of the corporation as a whole. So corporate performance should be one of the elements which determine incentive awards. The degree to which it should be determinative is involved in the question of weighting, which we will come to shortly.

Some companies' incentive plans are based on corporate performance entirely, with individual performance not even being included as a separate determinant. This is a minority practice, but it has some proponents. Their premise is that corporate achievement is a visible, unifying purpose. Participants in an incentive plan will move toward corporate goals more effectively if they are not distracted by considerations of their individual contributions. Within one management style this would be appropriate; within another it would be entirely foreign.

My own preference is to include individual performance significantly, since specifying goals and measuring the achievement of each person allows both the individual and management to make a sound evaluation of his contribution to the company. The exact weight to be given individual performance should be a function of a number of considerations—e.g., the degree to which overall corporate results are the product of interwoven group efforts rather than the sum of independently operating units and people, the extent to which the company wants to emphasize teamwork, etc.

In determining whether or not to include divisional performance, a company should consider the basic nature of its business. If divisions are highly interdependent, it may be counterproductive to try to emphasize separate contributions of divisions. If divisions are largely independent of each other, as is likely in a highly diversified company, it is both possible and more desirable to give separate weight to divisional performance.

Weighting of Performance Elements.   Let us assume that corporate, individual, and divisional performance are all to be included in the design of an incentive plan. The relative weightings among them are partly a function of management style, as indicated above. But there are other considerations.

These include organization structure, relative centralization or decentralization of operations, similarity or dissimilarity of products and businesses, existence or absence of corporate staff functions, and so forth.

To illustrate, most managers would readily agree that corporate performance should have some weight in any situation. But the appropriate weighting for corporate performance would differ greatly as between (1) a company with a few, highly interdependent divisions located close to one another and co-ordinated from a strong corporate staff and (2) a company with a large number of divisions in unrelated businesses, widely dispersed geographically, operating within a semi-holding company organization with a small corporate staff.

Just as weightings should vary between different types of corporations, so might they vary within a corporation, in relation to differences in its individual components and in kinds of jobs. To illustrate, the relative weightings of corporate, divisional, and individual performance logically should not be the same for, say, a group vice president over four divisions and a sales manager of a given division. Similarly, corporate staff jobs would be weighted differently from jobs in divisions, with all the weight in corporate jobs logically divided between corporate and individual performance.

As with virtually all other aspects of incentive compensation, there is no science that indicates a particular arrangement of weightings of the several elements of performance. What is required is thoughtful and imaginative analysis of the particular business of a company, of its individual components, and of what is being sought through incentive compensation.

Objectives and Measurement.   Chapter 27, "Appraising Performance for Incentive Purposes," details a sound and useful approach to setting and weighting objectives and measuring performance, and therefore in this chapter we will not attempt to deal with objectives and performance measurement in any detail. The only point to be made here is that objectives should be set and measurements made for any element of performance which is included in an incentive plan. Thus, if corporate performance is included, for example, some means of defining and communicating corporate objectives and their effect on incentive awards is needed. This may be accomplished through a formula for an incentive fund, as discussed earlier, or through announcement of specific corporate objectives year by year. Similarly, the relationship between divisional performance and incentive awards needs to be defined and communicated. And, of course, the same is true of individual performance.

PAYMENT OF INCENTIVE AWARDS

The basic considerations involved in payment of incentive awards are the timing of award payments and the medium of payment. Thus, payment may be current or deferred or a combination of current and deferred; and awards may be paid in cash or in stock. Each choice of medium may be associated with any choice of time.

The guiding principle in this area is to allow as much choice as possible to individual participants. Certainly this should be to the individual's advantage, and in most instances the company sacrifices nothing of value in extending these choices to individuals. The most basic purpose of an incentive plan is to reinforce motivation. Anything which can be done reasonably to permit incentive plan payments to be tailored to individual preferences and needs should strengthen this basic purpose.

Companies quite often establish particular forms of payment, rather than permit choice, because of advantages which are felt to accrue through them either for the company or for the individual, or both. One commonly used arrangement is the so-called "rollover" of incentive payments, in which each year's award is paid in three or five or some other number of annual installments. To the individual this is often said to have a tax advantage because it spreads part of his income over more than the year in which it is earned. To the company it is often said to have the advantage of retaining people, since an executive would forfeit the unpaid installments if he left the company.

Neither of these advantages holds up well on close examination. So far as the tax advantage to the individual is concerned, if it exists at all, it exists for only the first few years of his participation. After that the accumulated installments due from previous years, added to the current year's installment, wash out any tax advantage. So far as the assumed advantage to the company is concerned, rather than anchoring a person to the company, the unpaid incentive installment simply becomes one of the elements in the package another company must offer to hire the executive away. In this arrangement, the individual would be better off to have free choice and the company would suffer no disadvantage in extending it to him.

Free choice is a nice thing to have, though it is sometimes difficult to employ it intelligently. What is a sound choice or set of choices for an individual depends, of course, on his individual circumstances. But making a sound choice depends also on an understanding of things which most people do not understand fully—for example, provisional tax legislation or details of company benefit plans.

To provide the executive with expertise in these matters, many companies are beginning to make available to their executives authoritative and objective financial advice on the management of these personal affairs. Such a service recognizes that a busy executive does not have the detailed knowledge, nor the time to acquire it, that is necessary to use most effectively the various elements of his compensation package. This kind of service is a logical adjunct of the principle recommended here of giving incentive plan participants as much choice as possible as to the form of their incentive payments.

GENERAL COMMENTS

The purpose of this chapter has been to identify the issues about which decisions have to be made in designing an incentive compensation plan, and to discuss the bases for making these decisions. Unavoidably this has required an emphasis on the mechanics of incentive compensation. That is as it should be for a chapter in a book designed to be a manual for specific guidance.

As regards incentive compensation, however, this emphasis risks understatement of the view that incentive compensation is the financial expression of a mode of managing, rather than just a system of compensating people. In support of this broad view of incentive compensation, it is important that decisions about design issues should not be based merely or even primarily on the simplicity or convenience of this alternative versus that one. Rather, design decisions should be based on how effectively each alternative fulfills and reinforces the management purposes for which incentive compensation is initially undertaken. Also implicit in this broad view is the understanding that incentive compensation is a system of communicating corporate and individual objectives and progress toward them; and further, that the communication system needs constant monitoring and fine tuning to assure that the right things are being communicated and that they are being transmitted and received with fidelity.

chapter 37

Designing Incentives
for Commercial Banks

GRADY E. JENSEN *Director of Organization and Manpower Development, American Express Company, New York, New York*

THE NATURE OF COMMERCIAL BANKING

The banking business may be defined briefly as dealing in money and instruments of credit. The term "commercial bank" is usually applied to a lending institution which accepts demand deposits—deposits which can be withdrawn by the depositor without previous notice to the bank. In the United States commercial banks are distinguished particularly from mutual savings banks and savings and loan associations, which accept only time deposits or their equivalent.[1]

Functions of Commercial Banks. The commercial banking system of the country consists of nearly 14,000 banks. These banks are large and small, urban and rural, and they vary in many other respects. Collectively they can be considered the keystone of the nation's financial system. They hold deposits for millions of individuals, businesses, governmental units, schools and universities, trade unions, and foundations. Through their lending and investing activities for borrowers and customers of many types, they facilitate the flow of goods and services from producers to consumers as well as make possible the financial activities of governments. Commercial banks provide a major portion of our medium of exchange and are the mechanism through which

[1] *Financial Handbook,* 4th ed. rev., ed. Jules I. Bogen, The Ronald Press Company, New York, 1968.

monetary policy is effected. They are unquestionably one of the more critical agencies in the operation of our economy.[2]

Classification and Regulation of Banks. Commercial banks may be classified in three ways: by type of charter, by membership or nonmembership in the Federal Reserve System, and by relationship to deposit insurance. Banks chartered by the federal government ("national banks") are supervised by the Comptroller of the Currency. Banks chartered by individual states ("state banks") are subject to the regulations of their respective state banking authorities. All national banks, and state banks which are members of the Federal Reserve System, are subject to the regulations of the Board of Governors of the Federal Reserve System and are supervised by the Federal Reserve Bank of the district in which they operate. Membership in the Federal Deposit Insurance Corporation (F.D.I.C.) is compulsory for all Federal Reserve member banks but optional for nonmembers. However, nearly all state banks which are not members of the Federal Reserve System are members of and are supervised by the F.D.I.C. A small number of state banks are neither members of the Federal Reserve System nor insured by the F.D.I.C.

It is obvious that commercial banks, as a group, are subject to extensive, and frequently overlapping, governmental supervision of one sort or another.

Recent Changes Affecting Banks' Management Climate. Since the mid-1950s, and particularly during the last 10 years, there has been an unprecedented growth in the nation's economy. While banks have been a principal contributor to this growth, they have also been deeply affected by it. Some of the major changes which bear directly on and affect the quality of bank management are:

1. Accelerated competition for deposit dollars and allied banking services
2. Increased growth of banks through mergers, acquisitions, and formation of multibank holding companies
3. Major shifts in emphasis from wholesale to retail banking
4. Marked expansion of banks' international operations
5. Development of additional in-bank and parallel, complementary services, such as investment funds, credit cards, leasing companies, factoring organizations, and computer service bureaus
6. Emphasis on and significant contribution of youth
7. Development of sophisticated cost systems which can be used to measure the effectiveness of bank performance and the profitability of specific customer relationships
8. Increasing recognition of the necessity for and value of corporate planning, with concurrent use of integrated management information systems[3]

Changes of the type enumerated above have had, and will continue to have, a marked impact on banks' ability to recruit and retain the kind, number, and caliber of officer personnel necessary to produce and sustain profitable growth. During the 1960s banks found themselves at a disadvantage in both recruiting and holding qualified officer personnel. Although it is not true of all banks, generally banks have the reputation for emphasizing security and conservatism in both compensation practice and management approach. This aura of conservatism, although now diminishing, has not appealed to business school graduates or men in their thirties and early forties who are accustomed to, or

[2] Edward W. Reed, *Commercial Bank Management*, Harper & Row, New York, 1963.
[3] Edward N. Hay & Associates, *Incentives for Bankers*, prepared for the Trustees of the Banking Research Fund, Association of Reserve City Bankers, Chicago, 1969.

want, a creative environment, genuine decision-making responsibility, and immediate or near-term financial rewards geared to successful performance.

Competition for Personnel. In recruiting and retaining the new breed of managers, banks are unquestionably in direct competition with industry. This fact of life is becoming increasingly apparent, as evidenced by the following:

1. Banks and industrial companies often compete for the same college and business school graduates, who no longer are interested in the long periods of stewardship, slow promotions, and modest, if secure, compensation which have been the hallmark of banking for decades.

2. Banks and industrial companies have increasing needs for persons with specialized expertise, e.g., in data processing, who are more interested in improving their professional capabilities and their incomes and in the respect of their peers in a particular specialty than in a career in any single business. "Loyalty" frequently has been transferred from the enterprise to the discipline.

3. One-bank holding companies are finding themselves in direct competition with industry for various types of specialized and managerial talents.

4. Banks are recruiting trained manager-specialists in such areas as finance, marketing, and personnel from industry, and this practice is growing.

5. As bankers become increasingly sophisticated in the management arts, other businesses will begin seeking to employ top banking personnel, just as the reverse has been true during the past decade. Already this trend is apparent in the stock brokerage, investment banking, and other financial businesses.[4]

The Need for Improved Compensation Practices.   The unique nature of commercial banking, with its great reliance on public confidence and its influence on the nation's economic life, makes it mandatory that the quality and efficiency of banks' management be of high degree. Banks depend on the abilities, initiative, and energy of their employees and, in particular, of those charged with their management—the official staff. The continuing growth of the commercial banking system, its changing structure, interaction with the federal government in matters of fiscal and monetary policy, the marked expansion of business abroad, and the ever-increasing complexities of local, national, and international fiscal problems all point to an increasing need for a well-educated, trained, and experienced corps of bank management. There is no question but that modern, sophisticated, and competitive forms of compensation for bank officers are a prime requirement for ensuring a continuing supply of quality executive talent.

FORMS OF COMPENSATION USED BY BANKS

Commercial banks, as a group, use four general types of executive compensation.[5]

Straight or Base Salaries. A straight salary is an arrangement under which the bank agrees to pay an officer a fixed amount in monthly, semi-monthly, or other regular periodic payments, either for a stated number of years or so long as he is employed. There may or may not be a formal contract between the officers and the bank. When such contracts do exist, they usually apply to top management.

[4] *Ibid.*

[5] *The Executive Function and Its Compensation,* prepared by the University of Virginia Graduate School of Business Administration for General Dynamics Corporation, Charlottesville, Virginia, 1958.

Supplemental Compensation. The supplemental pay plans in operation are many and varied, including bonus, profit-sharing, stock acquisition, and incentive plans. More significant than the names and differences in approach are the philosophies underlying the arrangements. The general purpose of supplemental pay plans should be to stimulate executives to make more profitable use of the resources available to them and to inspire behavior that leads to constructive expansion and profitability.

Supplemental pay plans may be simple or complex, depending on their provisions. Bonus or incentive payment plans may be administered on completely discretionary bases by top management, or they may involve varying rewards based on appraisals of individual performance. Allocations may be made to individuals on a bankwide basis or they may involve, initially, varying allocations to specific segments of the organization for subsequent by-man distribution therein. The method of determining the total bonus or incentive fund pool varies from bank to bank.

Protective Compensation. Despite their varied forms, deferred income plans, pensions, and most bank insurance programs are usually contractual arrangements that pay money to the officer (or his estate) following completion of his term of full-time, active service. Deferred income and pensions level out the earning curve of an executive's life instead of concentrating his earnings in his working years. Usually, the deferred compensation has a dual purpose: to provide a postretirement income and to reduce the tax burden of the individual during his period of active service.

Protective compensation also has the value of helping relieve the employee of worries about an income after retirement. Compensation plans which include provisions for pensions, insurance, and disability give the individual more stable guaranteed income over a longer period of time than plans which include only salary and possible incentive pay.

Perquisites. Perquisites can be a substantial element in total compensation even though they are not a direct monetary reward for services performed. Perquisites in banks include such things as scholarship or tuition funds (and perhaps paid leaves) for outside study, a bank car, club memberships, expense allowances, use of the officers' dining room, longer vacations for more senior officers, bank-paid expenses of wives traveling with husbands on business trips, and the like. These are symbols of status and can have a prestige value that may be of real significance in recruiting and holding personnel.

INCENTIVES IN BANKING

"Incentive compensation" as applicable to banks is basically the same as for other types of business. It is additional compensation, over and above base salary, given as a reward for above-standard or superior performance. When applied properly, incentive compensation is aimed at improving operating results by individually stimulating to extra efforts those members of management whose actions bear strongly on these results.

Bankwide profit-sharing plans and fringe benefits and emoluments have no particular incentive value, simply because they are generally made available to all employees and include no selectivity predicated on performance.

Pros and Cons of Bank Incentive Plans in General. Arguments in favor of incentive plans in banks are generally self-evident and are basically the same as those put forth for such plans in other types of businesses. Either individually or collectively, incentive compensation is aimed at and can result in:

1. Attracting and retaining top men
2. Stimulating key executives to peak performance and thereby increasing bank income and profits
3. Rewarding outstanding performance
4. Tying key executives' compensation closer to operating results and to individual performance
5. Instilling a sense of partnership
6. Reducing turnover
7. Providing an opportunity for participants to develop significant estates[6]

Arguments against bank incentive plans, if examined carefully, are usually based on weaknesses that stem from inadequate planning or faulty administration of the plan, rather than from the concept of incentives. Major pitfalls which cause incentive plans to fail or to be ineffective are:

1. Carrying plans too low in the organization. Incentive compensation should be applied only to those officers whose positions in the organization enable them to have a real impact on profits.
2. Rewarding all participants equally regardless of performance
3. Awarding equal bonuses or other incentive compensation awards to two officers simply because they are on the same organizational level or have the same title
4. Awarding equal incentive payments to two officers simply because they earn the same base salary
5. Awarding incentive payments on the basis of windfall returns, where the recipient had no control over the results
6. Lack of a clear understanding by participants as to the factors on which they are being measured or evaluated
7. Failure to inform participants as to what effect changes in the bank's business and operating results may have in their areas of operation. This is particularly true in the case of "negative windfalls," that is, outside economic forces which can negatively affect a bank's profits.
8. Using incentive payments—even unconsciously—as a substitute for a sound salary program
9. Unwillingness of the chief executive or senior management to use incentives objectively to distinguish between good and poor performance, that is, a tendency to avoid hurt feelings in denying or reducing incentive awards to key officers who have not performed well

Stock Options as Incentives. There is a difference of opinion as to whether stock options can properly be considered incentive compensation. Any monetary benefits inherent in stock options accrue to the holder only if he exercises his options by investing personal funds, and then only if the market value of the stock advances beyond the price at which the options were granted. Nevertheless, because stock options are given in order to encourage selected employees and to enable them to have a proprietary interest in the enterprise —and thereby induce in them an added incentive to produce profits and corporate growth through current decisions—it is appropriate to consider them a form of incentive compensation.

Pertinent arguments have been made both in favor of and against the use of stock options by banks.

Arguments in Favor of Stock Options. Rothschild and Reichler have stated that bankers' chief reason for desiring the authority to grant options was to

---

[6] Hay, *op. cit.*

compete with other businesses for executive personnel.[7] The same reason was given by a Senate Advisory Committee for its proposal to authorize stock option plans during consideration of the Financial Institutions Act of 1957. And it was used by the Advisory Committee on Banking to the Comptroller of the Currency in 1962 to justify its recommendation that national banks be granted authority to utilize such plans.

Proponents of stock option plans for banks have argued that option stock is the most feasible means of ensuring that the bank is not deprived of the incentives to produce which result from granting key employees a proprietary interest in the business. They point to the fact that most banks are, normally, closely held corporations, and that when there is any trading in bank stock, it is usually thin and takes place in the over-the-counter market. For these reasons, bank employees find it difficult to purchase on the market at a reasonable price any significant proprietary interest in the bank in which they work. Before the Comptroller permitted authorized but unissued stock in 1962, the lack of availability of stock for officers and employees was particularly stressed by some of the smaller banks.

Comments to the Comptroller's Advisory Committee indicated that stock option plans were favored because they would permit a bank to offer competitive compensation to key employees without distributing cash needed by the bank. This advantage was deemed particularly appealing to the smaller bank which could not hope to compete on a cash salary basis with larger competitors.[8] In favor of options, Parker has stated:

> In competing with industry for this valuable and scarce executive talent, banks, which have traditionally never been charged with overpaying management, found themselves at a competitive disadvantage in not being able to offer to officers or officer material the type of inducement to become shareholders that industrial firms could offer. With federal and state taxes and an inflation-ridden cost of living consuming most of an executive's salary, the ... stock option is more than merely a form of compensation with the fringe on top. It gives a bank officer, argue its proponents, a true incentive to grow with the bank, an opportunity to hedge aginst inflation, and to build an estate for his survivors in what has been termed about the only way left for a talented individual without capital to "go from poor to rich in one lifetime."
>
> Stock options also provide an opportunity for the smaller bank to offer substantial attractions to needed key executives without depleting essential working cash or establishing an unrealistically high salary for one favored executive that would create obvious inequities and dissatisfaction among other personnel.[9]

Arguments against Stock Options. Against stock option plans, some bankers argue that since the executive's reward is related to the vagaries of the stock market, options have little real incentive value. Additionally, Rothschild and Reichler have stated:

> Many bankers, in one way or another, echo the opposition of the Federal Reserve Board to the stock option plans provision in the proposed Financial Institutions Act of 1957: option grants to key employees might result in a "profit motive expansion-type management." Other arguments made by opponents ...

[7] V. Henry Rothschild and Richard Reichler, "The New Executive Stock Option and the Smaller Bank," *The Bankers Magazine,* Spring, 1966.

[8] *Ibid.*

[9] Allan J. Parker, "Stock Options for Bank Officers," *The Bankers Magazine,* Winter, 1964.

include the fear that, under option plans, key employees would become more interested in increasing earnings at the expense of the quality of assets; and that such plans "might lead to rigging of operating results, and in unwillingness to charge down unsatisfactory loans and investments."

One objection, which focuses on the difficulty of financing the purchase of option stock, is the fear that key employees might overextend themselves in acquiring option stock. There is the added fear that these executives might bring pressure on correspondent banks or other financial institutions with whom they deal to assist in financing their option stock purchases.[10]

Restrictions in regulations having to do with holding periods before option stock may be sold, the necessity to exercise prior options before subsequent ones may be acted upon, market risk, margin restrictions on borrowed funds, and amount and time limitations on borrowings by officers from their own banks, all add possible other negative factors to the use of stock options as incentives.

Finally, Parker made a particularly provocative comment when he said that "it has not been and probably cannot be mathematically demonstrated that banks (or any other corporations) with stock option plans will necessarily prosper more than banks without such plans."[11]

CURRENT INCENTIVE COMPENSATION PRACTICE IN BANKS

While many books, reports, periodicals, and surveys are available on general business use of incentive compensation, relatively little has been published on bank compensation. Such information as is available on banks is summarized here.

The Conference Board. The Conference Board (formerly The National Industrial Conference Board) is a research and educational institution for cooperative study by economists and businessmen of the economic and administrative problems of American business. Its biennial research report on top executive compensation includes commercial banking as one of six major industry categories covered. Data regarding banks in the most recent (1969) NICB report are limited to the three highest-paid executives in the banks covered.[12] The data are based on 1967 compensation information from 208 banks (of 420 polled), each with deposits of $100 million or more. Banks included in the survey and their sizes in terms of deposits are shown in Table 1.

[10] Rothschild and Reichler, *op. cit.*
[11] Parker, *op. cit.*
[12] *Top Executive Compensation* (SPP 213), National Industrial Conference Board, Inc., New York, 1969.

TABLE 1   Banks Participating in 1969 NICB Survey

Total Deposits	Number of Banks
$1 billion and over	39
500–999 million	36
300–499 million	37
200–299 million	28
100–199 million	68
Total banks	208

Executive Bonus Awards. Of the banks responding to the survey, 10 percent (21) had some type of executive bonus plan. The incidence of a plan did not appear to have any relation to bank size, insofar as this could be judged from the size of the sample.

Seventy-three banks reported 1967 bonus awards for one or more of their three highest-paid executives. However, despite the fact that bonuses were paid to a total of 210 executives, in 58 of the banks the bonus was paid under an arrangement that the bank did not consider a "plan," or under a profit-sharing plan that covered other employees as well.

Bonus awards ranged from 2 percent of salary up to 90 percent of salary; the median award was 8 percent of salary, with the middle half ranging between 5 and 13 percent of salary. Bonus amounts for all recipients, regardless of salary level, are shown in Table 2.

Stock Option Awards. Almost 25 percent (47) of the 208 banks had a qualified stock option plan for executives in 1967. The incidence of these plans tended to increase as the size of the bank increased. For example, 12 percent (13) of the 96 banks with deposits under $300 million had a plan, compared with 24 percent (9) of the 37 banks with deposits of $300–499 million and 33 percent (25) of the 75 banks with deposits of $500 million or more.

American Management Association. The American Management Association is a nonprofit organization concerned with finding, developing, and sharing information on new and better methods of management. AMA's Executive Compensation Service, a specialized division of the Association, publishes annual and periodic studies on the compensation of top and other levels of management and on incentive compensation, stock purchase plans, and salary administration and control.

The 1969 edition of the *Top Management Report* reported on various facets of the compensation of 3,797 companies in eight broad industry categories, including average salary and bonus payments to 2,470 executives in 21 senior positions from 195 banks and trust companies. All bank and trust company data are presented in seven categories according to size in terms of assets, ranging from $25 to $50 million to over $1 billion for 1968 or the comparable fiscal year

Of the 195 participating banks, 72 reported making payments under some form of bonus or incentive plan, excluding profit-sharing retirement plans. For the entire group, bonus payments were 12.2 percent of the salaries of execu-

TABLE 2   Bonus as Percent of Salary

1967 bonus award (percent of salary)	Officers	
	Number	Percent
Less than 5	27	13
5–9	91	43
10–14	40	19
15–19	18	9
20–24	10	5
25–49	15	7
50 or more	9	4
Total officers	210	100

tives who received them.   The information is strictly numerical and does not discuss the policies or practices used in awarding bonuses.[13]

The AMA also publishes a *Report on Current and Deferred Incentive Compensation*.   Although not organized by type of industry as is the *Top Management Report*, bonus use is broken down by industry type in a table entitled "Analysis of Bonus Payments by Industry."   This table indicates that, of 176 banks and trust companies for which data were obtained, 106 had bonuses. In total, bank and trust company bonuses amounted to 6.2 percent of total pay (the sum of all salaries, bonuses, and pension contributions for all positions reported) and 10.8 percent of salaries alone for all positions reported. This is the only reference to banks in this volume.[14]

The American Management Association considers stock plans, including stock option plans, as something separate and apart from incentive compensation as discussed in this chapter.   The AMA *Report on Stock Purchase Plans* is a detailed and comprehensive study of all facets of stock option, stock bonus, and other stock purchase plans, but it does not provide a breakdown by industry[15]

Bank Administration Institute.   Biennially, Bank Administration Institute (formerly NABAC) publishes the results of a survey of bank personnel policies and practices.   The 1968 report contains information on bank uses of bonuses and stock options as well as on a number of other personnel practices.[16]

A total of 3,580 banks participated in the 1968 survey, representing 45.4 percent of B.A.I. membership.   For purposes of tabulating replies, all participating banks were categorized into two broad groups—those with less than, and those with more than, $25 million in resources.   Within these two groupings, the banks were subcategorized into eight and seven groups, respectively, according to the number of employees.   For the 1,002 banks in the $25 million and more resources group, the seven subgroups ranged from those with less than 50 employees (Group 1) to those with 2,500 and more employees (Group 7).   The following data summarize the B.A.I. 1968 study findings regarding use of bonuses and stock options.   Because not all banks answered all questions, totals will vary.

Bonuses.   Of the 1,002 larger reporting banks, 991 replied to the question regarding bonuses paid; 591 (60 percent) stated that they paid a bonus in 1967; 400 did not.   Bonus plans were more prevalent in the smaller banks in the survey: of the 591 banks that paid bonuses, only 23 had more than 1,000 employees.

Banks that did pay bonuses reported their criteria for payment as shown in Table 3.   Table 4 shows the percent of total staff members participating in the 1967 bonus in the 586 banks which reported their number of participants. Of the 587 banks responding to a question on the medium in which the bonus was paid, 569 paid the bonus entirely in cash; 18 did not.   In 81 percent of the banks, bonuses were restricted to full-time employees.

Stock Options.   Of the 1,002 larger-sized banks, 978 replied to questions

---

[13] *Executive Compensation Service—Top Management Report*, 20th ed., American Management Association, New York, December, 1969.

[14] *Executive Compensation Service—Reports on Current and Deferred Incentive Compensation*, American Management Association, New York, June, 1969.

[15] *Executive Compensation Service—Reports on Stock Purchase Plans*, American Management Association, New York, October, 1969.

[16] *Personnel Policies and Practices Survey*, vol. IV, Bank Administration Institute, Park Ridge, Ill., 1968.

TABLE 3   Bank Criteria for Incentive Payments

Criteria of Payment	Number of Banks
Salary	461
Length of service	259
Position	70
Performance	64
Other	39

regarding stock options; 121 stated that they had a stock option plan; 857 said they did not. Eligibility criteria used by banks which had stock option plans are shown in Table 5. Of the 121 banks with stock option plans, only 28 had 1,000 or more employees.

TABLE 4   Staff Participation in Bonus Plans

Percent of staff participating	Number of banks	Percent of banks
1–25	42	7
26–50	14	3
51–75	20	3
76–100	510	87
Total banks....	586	100

CURRENT INCENTIVE PRACTICE IN LARGE BANKS

At the end of 1969, there were 13,683 commercial banks in the United States. Their total deposits amounted to nearly $412 billion. Fifty-six percent of the total deposits were held by the 100 largest banks, with 46 percent being held by the 50 largest. Stated another way, slightly over 0.3 percent of all commercial banks hold 46 percent of total deposits; slightly over 0.7 percent of all commercial banks hold more than one-half of the nation's total deposits. The impact of the 100 largest commercial banks, their managerial practices, and the quality and compensation of their managements is obvious.

In 1966 and 1967 the writer conducted a detailed study of the use, by the nation's 50 largest commercial banks, of stock options and bonuses as incentive compensation for officers. Late in 1969 and early in 1970, the 50 largest banks again were queried on the subject. As shown in Table 6, the comparative figures indicate that interest in incentive bonus plans increased during the three-year interval. Whereas no additional banks had adopted stock option plans, nine had installed bonus plans during the interim.

In addition to updating information about the 50 largest banks, the recent study surveyed the second 50 banks. Thirty-seven of these responded: 13 had stock option plans, four others had bonus plans, and 20 had neither.

To recap, of the 100 largest banks, 49 are known to be using some form of extra compensation as, presumably, a form of incentive: 27 have stock option plans, 15 have bonus plans, 7 have both. Thirty-eight banks have neither stock options nor bonus plans.

Large-bank Practices in the Use of Stock Options. Generally, stock option

TABLE 5   Eligibility Criteria for Stock Option Plans

Eligibility Criteria	Number of Banks
Salary	16
Length of service	19
Position	64
Other	31

plans have been designed and administered in ways that minimize their value as true incentives:

1. Eligibility for stock option plans has been based primarily on title, or salary level, or a combination of the two.

2. The proportion of officers awarded options has exceeded the number who fall into the key, profit-impacting group.

3. Amount of individual option awards has been determined on subjective, discretionary bases by banks' chief executive officers, senior management, or a board committee responsible for administering the plans.

4. Very few banks have used any type of formula to relate the value of option shares to the officer's position, title, or salary. Only one bank has utilized a firm, precise formula to relate the number of option shares (and their value at the time of award) directly to both salary and the officer's performance rating. The prevalence of the criteria of salary, length of service, and position in making option awards is borne out by the Bank Administration Institute survey mentioned above.

The appeal and value of stock options as a means of incentive compensation usually depend on the growth potential of the business involved and the personal financial situation of the individual executive. It has been observed that the value of stock options is probably greatest when:

1. There are reasonable prospects of corporate growth

2. Factors beyond the control of the executive do not often play a significant part in shaping the success of the company

3. Stockholder relations are amicable

4. Other, more basic compensation factors (immediate cash needs, retirement, and the like) are already provided for

5. Annual income of each participating executive is high enough to make the capital gains factor a significant consideration

6. Eligibility is restricted to executives who have obvious and significant impact on the success of the company

7. There is a pressing need for additional executive and professional talent[17]

[17] N. B. Winstanley, "Keeping Executive Compensation in Balance," *Personnel*, March–April, 1965.

TABLE 6   Incentive Use in Large Banks

Banks with:	1966–1967	1969–1970
Stock option plan	14	14
Bonus plan	4	11
Stock option and bonus plan	5	7
Neither	27	18
Total	50	50

Because of the deferred and problematical benefits in stock options generally and the personal monetary investment and risk required, it seems highly questionable that stock options have a significant place as incentives for any but the most senior, highly paid bank officers.

Large-bank Practices in the Use of Bonuses.   Twenty-two of the 100 largest banks are now known to be using some type of bonus arrangement for officers. There is a marked diversity in the broad parameters within which the 22 plans are operated.   Some are completely informal, and the majority are highly discretionary in their application; others are highly structured, with detailed, written procedures for administration.   Several are actually used as *de facto* profit-sharing arrangements for all officers, and two of these include nonofficial employees in the plan as well.   One is used as a temporary substitute, in cash, for profit sharing for officers who are not yet eligible to participate in the bank's deferred profit-sharing plan.   One plan is applicable only to bond department salesmen.   While most pay bonuses in cash at year-end, one permits recipients to elect current cash, postretirement receipt, or restricted stock.   Of the 22 plans, only eight can be considered comprehensive, objective programs which:

1. Establish the total bonus fund by formula
2. Utilize predetermined, by-man objective setting, against which performance is measured and is related by formulas to individual bonus award payments

A number of the 100 largest banks which responded to inquiry—both with and without any forms of incentives—expressed considerable interest in the idea of incentive compensation.   In a number of cases, however, it appears that such banks have not incorporated into their management processes many of the basics which should precede consideration of incentive compensation.

PREREQUISITES FOR AN INCENTIVE PROGRAM

Prior to embarking on developing and implementing an incentive plan, several basic managerial programs should be in good working order.

Corporate Objectives.   Clearly stated long- and short-range objectives for the bank as a whole and its various organizational components, in terms of profits and/or services, should be in hand and updated at regular intervals. If an incentive program is to reward exceptional or better-than-average performance by individuals, then norms of satisfactory performance must be known.   And these must be related to and compatible with what the bank as a whole has decided it wishes to accomplish.

Organization Structure.   The organization structure should be committed to chart and written form and be kept current.   At one end the structure must reflect the corporate arrangement for doing business and providing service— in concert with the objectives referred to above.   At the other end there should be an exact meshing of specific segments and functions of the corporate structures with individual officer position descriptions.   Each position is, in effect, the smallest box on the chart of organization.

Organization planning is never a static effort, since corporate and departmental objectives and functions frequently change or are realigned.   In order to ensure that changes in structure, function, and responsibility are reflected in position duties and responsibilities, one office of the bank should be assigned to ascertain that changes in objectives and functions are reflected in the organization structure.   Organization planning should never be ignored simply because "charts are difficult to keep current."

Salary Administration.   A sound plan for administering officers' salaries is a *sine qua non* for any comprehensive compensation program. While there are a number of different approaches to salary administration, the plan for officers should include:

1. Written position descriptions for each job, emphasizing key responsibility and accountability factors, rather than merely listing duties

2. An acceptable method of determining the relative ranking of the bank's various officer positions

3. A level of salaries comparable to that paid by employers with which the bank must compete for executive talent

4. A consistent bankwide approach to officer performance appraisal

5. A consistent bankwide approach to the administration of individual salaries within the applicable salary ranges, with performance as a major consideration. Salary ranges should be based on job content as well as on horizontal and vertical relationship of jobs internally, and not on what individual incumbents demand or on other subjective approaches.

The Bank Administration Institute study, referred to above, indicated the following for reporting banks in the $25 million or more resource group:

1. Three hundred banks had written job descriptions for officer positions; 684 did not.

2. Two hundred seven banks had formal job evaluation plans for officer positions; 771 did not.

3. Two hundred sixty-nine banks had formal performance appraisal programs for officers, 713 did not.

ATTRIBUTES OF A SOUND INCENTIVE BONUS PLAN

Once the prerequisites enumerated above are firmly established and "working," the factors of the incentive plan itself can be considered.

Objectives. The objectives of the plan should be clearly thought through and stated in writing. Why is an incentive plan being considered? How would the bank really benefit from an incentive plan? What would be accomplished by such a plan that is currently not being done?

Financial Capability. The dollar capability to support an incentive plan should be ascertained. Are there perhaps other, higher-priority programs which should be provided for first? For example, should a bank with no form of employee profit sharing or without an adequate pension program be considering an officer bonus arrangement? Or, can a bank with a profit-sharing plan realistically afford the additional expense of a bonus plan sizable enough to provide substantial incentive payments for officers?

Total Bonus Fund. The total incentive bonus fund should be established by means of a formula appropriate to the particular corporation. The money for a bonus fund comes, obviously, from profits. The reason for having an incentive compensation plan is to increase profits over what they would be in the absence of such a plan. Since there must be evident in the plan's construction a genuine inducement to superior performance as measured by bank profits, the stockholders should be guaranteed a reasonable return on their investment before any provision is made for incentive awards to executives. Conversely, if a reasonable return to stockholders is not attained, there is no justification for paying any incentive rewards to executives. Thus, a formula to reflect varying profit levels and a reasonable return to the owners is necessary to establish the bonus fund.

Eligible Participants. Eligibility for the incentive program should be limited to persons in key profit-impacting positions. There is no point in making eligible for incentive payments an officer whose work—regardless of performance—has minimal or no effect on bank profits. Such officers should be rewarded for high performance through the salary program.

This does not mean that only executives whose responsibilities and performance are measurable in quantitative terms should be eligible. Significant contributions and accountabilities of key corporate planning, finance, personnel, and research officials are as important to an organization as the work of those in charge of customer interface areas.

Individual Bonus Awards. The amount of each bonus award must have an obvious and valid relationship to performance. Although qualitative measures are admittedly more difficult to define than quantitative ones, utilization of the goal-setting or management by objectives approach makes this feasible.

Bonuses must be related to base salaries so that total earnings compare equitably by both internal and external standards. Bonuses should truly be "supplemental" compensation, and not simply substitutes for an adequate salary plan. Also, there is no advantage in awarding bonuses widely throughout the organization, even if they are arived at objectively.

Individual awards should represent, after taxes, a noticeable increase over base compensation. Also, the higher the participant's base salary, the larger the bonus percentage must be to have a noticeable impact.

Bank Performance. Bonus awards must rise and fall noticeably with bank performance and profitability, thus underscoring the relationship between bank profits and individual and group performance.

Individual Performance. Bonus awards must reflect, clearly, a falling-off in individual performance in any one year. This is certainly one of the more difficult requirements to carry out. It necessitates candid discussions between superior and subordinate of the latter's performance, and the courage on the part of the superior to tell the subordinate when he has not performed up to standards and goals set by, with, and for him.

Communication. Each officer must be personally and fully informed of the relationship of his bonus—or lack thereof—to his performance. The philosophy and details of the incentive plan must be communicated to all participants so that they can recognize cause-and-effect relationships.

Keeping the Plan Current. The plan must be kept up to date. Changes in corporate objectives, in the competitive picture, or in organization structure will necessitate changes in objectives of the bank as a whole and in goals set for individual participants. Such changes may require revisions in the incentive plan.

DEVELOPING THE INCENTIVE PROGRAM

A bank which has determined that it posseses the prerequisites for an incentive program (clearly defined long- and short-range objectives, sensible and codified organization structures, and a viable salary administration program), which has determined that such a plan would be of definite benefit, and which has the dollar capability to support an incentive program will next be faced with the following questions:

1. How much money should be earmarked annually for the total incentive bonus fund?

2. Which officers shall be considered eligible to participate in the incentive plan?

3. How shall individual awards be determined?

4. In what form and under what timing shall awards be paid?

Establishing the Incentive Bonus Fund. A prime requirement of incentive compensation plans is some means for determining (and limiting) the aggregate of incentive awards in any one year. The most common means is to establish and apply a formula which creates an incentive fund. The fund may or may not be paid out in its entirety, depending on circumstances and management's judgment. Unused portions may or may not be carried over to be available for distribution in subsequent years. It is particularly important that the formula establish the maximum amount that may be paid.[18] Formulas are used in incentive compensation plans to:

1. Measure corporate achievement
2. Safeguard stockholders' interests by (a) ensuring a reasonable return on their equity before any incentive compensation is paid to management and (b) stipulating above this level a reasonable allocation of earnings between stockholders and management[19]

There are a number of ways for a bank to establish the total bonus fund. Several of the top 50 banks which currently have well-planned and administered incentive programs use approaches such as the following:

Bank A. Provided net operating earnings do not fall below $X million, the incentive fund will be equal to 25 percent of adjusted net operating earnings in excess of 10 percent of equity capital at the beginning of the incentive year, but may not exceed 15 percent of the total salaries of the participants.

Adjusted net operating earnings is net operating earnings as reported to shareholders reduced by average annual net loan losses during the most recent five years (including the current year) but before any provision for this incentive plan. Expense related to the employee profit-sharing plan will be deducted before arriving at adjusted net operating earnings.

Bank B. The amount of the incentive compensation fund shall be computed as follows: (a) from net operating earnings for the preceding fiscal year after federal income taxes and any surtax, subtract an amount equal to 10.5 percent of the daily average of the aggregate capital, surplus, and undivided profits for such fiscal year; (b) the difference, if any, thus obtained shall be converted to a pre-tax equivalent by adding to such difference a sum equivalent to the ordinary corporate federal income tax and any surtax which would have been payable had there been net earnings after taxes in the amount of such difference; (c) subtract from such equivalent sum the greater of (i) actual loan losses less recoveries incurred in such fiscal year, or (ii) an amount equal to the product of (xx) the average annual percentage loan loss (net of recoveries) with respect to outstanding applicable loans for the 10 years immediately preceding multiplied by (yy) the total principal amount of applicable loans outstanding at the end of such fiscal year; and (d) subtract from the difference so obtained any losses on the sale of investment securities incurred during such fiscal year after amortizing any such losses over the remaining maturity of the securities so disposed of, the figure so computed being hereinafter referred to as "base amount."

The fund for any fiscal year shall be an amount equal to: (i) 12½ percent of that portion of the base amount which is $1 million or less; (ii) 15 percent of that portion of the base amount which exceeds $1 million but is $2 million or less; (iii) 17½ percent of that portion of the base amount exceeding $2 million; and (iv) any amounts formerly awarded to any beneficiary which were declared by the committee to be forfeited to the fund during such fiscal year;

---

[18] *Incentives for Bankers, op. cit.*
[19] *Ibid.*

provided, however, no sum shall be allocated to the fund which, if subtracted from net operating earnings of bank for such fiscal year, would cause such net operating earnings to be less than 5¼ percent higher than the net operating earnings of the previous fiscal year of bank. Any portion of the fund not distributed in any plan year shall not be awarded in any subsequent plan year.

Bank C. Each year the officers are authorized to accrue for payment under the plan 5 percent of net operating earnings, less the past 10-year average of net loan losses, after deducting 6 percent of the capital accounts (capital stock, surplus, individual profits, and reserve for contingencies) with no adjustment for gains or losses on securities or capital assets or other nonoperating additions or deductions. Net operating earnings for the purpose of computing the accrual shall be before deduction for such accrual.

Bank D. The "incentive compensation reserve" for each calendar year shall be equal to such percentage of the consolidated net operating earnings of the bank for the preceding year as may be fixed by the committee during March of the preceding year. For this purpose, "consolidated net operating earnings of the bank" shall be as reported in the bank's annual report, excluding any nonrecurring or extraordinary deductions or items of gain, income, or loss. The reserve may be reduced any year by such amount, if any, as the committee determines should not be allocated with respect to such year.

It is difficult, if not impossible, to develop a formula that can stand unchanged over a long period of time as a satisfactory measure of corporate achievement. Yearly bank results are sometimes affected by events outside the immediate control of management, e.g., prime rate increase, loan or bond loss write-offs, etc. This would seem to argue in favor of establishing standards of corporate performance year by year, but within a formula approach to minimize subjectivity. Achievement, both corporate and individual, is more validly measured in relation to existing opportunities than to absolutes. Opportunity may differ from year to year and from circumstance to circumstance, and to the degree that it does, the same absolute results in two years may well constitute different achievements.[20]

Determining Eligible Participants. Bank incentive plans vary widely with regard to the number and level of officers participating. Too broad an inclusion simply turns the bonus plan into a disguised form of profit sharing, with little if any noticeable incentive impact. It is imperative that the plan include only those positions which will have a significant opportunity to influence important corporate results. Or, stated another way, no amount of supplemental, incentive compensation can be justified where the opportunity of the incumbent to contribute to bank profits is remote.

Objectivity in determining which executives should be eligible to participate in the incentive plan is best ensured through a system of job descriptions and job evaluation which clearly points up those positions heaviest in terms of accountabilities and end results. Accountability may be defined as the measured effect of the job on accomplishments (end results) that mean most to the bank's survival and progress.

The degree of accountability in a position constitutes a man's opportunity to affect profits, from which the bonus is to come. It is certainly a much more meaningful indicator of who should, and should not, be eligible for participation in the incentive system than, say, actual salaries, titles, organization level, or measures of total job content.

In the initial stages of implementing the incentive plan—assuming the ac-

[20] *Ibid.*

countabilities or profit-impacting content of all jobs have been established by job evaluation—it is highly desirable to limit the first participants to a very small number. Banks which have in operation effective incentive plans began with only the most senior officers, such as the chief executive officer and major departmental or divisional heads. This group will, of course, comprise those officers with the highest accountability scores under the job evaluation plan. Limiting the first participants to perhaps 12 or 18 officers, for the first several years, not only provides for testing the plan but also facilitates debugging of concepts and mechanics. Only when the plan is operating effectively for the bank's senior management should it be expanded downward into the organization.

Determining Individual Incentive Awards. The fact that a particular position is inherently high in accountability or profit-impacting factors does not mean that the incumbent will automatically receive an incentive award. Whereas the accountability factor of a job indicates the incumbent's level of opportunity to participate, this does not necessarily reflect his actual performance in his job, that is, how well he took advantage of his opportunity.

The level of a man's performance cannot be measured accurately unless goals or objectives have been established in advance with which his results can be compared. For example, the fact that a major division or branch had a profitable year does not reveal whether the profit was high, low, or simply adequate. A method must exist to determine that the profit was high, low, or adequate in terms of a predetermined target. Individual awards should be based on (1) the bank's overall profitability and (2) the attainment of previously agreed-upon goals or objectives tailored to each participating officer's specific responsibilities.

Management Performance Objectives. The use of management performance objectives is an effective means of gaining the commitment of individual managers to specific results—results which, when taken together, are necessary to achieve the annual and long-range objectives of each organization unit and the bank as a whole.

This approach involves the development of specific performance objectives for a specified time period for each key manager. These performance objectives constitute a target plan for the individual officer. The target plan for each officer is related to the target plan of his superior, and the target plans for all officers in an organization unit, taken together, constitute an integrated plan for meeting or exceeding the objectives of that organization unit. Attainment of the objectives of each organization unit results in meeting or exceeding the objectives of the bank as a whole.

In adopting a management by objectives approach, it is recognized that, because of the nature of the banking business, it is not always feasible to use profit center performance as the sole or principal basis for determining individual awards. On the other hand, subjective performance appraisals or merit ratings are too often a measure of effort expended rather than results achieved and, at best, are not a very effective basis for determining incentive awards.

Guidelines for Establishing Target Plans. Individual target plans should be kept as simple and specific as possible. A relatively few specific objectives which can be kept clearly in mind are better than a long, complicated list of things to be done. In identifying appropriate goals, the officer should consult with his immediate superior in advance of firming them up. In most instances targets should be limited to three principal objectives. In any event, they should not be less than one nor more than six.

Achievement of the target plan by an individual should result in a distinct improvement in performance of the organization unit as a whole and of the part he manages. Therefore, the target plan for an individual should be related to the near-term and long-range objectives of both the unit and the bank.

Specific performance objectives established for an individual should be those for which he can be held directly responsible. Specific performance objectives which comprise an individual target plan are of two types—quantitative and qualitative:

1. *Quantitative objectives* are those expressed in terms of "how much" and "when." There is usually more opportunity for the establishment of quantitative objectives for a line position than for a staff position, but quantitative objectives can be established for all positions.

2. *Qualitative objectives* are necessarily expressed in more general terms—frequently, by "how well." These are not normally capable of precise measurement but relate to the accomplishment of improvements which will favorably affect the bank's near-term or long-range performance and profitability.

Experience in the development and use of target plans indicates that the most effective plans are developed jointly by the individual and his immediate superior. The individual's proposed performance objectives should be agreed to by both levels as the target plan for the individual.

Measurement of Performance. There are a variety of approaches and refinements to the "mechanics" of determining the dollar amount of incentive awards to participants at year end. However, the most equitable technique is that which uses accountability, or "opportunity," points as the bases against which performance ratings—in numerical terms—are applied. Performance ratings are determined by the man's superior and a "bonus committee" as an evaluation of his degree of success in meeting his predetermined goals.

A four-point rating scale is a typical approach, in which, for example:

75% represents below-expected performance

100% represents expected performance

125% represents good performance

150% represents superior performance

In a theoretically ideal top management team of four men, all performance measurements would be equal at 100 percent, i.e., expected performance. In such a situation the distribution of the bonus fund would be the same as the relationship of accountability, or opportunity, points. However, because individuals vary from one to another in their respective successes in meeting management objectives, adjustments are made, such as in the example shown in Table 7. If the total bonus fund were equal to 100 percent, then officer A would receive 12.1 percent of the total as his bonus; officer B, 13.6 percent of the total as his; etc.

The example in Table 7 is oversimplified to illustrate the manner in which

TABLE 7 Incentive Distribution According to Accountability and Performance

Officer	Accountability points	Performance factor	Raw distribution	Distribution percentage
A...............	200	100%	200	12.1
B...............	300	75%	225	13.6
C...............	400	150%	600	36.4
D...............	500	125%	625	37.9
				100.0

performance ratings are applied to participants' accountability points. Plans can be made more sophisticated to reflect or include:

1. Appraisal of the performance of major organizational components as units, that is, the success of components themselves in meeting their objectives. Whereas corporationwide and individual performance measurements are mandatory in any genuine incentive plan, the inclusion of major departmental or divisional objectives and goals—and performance appraisal thereof—is somewhat more difficult in banking. This is so primarily because of the marked interdependency of major functions in banking. Also, until banks become more adept at determining and refining their cost accounting techniques, measures of component performance, for incentive use as well as for other purposes, had probably best wait.

2. The relative weight of organizational components in terms of the aggregate accountability points of the officers therein or key officers thereof who are to participate in the incentive plan. In this approach, the total bonus fund will be allocated among organizational units, based on units' success in meeting objectives. The portion of the total corporate bonus fund distributed to a major organizational unit becomes the total fund to be distributed to the participants in that unit, in a manner similar to the example given above.

3. Different weighting of performance appraisal factors as between various types of officer jobs. One large bank with detailed management by objectives, performance appraisal, and an incentive bonus plan classifies participating officers into three broad categories:

(a) COMMERCIAL DEPARTMENT AND BANKING OFFICES: President; division heads in charge of state, national, and international commercial banking; senior officers in city branch system; senior trust department officers; senior officer in charge of investments and credit

(b) ALL OTHER INCOME-PRODUCING DEPARTMENTS: Senior credit officer; senior investment management officer; senior customer investment advisory officer; officer in charge of bank's operating services; officer in charge of data processing services for customers

(c) STAFF DEPARTMENTS: Senior officers in charge of: marketing and public relations; financial planning and control; comptroller's office; personnel and general services; corporate planning and management services

Use of categories such as these permits the bank to recognize and reflect, in performance measurements, the heavier quantitative factors in pure income-producing, or line, jobs versus the qualitative factors necessary in appraising staff-type jobs.

Method and Timing of Incentive Bonus Payments. There is considerable diversity among the major banks in the method and timing of incentive award payments. Several make entire annual awards only in current cash. Two permit recipients to choose between current cash, deferred cash (invested in a pooled investment fund), and restricted stock, or combinations thereof. Two award only restricted stock. One makes awards only in deferred cash. One permits the award to be made in bank stock or in any other stock traded on stock exchanges or over the counter.

While there certainly is no single best way of determining the form and timing of incentive bonus payments, there is a growing trend—mainly in non-banking businesses—to consider individualized compensation plans. This approach recognizes differences in compensation and benefits needs as between executives in, for example, the 30 to 40, 40 to 55, and 55 and up age brackets. Younger and middle-career men with young and college-age children have greater needs for maximum life insurance coverage and maximum take-home pay.   Older men have reduced current income needs and higher tax bracket problems.   It would appear worthwhile for banks to consider the individualized compensation approach and to incorporate this concept by permitting officers to take annual incentive bonus payments in whatever form is most useful to them at the time.

Some system of special awards payable at any time during the year for critical-incident accomplishments is used with success by a small number of banks.   A sizable cash award, paid unexpectedly following a one-time major achievement, can be of great incentive value, both to the recipient and to others who hear about it.   Adequate safeguards to ensure objectivity and fairness in such selections are, of course, extremely important.

Part 8

Special Compensation Programs

chapter 38

Designing an Integrated
Sales Compensation Program

R. G. JAMISON *Corporate Manager of Compensation, General Mills, Inc., Minneapolis, Minnesota*

In spite of the knowledge that has made it possible for man to walk on the moon and explore space, our understanding of the relationship between human behavior and financial rewards remains pitifully small. Sales managers and compensation specialists are more intuitive than scientific in designing salesmen's compensation plans. To quote General E. W. Rawlings, former president of General Mills, Inc., "In this highly competitive world, it is clear that in motivating our sales force, we have no exact formula or exact science to guide us. Human judgment is still involved. You can't use computers to do this job; they may help, but they won't do it for you."

Sales managers appear to be destined to continue a never ending search for the panacea that will provide the ideal in motivation and sales results. Too frequently, national sales conventions stimulate dissatisfaction with the current plan in favor of looking for that perfect plan. Unfortunately, companies often fall victim to novel, untested approaches. Even worse, many plans proliferate because the sales manager of one company exudes enthusiasm about the results achieved with the plan at his company, and his listeners never give second thoughts to the fact that their own companies have a different product mix and different management and sales objectives, or that they are even in entirely different industries. Despite dramatic advances in our technological know-how, our approach to salesmen's compensation remains quite like that used in the 1940s—maybe a little more sophisticated, but essentially the same. There have been changes, of course, for the subject has been far from neglected.

Many good minds have spent long hours pondering the problems and opportunities of salesmen's compensation. What has not emerged, however, is that one single truth that can be applied to all salesmen's compensation plans in all fields and circumstances with equally good results. Therefore, salesmen's compensation becomes as individualized as the company's products, objectives, size, and profitability make it.

The cost of a sensible, effective incentive plan is actually not an expense. Such a plan is a good, sound investment for which a fair return is expected. It should help to stimulate sales, add profits, attract topflight personnel, and, of course, build for the future. Only poorly planned and badly executed programs are really costly. An important fact to remember is that the salesmen who are expensive to the company are usually those in the low-income group, while the cheapest salesmen are the few top earners.

LEVELS OF COMPENSATION

Numerous surveys indicate rather significant differences in compensation levels of salesmen in various industries. One cannot help being impressed by the difference between the compensation levels of pharmaceutical product salesmen and those of jewelry salesmen. However, these industrial differences seem to be getting smaller. Surveys by industrial groups may tend to perpetuate the status quo in that unsound compensation practices can be supported by comparisons within each industrial group.

To determine a company's relative position with regard to compensation of its salesmen, one needs to conduct a survey or analysis of a number of reliable surveys on salesmen's compensation. Such an evaluation, however, must consider the total compensation of the salesman, not just base salary alone.

In designing a salesmen's compensation plan, management needs to make some basic decisions regarding the amount of money a salesman might earn. That is, what is the most that the company would be willing to pay for truly outstanding performance? There is the age-old question of whether a salesman should ever be allowed to earn more than his boss. Many times, one hears a sales manager tell with great pride of the salesman who earns a great deal more in total compensation than the president of the company. At first blush, this sounds very exciting, for there can be no question about the incentive opportunities available in these companies. One cannot help but wonder, however, how many of these situations simply reflect a poorly designed incentive plan that permitted exorbitant and unreasonable amounts of compensation to occur.

"Sound travels faster than light" seems to be true within a sales organization, regardless of what happens in the world of physics. Unreasonably high earnings by certain salesmen because of inconsistencies or indiscriminate use of sales credits in the compensation plan are much discussed within sales organizations. Managers sometimes delude themselves into thinking that sales compensation can be kept confidential. It cannot.

In considering compensation levels for salesmen within a company, some rather elementary questions need answering:

1. Can the company afford to hire untrained and inexperienced salesmen, or does it have an immediate need for highly experienced professionals?

2. To what extent does the salesman have a direct and final impact on sales?

3. Will the company be able to afford to bring its more successful salesmen into the sales management group without destroying appropriate internal relationships?

4. Does the company want to compensate its salesmen at its own industry level, or at the level of salesmen in all industries?

ELEMENTS OF COMPENSATION

Base Salary. Base salary provides the security and opportunity for a salesman to establish a desirable level of living and social participation. It removes concern for the peaks and valleys which unfortunately do not appear on monthly mortgage and other fixed payments.

In 1946, over one-third (37 percent) of the 443 manufacturers in a National Industrial Conference Board study used a salary-only plan for salesmen.[1] Twenty years later, only 22 percent of 665 manufacturers surveyed by NICB reported salary-only plans.[2] Nevertheless, a number of companies are still enthusiastic about such plans—and rightly so—for their particular situations.

Adequate compensation for performance of essential nonselling tasks required of salesmen may be overlooked in compensation plans that put undue emphasis on incentives. These tasks include missionary work, new accounts, service, complaints, meetings, travel, conventions, training other salesmen, record keeping, etc.

Compensation plans which provide for base salary only may provide more realistic and fairer compensation relationships between salesmen on the basis of their performance and experience, etc., rather than on the serendipity of a particular sales territory. Another reason why companies look favorably on the salary-only plan is that with it changes can be made within the sales territories without detriment to the compensation of other salesmen. The sales manager is more directly in control of these kinds of changes.

Therefore, management must at least consider some of the advantages of salary-only plans. Since straight-salary plans do not use supplemental compensation to motivate salesmen, the responsibility falls on sales management to provide this motivation. Some advantages worth considering are:

1. The salesman has a steady and predetermined income. The salesman can establish a living level without the uncertainties of varying income.

2. Salesmen are more easily controlled and directed. For example, a salesman may carry out assigned nonselling tasks without loss of income.

3. The sales force is more willing to engage in teamwork.

4. There is reduced likelihood of overstocking customers by using high-pressure selling methods.

5. The accent is on continuing service to an account.

6. Inequities because of differences in the time necessary to make a sale are reduced.

7. The differences in the level of education and the length of training required for various types of selling receive recognition.

Base salary is also important in salary/commission and salary/incentive plans. Clearly, a base-salary structure must be sound if it is to serve as the underpinning of an effective incentive plan. Moreover, a company's base-salary levels affect its ability to attract outstanding salesmen. Base salary should reflect the long-term values of both the salesman and his job, and it should be high enough to free the salesman from his more serious money worries while

---

[1] National Industrial Conference Board report, "Salesmen's Compensation Plans," *Studies in Personnel Policy*, no. 81, 1946, p. 13.

[2] National Industrial Conference Board, "Changing Patterns in Salesmen's Compensation," February, 1966, p. 37.

he is building up his territory to productive, profitable levels. Ideally, it should also be part of an established range that will offer room for promotion and not impede desirable transfer of men between sales and other functions in the company.

Draw. A drawing account provides money advances to a salesman to be paid regularly like salary and later deducted from his total commission earnings. If a salesman fails to earn sufficient commission to cover his draw, he is expected to reimburse his employer for his overdraft before receiving additional commissions.

The drawing account is, therefore, used only where neither base salary alone nor salary in combination with incentive or commission is paid. A drawing account does provide greater stability in the salesman's income, but at a risk. The drawing account was far more popular at the turn of the century than it is today.

Commission. Technically, a commission program pays a calculable amount for achieving quantifiable objectives. A commission is generally a specific percentage of the dollar volume generated by the salesman's efforts. It always deals with specific measurable factors.

Between 1946 and 1966, companies with straight commission plans dropped from 15 percent to 11 percent of those surveyed by the National Industrial Conference Board. One of the reasons cited for the decline was the dramatic overpayments and underpayments to straight commission salesmen.

There seems to be a common frustration among sales managers because commission salesmen, as a group, feel they are free agents and consequently lack loyalty to the company. It is interesting that furniture and apparel manufacturers traditionally use the straight commission plan.

The commission plan does not provide salesmen enough earnings when the orders dry up. Conversely, earnings may rise unduly in periods of prosperity. Sometimes a straight commission plan has a built-in bias to build volume on easy sales while ignoring the most profitable items. When a company wants to open up sales in new outlets, it is very difficult, if not impossible, to induce the commission men to do the necessary missionary work.

Some of the advantages found in a straight commission plan are:

1. With its all-or-nothing approach, it tends to attract professional salesmen. High performance levels result in high earnings and a complete freedom of action.

2. Especially with new companies, the salesman is asked to share the risk with the company and conversely to participate more favorably in the rewards of the company if it becomes successful.

3. Commissions allow unit cost of sales to be predetermined. This is especially good for a small, struggling firm.

4. Straight commission plans are probably most effective in taking care of incompetent salesmen; they eliminate themselves.

5. Commission plans have worked well in highly competitive industries where aggressive selling and strong incentive are needed.

Bonus. Bonus plans are almost always measured in subjective terms or else consider quantified results at a distance. Generally, they work in the following manner: At the conclusion of the sales year, a judgment is made by the sales manager on the quality of performance of the salesman. It might consider number of sales calls, training of new salesmen, and quality of sales produced. Usually there is no precise formula, and therefore bonus plans are effective where it is difficult to measure precisely the effect of a salesman's activities on sales. The amount of the bonus reflects the manager's judgment on the salesman's job performance for that year. Bonus plans are common in technical service/sales positions, where the salesman may spend a large part of his time on nonselling activities. A bonus plan is almost always used in combination with a base-salary plan. Some of the advantages include:

1. Salesmen are encouraged to pay appropriate attention to both selling and service or other nonselling activities.

2. Rewards accrue on the basis of accomplishment of objectives.

3. Bonus plans promote teamwork among sales and service functions.

Commission-Bonus. Commission-bonus compensation usually considers the combination of subjective elements and quantifiable objectives. Normally, a certain percentage of the man's earnings is determined by precise sales accomplishments and may relate to a quota or be based on a percentage of sales. In addition, a portion of the incentive is based on other factors such as new accounts, expense reduction, and other nonsales performance measures. Individual earnings, therefore, reflect the combination of specific sales results and other performance criteria.

A company may gauge a man's record—in part, at least—by customer service, numbers of calls made, organization of territory, and customer potential. The company can then base incentive payments on the results achieved in these areas as well as on sales volume.

Some of the advantages of commission-bonus plans are:

1. Such plans seem to be a happy marriage between the straight commission and bonus plans, recognizing the importance of sales results as well as nonselling activities.

2. They provide an understandable target for salesmen to use in accomplishing the sales objectives of the company.

3. They establish a direct relation between individual performance and compensation.

4. While usually not affording the same earnings potential as straight commission plans, commission-bonus plans do allow better earnings when sales are poor—if the salesman has done other important functions well.

Combination Plans. A survey conducted in 1966 by the National Industrial Conference Board showed that 83 percent of the 665 manufacturers surveyed provided compensation programs that combine salary and commission or salary and bonus. This compares with 38 percent of 443 similar companies surveyed by NICB in 1946. Obviously, companies are striving to tailor their compensation plans to fit their own particular objectives.

Combination plans recognize the importance of the fixed portion of a man's earnings and the incentive value of a variable such as bonus or commission. As was discussed earlier, base salaries can be used to reflect the long-term values of the employee and to protect him while he is building his territory. The variable provides a reward for specific accomplishments over a predetermined period of time.

Compulsion for uniformity in sales incentive plans may be disastrous. Within one multidivisional company, a number of different plans may be equally effective in achieving sales goals for various divisions.

Judging from the trend toward combination plans, it does appear that managers must be concerned, not only with the type of plans, but also with the percentage they want to pay in more or less fixed amounts (salary) and the percentage they are willing to pay in variable amounts (incentives).

Automobiles. There is sometimes a question as to whether automobiles should be considered as part of a salesman's total compensation. Automobiles are generally thought of as necessities in today's culture. and having an automobile provided is, in truth, meaningful compensation. But, are automobiles any different to a salesman from what expensive and complicated equipment might be to quality control men? Both are tools of the trade, required to accomplish job accountabilities. Generally, however, automobiles are considered compensation.

Since most companies now provide their salesmen with automobiles, the value of the cars should not be included in the total compensation figures when comparisons are made with compensation in other companies. This is not to suggest that a company should ignore the automobile when talking to the salesman about his total compensation.

BALANCING FIXED AND VARIABLE PAY ELEMENTS

Pay plans are in a state of flux. Only 14 percent of all companies rate their current sales compensation plans as "excellent," while 13 percent actually label their plans "unsatisfactory." In the milling and shuffling around, nearly three changes out of every four involve the proportions of salary and incentive.[3]

When Research Institute of America asked today's salesmen how they wanted their compensation paid, salesmen voiced an interest in the security of a fixed base plus some opportunity for additional income in the form of incentive. Half the salesmen surveyed believe salaries should be 75 percent or more of their total compensation, and nine out of ten want at least 50 percent of their earnings in guaranteed salary.[4]

Because there is no one compensation plan that is best for all firms, each company tries to find the one best suited to its own purposes. There is no single ratio of salary to variable pay that would or should apply. Therefore, after determining the total compensation level for a salesman, a company must decide the method of paying it. Some basic requirements must be met if a salesmen's compensation plan is to be effective. The plan should:

1. Provide a method of payment that motivates personnel to work toward the specific objectives determined by management

2. Have flexibility that operates equitably for both the salesman and the company in all stages of the business cycle

3. Give realistic recognition to the relative impact the salesman himself has on the final sale and the extent to which his sales results are influenced by marketing and service support

4. Be relatively and appropriately consistent with practices used by other companies in the industry

5. Provide for fair treatment during foreseeable future developments, such as introduction of new products, changes in territory or method of distribution, and split-territory sales

6. Be understandable and acceptable to the sales force

7. Provide an equitable level of compensation commensurate with both the size and the profitability of the company

The portion of a man's total compensation that is commission, incentive, or bonus should reflect the degree to which the individual can directly influence the actual sale of the product. For example, certain technical salesmen must have a heavy technical background and often spend much time in a service

---

[3] "Sales Compensation Practices," 1968. Reprinted by permission of the Research Institute of America. Copyright, 1968, by the Research Institute of America, Inc.

[4] *Ibid.* Reprinted by permission of the Research Institute of America. Copyright, 1968, by the Research Institute of America, Inc.

role. It would be foolish to place a large portion of such men's compensation in a variable form which could fluctuate wildly with sales volume.

The weight of salary versus incentive or bonus should and does vary greatly between industries. Perishable or limited-shelf-life products do not lend themselves to the same degree of commission or incentive payment emphasis as heavy equipment, insurance, hardware, and other nonperishable products. Food companies must consider turnover and freshness of product among factors influencing the balance between salary and incentive pay components.

Other factors also influence the balance between fixed and variable components in the total compensation package for salesmen—especially the type of selling to be done and the basic objectives of the company.

Isolating the company's particular needs and objectives is an important first step. It is critical because it requires a precise definition of the selling task at hand. Moreover, going through the exercise of defining the sales task tends to get all members of sales management to thinking the same way about today's selling job. In the absence of the discipline of writing down a sales specification, company sales executives often think that each understands the other's views of the selling task when in fact there is a wide variation in the understanding of what is basic.

Objectives must then be communicated to the sales field. Trite as it sounds, it is nevertheless mandatory that a salesman understand his accountabilities precisely. This understanding may come through an effective manager, a position description, or a well-designed incentive plan. But he must understand what he is to do.

Behavioral scientists write much about the motivational aspects of incentive plans. In addition to being motivating, a well-conceived incentive plan is one of the most effective communications devices we have. A good incentive plan, properly designed, will tell the salesman in very precise terms how the company expects him to spend his time and what results will be most favorably regarded by the company. A plan designed strictly on the basis of volume tells the salesman that the company is most concerned about total dollar sales as opposed to the mix of the product sales or the development of new accounts. The name of the game in this particular company would be: Obtain sales volume.

A well-designed incentive plan provides a mutual understanding between sales management and salesmen of key objectives and priorities. The compensation program should reward each individual to the degree he has accomplished these desired objectives. Conversely, failure of a salesman to perform well should mean a penalty in the form of decreased compensation.

Low incomes resulting from lack of industry, ineptitude, lack of skill, or lack of planning may be regrettable, but the responsibility must be placed on the salesman, or the sales management, and not on the compensation plan. Administrative decisions to protect below-average salesmen are detrimental to the motivation of good salesmen and foolish from a business point of view.

As a general rule, therefore, the more directly a salesman can actually influence the sales result, the greater should be the opportunity for a higher variable in his compensation. There is no balance in the percentage of salary and variable that applies equally in all companies. Even within a multidivisional company, the design and the percentage of base to variable will differ.

One study shows that direct-contact salesmen can expect to earn an average of 29.5 percent of their compensation in incentive, compared with 20 percent for promotional salesmen. This same study showed that while the total compensation for sales engineers was greater than that of direct-contact salesmen, the percentage of incentive for the sales engineer was less than that for the direct-contact salesman.[5]

MANAGING SALARIES FOR SALESMEN

Modern job evaluation techniques make it possible to evaluate a sales position in the same manner as other management jobs. These evaluations consider and weight a number of factors, such as the amount of knowledge that is required in the position, the human skills requirements, the extent of problem solving, measure of the size of dollar impact, etc.

If the organization is properly structured, there will be a reasonable ladder of progression of positions. This offers the beginning salesman an opportunity for movement through the sales organization to reach his optimum management level. There should be a distinguishable difference between jobs. Often a temptation exists to describe and evaluate jobs which simply reflect that one salesman is more experienced than another. Unless there is a distinct difference in the requirements of the positions, experience is best recognized by movement within the salary range. Once the positions have been correctly evaluated, a dollar value for the jobs can be assigned. Most companies include sales positions in the same schedule as is used with other management jobs. A company is well advised to confirm the competitiveness of the assigned job values. In certain industries it may be necessary to use a structure that is different from the management structure in order to recognize competitive practices.

Typically, companies work with ranges having a 50 percent spread from minimum to maximum. This seems to give enough flexibility for movement of salaries while still protecting the proper salary relationship between jobs.

General Mills does not assign a minimum and a maximum for any of its exempt positions. It carefully determines for each job a value which is competitive for similar positions in other companies. Managers then administer salaries around the market value without the restrictions of an artificial minimum or maximum.

Let us consider this example: Sam Spade, a salesman for a cosmetic firm, currently earns $900 a month. Last year he was his company's leading salesman, eclipsing his quota by some 20 percent. Because of his sales results, he earned $4,800 in commission payments. His total earnings were a respectable $15,600. His manager must now decide whether Sam should be given a merit increase, and how much. It could be argued that his performance has been outstanding and that he deserves a high adjustment. However, his manager is fearful that if he raises Sam's salary too high, he will not be able to move Sam to a district supervisor's position. Such is the dilemma of many managers who must decide how much consideration should be given to the amount of incentive earned in arriving at a man's base salary.

In Sam's case, we need first to know what the policy guideline is for the job. His salary in relation to the guideline should be based on his overall performance. Now the manager can give consideration to many factors that may not be included in the incentive or commission plan, such as sales management potential, constructive ideas submitted, or other special criteria.

One division of General Mills requires a ranking of salesmen in each of its districts (see Figure 1). On the basis of these appraisals, the sales manager

---

[5] National Industrial Conference Board, "Incentive Plans for Salesmen," *Studies in Personnel Policy*, no. 217, p. 78.

Figure 1.   Performance review and salary budgeting program.

District _____   Performance Review and Salary Budgeting Program

Date _____

Name	Accomplishment against objectives	Use of innovation and new ideas	Mgt. of terr.	Selling complete line	Customer relations	Keeping up-to-date on company, competitors, and customers	Overall perf.	Health status	Sales mgt potential

3 best professional salesmen

_____

_____

_____

3 who need most improvement

_____

_____

_____

Definitions

Accomplishment against objectives
- Achieving or exceeding quota
- New product deliveries
- Generating new business

Keeping up-to-date on company,
competitors, and customers
- GMI organization and policies
- GMI products, services, and related technical information
- Competitors' policies, prices, tactics organization, and sales trends
- Each customer's operations, products, and market requirements

Management of territory
- Credit control
- Control of expenses and care of auto
- Developing sales plans
- Submitting required reports and keeping district manager informed of conditions in territory
- Effective use of time

Customer Relations
- Servicing customers by prompt handling of claims, technical assistance, expediting orders, etc.
- Cultivating those within a company who influence a buying decision

makes decisions regarding the man's base salary.   A man may receive a relatively small incentive yet receive a large merit increase.   Conversely, a man might receive little or no merit adjustment, even though his actual sales results were good.

It is a mistake to pass over a change in the salesman's base salary simply because his incentive was good and consequently he had a relatively high level of total compensation for any year.   As much as is possible, incentive results should be kept separate from base-salary considerations.

Consideration for merit adjustments in sales positions should be on the same time schedule as in other management positions.   If the salary structures are reviewed and updated each year, the assigned job values will reflect the current competitive salary level of the jobs.   The size of the merit increase is then determined by the salesman's performance rating and his salary relationship to the market value.   This salary relationship is often referred to as the man's "compa-ratio."   Generally, a salesman who is fully satisfactory in his position would have a compa-ratio of 100 percent.

By definition, a promotion is a movement to a higher-level position.   It therefore seems reasonable to give a promotional increase to recognize the greater responsibilities.   The size of the promotion increase will typically be in the range of 10 percent to 20 percent.   The actual amount should be determined by a review of job value for the new position, the length of time since the candidate's last adjustment, and his qualifications for the new job.

TRENDS IN SALESMEN'S COMPENSATION

In the 1968 survey by the Research Institute of America cited above, 36 percent of the companies reported recent changes in incentive plans. Of these, 37 percent moved toward more salary and less incentive pay; 33 percent toward more incentive and less salary; 30 percent, while making compensation adjustments, retained proportionately the same mix of salary and incentive. This continual rate of change, the study says, coupled with a lack of a clear trend, indicates that management is continuing to grope in the sales compensation area.

Today's salesman worries about the *way* he is paid. While money is certainly a factor, the opportunity for a positive measurement of performance by the salesman himself is an even bigger and more desirable element of incentive compensation. Everybody likes to keep score, even for fun. The salesman's earnings provide a yardstick the salesman can use to measure the type of job he is doing.

The job of the salesman is changing. The days of the Willy Lomans are gone. Salesmen in the future will become problem solvers rather than order-takers. The salesman will be much more of a manager and will have a much greater influence on the management of his time, territory, sales efforts, etc. As these changes occur, it is entirely likely that the amount of base salary will increase at a greater rate than the amount of incentives. As a greater amount of advertising support is given, there will be less of a need for commissions to motivate the salesman. Sales management will have to be looking for better ways to motivate the salesmen than money. Therefore, the base-salary aspects of salesmen's compensation will take on increasing importance in the years ahead.

chapter 39

Designing a Compensation Program for Retail Sales Personnel

ALAN LANGER *Senior Associate, Edward N. Hay & Associates, Boston, Massachusetts*

No compensation program can hope to be effective unless it takes into account the unique and multifaceted problems inherent in the industry within which the company operates. In order to get a better perspective on the retail industry, let us step back for a moment and look at its current problems in light of the changes that have taken place over the last 10 to 20 years—a series of changes which, I might add, have seen this industry expand its physical facilities, broaden its merchandise scope, increase its profit margin, shift major functional emphasis from the retailer to the supplier and the consumer, and in general try to follow (albeit sometimes under great duress) the trends of the times.

Decline in Retail Profits. Any attempt to follow the trends through the 1950s and 1960s will no doubt give social historians many sleepless nights, so suffice it to say we have seen phenomenal growth in all areas of our lives. In the retail field alone, sales rose $8 billion annually, or by 22 percent a year, between 1958 and 1963. And yet, as E. B. Weiss noted in 1964, "despite the healthy economic climate, the population explosion and a fantastic increase in discretionary purchasing power, most traditional chains (except for Sears and J. C. Penney) have failed totally to profit in proportion to the increases. Capital return and net profit ratios either show a steady decline or hold steady near or at their lows."[1] And *The New York Times* reported in 1969: "Retail profits or return on capital invested continues to run below those of other industries. The rate of return is 11.6 percent below that of all manufacturing companies."[2]

There are many reasons why this condition exists, and an equal number of opinions regarding the methods of correcting or at least ameliorating the situation. The fact is, however, that instead of developing new and creative approaches, the retail industry has further traditionalized its response, and it has thereby compounded its problems.

Weiss goes on to point out that, despite the clarity of the handwriting on the wall, "most of our retail chains were forced reluctantly into most of their major changes: (1) moving to the suburbs; (2) night hours; (3) extension of credit. And most of them are still 'talking' about the vital importance of training their salespeople."[3]

Service Cutbacks. In order to counteract the effects of decreasing net profits, certain steps were taken to "shortcut" some traditional retail services.

- Shoppers were urged to "pay cash and carry" rather than rely upon delivery systems which proved costly to the retailer.
- Stores began to charge for services formerly performed for free, such as for estimates for repair of large items purchased from the store.
- Standards of personnel service at the retail floor level dropped to new lows. In some instances, salespeople were asked to cover wider areas of the floor and handle merchandise with which they were not familiar. Low salaries and minimal benefits combined with long hours and poor working conditions to decrease the quality of the personnel attracted to the retail sales field.

Growth of Discount and Self-service Stores. While these steps may have reduced retailers' costs, they also sent customers scurrying to find better and less frustrating ways of fulfilling their consuming needs. Thus, the discount store has had substantial effect upon the retail industry's direction. While the magnitude of the impact varies between urban and suburban areas, the results are relatively the same.

In addition, self-service—already the rule in most food stores—is being extended rapidly to drug, variety, and discount stores. At the same time, however, rising income levels will increase the demand for merchandise which requires the salesperson to be better trained and more knowledgeable and to spend more time with the customer. Despite the need for better service on bigger purchases, the discount and self-service trends seem to indicate that the rate of sales employment will not keep pace with the volume of sales.

Changing Consumer Attitudes. The advent and growth of discount and self-service stores, coupled with the decline in service levels at the traditional department stores, have had a profound effect on consumer attitudes, as reported in *A Study of Consumer Frustrations,* conducted by Charles Collazzo, Jr., in 1963. Relative to sales service, Collazzo reported that:

A free word association showed the shoppers' greater preference for self-service than clerk service both in terms of number of favorable responses as well as in

[1] E. B. Weiss, *A Reappraisal of New Retail Trends,* Doyle, Dane & Bernbach, Inc., 1964, p. 6.
[2] "Retailers Are Facing Up to Sweeping Social Changes," *The New York Times,* Jan. 5, 1969, sec. 3, 1:1.
[3] E. B. Weiss, *op. cit.,* p. 9.

terms of intensity of feeling expressed.... The expressions used which were unfavorable to clerk service were very strong in intensity. They used words and phrases such as "pain-in-the-neck," "lousy," "slow," "impolite," "frustrating," etc. On the other hand, words favorable to clerk service were not as strong (e.g.: fair, good, agreeable).[4]

Asked to specify the nature of their unsatisfactory sales experiences, consumers found service bad on all counts, as shown in Table 1. In view of their sales experience it is not surprising that, in a forced-choice question, Collazzo's consumer respondents chose low prices and no sales help over regular retail prices and excellent sales help. After all, is "excellent sales help" a realistic alternative?

Nonetheless, when questioned on the major reasons why they chose to shop a particular store, customers frequently cited competency of sales help. And in a forced-choice question on sales service, respondents overwhelmingly indicated they would like competent sales help, particularly for big-ticket items. This near unanimity of opinion prevailed, with the proviso that they would not have to undergo the frustrations associated with existing service. Actually, many respondents who felt favorably toward sales service also thought clerks were poorly trained, incompetent, disinterested, and satisfactory only as an alternative to no help at all. Interestingly, the larger the consumer's income, the less he felt the need for assistance.

In an effort to accommodate the consuming public, and to win back some of the business lost to discount stores, department stores are accelerating their programs involving small specialty shops. These shops are in effect fine specialty stores.

Ultimately they will radically change department store operating procedures. The specialty shop concept is taking hold rapidly among the better department stores, and in several stores this trend has already brought about rather radical changes in buying authority and merchandising programs, etc. The fact is that the prestige department stores intend to become mass merchandisers to an aristocratic market.[5]

TABLE 1   Customers' Complaints about Sales Service*

Service Failure	Percent of Respondents
No refund on faulty goods.............	90%
Not courteous.......................	80
Sold too aggressively.................	77
Don't know job......................	75
"Pounce" on you.....................	74
Not around.........................	72
Slow...............................	72
Errors in writing up sale..............	56

* Charles J. Collazzo, Jr., *A Study of Consumer Frustration*, Retail Research Institute, 1963, p. 85.

[4] Charles J. Collazzo, Jr., *A Study of Consumer Frustration*, Retail Research Institute, 1963, p. 29.

[5] E. B. Weiss, *op. cit.*, p. 33.

Middle-class Migration to the Suburbs. Another major trend affecting the industry has been the marked shift in population which began after World War II and is still continuing. Middle-income families, predominantly white, began moving to the suburbs in large numbers. The widespread ownership and use of automobiles and the economic boom that accompanied the end of the war helped pave the way for this migration. Trade followed the trend, and sometime after 1950, the shopping center complex really began to expand, with the result that " 'interceptor' rings of stores surrounding central business districts began to curtail urban business."[6] This suburban or, more precisely, interurban consumer no longer has to travel into the urban complex to do his shopping. He is generally younger and more affluent, owns his own home, is better educated, and tends to have a larger family than the city dweller. While reducing the middle-class population from which the urban store could draw its business, the move to the suburbs also reduced the middle-class pool of available talent from which the industry could draw its personnel. The pattern is established: the suburbs have become almost the exclusive areas of child rearing, and the central city, by contrast, has become the domicile of minority-group members, the wealthy and the poor, the unmarried and the aged. As long ago as 1966, the U.S. Department of Labor reported that at least one-third of all retail sales were made at the suburban shopping centers, and that the trend was increasing.[7]

THE NEED FOR SERVICE AND THE PEOPLE TO PROVIDE IT

Changes like these in an industry's universe require substantial changes in approach to the public as well as to the employee—not only, as has been indicated, in terms of buying authority and merchandising, but in terms of the personnel practices and compensation programs, which in turn have an effect upon the employees who meet the public and provide them with service. For example, *The Wall Street Journal* reported in 1969 that Sears, J. C. Penney, and Lazarus Department Stores were instituting an "Open Sunday" policy in Ohio in an effort to buy back some of the business lost to the discount stores. But implementing the policy was no easy matter; as one retail department manager said, "It's murder because my female employees have families who don't want her to work on Sunday."[8] Inasmuch as women occupy one-third of all retail sales jobs in general merchandise and apparel stores, seven of ten in department stores, and eight of ten in variety stores, it is clear that answers to problems like this one will have to be found if the retail industry—and particularly the department stores—are to survive in our mechanized, mass-produced society.

We know, therefore, that one of the major problems facing the retail industry today is the recruitment, retention, and training of personnel adequate to the job of serving the public. Obviously, I am not suggesting that all of the other problems facing the industry will suddenly disappear overnight if the "people" problem is solved. What I am saying is that retailers must become more aware of the important role the salesperson plays in this time of growing demands for consumer goods and services; and, upon developing this awareness, they must

---

[6] James D. Taylor, *The Effect on Retail Trade of Outlying Shopping Districts,* Business Research Bureau, School of Business, State University of South Dakota, June, 1961, p. 16.

[7] E. B. Weiss, *op. cit.,* p. 15.

[8] "Shopping on Sunday," *The Wall Street Journal,* Dec. 10, 1969, 1:1, 19:1.

act positively to ensure recruitment of the best-motivated, best-trained, most responsive (to the needs of the customer) sales force from the population available to them.

Although some steps have been taken in this direction, much more needs to be accomplished before the retailers can begin to see the light at the end of the tunnel. As James Bliss, Executive Vice President of the National Retail Merchants Association, said in *The New York Times,* "the overall recruitment problem that confronts retailers over the next decade is to challenge the curiosity and energy of young people."[9]   In fact, by 1975 two of every five people will be under 17 years of age, and about 114 million (approximately one-half of the total population) will be under 25. In addition to being young, the urban labor pool for positions like retail salesclerk is becoming increasingly black. It has been predicted that by 1980 blacks, Puerto Ricans, and Orientals will comprise half of New York City's population. This trend is not confined to New York—it is nationwide.

It is interesting to note that in the late 1960s, San Francisco stores more than doubled the number of black and other minority-group workers they employed, and the percentage of minority people serving in supervisory positions was up from 3.5 percent to 9 percent.

While it is true that some retail stores are beginning to streamline their training programs and provide their sales staff more informational material to aid in serving the customers, it is also painfully clear that there is a gap between what retail management hopes is happening to customers in their stores and what is really happening in front of the counter. And retail executives are well aware of this gap. Lee Thompson, a Sylvania Sales Vice President, summed it all up when he said recently, "The key is service."[10]   The question is how to get the service—who will provide it.

A 1969 study involving 123 female salesclerks in a large department store provides some insight into this problem. The aim of the investigator, Charles N. Weaver, was to determine what relationships exist between age, education, and marital status and selling performance and sensitivity to sales incentive. Weaver found that the high producers tended to be older, better educated, and either married or divorced. The low producers tended to be younger, less well educated, and either single or separated.[11]   This is not a happy finding for urban stores, in view of the fact that their manpower market is increasingly young, unmarried, elderly, uneducated, and poor; and the growing proportion of the under-25 group (by the mid-seventies, 50 percent of our population will be under 25) means that all stores will be increasingly dependent on younger manpower.

How then can these facts be reconciled with the studies made regarding performance and motivation? Perhaps an entirely different approach is necessary in order to turn the tide. Perhaps the traditional view of the salesclerk needs a new perspective. Perhaps the standard "compensation" plans are not sufficient to attract the type of people who are now available to the industry. Currently, the industry is suffering from what R. Marin calls "personnel

---

[9] "Retailers Are Facing Up to Sweeping Social Changes," *The New York Times,* Jan. 5, 1969, sec. 3, 1:1.

[10] J. Blood, "Business as (Un)usual," *Merchandising Week,* vol. 101, June 23, 1969, pp. 30–31.

[11] Charles N. Weaver, "An Empirical Study to Aid in the Selection of Retail Salesclerks," *Journal of Retailing,* vol. 45, no. 3, Fall, 1969.

piracy,"[12] a less than satisfactory solution surely, and a malady that is growing worse rather than better.

THE CURRENT PERSONNEL PICTURE

If it is accepted that courteous, efficient service from behind the counter or on the sales floor does much to satisfy customers and to build a store's good reputation, it must also be accepted that recruiting, training, and retaining a good sales staff are of the utmost importance to the success of a traditional department store.

Historically, however, the salesperson has been the low man on the retail totem pole. Salespeople are poorly trained and their compensation programs provide little incentive for them to either stay with a particular store or improve their customer service. Moreover, retail salesclerks are poorly paid by external standards as well. For example, compare the retail employees' (one-third of whom are salespeople) 1965 median weekly salary of $82 with the median salaries for nonretail white-collar jobs shown in Table 2. Only the mail clerk and the messenger fall substantially below the retail pay level; the receptionist, typist, and file clerk are at a level approximately equivalent with that of the retail employee. Although dollar amounts have gone up since 1965, the relationships have remained relatively stable. And even the increases that have been granted have not been the result of more enlightened, long-term planning on the part of managements but the result of external pressures—increases in the minimum wage and union contracts.

Given the poor pay and poor training, it is not surprising that turnover industrywide averages 60 percent a year, a fact that only further aggravates the difficulty of providing customers with good service. An additional factor undermining any attempt to improve service is the prevalence of part-time help among retail sales employees. Although many retailers pay their full-time personnel time and a half for overtime, most employees are unwilling to work three or four evenings a week plus Sundays; thus, the stores are forced to take on part-time help.

Despite the seasonal variations in retail employment and sales and the fact that there may always be a need for some part-time help, particularly around

TABLE 2   Median Weekly Salaries for Nonretail Jobs*

Job	1965	1970
Addressograph Operator—Senior.....	$85	$111
Duplicating Machine Operator......	97	128
File Clerk—Senior.................	80	100
Mail Clerk.......................	69	91
Messenger.......................	64	84
Receptionist.....................	82	107
Purchasing Clerk.................	98	116
Typist—Senior...................	79	102

* Commerce and Industry Association of New York, *Office Salaries and Personnel Practices in New York*, 27th Annual Survey, April, 1970.

[12] R. Marin, "Personnel Piracy Grows," *Merchandising Week*, vol. 101, Nov. 10, 1969.

TABLE 3   Distribution of Working Population by Industry*

Industry	Percent of Total Employed Population
Manufacturing.	65%
Transportation.	11
Retail.	10
Finance, insurance, and real estate.	9
Wholesale.	4
Selected scientific services.	1
	100%

* United States Department of Labor, Bureau of Labor Statistics, *Professional Administrative and Technical Pay (Regional Reports)*, March, 1969.

the peak periods of April–May, September, and December, it is not unreasonable to believe that better year-long planning and a greater commitment from full-timers could substantially reduce the need for such help. For example, in 1966 the proportion of employees working part time ranged from 23 percent in stores with gross sales between $500,000 and $1 million to as much as 36 percent in stores with gross sales of under $250,000.[13] In some department stores, the part-timers far exceeded the full-time personnel. Obviously, a person who is working part time cannot have the sense of loyalty and commitment to the store that a full-timer can, nor can he (usually) have the depth of knowledge of the merchandise and the changes in style, etc., that is necessary to provide the customer with the kind of service that will satisfy him.

All of these factors—the low pay, the poor training, the high turnover, and the wide use of part-time help—must be dealt with if the retail industry is to be able to recruit and train the number and kind of salespeople necessary to provide customers with adequate service. Adding to the situation is the fact that retail's manpower needs are growing. According to figures reported by the Bureau of Labor Statistics in 1969 (see Table 3), the retail industry now employs approximately 10 percent of the working population in the country, and "approximately one-third (⅓) of them are in the sales field. This population group numbering about three million people (⅗ of whom are women) were employed last year in close to 100 different kinds of retail businesses."[14] Current growth and attrition projections indicate that the number of salespeople employed by the retail industry will increase 150,000 a year during the 1970s—this in response to increases in population and disposable income and concomitant increases in sales volume, consumers' demands for longer store hours, and employees' unwillingness to extend their working hours.

NEW APPROACHES TO RETAIL SALES COMPENSATION

The variables affecting the retail industry would make a 10-dimensional matrix. At this point, three areas of change are critical:

1. Changes in the industry's methods of doing business—the emergence of

[13] Bureau of Labor Statistics, United States Department of Labor, *Employee Earnings and Hours in the Retail Trade*, June, 1966.

[14] Bureau of Labor Statistics, United States Department of Labor, *Occupational Outlook Handbook*, 1968–1969 edition.

discounts, the wide extension of credit, evening and Sunday hours, and specialty shops within large department stores

2. Changes in consumer attitudes—the dissatisfaction with current levels of service, the willingness to trade off service for price advantages and to drive farther to shop at a less expensive store, and the disinclination to come into the city to shop

3. Changes in the manpower pool—the middle-class move to the suburbs, resulting in the city population becoming increasingly young, unmarried, black, elderly, and poor

Added to these factors are the low pay and high turnover characteristic of retail sales positions, the great reliance on part-time help, and, not least important, the customers' demand for better service from the nondiscount stores.

The retailer, then, is at a crossroads. He can continue his traditional methods of recruiting, training, and paying salespeople, thus foregoing the chance to motivate his people and improve service. Or he can recognize the new manpower pool with which he is dealing, gear his compensation and training programs to their needs, and thereby improve his customer service. It is really not an either/or situation, but it soon will be if retailers continue to cling to old attitudes and methods.

This is not to imply that everything that has gone before is obsolete or worthless. On the contrary, current compensation practices vary widely, and some have been effective in meeting the needs of employees and motivating them. By and large, however, retailers' thinking on sales compensation has been confined to what the hourly rate should be and on what items commissions should be given. Thus, retail salespeople may be paid straight salaries (usually for small-ticket items in department and self-service and discount stores), salary plus some commission (on big-ticket items such as fur coats and white and brown goods), or straight commission (in a few large chain stores). A few retailers have gone beyond this formula in an effort to motivate their people. Sears, Roebuck, for example, has for years provided its permanent employees with profit sharing. While Sears' profit-sharing plan has been a far-sighted, imaginative means of gaining the commitment of employees and motivating them, it does not address the employee's nonmaterial needs, needs which—for people among whom the retail industry must now do its recruiting—may be even more pressing and whose fulfillment may be prerequisite to even considering a job. Examples are transportation to and from work and child care during working hours.

An article in the summer, 1970, issue of *World*, a publication of Peat, Marwick, Mitchell & Co., confirms the critical nature of these needs. The authors reported a study conducted among welfare mothers by F. & R. Lazarus & Co., a part of the Federated Stores chain. Of the 5,700 welfare mothers interviewed, approximately 2,000 could not accept jobs because they had a group total of 6,000 children to care for at home. The article pointed out that the problem of day care is not unique to people on welfare: "though ten million mothers were working and 4.1 million had children under six, licensed day care was available for only 530,000 of those children."[15] The costs of hiring private baby-sitters—let alone the difficulty of finding reliable baby-sitters—make it impossible for many mothers to accept retail sales positions at the present low pay; by providing day care for the preschool children of female employees, a store would not only substantially enlarge its manpower pool, but it would go

[15] John A. Fiorillo and Ira G. Asherman, "A New Challenge for Industry—Child Care Centers," *World*, Summer, 1970, Peat, Marwick, Mitchell & Co.

a long way in gaining the commitment of these employees and motivating them to do a good job.

Another major factor which retailers have largely ignored is psychic need. Reams have been written on the psychological needs of executives, production workers, etc., and how an understanding of these needs can help companies to motivate people.   But the needs and satisfactions of retail salespeople have scarcely been considered, partly because it has always been felt that anyone can sell on the retail floor and partly because the industry has come to think of these jobs as filled by transient workers, upon whom no effort should be spent. These assumptions may have been correct when customers did not have the discount and self-service alternative, but now that service has become one of the critical factors differentiating a department store from a discount store, it is important to understand what motivates employees to provide that service.

Insight into this problem is provided in an article, "Self-actualization among Retail Sales Personnel," by Grady D. Bruce and Charles M. Bonjean, which appeared in the Summer, 1969, *Journal of Retailing*.   Bruce and Bonjean describe the effects of low self-actualization on an employee's performance:

1. Likely to daydream
2. Likely to have aggressive feelings towards supervisor
3. Likely to have aggressive feelings towards his co-workers
4. Less likely to show interest in his work
5. More likely to restrict his output
6. More likely to make errors
7. More likely to postpone difficult tasks
8. More likely to be concerned with material rewards
9. Less likely to indicate they are satisfied
10. More likely to think of doing other types of work[16]

In addition I think it can be extrapolated that low self-actualization is associated with high turnover.

Bruce and Bonjean's description fits many I have heard from supervisors and personnel executives about their employees.   To paraphrase an applicable line, the fault with our salespeople may not be in their stars, but in ourselves.   We may not be structuring the compensation programs or the working environment of these positions so that there is a real opportunity for self-actualization.   The trick, of course, is to determine precisely what an individual desires to actualize while at work.   Self-actualization may relate to wages, job security, or more subjective factors.   A Bonjean-Vance study of self-actualization in a large department store indicated, "One cannot generalize that employees receiving higher wages experience greater self-actualization."[17]   In fact, the variable most often positively associated with self-actualization was "feeling of productivity." Bonjean and Bruce go on to say that the formality of the organizational structure relates inversely to the degree of personal relationships, and that personal relationships tend to increase the possibility of self-actualization.   Further, they indicate that knowledge of employees' predispositions is crucial to motivating them.   For example, incentive compensation plans operate on the assumption that employees are favorably predisposed to high wages.

However, the climate in most retail stores is almost the exact opposite of what Bonjean and Bruce have found to stimulate motivation.   There is an over-

[16] Grady D. Bruce and Charles M. Bonjean, "Self-actualization among Retail Sales Personnel," *Journal of Retailing*, vol. 45, Summer, 1969, p. 75.
[17] *Ibid.*

abundance of structure—a great many routines, rules, and regulations which must be followed. Interpersonal relationships are rare—certainly between the supervisor and the salesclerk. Training of either the neophyte or the long-term veteran is almost nonexistent. Supervisory training until just recently has been a myth. Longevity rather than productivity on the job brings the greatest rewards. The prestige factor has all but been eliminated, because no matter what you say to an employee, it is what you *do* that indicates the esteem in which you hold him and his job. Virtually none of his sociological or psychological needs are being addressed, and, to make matters worse, few if any executives are conversant with these needs as they relate to youth, blacks, and women—the three groups from whom the retail industry will be drawing the majority of its sales personnel in the next 10 years.

SUMMARY

The retailers' universe has changed. Deep inroads into the market have been achieved by the discount and self-service stores. The population base from which retailers must draw their salespeople is becoming increasingly young, black, and female (mostly married women with children). If the response to the discount challenge is service, the problem before the retailer is to find and keep employees who will provide the service.

To attract and retain competent sales personnel, retail managements must construct total compensation plans geared to the needs of the potential sales force—and this means going beyond consideration of just salary. The pay structure, of course, must be sound—it must be internally equitable and competitive with the marketplace; policies and procedures must be established for handling pay increases and performance evaluations; and provisions must be made for incentives where they can help upgrade sales performance. The point is, however, that salespeople need and want more than cash, and these needs must also be considered in designing a compensation program. Traditional extra-compensatory devices in the retail industry have included fringe benefits, discounts, and goods. But given the changing manpower market and the overriding need to motivate salespeople to provide good service, retail managements must take a broad view of compensation. To successfully recruit people, they must be able to speak to their immediate needs, such as for day care and transportation; and to motivate them on the job, they must create a working environment which facilitates self-actualization.

This is a big order, but steps are already being taken to fill it. Abraham and Straus in New York has tried to redistribute its internal equity by hiring large numbers of minority-group members—however, much more must be done in the areas of supportive services, compensation, and training before such a program will be successful. Korvette's central office in New York City has tried to be responsive to the changing population base as well. The Spartan Industries (the parent company) board has charged the retail stores with becoming, in reality, "an equal opportunity employer," and yet, as a result of organizational problems and lack of commitment at lower levels of management, little has been done to achieve the objectives. Some moves, however, have been more successful: a group of New York City department stores have joined in a special summer intern program designed to attract black college students into retailing upon their graduation. Some stores in the Midwest are considering establishing a day care facility for their employees; the Melville Shoe Corporation has recently opened a clothing chain aimed at the youth market called Chess King, and the stores (boutiques) are staffed and managed by members of the group-to-be-served.

The solutions to the major problems facing the retailers lie not out there somewhere, but in the minds and hearts of the kind of men who had the courage and foresight to build the industry to what it has become today. While the chapter has dealt in large measure with its ills, there is much which is positive about the industry. It is through the examination of its weaknesses, however, that I feel a greater effort will be made to reassess its current course in the light of the predictable changes which are bound to have an effect on its well-being.

BIBLIOGRAPHY

Blood, J.: "Business as (Un)usual," *Merchandising Week*, vol. 101, June 23, 1969.

Bruce, Grady D., and Charles M. Bonjean: "Self-actualization among Retail Sales Personnel," *Journal of Retailing*, vol. 45, Summer, 1969.

Bureau of Labor Statistics, U. S. Department of Labor: *Employee Earnings and Hours in the Retail Trade*, June, 1966.

Bureau of Labor Statistics, U. S. Department of Labor: *Occupational Outlook Handbook*, 1968–1969 ed.

Bureau of Labor Statistics, U. S. Department of Labor: *Professional Administrative and Technical Pay (Regional Reports)*, March, 1969.

Bureau of Labor Statistics, U. S. Department of Labor: *Retail Trade*, 1966 (an interim study of the effects of the 1961 amendments).

Cleaves, Herbert M.: "Mass Sell Termed Mass 'Gap' Issue," *Merchandising Week*, vol. 101, Nov. 3, 1969.

Collazzo, Charles J., Jr.: *A Study of Consumer Frustration*, Retail Research Institute, 1963.

Commerce and Industry Association of New York: *Office Salaries and Personnel Practices in New York*, 27th Annual Survey, April, 1970.

Dartnell Corporation: *Wage and Salary Administration*, A Dartnell Survey, The Dartnell Corporation, Chicago, Ill., 1969.

Fiorillo, John A., and Ira G. Asherman: "A New Challenge for Industry–Child Care Centers," *World*, Summer, 1970, Peat Marwick, Mitchell, & Co.

Marin, R.: "Personnel Piracy Grows," *Merchandising Week*, vol. 101, Nov. 10, 1969.

"Retailers Are Facing Up to Sweeping Social Changes," *The New York Times*, Jan. 5, 1969, sec. 3, 1:1.

"Retailers Heeding Consumers Act to Improve Sales Personnel," *The New York Times*, Aug. 11, 1969, 47:6.

Schell, Eileen: *Changes in Boston's Retail Landscape*, Retail Research Institute (Graduate School Department of Geography, Boston University), 1964.

"Shopping on Sunday," *The Wall Street Journal*, 1:1, 19:1, Dec. 10, 1969.

Stephenson, P. R.: "Identifying Determinants of Retail Patronage," *The Journal of Marketing*, vol. 33, July, 1969.

"Students Flunk Retailers," *The New York Times*, Nov. 16, 1969, sec. 3, 14:3.

Taylor, James D.: *The Effect on Retail Trade of Outlying Shopping Districts*, Business Research Bureau, School of Business, State University of South Dakota, June, 1961.

Weaver, Charles N.: "An Empirical Study to Aid in the Selection of Retail Sales-clerks," *Journal of Retailing*, vol. 45, no. 3, Fall, 1969.

Weiss, E. B.: *A Reppraisal of New Retail Trends*, Doyle, Dane & Bernbach, Inc., 1964.

"What Customers Feel about Retailers Today," *American Druggist*, vol. 159, June 16, 1969.

chapter 40

Designing Compensation Programs for Scientists and Professionals in Business

LLOYD E. FULLER   *Manager, Compensation Department, Sandia Laboratories, Albuquerque, New Mexico*

While science and technology advanced rapidly in the post-World War II period—a period marked by highly imaginative and innovative technical performances—salary administration has for the most part remained somewhat less than scientific and largely geared to other environments and to another time.

Certainly any scientist-professional pay system based almost exclusively on job content could be accused of relating too strongly to the shop-office environment, where creativity is not the mainstream activity. On the other hand, it must be recognized that not all technical jobs have the same weight or professional depth. Although the research physicist and the electrical engineer are teammates in their basic college education, they play out their careers in different ball parks.

Among companies specifically recognizing differences in jobs, some do so on a gross basis, grouping activities under a few broad classifications. Others use more elaborate systems of position evaluation with assigned point values in an effort to reveal discrete differences in job requirements. Organizations committed to a formalized position-evaluation/salary-range approach to scientist-professional compensation have accepted the philosophy that such evaluation need not be fundamentally different from that of nonscientific or even non-technical jobs.

Although an established evaluation system may accommodate the activities in the research and development area, it may need elaboration to reflect the technical depth and problem-solving requirements of specific positions. It is difficult to compare the research activities performed by scientists at different companies without resorting to the subjective judgments that the more formal evaluation systems are supposed to eliminate.

Some of our larger research-oriented organizations prefer to reward the accomplishment of the scientist-professional staff under a system emphasizing comparative performance within groups of equally mature professionals. They have accepted a curve approach involving considerations of maturity and relative contributions (of which a subjective evaluation of job worth can be a consideration) as the most appropriate tool available for compensating scientists and professionals. They feel that a system which can recognize current differences in assignments yet place the greater stress on the contribution of the individual is more appropriate for the compensation of those involved in various disciplines and evidencing varying competence. That a man does his work well is a factor increasing his worth to the company. That his supervision has seen fit to give him one of the heavier assignments also enhances his worth to the company.

Even a cursory survey of the literature on compensation of scientists will impress the reader with the deep convictions of both the proponents of job-oriented systems and the champions of the maturity curve approach. What seems to get lost in the verbiage is a recognition that any system of evaluation, carefully applied and maintained, will disclose the same differences in relative worth of an individual's contribution. Neither position evaluation nor performance evaluation operates in a vacuum when applied to professional endeavors. When the systems are changed (in either direction), the similarity of end positions is amazing.

EXTERNAL COMPARISONS

Regardless of the compensation system it uses, a company usually attempts to compare favorably with other organizations similar in science and technology and nature of professional staff rather than seek comparability with industry in general. It may do this by exchanging salary information on an individual basis and by participating in the large nationwide surveys of professional salaries, such as the survey conducted by the Engineering Manpower Commission of the Engineers Joint Council. The 1968–1969 survey covered 979 employers with 191,042 engineering graduates, or an estimated 30 percent of the market.[1] Although the information presented in this survey is in maturity curve format, as are most large surveys in this area, individual companies using other bases for salary administration are still able to interpret the data and apply them to their own situations, sometimes as a check on established salary ranges under a job-oriented system.

Arriving at valid interpretations of the survey statistics and other salary data is quite a difficult exercise, and it can be done, at best, only semiquantitatively after considerable selective study. For instance, definitions of such terms as

---

[1] *Professional Income of Engineers, 1968–1969,* Engineering Manpower Commission of Engineers Joint Council, 345 East 47th Street, New York, N.Y. 10017, April, 1969, p. 7.

"engineer," "scientist," "professional," and "research" vary from one organization to another, and it requires care to match a particular company's situation with the survey data. In addition to survey information, a company must also include in its overall judgments pertinent data resulting from studies of college recruiting, market hiring, and resignations.

External comparisons of the salaries paid to a company's scientist-professionals usually lead to the establishment of a salary philosophy or goals. The basic decisions the salary administrator must make concern the relationship his company's salary levels will have to the market. Further decisions are required to answer such questions as: How will our company achieve and maintain this position? How much does our company need to spend during the next salary review period? How can we allocate these funds to assure that our goals are achieved?

After these decisions are made, the economic adjustment factor of a salary review must be considered. Any pattern of inflation or deflation in the economy becomes significant. Another factor needing careful consideration is any marked increase or decrease in the demand for scientist-professionals. In the past several years, we have witnessed jumps in the salary levels offered to new graduates or to experienced engineers with specialties suddenly in demand. Deliberate prudence must be used in responding to any of these barometers of market value in order to keep a company's internal salary relationships equitable.

A third factor to be considered in developing the salary increase budget may be called a "growth" factor. As time passes, the employee's value to the company tends to increase gradually. In an economy with no inflation or deflation and no supply-and-demand pressures, this gradual increase in value would probably be the only factor to consider when making out the salary increase budget.

INTERNAL COMPARISONS: PERFORMANCE EVALUATION

While there are those who express doubts as to the compatibility of performance ratings with professional endeavor, quantitative comparisons are inescapable. As long as ours is a society in which financial rewards are distributed in some relation to individual contributions, performance ratings will remain basic to our social structure.

Before the annual salary review, and independently of it, supervisors should rate each scientist-professional on his performance relative to that of his associates. Consideration should be given to his potential for continued growth as well as to the excellence and worth of his current assignments.

Most systems of job-based performance evaluation use such terms as "outstanding," "good," "acceptable," and "unacceptable." Some control of the application of these evaluations is also normally provided. Limitations on the application of "outstanding" evaluations, for instance, are usually on a percentage basis.

One method would provide a distribution of performance ratings within company organizational groups on the basis of a bell-shaped curve, with the requirements that outstanding performances be matched with acceptable-unacceptable evaluations and that the larger group comprise good ratings (e.g., 20 percent outstanding, 60 percent good, and 20 percent acceptable-unacceptable). The group being evaluated must be of sufficient size to make this method practical. A further refinement is to use a high–mid–low range within the broad performance evaluation rating (e.g., high = acceptable, or AO in Figure 1), which will allow for more discretion on the part of the evaluator.

The salary range of any particular classification or point level must be sufficiently broad to accommodate the outstanding as well as the average performer. In this heavy area of professionalism, broader salary ranges are more appropriate than they are for more routine, circumscribed tours. Ranges of 30 to 50 percent are fairly standard. Some method to identify that portion of the range designed to accommodate the various levels of performances should be established. The midpoint of the range might be looked upon as a control rate and the logical place to pay the lower good or top acceptable scientist-professional who is fully mature on his job. Figure 1 illustrates one system of job-related performance evaluation which provides performance bands and uses a concept of years "in level" (years in the same or an equal position) as an additional consideration.

The figure provides three performance bands for different rates of advancement. The individual who is performing in a completely acceptable manner should reach the control rate for his position in seven years. Employees who have top good-performance rankings should reach it sooner (about one-half the time). People ranked outstanding should progress still faster and should be paid toward the top of the range. The 80 to 120 percent of the control rate represents a salary range of 50 percent. Thus, considering the three variables, (1) percent of control rate, (2) years in level, and (3) performance ranking, it is possible to have two men in the same position, each ranked 0–0, but one being paid at 88 percent of the control rate and the other at 120 percent. The reason would be that one man had seven years "in level" whereas the other had only one year "in level."

Unless some sort of maturity factor is considered within the framework of a job-based compensation system, it is difficult to maintain internal equities between the new hire and the experienced professional. Many job evaluation-based systems recognize varying levels of the same activity as separate jobs. There may be quality control engineers A, B, and C, for instance, each with a separate rate range. Such a system gives additional consideration to maturity within the profession and at the same time recognizes a ladder for career development. Upward movement on this ladder is controlled by two factors:

Figure 1.   Performance review chart.

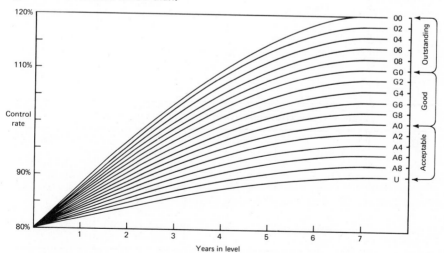

Years in level

(1) openings in the higher-level activities, and (2) demonstrated performance of employees at the lower levels as an indication of their potential for more complex, in-depth assignments.

Utilizing both techniques—job levels based upon progressively more involved and technically challenging professional assignments, and time-in-level consideration at each job level—gives management a method for professional treatment of professional employees and provides an appropriate means to recognize career development in a job-related system.

If the maturity curve approach is utilized in salary administration, performance ratings can be expressed in terms of octile positions (or quartile positions if the population is not large) relative to the other scientist-professionals. Thus, a performance rating of Octile 1 indicates that the individual is judged to have a performance among the top one-eighth of the group.

Unlike the position evaluation system, performance rating under the maturity system must take into account the worth of the job as well as the individual performance on the job. In other words, it entails the overall worth-to-company concept.

In general, meaningful comparisons of individual performance can best be made when the groupings consider age or experience as a prime factor. For example, age bands could be 30 and under, 31 to 40, 41 to 50, and 51 and over or some similar combination that would tend to group individuals with the same general experience levels together.

When individuals have been placed in the appropriate age-experience groups, they are ranked from highest to lowest within each group (see Figure 2, Example A). Then, comparisons are made between individuals in adjoining age groups to rank the entire group. No attempt should be made to compare indi-

Figure 2.   Ranking performance.

RANKING WITHIN AGE-EXPERIENCE GROUP

	30 and under	31 to 40	41 to 50	51 and over
Highest	Smith	Daniels	Connolly	Kelly
	Peters	Cassidy	Austin	Johnson
	X	X	X	X
	X	X	X	X
	X	X	X	X
	X	X	X	
		X	X	
Lowest		X		

RANKING AFTER COMPARISON BETWEEN ADJOINING AGE GROUPS

	30 and under	31 to 40	41 to 50	51 and over
Highest		Daniels		Kelly
	Smith		Connolly	
		Cassidy		Johnson
	Peters	X		X
	X	X X	Austin	X
		X	X X X	
	X X	X X	X	X
	X	X	X	
Lowest	X		X X	

TABLE 1   Organization Performance Slots

Performance slot	Number of employees Organization A	Organization B
1.............	3	8
2.............	3	10
3.............	7	7
4.............	14	3
5.............	10	2
6.............	6	
7.............	5	
8.............	5	
Weighted average performance.	4.6	2.4

viduals in widely different age-experience bands.   After this multiple ranking and comparison, the end result may look something like Example B in Figure 2. Each first-line supervisor should rank his own professional staff.   Following this, each successive level of supervision should meld the rankings of his staff until the organizational level where the performance review can still be meaningful is reached (perhaps the third or fourth level).

It cannot be assumed that all organizational divisions of a company have identical levels of work.   Therefore, translation from rank positions in a given organization to positions on the octile curves cannot be guided by any pattern of symmetry.   Instead, the first approach is to allow each organization the same aggregate of positions as its people currently occupy.

Before the scheduled performance review, this involves plotting each individual's current salary position as a performance "slot."   The aggregate of performance slots for each organization can be listed as shown in Table 1.

As supervisors rank their subordinates' performance, changes in performance rankings upward are matched by changes downward, a procedure which acts as a control mechanism.   It is not necessary from a salary administration standpoint that the same numbers of individuals occupy the same performance slots. It is only necessary that the average performance position of the organization remain the same, so that organizational differences are retained.   Changes in staffing and organizations will be reflected when the next cycle of performance evaluation takes place.   Supervisors should be encouraged to fight the tendency to rate everyone the same, which would ultimately lead to paying everyone the same.

In the illustration in Table 1, Organization B has a higher average performance ranking than Organization A.   It would be assumed that the level of competence needed to perform the work in Organization B was higher than that required in Organization A.

DEVELOPING THE COMPENSATION SYSTEM

The typical compensation program for scientist-professionals may be based on a traditional job evaluation approach or on a maturity curve system.   Job evaluation has already been covered in detail in Part 2, and therefore we will discuss it here only briefly.   The maturity curve system will be described fully, since it is uniquely well suited to scientists and professionals.

Job Evaluation: Classification.   Job analysis involves determining what the employee does and the skill and ability required for this.   This information is usually obtained through questionnaires, interviews with employees, or discussions with supervisors. Questionnaires are the simplest and least expensive method; however, the data can be misleading. Employee interviews, while the most effective method of obtaining the necessary job information, also require the most time and expense. While the analysis and evaluation of jobs and job structures can be based on second-source information (from the supervisor), this method may lead to inequities. It is often appropriate to utilize all three techniques in part.

When the job information relative to scientific-professional activities has been collected and organized in the form of job descriptions, it must be evaluated under some established and orderly system. A broad range of the company's activities should be evaluated at one time. Not only will the evaluation plan be applied with some consistency, but the internal relationships of jobs will also play a part in the evaluation process. Evaluating scientific and professional jobs without regard to other positions may seem only proper to research management, but other groups will not be convinced of the validity of the relationships. Once positions have been evaluated, a salary structure may be developed to show the relationship between different activities and the salaries paid individuals. A scattergram plot will provide an easy means of comparison and will reveal any differences or similarities in the salary treatment of those in different functional activities or with different educational backgrounds. A line of central tendency can be determined. The upper and lower limits can be set using a predetermined percentage spread; the upper limit may be 50 percent above the lower limit.

The Maturity Curve. Figure 3 is a salary octile chart. Coordinates on this chart are annual salary dollars and chronological age. Work experience, years since first degree, or some other measure of maturity could be used instead of age. The seven curves designated ½ through ⅞ are boundary lines dividing the chart into eight octile groups, each containing approximately one-eighth of the total population. The 1M curve represents the median of the upper-octile group.

Each company may prepare its own curves by using as raw data the actual salaries of all scientist-professionals at a given point in time or the projected salaries of the group through a salary review period. The grouping may be composed of those with specific educational disciplines or specific organizational assignments, supervisors only, nonsupervisors, or any combination that fits the particular circumstance. All supervisors and nonsupervisor scientist-professionals are included in Figure 3. Not only does the grouping of everyone on the same chart afford enough data to be statistically meaningful, but the relationships of the various subgroupings to the total population can also be identified through the use of colored dots or some other means.

The raw data are plotted for the population. Salary values corresponding to median, quartile, and octile division points can be readily determined for each age. Connecting the corresponding octile points results in a set of irregular "curves," as shown in Figure 4. For most purposes, a set of smoothed curves is desirable (see Figure 3). These smoothed curves retain the position and general shape of the original plottings, but they have been adjusted to eliminate the ragged features caused by statistical fluctuations. A least squares method of fitting curves to the data may be used and, depending on the need, second- or third-degree curves may be used. The main criterion is that the curves be developed from the data in a statistically sound manner. This means that (1) there must be a sufficiently large population, and (2) when the curves are smoothed, each band must retain a population representing its proportion of

Figure 3.   Salary octile chart for scientist-professionals.

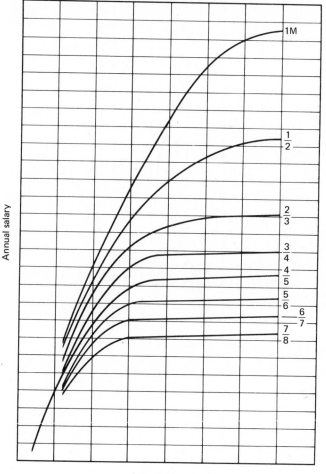

Age or experience

the total population, i.e., each octile band must have one-eighth of the total population, although any single age group may not have one-eighth of the entire age group.

The octile boundary lines show, of course, only the statistical distribution of salaries as of the dates indicated. They are not salary histories. The year-by-year salary history of an average individual shows a much steeper slope than that shown by the curves of salary-age relationship for any single year.

This concept is illustrated schematically in Figure 5. The six curves represent medians for the six dates indicated. The sharply rising line intersecting the curves represents the movement of the salary of a hypothetical individual whose position was median in every year and whose age changed from 30 to 40 over the 10-year period. Notice that it would be impossible to predict his salary at age 40 from the curve that was in effect when he was 30 years old.

Figure 4.   Raw salary data for scientist-professionals.

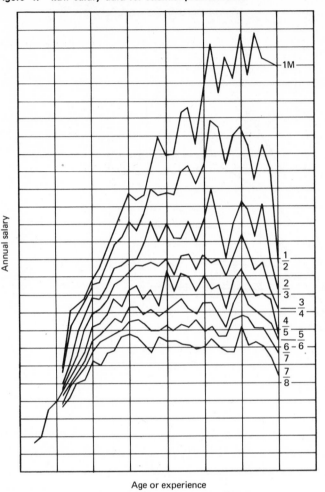

Age or experience

Whether an individual stays at the same relative position (the median, as assumed in this example) depends upon his career development and how it compares with that of his on-roll contemporaries.   If he developed into an upper-octile performer, his personal salary curve would rise even more steeply; and conversely, if his performance decreased relative to that of others, his salary curve would rise less steeply.   Figure 5 illustrates the effect of yearly economic change on the salary structure as well as the effect that the salary increase allocation policy has on the shape of the curve.

PERIODIC SALARY REVIEW

Following the survey of the market, which will give direction to a company's external relationships, the periodic performance review, which determines the internal relationships, and the preparation of the salary increase budget, which is the basis for money allocation and implementation of management's salary philosophy, the periodic review may proceed in a systematic manner.

The actual computation of the salary increase budget considers the amounts needed to take care of market movement and maturity growth. Varied statistical systems are available for the application of budgeted funds, either within the rate ranges or within the maturity curves. One is the compa-ratio, which is a ratio of actual salaries in each pay grade to the midpoint of the grade. Midpoint techniques are used under other systems also as a balancing mechanism to ensure appropriate distribution of funds.

The purpose of the periodic salary review is to correct discrepancies between an individual's present salary and the salary he should be paid. It also offers

Figure 5. Diagram illustrating ten-year salary history of a scientist-professional constantly maintaining a median position.

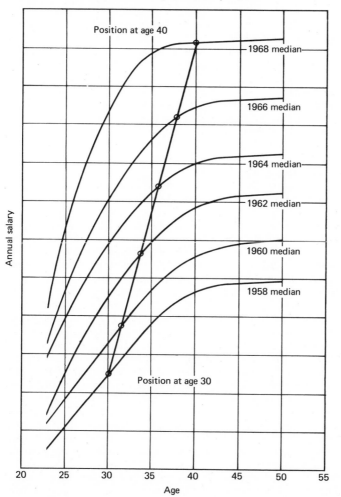

a systematic approach to maintaining the normal salary growth of the scientist-professional for his particular maturity and performance range and to making changes in the salary structure of the whole group as determined by management.

Once the decision is made concerning funds to be expended to achieve the company's objective, these funds should be divided among age-experience groups and salary ranges. Large dollar amounts may be allocated to younger employees to recognize their initial fast growth as they develop into mature professionals. Variations in the dollar amounts allocated for different performance ranges can combat the tendency for salary levels to move toward the average. By requiring that funds allocated to a given group be used for that group, management can control not only the change in the average level of salaries for a group, but also the salary spread and the gross variation within age-experience groups. By issuing generalized guides on salary allocations, management maintains controls but allows local supervision to exercise judgments on the amount to be granted to each individual.

The following sequence of events illustrates one approach to conducting a periodic salary review. It also gives some indication of the forms and paper work control that must be considered.

1. Performance evaluation worksheets are distributed by the appropriate organization unit listing name, salary octile position, and other pertinent information. Each organization is given the information that will enable it to balance its performance positions.

2. Evaluation worksheets are returned to the salary organization, audited for balance, and then reviewed by the appropriate levels of management.

3. At a later date, salary review sheets including all employees eligible for review are distributed to organizations. Special consideration may be given to new hires who might not be included in the periodic review or to employees who are not considered regular, full-time employees.

4. Recommendations of various line organizations are returned to the salary organization for audit and presented to higher levels of management for review and approval.

5. Individual salary adjustments are implemented through a listing sent to the payroll organization at each appropriate time throughout the review period. The indicated change in an individual's salary may range from a significant percentage to no change at all. To smooth out variations in performance rankings, full corrections for large differences in performance position and salary position are not made at one salary review but are spread over a two- to three-year interval.

For example, a median performer who maintains this position through the years (Figure 5) would have a salary growth pattern consisting only of the amount allocated for additional maturity and for salary structure change. Another individual whose performance rank changes from Octile 5 to Octile 3 receives not only the above treatment but also an additional amount to reflect his performance change. Table 2 illustrates the possible difference in salary review treatment for two individuals at the same maturity level. In the case of A, the proposed increase is 6.25 percent of current salary, while B's proposed increase is 18.75 percent of current salary. For further discrimination between these salary increases, a time interval between increases can be used as a variable. This involves relating the time interval between increases to the percentage amount of increase, allowing local supervision discretion to recommend raising these levels. The underlying assumption is that larger amounts and shorter intervals are related to improving performance ratings, and smaller

TABLE 2   Peformance-based Salary Review

	Employee A	Employee B
Current salary..............	$16,000	$16,000
Proposed increase:		
Maturity factor...........	400	400
Structure change..........	600	600
Performance change.......	0	2,000
Total proposed increase......	$ 1,000	$ 3,000

amounts and longer intervals are related to no change or to decreasing performance ratings.

CAREER DEVELOPMENT

Whether position evaluations or maturity curves are used as a basis for salary administration of scientist-professionals, the question arises of how to provide an appropriate means of recognizing normal career development. This refers to the expectation that the scope and complexity of work assignments will increase as the new hire progresses toward mature professional status.

When position evaluation is the basis for salary administration, differences in work assignments are reflected in different salary ranges paid according to position worth. One approach would be to accept upward movement as normal career development and treat the change in positions at the annual salary review as an additional factor to be considered in determining an appropriate increase.

When maturity curves are the basis for salary administration, promotional increases may not be granted as a matter of course. Those being advanced to higher levels of responsibility or classification would be expected to come from the population with high performance rankings, and they would therefore be compensated accordingly. One of the considerations at the annual performance review is the individual's contribution. Therefore, his change of status can be recognized by changing the increase amount or adjusting the time interval.

Any system used in the compensation of scientist-professionals must not only have intuitive appeal, but also must survive the searching inquiry to which this group will subject it. Money is a symbol of success no less with this group than with any other; however, it is traditional in this area to demand recognition (of which financial reward is certainly a part) based primarily upon individual professional contribution. The compensation system, then, should provide means of judging these contributions and determining relative rewards.

chapter 41

Designing Compensation
Programs for Public Employees

KENNETH O. WARNER *Executive Director, Public Personnel Association, Chicago, Illinois*

KEITH OCHELTREE *Public Personnel Association, Chicago, Illinois*

FACTORS INFLUENCING GOVERNMENT SALARIES

Governments set salaries for their employees on the basis of approximately the same factors as do private businesses. While some factors may receive greater emphasis in government than in private industry, and varying emphases may be given among different governments as well, the elements that go into structuring a wage and salary plan are the same. Although geographical location, degree of employee unionization, level of government, tradition, and other factors may cause some difference in emphasis, some factors play a significant role in determining salaries at almost all levels of government, and these are discussed below.

Job Evaluation. As in industry, governments use various methods to evaluate the relative worth of jobs. Most commonly used is the position classification system, in which positions are assigned to classes of positions on the basis of their similarity with respect to kind and level of work, background required, and other factors. Specifications describing the classes of positions are grouped together and designated as the "classification plan." On the basis of the classification plan and its descriptions of the differences and similarities among jobs, classes are assigned to ranges in the salary plan.

Salary Surveys. Salary surveys are an extremely important part of the wage determination process in government and are conducted with some regularity by governments attempting a rational approach to salary administration. Such surveys commonly cover only "key" classes in the classification plan—that is, classes that are easily identified as having fairly obvious counterparts in other employment and to which nonsurveyed classes can be easily related.   After rates for key classes are established on the basis of survey data, therefore, the salary structure is built up on the basis of knowledge of the occupational content of the various other classes and an evaluation of their worth in relation to the key classes.

Construction of Salary Ranges.   Salary ranges must be designed that are suitable to the various kinds of occupations covered.   Most governmental employers have, in the past, used a single schedule of overlapping salary ranges for all positions, occasionally lengthening or shortening the range for individual classes when the nature of the work called for it.   The standard salary range usually consisted of five or six rates, each one about 5 percent larger than the one immediately below it.   More recently, there has been a trend toward the establishment of salary ranges specifically tailored to individual occupational groups. Using this approach, salary ranges are shorter for occupations where there is little opportunity for growth on the job, and longer for occupations where the opportunities for growth are greater.

Union Relationships.   In the past, unions did not play as big a part in wage determination in the governmental sector as they did in private business, although they were long present to some degree.   During the 1960s, unionization of public employees grew at the fastest rate in history, and formal arrangements for dealing with unions and other kinds of organized employee groups proliferated.   During this period, a sizable minority of states passed legislation either permitting or mandating local governments to bargain collectively with their employees; in a much smaller number of states, state governments were required to do the same.   Even where formal collective bargaining is not permitted, governmental employers frequently "meet and confer" with unions on an informal basis.

Political Factors.   In contrast with union wage settlements in private industry, government salary plans may have an immediate effect upon tax levels, water rates, and other governmental levies.   Salary setting in the public service therefore may be influenced by considerations of political feasibility and the political futures of the officials directly involved in approving the level of wages.

Constitutional and Legal Limitations.   Especially in state government, there may be constitutional or statutory limitations on the salaries that can be paid to public officials.   These limitations can have a depressive effect upon salaries at the middle and upper levels of the career service.   Fortunately, the trend is for these ceilings either to be raised or to be eliminated entirely.

FEDERAL EMPLOYEES

Federal employees, for compensation purposes, can be classified into two broad groups: (1) employees subject to the Classification Act, and (2) the so-called Wage Board employees.

Classified Employees.   The pay of employees subject to the Classification Act is established by Congress, which acts to raise, lower, or otherwise modify through legislation a schedule of 18 salary grades to which are allocated all positions subject to the Classification Act.   Since the early 1960s these salary schedules have been subject to the comparability principle, the goal of which is to make federal pay levels equal to those for work of the same kind and level in the private sector.

While there is a measure of collective bargaining in the federal service on certain conditions of employment and other matters, there is no bargaining on wages for employees under the Classification Act. There has been, however, heavy political pressure on Congress from certain employee groups, most notably those in the postal service, which at times amounts to a type of quasi-bargaining. These pressures on Congress are likely to increase unless all-out bargaining on wages is authorized, as it has been for postal employees under the new organizational setup.

Wage Board Employees. Wage Board employees are for the most part those in the construction and other skilled trades. Their pay rates are set by federal wage boards in each locality on the basis of rates prevailing for similar work in private industry. Some negotiation may take place in the process of establishing these wages.

STATE GOVERNMENT EMPLOYEES

Constitutional and Other Limitations. As stated earlier, maximum salaries for specific state government positions often are designated either in the state constitution or in legislation. Problems of external comparability and internal equity frequently result.

Patronage. Political patronage is still a factor in a large part of the public service of nearly 20 states, both in appointment and in the setting of salaries. Under these circumstances the establishment of rational overall salary plans becomes extremely difficult even when the attempt toward it is made.

Rights of Constitutional Officers. The incumbents of offices named in state constitutions frequently have the right to appoint and establish the salaries of employees under their control without reference to any central personnel authority. Court decisions in some states have modified the effect of these provisions, as have agreements to submit voluntarily to an overall salary plan.

Legislative Action. In some states, salary plans may be established by the governor and his cabinet or some similar body, within broad limitations set by the legislature. In others, the salary plan must be approved by the legislature itself, thus introducing political factors on occasion.

Federal Grants. Federal grants to support certain state and local activities, especially in the areas of health, education, welfare, and social security, may be a factor in enabling state and local governments to pay competitive salaries.

LOCAL GOVERNMENT EMPLOYEES

State Requirements. State governments may occasionally become involved in wage setting in local governments through the establishment of minimum salaries for all or certain categories of employment, such as policemen and firemen.

Collective Bargaining. Collective bargaining is more common at the local than at the state level, with consequent impact upon local salaries.

Political Patronage. Patronage is also a powerful factor in many cities, especially those not operating under the city manager plan, with the same effects as in the states, mentioned earlier.

Debt and Tax Limitations. States frequently limit the amount of debt that can be incurred by local governments, as well as their tax rates. These limitations can effectively prevent local governments from paying equitable and competitive salaries.

SPECIAL CLASSES OF EMPLOYEES

Certain classes of governmental employment deserve special mention because of peculiar characteristics, traditions, and problems.

Teachers.   Characteristics of the teaching profession which affect salary administration procedures and practices for this group are discussed in the following sections.

Salaries Tied to Education.   In teacher salary plans, the individual's salary is frequently tied closely to the amount of postgraduate education the teacher has obtained.   A base salary is established that is suitable for the minimum educational requirement—usually a bachelor's degree in an appropriate field for the classroom teacher—with assignment to higher ranges contingent upon the completion of further course work.   Increments are also granted for years of service separately from the increment for additional education.   This practice runs counter to that of other areas of local government, where all persons in the same classification are usually in the same salary range regardless of individual differences in education and training.

Collective Bargaining.   The use of collective bargaining is probably spreading faster in public education than in any other area of local government.   The effect on salary levels and salary relationships has been considerable.   There is also a trend toward extending the areas subject to negotiation from simple economic matters such as salaries, hours of work, leaves, and other conditions of employment to such issues as teaching methods, textbooks, and size of classes.

Lack of Promotional Opportunities.   The organizational structure of a typical school system is a flat pyramid with many people at the classroom teacher level and relatively few opportunities for advancement to supervisory positions. Salary plans for teachers recognize this reality by providing yearly increments for a longer time than do salary plans for other public employee groups. Trends toward greater community control of individual schools may tend to create more levels of supervision, with consequent effect upon salary ranges.

Police.   Salary plans for the police have also reflected the peculiar characteristics of this segment of public employment.

Growing Professionalization.   The police in the United States traditionally have not enjoyed a level of prestige commensurate with their importance to the community.   Educational requirements have been lower than desirable, affecting both salaries and the quality of police service provided.   With growing recognition of the professional nature of police work and its increasing complexity, entrance-level requirements for police work have been raised and the tempo of in-service training has been stepped up.   The number of university offerings in police science of both the short-course and the degree variety has increased greatly.   Thus, although a high school education is still the most common requirement for members of the police force, some college work is beginning to be required in many places, with consequent enhancement of police professionalization and pressure for increases in salary levels.

Unionization.   Although fraught with constitutional and political problems, many people feel that the recent trend toward unionization of public employees has also affected the police.   While police officers are cognizant of the peculiar nature of their public responsibilities, they have not failed to notice the advantages gained by other types of public employees through unionization.   There are, therefore, increasing demands for unionization and collective bargaining, which are bound to affect salary levels, both absolutely and in relation to other groups of public employees.

Organizational Structure.   As in the case of public education, the typical police organizational structure consists of a great many working-level employees with relatively few people in supervisory ranks.   As a result, the top of the traditional four- or five-step salary range is reached relatively early in a lifetime career.   Consequently, there is constant pressure for wage increases as well as for longevity and other kinds of supplemental pay.   Another solution has been to create additional ranks with higher salary ranges for members of the force having special proficiency or longer service.

Educational Incentives.   Related to the increasing professionalization of police personnel is the growing tendency to establish formal systems for granting salary increments to policemen who have completed a specified number of academic credits in police science.   This is similar to practice in the teaching profession.

Community Relations Problems.   Especially in larger cities, the job of the policeman is increasingly centered on sensitive human relations problems.   The policeman's work is also more hazardous, on the whole, than it was a few years ago.   The need to attract people with the necessary attitudes and background for these changed conditions, as well as the hazardous nature of the work, is exerting upward pressure on police pay scales.

Police and Fire Parity.   There has long been a tradition that equivalent ranks in the police and fire services receive the same salary.   This situation has obtained in spite of the quite different nature of the work in the two occupations, and in spite of the difference in working hours.   This tradition is, however, slowly beginning to be breached in favor of the police, as a result of careful job analysis and analysis of background requirements, recruitment experience, turnover statistics, and other factors.

The Fire Service.   The fire service also has its peculiar characteristics, some owing to the nature of the work, others owing to tradition.

Similarities with Policemen.   The parity principle naturally operates with respect to firemen, as mentioned above.   Also, the fire service organization is another flat pyramid, with the same effects on salaries as mentioned for policemen.

Working Hours.   The work schedule of the typical fireman is probably like that of no other in public service, since it is basically a standby service.   The most common work shift for firemen is the 24-hour duty period (including time for sleep) followed by one or more 24-hour periods off.   The most common work schedule for firemen provides a weekly duty period of 56 hours averaged out over the course of a year.   Since this kind of work schedule results in extended periods of time away from the job, firemen are probably the most likely employees to supplement their incomes through outside employment.   This fact, however, should not be considered when establishing rates of pay for the firefighter's job.   Also, the number of hours spent actually working during each 24-hour duty period is difficult to determine, a fact that complicates comparison of the fireman's work with that of other municipal employees.

Relationship to Skilled Trades.   Many of the duties of the fireman require a knowledge of hydraulics, mechanics, automotive maintenance, and other skilled trades, as well as proficiency in first aid and rescue work.   For these reasons, salary comparisons between the firemen and these other groups of employees are appropriate.

Sanitation Workers.   The pay of sanitation workers is subject to unique considerations, discussed below.

Unionization.   Sanitation work is another area of public service where unionization is growing, and in a very militant way.   Some of the most dramatic instances of public employee strikes have occurred in this area. The principal reason is, of course, the traditionally low wages that have prevailed in this field.

Ethnic Problems. Salary problems in sanitation activities are very likely to be involved with problems of race, civil rights, equal opportunity, and related matters. For this reason, salary setting may carry emotional overtones.

The Disadvantaged. Programs to recruit and train persons from the underprivileged segments of society may require the establishment of special wages, such as trainee rates, on at least a temporary basis. These may create salary relationship problems with other classes in the regular salary plan and may cause dissatisfaction among other workers.

White-collar Employees. This group is the least likely of any to be unionized in the public service, as elsewhere, but unionization is growing and may be a factor in salary setting in some jurisdictions.

Public Works Employees. Certain segments of public works employees, especially those involved in skilled and semiskilled trades, have been unionized for some time, although there has been no authority for collective bargaining until recently and there still is no authority in many jurisdictions. Moreover, some groups, especially unskilled laborers, may be exempt from the merit system and therefore their pay rates could be susceptible to political influence. Furthermore, since public works activities may involve the employment of skilled tradesmen, the need to meet the rates prevailing in industry may be more pressing than in many other areas of governmental employment. Ethnic problems may also be present, as in the case of the sanitation workers.

Welfare Employees. Case workers and other types of social workers have been poorly paid in comparison with other professions requiring equivalent training. For this reason, unionization among these people is growing and strikes are becoming more common.

Paramedical Employees. As in the case of the public welfare workers, salaries have traditionally been low among this group. However, under the influence of unionization, salaries may be expected to increase absolutely and in relation to other groups. Union militancy is also increasing.

Administrative, Professional, and Technical Personnel. Because of shortages of skilled people in these fields and the higher salaries paid for similar posts in private industry, there is considerable upward pressure on the salary scales.

ROLE OF UNIONS, CIVIL SERVICE COMMISSIONS, AND POLITICAL APPOINTMENTS

As was indicated earlier, unions, civil service commissions and political appointments often play an important role in the determination of salaries within the public service.

Unions. The influence of unions in public employment is growing rapidly and bringing pay practices here close to industrial practice in some jurisdictions. However, the status and power of unions vary from state to state, depending upon state laws. Union influence is forcing the development of a new approach to public management and has obvious effects upon both the general level of pay and relative salary rates within a given governmental jurisdiction. Systematic salary setting, as it has been unilaterally practiced in the past in many jurisdictions, is becoming a more and more difficult exercise.

Civil Service Commission. The civil service commission has been the traditional administrative body for public personnel systems in the United States. Among the functions of the civil service commission may be included the responsibility to review and approve the salary plan for public employees before it is submitted for final approval to the legislature or the governor's cabinet. At least one state civil service commission (that of Michigan) has final authority to approve the salary plan.

Political Appointments.   Political appointments have a legitimate role, even in jurisdictions which have a merit system covering the majority of employees. It is generally held that the chief executive has the right to appoint his chief assistants and the heads of major departments.   Political factors, especially relationships with the salary of the governor and other elected officials, may play a role in the setting of these salaries.   In the case of these salaries, there is frequently no objective attempt at rational salary setting; salaries are set at a politically feasible level.   There is the additional factor that these positions are frequently not susceptible to comparison with jobs in private industry, since they are so completely different in their functions and operate in such a different kind of environment.

GOVERNMENT VERSUS INDUSTRY COMPENSATION PRACTICE

Lower-level Salaries.   In jurisdictions which have attempted to systematize salary setting, the most common approach is to set up a series of salary ranges consisting of a beginning rate and four or five increments, with each class of positions assigned to one of the ranges through one or another process of job evaluation.   The objective of this approach is to create a salary structure which is competitive with pay for similar jobs in private industry, as well as internally consistent and fair.   Following are some of the specific ways in which salary administration for lower-level jobs is similar to and different from practice in private industry.

1. When a systematic pay plan is established in government, most commonly a range of pay is established rather than a single rate.   Employees are usually hired at the lowest rate in the range, with periodic increases for at least satisfactory performance.   Single-rate jobs are seldom set up in jurisdictions which have a systematic approach to compensation, although ranges may be of varying lengths, depending upon the type of work.

2. Pay rates are based on job evaluation through the position classification method, using pay surveys to set the rates for key classes and working other classes into a pay structure in accordance with their relation to the key classes. Quantitative systems such as point rating and factor comparison are sometimes used to evaluate jobs, but these are not so common as in private industry.

3. The piecework approach to wages is seldom used in government since there are relatively few production jobs where this would be appropriate.   However, it has been tried in a few activities, such as the repair of water meters.

4. Because governments deal in services rather than in commodities, production incentives, either individual or group, are seldom used.

5. Since the profit motive does not exist in government, the year-end bonus and profit sharing are unknown.

6. Except for a few cases where it may have been negotiated as a part of a union agreement, formal severance pay is practically unknown, except for payment for accumulated vacation leave and sometimes for all or part of accumulated sick leave.

7. The most common pay periods in government employment are semimonthly or biweekly.   However, monthly or weekly pay periods are not unknown.   Hourly pay is common in the case of casual, seasonal, and part-time jobs and for occupations that are customarily paid by the hour in private industry.

8. Automatic cost-of-living pay adjustments have been installed in some jurisdictions but with mixed success. However, the growing influence of unions may compel the adoption of such plans in a greater number of jurisdictions.

9. As in private industry, white-collar positions are less likely to be unionized. However, white-collar unionization is growing, largely through the efforts of the American Federation of State, County, and Municipal Employees, which has as its goal the unionization of all kinds of public employees.

10. Some additional forms of pay available to public employees include: longevity pay, either for total length of service with the jurisdiction or for a given number of years of service at the top of the salary range without promotion; payment for unused sick leave either in cash or through the addition of a specified number of days to vacation leave; and awards for outstanding performance or meritorious suggestions.

Management Salaries. "Management" in the public service is more difficult to define than in the private sector. Many high-level employees who would not belong to the union in private industry are under civil service and are included in the same salary plan as the rank-and-file employees. Thus, their compensation treatment is similar to that of lower-level employees with respect to number of incremental steps in the range, and so forth. Normally, only a handful of top management positions, including that of chief executive, are outside civil service and thus outside the regular pay plan. Since high-level employees are paid according to the same plan and included in the merit system, their salaries are established on the same basis as those of lower-level employees, namely, on the basis of job evaluation and salary surveys. Generally, they receive about the same adjustments in terms of percentage of salary and have pay ranges of about the same percentage difference between minimum and maximum as do lower-level jobs.

In spite of attempts at comparability by the federal government and a few state and local jurisdictions, compensation for management positions in the public service is generally much lower than that for positions of equivalent responsibility in private industry. In view of the service orientation of government, it is unlikely that there will ever be complete comparability, although it can be achieved for certain positions (such as accountants, architects, lawyers, and other professional occupations) which, because of their definable professional nature, can be compared with relative ease. There is also the problem of constitutional and charter limitations on high-level salaries, as mentioned earlier, although these will probably disappear as time goes by.

Under the impetus of the unionization of lower-level employees, separate pay plans for executives and exempt supervisors have been developed in a number of jurisdictions. In some cases, these special management pay plans have no precisely defined steps, and increments are based on individual evaluation of performance by the city manager, department head, or other top executive.

For obvious reasons, public service management jobs do not receive bonuses, profit sharing, stock options, and similar benefits available to managers in private industry.

One problem in setting salaries for managers in the public service is that of salary relationships between political executives and top career people. There may be public policy reasons for keeping salaries of political executives relatively low, whereas the market may require that top career executives receive a relatively high salary. For this reason, it is not unusual to find top career people earning as much as or more than the political officials to whom they report. This is especially likely to be true in cities operating under the council-manager plan.

Fringe Benefits.   On the average, fringe benefits in government now amount to about 24 percent of payroll.   The industrial average differs to a negligible degree.   On the whole, it is safe to say that management people, except for those in political posts, get approximately the same fringe benefits as do the rank and file.   Distinctions are seldom made, although in insurance plans—for example, where the amount of insurance varies depending upon salary—the higher-salaried executives would be more heavily insured.

The most common benefits in governmental employment are the following:

1. Pension plans.   These may be totally independent of the social security system or integrated with social security.   Some jurisdictions still provide only social security for their employees.   Most governmental employee retirement plans provide for retirement at age 65, although occasionally earlier retirement is permitted at a lower pension.   Disability and survivors' benefits may also be included.   Pension benefits are commonly computed as a percentage of the average salary for a specified number of years immediately prior to retirement, plus a factor based on total years of membership in the plan.

2. Insurance, including health and life insurance.   Costs of these plans may be shared jointly between the employee and the employer.

3. Various kinds of leave, including vacation, sick leave, maternity leave, jury leave, military leave, and personal leave.   States and local governments commonly grant 10 to 12 working days of vacation and 12 to 15 working days of sick leave per year.

4. Educational leave, with or without salary or stipend, for the purpose of improving performance on the job

5. Rest periods (coffee breaks).   Fifteen minutes two times a day is the most common practice.

6. Holidays, in which respect governmental employers are probably somewhat more generous on the average than is private industry (nine to ten days per year, as compared with a private-industry average of six to nine days)

7. Tuition reimbursement plans for employees who are pursuing courses of study on their own time that are intended to improve their work performance

8. Clinics and medical examination programs for employees at the employer's expense.   These programs may include periodic examinations throughout the employee's career.

9. Credit unions, to provide an easy and safe place for savings as well as a convenient place to borrow modest sums of money at moderate interest rates

10. Social and recreational programs and employee newsletters for the enhancement of *esprit de corps*

11. Unemployment compensation, required for the employees of 14 states and for local employees in seven states, with coverage elective for state or local employees, or both, in the rest of the states

12. Workmen's compensation, which is compulsory for state employees in 41 states and voluntary in nearly all the others

COMPENSATION AND PROMOTION OPPORTUNITIES

The presence or lack of promotional ladders within the organization affects compensation practices in government just as it does in private industry.   In both cases, small organizations have different kinds of problems from those of large ones.   Also, differences in the kinds of activities carried on can create salary problems both in business and in government.

In general, in those organizations where promotional opportunities are limited (such as in the police and fire services and in teaching), means other than promotion have to be found to provide the incentive of higher pay. This may involve the creation of new ranks that recognize the special proficiency or long experience of the individual, or the establishment of a system of longevity pay for those who have been in the service for a long period of time or have been at the top of their pay range without promotion for a specified number of years. A few jurisdictions have experimented with longer pay ranges for those positions where there is little likelihood of promotion.

Conversely, in organizations where the nature of the work and the structure of the organization make for rapid upward mobility, little attention needs to be paid to such matters as lengthening pay ranges or longevity pay, since it is unlikely that they will ever be needed.

COMPENSATION, MOTIVATION, AND GOVERNMENTAL ORGANIZATION CLIMATE

Government's purposes are different from those of private industry. The goal of government is to provide services that have been mandated by the legislature, not to make a profit. Since government deals in services rather than in things, the contributions of government employees are not so directly measurable as those of many persons in private industry. The salesman who is paid a commission on each item that he sells has almost no parallel in government organizations.

Therefore, high-level government employees do not expect the same monetary rewards as they might get in a position of comparable responsibility in private enterprise. The emphasis on public service tends to depress salaries and to emphasize the psychic rewards of the work. While attempts to attain the comparability goal will continue, it is unlikely that complete comparability will ever be attained, although salaries of governmental officials have risen markedly in recent years.

These factors apply almost exclusively to the professional and technical employees at the upper levels, however. The rank and file of government employees, even including the first several levels of professional and technical employees, probably do as well financially as their counterparts in the private sector. Conversely, the profit motive probably has only limited effect on the paycheck of the rank-and-file worker in private industry and has its greatest effect at management levels (as does its absence in government). Lower-level employees do about as well working for either government or private industry, with the presence or absence of the profit motive or of psychic rewards playing a very small part in either case. The public service environment, therefore, is most relevant when discussing high-level officials who have a definite professional commitment to the public service.

chapter 42

Designing Compensation
Programs for Top Executives

ALVIN O. BELLAK, Ph.D. *Partner, Edward N. Hay & Associates, Philadelphia, Pennsylvania*

In the earlier years of our capitalistic society, compensation was a rather simple matter: for the workers, it meant some amount of cash and whatever benefits a paternalistic employer might care to bestow; for executives, it meant cash, again some volunteered benefits, and perquisites which clearly separated the workers from the gentlemen-executives.

Times change, of course, and with time has come a sort of people's capitalism (some have worse-sounding names for it). Individuals, whoever they may be, are now viewed as having inherent worth; previously volunteered benefits have become rights; and so forth.

Instead of workers and executives, with the latter commonly being also substantial owners, we have now several distinct populations on the payroll: organized hourly, unorganized hourly, organized exempt, unorganized exempt, and executives who are only infrequently substantial owners.

In the past, motivation was a simple matter: one worked to the satisfaction of his superior or faced peremptory dismissal. With the new times and values, with the new laws and edicts of regulatory authorities, and with the multiplicity of unique subgroups, we now have hordes of experts from many disciplines working hard to develop and implement means of attracting, retaining, and motivating people.

Compensation has become one of these means, and a complex one at that. With the appearance and evolution of the subgroups and their individual and collective rights, powers, and freedoms, we have learned that they cannot be treated uniformly. Their values and goals are different, their perception of their own role and that of the company is different, and, therefore, the compensation package to be offered them must also be different.

While there are only a limited number of ways of paying people with cash and its equivalents, some ways are more useful with a given subgroup than other ways. Further, for a given subgroup, while there are a finite number of choices, there are numerous permutations and combinations which vary with the nature of the company (e.g., its industry, its market share, and its state of maturity), the state of the economy, federal tax laws, etc.

THE TWELVE ELEMENTS OF COMPENSATION

Let us take things one at a time, and start with a review of the basic categories of compensation available and suitable for attracting, retaining, and motivating the subgroup of concern in this chapter, that is, top executives.

Salary. As Figure 1 indicates, salary is the core of the total compensation package. Usually, it is by far the largest element (excluding the occasional monumental payoff of a stock option plan) and must be carefully related to internal salary practices, the external market for executives, and the remainder of the compensation package.

It may be obvious to say this, but top executives care about what their salaries are even in the face of the equally obvious fact that it would take a substantial salary change to have significant impact on their style of living. Their salaries, relative to those of associates inside and outside the company, reflect on their sense of status, their position in the race, and their sense of personal worth, if not on their personal bank account.

There is one additional note of caution, and this will become more apparent later: be careful in chipping away at the salary level as you add compensation elements that may have big payoffs. Salary should be able to stand by itself as a meaningful, competitive amount of money apart from any other payoffs which may or may not occur. The only general exceptions to this, during reasonably good economic times, are the cases of new companies or high-risk situations elsewhere where the top group is practically shooting crap, with very little cash being received now but enormous rewards to come later if they pull it off.

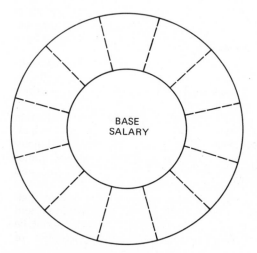

Figure 1. Salary: the core of the compensation package. An effective salary structure must be internally equitable and externally competitive.

For all practical purposes, salaries are virtually guaranteed incomes, assuming individual performance is reasonably satisfactory and company circumstances do not change too drastically. However, there are instances where the guarantee is in writing. These contracts usually specify a minimum amount to be paid annually over a period of years whether or not the individual continues as an active employee. This is not a standard practice and is found only in special circumstances—for example, when a very successful executive is lured away from a secure situation into a risky one, or in the case of an acquisition where the buyer wants some assurance that he can keep management for a while (or where managers want some assurance they will not be dumped unceremoniously after they are acquired).

Figure 2 shows the other elements which go with the salary to make up the total compensation package. They are all easily made available to the top executives. Some are intrinsically more valuable than others, but the real impact comes from the combinations rather than the individual items. But more about this later. First, a brief mention of the items by category (see other chapters for detailed definitions and descriptions of the 11 elements shown in Figure 2 and to be simply noted below).

Basic Rights.   Paid vacations and holidays have now become the right of just about all full-time salaried employees and the majority of hourly employees in this country. To our top executive group, this is the least valuable of benefits, and they would hardly recognize these items as forms of compensation at all. This is a highly motivated group which may or may not take any vacation, may take an afternoon off to play golf, or may work 10 or 12 hours a day without thinking much about any of it. But for the record, the trend is for the top group to be authorized three to six weeks' vacation.

What is important to this top group is not the paid time off but the freedom

Figure 2. The total package: salary plus other elements weighted to achieve specific organizational objectives.

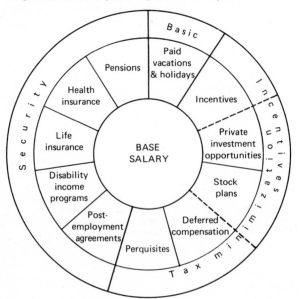

to work or not work on a schedule (of hours per day and weeks per year). If you want to design some basic rights into the top executive package, rather than think of paid vacations and holidays, you might better think of time off for self-renewal (e.g., going to the institute at Aspen) or a sabbatical to take on a government project (with company protection against loss of income).

Security Elements. There are five elements directed toward giving top executives a sense of security, that is, toward freeing them from some concerns so that they can concentrate on their jobs and not on their protective financial fences. These include pensions, health insurance, life insurance, disability income, and post-employment agreements. At proper levels, these tell the executive that whether he lives, dies, or anything in between, he and/or his family will have at least an adequate degree of financial comfort. These elements are all well known, so they will not be labored here; however, a few words about each are in order.

Pension. The pension continues to be the only near guarantee of ultimate financial security, and, therefore, it remains the foundation of retirement income. Estate building plans, deferred income, payoffs from options, and stock purchase plans may or may not be adequate and hence should not be relied upon. There are endless features to pension plans, but keep in mind that, whatever the features of the plan you have, you can supplement the payout for your top executive group by purchasing annuities (for example, for the outsider brought in to a top position at an advanced age).

Health Insurance. There are many plans available, and more that can be specially packaged to cover the medical expenses incurred by the executive and his family. As long as there is coverage for the catastrophic illness, you will find the top group not overly concerned about the details.

Life Insurance. As any insurance agent will tell you, this is estate building the quick way. In the case of company-purchased group insurance, there are double benefits: the executive gets the coverage at rates lower than he can obtain himself, and the payment is in before-tax dollars.

Disability Income. For top executives, most companies are self-insuring for the short term (i.e., they will continue the executive salary in full) and third-party-insured for the long term (e.g., some percent of salary after six months of disability).

Post-employment Agreements. These agreements permit an executive to continue to receive income from the company after he has left his position. Their intent is to delay his legal termination for any of a number of reasons, e.g., to prevent him from engaging in competing activities or to permit vesting or other qualifying acts for pension or deferred income plans. It should also be added that boards use such agreements for gracefully dismissing some executives.

Incentives and Tax Minimization Elements. Salary is earned through day-in, day-out performance. It is motivating in and of itself but not in potentially dramatic ways for the top group. The security elements are rather static. One does not deliberately work to get them; they sort of come along with everything else and serve to relieve the executive of worries extraneous to his job. The remaining elements shown in Figure 2 are intended to have maximum motivational pull.

Incentives. About two-thirds of the manufacturing companies and about 10 percent of the nonrural banks have incentive plans which pay off in cash (in hand or deferred) and/or stock. The basic idea of an incentive plan is to motivate extra performance and to share the results of that performance with the executive. The idea is sound but the implementation often leaves something to be desired. Nonetheless, the motivational potential is considerable if the plan is properly designed, clearly links individual performance with size of award, and pays off in cash (in view of the 50 percent maximum tax on earned income).

Stock Plans. Before the successive tax law changes in the 1960s, stock option plans in many companies had great potential for creating considerable personal wealth. Bolstering this potential was the long bull market in securities that started after World War II and continued with only modest interruptions (by historical standards) almost until the end of the 1960s. New taxes and the rediscovery of the possibility of prolonged bear markets have damaged but not destroyed the motivational value of stock plans.

Deferred Compensation. This element is intended to put off the receipt of earnings until a later and presumably more beneficial date, viz., a time when the executive will be in a lower tax bracket. The element has value as an option to be offered to top executives, and it *may* have its intended value as a means of minimizing taxes.

Perquisites. Rank still has its privileges, but the IRS continues to make them harder to come by, and vocal shareholders still like to talk about them at annual meetings. Typical items like automobiles, club memberships, and handsome offices have value in making the executive's life more pleasant and affording him a measure of status even though they do not have striking cash value.

Private Investment Opportunities. The days when an executive could do quite well by selling a piece of land to his own company or holding an interest in one of his company's suppliers are gone, but there are still legitimate, side-bar opportunities which are not company-related. When one is a member of the top executive club and has access to his peers in other companies, invitations to invest can be arranged. At the time of this writing we see such opportunities as the formation of syndicates to invest in drilling for oil, in real estate, and in cattle raising. The effect of these opportunities, aside from possibilities to minimize taxes and/or achieve capital gains, is to consolidate the executive's economic interests with those of other members of the club. Needless to say, extreme care must be taken to avoid conflicts of interest.

TAILORING THE TOTAL PACKAGE: TWO EXAMPLES

Having reviewed the elements in the compensation package, we now come to the strategic choice:

1. Do we offer each of your top executives each of these elements in amounts comparable to those awarded in other companies?

2. Or, do we distort the package, i.e., offer much more of some elements than others, for one reason or another?

In either case, do we treat each of your top executives exactly the same (i.e., offer the same package varied only by size relative to the value of each one's individual job)?

Put another way, what combination of salary, security, and incentive elements should your company have?

But there is really a prior question to answer which is not so obvious: What is your company today, and what can it be or what do you want it to be tomorrow? Keep in mind that compensation is a primary motivating and reinforcing device and is subject to deliberate manipulation. If you can define your company's position and its goals, you can design a compensation package that is truly meaningful for your company.

Let us illustrate the possibilities by looking at two kinds of companies: the large, mature one in traditional markets, and the small, new one with products of significant potential in either traditional or new markets.

Compensation in the Large, Mature Company. Many blue chips fall into this category. "Large and mature," in this illustrative case, means a company with a long history of satisfactory success, with substantial positions in a number of traditional product and/or market areas which supply the bulk of its earnings, and where size makes it unlikely that internal developments can have substantial short-term effects on company performance.

Companies like this might well consider emphasizing the salary and security elements and giving modest weight to the incentive elements, except for top management, perhaps about as follows:

1. *Salary:* A salary structure at about the 75th percentile or higher (in relation to the pay practices of similar companies) for the company's management group as a whole but with the structure bending toward the 50th percentile for the top executive group

2. *Pension:* For the long-service executive, 50 to 70 percent of the last five years' average salary. Also, unreduced benefits at age 60

3. *Health insurance:* The most generous you can find, and continued for the *life* of the executive and his family

4. *Life insurance:* At least $150,000 and possibly as high as $500,000, with features that taper it down over five to ten years *after* retirement

5. *Disability income:* Fifty percent of salary after six months' disability. Company pays full salary for the first six months.

6. *Stock plans:* Annual, modest awards of qualified options rather than larger occasional ones. This would be for estate building over a long period of years.

7. *Incentives:* Fifty to 75 percent of salary when corporate results warrant such awards

8. *Deferred compensation:* Optional provision for deferring part of salary and cash incentive

9. *Perquisites:* The usual, plus company-paid financial counseling by an outside agency

10. *Private investment opportunities:* As available, possibly through the offices of the financial counselor

Obviously, this is a sketchy rundown of major features, and there are many variations of the subelements which could be noted. The point is that the package is designed to offer virtually the maximum cash and protection (by today's standards) that a large and profitable company might reasonably put together. Its motivational value is its size and comprehensiveness. It is worth striving for to those down the line; it is worth working to protect for those who are receiving it.

It is also to be emphasized that the illustration is of a theoretical model. Current practices for such companies show every conceivable deviation from this model, including, for example, incentive awards over 100 percent of salary, phantom stock that pays "dividends" (in cash, current or deferred) or cash equal to appreciation (or *both*), and so forth.

You might note the subelement of company-paid financial counseling. This is a perquisite which is growing in use. Essentially, it involves employing the services of some outside agency to advise the executive in the management of his financial affairs. For all his knowledge of the world of business and finance, the evidence is that most executives do badly by themselves because of either a surprising lack of know-how or the limited time they have to devote to their own affairs (usually both). The counselor's role is to help in two ways: estate planning and estate building.

There is one additional aspect to the compensation package that the mature company might consider and that is giving the top executive some degree of choice in his compensation. This is known as "cafeteria compensation." Since executives can differ considerably in their personal circumstances, as, for example, in age, number of dependents, and size of estate, it can be very profitable for the executive, perhaps with the aid of his financial counselor, to pick and choose among the elements he is entitled to. For example, if he is over 55 and his children are all married and gone, he might choose to defer his cash incentive and perhaps all future salary increases. If he is something of a financial swinger and the company does not object to transactions in company stock, he might prefer nonqualified rather than qualified options to give him more flexibility in the marketplace.

Compensation in the Small, New Company. Examples here include the science-oriented companies, the company that has found a gap in traditional markets, and the occasional company that takes the establishment head-on because it believes it has better ways of doing business.

These companies are characterized by little cash and great expectations, so they ought to go easy on salary, moderate on security elements, and heavy on incentives, perhaps as follows:

1. *Salary:* About the 50th percentile—possibly less, if the team can stand it

2. *Pension:* None. A pension plan that is really worth anything is expensive. The company might consider a profit-sharing plan so there will at least be a little protection.

3. *Health insurance:* Ordinary coverage but with major medical of at least $20,000. Company and individual might split the cost.

4. *Life insurance:* Group life is not terribly expensive, and there should be protection in lieu of substantial salaries. Coverage at three times salary would be satisfactory.

5. *Disability income:* As good as you can afford. At least 50 percent of salary after six months

6. *Stock plans:* This is really the name of the game. Large qualified options prior to a public offering of stock, modest qualified options afterward

7. *Incentives:* Probably unnecessary in view of the stock options, but it might be wise to provide for awards at the discretion of the board of directors. The board might want to keep salaries on the low side and make incentive awards in the form of stock through the first few years of real company success.

8. *Deferred compensation:* Other than through a profit-sharing plan, none

9. *Perquisites:* Modest.

10. *Private investment opportunities:* This is *it*.

11. *Post-employment agreements:* Yes, but for the protection of the company rather than as a benefit to the executive.

The scheme here is simple: forego immediate cash for enormous gains later, but give as much inexpensive security coverage as you can afford.

TAILORING THE TOTAL PACKAGE: YOUR COMPANY

It is worth repeating that these are oversimplified, extreme examples conjured up for illustrative purposes. In applying the material in this chapter to the situation in your company, you might start by conducting an audit. What are the compensation elements now offered to the top group? What could be offered which is not now in the package? What is the company's current position—are we secure in our industry? Do our results fluctuate significantly with the economic tides? Are there plans to significantly change the company and its directions? Do we have, or are we growing, the kind of people we need at the top? If you can accurately see the company as it is and as top management plans it to be, then you can critically examine the compensation elements against useful criteria. Let us take two of the most badly handled elements for illustrative purposes: incentives and stock options.

Incentives. Generally, the purpose of a cash incentive system is to help bring about desired short-term results. Does your incentive system do this? Most systems do not. For example, in the building products industry, where earnings are largely affected by external factors beyond company influence, like interest rates, an incentive plan tied to absolute earnings can be misleading. It will pay off when rates are low, when mortgage money is available, and when employment is high; it will not pay off in depressed times or when mortgage money is very expensive and not easily available.

In other companies, where earnings are consistent and reliable, the incentive plan pays off like clockwork. But what the company really has is an additional salary plan, i.e., the salary is paid monthly with a thirteenth installment at year end.

An incentive plan for top people will be most meaningful if there is a clear connection between individual performance and the payoff. If this is not the case, consider abolishing the plan or devising a new one. Alternatively, keep the plan but lower salaries, thereby lessening the drain on company revenues in bad years and paying out in good years when the company is better able to afford it.

Keep in mind that incentive plans for the very top executive group should not necessarily be the same as for other executives. For the lower-level executives, payoffs tied to achievement of preestablished annual goals (not necessarily absolute earnings) are usually most desirable. For our very top group, who answer for the company's results come hell or high water, it may be desirable to hook their incentive to absolute results even if external factors do influence those results. After all, their accountability is to consider and plan for such factors, and a well-thought-out incentive plan can motivate the top group to make the strategic moves that can materially change these absolute results.

Stock Options. The cynics say there is little connection between company performance and the price of its stock. This is certainly possible at any given time and can be possible for extended periods, but over the long run consistently increasing earnings usually bring higher stock prices. The possibility that prices will be much higher in the future is obviously what makes options desirable even with the tax law changes of 1964 and 1969. But options can really be oversold as a compensation element.

What is the historical price performance of your company's stock? Are changes in the works that could cause Wall Street to reappraise your price-earnings ratio? Does your company actively promote its stock? Does your board approve of executives who sell when the price is right? These are among the questions that should be considered in determining the role of stock options in your compensation package. It is not enough to work out the number and kind of options; their motivational value must be established.

There are many sad stories of options exercised at high prices with borrowed money and sold at low prices to pay off the debt. Also disappointing are the cases where options are exercised at 100 percent of market value only to have the stock price fluctuate around the option price for 15 or 20 years. You are not expected to be a seer, but you can do more than recommend a stock option plan just because everybody else has one. You can at least give it a well-reasoned place in the compensation package.

SUMMARY

The point of this chapter is that you must design the compensation plan for your top executive group, not just let it happen. If you trust in the natural course of events, you will find that you will match the manpower marketplace more or less on all elements and everybody will be offered just about everything. Of course, such a plan will pay people, but it will do little in the way of motivating and reinforcing them. It will not serve your company. It will just be there as an expense.

chapter 43

Developing Compensation Programs for International Organizations

C. IAN SYM-SMITH *Vice President, Edward N. Hay International, Inc., Paris, France*

Direct business investment abroad by United States companies has grown since 1960 at a faster rate than capital expenditures domestically. This is true despite the tremendous growth in recent years of the United States economy. For the year 1966, for example, foreign investment by United States companies increased over the previous year by 23.5 percent. The increase in domestic plant and equipment expenditures for the same year was 16 percent. Absolute domestic investment was, of course, much larger than absolute investment abroad ($60.6 billion versus $8.7 billion), but the greater *rate* of increase in investment abroad was part of a trend which has been in evidence for some years. It is not unrealistic to suggest that before the 1970s are over, United States enterprises may be doing business in what is now thought of as the non-free world—not just export business (which is being carried on already and will increase in the 1970s), but also business resulting from direct investment in some of these countries.

The international trend is not confined to United States companies: organizations such as Shell, Nestlé, Bayer, Pirelli, and Sony have been aggressively international for years. This chapter, however, is written from the perspective of United States companies operating abroad. Their international expansion has been accompanied by rapid growth in number of overseas employees and the problems of paying them.

International employees normally are categorized into three subgroups: (1) United States expatriates—United States nationals working outside the United States; (2) third-country nationals—a native of country A working in country B for a parent company headquartered in the United States; and (3) local nationals—employees of a United States corporation working in their native countries. Statistics are not available on the relative proportions of these subgroups in the overseas operations of American companies, but even considering only the equivalent of the exempt work force, it is probably safe to assume that expatriates and third-country nationals are practically always well under 10 percent (and on an average even well below 5 percent) and the nationals well over 90 percent in any individual company and for all companies as a group. In the past, United States companies tended to concentrate on the expatriate and third-country national populations, but the sheer size of the local national group and the fact that more of them are in high management positions indicate they must be given more attention—commensurate with their importance to the company.

COMPENSATION OF EXPATRIATES

The matter of base salary for expatriates is not an issue: they are logically, and almost without exception, paid on a job content basis according to their companies' United States salary structures. In addition to the base salary, a number of premiums or allowances may be paid separately or in combination. In considering the various kinds of allowances and premiums and whether they are appropriate in individual situations, it is important to distinguish three types of expatriates:

1. The career international employee. This man has chosen to pursue his career abroad and is typically in a company which has an international division.

2. The temporary international employee. This man has taken an overseas assignment as one step in his career path; his immediate goal is training and experience to enhance and accelerate his career growth. In modern international companies, foreign service is more and more a requirement for attaining top management positions.

3. The short-term international employee. This man is assigned foreign service only for a specific project (e.g., for a plant start-up) and expects to return to his old job in the United States when the project is completed.

Foreign Service Premium. Traditionally, expatriates have been paid a special premium just for working abroad. Usually this premium is a percentage of pay, but occasionally a flat dollar allowance is used. When necessary, the foreign service premium may be increased by a supplement for hazardous duty or hardship.

Originally, when travel was slow, uncomfortable, and even hazardous, and when duty assignments were the same, a foreign service premium was the minimum required to persuade even the most adventurous to accept foreign assignments. More recently, however, the foreign service premium has come to be viewed as a payment for "cultural differences" that must be borne—as well as a catch-all for other allowances not computed separately.

Recently, across-the-board foreign service premiums have come under attack for several reasons:

1. A premium is in many cases something for nothing—why should a premium be paid for service in Puerto Rico, Jamaica, London, or Paris?

2. Extra pay as a basic right tends to be counterproductive, attracting employees for the wrong reasons and retaining the mediocre employees.

3. Growing nationalistic feeling and the increase in professionally trained managers in other countries focus greater attention on salary inequities created or magnified by foreign service premiums.

4. Foreign service premiums are costly—particularly when added to other allowances needed for expatriates.

These considerations indicate that the foreign service premium probably will endure but with limitations. For the career international employee and the employee working overseas for career development purposes, going abroad is a way of life. Hence, they should not receive a premium for service in most Western countries. The man who goes abroad to work on a short-term project, however, is in a different position—and the foreign service premium is the logical way to compensate him for his inconvenience.

Cost-of-living Allowance. Figuring cost of living for an expatriate is not an easy task. First of all, there is cost of living for locals in the community—food, housing, and transportation. Second there are the costs of the goods and services to which an American has become accustomed, e.g., the cost of a refrigerator, an automobile, a house with two baths, and foods such as fresh eggs, choice beef, oranges, and lettuce. Thirdly, there are costs related to the special status of the expatriate in the foreign community—e.g., the manager of a small plant represents the company to the community, and, as such, the demands on him and his family—for entertaining, etc.—may be well beyond those of a comparable United States plant manager.

Until recent years, a cost-of-living allowance as such was rarely needed. Very few areas were basically more expensive to live in than the United States (and most of those were also clearly hardship areas). The foreign service premium usually was considered to be sufficient compensation for meeting the peculiar needs of the American, and the costs associated with status as a company representative could normally be handled through liberal expense account practices.

Now, however, many areas of the world cost as much as or more than the United States, and elaborate procedures have been developed to determine extra costs for an expatriate and to reimburse him for these. The primary problem, of course, is to determine even approximately the *real* cost of living in a given community. Normally companies separate housing from the cost-of-living allowance, as discussed below, and use the concept of spendable income, i.e., the actual portion of income spent on goods and services in the country (i.e., not used for taxes or savings). This then creates the problem of selecting the items to be considered.

The most common reference source is the State Department of the United States. The State Department Allowance Section computes costs for spendable-income items for government employees in foreign service and makes these costs available to the public.[1] Unfortunately, the State Department index is designed for application to government employees, thereby limiting its usefulness for private industry. Government employees generally receive lower salaries than the typical expatriate, but they enjoy tax breaks not available to the expatriate. Also, government employees tend to be clustered together geographically, and thus they can take advantage of advice and assistance from the diplomatic community, whereas business expatriates are typically more widely dispersed in a country and have only limited access to the diplomatic community. Further, the spendable income comparison of the State Depart-

---

[1] Published quarterly in *Labor Developments Abroad*. Available from the U. S. Government Printing Office.

ment index does not reflect the changes in living and consumption habits required of an expatriate in private industry, nor does it attempt to define a relationship between salary and expenditures that is valid for Americans living abroad (since it is based on the average expenditure in the United States).

Because of these weaknesses, many companies rely on other data, including indexes from organizations such as Industrial Relations Counselors, Inc., or Associates for International Research, Inc., which provide data better suited to private industry for most major cities of the world. These indexes, too, must be adapted before they can be used, chiefly to add a cost increment for the permanent expatriate's real need to maintain peculiar and expensive United States standards.

In general, the best current thinking seems to be that, insofar as possible, allowances should be very carefully tailored to each individual situation. Employees sent overseas for a specific project should normally receive an allowance for the duration of their tour. The allowances of long-term expatriates, however, should probably be decreased over a period of time as they become acclimated to the country and more sophisticated about living abroad.

Housing Allowance. Since housing is the largest item in the expatriate's cost of living, most companies compute and pay a housing allowance separate from the cost-of-living allowance. Among other things, housing with the comforts and conveniences to which Americans are accustomed frequently is beyond the means of even the most highly paid, and in many areas severe shortages make housing excessively expensive by any standards. Because of the temporary nature of most assignments, housing usually is rented. In any case, purchasing a house is often very difficult either because of severe restrictions on house purchases by foreigners or because of scarcity or nonexistence of mortgage funds and the high rates of interest.

Generally, companies either provide a flat allowance or reimburse the expatriate for all costs above a certain percentage of salary. Both methods have advantages and drawbacks, and both must be well administered to maintain equity. If possible, a company should be willing to use either approach— whichever is most appropriate to the specific situation. In large metropolitan areas where housing is relatively easy to find, a flat allowance permits better cost control and usually involves fewer arguments. In areas where housing is extremely expensive or in short supply, the reimbursement allowance is usually necessary, even though the employee has less incentive to find housing compatible with his means or his real status.

Education Allowance. Most companies find it necessary to pay specific costs of education for children of expatriates. These can range from simple tuition in a local American school to tuition, room and board, and transportation to a private boarding school if there is no American school near by. Normally companies limit allowances to elementary and secondary students, providing only an extra transportation allowance for college students—typically, one round trip per year (sometimes for either the child or a parent).

Taxes. For many years, tax advantages were a major inducement to Americans considering work overseas; foreign taxes were nominal (for the expatriate at least), and income earned abroad was not subject to United States taxes. Now, however, the United States has placed a ceiling on the amount of income earned abroad which can be exempt from United States taxes; and in many countries, expatriates are taxed at a higher rate than they would be at home.

These changes have made it necessary for companies to develop allowances for taxes. There are two basic approaches: tax protection and tax equalization. Under the tax protection concept, the employee is guaranteed that he will not pay more taxes as a result of his foreign assignment than he would have paid had he continued to work in the United States. In effect, he receives foreign service premiums and allowances tax-free; the company pays the taxes on these items. The taxes to which he would be subject were he resident in the United States are calculated only on his base salary and bonus, if he receives one. (Some companies include foreign service premiums in this calculation.) If foreign taxes on company-earned income exceed the hypothetical United States tax on this income, the employee is reimbursed by the company for the extra taxes. The expatriate is responsible for filing his own tax returns.

Under the equalization concept, the company usually withholds monthly an amount approximately equivalent to the home-country tax on the employee's base salary. When the time comes for the payment of taxes, either foreign or at home, the company will either pay the actual taxes directly or let the employee pay the bill and then reimburse him. This method involves the company more directly, but the employee does not stand to gain from any savings from lower local tax structures or from inclusion of specific premiums, since amounts equal to United States taxes are deducted from his United States-equivalent income. Companies which use this approach feel that it is more equitable and also that it may encourage the employee to be more conscientious about paying local taxes (to the benefit of the company's image).

In either method, a certain amount of multiplication of costs is involved since the taxes paid are income to the employee in the year (the next year), so that each succeeding year's income includes extra taxes for the tax-reimbursement income. We believe a company is usually better advised to use the tax equalization approach if large numbers of expatriates are involved, but the tax protection device is much simpler and easier to administer where the costs are not as significant.

Moving and Travel Allowances. Normally, moving allowances for foreign service employees are handled on the same basis as for United States employees, except that often specific major-weight items are excluded (boat or machine shop) and overall poundage is restricted. However, special payments are frequently made in lieu of moving items such as cars—i.e., many companies pay the difference between the value of the United States car and a foreign-purchased car, rather than move the United States car. (Also, many expatriates are furnished company cars in positions which would not qualify for cars in the United States.)

Travel allowances usually are granted for home leave and/or vacation. In the past, home-leave policy typically permitted travel to point of origin in the United States for the entire family every two or three years—and some companies required the trip to help the expatriate family keep in touch with the United States environment. In recent years, the trend has been toward eliminating extra vacation for home leave but permitting a company-paid trip every year, or every two years at the least. Often companies schedule home-office visits for the expatriate executive to coincide with his vacation so that the family can extend its visit. Some companies permit use of the home travel allowance for non-United States vacations.

Miscellaneous Allowances. For a company that is conscientious in segregating allowances, additional allowances may be appropriate or necessary, depending on the local situation—for example, allowances for language instruction.

Finally, it should be noted that policy decisions must be made in many other compensation-related areas: splitting of income (most countries tax only income that is actually received in that country); handling of domestic financial affairs or at least providing liaison in handling them, preparing or auditing tax returns, and providing legal advice.   Many of these actually represent additional allowances for foreign service.

COMPENSATION OF THIRD-COUNTRY NATIONALS

Compensation practices for third-country nationals vary widely, probably because, until recently, most companies had only a small number of employees in this category and therefore tended to deal with their compensation on an ad hoc basis.   As their numbers grow, however, policies will need to be established.

Basically, there are four approaches which can be taken.   The third-country national can be paid: (1) on United States standards for salary and benefits, which, in effect, eliminates this classification of employee and joins him to the expatriate group, a practice followed by a number of companies; (2) on standards of the country of his citizenship; (3) on standards of the country to which he is assigned; or (4) on an artificial standard created to facilitate transfers within a given geographic area, e.g., the Common Market.   The choice among these alternatives should be based first on whether the person in question is hired by the corporation as part of its reservoir of international talent available for assignment anywhere or whether he is hired by a subsidiary for its own needs.   A second consideration is whether, regardless of his citizenship, he is hired within the country to which he is to be assigned or is hired within his own country for assignment elsewhere.   A third consideration, which may or may not be controlling, depending on the first two considerations, is whether he plans to retire to his own country or elsewhere.

The area of third-country national compensation is filled with contingencies, which is the primary reason why an underlying pattern is not readily apparent. For example, if the employee is a superior executive, he is often simply placed on the expatriate roll and treated as an American regardless of his actual nationality.   On the other hand, if the salary structure in the country of employment is higher than in his home country, he may be treated as a local national with no premiums or allowances (except possibly a commitment to offset losses of local social security upon retirement).   Often the decision as to status is made on the basis of original employment—if he is hired in the local country, he is considered a local employee, and if he is recruited from his country of origin (or the United States), he is considered an expatriate.   (This policy also typically applies to United States citizens who may be residing abroad at their own choice.)

However, if the individual is recruited from a third country, and particularly if he is recruited for a job typically held by an expatriate, the question of expatriate allowances inevitably arises, sooner or later.   Because of this, many companies establish special sets of allowances using a separate salary structure for third-country nationals.   The salary structure may be that of the local country or the home country, or a special structure may be developed for the situation.   Usually a foreign service premium is paid only for real hardship stations (but still on the non-United States base) and allowances are more restrictive.

A growing trend in handling retirement needs is the development of special offshore pension plans which may also apply to expatriates.

It appears that the increase in third-country nationals will encourage a pattern already developing in a few international companies: merging all international top management—United States expatriates, third-country nationals, and local nations—into one international management group in which few premiums (if any) are paid and allowances are limited to special situations, e.g., housing and taxes.   Obviously, such a policy requires the company to maintain salary levels competitive with compensation practices typical of any country from which top management members may originate. In the short range, however, we believe that most companies will formalize a third-country national program, which will then drift toward merger with the United States or local situation as appropriate.

COMPENSATION OF LOCAL NATIONALS

Most companies tend to place compensation of local nationals last in order of priorities, usually leaving it entirely to the discretion of local managers. Thus, long-established operations tend to follow local compensation patterns, and companies new to a country tend to make judgments which seem expedient (and which often disturb local patterns).

There are many reasons why parent organizations—even those that follow sophisticated compensation practices in the United States—have neglected local policies and practices. First of all, uniformity of practice is impossible in a multinational situation—and even consistency is difficult.

Compensation practices in highly industrialized countries vary widely. If the total amounts paid do not differ significantly, the forms the payment takes can be very different. Even considering only base salary, one will find in some countries a general use of a thirteenth month (and sometimes a fourteenth and a fifteenth), besides obligatory (or customary) Christmas payments and double vacation pay. One cannot, as in the United States, take the monthly salary, multiply it by 12, and call everything else either bonus or fringes.

Base salary is always the principal form of payment, but the social and taxation climate/practices of a country can and do influence significantly its relative importance. If taxes are high, other forms of compensation become more critical within the total package—hence the emphasis in a Dutch or British executive's pay package on cars and pension programs (which generally include widow's benefits and, to counter the effects of inflation, are geared to terminal salary).

Another significant difference is the relatively high rate of change of salaries abroad. Whereas salaries in the United States rose about 3 percent a year between the Korean War and 1970, salaries in Europe tended to increase at two or three times that rate.

Salary structures and practices in different countries differ not only in amount and form, but also in the slope of the structure (the relationship between increases in job size and increases in compensation). Thus, one cannot use a single (multiplier) factor to convert from amounts in one country to those in another. Compared with the practices of most other countries, the slope in the United States is flat. While salary structures abroad tend to be steeper than in the United States, in some countries the structures are considerably steeper than in others (being largely dependent on social and taxation mores). The result can be that whereas wages in country A may be significantly higher than in country B, the reverse may be true for management salaries.

Thus, compensation abroad is very different from what it is in the United States, and practices and customs vary widely from country to country. Because of this, it is very difficult for the United States salary administrator to make valid judgments about local national compensation, a fact that only reinforces his tendency to neglect this area.

A second factor discouraging United States companies from becoming involved in local national compensation is the difficulty—especially for an outsider—of getting an accurate picture of local practices. Reliable survey data are expensive and difficult to obtain, so that the best advice available at a reasonable cost often consists of the judgments of those on the scene.

Thirdly, the consequences of poor compensation administration usually are not evident for a period of years, and many managers are tempted to ignore the potential problems until action is necessary. Managers of new international operations are particularly susceptible to this danger: starting up will require many ad hoc decisions anyway, and the effects of inappropriate pay practices will be blurred by the rapid expansion and constant change inherent in new operations.

However, as international operations grow, sheer size will require that the parent organization take steps to ensure that the system under which local nationals are paid is properly designed and administered. The needs which a system of compensation must serve abroad are exactly the same as those at home: to assure that compensation is (1) consistent and equitable within a company, (2) competitive externally, (3) personally motivating, and (4) under adequate control as to cost and policy. An international company's management should have the same concerns in those regards for its subsidiaries abroad as it has domestically—and for the same fundamental reasons. But whereas in domestic operations companies have, within limits, a choice between operating in a relatively centralized or a relatively decentralized fashion, in international operations the range of choice is considerably narrower. The distances and differences involved naturally dictate a high degree of decentralization in all areas of management. In the compensation area, the aim should be to delegate authority for local compensation to local managers, thus allowing them the widest possible latitude in designing and administering a program that accomplishes the objectives specified above.

Although the following paragraphs focus principally on cash compensation, much of the discussion applies equally to benefits. This is important to note, since in many countries benefits such as cars and pension programs are much more important in the total compensation package than they are in the United States.

The Headquarters/Subsidiary Relationship. If compensation actions are to be decentralized effectively, corporate and foreign subsidiary management must understand each other's needs and, on the basis of this understanding, develop a sound, workable relationship.

Corporate management must set compensation for the top executive of each of its subsidiaries and, in addition, must review, before the fact, the top executive's recommendations on compensation for each of his key lieutenants. To make these decisions, corporate management needs reliable standards against which to test its compensation judgments. The subsidiary's top executive needs the same standards to guide him in formulating his compensation recommendations to corporate management. Standards for the top jobs, therefore, must ensure that the job relationships established are appropriate and the pay levels are competitive—i.e., sufficient to enable the company to attract, retain, and motivate the kinds of people it needs. Up to this point, corporate and subsidiary needs are the same.

Below the top people, at whatever level that cutoff is defined, the needs of corporate and subsidiary managements differ, not in principle, but in detail. Corporate management needs to know enough to be sure that what is being done is sound and effective, but not in the same detail it needs for matters on which it must make the decisions. Subsidiary management needs the same assurance of soundness and effectiveness but needs, as well, detailed standards to guide it in individual compensation decisions.

Thus, subsidiary management must develop and be able to use a sound method for establishing job relationships; corporate management needs only to know that the job is being done.   Corporate management must be satisfied that the general level of compensation is both adequately competitive and not too costly, but it can delegate to the subsidiary the task of determining how these conditions are met.   Subsidiary management, in fulfilling this delegated accountability, must do whatever is necessary to ensure that the unique characteristics of the national environment, and the subsidiary's competitive position therein, have been properly identified and measured in fixing the general level of the subsidiary's compensation and the form it is to take.   Finally, corporate management must assure itself that the subsidiary has some effective means of relating opportunity and performance and reward.   But, again, it does not have to prescribe the means; it confines its involvement to establishing criteria of effectiveness, which the subsidiary can meet as it sees fit.

Establishing the Pay Structure.   Given this relationship between the parent organization and its overseas operations and the concomitant necessity for decentralization, it is necessary to provide corporate management with some assurance that the local compensation structure is appropriate.

The first step is to evaluate at least the top jobs in subsidiary companies on a common basis, and on the same basis used for domestic jobs.   This helps establish compensation standards needed by both corporate and subsidiary managements.   It is helpful for noncompensation purposes as well.   Interchanges of personnel among subsidiaries are most likely to take place at the highest levels, and job evaluations are helpful in deciding whether a particular transfer represents good utilization of manpower and management talent.

Evaluations of the top jobs are also essential to decentralization.   Salary ranges developed on the basis of these job evaluations establish ceilings to which all lower jobs must be related in some sensible fashion.   Once corporate and subsidiary managements agree on proper compensation for the top jobs in subsidiaries, they have gone a long way toward giving corporate management the assurance it requires about the adequacy and propriety of compensation for jobs below the top, and toward giving subsidiary management the reference point it needs to establish compensation for these lower jobs.

It is important for subsidiary management to be involved in these evaluations for several reasons.   First, their knowledge of jobs in their companies and in the environment of the countries in which they operate is necessary to ensure the validity of evaluations.   Second, local managers must participate, since one of the chief purposes of evaluating these jobs is to arrive at mutually understood and agreed-upon standards to help local managers make intelligent recommendations which corporate management can approve.

Finally, the job evaluation process yields a common language for discussing compensation, job content, and related issues; overseas managers must be involved in the process to understand and use the language.

Sound evaluations of the highest jobs, then, are the first prerequisite to a decentralized compensation program.   The second is agreement on the general competitive level at which these jobs will be compensated.   (References to top subsidiary jobs exclude the top executive, since he should not help evaluate and price his own job.)

Corporate management should make the initial determination of where this level should be.   But to gain acceptance and to confirm that it takes into account both competitive pay practices and other environments of the particular country, the competitive level should be reviewed with local management, not just imposed upon them.

Benefits Plans. As was discussed earlier, in many countries (unlike the United States) the benefits package is provided primarily through government plans—i.e., a much expanded social security system, including health insurance and death benefits. Also, many countries require severance payments (typically one week's pay for each year of service) by law. Thus, the private sector is concerned principally with areas in which it can have a unique impact—that is, supplemental benefits, which are most often pensions. Typically, company pensions are geared to income at retirement in order to offset the effects of inflation, and they include provisions for survivor benefits. Moreover, since social security income limits are much higher, relatively, than in the United States, supplemental benefits for executives tend to be focused in the perquisite areas.

Because the patterns in benefits are so firmly established—by either law or custom—companies' choices in providing benefits are fewer. Group underwriting of insurance abroad, for example, does not yield the economies that can be realized in the United States, and employee contributions (up to a limit) are often tax deductible, thus encouraging individual underwriting. In addition, foreign operations are usually relatively small, so that the required separate underwriting sharply limits the bargaining power of the unit. In regard to pensions, the range of choices as to how they may be funded is considerably narrower than it is in the United States.

The entire benefits area, then, can probably be handled best by overseas personnel—always, of course, in keeping with the corporate objectives for the entire compensation package: that it be equitable, competitive, motivating, and financially feasible for the company. The contribution of an American salary administrator to the benefits plans of overseas subsidiaries is usually limited to providing ideas and technical assistance in developing new approaches where local conditions so indicate and to providing coordination for multinational personnel.

Bonuses. Very few United States companies have management incentive plans that extend to their foreign subsidiaries, except for United States nationals assigned to those subsidiaries, even though some companies include international earnings in the corporate results on which bonuses are based. In our opinion, incentive plans which make sense domestically should make just as much sense abroad.

chapter 44

Reconciling Compensation Programs in Merged Companies

ROBERT E. RADLEY   *Director, Salary Administration, Sperry Rand Corporation, New York, New York*

This chapter deals with the problems of the merged corporation which, from a personnel standpoint, continues to operate as a group of smaller, independent, and unrelated companies. Personnel philosophies are unchanged and policies and procedures retain areas of conflict, with the result that top management is unable to maximize strengths and minimize weaknesses in manpower applications as had been anticipated.

At this point, the corporation seeks to merge compensation programs so that the benefits of size can be realized. It is essential that top management communicate its compensation objectives to all concerned to emphasize its stand on the matter. The communication should take the form of a directive to accomplish a specific goal, and a continuing periodic review of progress toward that goal should be provided. The goal should be straightforward in its intent and generalized in its expression, and could be stated as *"the establishment of a compensation system to apply across the entire corporation, with basic similarities to reflect a single set of beliefs, attitudes, and concepts, but flexible enough to respond to the needs of different industries and/or geographic locations as applicable."*

However similar or different the existing compensation programs of merged or acquired companies may be, the job of consolidation is usually complicated by the sensitive nature of the subject. Compensation is more than just pay. It is an indication of the individual's status in the eyes of the company, and its improvement throughout the years measures his personal progress or lack of it. Further, there are no finite scientific formulas for the evaluation of a man or his services. The best we can do is order our judgments to create a system fair to employee and employer alike and administer that system impartially.

It may be that each party of the group to be merged has done just that but that each system is not quite compatible with the other's. This is the essence of the problem of merged compensation programs. It is extremely important that the goal be established, that top management support be obtained, and that all parties subject to the final outcome have a hand in the system's formation. The basic steps toward compensation reconciliation are (1) define the goal, (2) take inventory, (3) build the system, and (4) implement.

DEFINE THE GOAL

The first step toward goal definition is to identify the company as a single cohesive unit, with high potential for job interchangeability, or as a group of autonomous companies where job interchange is not anticipated.

If the corporation is such that little or no intercompany personnel transfer or communication is likely or desirable, the compensation systems can vary as widely as do the industry practices involved. In such cases, the establishment of a few basic ground rules concerning level of pay, bonus, and other administrative practices should suffice.

If, however, the corporation is one that requires executive and management interchange, and which encourages association of ideas between divisions, a cohesive and unified compensation system is required. Employees at all levels in such a corporation will be more likely to compare their personal job situation with that of their counterparts, and the expectation of equity will focus particularly on compensation levels and methods of administration. Recruiting efforts and efficiencies are heavily influenced by prospective and current employees' perception of their career opportunities within the organization. Of course, self-comparisons and expectations are present at all times with relation to outside companies, but the presence of other companies or divisions in the corporation presents an opportunity too tempting to resist.

Some of the concepts which need early identification, at least tentatively, revolve around the best method of executive pay: bonuses or straight salary; others, around how much to pay: to meet the market, to follow it, or to lead it; still others, around the method of keeping salaries current: merit increases, flat rates by job, increases by age, or some hybrid combination.

Certain decisions are dictated by how employees view the corporation's identity. The corporation which considers itself a single entity must conclude that certain commonalities are logical in the eyes of personnel. A common system of job evaluation or job grading must be adopted; a single salary policy should be developed, communicated, and applied to all levels where interchange is expected; and a single bonus plan should be developed and uniformly administered, if bonuses will be used at all. Some points of compensation philosophy or identity can be predetermined. Other decisions can be made but not yet implemented; still others cannot be made without a full investigation into the local situation. This realization leads us to the inventory and analysis of existing plans.

TAKE INVENTORY

The process of inventory and analysis will define in precise terms the task of reconciliation and should be undertaken with great care. During the initial inquiries into the practices of individual companies, personnel in the host company are certain to evaluate their visitors in terms of personal competence and in terms of corporate as well as personal intent. It is at this time that much of the groundwork is laid for a successful analysis and a lasting profitable relationship.

The inventory will define the size and nature of the reconciliation problem. Bonus plans, formalized salary plans and practices, the level of technical capability in salary administration, management's understanding and acceptance of existing salary programs, and the type and extent of noncash benefits offered to employees at all levels should all be considered. While it is not within the scope of this chapter to discuss noncash benefits, a full-scale reconciliation of compensation programs must recognize that full equity of treatment is ultimately possible only in terms of both cash and noncash compensation. The identification of similarities and differences in the pay plans and practices of each company or division, the pay philosophies upon which they are founded, and the nature of pay plan components, structures, regulations, and controls is a first order of priority in the inventory-analysis process.

Bonus Plans.   Some questions with which to begin the inventory of bonus plans are as follows: Does the member company pay bonuses at all? If so, are they considered a significant part of compensation, or are they simply frosting on the cake? Is the bonus plan thought of as an incentive plan, or is it an after-the-fact disbursement of funds unrelated to the individual's performance or contributions to the success of the enterprise? How extensive is the plan in terms of participation? What qualifies the individual for inclusion in the plan? How large are bonuses as measured against base salary or other criteria? How much variation in bonus size has there been from year to year?

Bonus fund accumulation formulas are somewhat similar among companies because of the usual requirements for stockholder approval, but disbursement formulas vary widely and in some cases are nonexistent. Where formulas or procedures are unavailable, it is well to analyze closely the bonus disbursements over a period of years. Usually a logical pattern of awards can be expected to exist because the bonus administrator must establish a position of equity among participants and must live with his decisions on a continuing basis. The pattern may be related to years with the company, salary level, position, performance, or a combination of these or other factors. Identification of the pattern is extremely valuable in helping avoid mistakes when designing and effecting changes at a later stage. When the analyst has become familiar with the bonus practices and plans of the member companies, his attention is directed to an examination of existing formalized salary plans.

Salary Plans.   The components of the salary plan include those elements which combine to make up total annual compensation, including base salary, bonuses, sales and production incentives, overtime pay received, and other forms of cash payment which may be discovered in the course of the analysis.

Overtime payments and some form of incentive, while usually paid to non-management employees, sometimes appear in surprising places, and they can be responsible for otherwise unexplainable pay practices at the management level. For example, the salary differential between managers and nonmanagers may appear excessive unless explained by a company practice of frequent or continuing extended work weeks, with managers on straight salary and subordinates earning premium time.

Base salaries are usually administered according to one of three systems: (1) a graded system, where several levels of skill or contribution have been established, each with its minimum or maximum allowable payment; (2) a smooth curve, where all jobs are assigned a point value which is in turn convertible to minimum or maximum rates through a salary formula; (3) the application of random rates, where salaries are paid against spot survey figures for individual jobs, or even at the whim of management, without benefit of market knowledge.

A variety of graded systems may cause the most problems in reconciliation, particularly if they are successful, are well communicated, and have the full support of local management. It may be that such systems should be left intact up to a level of potential job interchange. Jobs above that level would best be restructured with a common system which could be different from any of the lower-level structures. This is a difficult position to take, however, and it will later pose many problems concerning the amount of overlap between executive and nonexecutive systems or the propriety of policy pay levels at the point of intercept between the two structures.

Two aspects of the salary structure require regulation. One is the evaluation of jobs; the other is the pricing of jobs. The evaluation system establishes the pecking order in the organization in terms of value to the company. The administrator then seeks market values for selected benchmark jobs, establishes rates for those known points, and uses the evaluation system to interpolate values between those known points.

Job Evaluation. A well-ordered and effective evaluation plan will have an established procedure to govern the revision of old evaluations or the addition of new jobs, as well as a provision to record and control evaluation "drift." New or revised evaluations should meet the test of policy and/or market to be accepted as valid. That is to say, job evaluation alone is not enough. The new, or revised, job must bear up under close scrutiny when reviewed in the light of its relative position (rank) in the organization, and it should also relate well to survey data for similar jobs. Failure to employ such procedures may result in evaluation and, consequently, in rates far removed from reality.

Job Pricing. Jobs should be priced in accordance with a policy set by top management and related to appropriate salary surveys. Too many salary plans fail because management did not clearly define whether it wished to meet the market, follow it, or lead it, or because the salary administrator related to surveys which were irrelevant or poorly conducted, or because the ranges were not updated frequently enough or were updated on a "let's bump them up about 5 percent" basis. The absence of sound job pricing procedures can be a strong clue to the possibility of off-standard salary practice and offers the staff man a good opportunity to render a useful service.

Salary Administration Practice. It is also important to understand the company's salary administration practices and how deeply they may be established. Included are the practices of granting general increases, economic increases, merit increases, or others. Not to be overlooked is an assessment of the overall capability of persons charged with salary administration and of the level of understanding and acceptance of the salary program on the part of functional managers other than those in personnel.

Special Incentive Plans. Finally, it is of benefit to know the existence and extent of coverage of sales incentive plans or production incentives, primarily as they affect the relationship of jobs in these families to others in the same division. Incentives of this type are usually restricted to such specialized situations as to make consolidation and/or transfer of plans illogical.

The process of inquiry suggested here must, of course, be modified, reduced, or expanded to fit the situation in question. It is hoped that such inquiry would be conducted in a manner which would elicit full cooperation and constructive suggestions from all parties. A mutual appreciation of problems facing the operating activities and the central staff is essential to successful analysis and reconciliation.

BUILD THE SYSTEM

With the inventory of practices and policies completed, action can be taken to specify personnel goals reflecting past practice as well as the new direction established by top management. The general goal, it may be recalled, was "the establishment of a compensation system to apply across the entire corporation with basic similarities reflecting a single set of beliefs, attitudes, and concepts, but flexible enough to respond to the needs of different industries and/or geographic locations as applicable." Now in the light of a fuller understanding of division problems and practices, decisions governing the degree of division autonomy or corporate uniformity can be made, specific areas of application can be defined, and the goal can be more specifically defined in terms of bonus practices, job measurement systems, salary guideline policy, and salary increase policy.

The bonus plan, one of the most sensitive of personnel policies, is at the same time a part of executive compensation, a status symbol, and a report card of performance. Bonus plans usually accumulate funds under a profit-related corporate formula, and participants are alert to the plan's response to variations between years. Reassignment and promotion of participating executives provide the opportunity for accurate comparisons of bonus practices between divisions. The conclusions drawn through such comparisons can lead to serious morale and efficiency problems among key personnel if the plan is not designed properly.

In some cases, acquired companies may suddenly find themselves subject to the new parent's formula. If the parent's disbursement procedure can satisfactorily accommodate the new acquisition, the transition is simple. If not, it may dictate the need for an entirely new plan.

Division inputs concerning individual performance are critical to this kind of plan. The Sperry Rand Corporation, with companies engaged in widely divergent industries throughout the world, provides an example in the plan outlined in the following paragraphs.

Bonuses are considered a significant part of executive compensation. Participation is limited to those who the corporation believes are in a position to significantly affect business results and who can reasonably be expected to sustain a drop in earnings not due to reduced personal performance, should the availability of funds so dictate. Candidates recommended by division presidents are reviewed at the corporate level against established requirements for job level and approved or rejected by the corporate president. Candidates are qualified or denied on the basis of standards which provide equity across division lines. Bonus jobs are proprietary in nature to the extent that the corporation can reasonably expect the participant to sustain fluctuations in earnings correlated to fluctuation in profits.

Individual bonus awards reflect corporate performance, division performance, subdivision performance, and personal performance. Corporate performance determines the overall size of the bonus fund, a portion of which is allocated according to the size of the participating management team. The balance of the fund is allocated to divisions according to their performance, apportioned to subdivisions, and finally awarded to the individual on the job.

To effect the distribution of the performance portion of the fund, divisions are rated by the president and vice presidents at the corporate level according to profit performance, performance against plan, performance against prestated division goals, and return on assets. Each division is rated against the current year's performance and performance over the past three years as well. Finally, a single summary rating is agreed upon for each division and approved by the president for determination of the performance segment of the division bonus allocation. Division presidents rate their own subdivisions against the same factors to arrive at a bonus fund apportionment for each major profit center in the corporation. The profit center fund is then distributed among approved candidates in accordance with the bonus shares allocated to the job they hold, modified by the performance of the incumbent.

All bonus award recommendations are reviewed at the corporate level prior to actual payment to assure adherence to the principles of the plan and reasonable relationships between awards and performance, both personal and organizational.

Assuming a competitive accumulation formula, three problems must be dealt with in the installation of such plans. First is the absolute need for an available across-the-board job measure adequate for bonus qualification purposes. Sperry Rand uses its job evaluation system to provide that measure; it is possible to establish position values for bonus purposes separately from the job evaluation system, but they probably will not be as accurate.

Second is the possibility of having to reduce the size of the participating group. Management bonus plans have a way of becoming diluted over the years with the gradual inclusion of employees who are not truly in a position to personally influence the performance of the business as a whole. Dilution leads to smaller bonuses for true eligibles, requiring that higher salaries be paid to managers if they are to be kept within market. This situation undermines the incentive effect of the bonus plan, generating a need to reduce the number of participants until the gap between policy level for base salary and policy level for total compensation is small enough to be filled by the bonus fund generated by the accumulation formula.

The reduction can be accomplished by awarding those removed from bonus participation retroactive or current salary increases in an amount which will preserve their level of total compensation. The issue here is not how much will be paid, but how it will be paid. The advantages of this course of action are: (1) adequate funds are made available for a true executive incentive; (2) the assurance is given to nonmanagers that the level of their incomes is more dependent on personal performance than on business outcome over which they have no control; and (3) the opportunity exists for the company to administer nonmanagement total compensation against appropriate salary guidelines without being concerned over hidden factors.

The third problem area concerns the possible existence of significant differences between divisions in percentage relationship of bonus to base salaries. Adjustments to the proportion of compensation components may be required to bring about equity across the board. In cases where bonuses represent too large a proportion of the total compensation, a part of the bonus can be folded into base salaries. Where bonuses are too small in their proportion, it is best to increase the bonus level selectively and over a period of time until proper proportions are achieved.

In general, it can be seen that the circumstances of the case dictate the solution to problems of this nature. Some solutions may take several years to effect; others can be instituted immediately.

A common system of job evaluation is mandatory in the corporation which seeks to exchange employees between divisions. Such a system provides a yardstick against which to compare jobs when determining their relative value; it provides a measure to determine bonus eligibility and award potentials; and it provides a device through which policies defining the amount of base salary to be paid can be established. The system should be one that is applicable to all industries and to all levels of salaried jobs, including lower levels where interchange between divisions is unlikely or, at best, incidental. A system with that capability will provide equity at executive levels and avoid conflict or overlap which often occurs when separate systems are used for executive, exempt, and/or nonexempt salaried personnel. Edward N. Hay & Associates of Philadelphia provides an excellent system of job evaluation which fills these requirements and has the added advantage of being related to executive compensation surveys at home and abroad.

Whatever the mechanics of evaluation, the system should be applied impartially across the board, and preferably from the top down. The description of accountabilities for top positions and the evaluation of those jobs constitute a major step toward winning approval, understanding, and support for the entire program. At this initial stage, the impartial guidance of a competent consultant can be most helpful, even in companies which employ personnel strong in salary administration skills.

When description and evaluation of subsidiary presidents and corporate functional and line vice president positions are completed and approved, the precedents and upper limits have been set for application to subordinate levels within the division and/or member companies. This is a key point. The process of description preparation, interviews with executives, the self-examination required, and the discussion during evaluation will identify the composition of the corporation in terms of jobs and will elucidate many strengths and weaknesses of the organization.

At this point tentative decisions can be made on the size of the management group to be subject to central control. Certainly, the group should contain all employees eligible for management bonuses. Those potentially transferable between divisions and other key supporting positions, if not the entire population subject to national salary ranges, also deserve the attention of headquarters. Requirements for corporate approval over evaluations, direct compensation including bonus participation, bonus amounts, salary policy guidelines, and base salaries paid, as well as compensation in the form of pensions, insurances, options, and the like, can be established at this time.

IMPLEMENT

The completion of top executive evaluations, as described above, accomplishes one very important preliminary to further implementation of the plan. Properly executed, it establishes understanding and credibility for it in the eyes of top management. The need now is to establish that same understanding and credibility at successive organization levels as the plan is installed in member companies or divisions.

Installation of the System.   Understanding and credibility can best be achieved by fully involving the divisions in the evaluation of jobs subordinate to the general manager. The procedure used in the Sperry Rand implementation encompassed over 500 executives in six diverse divisions previously not subject to central headquarters influence in personnel matters. The principles used in that procedure can be applied to many companies with personnel merger problems, and they are described below.

After division personnel had completed the job description phase of the installation, a series of committees was formed to evaluate division-level jobs. The consultant and the corporate compensation director served on all committees. The division general manager and the division personnel director usually served on the committee for the evaluation of top division jobs. These sessions not only accomplished the top division evaluations, but also offered an opportunity for full-scale exchange of relevant knowledge. The evaluation sessions provided an excellent format for a full exposition of certain management principles, including accountability and organization delegation, and the jobs under analysis were used by the division committee members as focal points in explaining the characteristics of the business of that division as well as the nature of individual jobs.

After completion of the top division level, the division general manager withdrew from active evaluation in favor of a reviewing role. In some cases the vacated committee seat was filled by the controller or another member of the division staff, in some it was filled by the head of the function under evaluation, and in still other cases another member was drawn from the personnel department. These were the options open to the division.

Upon completion of the management segment of the implementation, that division's key scale of nonmanagement jobs was described and evaluated to provide a guide to future nonmanagement evaluations. The key scale consisted of some general benchmark jobs common to all or most divisions and some jobs peculiar to the division under consideration. Each division, in turn, was visited by the consultant and the director of corporate salary administration until all jobs considered of direct interest to top corporate management were covered. Before they were made official, committee evaluations were reviewed at the division general manager level, the corporate vice president level, and finally by the corporate president.

The above-described procedure offers control and accuracy in the installation of the plan. The control is inherent in the line of continuity offered by the consultant and the corporate representative as well as in the final top executive review of results. Accuracy is provided through the participation of division personnel who are in a position to obtain information concerning specific jobs if they do not already have that information.

Maintenance of the System. As is often the case, installation and maintenance are totally different problems. Reorganization, second thoughts about job relationships, pressures for higher salaries, pressures for greater bonus participation—all a part of the salary administrator's life—are frequent occurrences in the merged system. Without a systematized method of control, evaluations will drift upward in a continuous spiral.

The most suitable control is a capability to handle the gross detail so characteristic of salary administration. A computer program which lists job evaluations and salary data along with certain indicators such as volume of business, reporting level, scope of activity, and job profiles is of immeasurable value to the maintenance and integrity of the evaluation system. Of course, the system will not run itself. Division personnel departments must respond to real changes or inequities and resist imagined ones. Corporate headquarters must monitor the activities of each division to assure all concerned that the program retains its integrity.

Salary Policy Guidelines. Once jobs identified for corporate control are placed and maintained in relation to each other, we can establish salary policy guidelines which will assure payment in relation to the personnel market in which the jobs exist.

Salary guidelines should be established to reflect the policies of the corporation concerning its relationships to the appropriate market for employees. The guideline can take the form of ranges for salary grades or that of a line formula to be applied against evaluation points. In either case, it should apply to all positions in the personnel market in which it is used. The guidelines can be related to a single industry, a region, or a country—whatever is judged most appropriate for the company in question. Of course, where interchange of executives is expected, the policy guideline should reflect pay levels in all industries involved.

Assuming that the policy of the company is to meet its markets for personnel and that the company is a bonus-paying company, it would establish its policy for base pay in relation to the base pay in other bonus-paying companies in the appropriate personnel market. Its policy for nonbonus jobs would be set against statistics reflecting total compensation paid in nonbonus companies. This practice would yield a higher level of base pay for nonbonus jobs than for bonus jobs at the same evaluation-point levels, but it follows a single principle —that of reconciling each group with its own competition in the marketplace for people.

Past practice may make it impossible to realistically adjust executives' pay to the levels suggested by guidelines thus established. If such is the case, the evaluations should be held firm, with deviations from the desired salary guideline approved as necessary. Over a period of years the deviations can be eliminated.

chapter 45

Handling Unique Compensation Situations

C. S. DADAKIS   *Manager, Salary Administration, Union Carbide Corporation, New York, New York*

No matter how carefully conceived or executed a compensation program is, situations will arise which cannot be accommodated within the normal patterns of the plan.   The real test of the system and its administrators, then, is their ability to deal with these special situations without jeopardizing the operation and acceptance of the total program by the organization.

This is not to say that most variations in job market, employee performance, or grade structure cannot be handled within the context and procedures of the normal program.   Problems in compensation are usually a matter of degree. Judgment must be used to decide when the variations are sufficiently severe to tax the mechanics and logic of the existing procedure.

An effective program must be flexible enough to permit exceptions based on careful analysis and reason.   But the integrity of the whole compensation plan will depend on how well the exceptions are integrated into the system.   Caution should be exercised to avoid solutions which compromise any of the basic principles or challenge the fundamental equity of the program.

Most cases which require special consideration have one or more of the following underlying circumstances in common:

1. *Job Market Change:*   A sudden sharp change in the outside market for a specific function or a group of jobs

2. *Special Career Development:* A need to provide accelerated career paths for certain individuals beyond the salary limitations and normal promotional opportunities of the existing job

3. *Salary Compression:* A reduction in actual pay spread between levels caused by a disproportionate increase in such factors as starting salaries, hourly rates, or amount of overtime

4. *Professional Insulation:* A sense of detachment from the company salary scales affecting persons whose professional contribution is peripheral to the mainstream of the organization. Such persons usually identify more closely with the profession than with the company.

5. *Unique Performance Pattern:* Individual performance which varies sufficiently from the typical to require special attention

In any of the above cases, it is difficult to say precisely when the situation becomes unique and requires special handling. Problems arising from such circumstances have been encountered and solved by other companies. The few cases below will illustrate the sort of approaches which have been used:

Job Market Change.

Example 1: The Compensation Treatment of Computer Programmers and Analysts in a Rapidly Rising Job Market. Here we are dealing with rapid change in the market price of a specific function or profession, resulting from an acute imbalance of supply of and demand for trained personnel. (We are not, for the moment, considering the overall rise of the salary structure due to inflation or the increase in annual productivity which affects all groups in the salary population.)

Over the years, as companies sought to increase their computer capabilities, the demand for trained personnel in this field became extremely heavy. Job offers and salaries started an upward spiral which exceeded by a substantial degree the inflationary rise in the remainder of the salary structure.

At first, companies tried to maintain hiring rates and job ranges as originally evaluated, but this resulted in heavy attrition as employees sought better opportunities elsewhere. Companies then made it a practice to hire in the middle of the range and to pierce the top of the range for existing jobs in order to hold employees. In similar situations in the past, such temporary expedients seemed to afford relief until the supply-and-demand balance returned to normal. But in the case of computer personnel, the shortages continued year after year as computer operations were expanded. It became obvious to many companies that a more permanent solution was needed.

One way of meeting the problem was to remove the jobs from the regular classification tables and treat the group on an ad hoc basis. This did not work well, however, because it permitted employees with the strongest bargaining power to receive the greatest rewards. Also, managers were often at a loss to know whether their compensation practices were fair or in line with those of the rest of the industry. A more comprehensive solution was needed to achieve an acceptable and viable compensation plan for these employees.

One company solved the problem by removing the jobs from the salary evaluation procedure and setting up a separate ladder, distinct and apart from the regular program. This ladder was formed of typical nonsupervisory jobs somewhat as follows:

Junior Programmer
Programmer
Programmer Analyst
Senior Programmer Analyst
Consultant

The jobs were then compared with the outside market in a survey with careful regard for job content. On the basis of the survey information, realistic ranges, reflecting current market conditions in the area, were set for each level. This assured managers that the salaries they were offering were in line with the market. The ranges were reviewed every six months and adjusted to maintain market competitiveness.

However, the departmental problem was not only one of figuring valid ranges for each level, but also of defining criteria by which incumbents could be slotted into the levels. Many of the employees were seeking promotional opportunities based on their increasing experience and rising qualifications.

To meet this problem, a manning table was developed for the department which set forth the number of employees required at each level for optimum operating effectiveness. This was done for present operations and estimated for each successive year for the next five years.

Using this manning table as a guide, managers were able to appraise more precisely the promotional opportunities existing currently in the department and expected over the next five years. They could discuss current careers and future openings with the employees and indicate opportunities which would be available to those who qualified.

In effect, the managers' approach to stabilizing employment and improving morale in the department was twofold:

1. Realistic ranges in line with the market, on which merit increases could be based with the firm knowledge that the salary represented competitive compensation for each job

2. A reliable estimate of present and future promotional opportunities, based on the manning tables, which could reasonably be discussed with and provide incentives to the employees. Each employee could then relate these opportunities to his own rising qualifications and decide more intelligently how he would react to outside offers. Many such offers in the past were pseudo-promotions intended only to gain his services immediately. Now he could respond with a better knowledge of what his future would be if he chose to remain with the company.

The managers had the advantage of feeling more secure in their staffing at each level for both present and future operations. If they were unable to make a promotional offer to an employee who voluntarily terminated in order to accept a higher-level position outside, they did not feel as vulnerable as they had in the past. Previously, such a loss was looked upon as a major catastrophe. Often last-minute offers and promises were considered to entice employees to stay.

Under the new plan, with use of the manning tables, it was recognized that the loss of certain employees would not cripple the organization if the manning chart indicated that the department was sufficiently staffed at that level.   In fact, certain terminations could serve as a "safety valve" to provide openings and advancement for others in the department.

The experience with computer personnel is not the only example of a sharp change in job market conditions. At one time or another, this phenomenon has occurred for certain types of engineers, mathematicians, lawyers, and those in other specialized professions. In no case, however, has the shortage lasted quite as long or its impact been as severe as in the case of data processing employees.

However, the solution to the problem has always been more or less the same. The jobs have been segregated temporarily from the existing range structure. A separate evaluation and survey analysis has been undertaken to determine market values. Salary treatment has been in line with what was being paid in the market for comparable talents and contributions.

Usually a shortage in a particular trade or profession is neutralized within a few years by an influx of people into that field. As the supply-and-demand situation comes into balance, it is possible to place the jobs back into the normal structure, usually at the grade or point level at which they were originally pegged. Sometimes a slight change is needed either to correct an earlier error in evaluation or to allow for a permanent change in the market value of such jobs.

Example 2: *The Compensation of M.B.A.s.* For many companies, the hiring and salary treatment of selected M.B.A.s has become a major problem. These M.B.A.s are different from the business graduates in the past whom many companies assigned to well-defined jobs in accounting, credit, or related business departments.

Most companies engage relatively few M.B.A.s each year. Often a company is interested in finding the best-qualified young man available. Competition for these relatively few candidates can drive rates sharply upward. If the company can be satisfied with a slightly lower level of qualifications, the field becomes broader and the starting rates more reasonable. By having available a range of starting rates based on level of qualification, a company increases its chances for a successful recruiting effort.

If a candidate accepts employment, the company is faced with the problem of maintaining correct compensation to keep the man on the payroll. Although it is possible to administer salaries on the basis of the company's regular exempt program, merit increases are usually based on a special program for this particular group. In either case, it is important for the company to hold a candidate until it can be judged whether his contribution justifies his relatively higher starting rate and salary.

Attracting an M.B.A. may depend largely on the salary offer, but holding him requires more than salary. Of greater importance are the type of work he is doing, the environment in which he operates, and the challenge the job offers. Assuming that these variables are satisfactorily fulfilled, salary must be high enough so that the man will resist the temptations of the outside market. Demand for such people is heavy, and they tend to be more mobile than the typical exempt employee.

Special treatment accorded M.B.A.s may appear to confer on them "crown prince" status. This should be avoided as much as possible by discreet handling of salary matters as well as by firm insistence on performance equivalent to salary. Otherwise, the charge of favoritism may be justified. On the other hand, unless special treatment is granted to high-quality employees, it will not be possible to compete for them in the market, either in recruiting or in retaining candidates after they have joined the company.

Special Career Development.

Example 1: *Paying the Up-from-the-Ranks Foreman versus the College Graduate Engineer Who Starts as a Foreman.* There is a marked difference between the career paths of the up-from-the-ranks foreman and the trained engineer who starts as a foreman. It is therefore unwise to evaluate both on the same basis or to reward them according to the same criteria simply because they occupy the same job.

The foreman is generally at the top rung of his career. He may rise one more level (to general foreman), but most foremen in today's mass production factories accept their positions as career-terminal jobs. They are limited by their formal education and the technical demands of the higher-level positions.

The engineer, on the other hand, is at the beginning of his career. He has a vast reservoir of untapped knowledge and potential. The job of foreman is assigned to him more as a learning exercise than as a job in which he can demonstrate his full capabilities. Nevertheless, he is usually expected to perform the job more capably than his counterpart from the ranks.

At least for the first few years, the engineer in the foreman's job should be treated in the same manner as his engineering peers in the rest of the organization. That is, he should be treated the way college graduates in engineering, research, sales, or administration are treated within the company. Fortunately, the salary range for a beginning engineer in production is usually very close to that of a production foreman. In a typical job evaluation scheme, the experience and skills acquired by the foreman over his career often are equivalent to the academic learning of the engineer right out of college. Although the salary range may be similar, the merit increase treatment of the engineer will often differ from that of the foreman. The foreman is usually paid for a satisfactory and stabilized performance of the foreman's job. The engineer, on the other hand, is paid for performing a foreman's job but he is also recognized as one of the cadre of professionals within the company from whom further growth and contribution are expected.

In the early years, the engineer should be related to the college graduates in the company and receive any special merit treatments which are awarded to that group as a class. This means that his rate of pay will include normal merit increases as well as special adjustments influenced by new college hiring rates or unusual market considerations based on the supply and demand of candidates.

Sooner or later, however, a decision will have to be made whether the engineer will continue as a foreman indefinitely and cast his lot with the production hierarchy, or whether he will move to other areas of company operations to widen his background and experience. If the former decision is taken and he remains a foreman, he will have to climb the ladder of jobs as they exist in the production part of the business. His progress will depend on his own performance and the immediate openings which may occur in that part of the organization. If he remains a foreman for any protracted period of time (usually three years or more), he must begin to conform to the pay levels and salary treatment of the other foremen in the organization. Although at the start he may merit higher salary increases than his counterparts who came up from the ranks, after a few years such preferential treatment will have to be justified by his superior contribution on the job rather than by his technical background as a member of a college-trained group.

Example 2: Paying the Senior Bookkeeper versus the Entry-level Accountant. The salary structure of an accounting department is sometimes unsettled by the introduction of one or more entry-level college-trained persons. Much day-to-day accounting work is routine in nature, and it is hard for many staff members of the department to conceive that the new college-trained employee can make a different kind of contribution.

Yet, unless the college-trained accountant is called on to innovate and to participate in decisions which have meaningful impact on the total accounting function, the company is not fully utilizing the talents his formal education brings to the job.

Except for the initial training period, therefore, the college-trained accountant occupies a different position from the senior bookkeeper, and this fact should be recognized. The job description should reflect the difference in job content, and even the title should differ from that of the bookkeeper. Although there will be instances when the two seem to be doing the same work, the depth of application and the scope of the two will be dissimilar. The jobs should be evaluated separately and the merit treatment in each case should be related to the particular incumbent and job.

One word of caution. In setting up professional accounting jobs in the department, it should be remembered that college-trained employees expect to move up the ladder to more demanding and rewarding jobs. There have been many instances where a company has staffed lower job echelons in accounting with college-trained, eager incumbents only to have these employees discover in a few years that they had no place to go. Feeling stymied, many of the best candidates quit, causing disruption and temporary demoralization of the whole department. The years spent in early training were lost to the company solely because it had sought out overqualified employees for the lower-level jobs.

It is best to limit the number of professionals in the department to how many can reasonably expect upward movement and progress. The remaining jobs should be staffed as far as possible with people whose background and ability permit them to remain on career jobs over long periods of time.

Salary Compression.

Example 1: The Squeeze on Foremen's Salary as a Result of an Increase in Hourly Rates, Shift Allowances, or Overtime. In most companies, a foreman is considered part of management and his salary is tied to the managerial ladder (i.e., the exempt group in the structure). However, this often produces a dilemma because it is difficult to maintain a reasonable gap between the foreman's compensation and the compensation of his highest subordinate. At certain times, a foreman may earn scarcely more than his top operator, and sometimes, when unusually heavy overtime occurs, he may even earn less.

Companies have sought to solve this problem by continuing the foreman in the exempt ranks but tying his compensation to the hourly structure. This is usually done by relating a foreman's minimum or starting salary to a percentage above the rate of the highest-paid hourly worker he supervises. This percentage may be anywhere from 10 to 35 percent, but the most prevalent in industry is 15 to 25 percent. The top of the foreman's range, on the other hand, is usually related to the exempt salary structure, if possible. Where this causes a compression problem within the structure, the top of the range can be set as a certain percentage of the minimum rate. Usually the foreman's range spread is 35 percent, but this will vary and may be as high as 50 percent, depending on company policy.

When setting the starting salary or minimum of the range as a percentage of the hourly rate, it is usual to include any shift or holiday allowances which may be a permanent part of the hourly rate. Some companies also figure in "average overtime" to make sure the "total package" of hourly compensation is representative. However, where overtime is extremely heavy or erratic, its inclusion in the average hourly rate may distort the basis of the calculation. In such cases, it is best to adopt a policy of supplemental income payments to the foreman to counterbalance the effects of overtime.

Supplemental pay may be made at straight time or at time and one-half or a combination of both. The objective, of course, is to maintain a reasonable spread between the total compensation of the hourly worker and his immediate supervisor. Since the hourly worker is usually paid at time and one-half for all hours over 40, one way of maintaining the spread is to pay time and one-half on that portion of the supervisor's salary which is roughly equivalent to the hourly employee's base pay. For example, some plans provide time and one-half on the first $500 or $600 of his salary and straight time on the balance.

The plan often sets a limit on the amount of additional overtime compensation payable in any month regardless of how many hours have been worked. For example, the limit may be anywhere between $200 and $500 a month. Also, there is usually a salary cutoff, above which a person is not eligible. For example, foremen and general foremen might participate, but plant managers or assistant plant managers and their equivalent levels would not be eligible.

It is wise to stipulate that supplementary payments will be made for scheduled overtime only. Unless overtime is carefully controlled, the need for overtime may be interpreted too loosely, resulting in high costs and inefficiencies. In any supplementary plan, the need for overtime should be strictly controlled and authorized only by persons who do not participate in the overtime payments.

Another way to deal with overtime compression is to introduce a form of additional income for first-level supervisors. A bonus plan for foremen and other first-level supervisors need not be limited to considerations of overtime. Preferably, a bonus should be a reward for total performance which is measured rather precisely. For example, performance goals can be set for specific items, such as production costs, level of quality, percentage of scrap, or timeliness in meeting production schedules. This bonus can be calculated by simple mathematical formulas which measure how well the department meets these goals. Although such a bonus plan is not related directly to overtime, it does increase the foreman's total compensation and offers a means for providing a respectable spread between his overall reward and that of the people he supervises.

Where a company already has a bonus plan for middle management, the foremen can be made eligible to participate in the plan. Such middle-management bonus plans usually have the following characteristics:

1. They are selective in the people who are rewarded, so that a foreman may or may not get a bonus in any one year, depending on management's view of his total performance.

2. They are variable in the amount of payment to each individual. Most plans pay off at approximately one-half month's to three months' salary (4 to 25 percent of annual pay) to first-level supervisors.

3. The payment usually is not considered part of the base income on which benefit plans are predicated. Thus, a foreman cannot build up a greater stake in the pension plan or in the savings plan of the company through his bonus payments.

Some companies have attempted to alleviate the overtime compression problem by granting extra time off to the foreman. Theoretically, this does not cost the company any additional money. However, many busy foremen can hardly find enough time for their normal vacations and holidays, let alone schedule days off for overtime previously worked. In most cases, these foremen accumulate long backlogs of earned time off, which they are never able to exercise. As this builds up, companies find it necessary either to buy off the time by some type of cash equivalent or to gradually forget about it by quietly letting it drop into limbo. The problem usually cannot be solved by the latter approach. Although the foreman's reaction may not be overt, manipulating his earned time off usually undermines his loyalty to the company. The long-term result is often deterioration in the organizational health of the department.

Example 2: Compression of Salaries of Young College Graduates Due to Rapid Increase in Starting Rates for College-trained. Since most companies adjust the exempt salary structure over a broad spectrum of jobs, a serious compression problem arises when the starting rates of a particular group increase more rapidly than those of the rest of the structure.

Starting rates for college graduates have for many years increased at a faster pace than rates for the rest of the exempt population. As a result, graduates who have been out of school for two, three, or four years are often faced with the prospect of earning only nominal amounts more than the graduate just entering without any experience. For example, if starting rates rise 6 percent while the rest of the salary structure rises only 3 percent in a particular year and this is repeated for several years, the salary progression ladder for the first few years may well become uncomfortably flat. When this occurs, years of service are rewarded very slightly if at all.

To compensate for this, many companies set up a series of special payments to college graduates during the first one to five years. Other companies provide a special merit program which accelerates salary increases to keep a proper motivating distance between classes. Eventually, of course, all salaries must be melded into the regular structure, but this is usually done after about five years on the payroll.

Three ways by which yearly salaries of college graduates can be adjusted to keep up with starting rates are detailed below:

1. New graduates are granted a first increase in six months to bring them up to the hiring rate expected to be paid the following June. They then receive regular merit increases at the end of another six months. For the next two to four years, each class is kept a certain dollar figure ($25 to $50 a month) ahead of the previous year's class.

2. The first-year graduate is given an adjustment (in addition to merit increase) equal to the full amount of the rise in starting rates. Each successive class is given a decreasing percentage adjustment. For example, the size of the adjustments might be:

Years out of College	Adjustment
1	5%
2	4%
3	3%
4	2%
5	1%

Generally, after the fifth year is reached, adjustments phase out and the incumbent takes his place in the regular exempt salary structure.

3. The merit program is made strong enough to maintain a proper distance between classes, taking into account individual performance. This requires that management be alert to changing starting rates, and also courageous enough to give the size increases required to maintain equity. One way to help managers carry out such a policy is to provide a list of graduates with up to five years' service who have not kept reasonably ahead of the increase in starting salaries over the period of their employ. By using this list as a guide, managers can take the necessary action to bring young graduates into proper relationship with each other, assuming individual performance and contributions are satisfactory.

Professional Insulation. Certain professional employees, such as lawyers and doctors, often relate more closely to the pay structure of the profession than to that of the company.

Example 1: *Medical Doctors.* Doctors, whose duty it is to look after the general health of the employees, conduct physical examinations and handle emergency disabilities, are usually far removed in their interests from the line objectives of the enterprise. Although many companies have tried to incorporate evaluation of medical doctors into the overall company structure, such evaluations are often fictional and intended only to prove that all jobs can be evaluated under a plan rather than to determine the real worth of the medical job. It is far more realistic to try to relate the doctor's job to the going rates for similar jobs in that area. This cannot always be done by comparing him with the highly specialized market of industrial medicine. Depending on location, the market value of an industrial physician may be influenced more by local doctors' incomes than by industry rates for doctors.

A survey of the area should include both private and industrial physicians, if possible, to provide sufficient data to determine a fair level of pay. At best, such a survey will indicate a general range for the job. The actual pay level will depend on the individual, his skills, his reputation, and his experience, as well as the strength of his negotiating position based on the current supply-and-demand situation. Most companies do not want to compromise on the quality of a physician and would rather pay a reasonable amount above what appears to be an average rate to obtain a competent physician than to adhere rigidly to a preset range which would limit their choice and selection.

Example 2: *Lawyers.* Members of the legal profession are often found in various managerial and administrative positions in industry. Such jobs are evaluated like other company jobs, since they relate directly to the operations of the business. Where lawyers are used strictly to provide legal counsel and guidance to others who make decisions or take actions, their role is more nearly that of a member of an outside law firm who may be hired on a retainer by the company.

The most effective approach to compensation for this latter group of lawyers will vary from company to company. When the law department is large and there is a regular hierarchy of levels from beginning lawyer to senior attorney, the jobs can be evaluated as staff jobs, similar to other staff jobs in personnel, credit, accounting, etc., and related to the total structure. In this way, companies create a law structure which is part of the overall staff structure of the company. It is then priced as part of the overall company line, and the ranges for lawyers bear a relationship (i.e., are internally equitable) with the other professional, executive, and administrative jobs in the company.

When the number of lawyers is small and a hierarchy does not exist, companies have found it more effective to consider the jobs as specialists' jobs to be related to the outside profession rather than to the company structure. An area survey of rates for lawyers in law firms and in industry should provide sufficient background data to set up equitable ranges.

It should be remembered, however, that lawyers vary widely in professional ability and reputation. In many jobs, the man does make the job. His education, experience, and standing in the profession determine his level and his capacity to serve the company. It would be hard to evaluate a lawyer's qualifications or the level at which he serves without closely observing his *modus operandi.* Therefore, the exact pay level must be left to the person making the selection and evaluating the performance. A survey can serve only as a general guide. In most companies, the lawyer's actual compensation is related to the manner in which the company utilizes his services. In certain companies, law departments are equivalent to and comparable with the finest outside law firms. In others, the lawyer is intended only as an adviser to act as intermediary between the company executives and one or more outside law firms which conduct most of the company's law operations.

Over the years, the demand for legal services has risen so sharply that a shortage of lawyers has resulted. This has put upward pressure on lawyers' salaries in industry which has been more than matched by rising incomes in private practice and private law firms.

It would be wise, therefore, to develop separate market data on lawyers' income to ensure that company ranges and actual compensation are in line with the market. It should not be necessary to design a new structure to keep up with the market, but it would be helpful to have information on what is happening in the market so that the manager or the person administering the lawyers' salaries can act accordingly. Many companies include lawyers' positions in their bonus plans. They are, therefore, able to supplement the salaries with reasonable bonuses which reflect performance and also help to keep current remuneration in line with total compensation of professional counterparts in the outside market.

Unusual Performance Patterns. Although most merit programs operate with little difficulty and are able to distinguish variations in performance and award increases accordingly, there are indications that many plans are deficient in properly rewarding individuals when sharp differences in performance occur.

Example 1: *Extraordinary Growth in Performance.* Companies pay lip service to the concept of rewarding the outstanding performer but often back away when it comes time to actually pay the salary demanded by such performance. Much of this reluctance is understandable since companies closely examine present performance but also like to look at the employee on a career basis. However, certain managers, particularly those who have lived through the depression, suffer from a weakness which might be called "dollar fear"; i.e., the total amount of dollars required to bring an outstanding performer into proper relationship, particularly if he is young, frightens the manager. Philosophically, the manager goes along with the idea that a substantial boost in salary is needed to match the level of performance. But emotionally the "rend of parting" is too great for him to recommend the full amount of increase which is needed.

In order to help the manager meet this situation, some companies have set up certain percentages as guides for various levels of performance. For example, a typical merit increase guide might be:

> 5% for satisfactory performance
> 8% for commendable performance
> 15% for outstanding performance

By applying these percentages, the manager feels less "guilty" in awarding the amount of money which the situation demands.

Of course, percentage guides for merit increases should always be used in conjunction with time span considerations. A merit increase has two dimensions: money and time. If elapsed time since the last increase is disregarded, the percentage loses meaning. Therefore, it is best to specify elapsed time limits for each class of increase, or to designate the percentage as an "annualized percentage"—i.e., a percentage per year of time since the last increase. In other words, if it has been one and a half years since the last increase, and the incumbent is worthy of an 8 percent annualized increase, his real increase should be 12 percent. If he has been an outstanding performer, and his last increase was 15 months ago, his new increase should be 20 percent ($1\frac{1}{4} \times 15$ percent) to cover the time span since the last increase.

Example 2: *The Rapidly Promotable Individual.* Whenever possible, it is best to give an increase at or very close to the time of promotion. The old concept of "wait to see if he can prove himself on the job" has fallen into disfavor as a valid approach to rewarding promotable personnel. The reason is that much of the incentive generated by a promotion is wasted if the increase which should accompany that promotion is late. Furthermore, if the salary is below the minimum for the new job, there is a strain on the credibility of the salary program. In general, when there is a good reason to delay an increase and maintain a person below the minimum of the range, three months should be the maximum waiting time. Otherwise, the employee is not only underpaid in relation to his colleagues, but he may also be earning less than the people he supervises. Such situations very quickly lead to disenchantment with the salary program. The entire motivating impact of a promotion may be dissipated and the company will stand a good chance of losing a good employee in the not too distant future.

The situation becomes even more critical when the promotion is a substantial one. The employee may jump over the heads of two levels of subordinates—"a double jump promotion," as it is sometimes called. Here the gap between actual salary and the minimum of the range may be so great that a single increase to bring him up to the minimum may be unreasonable. In such cases, it may be better practice to give the increase in two awards—one at the time of promotion and the other approximately six months later. In other words, when a man's responsibility increases substantially, it is wise to look at his salary from the viewpoint of his total career. A single large increase at the time of promotion may make all subsequent increases of a more normal nature pall by comparison. Therefore, judgment should be used to provide a series of merit increases as a reward for his excellent performance.

Example 3: *A Sudden Downturn in Performance and Contribution.* There are occasions when a person who has been doing a good job over the years suddenly demonstrates a sharp downturn in performance. He may be assigned to a job which is beyond his capacity or he may have personal problems which prevent him from contributing on the job as would be expected. The obvious solution is to assign such a man to a job that is better suited to his capacity and in which he can do a satisfactory job. If he cannot be reassigned to such a job, then it is best to terminate the man rather than to continue him on a job which he does poorly.

On reassignment, most companies will permit the man to continue at his existing salary but hold to that salary as the structure moves upward until the salary is in line with the new range. However, other companies believe in giving the man a pay cut to put his current salary in line with the new job to which he has been assigned. Then, on the basis of future performance, the man is eligible for merit increases as he demonstrates his ability on the new job. Such action eliminates the need for waiting for the structure to catch up, and it often has a salutary effect on the man as he strives to do well on the new job. On the other hand, the shock of a pay cut often is severe, and unless the man is psychologically prepared and willing to take such a cut, it could have a devastating effect on his morale. The manager will have to select the best approach. Results have been good with both procedures, but the choice depends basically on the individual employee and the environment in which he works.

Example 4: *A Static Condition Where Growth Has Plateaued or Where the Employee Has Reached the Top of His Range and Cannot Be Promoted.* In both of these situations, we have what might be called a "stabilized performance" condition. In one case, the man's contribution remains satisfactory but there is very little, if any, growth in performance. In the other case, although growth may be present, the man is already bumping the ceiling on his job. Normally, the top of the range in any properly designed salary program is good pay for that job and is the level at which high performers on the job should be rewarded. It would be unwise to pierce the top of this range except for ex-traordinary career situations. Occasionally, some companies will pierce the top by a certain amount, usually a maximum of 10 percent. However, in most cases, the incumbent must await an opportunity for promotion to a higher-level job. In the meantime he continues to get increases equal to the movement of the structure, thus maintaining his position at the top of the range. Under these circumstances, it should be explained to him that he is already at the top of the range and that an opportunity for greater reward will occur if and when a higher-level job for which he qualifies becomes available.

The man who has plateaued in performance should receive increases no greater than the movement in the structure. This will keep him at the same relative level in the economy. Theoretically, his "real" dollar pay will be main-tained, since the structure tends to move in line with changes in the economy. However, in order for him to obtain a higher income in "real" money, it will be necessary for him to demonstrate a higher level of performance to justify a merit increase. This is hard to tell someone, but he will soon get the message. It is one of the built-in motivators of a good salary program.

❈   ❈   ❈

The examples we have given of unique cases requiring special consideration in compensation all revolve around the single factor of flexibility in the salary program. A successful salary program is fundamentally a system of job and performance measurement. The program enables management to set up a meaningful hierarchy of jobs and to set dollar ranges and actual salaries for these jobs which are both internally equitable and externally competitive.

By various schemes, most programs are able to set up these relationships to cover a wide spectrum of jobs and to permit managers to administer salaries fairly. In most cases, the system is self-sustaining and self-correcting. Whether the jobs are clearly defined line jobs or less distinct jobs with intangible content, ranges can be reviewed and changes made to maintain an up-to-date and work-able system.

Unfortunately, the job market never stands still. Career patterns of indi-viduals vary widely. Therefore, situations arise which cannot be adequately fulfilled by normal application of the rules and procedures of the program. Most of these problems can be solved if the program is built on understanding and has a built-in flexibility to allow variations. Such variations, however, should stand the test of "good common sense" and should not strain the credi-bility of the program merely to take care of special interests or petty differences of opinion.

chapter 46

Executive Financial Counseling

HAROLD N. CHADWICK   *Manager, Executive Financial Counseling Service, Edward N. Hay & Associates, Philadelphia, Pennsylvania*

CARL S. WEBBER   *Senior Principal, Edward N. Hay & Associates, Philadelphia, Pennsylvania*

Men usually start their working careers with relatively little in the way of financial assets. As they progress, their earnings tend to increase and, through a number of asset accumulation programs, they begin to build an estate. The most common forms of these savings include: cash savings in checking and savings accounts, equity in a residence, increasing cash values of insurance policies, the acquisition of securities, and, of course, the purchase of all those personal effects which, while not essential to life, make it more agreeable.

As time goes on and the man becomes older, it becomes appropriate for him to consider what portion of his assets will be needed to provide income for himself and his family when his working days are ended and what balance, if any, may be left for the benefit of his heirs. In many cases, his economic needs in retirement will be met by a company pension, social security payments, income from his income-producing investments, and the spending of his capital, should the need arise.

In the course of this human economic history, there are a number of useful steps which are commonly taken to ensure the achievement of the man's objectives. For example, in his earlier years some form of almost instant protection is needed to provide income for his wife and children should he become disabled or die before he is able to acquire sufficient working assets to generate replacement income. This problem is customarily met by the purchase of insurance. The man's overall investment program is usually designed to maximize asset growth consistent with reasonable protection against adverse economic developments. This requires a sound balance of liquidity, safety, and growth potential.

While taxation in its multifarious forms appears to be an inescapable concomitant of the exquisite benefits which we derive from participating in a highly organized society, taxation remains one of the principal obstacles to the successful accomplishment of the pattern of asset accumulation and disbursement described above. There are taxes on incomes, taxes on gifts, inheritance and estate taxes, and, of course, an endless variety of taxes relating to the sale and use of real and personal property. It is clear that any asset acquisition pattern which tends more to minimize the incidence of these forms of taxation would be the more successful.

In response to the challenges of various tax laws, a great variety of compensation patterns have been developed, including, among the most noteworthy, the use of various forms of stock options, restricted stock, phantom stock, and deferred income arrangements. And, in response to their development, the Treasury has designed further tax laws impairing their use. And so the game has continued, providing the spectacle of a kind of battle of economic wits between unenthusiastic, but imaginative, taxpayers and ever more tortuously effective tax collectors.

The result of this state of affairs is that the United States, for example, has what is probably one of the most complex set of tax laws in the civilized world. Indeed, for almost any given situation there are a multitude of exceptions and variations. A firm grasp of all the ins and outs of tax law is not granted to many mortals; in all candor, the laws of taxation are not among the most intriguing and compelling of reading materials, and by and large, only those who are professionally afflicted with the need to understand some part of them make it a point to do so.

To whom, then, may the man busy in the course of his working career usefully turn for advice and guidance? In practice, as might be expected, he is forced to rely upon those who have an economic interest in the provision of such counsel—for example, those who sell insurance, those who provide legal services, and/or those who derive an economic benefit from the construction and sale of various investment opportunities of whatever nature. Also, there are often experts in charge of the compensation practices of the company for which the man works, and, while their primary concern is to ensure that their company's compensation practice is internally equitable and externally competitive, they are also heavily involved in the development and implementation of many fringe benefit programs which, besides being advantageous to employees, also, because of their various tax consequences, are beneficial to the company and its stockholders.

The man himself, who is usually very busy working hard (and, we hope, becoming successful), is certainly too busy to devote much time to identifying and learning the multitude of facts and figures needed for the suitable and effective planning of all his financial affairs. Further, it is quite probable that this kind of activity will not be much to his liking and, almost by definition, he is just not going to be knowledgeable enough in the various financial, tax, and legal areas concerned to do a good job for himself.

It is in response to these obvious needs that the role of financial counseling has evolved: to put together all of the disparate elements of expertise necessary for effective life and estate planning. In this sense, a financial counselor must learn all that he appropriately should about a client's finances and his personal objectives. From the client's employer, if there be one, he should obtain necessary data on compensation, benefits, and retirement plans and other information that has a bearing on the client's financial standing. He must act as the catalyst and the coordinator of a team made up of the client's lawyer, his insurance counselor, his investment broker, his tax accountant, and similar specialists whose experience and in-depth knowledge are used to refine and carry out the overall program.

In the area of compensation, the counselor might well advise the client regarding restructuring the amounts and percentages of his base salary, his company-paid insurance, his deferred-compensation arrangements, his holdings of company stock, or his contributions to the firm's retirement plan(s).

With regard to estate planning, recommendations might be appropriate regarding the establishment or updating of wills, the setting up of trusts, the review of non-company-related life insurance programs, and the computation of personal tax projections. Working together with the client, and on the basis of his objectives and personal preferences, the counselor should develop capital building programs, not in fine detail, but with regard to such basics as the appropriate balance between risks and categories of securities investments and, if appropriate, the coordination and organization of the client's venture enterprises, tax shelter investments, etc.

One of the most important facts to be noted about effective financial counseling is that it must be individualized and personal in nature. For example, the client's family structure has a very strong influence upon his estate planning desires and requirements. His marital status, the number and ages of his children and their educational programs, the nature and number of any other dependents—elderly parents, in-laws, or minors—and the health of these parties are all significant. Is the client on good terms with his children? Does he feel any obligation to leave them with more than a token inheritance, or does he place a strong personal value upon the building up and transmittal of a significant financial estate to them? Is the client's spouse capable of managing an income-producing estate, and even if she is, should she be burdened with it? The answers to these questions are obviously highly idiosyncratic: there will be as many different views as there are clients.

Beyond these considerations, clients' economic situations will vary greatly: some may have a relatively large net worth with a relatively small current income; others may have negligible current net worth but a very large income. Some clients, through either good planning or good fortune, may be the recipients of a great deal of income which takes advantage of certain "tax umbrellas" such as oil depletion allowances, depreciation on certain real estate holdings, etc.

The financial counselor's basic function is to sort out all of the facts relating to the subject and to determine the extent to which they offer a reasonable prospect of fulfilling his life and death objectives, and to the extent that they do not, to suggest general steps by which they may more readily do so.

There are a number of things that financial counseling cannot and should not attempt to do: foremost among these is the practice of the professions of law and accounting. Financial counseling is, rather, the painting of a picture with a broad brush by an artist or, more appropriately, a team of artists acting in concert and who have expertise in all of the relevant subfunctions of which they speak. On the positive side, the financial counselors should be able to offer advice and guidance not only to their client and his professional team of lawyers, accountants, investment counselors, etc., but to the client's employer as well regarding the most suitable and appropriate compensation mix which the company itself might more profitably offer its top-level employees. In bringing together facts, functions, and knowledge in the diverse areas of personal income, gift and estate planning, and taxation and in relating them to various investment alternatives and to employment compensation patterns, financial counseling provides the busy working executive with the best possible guidance for the arrangement and planning of his life program of asset acquisition and distribution.

This is not to imply that this large and complex task, once done, is done forever. All of the circumstances which enter into the kinds of decisions described above are in a constant state of flux. Net worth changes in nature and size, as do the income pattern and the family structure. Because of this, the program and pattern developed by financial counseling should be carefully reviewed and audited on at least an annual basis and, of course, whenever significant changes occur. In a complex world, where all is in a state of change, no such financial plans may be regarded as immutable; the careful and timely modification of the individual's plans and programs to adapt them to changing circumstances offers, however, the best opportunity the individual has of attaining his objectives.

Part 9

The Compensation Program in Action

chapter 47

The Role of
the Compensation Manager

JAMES E. McELWAIN *Director, Compensation, National Cash Register Company, Dayton, Ohio*

Previous sections have discussed the principles, approaches, techniques, and procedures pertinent to the compensation field. It is at the level of the compensation manager that these various aspects are brought together to create a coherent whole—a coherent whole which must be tailored to the specific organization and the particular personnel serviced.

It is clear, for example, in the smaller company that a compensation function as such may not exist or be required as a distinct, specialized activity. Normally, compensation will be one of the many "hats" that a personnel manager who is a generalist will wear. Likewise, in the smaller company the service, sophistication, and formal system required are typically less. The same principles of internal equity between jobs, external competitiveness for jobs, individualized pay for performance, and so forth, continue to be applicable. However, because of its small size, it is likely that the company's individual jobs are known and understood by the line management in greater detail than is possible in a company with many divisions, many products, and large or far-flung operations. Less effort is required in job description; and similarly, job measurement (or job evaluation) to achieve internal equity can be approached more directly, since the number and type of internal relationships are fewer and more readily identifiable. In a word, under these conditions, line management is itself in a position to perform more of the compensation responsibilities, with less reliance on "system" and service from the specialist organization.

The compensation role in the smaller firm provides a good perspective from which to view the compensation manager's function in general, the point being that compensation is basically and principally a line management responsibility. This conditions the thrust or orientation of the compensation function under every set of circumstances. The corollary is that the compensation function exists to facilitate sound line management decisions concerning the relative worth of jobs and, in turn, the worth of individual performance and contribution compared with the job. The aim is to develop sufficient system, policy, and procedure to facilitate sound line management decisions—with the emphasis on line management decisions. As with any staff or service function, the tendency which is ever present, and the risk which is to be guarded against, is that of providing more system or policy than is necessary—the tendency to get involved in technique, methodology, and system to the point where these take on a life of their own independent of and well beyond the intended or required purpose.

This is a fundamental point. In the final analysis, the compensation function is a facilitating role. It is the centralization in a specialist organization of specific planning and control activities to meet the need for direction and coordination beyond that which is likely or possible if left entirely to each individual supervisor. On the other hand, each supervisor must be held accountable for accomplishing the work under his purview, and concomitantly, he must have the authority to secure, measure, and compensate performance and contribution accordingly. To the degree that the supervisor's authority is diluted or diminished in this area (as in others) his function and authority as a supervisor, in the eyes of his subordinates, are undermined.

This leads to another important, but sometimes overlooked, point about the compensation manager. Pay is the most basic and significant representation of the overall employment relationship of each individual. Additionally, the matter of pay implies "worth." Consequently, by nature this matter militates against system or centralization. It can be said that the company's compensation plan or compensation system is in reality determined and materialized at the point of the specific interaction of its management and the individual employee in the tens, or hundreds, or thousands of individual interfaces which take place over time. It is at that point that the company's compensation posture is translated into an individually meaningful context for better or worse.

It is all too easy for the compensation manager to veer from this perspective in discharging his responsibilities. It is all too easy to assume that the system or plan of classification, evaluation, and pay has a significance, or in fact an existence, apart from its application. The fact remains that the individual generally understands, interprets, evaluates, and judges the company posture on the matter of compensation only in terms of its application to him. The compensation manager therefore must guard against the assumption that the compensation system or salary plan is itself good or bad; that the plan itself will or will not accomplish something; that what the company needs is "system A" instead of "system B." This danger is equally likely if the line manager comes to depend on and expect the plan to do the job.

Thus, compensation is relevant only to the individual, and he judges the system according to the compensation decisions which affect him. The compensation plan is little more and little better than its actual use case by case. In view of this, the compensation manager's chief responsibility is to prepare each line manager to perform his compensation responsibilities most effectively. Techniques and systems do not by themselves provide the line manager with the tools to do the compensation job. Reliance on technique often leads to blind application of policy and substantial efforts to fit the man to the system, rather than translating the policy meaningfully with respect to the individual for his services performed.

What has been written to this point should not be interpreted as denigrating the importance and necessary contribution of the compensation manager. The intent is merely to place the role and function in a proper perspective as a basic starting point. We begin from that point because the importance of the matter of compensation needs relatively little emphasis. It is generally quite evident in its own right. The importance of pay in the operation of the total economy; the fact that the largest single component of national income is wages and salaries; the fact that in many businesses the largest single cost item is wages and salaries; the fact that among the most important decisions a company makes are those which will or will not afford it the opportunity to attract, retain, and motivate the people required to accomplish its objectives; the fact that pay decisions are remarkably complex in their elements and so far-reaching in their effects—all of these highlight the critical need for attention, expertise, and rational system, which are the substance of the compensation manager's role.

EVOLUTION OF THE COMPENSATION ROLE

The compensation function has emerged rather recently in business history in response to the growing size and complexity of business organizations. Because of its recent vintage, relatively little is understood generally of the role or functions of the compensation manager except by those closely associated with the activity. For the same reason, the compensation role as practiced in different companies will vary significantly in content and impact. Also, the speed with which the problems have emerged and the degree of change which has occurred have created a situation where the tools, techniques, and solutions have hardly been able to keep pace. For these and other reasons, the nature and scope of the compensation function vary from company to company. The compensation manager may simply take care of clerical functions—organizing and maintaining pay records; or he may have technical responsibilities—classification, grading, and surveying; or he may advise top management on strategic matters of policy dealing with human resources and labor economics.

Viewed from an historical perspective, the compensation role might be described as having evolved through three major stages. Any given organization might be, and might by design remain, at any of the three stages.

The first stage might be described as the records or information orientation. In this stage, one finds a centralization of pay data—data concerning base salaries, increases awarded, employee pay groupings, and so forth. The primary thrust is statistical, and the impact is related to the availability and reporting of information for analysis and decision. Often, and quite naturally, this phase leads to a control orientation, since the data generated and reported are typically put to that use by the management serviced.

The second stage might be described as the survey orientation. By utilizing the data available within the organization as a base for comparison, attention begins to be directed to the outside labor market. However, to ensure that the jobs surveyed are comparable with jobs in the organization, it becomes increasingly necessary to develop groupings or classifications of like activities and jobs similar to those in other organizations. The thrust at this point is often to build an internal structure (or microstructure) within the firm which will reflect or conform to the assumed external labor market (or macrostructure). At this stage, the limited informational and control orientation is exceeded and the service begins to take on an advisory orientation.

The third stage is, it would seem fair to say, one to which relatively few organizations have presently evolved, and then only to varying degrees. This stage might be described as the integrated professional compensation role. This is the stage where the function becomes one of explicit policy development, which includes elements of planning and control. It is this stage which seems most reasonable to treat and elaborate upon in any effort to define the role of the compensation manager.

Before proceeding in that effort, it might be worthwhile to note the implications of the evolution described above. It might be said that there is a pattern of evolution of staff roles which is applicable more or less in all cases. The emergence of the compensation function is but one example. When this pattern is considered from the point of view of responsibility and impact, there emerge what might be described as "plateaus of authority." There appear to be not only a chronological but also a natural progression from the "informational or recording plateau" to the "advisory plateau" and thence to the "policy plateau." There is, of course, a final plateau where the policy plateau is exceeded and actual operational decisions emerge. It is at this point that staff in effect becomes line. Although that final plateau may be necessary and desirable in certain types of activity because of an unusually critical need for control or because of the sophistication of technology, it would seem that in matters of human resources this last stage is generally not advisable and should be consciously avoided. This is particularly true in our view of the compensation function.

THE INTEGRATED PROFESSIONAL ROLE

As visualized here, the compensation manager functions at the "policy plateau," with considerable emphasis on planning and control. This role is integrated in the sense that it necessarily relies upon and welds together the theories, facts, discoveries, principles, and considerations of many allied fields and disciplines. It integrates these in arriving at sound, meaningful, and effective policy recommendations across a broad spectrum of compensation matters. It implies anticipating as opposed to simply reacting to existing conditions. It implies assessment of future conditions and their impact on the firm. It implies a depth and a breadth of analysis and action which go beyond studying the labor market, collective bargaining, and applying standard techniques. The compensation role as it functions in this context is multifaceted and, as such, will be discussed below as it relates to labor economics, organization theory, behavioral science, social science, and the total personnel function.

There is often some feeling of guilt or embarrassment in discussing the relationship between compensation and these disciplines—possibly because it has been suggested on occasion by members of those professions that compensation practitioners engage in the superficial and shallow pursuit of each of these disciplines. There is no doubt some truth to this. On the other hand, several facts remain: the compensation manager is not likely to be or become an expert in each field; secondly, the principles and findings of each of these fields have application to compensation issues; thirdly, if such findings are to get beyond the laboratory or theory state, the compensation manager is the one likely to see to that. In using theory to develop a practical working system in a real organizational environment, the compensation manager must deal with and relate such factors as cost of labor to price of services offered; the dynamics of organization design to relative job worth; the psychology of individual human needs to compensation rewards; and subtle institutional forces and changing social patterns, both internal and external to the organization, to appropriate monetary treatment.   Finally, he must consider the total mix of compensation in all of its elements, since no aspect of the employment relationship is entirely divorced from the matter of compensation (hours of work, seniority, transfer and promotion, perquisites, etc.).   As the words "practical working system" imply, compensation management is a double-edged sword: just as important as the dictums of his profession and the disciplines on which these are based is the need to identify and respect the peculiar mores and value system of his organization.

The Compensation Manager and Labor Economics.   A substantial portion of compensation responsibilities is related to labor economics, an area emphasized in the survey orientation.   Although compensation is now recognized as encompassing a good deal more, it still deals with the basic economic issue of setting a price for a factor of production.   From the employer's point of view, compensation must be treated as a cost which is associated with units of production. From the employee's point of view, compensation is a price which he establishes for offering his services.   Thus we have the concept of a labor market with the dynamic tension of supply and demand at work.

The compensation manager must first identify that segment of the labor market in which the firm deals both directly and indirectly; then he must measure and monitor as precisely as possible price fluctuations and movements as they occur.   If the pay level is too low relative to that labor market, the firm is likely to fail in attracting and retaining human resources of the proper number and quality.   If it is too high, the competitive position of the firm in terms of its product cost and selling price is likely to deteriorate.   Primary responsibility for the instrumentation which enables the firm to identify and maintain this delicate balance rests with the compensation manager.   This is one key and primary role.

This is not to imply, as is often assumed, that the labor market is in any sense a simple or perfect market.   Quite the contrary.   The problems of identifying and measuring the competition are substantial, and most of the present approaches are not adequate to the task.   The typical approach of identifying market practice on the basis of job title or a sketchy job description is hardly precise and less than satisfactory at best.   It makes basic assumptions concerning job comparability which are often subject to serious question.   Thus, for example, a nationally published survey recently reporting on salaries of EDP occupations showed quite astonishingly that the job identified and described as "director of EDP" ranged from a reported low salary of slightly more than $100 per week to a high salary of over $500 per week—a 500 percent range.   An average was calculated including these extremes.   This same survey showed the high salary reported for the junior keypunch operator as higher than the low salary for the "director of EDP" classification.   Although this type of market data makes interesting reading, the compensation manager must develop and use substantially more refined measurement techniques to provide the basis for critical decisions on pay policy.

The labor market is imperfect in many additional respects.   Not only is the employer's knowledge of the market less than perfect, but the employee offering his services is likely to experience even greater difficulty in determining the basis for establishing a price for his services.   Furthermore, there are traditional group relationships which tend to disregard the realities of supply and demand and collective bargaining—which in some cases is but remotely related to basic market factors. Beyond these, and possibly of more fundamental significance, is a recent trend which appears to discount the basic concept of a labor market —for example, a trend to have pay levels related to living costs, implying the concept of compensation based on need rather than on the type, level, or availability of work performed.

The compensation manager then must provide the firm with the tools necessary to maintain that precarious balance between a compensation level high enough to compete for needed human resources and low enough to allow the company to be profitable.

The Compensation Manager and Organization.   A sound compensation program must begin with and build from the work performed.   The nature of business organization is to take that work and segment and slice it into manageable elements which can be performed individually while being integrated toward a common objective.   Although certain basic organization principles are commonly followed, the division of work and the design of jobs in an organization are uniquely a function of the particular product or service it supplies, the specific skills and resources available, and the particular management style.   Further, since these factors are continually changing, the organization itself is constantly in the process of adapting and rearranging its design to accommodate and reflect these shifting requirements.   Occasionally, and at specific points, the organization is formally realigned.   However, more subtle and less evident shifts are continually in process as the organization acts and reacts over time.

Compensation, if it is to be meaningful, must relate to what people do, and what they do is intimately tied to the unique organization of work.   Thus, the compensation manager must have a thorough understanding of his organization's structure; a compensation program that is not grounded in the realities of organization relationships will be nothing but a paper program.

The compensation manager must ensure that the classification and compensation system is uniquely fitted to and reflective of the organization of work.   Of course, organization is inherently dynamic, and therefore it militates against the static description and classification of work; it is therefore essential to recognize that any such classification program is constantly dying.   It can maintain its vitality, usefulness, and meaning only to the degree that the compensation role is sensitive to the organization process.

Just as the matter and manner of compensation may encourage or discourage effective individual performance, the same is true of organization in terms of the division of work and job design.   The compensation manager must ensure that the factors of pay are selected and applied in such a manner as to facilitate effective organization patterns and to discourage ineffective patterns—e.g., under- or over-specialization, empire building, and the like.

The Compensation Manager and Behavioral Science.   Many behavioral scientists feel that the chief responsibility of the compensation manager is to spread dissatisfaction as evenly as possible throughout the organization.   There is possibly some element of truth in this viewpoint.   Recently a good deal has become known about the place of compensation in the employment phenomenon and its effect on individual behavior.   Enormously more has been hypothesized.   Although there is not complete agreement as to the nature and degree of the effect of pay on individual employee behavior, the very concept of pay for services performed inherently links the two.

The compensation manager must provide a compensation framework which positively reinforces effective performance and, equally important, discourages ineffective performance.   As was stated earlier, however, the compensation program itself does not accomplish this.   The proper and effective relationship of pay to performance is accomplished only by the line manager applying the compensation framework case by case in a highly individualized and personal setting.

In dealing with the matter of compensation and individual behavior, it would appear that historically the compensation practitioner has been concerned primarily with one aspect of motivation—the motivation to participate based on a competitive pay practice. Although the motivation to work in order to earn money is basic and important, equal attention should be given to pay in terms of its effect on the motivation to perform and the motivation to develop.

Similarly, the compensation manager must create and foster recognition of the fact that compensation in the work environment is enormously more than a matter of absolute dollars of purchasing power to the employees. It is a basic representation of the overall employment relationship. To state this another way, compensation, in addition to being a medium of exchange, is a symbol of how the firm views the employee's effort, performance, contribution, and potential. This is why very small differences or increments of pay take on a seemingly disproportionate significance.

The tendency to deemphasize compensation as a factor in motivation and satisfaction and to emphasize other factors, such as achievement and recognition, must take into account the fact that compensation is a symbol of these—it is part of the language (the most tangible part) which confirms, reaffirms, or denies these for the individual. The compensation manager's job, therefore, is to create an awareness and sensitivity to the behavioral implication of compensation and to ensure a compensation system which accommodates these considerations.

The Compensation Manager and Social Science. The compensation role has deep overtones in the matter of social patterns. In a mobile society and one which is economically advanced, social levels are strongly related to economic factors, notably employment income. The compensation manager must be sensitive to the social implications of compensation while at the same time being attuned to the implications of changing social patterns relative to compensation. Specific factors to be considered in this area include: the changing nature and makeup of the work force; the generally higher educational level; the emergence of the "knowledge workers" and the decreasing demand for raw labor; the effect of economic advances and affluence on the work relationship and motivation; increasing professionalism and its implications of group affiliation or scientific affiliation as a dimension additional to that of employer affiliation.

These changing social patterns will influence the role of compensation and the makeup of and approach to compensation much as did the emergence of collective bargaining in the past.

In addition to the changing social patterns external to the firm, the internal social system is of equal significance to the compensation practitioner. The firm is itself a complex of social institutions and groups striving to maintain traditional relationships in some cases or to secure more favorable relationships in others. These phenomena are closely associated and interrelated with the matter of organizational dynamics mentioned previously. As products change, product mix shifts, technologies disappear or emerge, organizational format shifts, and new authority relationships develop, the nature of the work of individuals, occupations, and groups is affected and their relative responsibility, impact, and contribution are modified accordingly. A compensation program which is not attuned to such matters or is not adapted to accommodate them will not remain internally equitable or externally competitive very long.

The Compensation Manager and the Total Personnel Function. The compensation role is characteristically found in the personnel or industrial relations organization in most large companies. This appears to be the case (despite the significant financial aspects of the function) because it deals primarily with the classification, evaluation, and pay treatment of the firm's human resources. Since no aspect of the employment relationship is entirely separate from compensation, the compensation manager must work closely with the various other personnel activities. The job description and job classification become a basic input and point of reference for the activities of the other personnel functions. Let us review the compensation manager's role as it relates to the other more typical personnel functions.

The *employment or placement activity* and the compensation activity require extremely close interaction. On the one hand, the employment function will rely directly upon job description and job specification to aid in the identification of potentially qualified employees. On the other hand, the employment function, since it is dealing daily in the labor market, can be a source of direct and immediate feedback to the compensation function concerning the competitiveness of the company's compensation posture. It will be recognized, however, that the difference in missions of these two activities means they often will be at variance. This is the case because the compensation function—through the establishment of wage or salary ranges—in effect places limitations upon that portion of the potential labor market which is actually eligible for employment with the firm. These constraints can easily be viewed by the employment function as obstacles to the accomplishment of its mission.

Compensation is also closely related to the *organization planning* activity—so much so that often these functions are found in combination. Sound, explicit, clearly delineated organization is essential to proper and equitable compensation. Difficulties in job description and job evaluation are often symptomatic of deficiencies or confusion in organization and job design. Similarly, the job description and job evaluation processes elucidate overlaps or gaps in organizational responsibility. The compensation manager can function effectively only when this association is close and continuing.

The compensation manager must also work closely with the *labor relations* or *employee relations* function. The labor relations activity is found primarily in those companies which operate under a labor agreement with a union. Of the bargainable items (wages, hours, and working conditions) the so-called economic issues—i.e., primarily wages—are most often the subject of the greatest contention and strife. A sound, well-conceived, explicitly defined, and properly administered compensation program is a prerequisite to labor harmony. Interestingly, although management and union groups often differ dramatically on other issues, both parties recognize and concur on the need to establish a reasonably formal and explicit basis for satisfying the requirement of internal equity and fairness. Where this is done effectively, a sound and workable framework exists for resolving differences on the key issue of wages. The compensation manager's role in labor relations is therefore quite critical, and he will normally function as either the principal representative or a key participant in the resolution of economic issues.

SUMMARY

This chapter has attempted to define the main characteristics of the compensation manager's role. Our description has projected the role as it might be performed in a highly professional context and typically in a large and complex organizational environment. This should allow for variations, of course, where size or other requirements dictate the need for expansion or contraction of the compensation function to meet particular circumstances.

In attempting to put it all together, the compensation manager's role might be summarized as follows: to perform a staff service which provides line management with a policy framework and a practical working system of total compensation which satisfies the economic, organizational, human, and social realities of the particular firm, its labor market, and its employees and which achieves necessary central control of labor costs, while reserving as fully as possible the operational decisions on individual compensation to line management.

chapter 48

Keeping the Compensation Program up to Date

W. O. LORY   *General Manager, Personnel Services, Aluminum Company of America, Pittsburgh, Pennsylvania*

JAMES H. DAVIS   *Manager, Organization & Compensation, Aluminum Company of America, Pittsburgh, Pennsylvania*

An effective corporate compensation program depends upon a compensation philosophy or state of mind as well as good administrative procedures. There are three different states of mind that produce certain physical and organizational structures. The first might be called "pyramid" thinking. The objective of the architects who built the pyramids was to construct a monument. No thought was given to possible renovation, updating, or modernization.

The management of a professional baseball team is representative of the second state of mind. Baseball teams have the same number of players from year to year. The manager's objective is to replace aging or less effective players with younger, more effective players. The team members still play the same positions and the manager's essential task is to improve on individual performance.

There is a third state of mind—response to changing conditions—that is illustrated by a homeowner's response to recent legislation on pollution control. It is now common in many communities to prohibit the burning of leaves and rubbish by homeowners. This requires the homeowner to do something different from what he used to do when the leaves fall, and it provides an opportunity to offer a new solution. One of the responses to that need has been the sale of polyethylene bags for leaves and refuse. Thus, a market enjoys new growth in response to a new set of conditions.

Compensation history has been dominated by pyramid thinking. This was a natural, but little recognized, outgrowth of poorly conceived compensation programs. The objective of most compensation programs was to establish or to administer relationships. It became increasingly clear that paying wages and salaries, particularly to large groups of people, without adequately devised and controlled programs, generally produced a variety of unsatisfactory situations. Random rates were common in the past; people doing the same work were paid different amounts, often for obscure and indefensible reasons. Favoritism was a charge frequently laid to salary and wage administration. High turnover of employees has often been due to poor understanding of adequate compensation practices or, indeed, to poor practices in spite of adequate understanding.

It was assumed that such problems could be relieved by adapting or revising the compensation program. The question of pay increases based on seniority versus pay increases for greater accountability has been long debated. Only recently has the weight of opinion swung in favor of accountability.

Compensation practice rests on a fundamental premise that the man who pays is the boss. A proprietor naturally and frequently resists sharing or explaining the compensation program because he recognizes this fundamental principle. In corporations, managers and administrators often vie for authority for determining pay because they recognize that it provides a base for their own accountability. In this atmosphere, inequities are often caused by an owner's or manager's style of compensation practice.

Undue secrecy or inadequate communication makes it difficult to convince employees they are properly paid. Whatever its cause, this lack of understanding has been a dominant producer of employee unrest, as expressed at the bargaining table, in management counsel, or in the rate of employee resignation. Contributing to the lack of understanding was the great tendency of the boss to delegate only what he did not want to do himself, usually the mechanical part of the compensation program. This has produced a generation of salary administrators dominated by pyramid thinking.

Pyramid thinking merely exchanges old problems for new ones and, indeed, ignores many identifiable problems. It produces a concern expressed by managers and employees alike that their jobs, careers, and compensation are boxed in by a job description, a salary scale, or a promotional table insensitive to their contributions.

Pyramid thinking does not easily adjust to economic changes, such as rises in the cost of living and inflation. It is insensitive to the change in people and jobs. It does not respond to organizational change, so common in industry today. It persists in tolerating and reinforcing the problems that the first mechanical salary administration program was supposed to relieve. Thus we conclude that something must be added to the pyramid approach.

Owners, executives, and compensation managers with baseball mentalities strive to keep the compensation program as good today as it was yesterday. This calls for diligent effort to maintain and administer yesterday's programs to achieve credible answers to today's problems. Obviously, job descriptions, job performance ratings, and job values must be current or this objective cannot be achieved. The implication is that yesterday's compensation program must be changed to keep pace with changes in the corporate environment. Included in such changes would be considerations of internal as well as external factors, such as company growth, diversification, organizational realignment, and governmental and legal regulations, in addition to the variable competitive relationships inherent in the marketplace. Yesterday's compensation program will not work today unless it has been revitalized by a subtle infusion of problem-solving modifications.

Owners, executives, and compensation managers should have a "smoke control" mentality to make programs do tomorrow what they did not have to do today. This suggests anticipating change and successfully planning the implementation of such changes. Assuming that the existing compensation plan is a good one, change should not be made lightly or capriciously. Dramatic changes must be either carefully planned for presentation to managers and employees or avoided altogether, because if they are not adequately explained, the reaction could be opposite to the desired effect. If dramatic changes are instituted, employees may reason that the previous system must have been pretty bad. Thus, proposed revisions must be pretested and explained carefully to ensure their being accepted and supported wholeheartedly by the management groups responsible for implementing them.

POLICY CONSIDERATIONS IN MAINTAINING THE PROGRAM

With state of mind identified and philosophy established for the compensation program, several factors are critical to maintaining it in an up-to-date condition.

Policy Approval. This fundamental requirement must exist before any meaningful compensation program can be maintained. History is full of the wreckage of compensation programs where the policy of the organization did not provide the guidance and support that could sustain the program under stress.

Competitive Position. A principal objective of a compensation program is to define the market in which a company intends to compete. For example, if a company chooses to compete with the top 25 percent of national industrial manufacturing companies, it provides itself a broad base with which to compare its own practice. Or, if it intends to compete with the retail stores of a particular geographical marketing area, it is provided a definable measure of comparison.

Promotion policy is a key factor in determining competitive objectives. The company that promotes from within must develop a compensation program that provides orderly progression and supportable differentials between jobs. The company that routinely hires for assignments at all levels has a different kind of hiring and compensating objective.

The transfer of employees also requires constant attention to the differences between a locally competitive and a nationally competitive program. This becomes more important if the company contemplates transferring people between countries.

Philosophy. The salary program is a management tool and, as such, must be designed to reflect overall corporate philosophy and the policies which embody that philosophy. Those responsible for corporate or institutional compensation programs should be responsible for devising or revising objectives which become part of approved policy. Objectives not in tune with approved policy are wasted effort. Policy not implemented by goal setting and the establishment of achievable objectives becomes so much verbiage.

PROCEDURAL MEANS OF MAINTAINING THE PROGRAM

The manager of compensation must be accountable for providing job descriptions that will meet the needs of the organization. Also, he must have accountability for approving the evaluation of all positions covered under the various evaluation plans of the company and for establishing the salary policy lines for nonbargaining employees.

Pay Relationships between Bargaining and Nonbargaining Employees. It is also important, for purposes of internal equity, that the compensation manager be involved in any bargaining to establish wage lines.   In the typical industrial company with a unionized hourly work force, the bargained agreement provides the basis of compensation for the existing hierarchy of hourly jobs.   These jobs represent a base-compensation group with which certain other similar, related, and associated personnel groups have logical and/or historical salary relationships.   By virtue of these relationships, salary structures for such personnel groups should be updated in a manner which recognizes equity in relation to the bargaining unit.   Comparison with hourly compensation is particularly important in establishing structures for *nonexempt salaried personnel* and *supervisory personnel:*

1. *Nonexempt Personnel:*   This is usually a nonbargaining group performing secretarial, clerical, or routine technical work and having job value levels corresponding to the hourly work force.   In businesses that do not have an hourly work force, the nonexempt salary structure is usually updated according to community wage practices as determined by local salary surveys.

2. *Supervisory Personnel:*   This group normally includes the direct supervisors of hourly and nonexempt salaried personnel.   Adequate salary differentials between supervisors and those supervised are required.   Typical practice in industrial organizations is to maintain differentials ranging from 15 to 25 percent.

Employee Performance Results.   Accurate and current evaluations of employee performance are essential to a well-ordered, up-to-date salary program.   This input is most difficult to achieve because it requires perceptive and unbiased managerial effort to obtain complete and useful results.   At the very least, each employee's performance should be appraised at the time salary action is being considered and as often as practical for each individual case.

Participation in Maintaining the Program.   How up to date a compensation program is will depend a great deal on who is involved in maintaining it.

The salary administrator or compensation manager can be a primary force in carrying out policy, meeting objectives, and monitoring the use of the compensation tools described above.   He can do this unilaterally to assure that the program is effective and up to date; if this approach is taken, the program's success will depend heavily on the salary administrator's own experience and his acceptance by other managers.

The department head can have the entire responsibility for evaluating people and administering salaries in his department in much the same way as the proprietor did in smaller and less complex situations in the past.   This plan has the advantage of providing the department head with some of the tools of the proprietor, but it has a conspicuous defect—which is magnified in a large organization—of creating or at least permitting wide variations between departments in the relationship of pay and contribution.

One device designed to give the compensation program the appearance or substance of top-level concern is the review of jobs, evaluations, and salaries by a *blue-ribbon committee* of key company executives.   In a small organization this is a proper role for a group of executives who have direct knowledge of the people and positions concerned.   In a large, multilocation organization the top executives often have little contact with the jobs or the incumbents.   Here it is a time-consuming artifice which may provide the illusion of concern by top management but very often results in the domination of the committee's action by one or another of its members.

A series of committees, each made up of managers in a specific area of the business (for example, a committee of sales managers), may be charged with the responsibility for maintaining the compensation program in their respective areas. This approach tends to allay some of the problems caused by having a single manager perform these functions, but the relief provided is simply one of degree. Although all the departments in the same area of the business will be in step with each other, there is still the risk that whole areas will be out of step with the rest of the company.

A corporate committee which includes the compensation manager, the manager of the position in question, and others who provide a broad base of experience with the job appears to be the best compromise. Such a committee is usually composed of a small permanent corps plus varying members, and tends to be more responsive to the levels of work being examined. The presence of the manager of the position in question assures him that his jobs are properly considered in relation to others, and the presence of other managers on the committee also assures him that problems in his department are being compared with problems in the other departments. In this arrangement the primary responsibility for results must remain with the compensation manager.

A probable dividend of this participative device is organizationwide communication and understanding of compensation policy and procedures. Also, key managers' firsthand knowledge is carried over to other employees, thus enhancing employees' understanding of the compensation program.

A NECESSARY CATALYST

To all the considerations mentioned in this chapter there should be added a needed catalyst: a generous application of openness, candor, and mutual respect. Those responsible for keeping a compensation program up to date need continuing endorsement of the program and honest feedback from managers who use it. Fairness and impartiality in the administration of a plan are musts even though they will produce unpopular decisions from time to time. For managers to accept these results, as well as more favorable ones, both managers and the compensation organization must recognize that a compensation program is not precise and neither is it controlled by a set of measures outside the tolerance of human judgment. Emphasis should be placed on reasoned usage of the systems involved and a seeking of facts as they exist. When this emphasis is achieved and all parties concerned are willing to review decisions and to amend previous results when new information is obtained or when the situation has changed, a truly responsive compensation plan can come into being and be used as a vital force in the effective management of the enterprise.

chapter 49

Adjusting Wages and Salaries

WILLIAM H. HRABAK *Director, Total Compensation, Owens-Illinois, Inc., Toledo, Ohio*

Many managers and supervisors, when first faced with responsibility for reviewing, recommending, and approving employee pay increases, approach the subject with less than a full understanding of the pertinent considerations involved. Typically, decisions by uninitiated managers are based on oversimplified, subjective, and either overly generous or tightfisted attitudes toward the subject. Allowed to continue, such practice will result in an inequitable, expensive, and generally unsatisfactory salary structure program in the units involved.

Because salary level and salary increase information is currently much more readily available to employees than it has been in the past, inequitable salary administration has a much higher probability of disrupting operations through dissatisfaction of employees with their pay treatment.

Salary increase decisions need not be based on complex analyses. However, there are several critical factors which are pertinent and should be given consideration to produce consistently satisfactory and equitable salary adjustment results.

BASE PAY REVIEWS AND INCREASES

Pay increase judgments should be made with consideration of the specific job level, the individual length of service, the date and amount of the last increase, the pay levels of others on the same or similar jobs within the company, the pay levels of similar jobs within the industry and among other companies normally used for comparisons, and—above all—the performance level and potential of each individual concerned.

How to Determine Amount of Pay Increase. From a purely mechanical standpoint, the amount of a pay increase should be influenced by the date and amount of the last increase, the position of the current salary within the salary range, if used, or the relationship of the present salary to outside salaries for comparable jobs.

With regard to administrative procedures, it is more practical to make salary increases effective at the beginning of a pay period rather than to be encumbered with increases given in the middle of the pay period, which will result in payroll administration complications.

Merit, general, or promotional increases should always be expressed as a percent of salary and adjusted to a weekly, monthly, or annual multiple. For example:

1. A nonexempt accounting clerk earning $5,200 per annum or $100 per week should have a pay increase presented as 7 percent—$7 per week.

2. An exempt supervisor earning $12,000 per annum should have a pay increase presented as 8 percent—$80 per month.

3. A manager earning $25,000 per annum should have a pay increase presented as 10 percent—$2,500 annually.

The amount of the increase should take into account individual performance (this item will be discussed more specifically later) plus the employee's salary history, his position in the range, and his *job level*. Assuming performance to be equal, a pay increase for an employee on a higher-level job with a salary in the lower part of his salary range should normally be higher in percentage but given after a longer interval than for an employee on a lower job level. As employees in higher-level jobs approach their range midpoints or approach a calculated median for the job, the increase percentage should normally be lower, unless economic conditions or other conditions take precedence.

Salary increases should always be made with consideration for the net amount that the employee's paycheck will be increased. In no event should small pay increases be granted where the net increase in paycheck amount will be extremely small or nonexistent. As a general rule of thumb, merit pay increases should be no smaller than 4 or 5 percent. If a manager wishes to recommend a smaller increase, he should consider lengthening the time interval between increases rather than reducing the percentage of increase.

Frequency and Regularity of Review. The frequency of review of an individual employee's pay level should be tied directly to the level of the job involved. Nonexempt jobs, such as clerks, secretaries, and technicians, should be reviewed at least every six to nine months. Exempt jobs, such as first-line supervisors, department heads, salesmen, engineers, exempt technicians, managers, and executives, should be reviewed no less than once each year.

However, a pay review should not automatically guarantee a pay increase. It is rather a process of investigating each individual employee's pay situation to determine whether individual salary pay levels are proper within the context of formal company pay policies, if they exist, or within accepted company pay practices. Also to be considered is the comparison of internal and external pay for similar jobs.

Review of Nonexempt Salaries. Reviews of employees in nonexempt salaried jobs should be made separately from reviews of higher-level exempt jobs.

The review of nonexempt salaries ought to be done with consideration for hourly pay changes experienced in the unit or company (whether the hourly jobs fall under union organization), specific economic conditions (whether the economy is in an inflationary or deflationary period), availability of people to fill nonexempt jobs (which will influence the marketplace), and prevailing salary rates in the particular company or locality. All of these factors have a bearing on pay review considerations at all levels of jobs but have a more profound influence upon nonexempt jobs, in which the incumbents tend to be much less mobile.

Employees in nonexempt jobs are hired locally and normally are not transferred. Therefore, their pay levels should be tied to prevailing salary levels for the specific locality and/or unit in which they work. General pay levels for nonexempt jobs will move in relation to the above-listed factors.

It is difficult to make merit increase judgments for employees in nonexempt jobs because only minor differences in the quality of performance can normally be observed, assuming the employee is performing well enough to remain on the job. Therefore, nonexempt salary increase practices should be more standardized than for jobs at exempt levels.

From a practical standpoint, it is generally agreed that of the two main variables associated with pay increases—the amount of the increase and the frequency of the increase—the latter is the more important consideration for nonexempt jobs. This is especially true for the lower or beginning level of nonexempt jobs. A higher degree of equity and employee goodwill will be created if increases for nonexempt employees are given more frequently, such as at eight- or nine-month intervals, but for smaller percentage amounts.

In some cases, depending upon the sophistication of a company's salary administration program, the more practical approach from an administrative and internal-equity concern would be to grant nonexempt pay increases according to a formalized progressional increase system. A typical salary progression system would be tied to a series of separate salary schedules developed to meet each location's competitive situation, with salaries administered automatically through a series of steps within the salary range for different job levels. For example, if a particular salary range is:

Minimum	Midpoint	Maximum
$400	$500	$600

the progressional steps could be established in $20 increments between the $400 minimum rate and the $500 midpoint rate. The progressional step range would appear as follows:

		$20 steps			
Minimum	1st	2nd	3rd	4th	Midpoint
$400	$420	$440	$460	$480	$500

As an alternative, progressional steps may be established as a constant percentage, for example, (4.5 percent):

		4.5 percent steps			
Minimum	1st	2nd	3rd	4th	Midpoint
$400	$418	$437	$457	$478	$500

The time intervals for administering increases can then be set at any point to conform with general company policy or philosophy. The intervals can be established at six, seven, eight, nine, or 10 months, or some other number of months determined to be competitive and reasonable.

It is important in such a system that the minimum of the progressional range be established as the minimum going rate, below which no incumbent would be paid. However, depending on individual qualifications and rates being paid longer-service employees, a new employee could be started at a step higher than the minimum rate.

The progression in the above example extends only to the midpoint rate, since a midpoint normally represents the company's judgment on its average rate for the job in relation to the local labor market. Thus, no automatic progression system should be carried to the maximum; the range between the midpoint and the maximum should be reserved for merit increases based upon individual ability and continued good performance.

A progressional increase system will avoid or help correct many equity problems and personnel relations difficulties which creep into nonexempt compensation programs. Some major advantages of such a system are that it:

1. Guarantees that each individual's pay is reviewed automatically at periodic intervals. There is no chance that the supervisor may forget or overlook review periods.

2. Ensures that each individual's salary is automatically increased on the scheduled effective dates unless that individual's supervisor countermands the increase by positive action properly substantiated.

3. Guarantees that new employees receive a fair and equitable minimum starting rate without regard for supervisory whims or for attitudes not based on good personnel management or compensation judgments.

4. Assures nonexempt employees of continuous and objective review of their salaries, provided that good job performance continues.

5. Enables employee recruiters and supervisors to clearly define the pay latitudes of specific jobs and the maximum pay potentials available.

6. Permits reduction of administrative detail and realization of cost savings, since this system is less time-consuming and eliminates unnecessary paper work.

Of course, any automatic program has disadvantages, and a nonexempt salary progression system is no exception; however, some can be avoided. The major pitfalls are:

1. Employees who do not deserve increases could receive them automatically under such a system. (This, however, would happen only through inaction on the part of concerned supervisors.)

2. All employees, regardless of performance, would receive the same amount of increase within the same time interval. (This is true only up to the midpoint of the salary range. This system can also be designed to permit a supervisor to delay an increase until the next review period or to advance an exceptional performer two steps within the progression range rather than one step.)

3. This system eliminates individual consideration and the personal contact between employee and supervisor on pay increase matters. (This may be true. However, a thorough examination of most companies will show that the personal pay relationships in a nonexempt area are not as meaningful or as well handled as many supervisors may believe. From a personnel relations standpoint, the improvement in internal equity will far outweigh any loss of so-called "individual" pay treatment.)

In essence, the most important aspects of good nonexempt pay increase administration are uniformity, consistency, frequency, and fairness. These are necessary in order to avoid inequities and assure competitiveness at each local level.

Review of Exempt Salaries below Management Levels. Exempt employees' salaries should also be reviewed in a uniform manner. However, since exempt jobs are not grouped in as narrow a hierarchy as nonexempt jobs, different factors must be considered in making salary increase judgments for different levels of exempt jobs. The lower exempt job hierarchy includes first-line supervisors, beginning salesmen, and junior accountants, while the next level includes senior salesmen, senior engineers, plant superintendents, territory sales supervisors, and accounting and office supervisors.

The traditional concept that the high degree of mobility of exempt personnel makes them part of a national market and that, accordingly, they should be assigned to a single exempt schedule, regardless of the number or diverse locations of company operations, is no longer considered correct by all companies. Individuals in lower-level exempt jobs tend to be hired locally and often remain in the same area. Therefore, these employees tend to compare their status and pay levels with comparable pay levels in their particular area rather than with the national level, of which normally they are not even aware. For example, an exempt junior accountant hired in the New York metropolitan area will tend to remain in the New York metropolitan area and should be paid commensurately with pay levels in that area rather than according to a national average pay schedule for junior accountants. Likewise, a junior accountant in Phoenix, Arizona, should be paid according to the prevailing salary levels in that area. Only in the upper exempt area, where jobs and people are truly mobile and are part of a national market, should salaries be compared with a national schedule. Companies which design their lower exempt schedule to be competitive nationwide will find the schedule to be higher than need be at some locations and lower at other locations.

Frequency and amount of pay increase for exempt employees should also vary with job level. Thus, although all exempt employees should be reviewed at least once a year, salary schedules should have a greater influence on pay increases in the lower exempt levels. Here again, for employees on lower exempt jobs, pay increase factors similar to those mentioned above for nonexempt jobs (union contract pay levels, company and general economic conditions, and, of course, specific comparisons with internal and external pay for similar jobs for each company location) must be considered. For example, in reviewing a first-line shift foreman, consideration must be given to the effect of pay increases granted in the hourly ranks, whether done under union contract or by unilateral company action. In addition, first-line foremen's pay ought to be maintained at a level sufficiently above the group of highest-paid hourly employees supervised to maintain an equitable differential between the different job hierarchies and to avoid pay compression problems. Nothing will defeat pay equity principles quicker than for a first-line foreman to receive total direct income that is not sufficiently above the highest-paid hourly employees he supervises. What is a proper differential will vary somewhat by company and/or industry but should be in a range of not less than 15 to 20 percent.

Pay increases for lower and higher exempt employees should be based on hard-and-fast merit judgments, and each increase should be substantial enough to have a definite motivational impact. For well-paid exempt employees approaching the maximum of their range, it is much better to lengthen the interval between increases to 18, 24, or more months but retain a reasonably high (7 to 10 percent) rate of increase.

It is self-defeating to a salary compensation program to promote a concept of general increases for exempt employees. Automatic annual increases of 4 or 5 percent will not substantially increase the net paycheck amount and will probably have a negative motivational effect on the employees. It is therefore best to review exempt salaries regularly but with the understanding that pay increases should not be automatic, especially in the higher exempt area, and that amounts should be substantial enough to make a significant improvement in individual take-home pay.

Review of Management and Executive Salaries. The review of management and executive salaries in a systematic and professional fashion is a new undertaking on the part of many salary compensation managers. Until very recently, the administration of executive salaries has been considered to fall within the private domain of the company's chief financial officer or chief executive officer. In many cases, companies have maintained separate executive payrolls to protect the "confidentiality" and "uniqueness" of top-level jobs. As a result of the isolation of top executive salary and pay practices in past years, many otherwise successful companies have found that their pay practices in this most important area have been chaotic and inequitable. As a result, more and more companies are coming to realize that good, objective salary administration serves as a valuable management tool in the administration of executive salaries just as it does for salaries at lower levels.

Salary administration for management and executive jobs, however, must reflect the fact that each position at this level is personalized, individual, and unique to itself and unique to the job incumbent. Therefore, in order to maintain equitable and competitive pay levels in the executive job hierarchy, more sophisticated and individualized administrative and job comparison techniques need to be employed.

Executive Job Surveys. The survey, which has been employed in the wage and salary field for many years, has just recently come into its own and gained acceptance by executives as a meaningful management tool. Various consulting firms and industry groups have developed systematic methods of surveying executive positions in order to provide companies with objective and meaningful data from which salary ranges and pay practices may be developed for their top executive employees.

It is most important in determining executive salary ranges and pay practices for a company treasurer, vice president of manufacturing, vice president of sales, personnel director, research director, president, and even chairman of the board to compare these jobs with their counterparts in other companies on the basis of industrial classification, size of company in terms of sales dollars, and even organization structure.

With regard to the latter, it is important in comparing executive jobs to know whether the company is completely decentralized, completely centralized, or divisionalized or operates in a manner which has been described as "controlled decentralization" (i.e., relatively autonomous divisions but with an overall corporate group responsible for developing, implementing, and administering overall policy).

When comparing executive positions, it is most important that company size enter into the picture. If a company's sales are $300 million, its top executive pay practices should be compared with those of other companies of the same size rather than with those of companies which have sales of $50 million or $5 billion.

In addition, it is important to recognize industrial groupings, because in executive compensation some companies have traditional (whether right or wrong) pay practices unique to their particular industry. For example, the automotive industry relies more heavily on bonuses than on base salary. Utilities rely heavily on base salary with very little bonus compensation. Other industries attempt to achieve a balance between base salary and bonus; and still others deliberately pay low salaries but extremely high bonuses in an effort to motivate executives to generate high levels of profit growth.

Also, in surveying executive compensation practices, it is important to look beyond individual job titles, which can be confusing and misleading. For example, the job of a treasurer in one company who reports to a vice president of finance will not be the same job as that of a treasurer in another company who reports to the president or chief executive officer. A sales manager in one company who has no marketing responsibility will not be the same as a sales manager in another company who has accountability for the marketing function.

In addition, it is becoming more important to understand the total compensation package of executives, since this has a bearing upon the base-salary or direct-pay package. Here again, some companies or industries establish high benefit and perquisite programs which may detract from salary levels, while others direct their executive compensation packages to heavy cash payments.

Another important factor to consider when surveying the executive field is the relative availability of executive talent as well as the mobility of this group. Do not base decisions on general top-of-the-iceberg comparisons, but delve as deeply into all compensation, organization, and company-size factors as are necessary to arrive at sound judgments in the executive compensation field.

Actual Executive Salary Pay Practice Guidelines. It is extremely important that a company's executive pay practices be formalized and documented in the same manner as pay practices for other employee groups. This is essential to provide top management and the board of directors with uniform and meaningful guidelines and policies on which to base individual executive salary increase judgments.

A formalized executive compensation program is important for purposes of attracting executive talent from outside the company. It is also an extremely important safeguard in the event that federal wage and salary controls should again be imposed on our economy. When such controls were established in the past, companies which did not have a systematic, formalized executive compensation program found it difficult, embarrassing, and complicated to increase individual executive salaries. Conversely, if a formal, documented program is in existence and working, wage control administrators will accept it as an ongoing means of administering executive salaries.

Executive salaries should be related to a salary range the same as are other salary jobs but with these differences:

1. Salary ranges should be wider than those in effect for other employee groups—at least 50 percent and as high as 66⅔ percent from minimum to maximum.

2. Performance increases should fall within the range of 7½ to 15 percent. The size of the increase is extremely important at this level since a small increase would have either no motivational effect at all or possibly a negative effect since the after-tax dollars would be insignificant in light of the income tax liability at the higher salary levels.

3. The term "merit increase" should not be used for executive salary increases. "Merit" is a term applicable to jobs at lower salary levels. At the executive level, *performance* is the name of the game and needs to be recognized and compensated. However, salary reviews should be made at least once a year for executive employees as they are for other exempt salaried employees.

Executive salaries, as many studies have shown, have not kept pace during the last 20 to 30 years with pay increases received by employees at most other, lower organization levels. This trend, however, does not justify pay increases for executives where the increases are not warranted. It is not uncommon for executives who have reached their top position and the top of their salary range to be passed over for salary increases for as long as three, four, five, or more years without any attached stigma.

A major problem in executive compensation is the case of the younger, fast-rising executive whose salary does not keep pace with his rapid job growth. In these cases, which are not uncommon, it is wise to pay the executive according to established company policies, even though the amount and frequency of the increases appear abnormally high. At the least, his salary should be brought up to minimum within a prescribed period of time as determined practical through good salary administration. There is no logical business reason to underpay a top executive if he truly is charged with the responsibility of the position and is performing the job in an acceptable manner. Below-minimum salaries not only invite dissatisfaction on the job but will tempt the executive to look for greener pastures and make him ripe bait for professional recruiters or "headhunters." This is especially true when executive talent is in great demand. In this same regard, it behooves any company to establish good pay practices for its executive employees, because true executive talent, regardless of the specific function or discipline involved, is readily transferable across company and industry boundaries.

An example for use in the administration of an executive pay increase program is shown in Table 1.

Relationship between Salary Reviews and Peformance Reviews. A definite relationship should exist and be workable between pay increases and employee performance appraisals. Nothing is more exasperating to a salary administrator or an operating manager than to see termination papers processed on an employee for reasons of incompetence when the same employee a month or two earlier had been granted a merit salary increase. This situation, which should not occur in a business organization, happens more often than management would like to believe, primarily because in most companies there is no direct relationship between individual employee performance appraisal and salary appraisal.

Formal appraisal programs have been in effect in some companies for many years but have been operated as separate entities with no relationship to pay practices. Personnel executives are finding, however, that pay practice and personnel appraisal systems must work in concert so that each can be more effective. Many new personnel appraisal programs have been developed and adopted by companies which merge individual performance with individual pay level.

TABLE 1   Salary Increase Guide

	If salary is—		
	Below range minimum	Range minimum to midpoint	Over range midpoint to maximum
1. Salary reviewed at least every......	6 months	12 months	12 months
2. Recommended salary increase range.	5–15%	5–12%	5–10%

It is important that a system linking performance appraisal with salary pay practices begin at the top of the organization, where performance is a truly measurable item, and be extended to all other job levels. Just as many companies have job evaluation plans to evaluate different job families and different job levels, it is important that performance appraisal systems be designed for different job levels. Performance appraisal systems for executives, management, and higher-level exempt jobs should be quantitative, business-goal-oriented, and merged with specific factors measurable in the individual job evaluation. For example, a sales manager can be measured on how well he meets his sales goals within price, quality, and service considerations. In the same sense, a manufacturing manager can be measured on how well he meets his production goal within cost and production efficiency and overall profit considerations. A salesman can be measured on his performance against sales volume goals in relation to price levels and market conditions, consistent with good supervisory support and guidance. Employees on lower-level exempt jobs and nonexempt jobs can be covered by a different appraisal system which would measure individual and/or group performance as part of a total group endeavor or specific skill levels.

The ultimate goal is a direct correlation between individual performance and salary pay level in which top performers would consistently receive higher salaries than low performers. Unless this is achieved, personnel appraisal will not have the muscle that it needs to be effective, and salary administration will be less equitable and consistent in its applications.

Administering Pay of Unionized Employees. Administration of a pay increase program takes on a different character for hourly or salaried employees covered by union contract. Union wage contracts are generally oriented toward the concept of one static base wage for specific jobs. The base wage can be identified as the job rate, the qualified job rate, the journeyman job rate as applied to skilled trade jobs, or in other terms unique to the union and/or company and industry involved. In most cases, management has little discretion during the terms of a contract in adjusting individual rates, since most union contracts provide for a negotiated advance to the qualified rate. However, two mechanisms are available which can be employed to distinguish between varying base rates in a union-organized situation.

The first is job evaluation, which has been described in Part 2. Job evaluation offers a systematic tool to be used in partnership with labor relations negotiators by which clear distinctions can be drawn between different levels of hourly job duties. Hourly job evaluation can establish rational pay rate differentials between different job and skill levels, but the qualified-rate concept will still prevail as the maximum job rate.

The second alternative is to establish a narrow hourly wage range. This approach is not foreign to hourly wage contracts and is desirable in that it helps to maintain management control. The range can establish a beginning hourly rate and increases in steps to a qualified or maximum job rate. An example of such a range is shown in Table 2.

The spread of the range from beginning to qualified rate should be very narrow—thus, the range depicted in Table 2 has an 11 percent spread. The step increments can be tailored to the particular union-and-company-negotiated agreements or other pertinent company factors. However, it is normally a good practice to establish the steps in time increments no greater than six months. It is also prudent to have only one or two steps in the lower unskilled classifications and to gradually increase the number of steps to four or five in the highly skilled classifications.

TABLE 2   Sample Hourly Wage Range

| Beginner rate | Steps | | | Qualified job rate |
	1st	2nd	3rd	
$3.00	$3.08	3.16	3.24	$3.33

The beginning rate should be used as a probationary hiring rate. In this case, no employee would be advanced beyond the beginning rate until a decision was made that he was qualified to become a permanent employee, at which time he would begin moving through the range according to established contractual procedures.

Another advantage of the hourly-rate-range concept is that a new hourly employee need not be hired at the beginning rate or the qualified rate. Instead, he can be started at an hourly rate commensurate with his ability as determined by supervision. For example, an employee assigned to a job for which he has no previous knowledge or job-related ability would be started at the beginning rate. Following this, his hourly rate would be advanced through the step progression as his abilities developed until he reached the fully qualified rate. Another employee assigned to a job for which he is judged to have satisfactory job skills to warrant the qualified rate could be paid the qualified rate immediately. Employees should be moved up in the range as soon as they have progressed to higher performance levels as determined through job standards and job measurement criteria established by the personnel department and as appraised and recommended by the employee's foreman or supervisor.

Movement within the range is not necessarily limited to one step at a time. If, in the opinion of the supervisor, the employee is moving faster in acquiring proficiency, he can be moved two steps at a time or be granted increases at shorter time intervals. This procedure would result in accelerated movement to the qualified job rate.

Employees who may have problems in learning the job should be moved less rapidly within the step progression. If the supervisor feels that an employee does not merit a step increase within the maximum period, he should consider transferring him to a lower-level job or terminating him. Of course, when a union contract is involved, delays in rate progression due to unsatisfactory performance should be carefully documented by foremen and supervisors involved, consistent with contract language and specific union-employer relations.

In summary, a pay increase program can be developed whether employees are organized or unorganized, but the system is more restrictive and limited in scope when a union is involved. In addition, it is advantageous for hourly wage administration programs and procedures to be as simple as possible so that day-to-day administration can be handled at the lowest possible operational level.

BUDGETING IN ADMINISTERING PAY INCREASES

Budgeting of pay increases on a calendar- or fiscal-year basis is a vital tool of salary administration. To be most effective, the pay increase budget and the methods by which it is developed and administered should be in keeping with the company's total financial control philosophy, accounting procedures and practices, and personnel policies. Essentially, however, there are two basic forms of budgetary systems.

The first is the formal control budget which is established after internal company and external job marketplace conditions are analyzed and company resources are appraised. The result is a total maximum amount of monies, usually represented as a percent of annual beginning payroll, which managers are authorized to grant in the form of pay increases to their employees in the following year. An example of a formal budget calculation is shown in Table 3. All the items shown in Table 3 must be analyzed to assure management that the 4.4 percent increase considers all relevant factors—employee promotions, turnover rates, inflation, increase or decrease in departmental operations, and mix of job levels.

The formal budget system is most practical in organizations where salary administration is decentralized. This system has the advantage of establishing definite cost projections which normally will not exceed the budgetary amounts, and in this regard it is strongly favored by financial management. However, it has the disadvantage of being inflexible. If later in the year the company needs to add or reduce personnel levels or to grant pay increases not anticipated when the budgets were developed, additional monies will not be available unless total budgets are revised with top management approval. A second disadvantage is that managers tend to use up all funds budgeted in any one year in order to justify subsequent years' increased budgets. A third aspect of the formal budget system, which can become a disadvantage, is that it delegates to unit managers broad authority for granting salary increases without review by higher management. This may result in inequitable pay situations. Of course these disadvantages can be controlled or avoided through alert financial and salary administration practices.

The second budgeting method utilizes accounting budgetary principles to estimate salary increase costs over a prescribed period of time—normally, one year. These estimated costs are built into accounting projections as a normal experience factor for cost control and overall cost and profit forecast purposes but are not established as rigid cost projection factors.

The accounting budgetary system has the distinct advantage of being flexible in its administration while at the same time retaining an element of cost control which requires managers to plan salary increases on an individual basis rather than on an overall cost projection basis. An example of an accounting budgetary analysis for salary increase purposes is shown in Table 4.

A shortcoming of the accounting budgetary system is that it cannot function equitably within reasonable cost boundaries unless other formal salary increase procedures are employed. These formal procedures should include time and percentage limits for granting salary increases, guidelines covering the use of the salary schedule, and a tie-in of personnel appraisal with merit increase administration.

In order for accurate cost projections to be developed under either budgetary system, the makeup of the employee organization must be thoroughly investigated by specific unit, department, division, and the total company.

TABLE 3   Annual Salary Budget Calculation

Total department annual salaries as of December 31 of previous year........	$69,840
Addition of new employee to payroll January 1...........................	14,400
New total salary as of January 1.......................................	$84,240
New year's salary increase budget:	
Percent and amount...(4.4%)	3,740
New year's total annual salary cost....................................	$87,980

TABLE 4 Programmed Salary Increases and Accounting Budget

Department A

Name	Job grade	1970 Dec.	1971 Jan.	Feb.	Mar.	Apr.	May	June	July	Aug.	Sep.	Oct.	Nov.	Dec.	1971 total annual salary
R. Jones............	4	$ 455									+$35 490				$ 5,600
J. Doe.............	5	515	+$35 550											+$35 585	6,635
J. Black..........	6	600				+$40 640									7,560
T. Williams.......	10	905		+$75 980											11,685
B. White..........	10	920											+$75 995		11,190
E. David..........	14	1,025					+$80 1,105								12,940
(New empl.)........	14	......	1,200											+ 90 1,290	14,490
C. Adams..........	20	1,400				+ 120 1,520									17,880
Monthly totals.....		$5,820	$7,055	$7,130	$7,130	$7,290	$7,370	$7,370	$7,370	$7,370	$7,405	$7,405	$7,480	$7,605	$87,980

A most important variable to be considered for either system is employee turnover rates for separate company units. Employee turnover, if not analyzed correctly, can have a disruptive effect upon a formal budget system. For example, a unit which has a high degree of employee turnover would normally need a smaller salary increase budget than a more stable unit which experiences low turnover. This conclusion is based upon the assumption that no general across-the-board increase would be granted. Of course, if general increases are planned, the cost effect upon the total budget can be easily projected. However, if the salary increase system is based entirely upon merit or performance, studies have shown that employees on the payroll longer than one year will, on the average, receive increases at least 3 percent higher than those given to employees on the payroll less than one year.

COMPENSATION ADMINISTRATION IN DECENTRALIZED AND CENTRALIZED ORGANIZATIONS

The administration for all types of pay increases takes on different forms depending on whether the organization is centralized or decentralized. Generally speaking, a decentralized compensation program provides much wider administrative latitude for operating managers but costs more to administer than a centralized program. From a practical standpoint, most companies do not have a completely decentralized or completely centralized program, but a combination of the two, consistent with the company's operations and needs.

A company's size, in terms of sales dollars or even diversity of product line, is not necessarily a good indicator of whether or not a pay increase system should be centralized or decentralized. The primary consideration will normally be the company's organizational philosophy and needs. These do not remain static but are influenced by industry position, marketplace, employee needs, and, most importantly, the basic "personality" of the company.

Some companies may find that as they grow beyond a certain size it becomes necessary to decentralize their direct compensation program. Other companies will remain centralized regardless of their size. Some companies may decentralize from an operational standpoint but find it wise to remain centralized for their compensation and, more specifically, for their pay increase programs.

It is clear, then, that no one particular system or program is best for all companies. In the sections that follow, we will discuss the primary characteristics of decentralized and centralized compensation programs, how they are run, and their advantages and disadvantages.

Administration in a Decentralized Organization. In a decentralized organization, wage and salary administration practices and programs, by necessity, are established to conform with the separate and individual nature of the organization units. If a decentralized unit is a separate and complete profit center and includes all operations of a staff and line nature within its structure, the administration of its employee direct-pay compensation program should also be decentralized. A decentralized pay practice operation need not be devoid of all corporate controls, but it does need to operate independently on a day-to-day basis. Normally the top corporate compensation function in a decentralized organization should guide the operating groups with research and development of new programs and techniques. The corporate group should also conduct periodic audits to assure that independent units do not deviate from broad company policy.

Unit management in a truly decentralized organization should have broad authority, within corporate policy guidelines, to establish direct-pay policies, including all necessary pay schedules, merit increase policies, and promotional increase policies, and also to develop and install job evaluation systems oriented to the decentralized unit's specific needs.

Normally, a decentralized company will not be concerned with job and pay equity between its major profit centers. This is true because, except at the very top management level, employees rarely are transferred between independent units of a decentralized company. The profit centers are established along separate and probably unrelated product lines, and even though they all are part of a total corporation in the eyes of the public, stockholders, and government agencies, the separate groups often are viewed by their employees as separate companies. In this regard, an employee hired for a particular level job in one unit of a decentralized company can move within that same group, be transferred to other plant locations within the same group, and rise to a management role in the same group, but can seldom have contact of an internal business nature with members of other units of the same company.

Most decentralized corporations do not operate in such a competely decentralized manner. Nonetheless, the point is well taken that in a decentralized organization it is more important that pay administration practices conform to the patterns of each particular unit and its relationship to the industry and geographical area in which it operates than to the standard and uniform patterns and practices of the total company.

It is extremely important in a decentralized organization that employee compensation costs be controlled through the use of a formalized budget system as described in the previous section. By necessity, corporate involvement in direct-pay programs focuses on broad financial aspects rather than on the individual worth or inter-unit equity of the programs. Program needs and equity needs must be left to the judgment of each unit's management, which is closer to the marketplace and therefore better able to appraise compensation needs. Conversely, corporate compensation management will deal primarily with total financial considerations—for example, increasing the corporatewide salary budget by 5 percent or decreasing it by 2 percent, and requiring each decentralized manager to live within the budget limitations. However, an overall cost increase factor does not necessarily indicate that all units will be affected to the same degree. The percentages normally vary depending on size of units, makeup of the employee job group, current profitability of each group, future sales and profit growth of each group, and, of course, not to be dismissed, the negotiating ability of the management of each group at the time when budgets are reviewed and finalized with corporate management.

Administration in a Centralized Organization. Administering a centralized employee compensation program involves the same functions as are performed for a decentralized organization, but, in addition, the centralized group plans and develops the total program and oversees and controls day-to-day administration. A centralized compensation program, being uniform throughout the corporation, is much less complex and less costly to administer than a far-flung, decentralized program. A centralized direct-compensation function can operate in a company that is essentially a one-product operation, or it can operate in a company engaged in the manufacture and sale of a multitude of products and having a product-division type of organization.

The essential characteristic of a centralized compensation program is its uniformity throughout the company. This is essential to assure equitable administration of direct-compensation policies.

Another prime characteristic of a centralized organization is internal pay equity. This is essential in a company which transfers exempt employees across organization lines.   In this regard, the company strives to establish an entire compensation program responsive to its own internal needs as well as to external considerations.   This does not, however, imply that a centralized company cannot compare its pay practices with those of other companies, but rather that, unlike decentralized companies, it is also concerned with corporatewide internal equity.   External pay comparisons are important to a centralized organization in order for compensation management to be familiar with all external elements which may influence internal pay relationships.   A centralized organization operating in more than one industry must establish a very sensitive balance between internal equity requirements and external competitive relationships.

A centralized compensation program is normally a highly structured operation which operates with formal and uniform compensation policies pertaining to job evaluation plans, pay increase systems, incentive programs, and related employee benefit programs.   Job evaluation or job ranking in a centralized organization will normally involve the use of one basic system or variations of the basic system, depending upon the job families or job hierarchies involved. This does not mean that only one plan is used to measure all jobs from top management to nonexempt clerks.   It normally does indicate that the same job evaluation system is used with variations built into separate plans to evaluate different levels of job families.   This technique also promotes the general theme of job evaluation consistency and pay equity in the determination of job values throughout the organization.

Salary schedules in a centralized organization need not be uniform or identical throughout the organization.   Some variation is always needed for nonexempt jobs in different operational areas of the country.   In addition, exempt salary ranges should vary according to the needs of different areas or industries in which the company operates.

A centralized direct-compensation organization does not mean one in which operating managers have no role to play in compensating their employees. Policies should be developed to permit managers sufficient latitude to make direct-pay and other compensation judgments based on individual performance, economic conditions, and unit performance.

An important element of a centralized program is an approval system designed to assure that general company policies are applied consistently and pay increases are granted judiciously.   All pay recommendations normally channel through a series of unit, divisional, and corporate management approvals and reviews prior to final authorization.

One advantage of a centralized compensation program is that it provides a constant, up-to-date flow of information at corporate headquarters so that all pertinent employee information can be maintained in a central data bank. Individual employee data can be used for many purposes in the personnel field beyond the basic direct-compensation needs.   In addition, centralized pay records facilitate close control of company pay increase trends and policy compliance and can be utilized for frequent reporting of cost data to management.

Hourly Compensation Administration in Decentralized and Centralized Organizations.   Hourly compensation administration, if covered by union contract, normally is not affected by whether the company is centralized or decentralized. A highly centralized company may be required to have a completely decentralized hourly pay program because of the number and type of union contracts that it may have or because of specific provisions contained in union contracts. In the same sense, a highly decentralized corporation with clear and distinct profit center organizations may have one major contract which applies to all units.   Similarly, an hourly job evaluation system can be used differently in a centralized or decentralized organization depending upon the type and number of union contracts involved. Hourly pay administration will follow union contract provisions and can follow administrative provisions, as covered earlier, without regard for company organization. However, if no union contracts are involved, hourly pay practices normally can be administered in accordance with either decentralized or centralized program policies and guidelines as described above.

Payroll Function. All pay increase programs, regardless of their makeup or of company organization, ultimately lead to the preparation of the individual employee paycheck.

In a centralized compensation program it is essential that the payroll function also be centralized and either directly controlled by or closely allied with the compensation department. A centralized program cannot function with the internal control and reporting mechanisms necessary without easy access to the records of a centralized payroll group.

In the case of the decentralized organization, each unit should have its own separate payroll function over which its management maintains direct supervision.

PAY TREATMENT WITH JOB CHANGES

Within the employee total compensation program, the individual direct-pay increase is the one major area in which supervisors and managers can influence employee pay levels. Very little discretion can be exercised by operating managers in the employee benefit area, i.e., pensions, group insurance, vacations and holidays, and premium pay, or in any other specific company programs which by necessity are established and controlled by inflexible formulas and are subject to legal and governmental regulations. This is not intended as a criticism; it simply states a fact of life that managers do not have complete control over an individual's compensation package except to the extent that an individual's salary level influences his benefit level.

Pension programs usually cover all employees and are normally based on salary level and years of service. Therefore, salary increases not only affect career income but also determine retirement income levels, either equitably or inequitably, depending on whether the employee's salary treatment has truly reflected his performance. The pension program itself does not and cannot determine whether one individual contributed more or less to the company's operations; it can only reflect the judgments implicit in his salary treatment during his career.

In the same sense, if a company observes 10 annual holidays, all employees, regardless of individual performance, receive 10 annual holidays. These programs, therefore, do not distinguish between good and poor performers; and furthermore, they should not, since benefit programs are established to meet employee security needs as well as competitive needs influenced by market conditions and socioeconomic factors.

Since direct-pay decisions not only increase or decrease individual employee pay levels but also directly influence most benefit programs, it behooves each supervisor and manager to use the pay increase program, as covered by company policy or practice, to make meaningful distinctions between individual performance levels. Usually the supervisor's salary decisions involve merit or performance increases, as described earlier in this chapter. However, in cases of promotion, transfer, or demotion, managers have wider latitude to reward or penalize employees through pay adjustments based on employee performance.

The single best motivational tool that any supervisor or manager possesses is the promotion. Promotion increases the employee's income, which it should in all cases, and, additionally, indicates his increased worth to the company, to his associates, management, family, and friends. A promotion, therefore, not only enhances the employee's material well-being but also is satisfying to his ego. In some cases it is difficult to determine which of the two provides the greater motivational mileage.

A promotional pay increase should be large enough to avoid being considered a hollow achievement in the eyes of the employee. The promotional increase should, in all cases, be substantially higher than increases given for reasons of merit or job performance. As a general rule of thumb, a promotional increase should be at least 50 percent higher than the upper level in effect for a merit increase. If the upper limit for a merit increase is 10 percent, a promotional increase should be a minimum of 15 percent. An alternative approach is to raise the employee's salary to the same position in his new salary range as it was in his previous salary range.

Promotional increases should not be combined with merit or general salary increases. It is sometimes a temptation for managers to schedule job promotions to fall on a merit review or merit increase due date and then grant the merit increase as if it were a promotional increase. However, this practice should be discouraged, because it detracts from the motivational impact of a job promotion and will classify the promotion as a sham in the mind of the employee. If a promotion must fall on a merit review date, one of two methods can be employed: the merit increase can be given separately in one month with the promotional increase to follow in the second month; or the total increase can be built up to include both the promotional and merit increase. The latter method is more practical and should be followed in order to avoid misunderstandings and administrative complications. In summary, a promotion should always be accompanied by a healthy increase in the employee's salary level so it is readily identified by him as a bona fide elevation in job responsibility.

An exception to the above may be justified if an employee is granted a public relations type promotion in which he is given a change in title but no change in job responsibilities. In this case the nature of the promotion should be clearly explained, and the employee should be made aware that the press releases do not warrant an increase in salary.

Transfer of an employee at the same job level should not necessarily be accompanied by a salary increase if the move is made to broaden the employee's exposure and experience within the organization. However, a lateral transfer in which the employee is required to change his residence should be reviewed very carefully by management to be certain that the move is necessary. If no salary increase accompanies a lateral transfer, and if the company has no other programs for compensating an employee required to change his residence, serious personnel and resultant direct-compensation problems will result. If at all possible, any employee job transfer should be organized and managed to involve a promotion so that the employee can be granted a pay increase. Any job transfer which involves a residence change results in short-term and/or long-term added expenses for the employee and his family. This is true no matter whether the new area has a higher or lower cost of living. Therefore, it is doubly important that managers carefully review the necessity of any lateral transfers which require a change of residence.

Employee demotion, accompanied by corresponding salary reduction, is one of the more difficult problems faced by a manager or salary administrator. In fact, it is more difficult than an employee discharge, because with a discharge the circumstances are generally clear-cut and justifiable. Many personnel experts contend that it is better from a total employee morale and management standpoint to discharge an employee than to reduce his pay. An employee who is discharged can often find employment opportunities that are as good as or better than those he left, whereas the employee who has had his salary reduced will more often than not continue to be a problem.

Demotions frequently are not clearly substantiated and can take many forms. The most common reason for a demotion, of course, is that the employee is not able to accept the responsibilities or perform the job to which he is assigned. Other reasons for demotions include changes in organization which eliminate jobs; change or elimination of some job duties which lowers the worth and evaluation of the job; and personality conflicts between the employee and his subordinates, superiors, or peers which prevent him from performing effectively. Whether or not an employee's pay should be reduced at the time of demotion should be a highly individualized judgment on the part of management in the light of all the circumstances.

As a general rule of thumb, salary should be decreased if the demotion is clearly the result of the employee's inability to accept his job responsibilities or to handle them in an effective manner. The size of the reduction should vary depending upon the circumstances, but in no case should it be greater than the promotional increase, if that was his last pay increase. It should be large enough so that his new salary will not be higher than the maximum of the job salary range to which he is demoted. If the demotion is for reasons of personality conflict, a decrease should not be made if it is possible to place the individual in another part of the company. If the demotion is the result of reorganization or elimination of some job duties, salary should not be cut unless a lower salary would make the employee available for a greater number of new job openings.

Because of the relationship between pay and benefits, a salary decrease as a result of the demotion should be investigated thoroughly to determine its effect upon the employee's benefit coverage.

Other types of "demotions" are: the transfer of a *competent* employee to a lower-level job in order for him to gain broader experience, and the transfer of a *competent* employee to a lower job where his talents can be utilized to correct a bad operation within a stated period of time. In these cases, it may be advisable to grant salary increases. The demotional increase may also be used when it is to the advantage of the corporation, associates involved, and the individual that the employee be moved to a nonsensitive, lower-valued job which may carry a prestigious title.

In summary, a manager does not have a great deal of latitude with regard to varying the benefit portion of an employee's total compensation package; therefore, he must utilize to the fullest the motivational tools available to him in the direct-compensation system—including the merit or performance increase, promotional increase, transfer promotional increase, and in rare circumstances, demotional salary changes.

chapter 50

Keeping Records for
Administration and Research

RICHARD C. FREMON *Director, Salary Adminstration, Bell Telephone Laboratories, Incorporated, Murray Hill, New Jersey*

The principal importance of record keeping and data processing in salary administration lies in the information they provide for decision making. Such useful information includes statistical descriptions of structural and paid salaries within and outside the organization and stable historical and trend data, as well as statistical answers to questions of all sorts.

In record keeping and data processing the scope of objectives that can be set realistically and the range of techniques that can be used are determined by the capabilities of computers and their associated apparatus. A brief description of computers and their uses, with particular reference to salary administration, is therefore included in this chapter prior to a discussion of record keeping and statistical procedures.

COMPUTERS

The principal value of a computer is its ability to do large numbers of ordinary arithmetic and other simple number manipulations at great speed and low cost. Computers are most efficient when used in procedures that involve manifold repetition of the same or very similar elemental steps. Computers thus make possible certain valuable kinds of mass data processing which would be impossible to do by hand. The peripheral equipment usually associated with a computer can offer a large variety of ways of feeding in, storing, and presenting data and thus extend the time and cost advantage to these operations as well.

The computer art is developing rapidly in terms of capacity, speed, efficiency, and input-output possibilities. To get the most service from a computer installation, one should rely on the advice of an expert who is familiar with the installation. To be able to use computers most effectively, a salary administrator should know at least their general uses and capabilities and their principal limitations.

Uses and Capabilities. Computers and associated equipment can be used to store information in a form which permits rapid and inexpensive access by and use within the computer. Information may be stored on magnetic tape, discs, or other magnetic devices, or in files of punch cards. These means of storage differ from each other in respect to ease of access, cost, and the volume of information they will hold, and each has its own mechanical characteristics and hazards.

The choice of a particular means of storage for large masses of data should be made by an expert. Factors to be considered include: (1) the amount of information or number of items, (2) how often the file will be updated, (3) how the information is to be used—i.e., what means of retrieval will be necessary—and (4) with what other collections of data the file is to be associated and in what ways.

For smaller amounts of information, particularly if the file is to be used infrequently, one should choose whatever means of storage are physically most convenient. The natural choices for small and medium-sized collections are magnetic tape and punch cards. Magnetic tape is easier to read into a computer, but punch cards are generally less expensive to maintain. Furthermore, the cards in a file may be selected and/or sorted at will to set up a desired input arrangement.

A large computer can be programmed to manipulate data in any way that is necessary in salary administration. All ordinary arithmetic operations can be performed with whole or decimal numbers, lists can be sorted, and computer decisions based on relationships among the data being processed can be made. Combinations of these elemental operations can be programmed to accomplish all kinds of standard mathematical calculations, as well as special procedures designed for particular problems.

Computer output is delivered in a number of different forms, depending on the peripheral equipment used. All installations have facilities for placing the output (i.e., any information that is in the computer at the time) on magnetic tape, punch cards, or paper. Some installations have the means to plot graphs and to record graphic or text output on microfilm and display it on a cathode-ray device. Remote input and output arrangements can be provided. Both paper and punch card outputs offer a wide variety of formats, which can be varied to suit specific needs or preferences.

Limitations. The most important limitation in computer applications is cost. A large computer installation is inherently expensive to operate per unit of time. Each routine used requires the preparation of a program, the cost of which must be justified by the extent of the program's use. Extensive manual preparation of data is expensive, as is the transformation of large amounts of data from one form to another—e.g., between printed or written copy and punch cards or between cards and magnetic tape.

Time scheduling also is often an important consideration. One should not forget that programming can be a slow process, particularly for large and complicated routines, and that the final preparation of a program for use (debugging) usually cannot be brought to an end at a predictable time.

All data storage devices are subject to partial or complete loss of contents. One should always be sure to have backup data so that lost material can be replaced or reconstructed. This means having duplicate files or being prepared to reassemble part or all of a collection of data in an efficient way.

Programming. Programming consists of all of the procedures that go into the preparation of a program or sequence of operations for a computer to perform. The steps are:

1. Analysis of the problem and the design of a system or logical procedure to solve it
2. Flow charting, i.e., making a schematic diagram of the system or procedure. (This step is often omitted in simple programs.)
3. Writing the procedure or program in a programming language or code
4. Testing and debugging, i.e., correcting logic and coding errors

For particularly demanding applications (large amounts of data or large numbers of operations), the programming should be done by a professional. The salary administrator should be prepared to provide: (1) a complete statement of the problem, (2) a description of the input data, (3) a detailed specification of the nature and format of the output desired, (4) an estimate of the expected volume of use of the routine, and (5) a statement of possible closely related future problems. The salary administrator should also participate in the analysis of the problem and the selection of approaches to its solution.

Most programming is done in one or another specialized "higher" language. A program written in one of these languages is subsequently converted in the computer, by means of a special, internal routine called a *compiler*. This routine transforms the higher language into the detailed steps which the computer will follow in actual operation. Programming languages are designed for specific kinds of applications, some primarily for scientific or technical work and some for business use. For a given computer installation one can use only the languages for which a compiler is available. For most ordinary applications, it is not critical which computer language is used. The choice of language is important only when esoteric procedures are required or huge amounts of data must be processed.

The rapid development of computer technology and applications and the consequent frequency with which many computer installations change equipment create a special concern about programming. When the machinery is changed it is often necessary to alter or even to rewrite existing programs. This process is less expensive if one uses general programs, each for a number of applications, instead of numerous specific programs, each designed for one application only.

RECORDS

Records pertinent to salary administration include organized collections of detailed data about individuals and historical statistics on past salary actions, market surveys, and other economic information. Both individual and statistical records should contain all items that might reasonably be used. Flexible and efficient retrieval arrangements are important.

Individual Records. An essential part of the arrangements for keeping records of individuals is a central or master file, containing a large collection of information about each employee, stored in some machine-readable form, from which working requirements for information are supplied mechanically. Accordingly, the first question bearing on the nature of salary adminstration records is whether they constitute the organization's master file or are derived from a master file kept for broader purposes. In the latter case the salary administrator need only provide storage for the items that he uses, whereas in the former he must be concerned with storing all kinds of information as well as maintaining its timeliness and accuracy. The following material assumes an interest in the whole process involved in keeping the master file.

In general, the master file should contain whatever information about each employee which might reasonably be found useful in managing the organization. Table 1 offers a list of possible choices. At any given time the master file should contain current information on each item for each person. It has been found useful to associate each principal item with its date of record so that the user can always judge whether he really has the latest information. Backup records are kept in the form of (1) master files of past key dates and (2) chronological lists of changes with suitable identifying data (also in machine-readable form). These backup records are, of course, also useful for studies of such personnel events as resignations, promotions, and transfers.

For economy of storage space, as much nonnumerical information as possible should be coded. It is not necessary that the codes be numerical. For some applications alphabetical codes are more efficient, and in any case mnemonic codes enhance accuracy. Coded information can be restored mechanically to plain language in the process of retrieval or analysis. Encoding of material en route to the master file can also be done mechanically, although not quite so easily as in the reverse process.

For efficiency and accuracy, input information for a master file should come directly from the primary written source via a single keyboard manipulation into a machine-readable form. Personnel forms should accordingly be designed with the machine record format information preprinted.

While hardware arrangements are available to permit almost instantaneous updating of a master personnel file, they are much more expensive than slower means. The maintenance cycle (daily, twice weekly, weekly) should therefore be as infrequent as the uses of the file will permit. If some applications need very rapid service (as for payroll department, mail distribution, or telephone exchange), this can be accomplished as a by-product of the first stage of a two-stage routine, in which the material for the master file is saved (on punch cards, for example) until the periodic running of the second stage, which is the main maintenance procedure.

Checking and auditing are of paramount importance in computer-kept records. Entirely new input (first recording of a new employee) should be confirmed with the source, preferably using data fed back from its ultimate

TABLE 1   Examples of Items in a Master Personnel Information File

Payroll account number	Regular/temporary
Name	Details of educational status
Sex	Completion of company training programs
Birth date	Present salary*
Citizenship status	Previous salary*
Company service date	Bonus status and history*
Social security number	Termination or leave category (if any)
Marital status	Selective service classification and expiration date*
Home address*	Military service record
Department number*	Job evaluation data*
Company location*	Performance rating*
Occupational classification*	Security clearance status*
Organizational rank*	How employed
Standard hours per week	Work limitations

  * These items should be accompanied by their date of record.

location in the master file.   A change in an existing record should be sent into the computer accompanied by several other associated items, particularly the expected present content of the item that is being changed, and, if these do not check, the change should be rejected automatically.   Consistency checks are useful parts of the maintenance computer program and might include, for example, a routine that will reject information that an employee is 10 years old or has a salary of an impossible size.   The maintenance program should also check the form of the input and should reject numbers where alphabetic characters belong, and vice versa.

Figure 1 is a schematic diagram of a working master file maintenance routine. Although the diagram does not show it, there should be a security mechanism included in the maintenance program.   This is an arrangement which keeps the master file itself in a changeable code and thus makes the information in the file available only to authorized persons who have the key.   Security coding should not be confused with coding to save storage capacity, mentioned above.

Recorded information liable to change—for instance, education and marital status—should be audited periodically. This is done by sending each employee a printout of the changeable data that appear in the file for him and asking for verification.

Retrieval.   One natural concomitant of the existence of a computer-oriented employee master file is the rapid expansion of management interest in using the file to obtain selected listings and categorical studies in an equally expanding variety of specifications.   This means that the retrieval routine must be flexible in all of its operations and, at the same time, highly efficient so that a large number of searches through a massive number of items can be carried out at reasonable cost.

The basic retrieval operations are (1) selecting a subpopulation specified by a number of parameters, (2) reading selected information about each member of the subpopulation, (3) sorting the data in a desired manner, (4) decoding, (5) making calculations from the selected data, and (6) delivering output in one or more forms (printout on paper or microfilm, punch cards, magnetic tape, etc.) with some flexibility as to titles, headings, and format.   The options available in the overall retrieval routine and the ways of calling for them can be organized so that the activity can be assigned to a clerk or clerks.

Historical Statistics.   As a resource for studies of relationships between current situations and actions and corresponding ones of previous times, standardized collections of compressed statistics kept in machine-readable form are useful. The computer reduction and analysis of the details of a personnel action or a collection of market data can, with minuscule extra cost, be made to produce a condensed statistical representation which can be stored cheaply and used as input in the computer analysis of a later action or survey of the same kind to give data about changes over time.   To set up such a statistical record, one should gather and record a relatively large number of categories of information so as to permit a flexible choice of groupings for later study and comparison. For example, for a salary survey that is repeated every year, one might choose to keep a record, on punch cards or tape, of the average salary and number of salaries reported for each combination of (1) occupational classification, (2) age, and (3) respondent organization.

STATISTICS

Formal statistical procedures are used in compensation administration to make generalized descriptions of detailed data, usually for the purpose of comparing

Figure 1. Master file maintenance system.

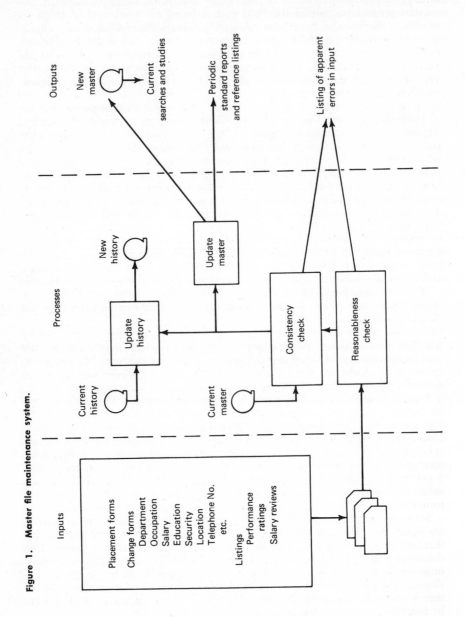

groups of people in some way, and to assess the precision of such generalizations and comparisons.

Among the most troublesome problems commonly encountered in developing statistics for use in managing are the maintenance of credibility and the avoidance of credulity. In the former interest it is better to adopt for regular use a relatively small set of generally explainable statistical techniques and always to be careful about the accuracy and relevance of the input data. For the latter, i.e., to combat the apparently natural human tendency to attribute undue accuracy to numbers as such, the analyst should cultivate the habit of estimating the statistical precision and the real significance of calculated results.

There are usually several good statistical approaches for any given situation. The selection of the one to use should depend on what feature of the data seems most meaningful in terms of the management decisions that are to be made or most interesting to those who will be responsible for making the decisions.

In designing a statistical analysis, the first question is, Which variables should be treated explicitly, and, of these, which one or ones are assumed to be caused (i.e., dependent) and which are assumed to be causes (i.e., independent)? The choice of independent variables usually involves a trade-off between showing more detail and making the presentation simpler and easier to absorb. If, in a given case, an additional independent variable does not improve the overall precision of the analysis, it should be rejected. Variables measured on continuous numerical scales are the most convenient, but discrete categories can also be analyzed either as such or by giving each a numerical value.

It often seems desirable to average together or otherwise combine data which come from different sources or which represent different categories of people. In making such combinations, one must always decide what relative weighting to use for each source or category. Sometimes a natural weighting is clearly the right choice—for example, equal weight to each category or weights proportional to the populations of the respective sources. On the other hand, the question of weighting is often so difficult or controversial that the data of the different categories are best reported separately and not combined at all.

Using a particular mathematical expression or graphical form to report the essence of a collection of actual measurements of some set of variables implies that the principal relations among the variables are described at least reasonably well by the chosen expression or form. Thus, if one speaks of the average salary of some classification of employees, he implies that a particular general level of salary is a principal characteristic of the classification. Likewise, using a curve of a given form to describe the relationship between experience and salary in some population suggests that that form of curve shows the main form of the relationship between those variables for such a population.

Measures of the dispersion of the actual data away from the generalized statistical statement (average, fitted curve, etc.) are related to the precision that may be attributed to that statement. In the practical case, the greater this dispersion, the poorer the precision. On the other hand, precision usually is improved by having larger amounts of data or larger samples of facts. One should, moreover, distinguish carefully between statistical precision and real significance. An observed difference between two averages, for example, might be highly significant statistically and utterly inconsequential in practical terms.

The following sections describe the more common ways of presenting statistical data, classified in terms of the number of variables that they involve.

Single Variable. Data on a single variable, such as the various individual salaries within a given occupational classification or the various market starting rates of the employers of a community for a particular level of skill, are most often reduced to some measure of central tendency. If the collection of items defined by the variable exhibits no central tendency, i.e., if no one value or range of values is more common than others, it ordinarily should not be expressed this way. Further, if there are two or more separate concentrations of data items among the values of the variable, one should suspect that the population represented by the data is really two or more different populations mixed together and seek ways of separating them.

The most commonly used measures of central tendency are:

1. Mean: the sum of the measurements divided by the number of them

2. Median: the middle of a list of the measurements put in numerical order. If there is an odd number of measurements, the median is the middle one. If there is an even number of measurements, the median is midway between the middle two of them.

3. Mode: the quantity or range of quantities which is found in the data more often than any other

For collections of data which exhibit a clear central tendency and in which the distribution of items is about the same on both sides of it, the mean, median, and mode are all about the same and the mean is usually the most accurate measure to use. Conversely, when the data items are distributed differently on the two sides of their central concentration, the three measures may be significantly different from each other, and one should use whichever one of them is consistent with the intended sense of the analysis.

The dispersion of measurements of a single variable is commonly expressed in terms of interquartile range or standard deviation.

The *interquartile range* is simply the difference between the value of the variable at the upper quartile and that at the lower quartile. The *upper quartile* is defined as that value of the variable which cuts off the highest one-quarter of the data items in an ordered list, and the *lower quartile*, the lowest one-quarter of them.

The *standard deviation* is the measure of dispersion which is most commonly associated with the mean, and it is estimated as follows:

$$\text{Standard deviation} = \sqrt{\frac{\Sigma(X - \bar{X})^2}{N - 1}}$$

where: Σ = summation over all items of data
X = each data item in turn
$\bar{X}$ = mean of data
N = number of data items

If one thinks of the data on hand as a sample of the data that would be obtained by measuring a very large population of the same kind, then the mean of the actual data may be viewed as an approximation of the mean that would apply to the larger universe. The precision of this approximation is estimated by the *standard deviation of the mean*, calculated as follows:

$$\text{Standard deviation of the mean} = \frac{\text{standard deviation}}{\sqrt{N}}$$

The connection between this quantity and the precision of the mean may be understood in the following way. Two-thirds of the time, on the average, the mean of the sample data will be within one *standard deviation of the mean* of the mean of the larger universe. Nineteen-twentieths of the time, on the average, the two means will be less than two *standard deviations of the mean* apart.

To estimate the precision of the difference between two means, one calculates the *standard deviation of the difference,* as follows:

Standard deviation of the difference =

$$\sqrt{(\text{std. dev. of mean } \# 1)^2 + (\text{std. dev. of mean } \# 2)^2}$$

The comparison of this quantity with the difference between the means indicates the *statistical* significance of the difference. If, for instance, the standard deviation of the difference is much larger than the difference itself, the variables in question might as well be assumed equal. If the standard deviation of the difference is equal to the difference itself, about one-sixth of the time the true difference between the variables is opposite in direction to the observed difference.

It must be noted that the estimates described in the preceding paragraphs are only approximations, which are better for larger samples. Textbook methods are available for assessing statistical significance more precisely, particularly for small samples.

Least-squares Method. Taking the mean of a set of measurements is the simplest example of a class of statistical techniques known as "least-squares methods." The name is taken from the fact that the estimates obtained have the minimum sum of the squares of differences from the actual data.

This least sum of squares of deviations corresponds to the idea of least error or best overall description of the data for a given form of representation.

Two Variables—Curve Fitting. Simplified representations of two variable (one dependent and one independent) data are obtained by fitting lines or smooth curves. The most common methods used are (1) visual smoothing, (2) group or moving averages, and (3) least-squares polynomials.

Smoothing by eye is the most flexible and least exact of these methods. It is particularly unreliable with respect to data that exhibit great dispersion.

Group averaging involves grouping the data in brackets or at intervals along the scale of the independent variable and then taking the mean of each variable in each group. The resulting group representations can be smoothed further by eye or by linear interpolation.

A moving average is constructed by calculating the mean of each variable at each of a progression of overlapping intervals of the independent variable. Usually these intervals are all of the same length along the independent scale, and each starts at a value that is one unit higher than the interval before it. An illustration of the calculation of a moving average is shown in Table 2. In this example the actual data are arranged in order of the independent variable (X), and the series of overlapping intervals is indicated by the numbered brackets. The values of the moving average for the first bracket are $X_a = 2$ (the mean of 1, 2, and 3) and $Y_a = 12.0$ (the mean of 11, 13, and 12). For simplicity, the example assumes equal weights for all of the data. Unequal item weights, on the other hand, would have to be included in the calculation of both the X_a and the Y_a.

Group averages and moving averages are highly flexible with respect to preserving the apparent fine detail of the data but often are harder to interpret than a properly chosen simpler form, such as a polynomial curve.

The algebraic statement of a polynomial of kth degree is

$$y = a + bx + cx^2 + \cdots + zx^k$$

The best-fit coefficients, $a, b, c, \ldots z$, are calculated by solving the simultaneous equations:

$$\begin{cases} aN + b\Sigma X + c\Sigma X^2 + \cdots + z\Sigma X^k = \Sigma Y \\ a\Sigma X + b\Sigma X^2 + c\Sigma X^3 + \cdots + z\Sigma X^{k+1} = \Sigma XY \\ \quad \vdots \\ a\Sigma X^k + b\Sigma X^{k+1} + c\Sigma X^{k+2} + \cdots \; z\Sigma X^{2k} = \Sigma X^k Y \end{cases}$$

where: X = independent variable
Y = dependent variable
N = number of data items
Σ = sum of values of expression to its right for all of data items

Standard computer programs are available for setting up and solving these equations for a variety of values of k.

The graphical representation of the equation for $k = 1$ is a straight line; for $k = 2$, a simple parabola; and for higher values of k, progressively more flexible and potentially more complex curves. The simpler polynomials tend to yield the truest fit around the midvalues of the independent variables, with wider variations from the actual data at the extremes. On the other hand, the higher polynomials, which generally improve the fit, sometimes introduce undesirable local peculiarities into the shape of the curve.

Figure 2 is an example of curve fitting by moving averages and by first-, second-, and third-degree polynomials.

More Than Two Variables. It is possible to fit algebraic expressions of two or more independent variables to observed data, reflecting the assumption that the dependent variable (salary, for instance) has two or more important causes (perhaps age, experience, and length of education). The expressions that work well, however, are generally complex, hard to understand, and difficult to show graphically. On the other hand, when a very precise idea of the relative influences of several causes is needed, these more complex algebraic expressions

TABLE 2   Calculation of a Moving Average

Actual data			Moving average	
X (Independent)	Y (Dependent)	Intervals	X_a	Y_a
1	11	(1)		
2	13	(2)	2	12.0
3	12	(3)	3	13.0
4	14		4	13.0
5	13	(4)	5	13.7
6	14	(5)	6	14.0
7	15	(6)	7	15.7
8	18	(7)	8	16.7
9	17			

give the best results. Their selection and calculation, however, should be left to a professional statistician.

For ordinary purposes, multiple-cause data can best be handled by grouping them into intervals or brackets of all but one of the independent variables and then studying the relationship between the dependent and the remaining independent variable, for each combination of the others, by the methods discussed above for the two-variable case.

Discrete Variables.   Some information falls naturally into discrete categories. Examples are levels of education, occupational classifications, and organizational ranks. Discrete variables can be assigned numerical values by judgment and thus made analyzable by continuous-variable methods (the preceding section discussed making continuous variables discrete by bracketing), or they can be analyzed as discrete variables.

A discrete dependent variable is usually reported in terms of the number or percentage of cases in the various discrete categories of the independent variables.

Figure 2.   Curve fitting.

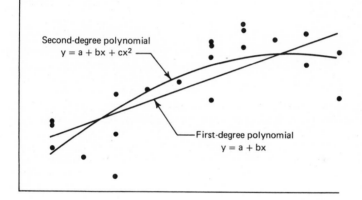

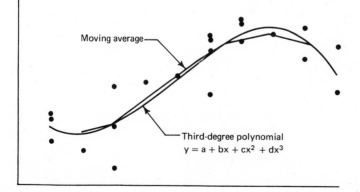

If the data represent a sample from a larger universe, precision may be estimated from the appropriate standard deviation, as follows:

$$\text{Standard deviation of the number in a category} = \sqrt{Np(1 - p)}$$

$$\text{Standard deviation of the percent in a category} = 100 \times \sqrt{\frac{p(1 - p)}{N}}$$

where: N = size of total sample
p = proportion of sample found in category

These formulas are reasonably good if the number in the category in question is at least 5 and the number in all the other categories together also is at least 5.

These standard deviations are related to the precision of the respective results (the number of individuals of the sample found in the category for the first and the proportion of the individuals of the sample found in the category for the second) in the same way that the *standard deviation of the mean* is related to the precision of the mean, as discussed earlier.

chapter 51

Communicating the
Total Compensation Program

ROBERT E. LUCE *Director, Training & Communications, Edward N. Hay & Associates, Philadelphia, Pennsylvania*

If an organization's top management embraces the idea that its personnel have a right to know something more about their compensation than the fact that they are paid at specified intervals by check, communication is called for. Communication is basically an *exchange of meaning* between a *sender* and a *receiver*. The exchange takes place through a medium, such as speeches, booklets, or slides, that carries a *message*.

Top management's openness—its willingness to share information with the organization as a whole—is the major factor determining exactly what is communicated to whom, in what detail, and with what intent. Top management's communication objectives for the total compensation program must be specified, and then, on the basis of these objectives, the communications planner can develop a program to achieve the desired results.

Communication of compensation programs is largely project-oriented work, related to installation of a new compensation program or a significant revision of an existing one. However, the best communications job involves continuous monitoring in order to assure that the right amounts of the right information are going to the right people at the right times. The communications program, therefore, although designed with the existing work force in mind, must also have built into it the ways the program will reach new people who join the company after the initial program launch.

Because these communications decisions must be made from the perspective of the total compensation program, the manager most familiar with compensation should manage communications, too. In addition to a comprehensive understanding of the compensation program, the communications planner must also know the organization's climate, its management style and philosophy, and other key factors, and he must be able to:

1. Make them a part of his overall communications program design
2. Demonstrate to top management that his program responds to specific organizational needs that cannot be ignored

Some of these responsibilities can be delegated to qualified personnel within the organization or assigned to outside organizations with specialized communications services. But the important point is that all elements of the communications program must be coordinated through one key decision maker. In a creative project, such leadership and centralized coordination are important for doing a quality job and for meeting deadlines.

BASIC CONCEPTS

To establish a framework for later discussion of the communications program preparation, this section presents the basic concepts which communications planners need as background for their work. The information also helps put in perspective the many factors which must be considered in communication of compensation programs.

Program Creation.   In this chapter, we recognize three overall stages of communications program creation:

1. *Program Planning.*   This is the stage in which communications needs are systematically analyzed and, on the basis of needs analysis, communications objectives are set.

2. *Program Design.*   In line with program objectives, the planner determines the media and methods that will be used for various audiences and establishes program timetables.

3. *Program Development.*   All writing, photography, artwork, editing, recording, printing, and packaging are done in this stage.

This chapter gives extensive treatment to the most critical stage—program planning—since this is the stage which launches the communications program planner into his task. Program design is given basic treatment, with discussion of the various media and their most customary and effective roles in communications programs. Program development is discussed only briefly; detailed coverage of such program development subjects as writing, art, and photography is beyond the scope of this handbook.

Program Implementation.   Once the program has been created, the communications planner is responsible for:

1. *Program Launch.*   This involves preparation and distribution of materials, handling of the logistics of any meetings involved, conducting of training activities for those who will handle parts of the program, and so on.

2. *Ongoing Program Administration.*   The planner should take steps to ensure that all new personnel receive the communications that have been given to the original communications audience.

3. *Continuing Analysis of Compensation Communication Needs and Renewal of Communications Program.*   As changes are made in the compensation program, the communications planner must adapt his program to reflect these changes. He must also consider the organization's needs for new or repeated communications efforts to ensure the maximum motivational impact of the organization's compensation package.

Levels of Communication.   In order to set the most appropriate communications objectives as he endeavors to design an effective program, the communications planner must know and be able to apply the levels of communication:

1. *Inform:* Creating awareness of facts, figures, and other information related to the subject being communicated. The receiver of such communications is not expected to answer questions about the subject or otherwise to demonstrate knowledge or skill.

2. *Build Knowledge:* Enabling the receiver of communications to articulate this knowledge to others, to answer questions about the subject, and to use the information in building related skills, as necessary

3. *Develop Skills:* Enabling the receiver of communications not only to demonstrate knowledge but also to apply it in performing specific tasks related to the subject

To illustrate with a simple example: some people know that the game of golf exists, but that is about it; some know the keys to a good swing and other golf facts but cannot translate this knowledge to effective action on the fairways; some have not only the necessary knowledge but also the skill to apply it. These differences express end behaviors produced by the three major levels of communication.

Put another way, at the first level of communication you can get away with just "telling 'em," but at the second and third levels you are "training 'em"— building knowledge and developing skill. Depending on top management's objectives for compensation communications, the communications planner has to reach the audience with the appropriate levels of communication to produce the desired end behaviors. Table 1 summarizes the most important factors related to the levels of communication.

Communications Objectives. Communications program objectives are developed in the program planning stage, and the levels of communication tie directly into setting communications objectives. That is, when top management is deciding on compensation program communications, they should recognize that some groups in the organization need only information (level 1), while others, because of varied management responsibilities and/or specific job duties, need to be able to explain parts of the program (level 2) or to contribute to maintaining and changing it (level 3).

Communications objectives are therefore set with respect to:

1. The level of communication desired for. . .
2. The audience receiving the communications and. . .
3. The subject matter being communicated

For example, the communications planner should conclude his program planning stage with objectives such as, "Inform (level 1) all personnel (au-

TABLE 1   Use of Levels in Communications Programs

	INFORM ▽1	BUILD KNOWLEDGE ▽2	DEVELOP SKILL ▽3
	For audiences who should know the subject	For audiences who must know the subject	For audiences who must be able to apply the subject
Communication elements produce { Individual involvement....	Slight	Extensive	Very extensive
Sender-receiver interaction......	Mainly sender to receiver	Partially two-way	Mainly two-way
Behavioral change.	Slight	Moderate	Extensive

dience) about the reasons for and format of job descriptions (subject matter)";
"Enable first-line managers (audience) to explain (level 2) vacation policy
(subject matter) to their subordinates"; "Enable middle managers (audience)
to apply (level 3) salary increase guidelines (subject matter)." Methods for
analyzing compensation communication needs so that objectives like these can
be set are presented fully later in this chapter.

COMPENSATION COMMUNICATIONS AND THE ORGANIZATION

This section explores potential impacts of compensation program communications on the organization. The communications planner should take these into
consideration as he plans and designs the compensation communications program. The information is also valuable as introductory material for his presentations of communications program rationale and plans to others, including top
management.

Ensure Consistent Understanding. Communications processes help assure
senders that their messages are received uniformly throughout the audience
group. Although it may be appropriate to communicate different elements of
the compensation program to different groups of employees—e.g., management
and hourly—and for some groups to receive more privileged information than
others, a planned across-the-board communications effort can give everyone
what he *needs* to know and ensures that the information provided various
groups blends together in a consistent, coherent whole.

This is particularly important in large organizations, where size itself increases the possibility that communications may be misinterpreted. The farther
an individual is from management, the less he knows about the whys of policy
and the more likely he is to interject his own biases, current rumors, and others'
opinions into what he receives from above. In the large organization many
layers of management and supervisory personnel lie between top and bottom,
and information becomes increasingly subject to distortion when received and
exchanged at ever lower, more populated levels.

Compensation is, of course, a subject that can stir strong emotions, and a
good communications program on compensation can help ensure that *every
individual in the total group receives the information he needs, should have,
and wants*—and that all parts of the communications program are consistent
with each other. By ensuring consistent understanding, the communications
process helps allay rumors and questioning and, at the same time, enhances the
motivational value of the compensation program.

Enhance Individual Motivation. An individual's compensation is a very subjective matter in that personal achievement, ambitions, desires for status, and
other factors are heavily involved. On the other hand, compensation is an
objective, formal link between the individual and the organization that may
not have continuous motivational value in and of itself if job satisfaction is not
also significantly present.

Information about his total compensation can motivate an individual by
giving him perspective on why he is paid the way he is and how he can improve
his compensation. Effective communication of total compensation can also
build job satisfaction in an area of organizational life directly related to individual needs.

The communications planner must ensure that the maximum motivational
potentials of compensation are being realized. He must do this at least partially by enlisting the support of top management for effective communications
about compensation—for a program of communication that keeps personnel

fully informed of compensation program changes and of advantages enjoyed through an enlightened compensation program.

Integrate the Compensation Program with the Management System.   If an organization uses a system of management that formally recognizes the appraisal and review of individual performance for manpower development purposes, as in management by objectives, then the relationships between this total system and compensation factors must be carefully delineated:

1. Performance appraisal and review, usually including joint goal setting by manager and subordinate, exist for systematic motivation and performance improvement of individuals in an overall management development process.

2. One use of performance appraisal results is to determine compensation actions, but this function should be separate from and subordinate to the development purposes for which the whole management system exists.

One means of emphasizing the distinction between these functions is to keep them separated in time: compensation actions are based on the latest performance appraisal, but the appraisal itself is a by-product of the performance review and goal setting process.

With a well-defined management system in use, compensation communications can discuss the use of performance appraisal for compensation purposes and, at the same time, reinforce the distinction between the developmental and compensation functions.   The effect, then, is to support the broader management system while meeting more narrowly defined communications needs.

Improve Compensation Program Administration.   The compensation program itself must, of course, be supported by well-defined policies and procedures, and one of the most important services a communications program can provide is skill development (level 3 communiction) in the policies and procedures area prior to implementation of the compensation system.   For example, if the program involves a new system of performance appraisal, management and supervisory personnel must be skilled in the new method to ensure that it will be applied with consistency throughout the organization.   Skills might also be needed in salary budgeting and in making actual dollar compensation decisions, and a systematic communications process can help meet these needs (if only by providing policy tables for reference).

In addition to developing skills needed for good compensation administration, the communications program can make managers aware of the availability of information that may be useful to them in discharging their salary administration responsibilities.   Communications can let managers know what information can be drawn from the compensation data base, ranging from the specifics of pay and performance appraisal records of people reporting to them to broader questions about:

1. Compensation practices of various units within the organization
2. Compensation practices of competitors
3. Pay for specific functions or jobs
4. Compensation trends
5. Specific problem areas that have been defined

In this way, the communications process can facilitate more effective management by making managers aware of the compensation data available to them.

Improve or Reinforce Organizational Climate.   Organizational climate, or environment, is the product of a number of forces at work as the organization pursues its goals.   The prevailing philosophy and management style of top management do much to determine climate, for these pervade the organization's life in many subtle ways.   If the communications planner understands the philosophy and style, he will have good insights into the kind of communication program top management will most readily endorse. Knowledge of climate is important for the communications planner also because it defines the setting into which communications will flow, thus enabling him to design communications that will reinforce or improve the climate, as necessary.

Since compensation program communications bear top management's signature, they represent organizational posture and therefore affect organizational climate. For example, if communications are viewed by employees as deliberately evasive, obscure, or incomplete, motivation and allegiance to the organization are undermined; however, if communications are considered open, informative, and useful, motivation and allegiance are reinforced.

An organization can therefore use its compensation communications program as a significant representation of its attitude about its people. In so doing, it can help contribute to a greater sense of organizational purpose and *esprit de corps* or it can help maintain this sense if it has already established a climate of openness, trust, and candor.

The communications planner must also be fully aware of the management-employee relationships characteristic of the organization. For example, the amount and type of union activity, the degree and causes of managerial turnover and other employee turnover, the success of the organization in its endeavors, and other such factors can help identify prevailing management-employee relationships. The nature of these relationships can tell much about the impact compensation communications will have; moreover, they can help the planner design a communications program that builds good relationships.

Improve or Reinforce Employee Attitudes toward Compensation. When a new compensation program is being launched, or when a current program is being updated, it is important that the communications planner know prevailing employee attitudes toward compensation. This helps him plan communications to meet real organizational needs. The major elements of attitude about compensation are described by how individuals view:

1. Their own wages, salaries, incentives, or benefits in their organization

2. The wages, salaries, incentives, or benefits of other people in their organization and in other organizations

3. The administration of wages, salaries, incentives, or benefits in their organization and in other organizations

4. The organization's desire and capacity to make real, beneficial changes in compensation

A questionnaire survey of the organization can provide this information. The survey should be conducted before a new compensation program is developed or the old one revised, for the information provided can be used in total program planning as well as in positioning and tailoring communications.

COMMUNICATIONS PROGRAM PLANNING

Planning is critical to creating the communications program, chiefly because it is in this stage that program objectives are set. The steps that precede objective setting must be carried out with sufficient thoroughness and accuracy to ensure that the objectives themselves point to the best possible program design (stage 2 of program creation). There are five steps in program planning, which are described below.

Step 1: Determine Subject Matter Areas. A typical compensation program is a blend of interrelated elements, each of which constitutes a potential subject matter area for communications purposes. The communications planner has to decide just how to break down the compensation program—what subjects stand out as discrete entities. For example, some subjects that might be covered in communications about a base-pay program for exempt salaried personnel would include the following:

1. Program objectives
2. Job analysis
3. Job evaluation
4. Determination of internal consistency
5. Determination of external competitiveness
6. Program policy and procedures

Step 2: Define Levels of Communication. Once the broad subjects have been determined, the communications planner should define the content to be included at each communications level for each subject matter area. As described earlier, three communications levels may be identified:

1. Inform
2. Build knowledge
3. Develop skills

Table 2 shows how communications of the illustrative subjects can vary depending on which level of communications is chosen.

Step 3: Determine Audience Groups. This step requires deciding first if there is, in fact, a logical division of the total audience into groups, such as overall management levels, or management levels by divisions in the organization, or management and nonmanagement. If the division seems possible, then the groups should be decided upon. It is not necessary at this point to be concerned with whether one group has the same information needs as another. Rather, the task is to sort out groups within the total audience that logically go together.

For example, a large bank communicating a base-pay program for salaried personnel (officers) might subdivide the total audience by officer (rather than title) groups:

1. Executive officers
2. Department executives
3. Managing officers
4. Supervising officers and officer specialists
5. All other officers

Again, the communications planner is in the best position to decide upon the way(s) to divide his organization for communications purposes.

Step 4: Construct and Use Communications Matrix. Steps 1, 2, and 3 provide the communications planner with inputs for a decision-making matrix that clearly delineates what should be communicated to whom. With subject matter (step 1) and audience group (step 3) as the horizontal and vertical variables, the level of communication for each item of subject matter is determined for each audience group and inserted in the matrix by numbers—1 (inform), 2 (build knowledge), or 3 (develop skills).

Table 3 shows such a matrix after it has been completed, using the examples given in steps 1, 2, and 3; the results are purely illustrative.

The communications planner can use the matrix in these ways:

1. As a personal or group decision-making tool for what communications go to whom. In the former case, it can become the focal point of the planner's analysis of compensation communications needs. When complete, it can be presented as part of a program proposal with objectives, media, and budgets worked out (see step 5 following, plus the final items in this chapter). In the latter case, it can help the planner assess top management's, or any other key

TABLE 2 Content of Illustrative Subject Matter Areas at Three Communication Levels

SUBJECTS / LEVELS	Program objectives	Job analysis	Job evaluation	Internal consistency	External competitiveness	Policy and procedures
1. Inform	1. What they are	1. Fact that job descriptions exist and their purpose	1. What it is and why it is done	1. What it is and fact that it has been achieved	1. What it is and fact that it has been achieved	1. Fact that they exist
2. Build knowledge	2. Above, plus why they were developed	2. Above, plus format and uses of descriptions and techniques used to write them	2. Above, plus method of evaluation	2. Above, plus methods used to achieve it	2. Above, plus methods used to achieve it	2. Above, plus full set of policy and procedures
3. Develop skills	3. Above, plus ability to set objectives	3. Above, plus ability to write job descriptions	3. Above, plus ability to evaluate jobs	3. Above, plus ability to determine internal consistency	3. Above, plus ability to determine external competitiveness	3. Above, plus ability to implement policy and procedures

TABLE 3 Communications Decision-making Matrix (Bank Example): Matching Levels to Audiences and Subjects

Communications levels matched to audiences by subject

SUBJECT AUDIENCE	Program objectives	Job analysis	Job evaluation	Internal consistency	External competitiveness	Policy and procedures
Executive officers......	3	2	2	2	2	3
Department executives.	3	2	2	2	2	3
Managing officers......	2	2	2	2	2	3
Supervising officers and officer specialists....	2	1	1	1	1	2
All other officers.......	2	1	1	1	1	2

Levels of communications   1—Inform.   2—Build knowledge.   3—Develop skills.

group's, thoughts and feelings about communications. Then these can be incorporated in the final plans that emerge.

2. As a blueprint for developing the actual communications program. The completed matrix not only shows what should be communicated to whom but also serves as a direct source of communications program objectives. With the level of communications specified for each subject and each audience group, objectives can be set and any booklets, films, meetings, and so on, that are then designed into the program can be tailored to the exact needs of the organization.

Step 5: Analyze Decisions and Set Program Objectives. With a completed matrix, the communications planner can study whatever patterns of communications needs it reveals, and he can then set objectives for the program. He sets the objectives horizontally, by audience groups, moving from one subject area to the next.

Analyzing the matrix in Table 3, here are the objectives that result in each subject matter area for two audience groups:

1. *Department Executives*

(*a*) PROGRAM OBJECTIVES: Enable the department executives to develop compensation program objectives.

(*b*) JOB ANALYSIS: Enable the executives to describe the purpose, format, and use of job descriptions and the techniques used to write them.

(*c*) JOB EVALUATION: Enable the executives to describe the purpose and method of job evaluation.

(*d*) INTERNAL CONSISTENCY: Enable the executives to describe what it is, the fact that it has been achieved, and the methods used to achieve it.

(*e*) EXTERNAL COMPETITIVENESS: Enable the executives to describe what it is, the fact that it has been achieved, and the methods used to achieve it.

(*f*) POLICY AND PROCEDURES: Enable the executives to implement policy and procedures for compensation program administration.

2. *All Other Officers*

(*a*) PROGRAM OBJECTIVES: Enable the officers to describe program objectives and why they were developed.

(*b*) JOB ANALYSIS: Provide information on existence and purpose of job descriptions.

(*c*) JOB EVALUATION: Describe job evaluation and its purpose.

(*d*) INTERNAL CONSISTENCY: Define internal consistency and show it has been achieved.

(*e*) EXTERNAL COMPETITIVENESS: Define external competitiveness and show that it has been achieved.

(*f*) POLICY AND PROCEDURES: Enable the officers to describe policy and procedures as necessary (in this case, reference to a policy and procedures manual is sufficient to meet the "as necessary" part of the objective).

With objectives completed, the communications planner knows what parts of the program will be for informing audience groups and what parts will be for knowledge building and skill development. He also knows what parts of programs will be the same for two or more groups. For example, it is probable that the same communications activities will be used for different groups which share common objectives in the same subjects.

COMMUNICATIONS PROGRAM DESIGN

The objectives developed from the matrix lead directly to program design—choices of methods and media. Although geared primarily to communications objectives, the choices of methods and media must also consider broader organizational needs and capabilities. For example, organizational priorities may indicate a major informing effort with other levels of communications deferred. Or budgets, meeting facilities, and/or hardware capabilities may dictate less ambitious communications than objectives indicate.

Given the existing organizational constraints, then, the communications planner can use objectives to design communications that achieve desired results. He can do so using combinations of the media and methods described below, and he can estimate exact costs of all elements, once his design is complete.

Media

The communications planner can employ many different media to reach program objectives. Naturally, some are better suited to one level of communications than to another; e.g., lectures are good for informing but meeting workshops are good for building knowledge and developing skill. Depending on program objectives, the media may be used separately or in combination. For example, to meet informing objectives, a booklet may be mailed to all personnel affected by the compensation program; and for skill development purposes, some members of this total group may also meet in a workshop on salary administration.

Meetings.   Many types of meetings can serve vital communications purposes by simply bringing people together to convey messages to them. Meetings in this context may include:

One-to-one sessions, e.g., between a manager and a subordinate, in person or even over the telephone. Such meetings can be very effective for informing as a follow-up to broader, less personal communications efforts.

Small-group sessions, with a leader prepared to conduct the session at any of the three levels of communications. For example, a slide presentation on a compensation program followed by a discussion can be very informative to a group of 10 to 15 or even 20. Meeting activities aimed at building knowledge and developing skills should have no more than 15 participants. Such meetings are usually some combination of audiovisual presentation, role playing, guided discussions, and so on, workshop style.

If field personnel are involved, as in sales organizations, then the benefits of carrying communications directly to the field should be fully considered. Small-group sessions for people in the field can have a great motivational impact.

Large sessions, usually called when there is a speech by an executive for informing purposes. The best of such sessions use some visual aid to make communications more effective, e.g., slides to illustrate the speech.

Written Materials. Some examples of written materials that are effective in the compensation communications context are:

Booklets for general distribution in the organization. Such booklets usually perform an informing function by covering compensation program information in minimal detail. Specific details are then communicated in other components of the program, e.g., through meetings.

Manuals covering compensation program policy and procedures. Such manuals can help perform both informing and knowledge building functions for program, administrators and others who need to know and be able to work with policy.

Self-instructional materials, such as programmed learning items, for high-level knowledge input as part of a training process. Such materials can be very effective as pre-meeting assignments for knowledge and skill sessions to bring trainees up to a higher knowledge level prior to involving them in workshop activities.

Audio and Audiovisual Materials. These are rarely used on their own, but instead help support individual and group communications activities. Some of the main ones are:

35mm slides and "super" slides, often used to illustrate speeches to large groups and also adaptable to special communicating activities in small groups. In the latter situation they are usually presented with prepared scripts that allow for discussion breaks.

Audiotapes and records, sometimes used to bring the voice of an unseen executive to outlying groups. Another effective use is in individualized communications where the tape or record can both present information and provide drill and practice as a self-instructional device. Reel-to-reel or cassette tapes can be used, depending on equipment capabilities.

Videotapes, useful mainly for "see yourself" training but also can be used like a motion picture in a pre-prepared format, e.g., an executive speech.

Closed-circuit television, very effective for reaching large numbers of people at once in disparate locations.

Videorecord cassettes, such as Electronic Video Recording and other video-processes, to perform the function of both individual slides and motion pictures in one format.

Motion pictures, either sound or silent, accompanied by tape sound track, or accompanied by live speaker with script. Super 8 formats provide good large-group projection potentials with stop-motion and other techniques useful at all communications levels.

Other aids, mainly used as meeting props, such as blackboards, flip charts, Hook and Loop boards, overhead projection cells, posters, and animations (movable devices, like special moving arrows, puppets, etc.).

Methods

Methods are the design components in which media are employed—the combinations and arrangements of media. A given communications program may employ several methods for each of several audience groups, depending on the objectives. To illustrate how methods are related to objectives, we will again use the bank example that was described in the preceding section (see Table 3 and subsequent discussion of objective setting):

1. A booklet is written at the first level of communication for distribution to all personnel included in the salary program. This meets informing objectives (level 1).

2. A presentation is given consisting of 35mm slides and a presenter's script, in two versions. The first version is tailored to executive officers, department executives, and managing officers, and the second to supervising officers, officer specialists, and all other officers. The first version is used in small-group sessions, allowing ample time for questions and discussions, while the second version is given to large groups with limited opportunity for discussion. Both meet knowledge building objectives (level 2), but the first allows more give-and-take in the communications to lay the groundwork for the skills development needed by executive officers, department executives, and managing officers in the policies and procedures area.

3. A two-day training meeting is held for department executives and managing officers in appraising performance and conducting performance counseling interviews. There is an audience of no more than 15 per meeting, and the meeting design includes such training techniques as a pre-meeting assignment, meeting discussion sessions, role playing, and use of the incident process for improving decision making and teamwork. This meets skill development objectives (level 3) in the policy and procedures area.

4. A policy and procedures manual is prepared for reference by all officers during and following the communications program. This meets knowledge building objectives (level 2).

5. Special preparation ("train the trainer" sessions) is given to all personnel who conduct communications workshops and presentations.

Note that this program has several different parts related to the differing levels of communication required by the audience groups. The program can also be developed and launched in "waves," in that the booklet can be developed immediately and sent to everyone. Then the slide presentation can be given, the department executives and managing officers trained, and finally the compensation program can be put on stream.

Components of the communications program can be used with new officers that come under the compensation plan, since administration to individuals or small groups is possible.

COMMUNICATIONS PROGRAM DEVELOPMENT

Actual development of the communications program involves extensive writing, editing, photography, artwork, and/or recording. It is therefore a major undertaking for the communications planner, which he can approach in one of three ways:

1. *Keep As Much As Possible Inside.* An organization that has extensive talent and facilities for developing program elements and getting them produced can usually do its own program development work, although it may occasionally seek outside help in photography, art, or recording, etc.

2. *Mix Inside and Outside Sources.* In this case the communications planner either does not have all the required facilities or he has them but goes outside for other reasons—for example, to meet a deadline. Most commonly in this situation, the planner does the design work himself, or he has it done internally under his guidance, and contracts out the artwork, photography, recording, printing, and/or other elements. He might even use outsiders to supplement his design and writing.

3. *Use Outside Sources for Most of It.* In this case, the organization has

little or no capability in communications and so engages an outside consultant in communications to work closely with the planner, usually in planning and designing the program as well as in developing the actual booklets, slides, scripts, etc., to be used. It is usually wise to involve the outside professional in all stages of program development to gain the fullest advantage from his expertise and to ensure that the program is tailored to the organization's unique needs. Sometimes consultants become directly involved in implementation by running meetings, training client personnel to implement the communications program, and so on. They usually coordinate all production of finished materials.

Each of the choices has unique advantages. The first approach is probably less expensive than the second and third. But many organizations feel they do not have the professional expertise necessary to create a good communications program and therefore call on outside professionals who make it their business to provide professional quality with assured performance measured against objectives.

COMMUNICATIONS PROGRAM IMPLEMENTATION

The compensation communications job really just starts with program creation. Once the program is ready, the communications planner has to turn to the following activities, described earlier:

1. Program launch
2. Ongoing program administration
3. Continuing analysis of compensation communications needs and renewal of communications programs

These activities ensure that the compensation program has maximum motivational impact on current employees now and in the future and on new employees brought in at any time in the future. The communications program must not be a one-shot affair. Once it has been created, the communications planner has to work at making it an integral part of organization life—from initial launch in administering it to new employees to updating it and repeating it with all employees as the compensation system changes.

Variations on the original program should be considered in order to keep the excellence of the organization's compensation program continuously before all employees. For example, if the initial launch involved highly specialized communications methods and media such as meetings, slide presentations, and home study materials, then "regular" organization communications channels might be used for refresher information—house organs, memoranda, bulletins, and others. Also, it is possible to issue page replacements for originally issued materials to bring information up to date.

An ongoing stream of compensation information helps drive home the main points the organization wants to make with employees. Thus, the organization has a solid motivational base that will provide employee support for changes employees recognize as management's commitment to make a good compensation program even better.

Index

1